The Archaeology of Ancient China

The Archaeology of
Ancient China

THIRD EDITION
REVISED AND ENLARGED

Kwang-chih Chang

NEW HAVEN AND LONDON
YALE UNIVERSITY PRESS
1977

Published with assistance from the foundation established in memory of Amasa Stone Mather of the Class of 1907, Yale College.

Designed by Sally Sullivan
and set in Bembo type.
Printed in the United States of America by
The Murray Printing Company, Westford, Mass.

Published in Great Britain, Europe, Africa, and Asia (except Japan) by Yale University Press, Ltd., London. Distributed in Latin America by Kaiman & Polon, Inc., New York City; in Australia and New Zealand by Book & Film Services, Artarmon, N.S.W., Australia; and in Japan by Harper & Row, Publishers, Tokyo Office.

Library of Congress Cataloging in Publication Data

Chang, Kwang-chih.
    The archaeology of ancient China.

    Bibliography: p.
    Includes index.
    1. China—Antiquities.   2. China—Civilization.
I. Title.
DS715.C38   1977   931   77-23212
ISBN 0-300-02144-5
ISBN 0-300-02145-3 pbk.

Contents

Illustrations

Tables

Preface

Chinese archaeological publications, suspended in mid-1966 with the onset of the Great Proletarian Cultural Revolution, were resumed in the beginning of 1972. Soon it became clear to the outside world that major archaeological discoveries were made in China during the hiatus years, and they are continuing. Hardly a single issue of any of the principal archaeological journals appears without containing some highly important report of some highly important find that in some way changes our view. Of particular consequence are the growing numbers of radiocarbon dates. In the previous edition of this volume I listed several "items for urgent research," and the first item was chronology. I had ventured that "several dozen well-placed radiocarbon dates" could very well drastically change our views of Chinese prehistory. Now faced with new data published in the last four years (1972–75), I find that this book must once again be extensively revised, not just to incorporate new finds but, especially, because some fundamental premises must now be reexamined in the light of new data and new dates.

The field of Chinese archaeology is certainly changing fast, and no practitioner can stay in business without a very open mind. The major difficulty with revising a book of this kind at this time is that positions on issues must be taken, however tentatively, at a time when no one, least of all this author, can really tell where new data and new studies are going to take us. Surprises may at any time be sprung upon us, not only in China but in adjoining regions as well, especially Southeast Asia, where new developments could affect our thinking about China itself. I would have preferred to wait a few more years before attempting a third revision. Nevertheless, as the author of one of the more widely used texts in Chinese archaeology, I do not feel I can allow my students to continue using the second edition of the book, knowing that parts of it have now become obsolete in a fundamental way. In this new edition, I have done my best to revise the book so that it conforms with the newest data and the best views of them. Where uncertainties must remain, the book leaves plenty of room to accommodate any additional data from the near future. New material that will appear after the manuscript of this edition is completed (mid-1976) but before the final proof is due at the printers will be summarized in appendix 3. This edition will, thus, be up to date through the end of 1976 and, compared with its predecessor, will have incorporated another whole decade of Chinese archaeology.

The preparation of the manuscript of this new edition has been aided by a Faculty Research grant awarded by the Concilium on International and Area Studies at Yale University, for which I am very grateful. Donna Conroy, my artist as well as typist, has been tremendously helpful; without her patient assistance this volume would not now have been completed. Illustrations that have been carried over from the previous edition were done by Ward Whittington and Susan Weeks. I thank Helena Bentz Dorrance of the Yale University Press for her wise and thoughtful editorial assistance.

In May and June of 1975 I returned to China (after an absence of almost thirty years from the mainland, which included my entire professional life thus far) as a member of the United States Palaeoanthropology Delegation, sponsored jointly by the Committee on Scholarly Communication with the People's Republic of China, Washington, D.C., and the Chinese Scientific and Technological Association, Peking. While in China I had the opportunity to discuss extensively many archaeological issues with my Chinese colleagues in Peking, Lin-fen, Sian, An-yang, Cheng-chou, Nanking, Shanghai, and Canton. Many of them also generously allowed me to photograph their unique collections. (No photograph of any object, however, is being used here, unless that object has been previously published both in picture and in words.) But more importantly I greatly benefited from their encouragement and advice. Whatever contribution I may have made to Chinese archaeology by writing this book pales in light of the gigantic but selfless efforts of the Chinese archaeologists in the past quarter century. To them, to their fellow archaeologists in Taiwan (among them leaders of Chinese archaeology in the preceding quarter century), and to the many generations of Chinese archaeologists before them all, I dedicate this book.

Kwang-chih Chang

June 1, 1976
New Haven, Connecticut

Abbreviations

AP   *Asian Perspectives* (Bulletin of the Far Eastern Prehistory Association), Hong Kong and Honolulu

BIE   *Bulletin of the Institute of Ethnology*, Academia Sinica, Taipei

BIHP   *Bulletin of the Institute of History and Philology*, Academia Sinica, Nanking, Lichuang, and Taipei

BMFEA   *Bulletin of the Museum of Far Eastern Antiquities*, Stockholm

GSoC   *Geological Society of China*, Peking

GSuC   *Geological Survey of China*, Peking

JZ   *Jenruigaku Zasshi*, Tokyo

KK   *K'ao-ku* (1959–), Peking

KKHP   *K'ao-ku Hsüeh Pao*, Peking

KKTH   *K'ao-ku T'ung-hsün* (title changed to *KK* after 1958), Peking

PS   *Palaeontologia Sinica*, Peking

QS   *Quaternaria Sinica*, Peking

TYKKPK   *T'ien-yeh K'ao-ku Pao-kao* (no. 1 of *KKHP*), Nanking

VP   *Vertebrata Palasiatica*, Peking

WW   *Wen-wu* (1959–), Peking

WWTKTL   *Wen-wu Ts'an-k'ao Tzu-liao* (title changed to *WW* after 1958), Peking

All Chinese words (except for some long-established place names) are romanized in this book in the Wade-Giles system.

Introduction

The following chapters outline a cultural historical framework into which the formative stages of Chinese civilization can be placed, and present the necessary data for its documentation. Much of the structure and practically all the data come from the results of other scholars' studies, which span several centuries, but some parts are original with this volume. In order to provide a historical background against which the present interpretation appears, and to introduce to beginning students in Chinese archaeology the essential traditions and idiosyncracies of this field of learning, I shall begin with a brief summary of the development of prehistoric and early historic archaeology in China.

Historical studies had an early start in China, and the study of bygone cultures and civilizations by means of their artifactual remains has also been a part of the historical method. Even in the Eastern Chou (ca. 770–221 B.C.) and Han (206 B.C.–A.D. 220) dynasties, when what to us is ancient history was contemporary event, and what to us are archaeological specimens of bronze, iron, and stone were still objects of daily use, and when prehistoric cultures remained faintly in the memory of the people in the form of legendary traditions, and their ruins and remains were still exposed on the ground or buried shallowly under the earth, there was already an archaeology of sorts. Han Fei Tzu (third century B.C.) says in *Shih kuo*:

> When Yao governed the world, people ate in clay vessels and drank in clay mugs;
> Yü made ritual vessels, painting the interior in black and the exterior in red;
> The Yin people ... engraved their utensils for meals and incised their utensils for drinking wine.

Wei Chü-hsien[1] thinks that Han Fei Tzu, a philosopher of the Warring States period (ca. 450–221 B.C.), must have seen some excavated prehis-

---

1. *Chung-kuo k'ao-ku-hsüeh shih*, Shanghai, Commercial Press, 1937, pp. 50–51.

toric ceramic remains and Yin bronzes and identified them with traditional ancient heroes, in order to have given such vivid descriptions of ancient artifacts. Ssu-ma Ch'ien of Western Han visited many ancient ruins and relics attributed to various preceding periods before he put the information that he considered verified and thus reliable into his great *Shih chi* (Historical Memoirs) (ca. 100 B.C.). An even more interesting "archaeological" approach to history is seen in Yüan K'ang's *Yüeh chüeh shu*. In the chapter on swords, Feng Hu Tzu, an Eastern Chou philosopher, is quoted by Yüan K'ang as saying to a king of Yüeh:

> In the Age of Hsüan Yüan, Shen Nung, and Ho Hsü, weapons were made of stones, for cutting trees and building houses, and were buried with the dead . . . ;
> In the Age of Huang Ti, weapons were made of jade, for cutting trees, building houses, and digging the ground, . . . and were buried with the dead;
> In the Age of Yü, weapons were made of bronze, for building canals . . . and houses . . . ;
> At the present time, weapons are made of iron.

In devising the Three Age system, Yüan K'ang's account of Feng Hu Tzu seems to have anticipated C. J. Thomsen of Denmark by more than a thousand years, and Yüan K'ang may thus rightfully rank with Lucretius as one of the world's first archaeologists to propose such a classification.[2]

But whatever credits one can give to these early scholars for utilizing material remains of ancient cultures to make historical studies, this archaeological fetus soon became undernourished during and after the Han dynasty, when the scheme of the ancient Golden Age of Three Dynasties and their legendary predecessors, systematized by the Confucian political philosophers and blessed by the royal governments, became the orthodox interpretation of ancient Chinese history. Studies of relics, largely confined to bronze vessels and stone tablets—hence the name *chin shih hsüeh*, or the "studies of bronzes and stones"—continued throughout the Chinese historical periods, but a different attitude prevailed. Bronzes were collected as curios and heirlooms for their artistic or fetishistic value, and whatever studies were made of them were largely confined to their

---

2. *Ibid.*, p. 58. George G. MacCurdy, *Human Origins*, New York, Appleton-Century, 1933, vol 1, p. 9: "In his poem *De Rerum Natura* Lucretius (about 98–55 B.C.) says: 'The earliest weapons were the hands, nails, and teeth; then came stone and clubs. These were followed by iron and bronze, but bronze came first, the use of iron not being known until later.'"

inscriptions, which provided confirmation of the Golden Age interpretation of ancient history or information of palaeographic interest. In addition,
bronze weapons, mirrors, chariot and horse fittings, porcelain and earthen-
ware vessels, tiles and eave tiles, jade, seals, and so forth, were also studied,
and since 1899, oracle bone inscription of the Yin dynasty have been
added to this list.

In general, these studies of ancient artifacts, which have appeared
throughout the historic period, either concentrated on the inscriptions as
supplementary data for literary history or focused upon ancient institutions recorded in existing literary documents, which these artifacts
confirmed or refuted. Little attention had ever been given to the historical
information the artifacts themselves could provide, or which their cultural
contexts, often unknown or neglected anyway, could suggest. In the
famous *K'ao-ku t'u*, compiled probably in the Northern Sung dynasty,
Lü Ta-lin recorded 211 bronzes in the palace and private collections and
13 jade objects, giving illustrations, place of origin if known, and dimensions and weight. Another book of the same period with noteworthy
archaeological descriptions and discussion is *Meng hsi pi t'an* by Shen Kua
(1031–95).[3] But these were rare books with few significant followers,
and their contributions were never fully taken advantage of by historians.
In short, China has had an indigenous tradition of archaeology, but this
tradition had not gone much beyond the scope and spirit of antiquarianism
before her contacts with the West.

Modern scientific archaeology was born in China in the early twentieth
century under the impact of Western civilization and scholarship. The
roots of the new inspiration are multiple, and a sheer enumeration of them
is necessarily arbitrary. But the following sources are clear.

First, of course, there was the tradition of antiquarianism and historiography in China, which represented both a deep-rooted scholarship of
past institutions and historical events and an unfailing interest in things
ancient, including early inscriptions. For a long period in the early decades
of this century, this tradition was under heavy fire from the new school
of historians and archaeologists, but it nevertheless provided a historic
foundation upon which new methodologies had to be based. When all
things against it have been said, new archaeologists still cannot disregard
the centuries-long experience of the antiquarians in dealing with objects
of the historical period.

Second, with the Nationalist revolution of 1911 and the May Fourth

3. Hsia Nai, in *KKHP* 1974 (2), 1–17.

Movement of 1919, the Golden Age interpretation of ancient China fell apart and a critical school of historical interpretation came into being, symbolized by the publication, in 1926, of *Ku shih pien*, or "Critical Reviews of Ancient History," edited by Ku Chieh-kang.[4] The well-known archaeologist Li Chi states:

> Their slogan, "Show your proof," though destructive in nature, did bring about a more critical spirit in the study of ancient China. Thus, if one wants to pay excessive tribute to the Golden Age of Yao and Shun, well, Show your proof; if one wishes to talk about the engineering miracles of the Great Yü of the third millennium B.C., proofs must also be given. What must be remembered in this connection is that written records alone were no longer accepted as valid proofs.[5]

Now that the traditional doctrines were being rejected and new substitutes were needed, Ku Chieh-kang proposed three new approaches to the study of ancient history: archaeology, critical reviews of false histories and pseudo-histories, and folklore.[6]

In this atmosphere, proofs were sought by the new historians to substantiate the literary records of ancient history, and proofs were at the same time being produced by an assortment of scholars, representing the Western methodology of historical study, who *excavated*, in various parts of China, artifacts dating not only from the historical periods but from the prehistoric periods as well. To such data and new techniques the new historians of enlightened China naturally turned for proof and for inspiration.

Western scholars came to China, a land of ancient civilization which they had admired in books, soon after the Manchu dynasty bowed to Western gunboats. To Chinese Turkestan came the Grum-Grzimailo brothers from Russia in 1889, M. Grenard and D. de Rhine from France in 1892, and Sven Hedin from Sweden in 1896. To southern Manchuria from Japan came Torii Ryūzō in 1895. But these places were distant from North China, and what these visitors produced were either historical documents or studies of apparently insignificant relics from border countries which used to be occupied by "barbarians," and thus their findings were of little importance to the historians of China. With J. Gunnar Andersson, a mining consultant hired by the Peiyang government of

4. Vol. 1, Peking, P'u-shê, 1926.

5. Li Chi, *The Beginnings of Chinese Civilization*, Seattle, University of Washington Press, 1957, p. 4.

6. Ku Chieh-kang, ed., *Ku-shih pien* 1, 57–77.

Peking in the early years of the Republic, things took a different turn.

In the early decades of the present century, study of the ancient history of China was indeed chaotic. Although Charles Darwin in his *Descent of Man* says that "there is indirect evidence of [flint tools'] former use by the Chinese and ancient Jews,"[7] this indirect evidence had never been substantiated, and such Western writers as Jacques de Morgan[8] and sinologists like Berthold Laufer[9] insisted that Chinese civilization had no prehistory. In China the critical school of historical studies found no assurance of even the Three Dynasties. But in 1920 Andersson discovered in Mien-ch'ih Hsien, western Honan, in the heart of Chinese civilization, a Stone Age site near Yang-shao-ts'un characterized by painted pottery, which was to be followed by his discovery of another Painted Pottery site at the cave of Sha-kuo-t'un in Liaoning in 1922 and many other Painted Pottery culture sites in Kansu in 1923–24.

In the meantime, in 1920 two Jesuit missionaries, Emile Licent and Pierre Teilhard de Chardin, found the first Palaeolithic implements at Ch'ing-yang, Kansu, and in the same year Andersson located fossiliferous sites in the Chou-k'ou-tien limestone hills near Peking. Bronze Age tombs were opened by farmers in 1923 at Hsin-cheng, in Honan, and at Li-yü-ts'un, in Shansi, which were soon investigated by antiquarians. Thus, within the short period of four years (1920–23), the existence of early man in China during both prehistoric and early historic periods could no longer be doubted. At that time the oracle bone inscriptions were also generally accepted as genuine Shang dynasty writing. This sudden appearance of proofs needed by historians for the study of ancient Chinese history deeply impressed Chinese scholars, who thus found in field investigations a new source of historic data.

After the early 1920s, when the field method was introduced to China by Western scholars, a new awareness of China's past, which was even more ancient than the Golden Age had traditionally held it to be, and a new historical school came into being, in which the new and the traditional were combined to the benefit of both. This new school of thought was symbolized by the founding of the Institute of History and Philology, Academia Sinica, in 1928, but was certainly not confined to this institution. Such scholars as P'ei Wen-chung, of the Geological Survey, Hsü Ping-ch'ang, of the National Research Institute of Peiping, and Kuo

7. New York, Crowell, 1874, p. 224.

8. *Prehistoric Man*, New York, Knopf, 1925, p. 293.

9. *Jade: A Study in Chinese Archaeology and Religion*, Field Museum of Natural History Publication 154, Anthropology Series, vol. 10 (1912), pp. 29, 54–55.

1. Some Chinese archaeologists who have made important contributions to the development of the field. *Top row*, Tung Tso-pin, An Chih-min, Hsia Nai; *bottom row*, Li Chi, P'ei Wen-chung.

Pao-chün, of the Research Institute of Honan Antiquities, worked in the same field with Li Chi, Liang Ssu-yüng, and Tung Tso-pin, of the Institute of History and Philology, at one in spirit and principle, if not always in sentiment (fig. 1).

Chinese archaeology made considerable strides during the decade from the mid-twenties through the mid-thirties, when the outbreak of the Sino-Japanese War halted its further growth. The Palaeolithic sites at Chou-k'ou-tien were excavated by the Geological Survey, and the human

remains and artifacts were ably studied by such geologists and palaeontologists as Teilhard de Chardin, Davidson Black, Franz Weidenreich,
Young Chung-chien, and P'ei Wen-chung. Although Palaeolithic remains
were known only from a few sites at Chou-k'ou-tien (mainly localities
13, 1, and 15, and the Upper Cave) and in the Ordos area, both middle
and upper Pleistocene occupations of men were now substantiated, and
a comparison of their physical types and cultures with other known
Palaeolithic men in East Asia, such as *Pithecanthropus* in Java, threw much
light on human origin in this part of the world. Elsewhere in China,
J. H. Edgar collected a few Palaeolithic-looking implements from the
Yangtze terraces in Szechwan, Russian and Japanese scholars collected
Mesolithic implements at Djalai-nor and Ku-hsiang-t'un in Manchuria,
the Geological Survey found some Mesolithic industries in limestone
caves of Kwangsi, and G. H. R. von Koenigswald found in Hong Kong
drugstores the giant anthropoid teeth that Weidenreich believed were
from ancestors of *Pithecanthropus* and modern man. These Palaeolithic
and Mesolithic data of varying importance, reliability, and quantity were
sufficient to give scientists some substantial ideas about man and his culture
in China during and immediately after the Pleistocene period. Toward
the end of this decade, Helmut de Terra, Hallam L. Movius, Jr., and
Teilhard de Chardin managed to pull together all the bits of information
then known to construct a total picture of Chinese Palaeolithic and Mesolithic cultures, and to tie this in with the Himalayan glacial sequence and
with the history of early man in most of the Old World.[10]

In Neolithic archaeology, Li Chi, a Harvard-trained anthropologist,
found and excavated another Painted Pottery site, in southern Shansi,
in 1926. By this time the existence of a Painted Pottery culture before the
dawn of Chinese history in North China had been generally accepted,
and the hypothesis had been advanced to identify this culture with that
of the legendary Hsia dynasty. The hypothesis was based on two assump-
tions: the first, which was beginning to be substantiated archaeologically
at that time, was that the Painted Pottery culture came before the Shang
and, thus, was apparently the Hsia, which had preceded the Shang
according to legends; the second was that the geographical distribution
of the Painted Pottery culture apparently coincided with the area of
activities of the Hsia in the legendary accounts. Moreover, many scholars,

10. Helmut de Terra, *Pleistocene Formation and Stone Age Man in China*, Peking, Institut
de Géo-Biologie, 1941. P. Teilhard de Chardin, *Early Man in China*, Institut de Géo-
Biologie, 1941. Hallam L. Movius, Jr., *Early Man and Pleistocene Stratigraphy in Southern
and Eastern Asia*, Papers of the Peabody Museum, no. 19 (1944), Harvard University.

particularly those who were aware of the Painted Pottery cultures in Western Asia, had noted a few similar decorative motifs in the painted ware of North China and that of western Asia, and it was considered without question by these scholars that the Yang-shao culture was an eastern offshoot of the Neolithic cultures of the West.

Against this historical background, the importance attached to and the interpretations given to the so-called Lung-shan, or Black Pottery, culture, identified in 1928 with the discovery of its type site, Ch'eng-tzu-yai, near Lung-shan Chen, Li-ch'eng Hsien, Shantung, can be understood. At this site, a different, wheel-thrown ware prevailed, characterized by its black color, thin wall, and lustrous surface. Together with this ware were found the *hang-t'u* ("rammed earth") structure and scapulimancy that were characteristic of the Yin–Shang culture but were not at all found in the Yang-shao culture. The two cultures were known to have different spheres of geographic distribution. Thus the "two-culture" theory gradually became generally accepted; if the Yang-shao culture was to be identified with the Hsia, then why should not the Lung-shan culture be identified with the Eastern I, known in historical literature to have been in the lower Huang Ho and along the Pacific seaboard? If the Yang-shao culture was derived from western Asia, then the Lung-shan culture, in which many Yin–Shang elements were found, could be indigenously Chinese. In 1931, the Hou-kang stratigraphy afforded the first real key to the formative cultural sequence of North China (see p. 148). However, because the two-culture theory fit what was then the understanding of ancient Chinese culture too well to be discarded, and because Andersson reported remains of both cultures, in western Honan, to be from the same stratigraphical position, the real significance of the Hou-kang stratigraphy was not fully realized until many years later. What Andersson said about this in 1943 may well sum up the majority opinion during the thirties:

> Owing to the Hou Kang section it has been held probable that Yang Shao is the older and Lung Shan the younger of the two. But the occurrence of black pottery with the painted ware at Yang Shao Ts'un, at Hsi Yin, at Sha Kuo T'un and some other sites, even in Kansu, raises the question whether it is not possible that the two are mainly synchronous in that painted and black ceramics occur together in the interior but the black pottery alone rules in the coastal provinces (Shantung and Chekiang?) and has there been given the name Lung Shan.[11]

11. Andersson, *BMFEA* 15 (1943), 292–93.

Further discussion in the present volume will, I believe, make clear the specific reasons that lie behind the insistence that Yang-shao and Lung-shan were two contemporary cultures of the Neolithic period in North China.

Elsewhere in China, Neolithic and Neolithic-like cultures were found and identified in Manchuria, Mongolia, Sinkiang, and South China. In the first two areas, Lin-hsi (1922), Pi-tzu-wo (1927), Ang-ang-hsi (1928–30), Yang-t'ou-wa (1933), and Ch'ih-feng (1935) were among the most important sites excavated during the period. A Microlithic culture was identified and formulated, and evidence of both Yang-shao and Lung-shan influences was brought to light. Their exact relationship was not yet clearly understood, however. From 1927 to 1934, Folke Bergman, of the Sino-Swedish expedition, located a series of prehistoric sites in Sinkiang, among which the Microlithic and the Painted Pottery culture sites drew most of the attention. In South China, the first stone implements were collected *in situ* from the lower Yangtze in 1930, and subsequently a Geometric Pottery culture was identified from many sites in the south-eastern part of China. Stone implements and pottery remains were collected extensively in the Red Basin by J. H. Edgar, D. S. Dye, D. C. Graham, and N. C. Nelson from the twenties onward, although the existence of prehistoric remains in this area had been known since 1886 when an Englishman, C. E. Baber, purchased two polished stone implements near Chungking. In the Hong Kong area and on the coast of Kwangtung, Neolithic stone implements and pottery were extensively collected during this period by C. M. Heanley, D. J. Finn, R. Maglioni, and W. Schofield. These investigations established the human occupation of South China from prehistoric times, but the time-space framework of prehistoric cultures and their relationships with North China and other adjacent regions in Southeast Asia were not at all clear.

Archaeology of the early historical civilizations of China probably made its most significant contribution during this period with the excavations of the Shang dynasty site near An-yang, from 1928 through 1937, under the auspices of the Archaeological Section of the Institute of History and Philology, Academia Sinica, and the able direction of Li Chi. Aside from the significance of the An-yang excavations for the study of early Chinese civilization, they were also important in the history of archaeology in that, during the ten years of excavations, many young archaeologists received their field training at this site, participating in one of the most complicated diggings ever undertaken in China. Most, if not all, senior Chinese archaeologists, such as Yin Ta, former director of the Institute of

Archaeology of the Academia Sinica, Hsia Nai, director of the same institute, and Shih Chang-ju and Kao Ch'ü-hsün, of the Academia Sinica in Taipei, received their training in the field at An-yang. So did the late Wu Chin-ting (discoverer of the Ch'eng-tzu-yai site), Ch'i Yen-p'ei, Li Ching-tan, and Yin Huan-chang, who made important contributions to Chinese archaeology during their lifetimes. Some of these people, for example Hsia Nai and Wu Chin-ting, subsequently broadened their background in foreign institutions, but it is clear that their An-yang experience helped shape their professional careers.

Aside from An-yang, Shang-like remains were reported from Shantung and Anhwei, but otherwise no well-established Shang dynasty sites were known. Chou dynasty sites were excavated here and there, such as the Hsia-tu of Yen (1929); the Warring States burials in Chün Hsien (1932), Chi Hsien (1935), and Hui Hsien (1935) in Honan; the Ch'u tombs in Shou Hsien, Anhwei (1934), and Ch'ang-sha, Hunan; and the Kuang-han find of jade artifacts in Szechwan (1934). Stray finds of bronzes were reported from Yunnan and Szechwan, but no cultural contexts were identified.

What I have described so far are some of the most important discoveries, from the mid-twenties to the mid-thirties, of prehistoric and early historic remains in China. Archaeological materials obtained during this period indicate a Palaeolithic and Mesolithic occupation of scattered areas, two Neolithic cultures in North China, a third along the northern borders (the Microlithic), still another in the southeast (the Geometric), and Bronze Age civilizations in North China and scattered regions elsewhere. These findings tend to confirm and enrich the literary records of the Shang and the Chou dynasties. The theoretical trends during this period can be characterized as follows: first, there was an establishment of a scientific discipline of field archaeology; second, a tentative grouping of cultures for the whole of China and for the various periods in her cultural history was formed along with a tentative alignment of the relationships among these different cultural groups in space and in time. Archaeological stratigraphy became a generally established principle of chronology, and typological comparison was the basic tool for the reconstruction of cultural sequences. The ultimate aim of archaeology in reconstructing prehistoric culture and society was recognized in theory,[12] and in practice,

12. Li Chi et al., *Ch'eng-tzu-yai*, Kenneth Starr, trans., Yale University Publications in Anthropology, no. 52 (1956), p. 19. Li Chi, *Bull. College of Arts, Nat'l. Taiwan University* 1 (1950), 63–79.

topical studies were not lacking. Many were particularly valuable, such as Kuo Mo-jo's studies of ancient Chinese society according to oracle bone and bronze inscriptions, Bernhard Karlgren's treatises on the stylistic development of Yin and Chou bronzes, and some others.

During and immediately after World War II, very little fieldwork was done in China. The enforced pause, together with the extremely difficult working conditions for archaeologists—several of whom died or became disabled as a consequence—provided opportunity for a synthesis of past accomplishments and for the formation of programs for the future. Many comprehensive volumes on Chinese prehistory and early historic archaeology appeared, and at the Institute of History and Philology a complete report of the An-yang excavations and several other monographs on relatively minor diggings were completed or underway.

Fieldwork was resumed soon after the establishment of the communist regime in 1949, and during the following quarter century archaeology in all its phases of operation flourished in China as never before. With a few notable exceptions—Chou-k'ou-tien and An-yang, among others—the bulk of the most important archaeological material for the ancient period has been uncovered during this interval, as is clear from a scrutiny of the footnotes of this book.[13] The Great Leap Forward of Chinese archaeology may be accounted for by several factors. Above all, the past twenty-seven years have witnessed a political stability in the country unparalleled since before the Opium War of 1839–42, and her industrialization has been unprecedented. "During the past ten years," said Hsia Nai in 1959, "in the course of economic construction, . . . sites of ancient dwellings and burials, where many important artifacts were found, have been discovered in many places. Archaeological advances have been brought about as a consequence."[14] Edgar Snow wrote in 1961 that "earth removals for construction of 180,000 miles of new roads, 12,000 miles of new railways, foundations for countless new buildings, reservoirs and thousands of local dams, canals and irrigation works, did incidental spade work for archaeologists, anthropologists, and general sinologists which would have required vast outlays and might not have been undertaken for years."[15] A notable example of archaeological discovery in the process of industrial construction is the large series of highly important Neolithic and Chou sites

13. A summary of the archaeological work from 1950 to 1960, with a useful bibliography, appears in *Hsin Chung-kuo ti k'ao-ku shou-huo*, Peking, Wen Wu Press, 1962. For brief accounts of new findings, see Hsia Nai, *KK* 1964 (10), 485–97; 1972 (1), 29–42.

14. *KK* 1959 (10), 505.

15. *Red China Today*, Random House (Vintage Books), 1971, p. 219.

found in and near the San-men Gorge region of the Huang Ho (Yellow River) in southwestern Shansi and northwestern Honan, the area of the much-heralded Sanmen Dam project.

Ideology, too, plays a significant part in the archaeological upsurge in China. As Gustorm Gjessing has pointed out, archaeology is often used in communist countries as a weapon for promoting solidarity of their peoples.[16] When a communist regime is also nationalistic, in a country whose people are proud of their ancient heritage, conscious of history, and possessed of an antiquarian tradition, archaeology cannot help but boom. Many important sites have been found by farmers, who are known to be in the habit of promptly reporting the finds to the proper authorities. A team of experts is soon dispatched, sometimes from a great distance, to investigate. The experts are organized in a nationwide hierarchy. At Peking, under the Chinese Academy of Sciences (Chung-kuo K'o-hsüeh Yüan), two national research institutes have been established for archaeological study—the Institute of Archaeology (K'ao-ku Yen-chiu Suo) and the Institute of Vertebrate Palaeontology and Palaeoanthropology (Ku Chi-chui Tung-wu yü Ku Jen-lei Yen-chiu Suo). Also concerned with archaeology is the National Cultural Relics Administration (Kuo-chia Wen-wu Shih-yeh Kuan-li Chü), which presides over the nation's thousands of museums. In many parts of the country and in each province and major city there is a Commission for the Preservation of Cultural Objects (Wen Wu Kuan-li Wei-yüan-hui) or a Bureau of Culture (Wen-hua Chü) or a museum or all three. Many of these institutions have field personnel, often organized into teams or task forces to tackle chance discoveries or to engage in planned excavations. The two institutes also have a number of field stations in the provinces. Many major local institutions have their own publications, but most of the important reports are published in Peking. Short reports are published in four major journals—K'ao-ku hsüeh pao (semiannual), K'ao-ku (bimonthly), Wen-wu (monthly), and Vertebrata Palasiatica (quarterly)—and long monographs are published in separate volumes (often in numbered series) by the Science Press and the Wen Wu (Cultural Objects) Press in Peking.

As these publications show, Chinese archaeology in the past twenty-seven years has undergone considerable progress in planning of fieldwork and in technical and theoretical sophistication. Three stages of development can be distinguished. During the 1950s, most of the field operations undertaken were salvage projects, and planned excavations were a rarity.

16. American Anthropological Association, Memoir no. 94 (1963), pp. 261–67.

One notices a substantial change, an improvement, in the quality of the archaeological work undertaken during the 1960s. In an important article on retrospect and prospect in Neolithic archaeology, written in 1963 by Yin Ta, then Director of the Institute of Archaeology, the "scientific" requirements of archaeology are greatly emphasized. In order to effectively advance Neolithic research, Yin Ta states, the archaeologist must carry out his work in three separate and successive stages:

> Scientific archaeological excavation and the preparation and public-ation of the excavation report are the most elemental task and the first important link of the whole process. The primary function of this step is to scientifically describe, in a total and systematic manner, the phenomena at single sites. Comparative and synthetic studies are a further step in depth on the basis of the scientifically excavated data, another indispensable step of archaeological research. At this stage one analyzes from a theoretical level the complex phenomena reflected by the archaeological data, and one seeks to solve scholarly and theoretical problems. For both of these stages of work, an archae-ological terminology is employed. The third stage can be reached only after the basic solutions to problems that exist in archaeology have been obtained, a stage of the study of the clan institutions on the scientific basis laid down in the two previous stages. At this point one must do everything possible to translate the archaeological terminol-ogy into a language customary in the historical social life—providing an atmosphere of humanity, life, and society—and to reconstruct material for whole and lively social histories from the fragmentary remains and relics.[17]

The first two steps are, according to Yin Ta, the basis of archaeological work; in this article he also discusses several important topics in scientific archaeological excavation and synthesis, stressing problems in the use of relative and absolute chronological methods, the reconstruction of whole societies and cultures, care in the use of archaeological terms, and the inter-disciplinary approach. This is by no means an archaeological manifesto of method and theory, but it does indicate a serious awareness of theory and methodological sophistication. This is further and more concretely shown by the publication in the 1960s of a number of major excavation reports, such as those of the sites in Pan-p'o-ts'un, Sian,[18] and on the west bank

17. Yin Ta, *KK* 1963 (11), 582.
18. *Hsi-an Pan-p'o*, Peking, Wen Wu Press, 1963.

2. Pan-p'o Museum, Sian, Shensi. A part of the Neolithic Pan-p'o-ts'un village of the Yang-shao culture (p. 100) left intact as of the final stage of excavation and covered by a permanent roof. This is an example of the many expensive efforts to preserve archaeological relics for the purpose of public education. (Photograph by Harold E. Malde, 1975.)

of the river Fen near Sian,[19] and the proceedings of the scientific papers delivered at a 1964 interdisciplinary conference on Cenozoic geology and palaeobiology and Palaeolithic archaeology in the area of Lan-t'ien.[20] There is no question that these publications, and the field and laboratory work they represent, qualify by any international standard for scholarly excellence.

The Great Proletarian Cultural Revolution, officially launched in the summer of 1966, marked the beginning of a new stage of Chinese archaeology. All archaeological works ceased to be published in mid-1966, and they were not resumed until early 1972. During the Cultural Revolution, the "Four Olds"—Old Thought, Old Culture, Old Customs, and Old Habits—were singled out to be destroyed, which may have led to the speculation as well as rumor reported in the foreign press that archaeological

19. *Feng hsi fa-chüeh Pao-kao*, Peking, Wen Wu Press, 1962.

20. *Shensi Lan-t'ien Hsin-sheng-chieh hsien-ch'ang hui-i lun-wen chi*, Peking, Science Press, 1966.

monuments were being vandalized and damaged by the Red Guards on a nationwide scale.[21] It is not possible for me as an outsider to know for sure what actually happened. But travelers in China in the 1970s have seen many of the previously known important archaeological monuments and could detect no evidence of any damage whatever (fig. 2). Furthermore, we are told that during the period of 1966–71 important archaeological work not only did not cease, it flourished more than ever, leading to many important discoveries.[22] Two archaeological exhibitions were put on the road in 1974 and 1975, one through Europe and North America and the other to Japan and Mexico, consisting entirely of art and archaeological pieces found during the Cultural Revolution period, as if to show the world that the Cultural Revolution was archaeology's blessing, not its foe.

But the archaeological life surely did not go on as usual. The Cultural Revolution apparently resulted in some fundamental changes in all spheres of Chinese society, including Chinese science and education. Article 12 of the Constitution of the People's Republic of China, adopted in January 1975, by the Fourth National People's Congress, states that "the proletariat must exercise all-around dictatorship over the bourgeoisie in the superstructure, including all spheres of culture. Culture and education, literature and art, physical education, health work, and scientific research work must all serve proletariat politics, serve the workers, peasants, and soldiers, and be combined with productive labor." Judging from the archaeological publications that have become available since early 1972, one gets the unmistakable impression that in archaeological writing a genuine effort is being made to make archaeology a part of the "scientific research work" that serves proletariat politics. The professionalism of archaeological writings of the 1960s is now replaced by a much closer, interweaving relationship of archaeology and politics (fig. 3). Data are faithfully recorded and described, to be sure, but invariably they are related to politically relevant themes (such as class struggles in history, Chinese culture in the northern border provinces' early in history, the Legalist-Confucian struggle, and so forth). There is no question that the past serves the present more now than before. This use of the past through archaeology is unprecedented in the history of archaeology, and it is the more noteworthy because of the Chinese civilization's great weight. Archaeologists every-

21. S. Pan and R. J. de Jaegher, *Peking's Red Guards*, New York, Twin Circle, 1968, p. 34.

22. *KK* 1972 (1), 29–42.

3. Chariot burials, Chang-chia-p'o, Sian, Shensi. The slogan on the wall ("Carry to the end the Criticize Confucius, Criticize Lin Piao struggle") is related to the burials because Confucius called for a "return to the rites," namely, a return to the institutions under which the chariots and their drivers (arrow) were buried in sacrifice. (Photo by author, 1975.)

where should watch the developments in China in the 1970s with great interest.

Outside the People's Republic of China, a wide diversity of work synthesizing the archaeology of ancient China has appeared. In Taiwan, under the leadership of the venerable Li Chi, scholars of the Academia Sinica and other institutions have embarked upon an ambitious project to compile a history of ancient China, using archaeological as well as literary data, and individual chapters of the book have begun to appear in draft form.[23] Many books on Chinese prehistoric and early historical archaeology have also appeared in English.[24] One might have assumed that, since these are for the most part written by impartial observers, these syntheses would be quite objective and their conclusions would essentially converge; but comparison of these works and their differences from my own and from one another will show that nothing could be farther from the truth.

This divergence of views, however, is no reason for sorrow, because

23. E.g., *Chung-kuo shang-ku shih*, vol. 1, *Shih ch'ien shih*, 1972.
24. See Recommendations for Further Reading, this volume.

competitive theories are a prerequisite for the eventual fruition of the archaeological synthesis of ancient China and also, more significantly, because the different points of view are the results of a number of necessarily different approaches to the same subject matter and the same corpus of data. Some of these recent works aim at summarizing the data without ambitious attempts at interpretation, thus providing invaluable material for study. Others stress the basic unity of human history as a whole and the pool of knowledge shared by the early segments of Chinese and Western cultural histories. Still others describe artifacts and their significance to the history of Chinese art and technology.

What has convinced me that a volume like the present one is worth writing, even in this recently prolific field of ancient Chinese archaeology, is the fact that still another approach, one that has proved capable of bringing about fruitful results elsewhere in the world, has yet to be applied to the Chinese data. By this I mean the method of developmental classification which has been used with considerable success by V. Gordon Childe and Robert J. Braidwood for the Near East, and also by Gordon R. Willey and Philip Phillips for the New World.[25] This volume does not intend to adopt a monolithic point of view in methodology, and the historical framework it tries to set up is intended to be a balanced one. The reader, however, will not fail to notice that the developmental approach is emphasized somewhat at the expense of all others. I do this with deliberation, believing that in the field of Chinese archaeology there have been sufficient hypotheses on the problems of art and origins, and enough descriptive analyses of artifacts, whereas the process of cultural and social growth remains to be discussed in a general theoretical fashion.

In the following chapters the archaeological data of ancient China will be interpreted, processed, and arranged with such a perspective in view. Chronological sequences and cultural groups will be formulated for the total area of China and its various regions, and questions will be asked, and answers sought, as to how such sequences and groupings came about, and why such distinctive historical developments occurred in this part of the world. To put this another way: How did civilization arise in China,

25. V. Gordon Childe, *What Happened in History*, New York, Penguin Books, 1942; *New Light on the Most Ancient East*, New York, Praeger, 1953. Robert J. Braidwood and Linda Braidwood, *Cahiers d'histoire mondiale* 1 (1953), 278–310. R. J. Braidwood and Charles A. Reed, *Cold Spring Harbor Symposia on Quantitative Biology* 22 (1957), 19–31. Gordon R. Willey and Philip Phillips, *Method and Theory in American Archaeology*, University of Chicago Press, 1958. Julian H. Steward, *Theory of Culture Change*, Urbana, University of Illinois Press, 1955.

and what course of development did it take? To describe is inevitably to interpret, and an interpretation complete in all aspects of this development is not intended. If, for instance, I seem to have treated the Palaeolithic period in an unceremonious and summary manner, it is because I believe this period is irrelevant to the particular direction and development of Chinese civilization except for providing a general foundation of basic cultures and populations. If I seem to have underplayed at times the role of external influences in shaping the events and the courses of cultural development in ancient China, it is because such influences have been more than adequately dealt with by previous authors. I wish, instead, to stress the growth process of civilization itself and its formative antecedents which, above all, must be accounted for by what took place *in situ*.

In this respect, I find myself in complete agreement with Cheng Te-k'un that "as long as plain archaeological facts are not properly established in their native contexts, any comparison with distant parallels tends to be farfetched," [26] and with Li Chi that "before we accept this [that the birth of all great civilizations is due to cultural contact] as true of any particular civilization, no effort should be spared to collect all available data in order to examine in detail the process of actual growth." [27] It is precisely around this process of actual growth of the Chinese civilization in its native contexts that the present study is centered.

26. *Archaeology in China*, vol. 1, *Prehistoric China*, Cambridge, Heffer & Sons, 1959, p. xix.

27. *The Beginnings of Chinese Civilization*, p. 17.

1 : *The Environmental Setting and Time Scale*

Geographic Subdivisions of China

In discussing the early history of man in China, we must constantly bear in mind that the area known as China is continental in dimensions (ca. 3,705,400 square miles, as against Europe's 4,100,000 and the United States's 3,615,000). This area contains a great variety of topography, climate, and vegetation, ranging from tropical jungles in the southwest to subarctic taiga in Manchuria; from the vast Tibetan plateaus to river-dissected hills of the southeast; and from the deserts and steppes of Chinese Turkestan to the temperate alluvial plains of the lower Huang Ho (Yellow River) valley. In most of these widely differing geographical regions man's progress has been traced in some detail, indicating invariably that human life in each area adapted to its peculiar ecological circumstances.

Largely speaking, the subdivision of China into a northern part and a southern part has been a significant demarcation throughout the whole period of man's occupation. Further, in view of the special importance of the Huang Ho valley in the early cultural history of China, North China can itself be divided in two. Thus, for the purposes of this volume, three ecological zones of the first magnitude are distinguished: the Huang Ho valley, the southern deciduous zone, and the northern forests and steppes.

The landscape of China is dominated by mountains and hills which, in prehistoric times, were presumably covered with thick woods and jungles.[1] The activities of the prehistoric inhabitants, therefore, were mostly restricted to the large and small river valleys. Furthermore, most of the great rivers lie horizontally, on a west-east axis, and flow into the Pacific Ocean. This results in a happy coincidence in that the great river valleys of concern to us seldom run through different major climatic and vegetational zones and hence can serve as a basis for a cultural as well as a geographical subdivision of China (fig. 4).

1. G. B. Cressey, *China's Geographic Foundations*, 2nd ed., New York, McGraw-Hill, 1934, p. 37.

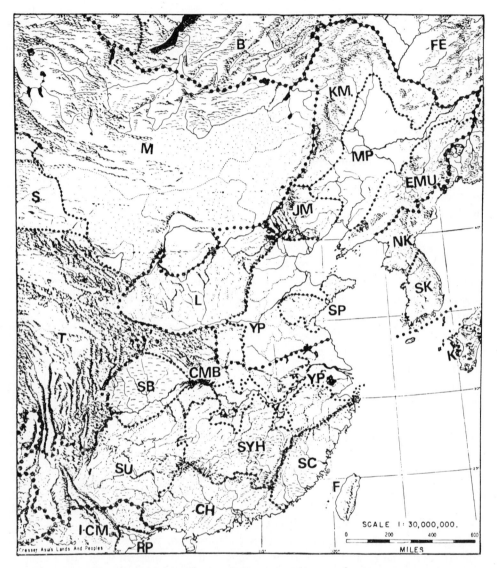

4. The geographic regions and landforms of China, divisible into three broad ecological zones. (1) The Huang Ho valley: L (loessland) YP (Yellow Plain), and SP (Shantung Peninsula). (2) The northern forests and steppes: MP (Manchurian plain), KM (Khingan Mountains), JM (Jehol Mountains), EMU (eastern Manchurian uplands), M (Mongolia), and S (Sinkiang). (3) The southern deciduous zone—YP (Yangtze plain), SB (Szechwan basin), CMB (central mountain belt), SYH (southern Yangtze hills), SC (southeast coast), CH (Canton hinterland), and SU (southwest uplands). (Base map by Erwin Raisz, courtesy Harvard-Yenching Institute. Adapted by Rowland Illick in George Cressey's *Asia's Lands and Peoples*, 2d ed., New York, McGraw-Hill, 1951.)

Table 1

Geographic Contrasts between North and South China

North	South
Limited, uncertain rainfall, 400–800 mm	Abundant rainfall, 800–1,600 mm
Cold winters, hot summers, a little snow	Cold winters, hot, moist summers; snow and ice uncommon
Semiarid climate	Subtropical climate, summer monsoon rains, and typhoons
Unleached calcareous soils	Leached noncalcareous soils
Kaoliang, millet, wheat, beans	Rice the dominant crop
4 to 6 months growing season, one or two crops	Nine months to a year growing season; two or three crops
Mixed deciduous forests and grasslands	Subtropical and tropical forests
Brown and dustblown during the winter	Green landscape at all seasons

The Huang Ho valley. This region includes the drainage of the Huang Ho and its tributaries, together with the upper courses of a few tributaries of the Yangtze River and several small independent drainage systems in the Hopei plain. The topography of the Huang Ho valley is further divisible into three more or less distinct regions: the loess highlands in the west, the alluvial plains in the east, and the Shantung Peninsula along the seacoast. Generally these are all in the temperate climatic zone, with warm summers and cold winters and with moderate (400–800 millimeters) rainfall. The vegetational cover of the entire area can be characterized as mixed deciduous-coniferous forests, though part of the area is now entirely deforested and part of it has become semiarid.[2]

The southern deciduous zone. The boundary between the Huang Ho valley and the southern deciduous zone lies midway between the Yangtze and the Huang Ho, near the thirty-third parallel. In the west, the line corresponds with the crest of the Ch'in Ling Mountains; farther east it follows the Huai River.[3] This division between the north and the south is clearly marked by climate, natural vegetation, soil, and crops, as shown in table 1.[4]

2. James Thorp, *Geography of the Soils of China*, Nanking, National Geological Survey, 1936. G. B. Cressey, *Asia's Lands and Peoples*, New York, McGraw-Hill, 1951.

3. Cressey, *Asia's Lands and Peoples*, p. 99.

4. Simplified after Cressey, *China's Geographic Foundations*, p. 15.

South China has a network of large and small river systems. These include the Yangtze, the Huai, the Pearl, and several smaller but independent drainages in the southwest and along the southeastern coast. Topographically, South China is divisible into three major regions: the hills, which cover most of the area and are drained by all the river systems mentioned above except the Huai; the Red Basin of Szechwan, drained by the upper Yangtze and its several tributaries; and the Yangtze-Huai plain, drained by the lower Yangtze and the Huai. There are two principal lacustrine areas in South China—one among the hills in the middle Yangtze consisting of the remnants of the ancient lake Yün-meng and including such major lakes as Tung-t'ing (Hupei) and Po-yang (Kiangsi), and another situated on the lower Yangtze-Huai plain, which includes such major lakes as Hung-tse and T'ai.

The northern forests and steppes. The area immediately north of the Huang Ho valley consists of the modern regions of Inner Mongolia and the Northeast (known in the West as Manchuria). Topographically this area may be compared to a horseshoe, opening to the south. The space at the center is the erosion plain of Manchuria, drained by the lower courses of the Liao River and by the Sungari, and originally covered with mixed deciduous-coniferous forests. The eastern branch of the horseshoe is formed by the eastern Manchurian uplands, and is drained by the T'umen and Yalu rivers and the lower Amur. The western branch is formed by the Khingan and the Jehol mountains and is drained by the upper courses of the Amur, the tributaries of the Sungari, and the upper Liao. These mountainous areas are covered with coniferous forests or parklands in the east and north, and steppes in the west. The latter extend westward into Mongolia and Sinkiang. Climatically, this entire area is extremely seasonal and continental, with long, severe winters and short, warm summers.

China of the Pleistocene Period

The geographic features of China as we see them today characterize only the geological present; some of them have been around for millions of years, but most are transitory. During the past two or three million years —the period geologically and palaeontologically known as the Pleistocene or Quaternary, when the human animal lived here and left the remains of his activities—China's landscape, vegetation, and climate have undergone demonstrable changes—minor or drastic—some cyclical and repetitive, others unique and passing. The study of such changes is properly the job of natural scientists, but students of early China must acquaint themselves with the results. To understand the life of the early Chinese

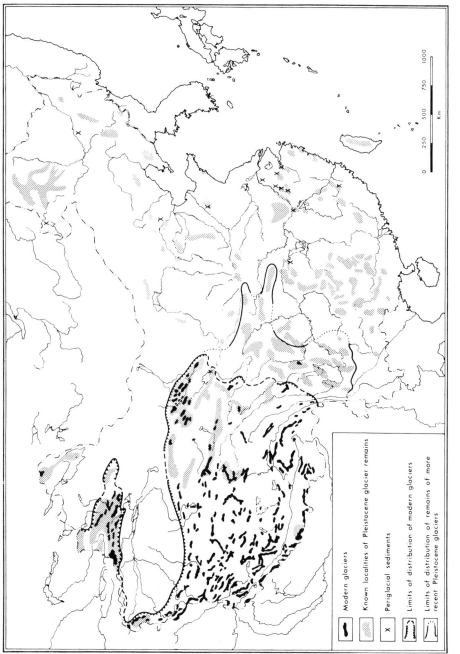

Legend:

Modern glaciers

Known localities of Pleistocene glacier remains

Periglacial sediments

Limits of distribution of modern glaciers

Limits of distribution of remains of more recent Pleistocene glaciers

0 250 500 750 1000
Km

5. Glacial and periglacial remains in China. (After *Ti-ssu-chi ti-chih wen-t'i*, Peking, Science Press, 1964, fig. 10.)

inhabitants, we must have at least a general idea about their environmental surroundings, which to varying extents and in various aspects differed from one epoch to the next. Moreover, macroenvironmental changes provide a convenient and practical time scale for the relative placement of the archaeological data: what came before or after, and what was contemporaneous with what else. The chronological sequences and contemporaneity thus arrived at are in most cases only approximate unless absolute dates like carbon-14 determinations are available, but these rough estimates are largely adequate for much of human history because, for the most part, it has changed slowly and in broadly defined steps.

The Pleistocene period, the last and the shortest of the geological epochs since the formation of our planet, and the interval characterized by the emergence and development of modern man and his nearest ancestors, is known to be a period in which a large series of interrelated upheavals in nature took place—tectonic movements, cyclical alternations of vastly contrasting climatic conditions, changes in the state and amount of water on land with resultant erosion and sedimentation cycles, and the movements and evolution of animal and plant groups adapting to shifting climatic settings, to mention only the most prominent. Evidence for such changes and movements makes it possible to characterize the Pleistocene events of various regions and to tie them together. The sequence that results can then serve as a time scale for generalizing the history of the period and dating assemblages of remains found at various localities.

In China such evidence is extensive. The most direct consists of glacial and periglacial sediments and deposits. J. S. Lee was the first to recognize such remains at Lu-shan, in Kiangsi, and to distinguish three glaciations: Poyang, Taku, and Lushan.[5] Another later glaciation, Tali, was recognized by H. von Wissmann in Yunnan.[6] During the last thirty years similar remains have been identified throughout the country (fig. 5), and the four glacial and three interglacial periods are widely accepted. The four glaciations may possibly be correlated with the four glaciations of the Himalayas[7] and the Alps sequence from Günz to Würm.

5. "Quaternary glaciation in the Yangtze valley," *GSoC Bull.* 13 (1933), 2–15. *Lu-Shan during the Ice Age*, Institute of Geology, Academia Sinica, Monographs, ser. B, no. 2 (1937). *Chung-kuo Ti-ssu-chi ping-ch'uan*, Peking, Science Press, 1975.

6. "The Pleistocene glaciation in China," *GSoC Bull.* 17 (1937), 145–68. "Die quartäre Vergletscherung in China," *Ztschr. Gessell. Erd Berlin* (1937), 241–62.

7. H. de Terra and T. T. Paterson, *Studies on the Ice Age in India and Associated Human Cultures*, Carnegie Institution of Washington Publication no. 493 (1939). For a new study of the Quaternary climatic changes in the Himalayas near Mount Jolmo Lungma (Everest), see *Scientia Geologica Sinica* 1974 (1), 59–78. A new attempt to correlate glaciations in various parts of China is published in *Acta Geologica Sinica* 1973 (1), 94–101.

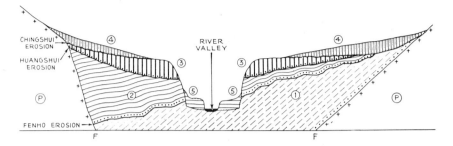

6. The structure of a late Cenozoic basin in North China. F = fault; P = Palaeozoic rocks.
(1) Pliocene deposits; (2) lower Sanmenian beds, lower Pleistocene; (3) Choukoutienian
red loam and basal gravel, middle Pleistocene; (4) Malan loess and associated deposits,
upper Pleistocene; (5) Panchiao alluvium. (From H. L. Movius, Jr., *Trans. Amer. Philos.
Soc.*, n.s., vol. 38, 1949, p. 344.)

Closely related to the glacial and interglacial intervals are the sedimentary
and erosional cycles recognizable in the Pleistocene formations throughout
China in river terraces and cave-fissure deposits (fig. 6). Animal and plant
(especially pollen) fossils from these formations are particularly useful for
chronological purposes, for, adaptive to climatic conditions, animal and
plant life often underwent appreciable change in severe cold conditions
and is thus indicative of broad levels of time to which the formations
belonged. According to the most recent studies of this evidence,[8] the
Chinese Pleistocene is subdivided into early, middle, and late.

8. *Ti-ssu-chi ti-chih wen-t'i* [Quaternary Geology Problems], ed. by the Institute of
Geology, Academia Sinica, Peking, 1964. *Shensi Lan-t'ien Hsin-sheng-chieh* [Cenozoic in
Lan-t'ien, Shensi], ed. by the Institute of Vertebrate Palaeontology and Palaeoanthro-
pology, Academia Sinica, Peking, 1966. P. Teilhard de Chardin, *Early Man in China*,
Peking, Institut de Géo-Biologie, Publication 7 (1941). Hallam L. Movius, Jr., *Early Man
and Pleistocene Stratigraphy in Southern and Eastern Asia*, Papers of the Peabody Museum,
Harvard University, vol. 19 (1944).
    In her doctoral dissertation, *The Archaeology of Pleistocene China* (1969, University of
Wisconsin), portions of which have since been published ("Relative dating of North
Chinese faunal and cultural complexes," *Arctic Anthropology* 9 [1972], 36–79), Jean Aigner
has made an attempt to collate available data on fauna and on palynology from Pleistocene
China and to use comparisons with current European sequences to provide "a more
refined relative dating of traditional Chinese geological sections and faunas, and of palaeontological and archaeological stations and sites." I prefer to stick to the broader scheme
adopted here—characterized by Aigner as oversimplistic and old-fashioned—because a
China-wide synthesis of a more refined nature is not yet internally ripe. The broader
scheme suffices for my purposes, and I distrust any forced imposition, on Chinese data,
of a European model in geology and palaeobiology as much as in archaeology. But
Aigner's works, along with the original Chinese technical reports, should be consulted
by those needing more technical details.

Early Pleistocene

Early Pleistocene formations lie directly above the late Pliocene Pao-tê (Pontian) beds in marked disconformity, indicating a tectonic uprising movement known as the Fenho erosion. Such formations are represented by the Ni-ho-wan or Lower Sanmenian riverine-lacustrine sediments found throughout North China, the red and grayish-green calcareous clays in scattered areas of North China, the Wuch'eng loess of the middle Huang Ho, and isolated occurrences of gravels and conglomerates in both North and South China. Associated with these sediments are mammalian fossils of the Ni-ho-wan fauna of the north (*Bison, Equus sanmeniensis, Archidiskodon planifrons, Paracamelus, Proboscihipparion* and *Postschizotherium*) and the Liu-ch'eng fauna of the south (*Trilophodon serridenstoides, Stegodon praeorientalis, Equus yunnanensis, Bubalus, Elephas* cf. *namadicus,* and *Gigantopithecus blacki*).

The early Pleistocene stage can be subdivided into two substages according to climatic changes marked in its sediments. An early substage is characterized by the lowered temperature and the advances of glaciers and ice sheets in the highlands and plateaus, and this corresponds to the Poyang glacial advance of J. S. Lee. Fossil pollens of poplar (*Populus bifolia, P. euphratica*) have been identified from sediments of this level in Shansi and Sinkiang. In some areas not covered by ice, moist pluvial conditions apparently prevailed, resulting in the riverine-lacustrine and conglomerate formations mentioned above. Corresponding retreats of seawater produced land bridges between continental Asia and Japan, and between Taiwan and many South Sea islands.

A late substage of the early Pleistocene is marked by interglacial conditions, an increase in temperature, and general aridity. The warming trend is well indicated by laterization of the red clay sediments, the deposition of warm-type coral limestone and foraminiferous fossils, and the occurrence of warm-temperature and subtropical fossil pollen species in central and North China. In terms of the Lushan glacial sequence, this warm interval corresponds to the Poyang-Taku interglacial.

Middle Pleistocene

The most violent tectonic upheaval of the Quaternary in China took place at the end of the early Pleistocene; the Huangshui erosion produced a major disconformity between the early Pleistocene and younger beds. A major sedimentary cycle (Chou-k'ou-tien), resulting from the uprising of the earth crust and growing aridity, came about in the form of clay and gravel deposits—gravels in the mountainous areas of the northwest, laterized gravels in the Yangtze Valley, the Lishih loess of the middle Huang Ho, and the reddish clay deposits in limestone caves and fissures. In association with these reddish clay, loessic, and gravelly sediments are the Choukoutien fauna of North China (*Hyaena sinensis, Machairodus inexpectatus, M. ultima, Dicerorhinus mercki, Equus sanmeniensis, Eurycerus pachyosteus,* and *Homo erectus pekinensis*) and the Wan Hsien fauna of South China (*Ailuropoda, Megatapirus, Stegodon orientalis, Pongo*).

Again two substages can be distinguished within the middle Pleistocene according to climatic data. The first is characterized by the most extensive glaciation known in the Chinese Pleistocene—Taku glacial. Outside the highlands the interval is indicated by sediments of a cold and moist climate. This was followed by an extended stage of interglacial climatic conditions during which lateritic reddish clay was deposited in areas as far north as 43° latitude. Pollen analysis of the sediments from which early forms of man were found (at Chou-k'ou-tien and Ch'en-chia-wo) shows a prevalence of warm, dry climatic elements suited to the Taku-Lushan interglacial interval.

Late Pleistocene

Toward the end of the long Choukoutienian sedimentation cycle, represented by Locality 15 and the upper strata of locality 1 of Chou-k'ou-tien, the warm, dry interval apparently came to a gradual end, and glacial conditions once again prevailed. Pollen analysis of a locality 1 sediment sample yielded results indicating a cold, moist climate,[9] and animal fossils began to include upper Pleistocene varieties. This period probably corresponds to J. S. Lee's Lushan glacial.[10] At the end of this sedimentary cycle a series of new tectonic movements cut into the flat surfaces of the Lishih loess and resulted in the disconformity between the Lishih loess below and the Malan loess above. This is the interval of Chingshui erosion, during which the 20- to 50-meter river terraces of North China were formed. Pollen profiles at two localities in the Lan-t'ien area of central-eastern Shensi in sediments of late-Pleistocene date indicate a cold, moist climate near the bottom and a warming, drying trend toward the top, very likely

9. B. Kurtén, *VP* 3 (1959), 173–75.

10. In a recent synthesis of Pleistocene geology of China (*Ti-ssu-chi ti-chih wen-t'i,* 1964), middle Pleistocene is considered to end with the termination of the Chou-k'ou-tien sedimentation, and the Chingshui erosion is made to correspond to the Lushan glacial. This division is not adopted here, and for now I continue to use the older system of subdivision.

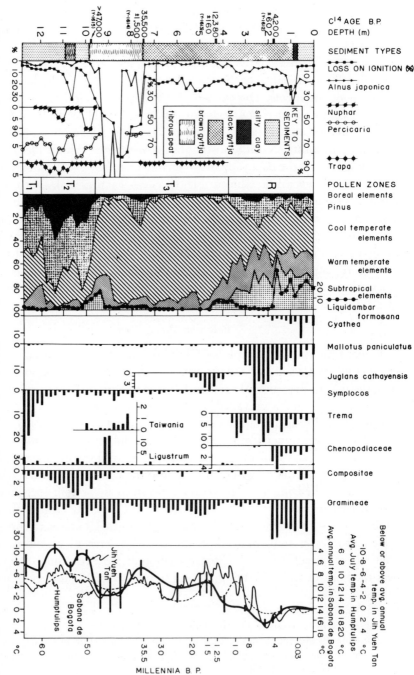

7. Pollen diagram for a 12.79 m core from Jih T'an (745.5 m), central Taiwan, showing sediment types in relation to loss on ignition, and pollen curves of *Alnus*, water plants, climatically grouped elements, and other selected species. *Right*, temperature curves from the present site, from Sabana de Bogota, Colombia, and from Humptulips, Washington, with a uniform scale for time as well as temperature, as far as the data permit. (From Matsuo Tsukada, *Proc. Nat'l. Acad. Sci.* 55, 1966, p. 544.) In the column "Pollen Zones," R = Recent, T = Tali glacial.

coinciding with the change from the uppermost reddish clay deposits to the Chingshui erosion interval and suggesting an interglacial climate befitting the Lushan-Tali interval.[11]

The rest of the late Pleistocene stage witnessed the extensive deposition of aeolian loess on top of the Chingshui erosion beds, resulting in the Malan loess of the middle Huang Ho. Contemporary with the Malan loess are the sediments deposited at the same time but under different glacial conditions, such as the riverine-lacustrine sediments of the Ordos region. In association with these sediments are the Sjara-osso fauna of North China (*Crocuta crocuta, Coelodonta antiquitatis, Megaloceros ordosianus, Spirocerus*), and the Tzuyang fauna of South China (*Ailuropoda, Homo sapiens, Mamuthus*). Both the woolly rhinoceros of the north and the mammoth of the south indicate a cold, moist climate, and pollen analysis of a number of Malan loess localities shows conclusively that a cold vegetation prevailed, reflecting an annual temperature probably 8°C lower than it is at present, a conclusion confirmed by the palynological analysis of a core of sediments taken from Lake Jih-yüeh-t'an of Taiwan[12] (fig. 7).

Concluding the descriptions given above we can say that from geological and palaeontological evidence it is clear that the Chinese Pleistocene is marked by a series of climatic oscillations accompanied by changes in landform and animal and plant life; that four major cold-moist intervals are shown, probably correlatable with the four glacial advances of the highland areas; and that these oscillations and changes provide a practical time scale for dating human fossils and the Palaeolithic industries found in Pleistocene sediments. Table 2 gives a convenient summary of the time scale.

Climate in the Early Postglacial Period

With the retreat of the ice sheets and glaciers in the Himalayas and on other highlands at the end of the stage of the Malan loess, the Recent (Holocene) geological period came to eastern Asia. Many of the Pleistocene faunal forms became extinct, such as the mammoth and the woolly

11. This has been confirmed by more recent palaeontological work in Lan-t'ien; see Chi Hung-hsiang, *VP* 12 (1974), 226.

12. Matsuo Tsukada, "Late Pleistocene vegetation and climate in Taiwan (Formosa)," *Proc. Nat. Acad. Sci.* 55 (1966), 543–48; "Vegetation in subtropical Formosa during the Pleistocene glaciations and the Holocene," *Palaeogeography, Palaeoclimatology, Palaeoecology* 3 (1967), 49–64.

Table 2

Subdivisions of the Chinese Pleistocene

Stages	Glaciated Areas	Unglaciated Areas	Tectonic and Sedimentary Cycles	Pollen	Fauna
Late	Tali Glacial	Pluvial	Malan Loess — Riverine-Lacustrine Deposits	Cold	Tzu yang / Sjara-osso
	Lushan–Tali Interglacial	Interpluvial	Chingshui Erosion	Warm	
	Lushan Glacial	Pluvial	Lishih Loess	Cold	
Middle	Taku–Lushan Interglacial	Interpluvial	Chou-k'ou-tien Reddish Clay — Sedimentation	Warm	Wan Hsien / Chou-k'ou-tien
	Taku Glacial	Pluvial		Cold	
Early	Poyang–Taku Interglacial	Interpluvial	Huangshui Erosion / Wuch'eng Loess Red Clay	Warm	Liu ch'eng / Ni-ho-wan
	Poyang Glacial	Pluvial	Ni-ho-wan Beds / Fenho Erosion	Cold	

rhinoceros, while the modern faunal group, which began to appear during the upper Pleistocene period, came to dominate. There was probably a general rise in temperature and precipitation, together with an increase of vegetational cover, a gradual elevation of land, and a stage of erosion. These concurrent geological and palaeontological changes may have occurred in the different regions of eastern Asia with varying intensity and in different ways, but information from North and South China indicates that in these regions they were sufficiently intense to bring about widespread changes both in landscape and in the human cultures adapting to it.

The terminal Pleistocene period in North China, which was also the final phase of the Malan loess stage, was characterized by a generally cool climate. With the beginning of the postglacial stage there was probably a general uplift in the mean annual temperature of China, as indicated by the extinction of such "cool" fauna as the mammoth, the woolly rhinoceros, and *Bos primigenius*; the appearance of many southern species of modern fauna; the apparent thickening of vegetation and the increase of subtropical and warm-temperate species in a number of pollen profiles; and the erosion of landscape and the apparent abundance of water. During this warm, moist period Mesolithic and Neolithic cultures began and flourished throughout China. The relatively mild and moist climatic condition, however, began to deteriorate after the initial periods of the historic stage, until in the north the climate became cool and the landscape nearly barren, probably as a result of intensive and unrestricted deforestation and the gradual lowering of temperature.

With regard to erosion and the abundance of water during the early phases of the postglacial period, it is believed that beginning with the Holocene a new sedimentary cycle was initiated by the Panchiao erosion stage. According to Teilhard de Chardin:

> That a positive movement of the land is today still in process is confirmed by the fact that, since the deposition of the Malan loess, the last remnants of the Pliocene lakes have been largely desiccated in the interior: Sjara-osso-gol depression, Lower Fenho and Taiyüan basins, Sungari Basin, Djalai Nor (and a number of other nors in Mongolia).[13]

During the Late Pleistocene, the distribution and local facies of the modern deserts are fully recognizable. Yet their depressions are

13. Teilhard de Chardin, GSoC Bull. 16 (1936/37), 199–200.

abundantly filled with temporary lakes, not so temporary however that they could not feed at places a rich population of Mollusks. Heaps of *Lymnaea* and *Planorbis* occur in the high terraces along the "nors" of East Mongolia. . . . The continuation of this regime, or even a somewhat moister period, is necessary for explaining the distribution of human industry during Neolithic times. Since the Neolithic, an increasing aridity is positively indicated by a general extension of the sand dunes, a general reduction of the "nors," and a general deflation of the Late Pleistocene silts. The influence of human agency . . . seems to be, on the whole, insufficient for explaining the main phenomenon.[14]

These "nors" in Mongolia are now largely desiccated, but the windblown cultural remains in this region "occurred with such regularity in the various basins and hollows, large and small," as to suggest that their formation took place under climatic conditions decidedly different from those of the present day and when these basins were filled with water.[15] Similar climatic peaks during the early post-Pleistocene period are also indicated by peats at San-ho and Chi in the Hopei plains area, and by the high water levels near prehistoric sites in Honan,[16] as well as by the literary records of the existence of nors in Honan, Shansi, and Shensi in the western loesslands.[17]

The decline of the moist climatic conditions in North China was accompanied by the disappearance of a thick vegetational cover in areas that are now barren and semiarid, as indicated by a black-earth horizon at some localities in the north. At Lin-hsi (Liaoning), Sha-kang in Hsin-min Hsien (Liaoning), and Ang-ang-hsi in Heilungkiang, cultural deposits were found in a black-earth layer which lies beneath a yellowish, sandy layer of Recent formation and above the loess deposits of Pleistocene origin.[18]

14. *Ibid.*, p. 219.

15. N. C. Nelson, *Natural History* 26 (1926), 250. John Maringer, *Contribution to the Prehistory of Mongolia*, Stockholm, 1950, pp. 207–08.

16. J. G. Andersson, *Essays on the Cenozoic of Northern China*, GSuC, Mem., ser. A, no. 3, 1923; *BMFEA* 19 (1947), 20–21.

17. Andersson, *BMFEA* 15 (1943), 40–41. Meng Wen-t'ung, *Yü-kung* 1 (Peking, 1934), 14–15. Hu Hou-hsüan, *Chia-ku-hsüeh Shang-shih lun ts'ung*, 2 vols., Ch'i-lu University, 1944/45.

18. Liang Ssu-yung, *BIHP* 4 (1932), 5; *TYKKPK* 1 (1936), 9. Teilhard, *Mém. Soc. Géol. France*, n.s. 3 (1926), fasc. 3, 24. Wang Tseng-hsin, *KKTH* 1958 (1), 1.

This black-earth layer, marking the transition from the semiarid loess stage of the terminal Pleistocene to the semiarid condition of the present day, probably represents an ancient forest cover.[19] The existence of a thick forest in the river basins of North China and on the Manchurian plains is further indicated by such cultural remains from prehistoric sites as an abundance of charcoal and woodworking implements (ax, adz, chisel, etc.), and by the frequency of bones of wild game.[20] Some of these bones are definitely from forest-dwelling animals such as tigers and deer.

Of even greater importance is the fact that there were, in the woods of that time, certain faunal and floral forms indicating a climate warmer than that of present-day North China. At the Upper Cave of Chou-k'ou-tien, which dates from the terminal Pleistocene, there appeared such warm-climate species as *Cynailurus* cf. *Jubatus* and *Paguma larvata*.[21] According to the reports of some early postglacial geological deposits and Neolithic and early Bronze Age archaeological sites,[22] there is evidence of the following "warm" species:

Bamboo rat (*Rhizomys sinensis; R. troglodytes?*): Yang-shao stage sites, An-yang

Elephant (*Elephas indicus*): An-yang

Rhinoceros: Ma-chia-yao

Bison (*Bos namadicus*): Ma-chia-yao

Tapir (*Tapirus* cf. *indicus*): An-yang

Water buffalo (*Bubalus mephistopheles; B. indicus*): San-ho

Water deer (*Hydropotes inermis*): Pan-p'o, An-yang, San-ho

Père David's deer (*Elaphurus davidianus*): San-ho

Menzies' deer (*Elaphurus menziesianus*): An-yang

Porcupine: Peking

Squirrel (*Tamiops*): Peking

19. Teilhard, *Early Man in China*, pp. 38–39.

20. Andersson, *BMFEA* 15 (1943), 34.

21. P'ei Wen-chung, *PS*, ser. C, 10 (1940).

22. Andersson, *BMFEA* 15 (1943), 35–40. Carl W. Bishop, *Antiquity* 28 (1933), 389–404. Arthur de Carle Sowerby, *Jour. North-China Branch, Royal Asiatic Soc.* 53 (1922), 1–20. Gad Rausing, *Bull. Soc. Lettres Lund* 3 (1956), 191–203. Li Chi et al., *Ch'eng-tzu-yai*, Academia Sinica, Nanking, 1934. Teilhard and C. C. Young, *PS*, ser. C, 12 (1936). Teilhard and P'ei Wen-chung, *Le Néolithique de la Chine*, Peking, Institute de Géo-Biologie, 1944. F. S. Drake, *Proc. 4th Far Eastern Prehist. Congr.* 1 (1956), fasc. 1, 133–49. *Hsi-an Pan-p'o*, Peking, Wen Wu Press, 1963.

Warmth-loving mollusks (*Lamprotula tientsiniensis; L. rochechouarti;*
 L. leai): Tientsin muds, Ch'eng-tzu-yai
Rice (*Oryza sativa*): Yang-shao-ts'un, Liu-tzu-chen(?)
Bamboo: inferred from the form of pottery and mentioned in early
 literary records

The existence of rice, bamboo, and elephants is corroborated by the
written records,[23] while the presence of elephants and rhinoceroses is
further confirmed by sculptures and some zoomorphic bronzes from the
archaeological site at An-yang.

Finally, palynological study—commonly regarded as the most reliable
means of determining ancient vegetations and thus the history of ancient
climates that supported the various plant species—has recently been
brought to bear on the problem of postglacial environment in China,
with significant results. The pollen analysis of lake sediments collected
in Taiwan by Matsuo Tsukada, formerly of Yale University, shows a
postglacial "climatic optimum" (postglacial hypsithermal interval) carbon-
dated to the period between approximately 8,000 and 4,000 years B.P.,
during which the annual temperature in subtropical Taiwan was probably
two or three degrees centigrade higher than the present level[24] (fig. 7).
Similar work has been undertaken with peat deposits near Peking[25] and
with the Manchurian black-earth sediments in Liaotung Peninsula,[26]
with identical results. The palynological sequence based on the Liaotung
peats is beginning to be supported by carbon–14 dates,[27] and for the
southern part of the Soviet Far East, from data based on the pollen content
of five peats in the Amur-Ussuri region, M. I. Neishtadt has divided the
post glacial period of that area into four stages:[28] Archaic, 12,000–9,800
B.P.; Early, 9,800–7,700 B.P.; Middle, 7,700–2,500 B.P.; Late, 2,500–0
B.P. The peak of broad-leaf forest lies in the Middle stage, whereas from
2,500 B.P. on, the Korea pine (*Pinus koraiensis*) begins to dominate the
local vegetation, indicating a postglacial hypsithermal and a subsequent

23. Ch'en Meng-chia, *Yen-ching hsüeh pao* 20 (1936), 485–576. Hu Hou-hsüan, *Chia-
ku-hsüeh Shang-shih lun ts'ung*, vol. 2, 1945. Meng Wen-t'ung, *Yü-kung* 1 (1934).

24. Tsukada, *Proc. Nat. Acad. Sc.* 55 (1966), 543–48.

25. Liu et al., QS 4 (1965), no. 1. Chou, QS 4 (1965), no. 1.

26. Ch'en et al., QS 4 (1965), no. 2.

27. *Geochimica* 1974 (1), 25–27.

28. M. I. Neishtadt, *Istoriia Lesov i Paleogeografiia SSSR v. Golotsene*, Moscow, Isd.
AN. USSR, 1957.

climatic deterioration similar in trend and in age to the Taiwan sequence. Since the interval 8,000 to 2,500 B.P. covers much of the late prehistoric period, the importance of such studies for students of early China cannot be overemphasized.[29]

These bits of evidence together prove beyond a doubt that the beginning of the postglacial stage in China was marked by a gradual rise of the mean annual temperature, accompanied by an increasing vegetational cover and corresponding faunal and floral assemblages. This conclusion is broad, but any finer conclusion will have to depend upon future investigations.

It is perfectly clear, however, that the climatic amelioration in China during the early postglacial period must have had considerable influence upon the human industries previously adapted to the cool, semiarid loessic conditions. The inhabitants were now confronted with a changed environment and a widened range for development. Moreover, the higher temperature must have had different effects in different regions. We may infer that in prehistoric times most of the eastern low plains of North China, for example, were wet and marshy (Shantung Peninsula was probably an island surrounded by marshes and lakes if not by seawater),[30] while the western high loesslands were dissected by watercourses that were able to support thick vegetational growth in the lowlands and the valleys. If this is true—and the scanty evidence at out disposal leads us to think it is—it unquestionably had great bearing on the emergence and distribution of human cultures in postglacial times.

29. It should be noted that the interpretation of pollen profiles from sediments deposited after the beginning of agriculture must take into serious account the part played by human and cultural factors in the local histories of vegetation. On the basis of analysis of pollen grains taken from the Neolithic habitation site of Pan-p'o-ts'un, near Sian, Shensi, for example, Chou K'un-shu (KK 1963, no. 9) concludes that, since the pollen grains were predominantly from grassy species, the climate of the environs was "cool and dry," as it is today—a conclusion at considerable odds with other evidence, notably zoological. It is possible that local variations existed in ancient climate as in culture, but Chou's interpretation did not take into account the factor of deforestation by agriculturalists.

It should also be mentioned that in his recent book *The Cradle of the East* (1976) Ho Ping-ti again takes issue with the view of a warmer and more moist North China during the early postglacial period, although almost all of his data in support of his argument had come from either earlier Pleistocene periods or later historical periods. See also Richard J. Pearson, in *Antiquity* 48 (1974), 226–28, for a cautionary note on the use of pollen data for cultural interpretation.

30. W. S. Ting, *BIE* 20 (1965), 155–62. Li Shih-yü, *KK* 1962 (12), 652–57.

A Note on Postglacial and Historical Chronologies

For an area as large and as complex in cultural variations over time as China, prehistoric events can hardly be pieced together in any coherent manner without a tight and accurate chronological control. The most commonly employed chronological methods that one can use for China as a whole, prior to the beginning of historic dates, are relative chronological methods such as stratigraphy, synchronism, and typological sequences and comparisons. In addition, absolute chronologies known from other areas of the world, where available and pertinent, could provide ranges of time for comparable events in the area of China.

As mentioned above, the progress of Palaeolithic man and his work was extremely slow and can be measured in geological terms. The Pleistocene subdivision described above certainly lacks refinement, compared with such well-studied regions as western and central Europe, but for our purpose here, dealing with a small amount of data for all of China, it is not entirely inadequate for seriating and synchronizing major events of the Chinese Pleistocene into an intelligible picture for the time being.

For the postglacial period, however, the situation drastically changes. Human progress in cultural achievements can no longer be measured in geological terms. The entire postglacial period, up to the present, is only about ten thousand years, but human accomplishment during this time consists of a series of quantum and accelerated jumps, and a difference of a millennium, a century, or even a decade might give rise to drastically different pictures, in which various events over time and space are delicately structured.

Fortunately, precisely because of the rapid rate of cultural change, it is now possible to formulate microchronological segments according to minute cultural shifts and changes—a decorative motif on a pottery vessel may undergo appreciable transformations in a generation, as against a minute improvement in the preparation of a striking platform of a flint core that took millions of experiments and a quarter of a million years to perfect during the early part of the Pleistocene. It is therefore possible for later prehistoric periods to reconstruct cultural groups and sequences, even without any absolute age data, by means of careful manipulation of the principles of stratigraphy, synchronism, and typology. Such archaeological concepts as culture, phase, regional chronology, horizon, and tradition may and will be fruitful if they are applied with care and caution. Most of these concepts have yet to be employed on the Chinese data, which have often been handled with an assortment of idiosyncratic

Table 3

Chronology of the Shang and Chou Periods

Dynasty	Subdivisions	Events	Absolute Dates (B.C.)
Shang		Founding of dynasty by T'ang	? $1722^{+}-1514$
		P'an Keng moves capital to An-yang	? 1397–1291
———————————		Wu Wang conquest ———	? 1122–1018
Chou	Western Chou	First year of the Kung Ho era	841
		P'ing Wang moves capital to Lo-yang	770
	Eastern Chou		
———————————		Ch'in unification———	221
Ch'in			

methods and systems of terminology that are difficult to evaluate and use for comparative purposes.

Furthermore, since 1965, archaeological samples have begun to be subjected to radiocarbon dating in laboratories in Peking (Institutes of Archaeology and Geology, Academia Sinica), Kuei-yang (Institute of Geochemistry, Academia Sinica), and Taipei (Department of Physics, National Taiwan University), and more than a hundred determinations have thus far been reported.[31] (Appendix 1 lists all important dates available thus far). Considering the size of China and the volume of her archaeological relics, these dates are yet insufficient for an absolute chronology of the land, but at least we are on a much firmer footing now than a decade ago insofar as a chronological arrangement of late prehistoric cultures is concerned.

The latest four thousand years or so are a different story again. The emergence of the Shang civilization means the dawn of written records.

31. *KK* 1972 (1), 52–56; 1972 (5), 56–58; 1974 (5), 333–38; 1976 (1), 28–30, 58. *Geochimica*, 1973 (2), 135–37; 1974 (1), 28–31. *Scientia Geologica Sinica* 1974 (4), 383–84. *Radiocarbon* 12 (1970), 187–92; 15 (1973), 345–49.

From about 1750 B.C. onward, textual materials are available so that historical events can be pieced together in calendrical language, and a useful chronological subdivision is possible for both the Shang and the Chou (table 3).[32] For reasons to be given later, this volume will arbitrarily end at 221 B.C. when the first unifier of China, Ch'in Shih Huang Ti, subjugated the last opposing state. For this millennium and a half, chronological segments as fine as necessary become available within the domain of civilized China. Even outside it, in areas peripheral to or even distant from the Chinese civilization, the historical chronology—the earliest available historical chronology in all of Asia east of the Urals—serves as a frame of reference for events that took place within the period. In these areas, however, where many things of relevance to Chinese civilization happened somewhat slower and later and persisted long after they had ended in North China, a clean break at 221 B.C. is more often than not impossible to make, and these events will be followed through to their ends, often into the Han dynasty (second century B.C. to second century of the present era). As far as possible, however, this volume describes the history of cultures in China up to the beginning of the Ch'in and Han empires—the cutoff point that in historiographic tradition concludes China's ancient period.

32. See Ho Ping-ti, *Cradle of the East*, pp. 1–21.

2 : Palaeolithic and Mesolithic Foundations

Following general Old World archaeological usage we refer to human culture during the Pleistocene period as Palaeolithic, and to that from the beginning of the postglacial stage up to the advent of agriculture as Mesolithic. A "Chinese" culture tradition as we now know it did not become manifest in the archaeological record until after the emergence of farming villages, but its foundation was laid, and the stage set for its occurrence, during the Pleistocene; and the populations and cultures during that period in China were part of significant worldwide events.

The concept of the so-called Palaeolithic culture of the Pleistocene in the area of China is a new one that did not emerge until this century. According to the legends upon which traditional Chinese history was based, the universe was made by P'an Ku, and mankind was created by Nü Wa. Then the world was ruled by a long series of sage kings, grouped into San Huang, the Three Sovereigns, and Wu Ti, the Five Emperors. These were followed by initial historical periods, the last two millennia B.C., which comprised the reign of the Three Dynasties—the Hsia, Shang, and Chou. A cumulative chronology of the reigns of the ancient sages would place the legendary beginning of Chinese ancient history well within the Pleistocene period, and, in fact, some historians have tried to reconcile the new and the old by attempting to identify remains of fossil man with legendary sages.[1] In scientific Palaeolithic archaeology, however, human and cultural *remains* must be recovered from Pleistocene deposits to be counted, and ancient artifacts themselves were not known in China from demonstrably Pleistocene contexts until 1920.[2]

During the half century since their first discovery, Palaeolithic sites and relics have been brought to light throughout China and from many different periods, including findings of great world significance (fig. 8). The Pleistocene period is over two million years long, and the sites,

1. Hsü Liang-chih, *Chung-kuo shih-ch'ien-shih hua*, Hong Kong, Asia Press, 1954.
2. P. Teilhard de Chardin, *Anthropologie* 33 (1924), 630–31. Teilhard and E. Licent, *GSoC Bull.* 3 (1924), 45–50.

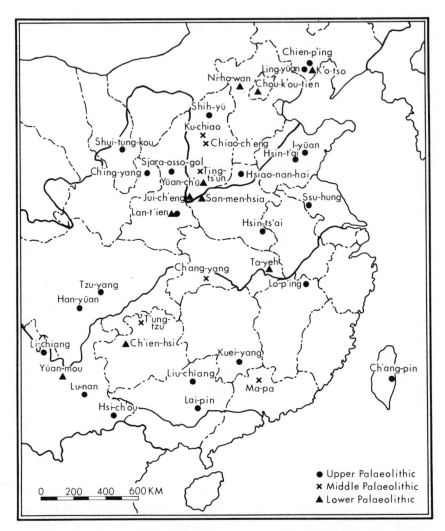

8. Major sites of Palaeolithic cultures and fossil man remains in China. (Based on map prepared by Institute of Vertebrate Palaeontology and Palaeoanthropology, Academia Sinica, May 1975.)

although numbered in the hundreds, are few and far between. Because of the slowness of change during this ancient period, however, a brief sketch of the human and cultural developmental history in China is possible, and in places the story is even filled with significant and interesting details.

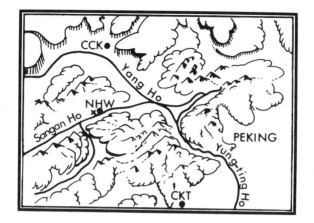

9. Palaeolithic locality (x) at Ni-ho-wan (NHW). Other localities nearby include Chou-k'ou-tien (CKT) and Chang-chia-k'ou (CCK).

Man of the Early Pleistocene Stage

Archaeologists and human palaeontologists used to hold to the view that during the Villafranchian stage China was not occupied by man.[3] There is now evidence to the contrary, however. Some forty years ago in the Ni-ho-wan beds (generally thought to be Villafranchian) of the Sang-kan River valley of Hopei, in North China, Emile Licent and Teilhard de Chardin discovered a so-called faceted stone and some bone fragments. The Abbé Breuil believed that this stone and some of the bone fragments were modified by humans, but his view is generally rejected.[4] New investigations at the same locality in 1972 (fig. 9) unearthed a quartzite chopper, which, in the opinion of Kai P'ei and Wei Ch'i, was without question fashioned by humans.[5] Furthermore, a few humanoid teeth have been found in South China from the Villafranchian age. In the late 1930s G.H.R. von Koenigswald obtained in Hong Kong drugstores several human teeth that he believes were originally derived from South China Pleistocene deposits and that he has compared morphological-

3. F. C. Howell, *Science* 130 (1959), 833.

4. Teilhard, *Anthropologie* 45 (1935), 736. Henri Breuil, *Anthropologie* 45 (1935), 746. Movius, *Trans. Amer. Philos. Soc.* 38 (1948), 345.

5. *VP* 12 (1974), 69–72. A "few score of stone implements" have been reported since 1961–62 from a similar geological stratum at Hsi-hou-tu village, Jui-ch'eng, Shansi, but details of the find are as yet not available; see Chia Lan-p'o, *The Cave Home of Peking Man*, Peking, Foreign Languages Press, 1975, p. 47.

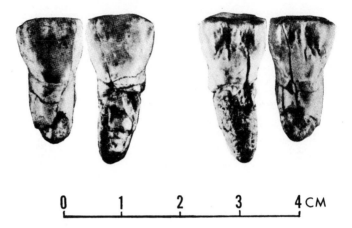

10. Yüan-mou incisors, frontal (*left*) and lingual (*right*) views. (From Hu Ch'eng-chih, *Acta Geologica Sinica* 1973, no. 7, p. 70.)

ly with the *Paranthropus* of South Africa. These he has named *Hemanthropus peii*.[6] In 1968, scientists from the IVPP (Institute of Vertebrate Palaeontology and Palaeoanthropology), Academia Sinica, collected a hominid molar from a drugstore in Pa-tung, western Hupei. In 1970, three additional molars were excavated from a cave in Chien-shih. These were associated with lower Pleistocene fauna, and they are morphologically compared with *Australopithecus africanus*.[7] The taxonomic position of both *Hemanthropus peii* and the Hupei teeth is, however, still uncertain; the possibility of their belonging to some species of *Homo* cannot be ruled out. More significant still are two incisors (fig. 10), described as *Homo*

6. G. H. R. von Koenigswald, *Koninkl. Nederl. Akad. Weternschap., Amsterdam, Proceedings*, ser. B, 60 (1957), 153–59.

7. Kao Chien, *VP* 13 (1975), 81–88. In the Chien-shih cave they were found associated with teeth of *Gigantopithecus blacki*. Concerning this creature, see G. H. R. von Koenigswald, *A Giant Fossil Hominoid from the Pleistocene of Southern China*, Anthropological Papers, American Museum of Natural History, no. 43 (1952), 301–9. Franz Weidenreich, *Giant Early Man from Java and South China*, Anthropological Papers, American Museum of Natural History, no. 40 (1945), pt. 1; *Apes, Giants and Man*, University of Chicago Press, 1946. P'ei Wen-chung, *VP* 1 (1957), no. 2, 65–70; *Amer. Anthropologist* 59 (1957), 834–38. W. C. P'ei and Woo Ju-k'ang, *Acta Palaeontol. Sinica* 4 (1956), 477–89. W. C. P'ei and Li Yu-heng, *VP* 2 (1958), 193–97. Woo Ju-k'ang, *VP* 6 (1962), 375–83. Hsü Ch'un-hua, Han K'ang-hsin, and Wang Ling-hung, *VP* 12 (1974), 293–304. David Pilbeam, "Gigantopithecus and the origins of Hominidae," *Nature* 225 (1970), 516–19.

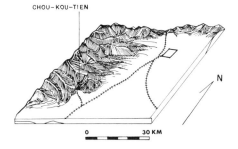

CHOU-KOU-TIEN

N

0   30 KM

11. The caves of Chou-k'ou-tien in relation to the city of Peking and the West Hills. (After J. G. Andersson, *BMFEA* 15, 1943, p. 21.)

erectus, that were reportedly recovered in 1965 from lower Pleistocene deposits in Yüan-mou, in Yunnan.[8]

Lower Palaeolithic Culture of Chou-k'ou-tien

The Chinese Palaeolithic can be broken down into lower, middle, and upper stages. The Lower Palaeolithic—the longest in time, spanning the entire middle Pleistocene and at least the earlier third of the upper—was a stage of crude beginnings of a stone industry characterized by relatively slow development of generalized, all-purpose implements. It is represented in China by several major archaeological sites—among them Chou-k'ou-tien, Lan-t'ien, and K'o-ho, all in North China in or near the Huang Ho valley. Human pithecanthropoid fossils have been found at the first two sites. The earlier, Yüan-mou incisors are of the same type.

Chou-k'ou-tien site, the first found of the three and still the best known, is near a small village 42 kilometers southwest of the center of Peking at the foot of the West Hills (fig. 11). The limestone caves and fissures west of Chou-k'ou-tien have been known archaeologically since 1918, and no fewer than twenty-two fossiliferous localities have been identified. At four of these, localities 1, 4, 13, and 15, Palaeolithic implements were excavated from 1921 to 1937 and again from 1959 to date.[9] Locality 1, the Ko-tzu-t'ang ("Hall of the Pigeons") cave, is the most important, for from it have come not only the largest number and the longest series

---

8. Hu Ch'eng-chih, *Acta Geologica Sinica* 1973 (I), 65–71. Yu Yü-chu and Ch'i Kuo-ch'in, *VP* 11 (1973), 66–80. According to a New China Agency dispatch of 25 July 1976, the geological stratum from which the Yuan-mou teeth were derived had been dated by palaeomagnatism to 1.7 million years ago.

9. For a bibliography of the Chou-k'ou-tien excavations, see K. C. Chang, *Arctic Anthropology* 1 (1963), 2, 31. Excavations in 1966 were reported in *VP* 11 (1973), 109–24. A recent synthesis is Chia Lan-p'o, *The Cave Home of Peking Man*, Peking, Foreign Languages Press, 1975.

Sinanthropus cave

12. Ko-tzu-t'ang Cave, locality 1 of Chou-k'ou-tien. (From J. G. Andersson, *BMFEA* 15, 1943, p. 21.)

of stone artifacts but also a large number of human fossils.

The cave opened to the northeast at the time of its occupation and was about 175 meters long and 50 meters wide, filled with occupational debris and éboulis more than 40 meters deep, accumulated over a very long time (figs. 12, 13). About one-third of the cave has been excavated, and altogether thirteen natural strata are distinguished, numbered 1 to 13 from top to bottom. Three cycles of deposition are manifest: (1) basal gravel, consisting of strata 11–13, a zone of red clay in which sands and gravels are embedded; (2) lower and middle breccia, strata 8–10, containing the fossil remains of *Hyaena sinensis*; and (3) upper breccia, strata 1–7, with remains of *H. ultima*. There have been lengthy discussions about the respective ages of the three depositional cycles of locality 1,[10] but a recent palynological profile taken from the sediments in the cave from 9.3 meters to 40 meters, cutting through all three divisions, is most revealing. Three pollen zones are distinguished, corresponding to the three depositional cycles:[11]

> The first stage (I), ranging from 40 meters to 36 meters, is represented by the basal gravel. . . . The pollen of herbs is far above that of woody plants in numbers. . . . It is represented only by Chenopodiaceae, *Artemisia*, and other members of Compositae. Spores of *Selaginella* and Bryophyta are abundant. The presence of spores of *Botrychium lunaria* is rather significant. At present . . . in North China [*B. lunaria*] grows only in high altitudes above 2,400 meters, [and is] often associated with lichens, mosses, and grasses. So the climate then must have been much cooler than that of the present.
>
> The second stage (II), ranging from 36 meters to 20.5 meters, is mainly represented by the second cycle of deposition. The relative

---

10. D. Black et al., *Fossil Man in China*, Peking, 1933. H. L. Movius, Jr., *Trans. Amer. Phil. Soc.* 38 (1948). L. P. Chia, *VP* 3 (1959), 41–45. T. K. Chao and Y. H. Li, *VP* 5 (1961), 374–78. H. D. Kahlke and P. H. Chou, *VP* 5 (1961), 212–40.

11. J. Hsü, *Scientia Sinica* 15 (1966), 412.

13. Ko-tzu-t'ang Cave, locality 1 of Chou-k'ou-tien. (Photo by author, 1975.)

dominance of NAP [nonarboreal pollen] is rather characteristic. . . . At the beginning of this stage, trees of cold temperate zone like *Abies* and *Betula* existed. Afterward there was a rapid immigration of warm temperate elements, such as *Pinus*, *Quercus*, *Alnus*, *Salix*, *Celtis*, *Pistacea*, *Ulmus*, and *Fraxinus*, indicating that at that time a mixed forest [was] flourishing in the hills. At the end of this stage, there was a gradual decrease in the number of pollen grains of *Betula*, as well as that of the shrubs and the herbs, and a sudden appearance of the thermophile *Symplocos*. This indicates a tendency of rise in temperature.

The third stage (III), ranging from 20.5 meters to 9.3 meters, is represented by the third cycle of deposition. It is characterized by the presence of some warmer temperate elements such as *Carpinus*, *Carylus*, *Ostrya*. At the same time, *Symplocos* still existed. At present, *Symplocos* generally lives in regions almost 5 degrees south of Peking. . . . This indicates that at the beginning of this stage the climate would be warmer than that of the present, and probably represents the "climatic optimum" of the *Sinanthropus* [Peking man] period. . . . At the latter part of this stage, *Betula* reached its maximum. That was the time of declining warmth.

From another sample, probably collected at less depth than 9.3 meters, a palynological spectrum was obtained that led B. Kurtén to conclude that at the time of the sample the climate of Chou-k'ou-tien was cooler than it is today.[12] Thus, the entire Chou-k'ou-tien sedimentation cycle began and ended in climatic phases colder than now, through a middle phase warmer than the present. This is in complete accord with the geological placement of the Chou-k'ou-tien sedimentation within the period represented by Taku glacial, Taku-Lushan interglacial, and Lushan glacial; the entire collection of human fossils came from the breccia deposited toward the end of the Taku glacial; the lower and middle breccia during the Taku-Lushan interglacial; and the upper part of the upper breccia probably was laid down in the beginning of the Lushan glacial. Locality 13 of Chou-k'ou-tien[13] can be synchronized with the basal gravel of locality 1 on zoological grounds, and localities 4[14] and 15[15] with the latest upper breccia or later. The bulk of Palaeolithic stone

12. *VP* 3 (1959), 173–75.
13. W. C. P'ei, *GSoC Bull.* 13 (1934), 359–67.
14. *Ibid.*, 19 (1939), 207–34.
15. *Ibid.*, pp. 147–87.

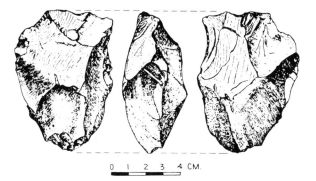

0 1 2 3 4 CM.

14. Chopping tool from locality 13, Chou-k'ou-tien. (From H. L. Movius, Jr., *Trans. Amer. Phil. Soc.*, n.s., vol. 38, 1949, p. 391.)

materials was excavated from the breccia strata of locality 1 and from locality 15, thus dating from the Taku-Lushan interglacial and the Lushan glacial; the entire collection of human fossils came from the breccia zones of locality 1. One piece of stone implement was known from locality 13 (fig. 14), and two pieces of stone of debatable artificiality were collected from the basal-gravel strata of locality 1.[16]

Human fossils found at locality 1 consist of bone fragments—including fourteen skulls, over a hundred teeth, and isolated postcranial bones—that belonged to over forty individuals.[17] Commonly known as Peking man, they have been variously latinized as *Sinanthropus pekinensis, Pithecanthropus pekinensis,* and *Homo erectus pekinensis.* Whatever the appellation, they were possessed of hominid features: erect posture, considerable cranial capacity (average 1,075 cc), and the capability of making and using tools and implements (fig. 15). On the other hand, other physical features distinguish them from *Homo sapiens*: the low skull vault, the great thickness of the skull wall, the bony crests around the skull's horizontal circumference, the receding chin, and other minute but important characters of dentition and tooth eruption. These place Peking man in the same league as *Homo erectus* of Java, to whom all physical anthropologists agree he is related. From the length of a femur, Weidenreich speculated that the stature of an adult male Peking man was only about 156 centimeters, and

16. L. P. Chia, *VP* 3 (1959), 41–45. T. K. Chao and Y. H. Li, *VP* 5 (1961), 374–78. But see S. S. Chang, *VP* 6 (1962), 278–79.

17. D. Black, *PS,* ser. D, 7 (1927), 1–28. F. Weidenreich, *PS,* ser. D, 12 (1936), 4; *PS,* ser. D, 7 (1936), 3; *PS,* n.s. D, 1 (1937); *PS,* n.s. D, 10 (1943). J. K. Woo and T. K. Chao, *VP* 3 (1959), 169–72. Ch'iu Chung-lang et al., *VP* 11 (1973), 109–24.

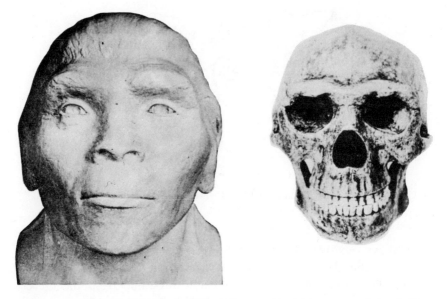

15. Reconstruction of the head of a *Pithecanthropus pekinensis* woman, and the skull on which the reconstruction was based. (From Franz Weidenreich, *PS*, n.s. D, no. 10, 1943, 1. 48.)

that the female was probably 144 centimeters tall. The life span of the Peking man population was brief by modern standards: 40 per cent died before the age of fourteen, and less than 3 per cent achieved the sixth decade of life.[18] Weidenreich believed that many of these people were cut down early in life by injuries.

> For the most part, only the skulls of Sinanthropus seem to have been brought into the caves at Choukoutien and, with the exception of the few fragmentary postcranial parts ... there are simply no long bones, vertebrae, etc. in the deposits. It appears that these skulls were trophies of head hunters, and, furthermore, that said hunters usually bashed in the bases of the skull when fresh, presumably to eat the brains therein contained. Many crania also show that their owners met their deaths as a result of skull fractures induced by heavy blows.[19]

Apparently some portion of Peking man's diet consisted of the flesh, brain, and marrow of their own kind. Their principal food, however,

18. F. Weidenreich, *Chinese Med. Jour.* 55 (1939), Peking.
19. E. A. Hooten, *Up from the Ape*, New York, MacMillan, 1949, p. 304.

was meat of wild animals—70 per cent being deer with very heavy horns (*Sinomegaceros pachyosteus*), to judge from the bony fossils found in the cave; the rest included leopard, cave bear, saber-toothed tiger, hyena, elephant, rhinoceros, camel, water buffalo, boar, and horse.[20] The many bits of charcoal in the cave, burned bony fragments, and hearths suggest that Peking man was capable of making fire and cooked his meat.[21] Trees in the hills were cut for fuel, and timber was used. Some nuts found in the cave, such as those from *Celtis*, probably came from branches and twigs cut for fuel, but Peking man quite likely also collected wild fruits and nuts to supplement his diet.[22] Primarily, however, he was a hunter of game, large and small, presumably using a variety of implements ranging from wooden throwing spears to traps and snares.

Other than pieces of bone that bear possible signs of incisions for use,[23] the artifacts of Peking man consisted mainly of some hundred thousand stone implements, which provide the essential body of data for any study of their culture.[24] According to a recent analysis of 5,897 specimens by Chang Shen-shui, of the Institute of Vertebrate Palaeontology and Palaeoanthropology (IVPP), the Peking man stone industry has the following characteristics (fig. 16):[25]

1. The stone implements were mainly made of flakes.
2. They were made principally by means of unilateral percussion and retouched by the hammer technique. The principal raw material was vein quartz.
3. Many flakes were unretouched but had signs of use.
4. The implements and flakes do not have conventional forms.
5. There is great flexibility of technique and variation in the levels of skill throughout the layers of deposition.

20. W. C. P'ei, *PS*, ser. C, 8 (1934), fasc. 1 and 3. Liu Hou-i, *VP* 11 (1973), 86–97.

21. D. Black, *GSoC Bull.* 11 (1931), 107–08. H. Breuil, *GSoC Bull.* 11 (1931), 147–54; *Anthropologie* 42 (1932), 1–17; *Anthropos* 27 (1932), 1–10.

22. R. W. Chaney, *Carnegie Inst. Wash. Bull.*, n.s. 3 (1935), 25, 199–202; *GSoC Bull.* 14 (1935), 99–113. Chaney and Daugherty, *GSoC Bull.* 12 (1933), 323–28.

23. H. Breuil, *GSoC Bull.* 11 (1931), 147–54; *Anthropologie* 42 (1932), 1–17; *PS*, ser. D, 6 (1939), 7–41. W. C. P'ei, *GSoC Bull.* 12 (1932), 105–08; *KKHP* 1960 (2), 1–9. L. P. Chia, *KKHP* 1959 (3), 1–4.

24. W. C. P'ei, *GSoC Bull.* 11 (1931), 109–39. Teilhard and P'ei, *GSoC Bull.* 11 (1932), 315–58. D. Black et al., *Fossil Man in China*, 1933. H. L. Movius, Jr., *Early Man and Pleistocene Stratigraphy in Southern and Eastern Asia*, Papers of the Peabody Museum, Harvard University, no. 19 (1944); *Trans. Amer. Phil. Soc.* 38 (1948).

25. *VP* 6 (1962), 271–79.

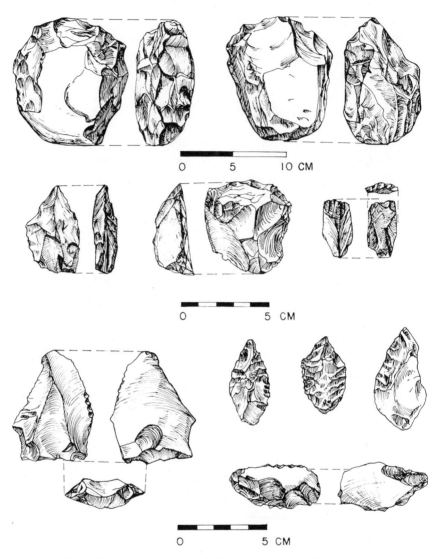

16. Lower Palaeolithic implements from Chou-k'ou-tien, locality 1 (*upper group*) and locality 15 (*lower group*). (After H. L. Movius, Jr., *Trans. Amer. Phil. Soc.*, n.s., vol. 38, 1949, figs. 35, 37–39.)

6. The retouched edges are in most cases curved, showing marked scars left by retouching blows, indicating a very primitive level of stone technology.

7. Types of artifacts are not sharply demarcated. The principal cate-

gories are scrapers, choppers, points, and awls; there are some end scrapers, engravers, balls, hammers, and chipped pebbles. Many artifacts, however, can be classified in more than one category, and there are many multiple-purpose implements.

The conclusion of S. S. Chang is that such a stone industry is characteristic of the Lower Palaeolithic level and is more like the Lower Palaeolithic assemblages of southern and eastern Asia than those of Europe and Africa. As early as 1944, Movius pointed out that Lower Palaeolithic industries of southern and eastern Asia, i.e., the Soan of Pakistan, the Anyathian of Upper Burma, the Patjitanian of Java, and the Choukoutienian of Peking, formed a so-called chopper–chopping tool complex and that, in contrast to the European and African Abbevillian and Acheulian industries with hand-axes and flakes struck from preworked cores with prepared striking platforms, the Asian industries were distinguished by implements struck from pebbles, with only a few scars and generally simple forms.[26] There is little question that the East Asian Lower Palaeolithic cultures have their distinctive features, but one now wonders if their differences from contemporary cultures to the west were not unduly exaggerated. A recent analysis of newer data has shown Chang Shen-shui's above generalizations to be somewhat simplistic. Several Chineae archaeologists—including Chang himself—now see the Choukoutienian industry as containing clearly defined artifact types of considerable sophistication, especially toward the upper parts of the deposits.[27] On the basis of twelve morphological features of Peking man—primarily the shovel-shaped incisors, the sagittal crest, and the mandibular torus—Weidenreich believed that some of the genes of Peking man were transmitted into the modern Mongoloid populations who inhabit the same area of the world, but this view is far from being generally accepted.[28]

Lower Palaeolithic Cultures at Lan-t'ien, K'o-ho, and other Sites

The Peking man fossils—bony remains of a small population including five nearly complete crania, excavated under close scientific supervision from well-documented depositional contexts in association with middle

26. Movius, Early Man.

27. Ch'iu, Ku, Chang, and Chang, VP 11 (1973), 109–31.

28. F. Weidenreich, PS, n.s. D, 10 (1943), 253–54. But see, e.g., Woo Ju-k'ang and N. N. Cheboksarov, Sovietskaia Etnografia, 1959 (4), 3–24.

Pleistocene fauna and a Lower Palaeolithic stone industry—were China's contribution to world scholarship and palaeoanthropology's greatest catch. Safely buried underground, untouched by the great physical upheavals of the subsequent half-million years,[29] these fossils were lost barely a decade and a half after their discovery. Although Peking fell to Japanese invaders in 1937, scientists at the Cenozoic Laboratory of the Geological Survey of China were able to continue study at Chou-k'ou-tien until 1939. Then, in 1941, decision was reached between the Chungking and American authorities to transport these fossils to the United States for safekeeping, and they were crated and moved to a warehouse in Ch'in-huang-tao, a small port city northeast of Peking, into the custody of the U.S. Marines. Just at this time Pearl Harbor was attacked. In the resultant confusion the fossils disappeared either from the warehouse or together with a sunken ship and have never been heard of since.[30] A few teeth, a skullcap, a mandible, and a few long bones of Peking man have been found since 1950 at locality 1, but these are small recompense for the immeasurable loss. We can, however, take comfort in the knowledge that only about one-third of the total length of the Ko-tzu-t'ang cave has been excavated and that, presumably, additional fossils still await future discovery.

The discovery of Lower Palaeolithic human remains in China has in any event only just begun. In 1963, scientists of the Cenozoic laboratory of the IVPP, Academia Sinica (Peking), discovered a pithecanthropoid mandible near the village of Ch'en-chia-wo, some 10 kilometers northwest of Lan-t'ien, in eastern-central Shensi, almost 1,000 kilometers southwest of Chou-k'ou-tien.[31] In 1964 a human skull of similar age was found at Kung-wang-ling, in the northern foothills of the Ch'in Ling Mountains, more than 10 kilometers east of Lan-t'ien.[32] Both the mandible and the skull were probably from females. Their morphological features indicate close affinity with Peking man, but they exhibit characteristics more "primitive" than their Peking counterparts—e.g., a more pronounced supraorbital torus, a thicker skull wall, a smaller cranial capacity (ca. 780 cc, as against *Australopithecine*'s 435–700 cc, Java man's 775–900 cc,

29. V. V. Cherdyntsev, *Voprocy Geologii Antropogena*, Moscow, Isd. AN. USSR, 1961, gives a uranium-thorium date of 210,000–500,000 + for Peking man.

30. For an account of the circumstances of the disappearance of Peking man fossils and some recent efforts to recover them, so far without success, see Harry Shapiro, *Peking Man*, New York, Simon & Schuster, 1975.

31. J. K. Woo, *VP* 8 (1964), 1–12.

32. *Ibid.*, 10 (1966), 1–16.

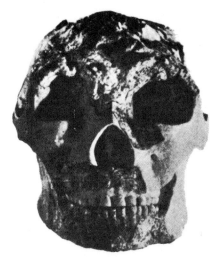

17. The Lan-t'ien skull, frontal view. (From *VP* 10, 1966, no. 1.)

Peking man's 850–1,300 cc, and modern man's 1,350 cc), and several other significant attributes (fig. 17). Woo Ju-k'ang believes that Lan-t'ien man was more primitive than either Peking man or Java's *Pithecanthropus erectus* and considers him most comparable with Java's *Pithecanthropus robustus*.[33] It may be interesting to note that the Lan-t'ien mandible lacked the third molar, a rare occurrence of agenesis in fossil-man specimens. According to Garn,[34] the highest occurrence of agenesis in modern populations is among some American Indians, the Eskimos, and many Asians.

Geologically the Lan-t'ien fossils occurred in strata broadly comparable with the Chou-k'ou-tien sedimentation. Both the mandible and the skull were found in sediments on the banks of the river Pa, a tributary flowing out of the Ch'in Ling Mountains into the Wei River near Sian (fig. 18). At Ch'en-chia-wo the mandible occurred in a reddish clay stratum, separated by a line of disconformity from lower Pleistocene deposits, in association with fossil remains of *Cuon alpinus, Felis tigris,* elephant, *Pseudaxis grayi, Sus* cf. *lydekkeri,* and *Mospalax fontanieri,* elements that recall the Chou-k'ou-tien fauna.[35] Palynological data from these sediments indicate prevalence of grassy species and broadleaf trees of an interglacial

33. *WW* 1973 (6), 41–44. For another opinion see J. S. Aigner and W. S. Laughlin, *Am. J. Phys. Anthrop.* 39 (1973), 97–110.

34. S. M. Garn, *Human Races,* rev. 2nd printing, Springfield, Ill., Thomas, 1962, p. 29.

35. *Shensi Lan-t'ien Hsin-sheng-chieh,* 1966, p. 17.

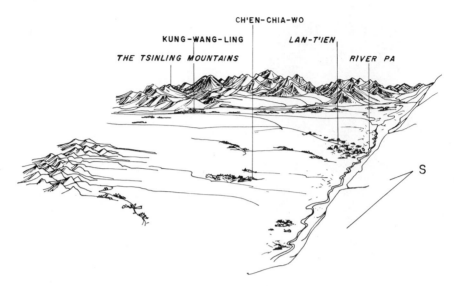

18. The Lan-t'ien Palaeolithic sites. (After *Shensi Lan-t'ien Hsin-sheng-chieh*, Peking, Science Press, 1966, p. 122.)

environment.[36] The Kung-wang-ling skull was found from Lishih-loess deposits, again above a line of disconformity that separates it from lower Pleistocene deposits below, in association with mixed Chou-k'ou-tien–Wan Hsien fauna, including *Ursus thibetanus kokeni, Hyaena sinensis, Equus sanmeniensis, Ailuropoda melanoleuca* cf. *fovealis, Cynailurus pleistocaenicus, Nestoritherium* cf. *sinensis, Leptobos, Macacus, Megantereon, Stegodon, Tapirus,* and *Sinomegaceros*.[37] The occurrence of many South China faunal species here north of the Ch'in Ling must indicate immigration during a warm interval, and both Ch'en-chia-wo and Kung-wang-ling were probably datable to the Taku-Lushan interglacial, contemporaneous with Peking man of Chou-k'ou-tien, though it is possible that there is minor temporal difference between Lan-t'ien and Chou-k'ou-tien, and between Kung-wang-ling and Ch'en-chia-wo. Excavations at Kung-wang-ling in 1965 produced mammalian fossils that suggest greater similarity with locality 13 than locality 1 of Chou-k'ou-tien.[38]

Habitation sites of Lan-t'ien man have yet to be located. Fewer than forty quartz and quartzite artifacts have been collected from the Lan-t'ien area from geological strata correlatable with the horizon of human fossils;

36. *Ibid.*, p. 172.
37. *Ibid.*, pp. 17, 287.
38. H. C. Wu et al., *VP* 10 (1966), 23–29.

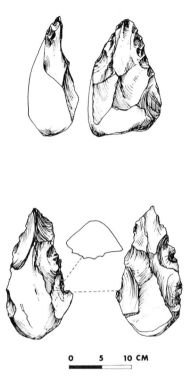

19. Two chopping tools from middle Pleistocene deposits in the Lan-t'ien area. (*Upper*, from *VP* 8, 1964, p. 155; *lower*, from *VP* 10, 1966, p. 31.)

these include cores, flakes, choppers, and chopping tools (fig. 19). Some of the choppers and chopping tools are relatively large and roughly prismatic in cross section, and are described as "heavy, pointed implements." [39] A small blade with a horizontal truncation appears to be much more advanced than the rest of the Lan-t'ien finds and the Choukoutienian ones, but it was found considerably above the human-fossil horizon and its age is uncertain. [40] The use of quartz and the prevalence of flake and pebble implements recall Choukoutienian characteristics, but they are distinguished by their large, pointed tools, large, discoidal choppers, alternately flaked choppers, scrapers, and stone balls. The "bipolar" technique, common at Chou-k'ou-tien, is not seen here.

Stone assemblages of large numbers of implements of comparable age are also known from no fewer than eleven localities near the village of K'o-ho, in Jui-ch'eng Hsien, southwestern Shansi, approximately 150

39. E. C. Tai and H. H. Chi, *VP* 8 (1964), 155. E. C. Tai, *VP* 10 (1966), 30–32. *Shensi Lan-t'ien Hsin-sheng-chieh*, pp. 151–52. E. C. Tai and C. H. Hsü, *KKHP* 1973 (2), 1–11.
40. E. C. Tai, *VP* 10 (1966), 30.

kilometers east of Lan-t'ien.[41] Palaeolithic implements were excavated in 1960 by scientists from the IVPP at all these localities from a layer of slightly consolidated gravels lying below a thick bed of reddish clay and above an erosion surface of a layer of marly clay. The associated fauna were *Coelodonta* sp., *Equus* sp., *Sus* sp., *Sinomegaceros pachyosteus*, *S. flabellatus*, *Pseudaxis* sp., *Bubalus* sp., *Bison* sp., *Stegodon zdansky*, *S.* cf. *orientalis*, and *Palaeoloxodon* cf. *namadicus*. The fauna more than the stratigraphy places the K'o-ho assemblage within the middle Pleistocene, but the assemblage was probably deposited earlier than the main phases of Chou-k'ou-tien locality 1 and was perhaps broadly contemporaneous with locality 13.[42]

Except for rare vein-quartz pieces, the K'o-ho stone industry was based on quartzite pebbles. Many of them retain the pebble cortex. Cores (53) and flakes (66) were collected from all localities, a few of them exhibiting signs of use and retouching. In addition, there are nineteen definitely retouched artifacts, divided into five types: chopping tools and choppers of cores and flakes (7); scrapers (7); a heavy, triangular point; a small, pointed implement; and stone balls (3). Like the Choukoutienian, the stone-making technique was extremely primitive, characterized by flaking, large scars, and the lack of core preparation. Typologically, both the Choukoutienian and the K'o-ho industry contained principally pebble and flake implements—characteristic of Movius's chopper–chopping tool complex—and both are at a Lower Palaeolithic level of development. The Choukoutienian, however, appears to be slightly more sophisticated technologically: a flaking edge, rather than the pebble cortex surface, was used for a striking platform, and there was greater refinement in retouching and in type control. On the other hand, the prismatic, pointed implements, found both at Lan-t'ien and K'o-ho, were absent in Peking. It is possible that even for the Lower Palaeolithic there were already, in North China, regional stone-making traditions, with recognizable and significant differences.

The Choukoutienian—Lan-t'ien/K'o-ho contrast is clearly manifest in other stone assemblages characterized as Lower Palaeolithic. A new stone assemblage, excavated in 1973 from the Ko-tzu-tung ("Cave of the Pigeons") in K'o-tso county, western Liaoning, 230 miles to the northeast

41. L. P. Chia et al., *K'o-ho: Shansi hsi-nan-pu chiu-shih-ch'i ch'u-ch'i wen-hua i-chih*, Peking, Science Press, 1962.
42. For chronological controversies of the K'o-ho site, see *ibid.* C. L. Ch'iu, *VP* 6 (1962), 291–94. L. P. Chia, *VP* 6 (1962), 295–98.

of Peking, has been compared with the stone industry at locality 15 in Chou-k'ou-tien and is an important member of the Choukoutienian tradition.[43] On the other hand, Lower Palaeolithic implements very similar to the K'o-ho industry (including flakes, choppers, chopping tools, heavy prismatic points, and stone balls) were unearthed at the sites of Shui-mo-kou and Hui-hsing-kou, in San-men-hsia, northwestern Honan, from geological strata identical with the K'o-ho beds, reinforcing the impression of a middle Huang Ho center of Lower Palaeolithic cultures broadly similar to but specifically distinguishable from the Choukoutienian.[44]

Besides the above regions of Lower Palaeolithic occurrence in North China, evidence of human occupation during the same Reddish Clay period is also known from several localities in South China. Excavated materials of a pebble chopper and flake industry have been reported from Hupei[45] and Kweichou,[46] and surface and incidental collections are known from Szechwan[47] and Kwangsi.[48] At the site in T'ung-tzu, Kweichou, two human teeth have been found; they are thought to resemble teeth of Peking man. This reminds us of the fact that another tooth that Koenigswald found in a Hong Kong drugstore in the late 1930s, from a hominid which he has termed *Sinanthropus officinalis*, was believed by him to have come originally from a reddish-clay stratum somewhere in South China.[49] The South Chinese "Lower Palaeolithic" finds and hominid fossils are of particular significance in tying the Peking and Lan-t'ien fossils to points south, where earlier hominid fossils are abundant. The dating of all these finds is not, however, sufficiently firm, because it is based on broad, palaeontological grounds. We know from Southeast Asian and Japanese experience that a "Lower Palaeolithic" typology without good geochronological evidence is no sure proof of middle or early upper Pleistocene date. Application of scientific chronological methods to these South China Lower Palaeolithic finds is imperative.

43. *VP* 13 (1975), 122–36.

44. W. W. Huang, *VP* 8 (1964), 162–77.

45. Y. H. Li et al., *VP* 12 (1974), 139–57.

46. W. C. P'ei et al., *VP* 9 (1965), 270–79. M. L. Wu et al., *VP* 13 (1975), 14–23.

47. D. A. Hooijer, *Southwestern Jour. Anthropol.* 7 (1951), 77–81. D. C. Graham, *Jour. W. China Border Research Soc.* 7 (1935), 47–56. H. de Terra, *Pleistocene Formations and Stone Age Man in China*, Peking, Institut de Géo-Biologie, 1941, pp. 36–37.

48. Teilhard et al., *GSoC Bull.* 14 (1935), 179–205.

49. Anthropological Papers, American Museum of Natural History, New York, no. 43 (1952), p. 308.

20. The Fen Ho valley at Ting-ts'un, in Hsiang-fen Hsien, Shansi. (Photo by author, 1975.)

Middle Palaeolithic

The Lower Palaeolithic human and cultural beginnings spanned in time the entire Chou-k'ou-tien sedimentation cycle that climatically encompassed the Taku glacial, the Taku-Lushan interglacial, and the Lushan glacial intervals. The Choukoutienian sequence, which was almost as long as the entire period in question, shows quite clearly that cultural development was slow but appreciable from beginning to end. The human fossils found in association with Lower Palaeolithic industries were invariably pithecanthropoid in type.

In the remaining geological stages of the Pleistocene, the pace of human and cultural development was very much quickened. The last glacial stage, Tali, witnessed the emergence of *Homo sapiens* and blade industries throughout China, and the change began to be appreciable during the Lushan-Tali interglacial interval. In this sense, the Palaeolithic cultures during this transitional interval—the Chingshui erosion—were Middle Palaeolithic. Human fossils attributable to this stage are generally described as neanderthaloid.

From deposits of the Chingshui erosion stage, Palaeolithic implements have been discovered in the Ordos area (from the so-called basal-gravels

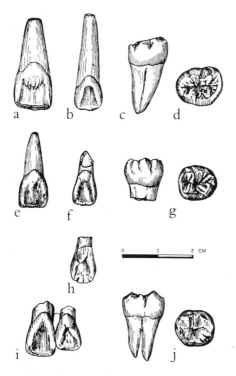

21. Teeth of ancient and modern North China inhabitants, showing the persistent occurrence of shovel-shaped incisors. *Pithecanthropus* (a–d): (a) left upper median incisor; (b) right upper lateral incisor; (c) right lower second molar; (d) left lower second molar. Ting-ts'un man (e–g): (e) left upper median incisor; (f) left upper lateral incisor; (g) right lower second molar. Ordos man (h): left upper lateral incisor. Modern northern Chinese (i–j): (i) right upper incisors; (j) right lower second molar. (From Kuo Mo-jo et al., *Chung-kuo jen-lei hua-shih ti fa-hsien yü yen-chiu*, Peking, Science Press, 1955, p. 44.)

strata at the base of the Malan loess) and in the Fen Ho valley (fig. 20) in Shansi.[50] Three human teeth also came to light in 1954 at locality 100 of Ting-ts'un, in Hsiang-fen Hsien, southern Shansi. The teeth, all probably from the same child, are said to exhibit neanderthaloid characteristics but also are similar to the dentition of Peking man—two of the three are upper incisors that have pronounced shovel-shaped lingual depressions (fig. 21). A parietal of a child was recovered at the same locality in late 1976.

50. Teilhard, *Early Man in China*, Peking, Institut de Géo-Biologie, Publication 7 (1941), p. 68. W. C. P'ei et al., *Shansi Hsiang-fen Hsien Ting-ts'un chiu-shih-ch'i shih-tai i-chih fa-chüeh pao-kao*, Peking, Science Press, 1958. L. P. Chia et al., *Shansi chiu-shih ch'i*, Peking, Science Press, 1961. T. Y. Wang, *VP* 9 (1965), 399–402. M. C. Chou et al., *VP* 9 (1965), 262–63. L. P. Chia and T. Y. Wang, *KKTH* 1957 (5), 12–18.

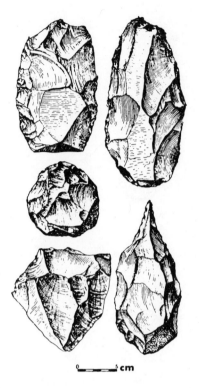

22. Ting-ts'un Palaeolithic implements.
(From *Hsin Chung-kuo ti k'ao-ku shou-huo*,
Peking, Wen Wu Press, 1962, p. 5.)

The stone industries from these deposits indicate a considerable advance over those of the Lower Palaeolithic. While the predominant technological traditions continue to be characterized by flakes and choppers and chopping tools, the skills of stone-making (in particular, in Ting-ts'un, with hornfels, a difficult rock to work) were markedly more refined, and the various types of implements included heavy triangular points, polygonal scrapers, and stone balls, as well as points, scrapers, choppers, and chopping tools (fig. 22). Bifacially flaked core implements increased in number, the striking platforms and the core surfaces were quite often prepared before striking, and, most important, there were some finely made parallel-sided flakes which were probably the forerunners of the blades of the next geological stage. The heavy prismatic points and the stone balls in the Ting-ts'un assemblages are particularly noteworthy; apparently they carry on the same typological tradition of the middle Huang Ho Lower Palaeolithic cultures.

Beside Ordos and the Fen Ho valley, Middle Palaeolithic industries are not significantly known from geologically established strata elsewhere in China, but human fossils described as neanderthaloid have been found in limestone-cave deposits in China. These include a left maxilla and a premolar from Ch'ang-yang, in Hupei, central China,[51] and a skullcap from Ma-pa, in Kwangtung, on the southern coast.[52] It is apparent that, by the Lushan-Tali interglacial, early man throughout China had begun to step onto the modern stage. Whether the transitional features of a Middle Palaeolithic stage were confined to the north or occurred universally remains to be shown by additional data from South China.

Upper Palaeolithic Cultures of North China

The last geological interval of the Pleistocene, during which the Tali glacial occurred on highlands of the southwest and on Taiwan, was the period of culmination of the Chinese Palaeolithic development. In contrast to the slowly developing and relatively homogeneous industries of the Lower Palaeolithic, the Upper Palaeolithic cultures found in the Malan loess and related deposits of the Tali-glacial stage were characterized by a gradual but sure emergence of regional phases of culture in which finely made blade implements of a variety of well-defined types occurred. The owners and makers of these implements were completely modern in physical characteristics—they were, in fact, *Homo sapiens*. The known sites of this stage form three clusters: loessic and sand-gravel deposits in the Ordos and in limestone caves on the lower Huang Ho and in the southwest.

"Ordos" is the Mongolian name of the northern grasslands of the middle Huang Ho where it flows northward, turns east, and returns toward the south; it includes the modern administrative units of eastern Ninghsia, southwestern Inner Mongolia, northern Shensi, and northwestern Shansi. Palaeolithic sites have been uncovered throughout the area, but particularly in the Huang Ho and the Sjara-osso-gol valleys since the 1920s, and are collectively known as the Ordosian culture. Associated human-fossil remains of Ordos man include an incisor (fig. 21), a parietal, a piece of facial skeleton, and a femur.[53] Besides some "primitive" features in the parietal, the morphology of Ordos man is insufficiently represented for any definitive study, but it must be noted that the shovel-shaped depression again occurs on the incisor.

Much is known, on the other hand, of Ordos stone industries. Although

---

51. L. P. Chia, *VP* 1 (1957), 247–57.
52. *WW* 1959 (1), 47. *VP* 3 (1959), 104. J. K. Woo and J. T. P'eng, *VP* 3 (1959), 175–82.
53. E. Licent et al., *GSoC Bull.* 5 (1926), 285–90. Y. P. Wang, *WWTKTL* 1957 (4), 22–25; *VP* 7 (1963). J. K. Woo, *VP* 2 (1958), 208–12.

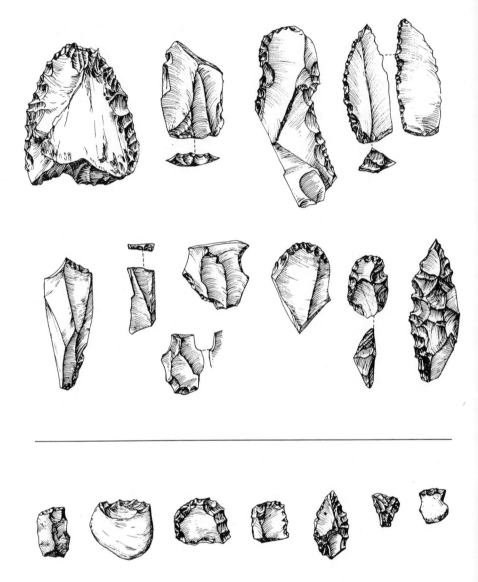

23. Upper Palaeolithic implements from the sites at Shui-tung-kou (*upper group*) and Sjara-osso-gol (*lower group*). (From M. Boule et al., *Le Paléolithique de la Chine*, Paris, 1928, figs. 30–48 passim.)

some seven or eight clusters of sites have been investigated and reported,[54] the best-known assemblages are those uncovered at Hsiao-ch'iao-pan in the Sjara-osso-gol valley in southern Inner Mongolia[55] and at Shui-tung-kou in eastern Ninghsia east of the Huang Ho.[56] According to the various studies of these assemblages,[57] the main features of the Ordos industries may be summarized as follows (fig. 23):

1. The two basic technological components of the Lower Palaeo-lithic—that is, the use of flakes and pebbles for tool fashioning—remained in the Ordosian.

2. Significant technological advances, however, are observed in the new industry. Choppers and chopping tools are so rare as to be insignificant. More important, flakes were struck from elaborately prepared cores. This is indicated by prepared cores (discoidal, tortoiseshell, and prismatic), the faceted striking platform, and the uniformity of flake shapes.

3. Two kinds of flakes are most common: triangular flakes struck from discoidal and tortoiseshell cores, and parallel-sided flakes (blades) struck from prismatic cores. The significant concurrence of pebble tools, triangular ("Mousterian") flakes, and blades is an Eastern feature similar to the Upper Palaeolithic of Siberia.

4. In the total stone assemblages, artifacts with secondary retouch formed a very small percentage, but several "types" had become definitely established. These include the triangular flakes retouched along one or both long edges—probably scrapers; points of triangular flakes retouched along both edges near the point; secondarily retouched blades; scrapers on ends of blades; and burins on ends of blades (of several varieties).

On the whole the blade artifacts of the Ordosian are identical with many Périgordian and Aurignacian types of western Europe, but the

54. K. C. Chang, *Arctic Anthropol.* 1 (1963), no. 2, 32–33.

55. Teilhard, *Anthropologie* 33 (1924), 630–31; *Natural History* 26 (1926), 239–42. Teilhard and Licent, *GSoC Bull.* 3 (1924), 46–48. Licent and Teilhard, *Anthropologie* 35 (1925), 220–28. M. Boule et al., *Le Paléolithique de la Chine*, Paris, Institut de Paléontologie Humaine, Memoir no. 4 (1928).

56. Teilhard and Licent, *GSoC Bull.* 3 (1924), 45–46. Licent and Teilhard, *Anthropologie* 35 (1925), 206–19. Teilhard, *Natural History* 26 (1926), 239. Y. P. Wang, *KK* 1962 (11), 588–89. L. P. Chia et al., *VP* 8 (1964), 75–83.

57. Including the author's own study in 1959 of the Sjara-osso-gol and Shui-tung-kou collections at the Institut de Paléontologie Humaine at Paris, whose courtesy is gratefully acknowledged.

rarity here of backed blades is conspicuous. Its comparative significance aside, the Ordosian stone industry exhibits a clear tendency to specialize: artifact types were no longer generalized, all-purpose implements, but each served a limited number of purposes. More specialized implements were obviously more effective, but each set of such tools must have had a more restricted range of uses and was adapted to certain kinds of environments and ecological situations. With these points in mind we cannot fail to recognize the potential significance of a very detailed study of the geological period in question—its regional facies and minute chronological divisions—and, in the meantime, the absence of such study in the current stage of our discipline in China. In comparing the Sjara-osso-gol and the Shui-tung-kou assemblages, W. C. P'ei and Y. H. Li have lately observed,[58]

> The Quaternary deposits in Sjara-osso-gol and Shui-tung-kou were formed at the same time, in the same basin, under identical conditions, and can be regarded as of the same geological stratum. Certain differences, however, in animal fossils and stone artifacts existed between the two sites, indicating that their geographic environments differed during the late Pleistocene stage. Specifically, a larger number of mammals lived in the Sjara-osso-gol region, which indicates that the area was more moist and more thickly vegetated, providing man with a larger number of game animals. But rock materials for stone manufacture were scarce here, and its inhabitants had to manufacture small stone tools. Living mammals, on the other hand, were fewer in the Shui-tung-kou region, which means the area was more arid and barren, and man's living resources were scanty. Rock materials here were more abundant, and a larger number of stone tools was produced.

P'ei and Li's inference here appears to be reasonable, but it may have given the human and cultural factors too passive a role. The differences between the Shui-tung-kou and Sjara-osso-gol assemblages may very well be the result of active adaptation. Microlithic implements became highly popular during early postglacial times, when the land was covered with heavy vegetation and game was abundant—favorable conditions for the development of composite implements made of bone shafts and microlithic blades. Quite possibly a microlithic complex was already coming into being, in relatively moist and vegetated areas like the Sjara-osso-gol,

58. *VP* 8 (1964), 114.

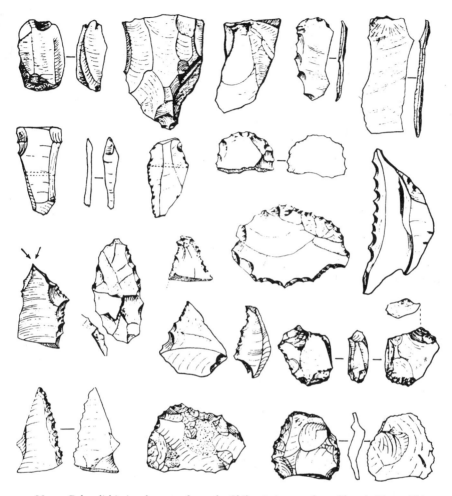

24. Upper Palaeolithic implements from the Shih-yü site, northern Shansi. (From Chia, Kai, and Yu, *KKHP* 1972, no. 1, p. 49.)

as early as the final Pleistocene stage. A cultural tendency to regionally different stone assemblages seems to have been well on the way within the Ordosian itself.

Both regionalization and microlithic development are again conspicuous features of other Upper Palaeolithic assemblages found outside the Ordos area. To the east of Ordos, in northern Shansi, an important new Palaeolithic site was excavated in 1963 near the village of Shih-yü. Brought to light were a human occipital, more than fifteen thousand pieces of stone implements and flakes, a polished stone disc, many burned stones and

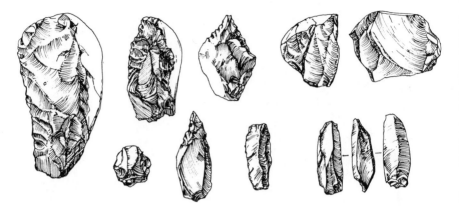

25. Upper Palaeolithic implements from Hsiao-nan-hai Cave near Anyang, Honan. (After *KKHP* 1965, no. 1, pp. 7, 10, 12, 14, 16.)

bones, pieces of animal bones apparently broken by man, and more than five thousand animal teeth. The animals represented include ostriches, Ordos deer (*Megaloceros ordosianus*), gazelles, woolly rhinoceroses, horses (*Equus przewalsky*) and donkeys (*Equus heminus*), and several kinds of cattle, indicating an upper Pleistocene date and an environment characterized by "broad steppes near mountains, interspersed with brush forests, with a wide temperature range summer to winter and an annual temperature lower than the present."[59] The stone implements include, in the terminology of the archaeologists reporting on the Shih-yü site, bipolar nuclei and flakes, polyhedral nuclei, flakes, microflakes, small choppers, points, scrapers, burins, and other types (fig. 24). Essentially these are the same types seen at the Ordosian sites, but the Shih-yü assemblage is larger and was excavated under better-controlled conditions. A piece of cattle bone found at the site has yielded a radiocarbon date of $28,135 \pm 1,330$ years ago.[60]

In a limestone cave in the hill region of Hsiao-nan-hai, 30 kilometers southwest of An-yang, in northern Honan, ancient habitation remains were discovered in 1960 in association with typical Sjara-osso-gol fauna.[61] More than seven thousand pieces of stone were excavated, about 90 per cent chert, but only about a hundred were secondarily retouched artifacts. Again there is a combination of implements of pebble, flake, and blade, similar to the Ordosian, but a microlithic tendency is even more pro-

59. L. P. Chia, P. Kai, and Y. C. Yu, *KKHP* 1972 (1), 47.

60. *KK* 1976 (1), 30.

61. C. M. An, *KKHP* 1965 (1), 1–27.

nounced than at Sjara-osso-gol. A few types—especially a variety of heavy scrapers on sides of flakes—are distinctive here, but burins are poorly developed (fig. 25). Farther down the Huang Ho another limestone cave site was discovered in Shantung in 1965. Heavy scrapers on sides of flakes are again distinctive of the stone assemblage here.[62] In 1966, a human molar was found among other late Pleistocene mammalian fossils in a limestone cave in Hsin-t'ai, in central Shantung.[63] Another site containing late Pleistocene mammalian fossils and a microflake and microblade lithic assemblage was found in 1972 and 1973 near Ling-yüan, in southeastern Liaoning.[64]

Upper Palaeolithic Cultures of the Southwest

Aside from scattered small finds of uncertain age in the upper Yangtze,[65] all Upper Palaeolithic discoveries in this region have been made in recent years. They include human-fossil remains found at Tzu-yang, in Szechwan,[66] and at Liu-chiang[67] and Tu-an,[68] in Kwangsi, and stone assemblages found at I-liang Hsien,[69] in eastern Yunnan, at Han-yüan Hsien,[70] in western Szechwan (formerly eastern Sikang), and at Liu-chou city, in Kwangsi.[71]

The Tzu-yang and Liu-chiang skulls were from deposits that are dated to the upper Pleistocene by the mammalian fauna found with them.[72] Both undoubtedly belonged to *Homo sapiens* but exhibit certain features

62. E. C. Tai and Y. C. Pai, *VP* 10 (1966), 82–83. For some reason the cave is referred to only as "a certain cave in Shantung," and no location is given.

63. H. C. Wu and K. F. Tsung, *VP* 11 (1973), 105–06.

64. Liaoning Provincial Museum, *VP* 11 (1973), 223–26.

65. Teilhard and C. C. Young, *GSoC Bull.* 14 (1935), 176. J. H. Edgar, *Jour. W. China Border Research Soc.* 6 (1933/34), 56–61; 7 (1935), 47–56. G. T. Bowles, *GSoC Bull.* 13 (1933), 119–41. Y. H. Li, *VP* 5 (1961), 143–49.

66. W. C. P'ei and J. K. Woo, *Tzu-yang Jen*, Peking, Science Press, 1957.

67. J. K. Woo, *VP* 3 (1959), 109–10.

68. Kwangsi Museum, *VP* 11 (1973), 221–23.

69. W. C. P'ei and M. C. Chou, *VP* 5 (1961), 139–42. Y. H. Li and W. W. Huang, *VP* 6 (1962), 182–89.

70. L. Yang, *VP* 5 (1961), 353.

71. *VP* 13 (1975), 137.

72. A piece of wood found associated with the Tzu-yang fauna has yielded a radiocarbon date of 7270 ± 130 B.P. (*KK* 1972, no. 1). On the basis of new geological observations, the staff of the Ch'eng-tu Geological Institute now places Tzu-yang man at early Holocene (*KKHP* 1974, no. 2, 111–23). Since the original condition of deposition has long since been irreparably lost, I am not convinced that the new dating is more acceptable than the old.

which recall both Peking man and the Neanderthaloid types. Moreover, the Liu-chiang skull has some morphological attributes that are comparable with Oceanic Negroid characteristics, and both the Tzu-yang and the Liu-chiang skulls show similarities to features of modern Mongoloid populations. On the basis of the two skulls one might be tempted to suggest that the population in South China during the Tali-glacial stage represents an early form of *Homo sapiens* which later differentiated into some of the principal constituent elements of the modern Mongoloid and Oceanic Negroid populations. In this connection one may recall the persistence of certain morphological features throughout the fossil record of man in this part of Asia and into its modern inhabitants (such as the shovel-shaped incisors, the sagittal crest, and the congenital absence of the third molar). C. S. Coon's recent attempt to trace some modern Mongoloid elements back to Peking man[73] may not have proved that mankind crossed the *Homo sapiens* threshold independently in the area of eastern Asia but has certainly brought serious attention to the need for further research into a highly important problem. As for the Tu-an teeth (an incisor and a molar), they are said to exhibit no apparent "primitive" features and are dated to the Pleistocene only on the strength of old fauna found in layers lower than the teeth.

Each of the Upper Palaeolithic sites in the southwest has its own peculiarities, which is understandable for this stage of cultural specialization and differentiation (fig. 26). The Han-yüan assemblage is one of microcores and microblades, closely similar to the Sjara-osso-gol component of the Ordosian. The stone artifacts of I-liang, on the other hand, are flakes struck from pebbles (retaining much of the cortex) and retouched by unilateral and bilateral blows in the chopper–chopping tool fashion. The Liu-chou find consists of a single pebble chopper. These finds are devoid of a general pattern, and their datings are largely uncertain; one can only observe that in southwestern China the archaic pebble and flake stone traditions persisted into the upper Pleistocene and, also, that a blade-microblade industry occurred. It is impossible to say which of these diverse industrial elements was associated with the Tzu-yang and the Liu-chiang skulls.

Final Palaeolithic and Mesolithic Cultures of North China

The fact that the lithic industry discovered at the Chou-k'ou-tien site and that at the Lan-t'ien and K'o-ho sites exhibit significant differences

73. C. S. Coon, *The Origin of Races*, New York, Knopf, 1963.

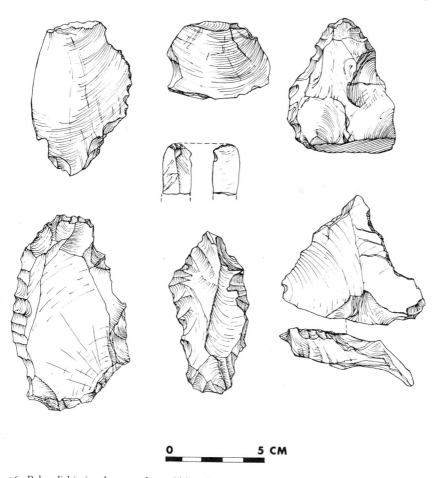

0   5 CM

26. Palaeolithic implements from Ch'ien-hsi (Kweichow) and I-liang (Yunnan). (*Lower half*, Ch'ien-hsi, from *VP* 9, 1965, pp. 277–99; *upper half*, I-liang, from *VP* 6, 1962, pp. 184–87.)

has been mentioned above. In recent years, seizing upon these differences, Chia Lan-p'o, Yu Yü-chu, and other palaeolithic archaeologists at the IVPP have proposed to view the differences between the two traditions— which they maintain were continuous and persistent throughout the Palaeolithic periods—as representing two adaptive patterns and two ways of life. The first tradition, the K'o-ho–Ting-ts'un series, or the "large flake chopper–large prismatic-point tradition," is characterized by large prismatic points, large choppers of various types made of broad and large flakes, and stone balls. Small ("microlithic") implements are few and include limited types in this series, which is typified by the sites at K'o-ho,

San-men-hsia, and Ting-ts'un. The second tradition, the locality 1–Shih-yu series, or the "keel-scraper–burin tradition," is distinguished by the small implements (microliths), of a great diversity of types, made of irregular small flakes and with small and careful retouch. Important sites of this series are locality 1 and locality 15 of Chou-k'ou-tien, Sjara-osso-gol, Shih-yü, and Hsiao-nan-hai.[74]

In the opinion of the above-mentioned archaeologists, this contrast persisted into terminal Pleistocene or even the postglacial period. A newly reported "Mesolithic" workshop site at Eh-mao-k'ou, in Huai-jen county, northern Shansi, with large flakes, thick, pointed implements, hand-axes, and "tortoise shell–shaped axes," is regarded as a late manifestation of the K'o-ho–Ting-ts'un series. Chia and Yu, in observing this persistence of the contrastive traditions, believe that

> such differences reflect the differences in their economic life-ways. Under the microlithic [locality 1–Shih-yü] tradition, people's livelihood leaned toward hunting and fishing, only to be supplemented with gathering and other means of subsistence. Early in the Late Palaeolithic period (e.g., at the Shih-yü site, in Shansi) chipped arrowheads appeared. In later periods, when microlithic elements became even more conspicuous, arrowheads became more abundant, indicating a heavier reliance upon hunting. Animal domestication eventually grew out of an intensification of hunting as a way of life. On the other hand, the large flake-chopper–thick point series suggests gathering as the primary way of life, supplemented by hunting and other means of subsistence. The subsequent beginning of agriculture was probably based upon a further development of gathering.[75]

These speculations are noteworthy in underlining the regional diversity of lithic assemblages throughout the Palaeolithic period of North China, as well as in calling attention to the adaptive aspects of the diversity. By the final stages of Pleistocene and early Holocene, North China was populated throughout by people manufacturing stone implements of great complexity, displaying different features at different sites, from the Mongolian steppes to the Manchurian and northern Chinese forests. During prehistoric times the Mongolian steppes formed a great oasis belt, and the early Holocene inhabitants of this area manufactured microcores, microflakes, and microblades. Apparently they engaged in fishing and

74. L. P. Chia, P. Kai, and Y. C. Yu, *KKHP* 1972 (1), 54.
75. L. P. Chia and Y. C. Yu, *KKHP* 1973 (2), 25.

hunting near the now-dry, shallow depressions which were then partially filled with water. Their main quarry seems to have been the ostrich, as shown by many ostrich-eggshell rings found at these and later cultural stations. From these sites very few arrowheads have been found, however, which indicates that hunting was probably of secondary importance. This inference is also supported by the scarcity of bone and antler remains and implements in the Mongolian sites, although this can partly be accounted for by the perishability of these remains and the unfavorable conditions for preservation.[76] The Mongolian Mesolithic tradition persisted in this region for a considerable time, even when areas to the south had become farmlands and when Neolithic techniques were introduced and gave the Mongolian Mesolithic a sub-Neolithic appearance. This will be discussed in a later chapter.

More is known about the forest dwellers of North China and Manchuria, who were clearly the direct descendants of the Upper Palaeolithic occupants of the area. One of the best known terminal Palaeolithic assemblages in this region was found in the Upper Cave of Chou-k'ou-tien. Its fauna, still yielding remains of such persisting Pleistocene forms as *Hyaena ultima*, *Ursus spelaeus*, *Elephas* sp., and *Paradoxurus*, definitely testifies to the introduction of completely modern forms: *Homo sapiens*, *Cervus elaphus*, *Siphneus armandi*, and *Struthio*, as well as some southern, warm-climate species: *Cynailurus jubatus* and *Paguma*.[77] The site was probably a burial place and gives no indication of intensive occupation. The industrial assemblage includes some stone tools (scrapers, flakes, and chopper–chopping tools), and abundant bone and antler artifacts (worked bone; bone needles; worked antler; perforated teeth of badgers, foxes, deer, wildcats, polecats, and tigers), together with mollusk shells and fishbones (fig. 27). According to W. C. P'ei, the Upper Cave man lived in calcareous caves.[78] Nearby there were woods in which tigers, leopards, bears, and wolves dwelt; there were steppes on which the Chinese deer, the red deer, and the gazelle roamed about, and plains and lakes in which gigantic fish swam. The man hunted in the woods and fished by the lakes and made abundant bone and shell artifacts. The marine shells in this site indicate also either extensive trade connections or long-distance seasonal migrations. In the cave were found skeletal remains of man, apparently

76. N. C. Nelson, *Amer. Anthropologist* 28 (1926), 307. John Maringer, *Prehistory of Mongolia*, Stockholm, pp. 90, 92, 140–43, 151–54, 201, 206.

77. W. C. P'ei, *PS*, ser. D, 10 (1940); *VP* 1 (1957), 9–24.

78. *Chung-kuo shih-ch'ien shih-ch'i chih yen-chiu*, Shanghai, Commercial Press, 1948, pp. 72–73.

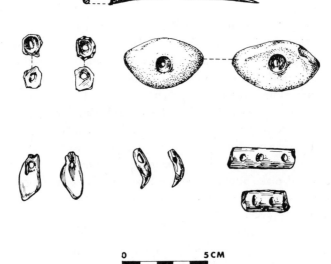

0   5 CM

27. Artifacts of the Upper Cave, Chou-k'ou-tien. (After W. C. P'ei, *PS*, ser. D, no. 9, 1939.)

seven individuals. Since skulls or skull fragments and lower jaws are preserved, Weidenreich has been able to determine that this population was composed of an adult male over sixty, a relatively young male adult, two young adult females, one adolescent, and two children. It is interesting to note that all of the remaining skullcaps show depression, fractures, or holes which, according to Weidenreich, "apparently have been caused by heavy blows with sharp and blunt implements delivered at a time when the scalp still covered the bones." Weidenreich thus infers that these were the remains of a single family who, being "victims of a sudden attack and dismembered, were thrown into the cave."[79] This suggestion is certainly plausible, but other explanations cannot be ruled out. The earth which surrounded the skeletons was partly covered with hematite, indicating that funeral rites probably took place. The damage to the skulls, as W. C. P'ei has suggested, could have been caused later by rockfalls from the cave ceiling. It is therefore entirely possible that the family, if it was one, fell victim to a local epidemic and was buried in the cave by kinsfolk or companions.

Another intriguing aspect of the Upper Cave skulls concerns their racial characteristics. Weidenreich's morphological analysis of the three best-preserved adult skulls has convinced him that "they typify three different racial elements, best to be classified as primitive Mongoloid, Melanesoid, and Eskimoid types."[80] This conclusion has led the late Ernest A. Hooton to discuss the Upper Cave population in his book *Up From the Ape*, under the heading "The Old Man of China who Married an Eskimo and a Melanesian."[81] Recent findings about Upper Palaeolithic man in South China, as mentioned above, has shed much new light on this problem. If Wu Hsin-chih is right in identifying the Upper Cave specimens as altogether Mongoloid, according to recent studies of casts,[82] it then seems that by the beginning of the Recent (Holocene) period the population in North China and that in the southwest and in Indochina had become sufficiently differentiated to be designated as Mongoloid and Oceanic Negroid races respectively, even though both of them may have evolved out of a common upper Pleistocene substratum as represented by the Tzu-yang and the Liu-chiang skulls. A piece of deer bone from the Upper Cave has yielded a radiocarbon date of $18,340 \pm 410$ years before the present.[83]

It is quite possible that Manchuria in the initial postglacial period was covered by woods, and its climate was probably cooler. Here, several surviving Pleistocene faunal forms are found in association with Mesolithic industries. From the Mesolithic sites at Ku-hsiang-t'un (and possibly Ta-kou), near Harbin, stone (scrapers, willow-leaves, microliths), bone (knives, spearheads, and barbed points), and antler implements were found, indicating that the Mesolithic inhabitants of this region lived in

79. F. Weidenreich, *Bull. Natural Hist. Soc. Peiping* 13 (1938/39), 163.
80. *Ibid.*, p. 170.
81. Hooten, *Up from the Ape*, New York, MacMillan, 1949, p. 401.
82. *VP* 5 (1961), 181–203.
83. *KK* 1976 (1), 30.

woods and hunted game.[84] Farther north, at Djalai-nor, implements of stone, bone, and antler, and willow basketwork have been found in direct association with remains of woolly rhinoceros, bison, and mammoth, indicating a similar ecology and culture.[85]

The Sha-yüan assemblage of Shensi is of uncertain age, but it is believed to date from early postglacial times. Cultural remains from fifteen localities were collected during 1955 and 1956 in the area of Chao-i Hsien and Ta-li Hsien, in the central part of eastern Shensi—an area in the western portion of a sand-dune region (referred to as Sha-yüan by the local inhabitants) of considerable dimensions.[86] Many of the flakes, stone implements, and bone fragments that were collected are badly rolled, and no habitation layers have been recognized, indicating that the original cultural deposits have been destroyed by strong sand-bearing winds over the centuries. The frequent movements of the sand dunes may also have disturbed the original distribution. The fifteen localities, therefore, are really nothing more than fifteen spots where cultural remains happen to have been concentrated.

Surface specimens, 519 in all, were signled out as representative by the investigators of the Institute of Archaeology, Academia Sinica. Most of these consist of chipped flakes and implements, of which only a few were secondarily retouched. The rest include two polished stone arrowheads—presumably later intrusions—a bone bead, a mollusk-shell ornament, and a fragment of a stone ornament. The chipped stones fall into two major categories. The microliths consist of small flakes and blades made of flint, quartzite-silicate sandstone, agate, opal, jade, and light-colored siliceous pebble by means of indirect percussion and pressure flaking. Retouching, when it occurs, is in most cases limited to a single surface. In typology, these microliths include cores, leaf-shaped points, microblades, points, arrowheads, and scrapers. The other category consists of flakes of quartzite-silicate sandstone and light-colored siliceous pebbles; agate also occurs occasionally. These flakes as a rule are larger than the microliths, but their maximum length is still less than 9 centimeters. According to the investigators, direct percussion was the principal technique for making this series of flakes and implements, which include such types as points and scrapers (fig. 28).

84. Tokunaga Shigeyasu and Naora Nabus, *JZ* 48 (1933), 12. *Manshuteiko Kitsurinshō Ku-hsiang-t'un kaiikkai hakkutsu butsu kenkyu hobun*, Tokyo, Waseda University, 1934.

85. V. J. Tolmatchov, *Eurasia Septentrionalis Antiqua* 4 (1929), 1–9. Teilhard, *Early Man in China*, p. 78.

86. C. M. An and J. T. Wu, *KKHP* 1957 (3), 1–12. S. S. Chang, *VP* 3 (1959), 47–56.

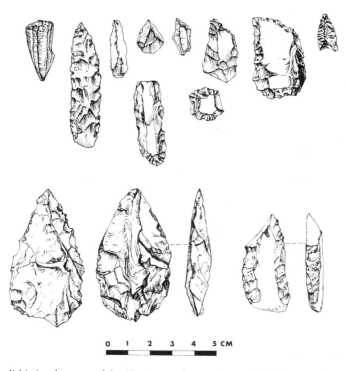

28. Mesolithic implements of the Sha-yüan culture. (After An Chih-min and Wu Ju-tso, *KKHP* 1957, no. 2, pp. 5, 8.)

Although more precise dating of the Sha-yüan assemblage is needed, it is one of the most significant discoveries in the prehistoric archaeology of North China in recent years. It is the first evidence in North China proper of a microlithic industry (probably of the early postglacial period) that shows affinities with the microlithic horizons in Manchuria, Mongolia, and Soviet Siberia and thus indicates a widespread cultural substratum in North China on which later cultural developments might have been built. On the other hand, the "Mousterian-like" flakes of this assemblage indicate an unmistakable linkage with the Ordosian industries of the upper Pleistocene period in the same region.

The lithic assemblage at Ling-ching, northwest of Hsü-ch'ang, in central Honan, collected in 1965 but not fully described until 1974, completes the link that places the microlithic industry into the center of North China. The 1,353 pieces of quartz, flint, and quartzite collected here include pebble implements, flake implements, and microliths, the last kind being the more numerous, including microcores, microblades, scrapers, and burins. Two pieces of human femurs were also found.

Mammalian fossils associated with the stones include such Pleistocene animals as woolly rhinoceros, ostrich, red deer (*Cervus elaphus*), elephants, horses, and donkeys, suggesting that the Ling-ching assemblage may be dated to the terminal Pleistocene, probably contemporaneous with Upper Cave.[87]

Final Palaeolithic and Mesolithic Cultures of South China

A different situation prevailed in the early postglacial period south of the Ch'in Ling Mountains and the Huai Ho valley. During the Recent period of Southeast Asia, there was widespread representation of the old pebble-tool technological tradition, generally known as the Hoabinhian pebble-tool complex. This can be characterized by chipped pebble tools, reminiscent of the older chopper–chopping tool tradition, including "hand-axes" and scrapers; the absence of blades, "Mousterian" flakes, and the microlithic industry; and the association of "Negroid" skeletons, in contrast to the north where a "Mongoloid" population seems to have prevailed throughout. This general Southeast Asian pattern manifests itself regionally in South China in widespread finds of chipped stone implements in Szechwan,[88] Kwangsi,[89] Yunnan,[90] and in the western part of Kwangtung as far as the Pearl River delta[91] (fig. 29). A paucity of reliable data still makes a classification of regional facies extremely difficult, but some significant assemblages from this area offer clues. In the Red Basin of Szechwan, the antiquity of the chipped axes is suggested by their geographical distribution,[92] but the stratigraphical evidence at Tai-hsi is scanty. Little is known about the cultural associations of these chipped axes in a preceramic context. More is known about Yunnan and Kwangsi, however, where chipped stone tools, shell middens, and charred animal bones have been found in limestone caves and rock shelters. In a cave at Ch'i-lin-shan, in Lai-pin Hsien, Kwangsi, cultural debris, charred bones, two quartzite flakes, one chopper made of quartzite

87. K. H. Chou, *KK* 1974 (2), 91–108. *VP* 10 (1966), 86.

88. Cheng Te-k'un, *Archaeological Studies in Szechwan*, Cambridge Univ. Press, 1957.

89. W. C. P'ei, *GSoC Bull.* 14 (1935), 393–412. L. P. Chia and C. L. Ch'iu, *VP* 4 (1960), 39. Y. M. Ku, *VP* 6 (1962), 193–99.

90. M. N. Bien and L. P. Chia, *GSoC Bull.* 18 (1938), 327–48.

91. *VP* 4 (1960), 38. W. Schofield, *Hongkong Naturalist* 5 (1935), 272–75. C. Mo, *KKHP* 1959 (4), 1–15. J. T. P'eng and W. Wang, *WW* 1959 (5), 75. R. Maglioni, *Hongkong Naturalist* 8 (1938), 211.

92. T. K. Cheng, *Archaeological Studies in Szechwan*, p. 130.

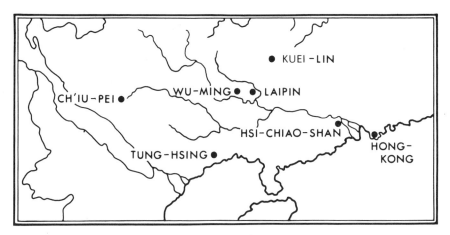

29. Mesolithic sites in southwest China.

pebble, and parts of a human skull were discovered in 1956, in a yellowish breccia stratum, in association with bones of deer, wild boars, and a large number of mollusk shells. The human skull fragments include a large part of the upper jaw, the hard palate, the right zygomatic bone, and the occipital bone; it is reportedly the skull of a male individual of advanced age. Its morphological features are certainly indicative of *Homo sapiens*, but the flat malar bone and a well-marked ridge at the entrance to the nasal floor are said to separate this skull from the Mongoloid pattern.[93] A rock-shelter site at Hei-ching-lung, near Ch'iu-pei in Yunnan, has yielded, in addition to charcoal and ash layers and two pieces of flint flakes, many seeds of *Celtis* and bones of *Canis gray*, Ursidae indet., Felinae indet., *Cervus* sp., Bovidae indet., and *Macacus* sp.[94] Similar assemblages were found in 1959 at Ya-p'u-shan near Hsi-chiao Ts'un and Ma-lang-ch'uan-shan near Ma-lang-chi Ts'un, both in Tung-hsing Hsien, western Kwangtung. Four strata are excavated at these two sites: top soil; shell bed with pottery and Neolithic implements; bed with shells and concretions with abundant chipped implements; and red sandstone basement rocks. The cultural remains from the third layer are characterized by core implements including hand axes, choppers, and so forth, most of which retain the original cortex of the pebbles. The associated fauna, all of modern species, is distinguished by such forms as *Rusa*, *Bubalus*, and various mollusks.[95]

93. L. P. Chia and J. K. Woo, *VP* 3 (1959), 37–39.
94. M. N. Bien and L. P. Chia, *GSoC Bull.* 18 (1938), 345–46.
95. *VP* 4 (1960), 38.

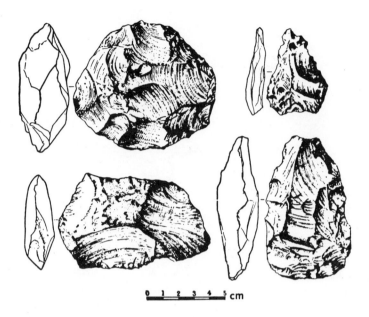

0 1 2 3 4 5 cm

30. Stone implements from Hsi-chiao-shan, Kwangtung. (From *Hsin Chung-kuo ti k'ao-ku shou-huo*, Peking, Wen Wu Press, 1962, fig. 15.)

Around the Pearl River delta area, open sites have been discovered where chipped stone implements were found in a preceramic context. In addition to the somewhat dubious finds in the Hong Kong area,[96] a highly important assemblage has been brought to light since 1955 at Hsi-chiao-shan in Nan-hai County, Kwangtung.[97] An inactive volcano called the Hsi-chiao-shan, approximately 12 square kilometers in area and surrounded by creeks and dried-up ponds, is about 70 kilometers southwest of Canton. Around the hill, fourteen prehistoric localities have been discovered. These can be grouped into three classes: preceramic, sub-Neolithic, and Neolithic. The last two will be discussed in a later chapter, but it should be remarked here that these three groups represent a common culture substratum characterized by chipped stone implements. The implements found in a nonceramic context, as well as those in association with pottery and polished stone tools, include both flake and core implements made of flint and sandstone. The core implements apparently

96. W. Schofield, *Hongkong Naturalist* 5 (1935); *Proc. 3rd Far Eastern Prehist. Congr.*, 1938, 243.

97. C. Mo, *KKHP* 1959 (4). J. T. P'eng and W. Wang, *WW* 1959 (5).

resemble the familiar chopper–chopping tool varieties, but some of the flakes bear faceted platforms and many of them fall into the categories of end scrapers, points, and flake blades (fig. 30). Further to the east, a similar lithic assemblage has been discovered in Taiwan, on the east coast of the island, near Ch'ang-pin.[98]

98. W. H. Sung, "Ch'ang-pin wen-hua," *Newsletter of Chinese Ethnology* 9 (1969), 1–27, Taipei.

3 : The Earliest Farmers

More than 99 per cent of the entire history of man, in China and elsewhere, belongs to the Palaeolithic period. During this era progress was slow—measured in terms of millennia and tens of millennia. Throughout the entire Palaeolithic and Mesolithic periods man had been a gatherer, acquiring his food from natural resources: game animals, fish, beetles, and grubs; and wild seeds, fruits, nuts, and berries, as these were provided in their natural states. The food gatherer's life is dependent upon nature's bounty, and he is usually mobile in order to follow the seasonal and cyclical changes of the natural resources. His culture is necessarily simple, because almost every member of the society must work hard to gain food. The invention of food production—the cultivation of plants and the domestication of animals—was thus a crucial turning point in human history. With resources of food under some degree of human control as to timing, quantity, and quality, man's life began to move toward a more complex and sedentary culture.

The importance of this great transitional process—the late V. Gordon Childe called it the Neolithic Revolution—was not lost on ancient man himself. In early Chinese legends one of the greatest heroes of all was Shen Nung, inventor of agriculture.

> Shen Nung cultivated plants and made pottery. [*Chou-shu*, as quoted in *T'ai P'ing yü lan*]
>
> Shen Nung invented wooden agricultural implements [*lei* and *ssu*] and taught the whole world his inventions. . . . He instituted the market held at noon. He administered all the peoples of the world and gathered their produce in the markets. The people went back to their homes after exchange and rested contented. [*Hsi-tz'u*, in *I*]
>
> During the Age of Shen Nung, people rested at ease and acted with vigor. They cared for their mothers, but not for their fathers. They lived among deer. They ate what they cultivated and wore what they wove. They did not think of harming one another. [Chapter "Tao-ch'e," in *Chuang tzu*]

These passages are sufficient to show that as late as the second half of the first millennium B.C., when they were supposedly written, the Chinese in North China had some knowledge, or image, of the Neolithic life of their ancestors. Concerning the invention of agriculture by Shen Nung, there are some stories of special interest. Some relate that the first plant cultivation was the result of necessity:

> The ancient people ate meat of animals and birds. At the time of Shen Nung, there were so many people that the animals and birds became inadequate for people's wants, and therefore Shen Nung taught the people to cultivate. [*Pai hu t'ung*]

In other stories, the cultivated plants were given by divine forces:

> At the time of Shen Nung, millet rained from Heaven. Shen Nung collected the grains and cultivated them. [*Chou shu*, as quoted in *I shih*]
>
> [At the time of Shen Nung] there was a red bird holding in its mouth a cereal stalk with nine ears. Some of the grains fell onto the ground. Shen Nung picked them up and cultivated them in the field. Those who ate the grains lived long and did not die. [*Shih i chi*, by Wang Chia of the Chin dynasty]

Although plant cultivation was in all likelihood independently invented in China, we do not know how the process was first established. It is significant, however, that Shen Nung, besides being the inventor of agriculture, was also the first and greatest herbalist. It is said that Shen Nung tasted a "hundred varieties of grasses" and knew the nature of them all. According to one folktale of the people at Szechwan, it was a highly poisonous grass that killed Shen Nung. Even today, Shen Nung, among his numerous other characteristics, is the patron divinity of the Chinese druggist and herbalist. Anthropologists have proposed many theories about the origin of agriculture, but to my knowledge none has suggested that the first cultivation of plants in some parts of the world might have been the work of a (or *the*) herbalist in the hunting-fishing stage of culture. The implications of the tale of Shen Nung the Herbalist seem to open an interesting line of study.

Whatever significance one attaches to the legends about the beginnings of agriculture in China, these passages are not very helpful for understanding the actual process of the Neolithic Revolution. Scientific archaeology has in the last thirty years or so all but established that this revolution took place independently in at least the Near East and Mesoamerica several thousand years before our era and that in both places the process was gradual and cumulative as the result of man's experience, over centuries or millennia, in experimenting with the domestication of wild plants and animals. In the Near East the experiments centered on wheat; in Mesoamerica maize was the focus of Neolithic life. In the Far East, the prominent crops in historical and ethnographical times are known to have been such cereals as millet and rice and such root crops as taro and yam. What can archaeologists tell us about man's first experiments with these plants? And what can they tell us about the animals that were domesticated at the same time? Unfortunately, they know very little so far about China.[1]

By Upper Palaeolithic times, with the technological sophistication of blades and microliths, man was able to develop specialized tool kits to take advantage of the diverse resources of his environment. The food-gatherers of the terminal Pleistocene had sets of techniques and tools for a great variety of sustenance needs and opportunities: animals of one kind or another, birds of different habits, fishes of various seasons, and all sorts of wild plants. Through many millennia and centuries of manipulative experience, man knew the nature of each plant and the outer limits and potential for its exploitation. In time, man learned that plants could be manipulated to a much greater extent than animals without undesirable ecological consequences, and agriculture became increasingly important to produce the so-called Neolithic Revolution—or at least so think a good number of archaeologists specializing in the history of plant cultivation.[2]

If the above hypothesis of the process of Neolithic beginnings makes sense, then Neolithic beginnings must almost invariably be based on familiarity with regional natural resources, and Neolithic cultures must first of all be understood in relation to the histories of the plant domesticates in their native habitats. On the other hand, the knowledge and idea of agriculture can diffuse: the hunting-fishing people of a region may

1. In his 1936 classic on the phytogeographic differential study of cultivated plants, N. I. Vavilov, the Russian botanist, lists China as one of the eight primary centers of cultivation of the world and assigns 136 cultivated plants (out of 666 for the world) to China (see his "The origin, variation, immunity, and breeding of cultivated plants," *Chronica Botanica* 13, 1949/51). Vavilov also assigns 172 other plants to his Indo-Malayan area, which should include a large portion of South China. Very few of these plants, however, have been archaeologically discovered as yet in China. See also Li Hui-lin, "The origin of cultivated plants in Southeast Asia," *Economic Botany* 24 (1970), 3–19.

2. See S. Struever, ed., *Prehistoric Agriculture*, Garden city, New York, Natural History Press, 1971.

learn about plant cultivation from their neighbors and begin experimenting with their own plants. Or when a farming people moves into a region with a different assemblage of native plants, they may come to utilize what the new place has to offer. For these reasons, to study Neolithic beginnings of any region one must very carefully study the data provided by both botany and archaeology.

How did the Neolithic way of life—characterized by a central reliance upon farming for food, use of pottery, and making of stone implements by grinding—begin in the area of China? Up until thirty years ago many scholars thought that it began late—in the third millennium B.C.—in North China, through cultural diffusion from western Asia. In the 1950s new archaeological finds from North China became numerous enough to show a culture of distinctive character, and many studies appeared— among them the first edition of the present volume—to establish the indigenous character of the Neolithic development in the Central Plain (Chung Yüan) area of North China. New archaeological data brought to light in the 1960s in the southeast, especially in Taiwan, indicate a parallel regional development of Neolithic cultures in the southeastern coastal area of China, a development with ties to the Neolithic cultures of Southeast Asia. The publication of the first radiocarbon dates of Neolithic sites from all over China, in the 1970s,[3] has further confirmed the parallel developments in the north and southeast, and further suggests a possible third early center of Neolithic growth (fig. 31). The important question is no longer, Was the Chinese Neolithic an indigenous development? It demonstrably was. Nor is it, Did Neolithic cultures begin in China in several regional universes? It apparently did, essentially in line with the process described earlier. Rather, the important current issue is the interrelationship of the several parallel lines of Neolithic development in and near the area of China.

Current archaeological material permits the identification of two groups of early farming cultures in China: the Yang-shao culture of the middle Huang Ho valley, and the Ta-p'en-k'eng culture of the southeastern

3. Principal reports are: *KK* 1972 (1), 52–56; 1972 (5), 56–58; 1974 (5), 333–38; Y. C. Hsü et al., *Radiocarbon* 12 (1970), 187–92; 15 (1973), 345–49; M. Stuiver, *Radiocarbon* 11 (1969), 545–658. For discussion, see An Chih-min, in *KK* 1972 (1), 57–59; 1972 (6), 35–44; Noel Barnard, *The First Radiocarbon Dates from China*, Monographs on Far Eastern History, no. 8, Australian National University, 2nd ed., 1975; Richard J. Pearson, *Antiquity* 47 (1973), 141–43; K. C. Chang, *Current Anthropology* 14 (1973), 525–28; *Bull. of the Department of Archaeology and Anthropology*, National Taiwan University, no. 37/38 (1975), 29–43.

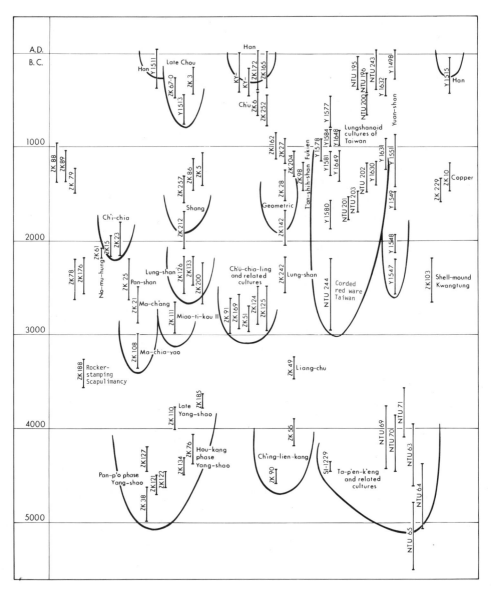

31. Time-space plotting of 87 radiocarbon dates (calibrated) in Chinese archaeology. (See appendix I for the sources.)

coast. Both appeared in the archaeological record by the fifth millennium
B.C., but they were probably formed much earlier. Slightly later in time,
the Ch'ing-lien-kang and related cultures emerged in the Huai Ho valley
and the lower Yangtze. Still others are conceivable, but these are the ones
that will now occupy our attention.

The Ta-p'en-k'eng Culture of the Southeastern Coast

In the last ten or fifteen years a number of archaeological sites with a
characteristic cord-marked pottery have been found in several areas along
the southeastern coast of China, from a time horizon best placed into the
early third millennium B.C. and earlier. The best studied of these sites are in
Taiwan, especially the site at Ta-p'en-k'eng, in T'ai-pei County, northern
Taiwan.[4] Other Taiwanese sites are found intermittently along the entire
circumference of the island. Only one radiocarbon date is available for
this culture (5480 ± 55 B.P., calibratable to 4450–4350 B.C.),[5] but the
dating could range from the third to the tenth millennium B.C.

The most conspicuous feature of this culture is its distinctive pottery
(fig. 32).[6] Fragile and often heavily eroded, potsherds of the Ta-p'en-k'eng
culture are usually fragmentary, thick, and gritty. The color ranges from
creamy buff to dark brown, and the principal shapes of the vessels are
large, globular jars and bowls. Low and perforated ring feet are found
attached to the bottoms of some jars. The rims have medium flare, and
many have a circumferential ridge ('carinated') below the lip. The entire
body of the vessel is invariably impressed with cord marks, probably
applied with a cord-wrapped stick (rouletting) or paddle (impressing), but
the rim is never so impressed. The rim surfaces and, frequently, the upper
part of the shoulder are decorated with incised designs composed of wavy
lines and short, parallel strokes, applied with a pair of (or occasionally
three) sticks bundled together.

Only a small number of stone tool types are known so far from this
culture, including worked pebble (perhaps net sinkers), bark beater with
polished and grooved surface, polished adz (with asymmetrical edge and
rectangular cross section), and small, triangular, perforated slate point.
The stone and ceramic inventory indicates a culture of considerable complexity, and although there is as yet no direct evidence of agriculture, their

4. K. C. Chang et al., *Fengpitou, Tapenkeng, and the Prehistory of Taiwan*, Yale University
Publications in Anthropology, no. 73 (1969).
   5. Huang Shih-ch'iang, *Bull. Dept. Arch. Anth.* 35/36 (1974), 66.
   6. K. C. Chang, "Prehistoric Archaeology of Taiwan," *AP* 13 (1970), 62–64.

32. Cord-impressed and incised sherds from the sites of Ta-p'en-k'eng and Feng-pi-t'ou, Taiwan. (Collection, National Taiwan University.)

culture undoubtedly included significant reliance on plants, and this is of importance in consideration of a wider area of Southeast Asia.

Several ethnobotanists and cultural historians have speculated about an early horticultural revolution in the tropical regions of Southeast Asia,[7] and they agree in characterizing the early garden culture as follows: (1) The area where the first plant domestication and cultivation took place was probably a permanently humid, tropical region with rich flora and an abundance of marine and, to a lesser extent, freshwater resources. (2) Some "progressive fishermen" dwelling on river banks or near estuaries in the Southeast Asian tropics were likely the progenitors of the earliest growers of root crops. (3) The first gardening in this area was probably done by individual farmers who propagated perennials (such as taro and yam) in fenced gardens. The technique was at most a swidden cultivation with periodic cuttings into the forests from the river banks and estuaries. (4) In this early stage of cultivation, when fishing had an important role, fiber was a material of prime importance for making fish lines and nets and as a kind of oakum for calking canoes. In fact, the first uses of plants in this area may have been related to the gathering of fibers. Furthermore, fibrous and edible barks were important items of material culture, and "barking"

7. See K. C. Chang, *Discovery* 2 (1967), no. 2, 3–10.

was probably the first technique of land clearing, perhaps discovered by accident through the gathering of fibrous material from wild plants.

The tropical region of Asia that scholars have in mind as a nuclear agricultural area includes all of monsoon Asia, from southeastern India to mainland and insular Southeast Asia. The archaeological material from the Ta-p'en-k'eng culture of Taiwan, a part of the area, has proved to be illuminating with regard to the problem of agricultural origins, and it merits consideration in this context. The great variety of cord marks on the pottery demonstrates the existence of highly sophisticated cordage techniques, and fibers for the cord must have been obtained from plants among the abundant local flora. The sites of this culture were near bodies of water from which the inhabitants obtained fish and shellfish, and the stone sinkers and carpenter's tools (adzes and chisels of various kinds) suggest the construction of canoes and deep-sea fishing, for which fibers and cordage were probably needed for calking, fish lines, and nets. Stone bark beaters are known and barking was probably one of the means for obtaining fiber from wild plants. All this contextual information at the cord-marked pottery sites suggests agreement with the conditions proposed by ethnobotanists for the early horticulturalists. The evidence at the sites shows beyond question that the inhabitants' principal mode of subsistence remained in the hunting-fishing-collecting category, but the probability of some form of gardening among these peoples is very strongly indicated indeed.

Taiwan, of course, was not the sole habitat of the ancient people who made the corded ware so characteristic of the Ta-p'en-k'eng culture, for cord-marked pottery is widespread throughout South China (fig. 33) and the Indo-Chinese peninsula as well as the Japanese islands. The Japanese Jōmon culture did not seem to be tied to the Ta-p'en-k'eng culture in any way, the latter instead extending in a western direction. In Fukien, directly facing Taiwan across the Formosa Strait, the only known site containing very early pottery is the Fu-kuo-tun shellmound on Quemoy (Chin-men) Island. Here the potsherds again show incised straight and wavy lines, but in addition to cord-marking, they exhibit impressions made by molluscan shells and fingernails (fig. 34).[8] A series of radiocarbon dates place this site again in the fifth-millennium B.C. range. Moving north to Kiangsi one encounters the very rich cord-marked pottery site at the Spirit Cave (Hsien-jen-tung) in Wan-nien County.[9] Here chipped-pebble

8. C. C. Lin, *Bull. Dept. Arch. Anth.* 33/34 (1973), 36–38.
9. Y. W. Kuo and C. H. Li, *KKHP* 1963 (1), 1–16.

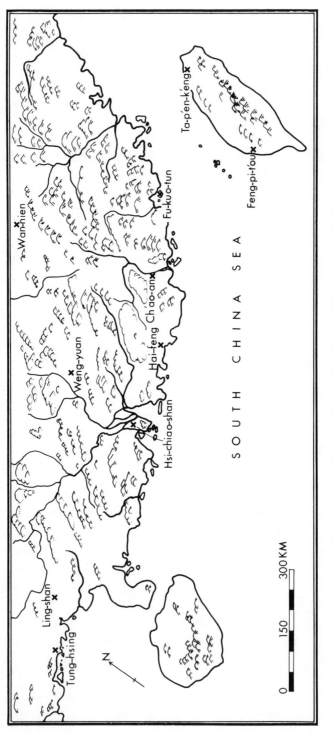

33. Map showing the location of sites of the Ta-p'en-k'eng and related cultures.

34. Potsherds from Fu-kuo-tun shellmound, Quemoy. (Collection, National Taiwan University.)

choppers, flakes and polished stone discs, points and chisels were found, together with bone points and harpoons, molluscan shells, and animal bones—again suggesting a culture predominantly hunting, fishing, and collecting for its subsistence. The dating of this site is uncertain but undoubtedly much earlier than the later Lungshanoid culture in the same area, several millennia before Christ.[10]

Many early cord-marked pottery sites are known in Kwangtung and southern Kwangsi, but published data are scanty. "Coarse" or "gritty" cord-marked potsherds from pre-Lungshanoid and pre-Geometric contexts have been reported from Ch'ao-an,[11] Hai-feng (fig. 35),[12] the delta

10. KK 1974 (5), 337. A Hsien-jen-tung sample date of 10,565 ± 240 B.P. is reported here. The sample, however, is reported as coming from the Geometric stratum overlying the cord-marked pottery layer and in that case must have been contaminated. It should not be used to date the earlier culture. (See appendix 3 for a new date.)

11. C. Mo, KK 1961 (11), 577–84.

12. This was determined by the author's examination of Father Maglioni's collection in the Fung Ping Shan Museum, University of Hong Kong, in 1966. For Maglioni's interpretation of Hai-feng's earliest ceramic phase, see his *Archaeological Discovery in Eastern Kwangtung*, Hong Kong Archaeological Society reprint, 1975.

35. Earliest potsherds from Hai-feng, Kwangtung. (From R. Maglioni, *Archaeological Discovery in Eastern Kwangtung*, Archaeological Society of Hong Kong, 1975 reprint, p. 32.)

area,[13] Ling-shan,[14] Nan-ning,[15] and Tung-hsing,[16] and from Tung-hsing the same kind of pottery extends into Vietnam[17] and is found in the so-called Hoabinhian culture. The site in Hai-feng yielded a rim sherd with incised wavy lines closely resembling Ta-p'en-k'eng rims, and at the Hsi-chiao-shan site in Nan-hai, on the delta, cord-marked sherds were found associated with chipped stone implements classified as "Mesolithic." These two finds make it certain that the Ta-p'en-k'eng culture was in fact an early ceramic culture found throughout the southeastern coastal area of China. The people were hunters, fishers, and gatherers, but there is little doubt that plants provided a good part of their food.[18] Many botanists

13. C. Mo, *KKHP* 1959 (4), 1–5. C. Mo and S. W. Li, *KKHP* 1960 (2), 107–19.

14. Y. M. Ku, *VP* 6 (1962), 193–99.

15. *KK* 1975 (5), 295–301.

16. C. Mo and C. L. Ch'en, *KK* 1961 (12), 644–49, 688.

17. See especially E. Saurin, *Proc. 3rd Far Eastern Prehist. Congr.*, Singapore, 1938, pp. 235–305. Also, H. Mansuy, Service Géologique de l'Indochine, Mémoire, vol. 11 (1924), vol. 12 (1925).

18. A Hoabinhian site in Thailand has yielded remains of food plants from strata radiocarbon-dated to eight or nine thousand years ago; see C. Gorman, *World Archaeology* 2 (1971), 300–20.

believe that taro and yam were among the first cultigens of Southeast Asia. If so, the people of the Ta-p'en-k'eng culture could be among the earliest cultivators of taro and yam as well as other tropical and subtropical fruits, vegetables, and condiments.

The Yang-shao Culture of the Huang Ho Valley

The Huang Ho valley is commonly regarded as another birthplace of agriculture—especially important for the first cultivation of several varieties of millet—and its Neolithic cultures are the best known in the area of China. The Chung Yüan area of the Huang Ho was not only the center of the Chinese empire throughout its history, it was also the location of the first three Chinese historic dynasties—Hsia, Shang, and Chou. Assumed to be the cradle of Chinese civilization, the Chung Yüan area naturally received the most attention, and it is also an area in China that has been most extensively eroded and cultivated, resulting in the exposure of more ancient relics than in the rest of China.

The Yang-shao culture, the earliest known Neolithic culture of this area, was discovered in 1920 by the farmers of Yang-shao village, in Mien-ch'ih County, northwestern Honan. Here is J. Gunnar Andersson's account of how the finds from Yang-shao-ts'un came into his hands:

'In the autumn of 1920 I had sent my collector Liu Ch'ang-shan to the district west of Loyang in Honan.... Liu's principal mission was to collect more of the Tertiary remains of vertebrates, but I had also asked him to keep his eyes open for the possibility of Stone-age discoveries.

Imagine my surprise and delight when on his return in December to Peking Liu unpacked a collection of several hundred axes, knives and other objects of stone, many of them exceptionally fine and well-preserved. The collection was the more remarkable as Liu related that he had purchased everything from the inhabitants of a single village, Yang Shao, where the peasants had collected the coveted objects in their fields.'[19]

The next year Andersson and several associates went to visit and excavate Yang-shao-ts'un, bringing to light a Yang-shao Neolithic culture characterized by red pottery painted with black decorative designs as well as

19. *Children of the Yellow Earth*, London, Kegan Paul, Trench, Trubner & Co., 1934, p. 164.

36. Map showing cities near which principal sites of the Yang-shao culture have been found. *Left to right*: (LH) Lin-hsia; (LT) Lin-t'ao; (P) Pao-chi; (WK) Wu-kung; (PH) Pin Hsien; (LTU) Lin-t'ung; (H) Hua Hsien; (HY) Hua-yin; (JC) Jui-ch'eng; (WC) Wan-ch'üan; (HH) Hsia Hsien; (S) Shan Hsien; (LN) Lo-ning; (LY) Lo-yang; Cheng-chou; (AY) An-yang; (TH) Tz'u Hsien.

polished stone axes and knives.[20] In the subsequent half-century, hundreds of sites of the Yang-shao culture have been found, and scores excavated, in a large area of the Huang Ho basin—from southern Hopei, northern Honan, and western Shantung in the east to eastern Kansu and Chinghai in the west; from northern Shensi and Shansi in the north to southern Shensi and Honan in the south (fig. 36).[21] Among the sites best representative of this culture are Pan-p'o-ts'un near Sian,[22] Chiang-chai near Lin-t'ung,[23] Yüan-chün-miao near Hua Hsien,[24] and Pei-shou-ling near Pao-chi,[25] all in Shensi; Hsi-yin-ts'un near Hsia Hsien,[26] Ching-ts'un near Wan-ch'üan,[27] Tung-chuang-ts'un and Hsi-wang-ts'un near Jui-ch'eng,[28] all in southern Shansi; Miao-ti-kou near Shan Hsien,[29] Ta-ho-ts'un near Cheng-chou,[30] and Hou-kang near An-yang,[31] all in Honan; Hsia-p'an-wang[32] and Tuan-chieh-ying[33] in Tz'u Hsien, southern Hopei; and Ch'ing-kang-ch'a near Lan-chou,[34] Ma-chia-wan near Yüng-ching,[35] and Ma-chia-yao near Lin-t'ao,[36] all in Kansu. Ironically, Yang-shao-ts'un itself is no longer regarded as a type site of Yang-shao culture, because its stratigraphy was never really clearly understood, and its main cultural component may belong to a post–Yang-shao Neolithic period. But the name Yang-shao stuck.

20. J. G. Andersson, *GSoC Bull.* 5 (1923); "Prehistoric sites in Honan," *BMFEA* 17 (1945).

21. *Hsin Chung-kuo ti k'ao-ku shou-huo*, Peking, Wen Wu Press, 1962, p. 7. An Chih-min, *Yang-shao wen-hua*, Peking, Chung-hua, 1964. For western Shantung, see *Ta-wen-k'ou*, Peking, Wen Wu Press, 1974, p. 120.

22. *Hsi-an Pan-p'o*, Peking, Wen Wu Press, 1962. *KK* 1973 (3), 146–48.

23. *KK* 1973 (3), 134–45; 1975 (5), 280–84. *WW* 1975 (8), 82–86.

24. *KK* 1959 (11), 585–87, 591.

25. *KK* 1959 (5), 229–30, 241; 1960 (2), 4–7.

26. Li Chi, *Hsi-yin-ts'un shih-ch'ien ti i-ts'un*, Peking, Tsing-hua University, 1927. S. Y. Liang, *New Stone Age Pottery from the Prehistoric Site at Hsi-yin-ts'un, Shansi*, Memoirs of the American Anthropological Association, no. 30 (1930).

27. K. C. Tung, *Shih-ta yüeh-k'an* 3 (1933), 99–111, Peking. C. W. Bishop, *Antiquity* 7 (1933), 389–404.

28. *KKHP* 1973 (1), 1–62.

29. *Miao-ti-kou yü San-li-ch'iao*, Peking, Science Press, 1959.

30. *KK* 1973 (6), 330–36.

31. *KK* 1972 (3), 14–25; 1972 (5), 8–19.

32. *KKHP* 1975 (1), 73–115.

33. *KK* 1974 (6), 356–72.

34. *KK* 1972 (3), 26–31, 53.

35. *KK* 1975 (2), 90–101.

36. B. Sommarstrom, *BMFEA* 28 (1956).

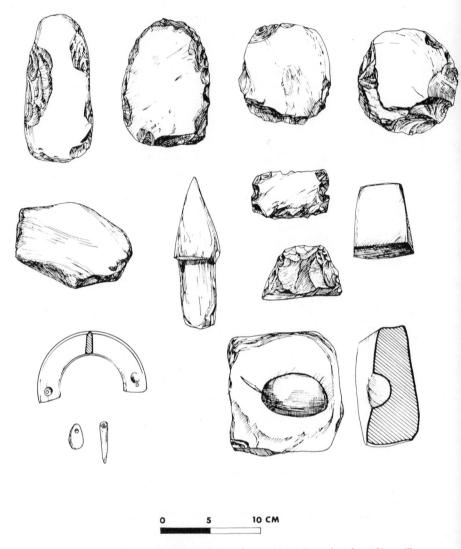

37. Stone implements from the Yang-shao culture site at Pan-p'o-ts'un, Sian. (From *Hsi-an Pan-p'o*, Peking, Wen Wu Press, 1963, pp. 61, 64, 65, 70, 71, 74, 90, 96, 192, 195.)

The Neolithic culture indicated by the remains of these scores of sites is that of settled village farmers inhabiting the large and small river valleys of the Huang Ho drainage, often making their abode on the lower loessic terraces along the river banks. The principal cultivated crop of the Yang-shao farmers was the foxtail millet (*Setaria italica* Beauv. var. *germanica*

Trin.), actual remains of which have been found at a number of sites.[37] Remains of cultivating implements include hoes, spades, and possibly digging sticks. Perforated stone disks, possibly the weights of digging sticks, have been found in considerable quantity. Other relevant implements are polished stone celts, often oval in cross section and presumably effective tools for field clearance, and polished or chipped rectangular and semilunar stone or pottery knives, which were probably fastened to the hand with string or leather ropes through a hole or around two side notches, and were used for cutting, scraping, weeding, and harvesting. Some of the pottery jars found widely in the Yang-shao context were presumably used for storing grains, the remains or impressions of which are sometimes found therein. Some of the harvest must have been prepared and preserved in the form of flour, for grinding stones have also been discovered (fig. 37).

The most important domesticated animals in this stage were dogs and pigs, whose bones have been unearthed from countless sites. Much less common were cattle (Ching-ts'un and Kao-tui, southern Shansi; and Hsing-yang, northern Honan),[38] and sheep and goats (Ching-ts'un and Lo-han-t'ang).[39] Hemp was probably cultivated,[40] and silkworms (Bombyx mori) were raised. A half-cut cocoon of the latter was found at Hsi-yin-ts'un in southern Shansi.[41] The many stone and pottery spindle whorls and eyed bone needles were probably used with hemp, silk, and other fabrics.

Wild-grain collecting, hunting, and fishing supplemented the diet. Remains of a kind of foxtail weed (Setaria lutescens) were found at Ching-ts'un, and seeds of vegetables were found in a pottery jar at Pan-p'o.[42] Bones of a variety of wild animals were recovered from the middens of the Yang-shao settlements: horse, leopard, water deer, wild cattle, deer,

37. Also reported in the literature were broomcorn millet (Panicum miliaceum L.) from Ching-ts'un, southern Shansi (Bishop, Antiquity 28, [1933]); grant millet, or kaoliang (Andropogon sorghum Brot.), also from Ching-ts'un; and wheat, from Wang-chia-wan, in Pao-tê Hsien, Shansi (C. M. An, Yenching Social Studies 2 [1949], 40). These are all unique occurrences and are, therefore, suspect. If the identification or stratigraphy is reliable in each case, they must have been extremely rare. See Ho, Cradle of the East, pp. 380–84, for a discussion of kaoliang.

38. J. G. Andersson, BMFEA 15 (1943). C. C. T'ung, KKHP 1957 (2), 9.

39. J. G. Andersson, BMFEA 15 (1943), 43. M. Bylin-Althin, BMFEA 18 (1946), 458.

40. Andersson, GSoC Bull. 5 (1923), 26. KK 1959 (2), 73.

41. Li Chi, Hsin-yin-ts'un shih-ch'ien ti i-ts'un, 22–23.

42. Bishop, Antiquity 28 (1933), 395. H. P. Shih et al., Hsi-an Pan-p'o, 1962, p. 223.

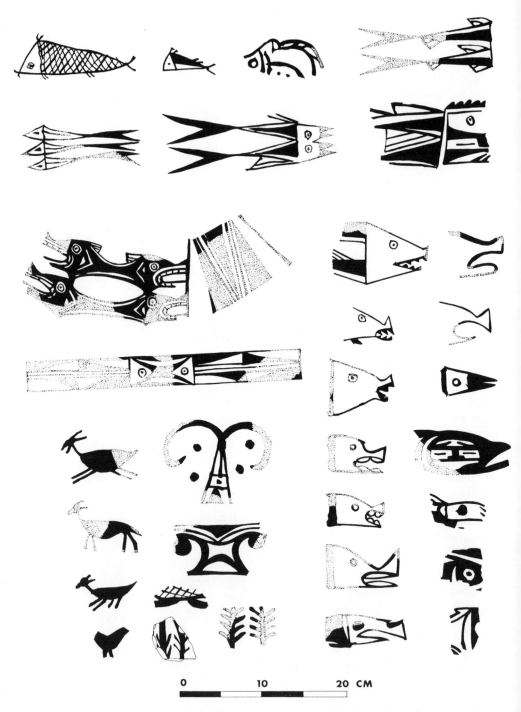

38. Fish, animal, and plant patterns in the pottery decoration of the Yang-shao culture site at Pan-p'o-ts'un, Sian. (From *Hsi-an Pan-p'o*, Peking, Wen Wu Press, 1963, figs. 121–22.)

rhinoceros, bamboo rat, antelope, hare, and marmot. The hunters must have used bow and arrow and spear, for remains of stone and bone points and arrowheads are numerous. Some roundheaded arrowheads were probably employed for shooting birds. Stone balls have been found occasionally, perhaps slingstones for the hunt. The importance of fishing is indicated by the abundance of bone fish spears, harpoons, and fishhooks as well as grooved pottery and stone net sinkers, fish designs on pottery, and the bones of fish. The decorative fish motif on pottery is particularly abundant in the Wei River valley sites[43] (fig. 38).

These early cultivators lived in villages. There are several indications that their village settlements shifted from one locale to another after a short period of occupancy, that some favorable locales were repeatedly occupied, and that the shifting and repetitive settlement pattern probably resulted from the slash-and-burn technique of cultivation. The deposits of the villages, often very thick, usually consist of multioccupational remains, which seems to indicate that these localities were occupied discontinuously but repetitively. A house at a site near Sian, Shensi, has a succession of three floors, apparently the result of three discontinuous occupations.[44] Furthermore, we find that in the same general neighborhood, the Yang-shao sites were widely distributed over a vast area, and each component consists of remains that show no marked changes in typology through time. In 1952 and 1953 twenty-one Yang-shao sites were located in the vicinity of Sian, Shensi (fig. 39). The investigators of these sites made the following remarks:

> The Yang-shao sites are many and widely distributed. Remains at a single locality are chronologically simple and neighboring localities can easily be given a relative dating on their respective cultural inventories.[45]

At Miao-ti-kou, Shan Hsien, Honan, similar phenomena have also been recorded.[46] And finally, the general cultural configuration gives similar indications which, taken together, point convincingly to the conclusion that the pattern of settlements was characterized by shifting and repetitive occupations. This conclusion is not in agreement with the former impression of most scholars, who considered that "Yang-shao" villages were large, sedentary communities.[47] We are now able to suggest that this

43. See, e.g., H. C. Chao, *KK* 1959 (11), 589.
44. Y. H. Chang, *KK* 1961 (11), 601–08.
45. P. C. Su and J. T. Wu, *KKTH* 1956 (2), 37. Cf. H. C. Chao, *KK* 1959 (11), 588–89.
46. *KKTH* 1958 (11), 68.
47. E.g., Cheng Te-k'un, *Prehistoric China*, pp. 69–72.

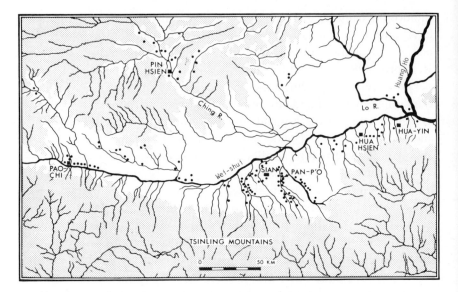

39. Distribution of Yang-shao sites in the Wei River valley of Shensi. (After *Hsi-an Pan-p'o*, Peking, Wen Wu Press, 1963, p. 3.)

impression is erroneous and that there are at least two sources of error. First, most of the large Yang-shao sites with apparently deep deposits were measured in a preliminary manner during a survey or survey excavations. Thus it seems likely that the large volume of Yang-shao remains represent discontinuous occupations which the surveyors or the excavators did not recognize. Second, granted that the measured village site represents one component—that is, a single-occupation village—these sites were probably of the very latest Yang-shao stage, which had already begun to show changes toward the next stage, such as the Yang-shao-ts'un site itself.

On this basis I presented an argument, in 1959, for a repetitive and discontinuous pattern of settlement for the Yang-shao farmers, a pattern concomitant with a shifting technique of cultivation.[48] This hypothesis was received by a few colleagues with some skepticism, and the Pan-p'o site has been used as a disproof of the view. Pan-p'o is a large village—50,000 square meters—and it is thought that such a large settlement could not have been occupied by farmers with primitive, shifting techniques.[49] An analysis of pollen specimens is supposed to have disclosed a "steppe-

48. *BIHP* 30 (1959), 268; *Harvard Journal of Asiatic Studies* 20 (1959), 167–68.
49. Cheng Te-k'un, *Antiquity* 38 (1964), 184–85.

like" vegetation, and it is thought that the shifting technique of agriculture was not compatible with the arid and treeless, northern Chinese landscape.[50] Contrary to this view, Pan-p'o-ts'un, certainly the best excavated and described of all Yang-shao sites, offers the best proof yet for the above interpretation of the Yang-shao settlement patterns.

The authors of the report on the Pan-p'o-ts'un site themselves have actually adopted the idea of shifting cultivation for the Yang-shao inhabitants: "Regarding cultivation, the Pan-p'o inhabitants possibly employed a slash-and-burn technique. After burning, the soil in the field becomes more fertile and easy to till. At the time, there was a great amount of land relative to the sparse population, permitting patches of field over wide areas to be fallowed and used in rotation."[51] Although the same authors do not tell us the precise reasons for this inference, the description of the site in the report contains very substantial evidence to support their view. Despite the size of the site and the apparently extensive remains, the debris was deposited during two to four successive occupations.[52] According to the changes in artifacts, two cultural components are distinguished: The early component includes remains of 22 houses and 43 storage pits; the late contains 24 houses and more than 160 storage pits. The authors estimate that the excavated portion of the site was about one fifth of the total area of settlement. This suggests that perhaps more than a hundred houses were built during each of the two cultural components. There is no question that both components were of the same culture, but minor changes in house construction methods and in artifact style are appreciable. Quite possibly the site was abandoned for a considerable interval between the two components. An explanation for this phenomenon is provided by a pollen profile taken from a 2.8-meter section of the site that represents both components.[53] Table 4, prepared according to the published pollen data, gives an interesting sequence of the change in the relative frequencies of tree and grass pollen.

This shows that at the beginning of settlement the Pan-p'o village was probably still surrounded by a considerable number of trees, whose pollen, transported to the village site from a notable distance, still accounts for 32 percent of the total. The scanty pollen in the next 80 centimeters suggests extensive clearance and open farming fields. The rise in tree pollen in the

50. Ho Ping-ti, *Huang-t'u yü Chung-kuo nung-yeh ti ch'i-yüan*, Hong Kong, Chinese University, 1969, pp. 33–34, 85–98.

51. H. P. Shih et al., *Hsi-an Pan-p'o*, p. 224.

52. *Ibid.*, p. 54.

53. *Ibid.*, appendix 3.

Table 4

Change of Tree and Grass Pollen During the Yang-shao Occupation
at the Pan-p'o-ts'un Site, Sian

Depth of Sample	Tree Pollen	Grass Pollen
(cm)	(%)	(%)
0–50	(0)	8 (100)
50–60	3 (37.50)	5 (62.50)
60–90	(0)	15 (100)
90–100	20 (27.78)	52 (72.22)
100–180	2 (1.70)	116 (98.30)
180–220	15 (31.92)	32 (68.08)

next level shows a cessation of agricultural activities at the site, allowing
for a considerable regrowth of trees. The soil of this layer is very dark and
compact and contains a large amount of organic materials, also indicating
a second growth of wild plant life. The next 90 centimeters above again
exhibit almost total absence of tall growth; apparently the village once
more served as the center of intensive farming activities. Thus this sequence
of pollen species, with an interval of forest growth in the middle, agrees
with the inference of two discontinuous cultural components, providing
an interesting support for our interpretation of the Yang-shao pattern of
settlement.

The physical plan of the Yang-shao villages is known only where the
sites were extensively excavated and the results were given in published
accounts. An interesting layout is attributed to the Pei-shou-ling site of
Pao-chi, in central Shensi, where two rows of houses faced each other
across a narrow lane, but detailed descriptions are absent.[54] A well-
described village plan is available for the Pan-p'o site. It is on a river
terrace about 800 meters east of the river Ch'an, a tributary of the Wei
River, and about 9 meters above the riverbed. The area of the settlement
is estimated at about 50,000 square meters, and its shape is an irregular
oval with the long axis north-south. The houses (forty-six of which were
excavated) and most of the storage pits and animal pens are clustered at
the center of the site in an area of about 30,000 square meters outlined by
a ditch 5 or 6 meters deep and wide. The village cemetery is in the northern
part of the village, outside the ditched dwelling area, and pottery kilns
are concentrated in the village's eastern portion (fig. 40). Within the

54. *KK* 1959 (2), 229–30.

40. Model of the Yang-shao culture village at Pan-p'o, Sian, at the Pan-p'o Museum. (Photo by W. T. Chase, 1973.)

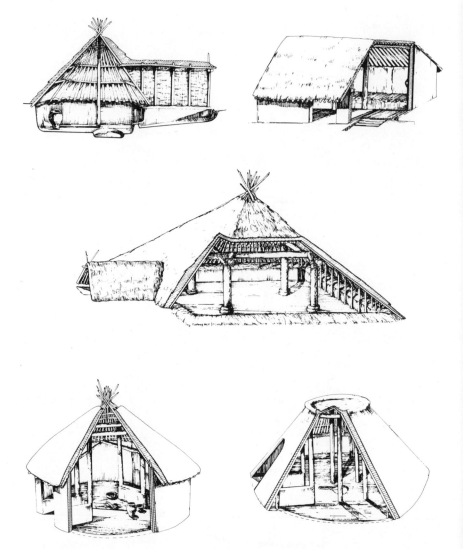

41. Reconstructed house types at the Yang-shao site at Pan-p'o-ts'un. (From *Hsi-an Pan-p'o*, Peking, Wen Wu Press, 1963, pp. 15, 19, 24, 27, 31.)

dwelling area, houses of fairly permanent nature were constructed. The most common kinds were 3 to 5 meters in diameter and were square, oblong, or round, with plastered floors. They were semisubterranean or at ground level, had wattle-and-daub wall foundations, and upper walls and roofs were supported by large and small wooden posts (fig. 41). During a latter occupation, a huge longhouse was constructed (over 20 meters long and 12.5 meters wide) divided into compartments by partition

42. Pottery kilns at Pan-p'o-ts'un. (From *Hsi-an Pan-p'o*, Peking, Wen Wu Press, 1963, fig. 118.)

walls. During this stage the communal house was at the center of the village plaza, with the small houses surrounding the plaza, their doors facing the center. Each house and each compartment of the longhouse was equipped with a hearth (a burned surface in the earlier occupations and a gourd-shaped pit in the later occupations).[55] The pottery-making center, east of the dwelling area, had no fewer than six kilns (fig. 42), in one of which were found some unfired pots. North of the dwelling area was the village cemetery, in which were found more than 130 adult burials— single, with the exception of one double and one quadruple burial—the skeletons lying face upward and stretched out (fig. 43). Infants and children were buried in urns between the dwellings.[56]

Chiang-chai—another Yang-shao site only 15 kilometers east of Pan-p'o, in Lin-t'ung County—excavated in 1972–74, is providing the best layout yet of a Yang-shao village:

'A ditch separated the residential area and the burial area. The former was inside the ditch, whereas the latter was to the east. Within the residential area houses were laid out in a regular plan: the houses in

55. According to Yang Hung-hsün, in *KKHP* 1975 (1), 39–72, the architectural history at Pan-p'o-ts'un—from semisubterranean houses, at an earlier stage, to ground-level houses, to, finally, large houses with many rooms—in fact represents a general pattern for Yang-shao culture as a whole.

56. H. P. Shih et al., *Hsi-an Pan-p'o*, 1962. H. P. Shih, *KKTH* 1955 (3), 7–16; *KKTH* 1956 (2), 23–30; *Rev. Archéol.* 2 (1959), 1–14. Hsia Nai, *Archaeology* 10 (1957), 181–87. *KK* 1973 (3), 146–48.

43. A Yang-shao burial at Pan-p'o-ts'un. (From *Hsi-an Pan-p'o*, Peking, Wen Wu Press, 1963, pl. 173.)

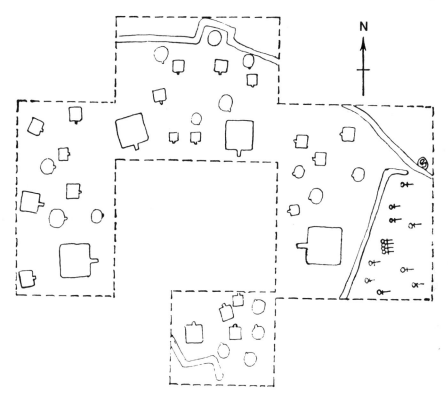

44. Yang-shao village layout at Chiang-chai, Lin-t'ung, Shensi. The circular form at right, above the grave sites, signifies the pottery kiln. (From *WW* 1975, no. 12, p. 76.)

the east opened their doors to the west, those in the north opened to the south, those in the west to the east, and those in the south to the north. In other words, all the houses opened toward the center of the village. The central area has not been excavated. In the eastern, western, and northern sections of the settlement, large houses were found, and near the large houses were medium-sized and small houses.'[57] [Fig. 44]

This pattern of subdividing a village into a dewlling area and cemetery recurs throughout the Yang-shao settlements that have been extensively excavated, such as those near Pao-chi[58] and Hua Hsien[59] in Shensi, and

57. *WW* 1975 (8), 82.
58. *KK* 1959 (2), 229–30, 241.
59. *KK* 1959 (2), 71–75; 1959 (11), 585–87, 591.

45. House floors at the Yang-shao village site at Ta-ho-ts'un, Cheng-chou, Honan (From *KK* 1973, no. 6, pl. 2, pic. 1).

Lin-shan-chai[60] and Miao-ti-kou[61] in Honan. More detailed information on small houses is known from the Miao-ti-kou site and the Ta-ho-ts'un site (fig. 45);[62] another huge communal building was found at Liu-tzu-chen, and the cemetery at Pao-chi has yielded abundant findings (fig. 46). But the general pattern repeats itself throughout, with such exceptions as that at Liu-tzu-chen, where the Yang-shao village did not have its own cemetery but seems to have shared a large one some distance away with neighboring villages. This is a very notable exception nevertheless, since the Liu-tzu-chen site belongs chronologically to a late phase of the Yang-shao stage, for this may indicate a tendency toward growth and fission on the part of the farming villages near the end of this stage. This tendency is made clear by J. G. Andersson's discovery, in 1923–24, of a cemetery area on the Pan-shan Hills, in the T'ao River valley in eastern Kansu. The prehistoric cultures of the Yang-shao stage in eastern Kansu, as will be described presently, are generally of a latter phase than the Yang-shao sites in the "nuclear area" of central Shensi, southwestern Shansi, and western Honan. The location of the Pan-shan sites is best described in Andersson's own words:

60. C. H. An, *WWTKTL* 1957 (8), 16–20. C. Y. Chao, *KKTH* 1958 (9), 54–57. P. L. Mao, *KKTH* 1958 (2), 1–5.

61. *Miao-ti-kou yü San-li-ch'iao*, 1959.

62. *KK* 1973 (6), 330–36.

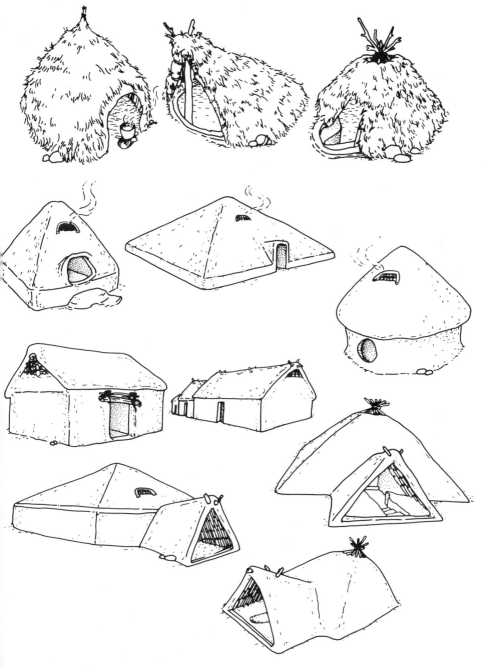

46. House types of the Yang-shao culture. (From *KKHP* 1975, no. 1.)

On both sides of the broad flat river-plain [of the river T'ao] the hillsides rise in terraces up to 400 meter above the river-valley, where
we stand upon a dissected peneplane, which, at a level of 2200 meter
above the sea, extends far to both sides of the T'ao valley. The Pan
Shan hills occupy a small area of this elevated plateau.[63]

Five burial areas have been located in the Pan-shan Hills: Pan-shan, Wa-
kuan-tsui, Pien-chia-kuo, Wang-chia-kou, and another, unnamed site.
Each is within a short distance (1,000–1,800 meters) of the others.

Each of the five grave sites is situated on one of the highest hills in the
district, surrounded by steep and deep ravines, 400 meters above the
floor of the neighboring T'ao valley. . . . These cemeteries must have
belonged to the habitations of the same period down on the valley
terraces. It then became clear that the settlers in the T'ao valley of
that age carried their dead 10 kilometers or more from the villages
up steep paths to hill-tops situated fully 400 meters above the dwellings
of the living to resting places from which they could behold in a wide
circle the place where they had grown up, worked, grown grey and
at last found a grave swept by the winds and bathed in sunshine.[64]

The custom of sharing cemeteries during the later phases of the Yang-shao
carries important social implications. It shows that toward the end of this
stage the population pressure had caused the fission of residential villages,
which probably has important bearings upon the further development of
the North China Neolithic culture into the next—Lung-shan—stage. They
also show that a strong lineage consciousness must have been behind the
custom of sending the dead to rest in the common ancestral ground. This
latter inference is substantiated by the community patterns of the Yang-
shao farmers. The longhouses at Pan-p'o-ts'un and Liu-tzu-chen, and the
planned layout of the Pan-p'o-ts'un, Chiang-chai, Pei-shou-ling, and Lin-
shan-chai villages, as well as the clustered pit houses at Sun-ch'i-t'un, near
Lo-yang in Honan,[65] suggest planned and segmented village layouts, and
on these grounds and others, lineage and clan types of kinship groupings
could be postulated. The graveyards were presumably burial places of kin
groups as well as of village residents.

63. Andersson, *BMFEA* 15 (1943), 116.

64. *Ibid.*, p. 112. Andersson's description of the Pan-shan cemeteries is still valid, but
his view that the Pan-shan cemeteries were the burial grounds for the Ma-chia-yao
culture was proved erroneous with the discoveries of Pan-shan living sites (*KK* 1972 [3],
26–31, 53) and Ma-chia-yao cemeteries (*WW* 1975 [6], 76–84).

65. *WWTKTL* 1955 (9), 58–64.

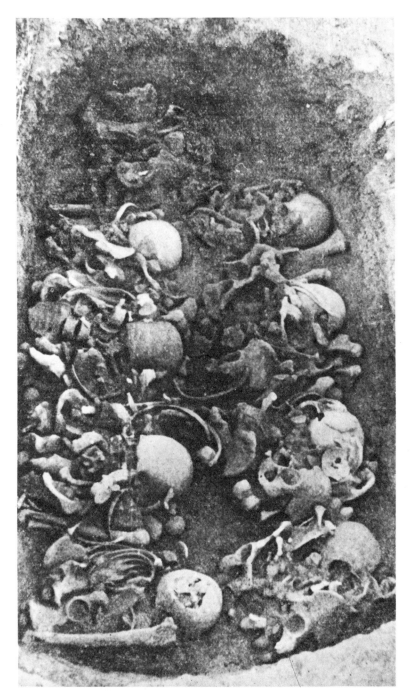

47. A group burial at the Yang-shao cemetery of Tung-chuang-ts'un, Jui-ch'eng Hsien, Shansi. (From *KKHP* 1973, no. 1, pl. 1.)

48. A bowl painted with human and fish figures, discovered at the Yang-shao site at Pan-p'o-ts'un. (From *Wu sheng ch'u-t'u chung-yao wen-wu chan-lan t'u-lu*, Peking, Wen Wu Press, 1958, pl. 1.)

The dead were inhumed in extended or flexed posture, singly or in groups (fig. 47), in rectangular or amorphous pits in the village cemetery. Infants were often buried in urns amid dwelling houses. Belief in an after-life is indicated by the utensils and stored foods buried with the dead. In several instances, some of the dead man's fingers or toes were removed and placed near another part of the body or within some of the mortuary pottery vessels.[66] The probable lineage arrangement in the village ceme-tery and the regularity of the individual burials within the cemetery in many cases make it highly probable that the cult of ancestors to symbolize lineage solidarity had already been initiated during the Yang-shao stage, although it was not until the Lung-shan stage that the evidence of this cult became remarkable in the archaeological record. There is also some evidence that the Yang-shao farmers may have performed in their villages some kinds of fertility rites for the sake of crop harvests and fishing and hunting gains. This is implied by their burials of deer,[67] the frequent occurrence of female symbols among their ceramic decorative designs, and a painted bowl discovered at Pan-p'o-ts'un, depicting on the inner

66. *Hsi-an Pan-p'o*, p. 202. *KK* 1973 (3), 135; 1974 (5), 301.
67. Andersson, *BMFEA* 15 (1943), 130.

surface a tattooed face, possibly that of a priest, wearing a fish-shaped headdress (fig. 48). Some of the beautifully painted bowls and miniature vessels also may have been used in this connection. Andersson, on the basis of some incised parallel lines on bone artifacts from Lo-han-t'ang, has also postulated a sort of "cryptic magic."[68]

Turning to the Yang-shao farmers' technological achievements, we have considerable data on their ceramics and on their stone, bone, and antler industries. Stone implements were polished, pecked, and chipped. The most frequently found types are axes and adzes, with cylindrical bodies or an oval or lentoid cross section, used for felling trees and for carpentry; hoes and spades, with flat bodies and often with a hafting portion, for cultivation; chisels for carpentry and possibly woodcarving; rectangular knives, with central holes or two side notches, for weeding, harvesting, skinning, and scraping; and arrowheads. Other stone-made artifacts are net sinkers, mealing, grinding, and polishing stones, spindle whorls, etc. Ornaments such as rings and beads were often made of semiprecious stones, including jade. Bone and antler were used for implements: needles, awls, fishhooks, arrowheads, spearheads, chisels, hoes, points, polishers, beads, etc. (fig. 49).

Their pottery was handmade and molded, and indications of coiling techniques were observed at many sites in Shansi, Shensi, Kansu, and Honan.[69] A turntable may have been used for finishing the rim, in the Shansi and Shensi regions.[70] Pottery-making implements recovered include bone scrapers, stone polishers, paint-grinding stones, and paint containers. Kilns were discovered at many settlements. Several classes of pottery were made for various purposes. For drinking water there were red or gray-brown, thick-walled, pointed-bottomed pots, containing a noticeable amount of sand or mica temper and decorated with thick and thin cord, mat, basket impressions. The tripods with solid legs (ting) were cooking utensils. For storage, coarse or fine red and gray pottery in the form of thin-necked, big-bellied jars were manufactured. Red and gray cups and canteens of a variety of pastes were made for drinking; and beautifully polished red and black designs were made of fine paste for use at meals or for rituals. In addition to these receptacles, spindle whorls, knives, sling balls, and net sinkers were also made of baked clay. The

68. Ibid., pp. 252–55.

69. L. F. Ho, KKHP 1957 (1), 5. Andersson, BMFEA 19 (1947), 54. H. P. Shih, KKTH 1955 (3), 12. P. C. Su and J. T. Wu, KKTH 1956 (2), 35. F. T. Yang and C. Chao, KKTH 1956 (2), 42.

70. C. M. An, KKTH 1956 (5), 5.

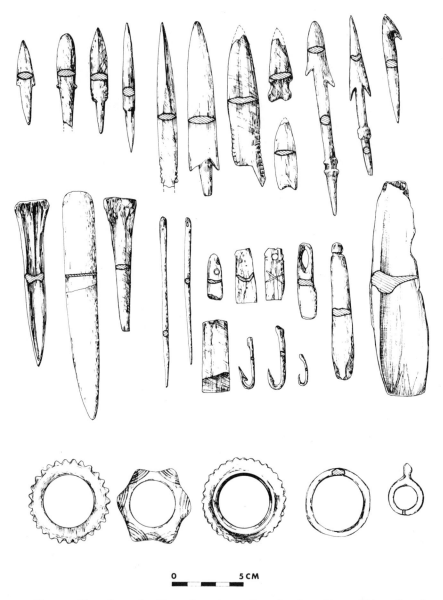

0   5 CM

49. Bone artifacts from the Yang-shao site at Pan-p'o-ts'un. (From *Hsi-an Pan-p'o*, Peking, Wen Wu Press, 1963, various figures.)

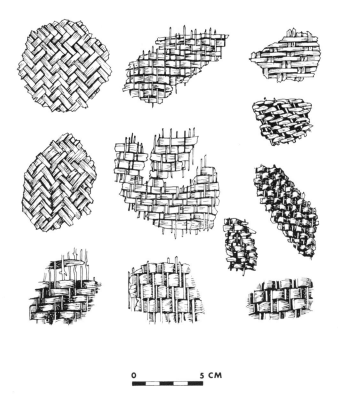

0   5 CM

50. Types of basketry at the Yang-shao village at Pan-p'o-ts'un, reconstructed from impressions on pottery. (From *Hsi-an Pan-p'o*, Peking, Wen Wu Press, 1963, fig. 119.)

prevalence of cord-, mat-, and basket-impressed decorations on pottery suggests a high level of development of fabric and basket technology, and a variety of basketry techniques is discerned from the remains at Pan-p'o (fig. 50).[71]

At several Yang-shao sites, Pan-p'o and Chiang-chai among them,[72] some of the pottery vessels had an incised sign or symbol on them (fig. 51), often on the black band near the rim of bowls. They all occurred singly, perhaps marking the makers of the pottery, or possibly the owners. Li Hsiao-ting and Kuo Mo-jo have convincingly shown that some of these signs are comparable with some numerals and clan emblems of the Shang.[73] There is not yet evidence for the Yang-shao people to claim any writing

71. *Hsi-an Pan-p'o*, pp. 161–62.
72. *Ibid.*, p. 197. *WW* 1975 (8), 82.
73. *Nan-yang University Journal* 3 (1969), 1–28, Singapore. *KKHP* 1972 (1), 1–13.

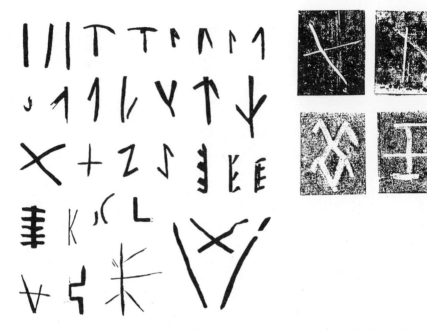

51. Incised signs on pottery from the Yang-shao culture sites at Pan-p'o (*left*) and Chiang-chai (*right*). (From *Hsi-an Pan-p'o*, Peking, Wen Wu Press, 1963; and *WW* 1975, no. 8, p. 82.)

system, but it may be said that the Yang-shao pottery signs were probably one of the sources of the historical writing system of North China.[74]

Chronology and Regional Subdivisions of Yang-shao Culture

The generalizations about the life of the Yang-shao farmers, despite brevity and unavoidable incompleteness, are sufficient to show that each of the villages was a self-sufficient community. Such communities during the earlier stages of the Neolithic period dotted the North China landscape in the river valleys and on river terraces, and their ceramic decorative art, throughout North China, constitutes a well-established horizon style of considerable overall uniformity. This style consists of plastic art and painting. The former is represented by only a handful of human figurines (fig. 52) and house models (fig. 53) discovered at few and scattered locations, but ceramic painting is universal and can be given an analytic treatment because of its infinite variety of composition.

74. See Ho Ping-ti's discussion in *Cradle of the East*, chapter 6.

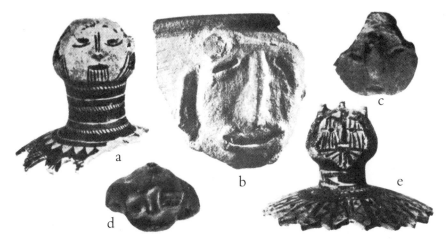

52. Clay heads found at Yang-shao sites: (a, e) Pan-shan (from J. G. Andersson, *BMFEA* 15, 1943, pls. 186, 187); (b) Chiang-hsi-ts'un, Fu-feng Hsien, Shensi (from *KK* 1959, no. 11, pl. 8, pic. 1); (c) Liu-tzu-chen, Hua Hsien, Shensi (from *KK* 1959, no. 2, pl. 2, pic. 12); (d) Pan-p'o-ts'un, Sian, Shensi (from *Hsi-an Pan-p'o*, Peking, Wen Wu Press, 1963, pl. 162). (Items not to comparable scale.)

53. Clay models of houses of Yang-shao culture, at Yu-feng, in Wu-kung, Shensi. (From *KK* 1975, no. 2, pl. 3.)

All the painted pottery of this period in North China has a brick-red or yellowish-brown base, which is then burnished or polished and painted with red or black pigment. Regional variations are to be expected. In some regions (western and northern Honan and, occasionally, central Shensi), white slips were applied before painting; in others (Kansu and Chinghai, southern Shansi and western Hopei), pigment was directly applied on the red or brown surface; black paint was used in all regions, but red was less common; and painted decor was applied on the inner surface of the pottery only in some of the areas (Kansu, Chinghai, and central Shensi).[75] However, a major contrast is seen between the painted pottery of Kansu (including Chinghai, for the sake of convenience) and that of Chung Yüan.

> In a very striking way the painted motifs of the Kansu group are different from those of the other groups. The colours are red and black, but the red is seldom so fresh and bright as it is in western Honan. Except at Hsin-Tien, the painting seems to have been done with the intention of covering the surface as much as possible, and not leaving any blank space, contrary to what is found in the Shansi and Honan groups. . . . The painted decoration, unlike that of the other groups, is intended to be viewed from the top, instead of from the side. The motifs are very complicated, though there are a number of stock designs, which frequently occur.[76]

Admitting the differences in decorative motif and form between the painted pottery of Kansu (represented by Ma-chia-yao) and Honan (represented by Yang-shao-ts'un), Andersson nevertheless considers these two phases as "strictly contemporary" regional variations.[77] In fact, Andersson would place Ch'i-chia culture, another prehistoric Kansu culture with some painted pottery, at an earlier position than Pan-shan culture, making the latter a derivative of the former. The whole Anderssonian scheme, contrived to lend credence to the view that the Yang-shao culture came ultimately from the West, has completely crumbled in light of the data we now have.

The excavations and studies of the Yang-shao sites in both Chung Yüan and Kansu, in the past twenty-five years, have evoked a far more complex

75. G. D. Wu, *Prehistoric Pottery in China*, London, Kegan Paul, Trench & Trubner, 1938, pp. 145–47. C. M. An, *WWTKTL* 1956 (8), 41–49; *KKTH* 1956 (5), 1–11. C. C. T'ung, *KKHP* 1957 (2), 7–21. S. Wu, *WW* 1975 (5), 59–72.

76. Wu, *Prehistoric Pottery in China*, p. 146.

77. *BMFEA* 15 (1943), 104.

picture of their chronology and regional grouping than was realized before. On the basis of available data, we now know that the Yang-shao farmers were distributed in an H-shaped area from eastern Kansu in the west, through the Wei River valley in the middle, to the Huang Ho valley of southern Shansi and northwestern Honan in the east (fig. 36). Within its area of distribution the Yang-shao culture exhibited differing features in the various regions and had considerable time depth susceptible to further subdividions.

Within the area of distribution of Yang-shao sites the contrast between the Chung Yüan Yang-shao and the Kansu Yang-shao, as noted by Andersson and G. D. Wu, remains valid. Purely on stylistic grounds Wu had felt that the Kansu group was probably later than the Chung Yüan (Wu's Honan) group because its decorative designs are more complicated and mature.[78] The sites of these two groups meet and overlap in the upper Wei River valley of eastern Kansu. Going into the Kansu area from Chung Yüan along the river Wei, we see a continuation of the Chung Yüan style into the T'ao Valley, especially at the sites in T'ien-shui Hsien, Kan-ku Hsien, Wu-shan Hsien, and Lung-hsi Hsien. However, starting from T'ien-shui Hsien in the upper Wei, remains of painted pottery of the Kansu style begin to occur and become increasingly dominant into the T'ao Valley and farther northwest. In the upper Wei and T'ao valleys the two styles overlap.[79] A key stratified site was found in 1957 at Ma-chia-yao in Lin-t'ao Hsien, where sherds of the Kansu style were found over-lying sherds of the Chung Yüan style:

On the First Terrace (10–30 meters) at the northern bank of the Ma-yü ravine, south of Ma-chia-yao, the cultural deposits are fairly deep. A clear section is seen on an exposed surface. The uppermost layer is a stratum of disturbed modern humus. Beneath the humus, about one meter in thickness, is a layer of prehistoric cultural deposits, about 3.5 meters thick. The upper meter and a half of this layer is composed of loose ashes, from which were derived a great number of potsherds. These are of fine or coarse paste, tempered or not tempered, some with painted designs. The paint was applied in black pigment. The designs are in most cases composed of thick lines and include many parallel lines and black dots. Sherds painted on the inner surface, and rim sherds with complicated painted patterns are also found.

78. Wu, Prehistoric Pottery in China, pp. 168–69.

79. T. Y. Kuo, KKTH 1958 (9), 72–73. H. C. Chang, KKTH 1958 (9), 41. C. M. An, KKTH 1956 (6), 13.

The forms of the painted sherds include bowls, jars, basins, and pots. The unpainted, fine-pasted red or gray sherds are mostly parts of bowls. The sand-tempered sherds are mostly cord-marked and are in the forms of pots and basins with flaring mouths that curve out. These types are similar to the Ma-chia-yao types excavated from Yen-erh-wan, near Lan-chou.

The ashy layers below this stratum consist of compact earth, about two meters thick. Cultural remains from this lower layer include polished stone chisels, bone artifacts, gray rings of baked clay, and potsherds. Some of the sherds are painted in black pigment with designs of wavy triangles, hooked dots, thin parallel lines, thick bands, and patterns. There are also some rim sherds with simple painted patterns, sherds of basins with inwardly curved mouths, plain fine-pasted red and gray sherds, and a great number of cord-marked pointed-bottomed jars and thick-rimmed basins and pots. In short, this lower cultural stratum is similar to the Yang-shao types of the upper Wei.[80]

According to such distributional and stratigraphic evidence, it appears clear that the Yang-shao culture of the Chung Yüan subdivision expanded westward as far as the T'ao River valley, where it developed into the Kansu subdivision.

Within the Chung Yüan and Kansu Yang-shao cultures themselves, further subgroupings are recognizable, each apparently localizing in a separate region and overlapping in time with other subgroups. Since the Chung Yüan region is quite large, it is not surprising that new materials make it apparent that, within it, the central Shensi–southern Shansi–western Honan region and the northern Honan region must now be discussed separately.

New data has also made it possible to discuss, for the first time, the absolute dating of the Yang-shao culture. Andersson's estimate of 2200–1700 B.C. for the Yang-shao culture[81] became an impossibility with the discovery of the Hou-kang (An-yang) stratigraphy in 1931, in which a Lung-shan culture was shown to be sandwiched between the Yang-shao, in an earlier stratum, and the Shang, which began in An-yang around 1400 B.C. The Shang were known to begin their dynastic rule in the eighteenth century B.C., and the Hou-kang stratigraphy was known to be repeated throughout Honan, which would make it impossible for the Yang-shao to last to 1700 B.C., as Andersson insisted as late as 1943. New

80. H. C. Chang, *KKTH* 1958 (9), 38–39.
81. Andersson, *BMFEA* 15 (1943).

data brought to light after 1949 made it increasingly clear that both Yang-shao and Lung-shan cultures possessed considerable time depth. In the previous edition of this volume I remained reluctant to chronologically place Yang-shao in absolute terms, but in a chronological chart of ancient cultures of North China I was sufficiently persuaded by the data and results of all the studies that have been made in the field to place the Yang-shao culture in Chung Yüan into the period 6000 B.C.–3000 B.C., and that in Kansu into 3000 B.C.–1850 B.C. In 1972–74, when the first radiocarbon dates of the Yang-shao culture were published, I was pleased to see that they essentially confirmed these estimates. I mention this merely to use it as another confirmation of the common knowledge that when the time is ripe all lines of evidence should point in the same direction.

Table 5, a more refined chart than its 1968 prototype, shows the regional subdivisions of Yang-shao culture, their internal chronological sequences, and the absolute dates based on radiocarbon dates.

The Chung Yüan Yang-shao Culture: Shensi, Western Honan, and Southern Shansi Phases

Chung Yüan, or the Central Plain, is a Chinese term of long-standing for the area regarded throughout Chinese history as the center of the Middle Kingdom, the area comprising the river basins and alluvial plains in the middle Huang Ho valley—central Shensi in the Wei River valley, southern Shansi, the northern half of Honan, southern Hopei and western Shantung. To rule China one must first take control of Chung Yüan, as indicated in such sayings as "to chase deer in the Central Plain" or "to go after the ritual *ting* cauldrons in the Central Plain." This is the area of the first three dynasties in Chinese history, and is commonly regarded by all Chinese (as a part of the Chinese ethos) as the cradle of Chinese civilization.

As we will be discussing later in the book, if we understand Chinese civilization to be the civilization that was first consolidated during the Ch'in (221–207 B.C.) and Han (206 B.C.–A.D. 220) periods, Chung Yüan was but one of its several major contributors, rather than its only ancestor. But there is little question that Yang-shao culture was in the direct ancestral line that eventually developed toward the Hsia, Shang, and Chou civilizations of North China. These early historical civilizations were without question the most important contributors to the Chinese civilization. In this light, Yang-shao culture was in every sense an early "Chinese" culture. Among its cultural elements one needs merely to enumerate the following as being characteristically Chinese in terms of their continued importance throughout Chinese history: the use of millets for food and

Table 5

Regional and Chronological Divisions of the Yang-shao Culture

Years B.C.	E. Kansu	Shensi – W. Honan	N. Honan
3000	Pan-shan and Ma-ch'ang phases		
	Ma-chia-yao phase	Miao-ti-kou phase	Ta-ssu-k'ung-ts'un and Ch'in-wang-chai phases — "Red-top bowl" style ← ?
	Chung-yüan Yang-shao	Pan-p'o phase	Hou-kang phase
4000			
5000		Pre-Pan-p'o phase	

for ritual; domesticated pig; vegetables of the *Brassica* genus; hemp and silk for fabrics; *ting* tripods and *tseng* steamers indicative of the beginning of a Chinese cuisine style; timber and wattle-and-daub architecture; and the use of signs and symbols on pottery, which may be among the forerunners of Chinese writing.

Because of the unique importance of Yang-shao culture in the history of Chinese culture, the origin of the Yang-shao culture is a most crucial issue in any exploration of the origin of Chinese civilization. While this is as yet an unresolved issue, we have had sufficient archaeological data to know this much: Terminal Palaeolithic and Mesolithic cultures are known in scattered regions throughout the Chung Yüan area, and it could only be among these people (who utilized a great diversity of natural resources, including wild cereal grasses that are found today in North China in many species and some of which are ancestral to the domesticated millets)[82] that the agricultural transformation took place, probably in the early millennia of Holocene. Since the earliest known Yang-shao culture sites have been confined to central Shensi, southwestern Shansi, and western Honan—the so-called nuclear area—there cannot be any doubt that the earliest events took place within this small basin area. The archaeological and palaeoecological substantiation (or revision) of this speculated process will be a central task for archaeologists in the coming years.

The earliest archaeological remains in this area with ceramics have been identified in a series of sites in the Wei River valley and the Huang Ho valley in western Honan, including the lower strata at Pei-shou-ling in Pao-chi and Yüan-chün-miao in Hua Hsien, and the sites at Lao-kuan-t'ai in Hua Hsien and on the banks of river Lo near Lo-ning, western Honan.[83] The types of artifacts that characterize this phase of Yang-shao culture include (fig. 54): "jars and pots of sandy paste with incised, fine-cord-marked, and incised and cord-marked decoration; bowls with quasi ring feet or ring feet; light-brown bowls of hard texture with indented rims; plain jars with small mouths and wide, globular bodies; and bowls with three short, solid legs."[84] Stratigraphic evidence at Pei-shou-ling and Yüan-chün-miao shows conclusively that this phase of Yang-shao culture antedates both of the other phases of this culture to be described below; the absence of painted decoration in this phase and

82. Y. L. Keng, ed., *Flora Illustralis Plantarum Primarum Sinicarum, Gramineae*, Peking, Science Press, 1959.

83. P. C. Su, *KKHP* 1965 (1), 55. N. Hsia, *KK* 1964 (10), 486.

84. P. C. Su, *KKHP* 1965 (1), 55–56.

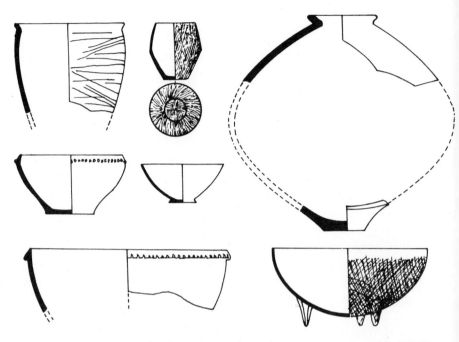

54. Pottery of the pre-Pan-p'o phase of Yang-shao culture. (From Su Ping-ch'i, *KKHP* 1965, no. 1, p. 55.)

the prevalence of cord marks point to the possibility that it is perhaps the earliest Yang-shao culture now known and is a first substantiation of the hypothetical earliest farmers mentioned above.

A second phase is represented by the site of Pan-p'o-ts'un, and identical assemblages are known from Pei-shou-ling in Pao-chi, Chiang-chai in Lin-t'ung, Yüan-chün-miao in Hua Hsien, and Heng-chen-ts'un in Hua-yin, all in the Wei River valley of Shensi.[85] The features that contrast the Pan-p'o phase most sharply with the others are pointed-bottom jars with so-called gourd-shaped mouths and bowls painted with blackish geometric and fish designs (fig. 55). The third, or Miao-ti-kou phase—typified by the lower stratum of Miao-ti-kou, in Shan Hsien of Honan, and the Ch'üan-hu-ts'un site in Hua Hsien, eastern Shensi—is characterized by pointed-bottom jars with double lip and small mouth, and bowls painted with bird, geometric, and plant designs (fig. 56).[86]

The temporal and historical relationship between the Pan-p'o and the Miao-ti-kou phases of the Yang-shao culture has been a focus of

85. H. P. Shih, *Hsi-an Pan-p'o*, p. 230. P. C. Su, *KKHP* 1965 (1), 61–63.
86. C. M. An, et al., *Miao-ti-kou yü San-li-ch'iao*. P. C. Su, *KKHP* 1965 (1), 57–61.

55. Pottery of the Pan-p'o phase excavated from Pan-p'o-ts'un, Sian, Shensi. (From *Hsi-an Pan-p'o*, Peking, Wen Wu Press, 1963. Items not to comparable scale.)

56. Pottery of the Miao-ti-kou I phase, Yang-shao culture. (From An Chih-min et al., *Miao-ti-kou yü San-li-ch'iao*, Peking, Science Press, 1959, various plates. Items not to comparable scale.)

57. Hua Mountain, Shensi. (Photo by Harold E. Malde, 1975.)

archaeological debate.[87] Some believe Pan-p'o is the earlier of the two; others insist it is the later. Shih Hsing-pang[88] and Su Ping-ch'i[89] are both convinced, however, that these phases represent two parallel and contemporaneous "tribal groups." Shih believes the Pan-p'o phase to be the remains of a Yang-shao tribe with fish totems and the Miao-ti-kou phase to be the remains of a tribe with bird totems · has brought attention to the flower designs of the Miao-ti-kou–phase pottery and the location of its sites in the neighborhood of Hua (Flower) Mountain (fig. 57) in Hua and Hua-yin counties, eastern Shensi—points that may be pertinent to the earliest name of the Chinese people, Hua.

This is very interesting, but more relevant are two items of information that have significant bearing on the temporal relationship of these Yang-shao–culture phases. The first is that stratigraphic excavations in 1959–61 at the Yang-shao site near Hsia-meng-ts'un in Pin Hsien, in the Ching River valley of Shensi, have disclosed that the Pan-p'o type of remains

87. *Hsin Chung-kuo ti k'ao-ku shou-huo*, 1962, p. 12. Y. H. Li, KK 1964 (7), 374–86.
88. KK 1962 (6), 326.
89. KKHP 1965 (1), 66.

was stratigraphically below the Miao-ti-kou type.[90] This would not rule out the possibility that the two cultural phases were contemporaneous, for Pin Hsien is closer to the Pan-p'o sphere of distribution than to the Miao-ti-kou, and this stratigraphy could indicate an intrusive situation. But the second fact is perhaps even more revealing. Comparing the various types and number of artifacts found at the Pan-p'o-ts'un and Miao-ti-kou sites,[91] Su Ping-ch'i has concluded that "the Pan-p'o inhabitants put equal emphasis on agriculture, fishing, hunting, and tree felling, whereas the Miao-ti-kou people engaged principally in agriculture, with only slight fishing and hunting activity. The Pan-p'o people used animal skins for clothing, but the Miao-ti-kou people relied more heavily on plant fabrics."[92] Su intends to show by this that the Pan-p'o and the Miao-ti-kou "tribes" engaged in different types of subsistence activities and could therefore be contemporary cultures with different styles. It is apparent, however, that the Pan-p'o phase was at an earlier stage of agricultural development, where fishing and hunting were still important to subsistence and forest clearance was a major agricultural activity. Finally, the newly available radiocarbon dates also firmly place the Pan-p'o in an earlier period than the Miao-ti-kou.

The Chung Yüan Yang-shao Culture: Northern Honan Phases

The dividing line between western Honan and northern Honan in terms of Yang-shao pottery styles is probably somewhere in the neighborhood of Lo-yang, where, at the Wang-wan site, an earlier Yang-shao stratum of apparent Miao-ti-kou affiliation was later intruded into by decorative elements of the Ch'in-wang-chai type.[93] Ch'in-wang-chai, in Hsing-yang (formerly Kuang-wu) county, west of Cheng-chou, was in 1921 among the earliest found Yang-shao sites.[94] The red ware here was highly polished or slipped in white, and the designs were then painted in purplish black and, sometimes, also in red. The designs are in general composed of parallel curvilinear lines, crosshatches, or broad ribbons

90. S. K. Li, *KK* 1962 (6), 292–94.

91. *Knives:* Pan-p'o 217, Miao-ti-kou 200; *stone axes:* Pan-p'o 313, Miao-ti-kou 27; *stone adzes:* Pan-p'o 71, Miao-ti-kou 5; *stone choppers:* Pan-p'o 59, Miao-ti-kou 0; *fishing spears, harpoons, and hooks:* Pan-p'o 36, Miao-ti-kou 0; *net-sinkers:* Pan-p'o 320, Miao-ti-kou 5; *arrowheads:* Pan-p'o 288, Miao-ti-kou 71; *spindle whorls:* Pan-p'o 52, Miao-ti-kou 100; *bone awls and needles:* Pan-p'o 996, Miao-ti-kou 26.

92. P. C. Su, *KKHP* 1965 (1), 66.

93. *KK* 1961 (4), 177.

94. T. J. Arne, "Painted stone age pottery from the province of Honan, China," *PS,* ser. D, 1, fasc. 2, Peking, 1925. Andersson, *BMFEA* 17 (1945).

58. Painted pottery at Ta-ho-ts'un, Cheng-chou, Honan. (From *KK* 1973, no. 6, pl. 1.)

forming recurrent units in a band around the vessel. The Ta-ho-ts'un site in Cheng-chou, mentioned before, has yielded almost identical painted pottery (fig. 58), associated with a charcoal sample giving a radiocarbon date of 4885 ± 100 B.P. (calibrated to 3760–3610 B.C.). This makes the Ch'in-wang-chai phase only slightly later than Miao-ti-kou, with whose style it was evidently affiliated.

To the north in the Chang Ho drainage of northernmost Honan and southern Hopei, there is a Ta-ssu-k'ung-ts'un style of Yang-shao pottery, very similar to Ch'in-wang-chai and probably contemporaneous. This style was first encountered at the Hou-chia-chuang site in An-yang,[95] but its significance was not recognized until 1958–59 with its discovery at Ta-ssu-k'ung-ts'un, also in An-yang.[96] The style, as now known from a number of sites in the An-yang[97] and Tz'u Hsien (Hopei)[98] area, is particularly characterized by decorative bands around the vessel consisting

95. C. T. Wu, *TYKKPK* 1 (1936), 201–11.
96. *KK* 1961 (2), 63.
97. *KK* 1965 (7), 326–38.
98. *KK* 1974 (6), 357–59. *KKHP* 1975 (1), 77–82.

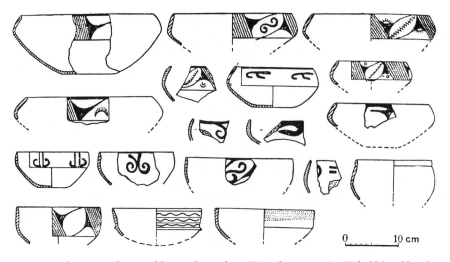

59. Painted pottery of Ta-ssu-k'ung-ts'un style, at Hsia-p'an-wang site, Tz'u Hsien, Hopei. (From *KKHP* 1975, no. 1, p. 80.)

of roundish units separated by parallel wavy lines. The units often consist of two adjoined semicircles, broad ribbons, S-shapes, "cowries," and "moth-antennae", most of which are also common Ch'in-wang-chai motifs (fig. 59). In both phases the prevailing vessel forms are basin, bowl, and jar.

The third Yang-shao phase to be distinguished by ceramic style in the northern Honan area is the Hou-kang phase, first identified in 1931 with the Hou-kang excavation.[99] Its most important elements are: red pottery bowls, basins, jars, and *ting* tripods; black-on-red painted pottery, with a few simple designs (broad band on bowl rim, groups of parallel lines, triangles filled with parallel lines and crosshatches); the "red-top bowl" (*hung-ting wan*), with a broad red band under the rim over a (mostly) gray lower half—the red and gray colors the result of differential oxidation during firing and not from painting; and incised and punctated designs[100] (fig. 60). Two radiocarbon dates associated with the Hou-kang style (5330±100 B.P., 5520±105 B.P., calibrated to 4370–4030 and 4490–4330 respectively) indicate that the Hou-kang phase is only slightly later than the Pan-p'o phase, antedating the Ch'in-wang-chai and Ta-ssu-k'ung-ts'un phases in the northern Honan area.

99. S. Y. Liang, *An-yang fa-chüeh pao-kao* 4 (1933), 609–25; "Hsiao-t'un Lung-shan yü Yang-shao," *Essays Presented to Ts'ai Yüan P'ei on His Sixty-fifth Birthday*, part 2 (1935), pp. 555–67, Peking, Institute of History and Philology, Academia Sinica.

100. *KK* 1972 (3), 15–18; 1972 (5), 10–12.

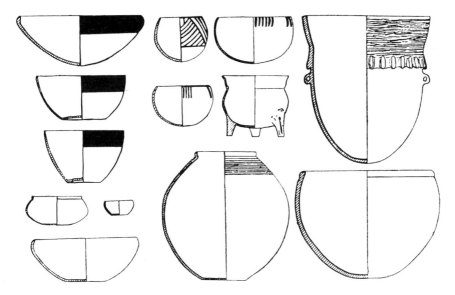

60. Painted pottery of Hou-kang style, at Hou-kang, An-yang, Honan. (From *KK* 1972, no. 3, p. 16.)

But elements of the Hou-kang style apparently lasted a very long time. In southern Hopei, in the same area as that of the Ta-ssu-k'ung-ts'un phase, several sites have been found with the red-top bowl, and these have sometimes been labeled "Hou-kang–phase sites."[101] But these sites lacked painted and incised pottery, and *ting* tripods have also disappeared from them. They appear to be later than Ta-ssu-k'ung-ts'un–phase sites, and their connection with the real Hou-kang phase remains unclear.

The Kansu Yang-shao Culture

In 1921–23 J. G. Andersson undertook a series of archaeological surveys in eastern Kansu in the Huang Ho valley near Lan-chou and in the T'ao and Tahsia river valleys.[102] The prehistoric sites he discovered he classified into six groups, three of which are Stone Age and were called Ch'i-chia, Pan-shan/Ma-chia-yao, and Ma-ch'ang. Actually these were four different phases, because the finds at Pan-shan were mortuary remains and those at Ma-chia-yao were habitation remains. Andersson, however, considered these two phases to be entirely contemporary and representative of two

101. *KK* 1974 (6), 359.
102. *Preliminary Report on Archaeological Research in Kansu*, GSuC, Mem., ser. A, no. 5 (1925).

61. Pottery of the Ma-chia-yao phase of Kansu Yang-shao culture. (From *KK* 1962, no. 6, 319.)

different types of assemblage. He thought this stage was strictly contemporaneous with the Yang-shao culture of Honan.

During the half century since Andersson's initial work in Kansu, many more sites have been investigated and several extensively excavated. Andersson's grouping of the four cultural phases remains valid but, besides the great amount of additional information they are each accruing, three important modifications must now be made. First, the entire Kansu Yang-shao culture has been shown to be later than and an offshoot of the Chung Yüan Yang-shao culture. Second, the Ch'i-chia phase must now be removed as an early phase of the Yang-shao sequence and placed in a later period (to be described in another chapter). Finally, the Ma-chia-yao and the Pan-shan assemblages are no longer generally regarded as contemporary complexes of different types but are thought by many to be two separate phases of the Yang-shao culture in Kansu. Stratigraphic and stylistic studies now suggest the following sequence of the Kansu Yang-shao phases: Ma-chia-yao, earliest; Pan-shan, following; and Ma-ch'ang, latest and farthest west.[103]

The three phases are best distinguished by their ceramics. The Ma-chia-yao pottery, best known from the site of Ma-chia-yao in Lin-t'ao Hsien,[104] is characterized by a number of distinctively shaped bowls, jars, and small-mouthed jars of fine paste and high luster, with black decorations painted on red or yellow. Characteristic designs appear on the inside of shallow bowls and beakers. The painted decorations consist of animals (frogs and birds) and geometric patterns, the latter being distinctively curvilinear and gracefully executed (fig. 61).

The sophisticated artistry of the Pan-shan painted pottery, found in museums around the world and typically from the Ch'ing-kang-ch'a site near Lan-chou[105] and the sites on the Pan-shan Hills in Lin-t'ao Hsien,[106] is characterized by the tall jar with small mouth, wide belly, two loop handles at the largest diameter of the body, and flat bottom. Most of the painted decorations are in red and black and form a wide band covering the upper part of the body; the basic motifs are a large

103. C. F. Yang, KKHP 1962 (1), 71–77. H. P. Shih, KK 1962 (6), 318–29. Among the available radiocarbon dates from Kansu, one is that of the Pan-shan culture (3900 ± 100 B.P.) and another that of the Ma-ch'ang culture (4010 ± 100 B.P.), raising the possibility that Ma-ch'ang was, in fact, slightly earlier than Pan-shan. I would reserve a final judgment on this issue until more dates are known.

104. Sommarström, BMFEA 28 (1956), 55–138.

105. KK 1972 (3), 26–31, 53.

106. Nils Palmgren, PS, ser. D, 3 (1934). Andersson, BMFEA 15 (1943), 104–40.

62. Pottery of the Pan-shan phase of the Kansu Yang-shao culture. (From *KK* 1962, no. 6, p. 323.)

variety of spirals and gourd-shaped units (fig. 62). The Ma-ch'ang phase, named after the type site at Ma-ch'ang-yen in eastern Chinghai,[107] is sometimes regarded as having followed the Pan-shan phase; it had similar pottery forms, but the decorative designs are less elaborate and generally are composed of anthropomorphic patterns (fig. 63).

107. Palmgren, *PS*, ser. D, 3 (1934). Andersson, *BMFEA* 15 (1943), 104–40. See also *KK* 1974 (5), 299–308, for an important, newly discovered cemetery of the Ma-ch'ang culture.

63. Pottery of the Ma-ch'ang phase of the Kansu Yang-shao culture. (From *KK* 1962, no. 6, p. 324.)

Ch'ing-lien-kang and Related Cultures of the Pacific Seaboard

The third center of early farming cultures in China is the Pacific seaboard of eastern China from Shantung to Chekiang, drained by the Huai Ho and the lower Yangtze. Until the early 1950s the earliest Neolithic culture known in this area was the Lung-shan culture, characterized by black pottery. In 1951 a new type of prehistoric culture was recognized at the Ch'ing-lien-kang site, in Huai-an county, northern Kiangsu, at which pottery of a red ware (some are even painted with decorative designs) (fig. 64) and flat, polished stone axes with a large hole at the center of the blade are particularly characteristic.[108] In the first report of the site the new culture was considered to have begun "after the rise of the Lung-shan culture" and to have ended "prior to the Han dynasty."[109] The stratigraphical relationship between the Ch'ing-lien-kang and the Lung-shan strata at the site at Erh-chien-ts'un, in the city of Lien-yün-kang on the coast of northern Kiangsu,[110] established for the first time that Ch'ing-lien-kang culture predated Lung-shan culture as a whole. The excavations in 1963 at Ta-tun-tzu in P'i Hsien, northern Kiangsu,[111] brought to light a long sequence of development within the Ch'ing-lien-kang culture itself, by now incorporating several subphases, and the excavators were bold enough to date the Ch'ing-lien-kang culture at an early age, "roughly contemporaneous with the Yang-shao culture of Chung Yüan."[112] This is beginning to be substantiated by radiocarbon dates—especially the one from the lower stratum at Ta-tun-tzu, 5625 ± 105 B.P., calibrated to 4580–4410 B.C.—only slightly later than the Pan-p'o-ts'un site.

108. *KKHP* 1955 (1), 13–24.
109. *Ibid.*, p. 23.
110. *KK* 1962 (3), 111–16.
111. *KKHP* 1964 (2), 9–56.
112. *Ibid.*, p. 49.

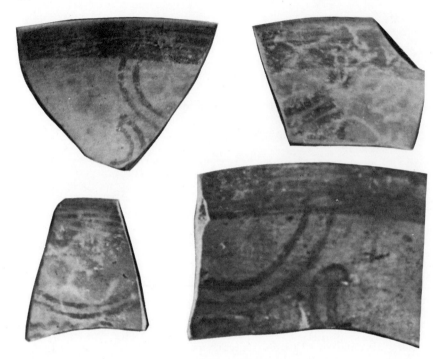

64. Painted potsherds from Ch'ing-lien-kang site, Huai-an, Kiangsu. (Collection, Nan-king Museum; photo by author, 1975. First photos of collection originally published in *KKHP* 1955, no. 1.)

The possible establishment of the Ch'ing-lien-kang culture in northern Kiangsu as a third early Neolithic center in China parallel to Yang-shao and Ta-p'en-k'eng is an important event in the history of Chinese archaeology, but it brings to the fore a number of questions that cannot yet be answered. For example: Was the Ch'ing-lien-kang culture confined to northern Kiangsu, or could it be defined so that it includes similar cultures in Shantung in the north and southern Kiangsu in the south? What was the nature of the relationship of the Ch'ing-lien-kang culture with the Yang-shao culture, on the one hand, and with the Ta-p'en-k'eng culture on the other? There are, as yet, no definitive answers to these questions.

In an important article, "Lüeh lun Ch'ing-lien-kang wen-hua" ("Briefly discussing the Ch'ing-lien-kang culture"),[113] Wu Shan-ch'ing presented in 1973 a first synthesis of the archaeological data pertaining to the culture

113. *WW* 1973 (6), 45–61.

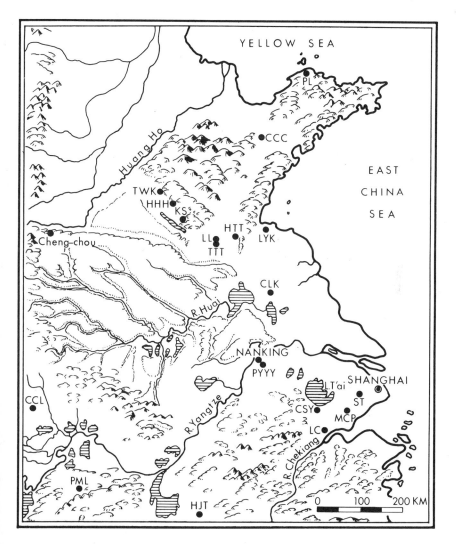

65. Important Neolithic sites (including those of the Ch'ing-lien-kang cultures) of the Pacific seaboard. *From top to bottom*: (PL) P'eng-lai; (CCC) Ching-chih-chen; (TWK) Ta-wen-k'ou; (HHH) Hsi-hsia-hou; (KS) Kang-shang; (LYK) Lien-yün-kang; (HTT) Hua-t'ing-ts'un; (LL) Liu-lin; (TTT) Ta-tun-tzu; Cheng-chou; (CLK) Ch'ing-lien-kang; Nanking; (PYYY) Pei-yin-yang-ying; Shanghai; (ST) Sung-tse; (CSY) Ch'ien-shan-yang; (MCP) Ma-chia-pang; (LC) Liang-chu; (CCL) Ch'ü-chia-ling; (PML) P'ao-ma-ling; (HJT) Hsien-jen-tung.

in question, in which he takes the broadest view possible and includes under the Ch'ing-lien-kang label prehistoric cultures not only of northern Kiangsu but also of Shantung and southern Kiangsu (fig. 65). Thus broadly defined, Ch'ing-lien-kang culture is then subdivided into a north-of-Yangtze and a south-of-Yangtze type, each of which is further subdivided chronologically (table 6). Wu Shan-ch'ing's synthesis is the first attempt to bring order to a vast body of data and may be used as a working hypothesis, but it is by no means the final word. The most serious problem in my judgment is the absence of a working definition of the Ch'ing-lien-kang culture that is applicable to all sites both north and south of the Yangtze River. An Chih-man pointed out that "the Ch'ing-lien-kang culture south of the Yangtze and that north of the Yangtze are not entirely the same in their cultural appearance. Was this because of temporal or geographical differences, or because they in fact belonged to separate cultural systems? This remains to be solved at the next step."[114] For this Wu provided a non-answer: "These two have both differences and similarities. Because there are similarities, we may call them both Ch'ing-lien-kang culture. But because there are also differences, which appear to have been caused by geographical factors, we may group them into two types."[115]

But there are very important differences between the so-called Ch'ing-lien-kang culture north of the Yangtze and the so-called Ch'ing-lien-kang culture south of the Yangtze. Undoubtedly both were heavily agricultural, but one cannot be sure that identical crops were planted in the north and in the south. Remains of rice have been uncovered in considerable quantity in the south, but none yet have been found in the north. The Huai Ho valley is on the same latitudes as much of Honan, and there is every likelihood that millets were as important in Shantung and northern Kiangsu as in Honan. Related to this is the fact that stone harvesting knives are common in the south but rare in the north, where a cutting implement consisting of a bone handle and two cutting hooks made of deer teeth is prominent. In ceramics, many common types are found in both areas, but the *kui* tripod, the high-stemmed cup, and the shallow, bowl-shaped body (instead of the deep, bowl- or basin-shaped body) that are common in the north are rare in the south, while impressed decorations (especially cord marks) that are common in the south are uncommon in the north. Both areas had painted pottery, but the designs are widely different.

114. *KK* 1972 (6), 40.
115. *WW* 1973 (6), 51.

Table 6

Regional Grouping and Subdivision of the Ch'ing-lien-kang Culture

Type	Stage	Major Sites
North-of-Yangtze	Ch'ing-lien-kang	Ch'ing-lien-kang (Huai-an, Kiangsu), Erh-chien-ts un (Lien-yun-kang, Kiangsu), Ta-tun-tzu, Lower stratum (P'i Hsien, Kiangsu)
	Liu-lin	Liu-lin (P'i Hsien), Ta-tun-tzu, Middle stratum (P'i Hsien)
	Hua-t'ing-ts'un	Hua-t'ing-ts'un (Hsin-i, Kiangsu), Ta-tun-tzu, Upper stratum (P'i Hsien)
	Late Ta-wen-k'ou or Ching-chih-chen	Ta-wen-k'ou, late stage (Ning-yang, Shantung), Ching-chih-chen (An-ch'iu, Shantung)
South-of-Yangtze	Ma-chia-pang	Ma-chia-pang (Chia-hsing, Chekiang), Pei-yin-yang-ying residential remains (Nanking, Kiangsu)
	Pei-yin-yang-ying	Pei-yin-yang-ying burials (Nanking)
	Sung-tse	Sung-tse (Ch'ing-p'u, Shanghai)

Source: Wu Shan-ch'ing, *WW* 1973 (6).

In the area of prestige goods, jade ornaments were remarkably abundant in the south, but in the north perforated and apparently decorated turtle shells are much more conspicuous.

In the light of differences like these, it appears unwise at this time to classify the early Neolithic cultures throughout the Pacific seaboard as all being Ch'ing-lien-kang. Until additional data become available and better analysis is undertaken, it seems prudent to adopt the following provisional terminology: (1) important assemblages are grouped as regional phases—the Ch'ing-lien-kang phase, the Liu-lin phase, the Hua-t'ing-ts'un phase, the Ta-wen-k'ou phase, the Ma-chia-pang phase, the Pei-yin-yang-ying phase, and the Sung-tse phase; (2) the Shantung and northern Kiangsu phases are assembled into an earliest Ch'ing-lien-kang phase and a later Hua-t'ing culture; and (3) the southern Kiangsu and northern Chekiang phases are put together into an earliest Ma-chia-pang phase and a later Pei-yin-yang-ying culture. In this chapter we will briefly describe only the earliest phase of each group, the Ch'ing-lien-kang phase and the Ma-chia-pang phase. The rest of the phases, under the names of Hua-t'ing and Pei-yin-yang-ying cultures, will be discussed in the next chapter.

The Ch'ing-lien-kang Phase

Remains of the Ch'ing-lien-kang phase are confined to northernmost Kiangsu and Shantung. According to Wu Shan-ch'ing, the following sites have yielded Ch'ing-lien-kang phase remains: Ch'ing-lien-kang, Yen-chia-ma-t'ou, and Hsi-han-chuang in Huai-an, Erh-chien-ts'un and Ta-ts'un in Lien-yün-kang, Hsiao-lin-ting in Hsin-i, Li-yüan in Fu-ning, and Ta-tun-tzu (lower stratum) in P'i Hsien, all in northern Kiangsu, and Liu-chia-chuang, in Ch'ü-fu, Shantung.[116] The Tzu-ching-shan site in P'eng-lai, on the northern coast of Shantung,[117] may be another manifestation of this culture (fig. 66). This is flat, low country drained by a network of freshwater lakes and small rivers. At the time of Neolithic occupation the area was presumably quite marshy,[118] and prehistoric sites were located on mounds, low hills, or river terraces at the foot of hills.

The subsistence pattern indicated by archaeological remains is diversified: farming, shown by stone axes and deer-teeth cutters; animal husbandry,

116. *Ibid.*, p. 46. See also *KKHP* 1964 (2), 48. Principal sites were reported in *KKHP* 1955 (1), 13–24; 1964 (2), 9–56; *KKTH* 1958 (10), 45–50; *KK* 1962 (3), 111–16.

117. *KK* 1973 (1), 11–15.

118. W. Ting, *BIE* 20 (1965), 155–62.

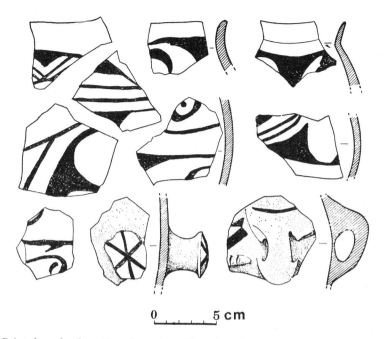

0 _____ 5 cm

66. Painted potsherds at Tzu-ching-shan, P'eng-lai, Shantung. (From *KK* 1973, no. 1, p. 14.)

by bones of dog and pig; hunting, by bones of cattle and deer and by arrowheads of stone and bone; and the use of aquatic resources, as indicated by remains of fish, molluscan shells, and turtles. As we pointed out above, there is no evidence as to the kind of crops that may have been planted. Nor are there data on housing, other than chunks of burned wattle-and-daub wall fragments that are flat and smooth on one side and exhibit impressions of reed matting on the other. Erh-chien-ts'un and Ta-ts'un yielded burials of this phase: sparsely furnished, single burials, with the body stretched out, supine, and the head pointing east. In many of the graves a large red bowl was used to cover the head of the body.

The pottery of the Ch'ing-lien-kang phase was almost all of a red ware, some of a fine paste and the rest sand-tempered. All were handmade. The forms of the vessels included bowl, round-bottomed beaker, jar with a spout, *ting* tripod with conical feet, small-mouthed jar with two shoulder loop-handles, and bowl on high pedestal without holes. Most pottery was plain, some were incised or appliquéd, a few were impressed with basketry designs or "comb-punctated," and some bowls were slipped in red and painted with dark red designs on the inside. The designs were relatively simple, consisting mostly of parallel strokes. Some of the bowls have a gray belly and a red top, calling to mind the red-top bowl in the Hou-kang phase of the Yang-shao culture. In fact, the ceramic forms (bowls and *ting* tripods), the painted designs of short parallel lines, and the incised and punctated decorations, as well as the red-top bowl, all recall the Hou-kang Yang-shao, which is less than three hundred kilometers to the west of the Ch'ing-lien-kang area. The radiocarbon dates from Ta-tun-tzu (5625 ± 105 B.P.) and from Hou-kang (5520 ± 105 B.P. and 5330 ± 100 B.P.) place these two cultures at just about the same time.

The Ma-chia-pang Phase

The Ma-chia-pang phase, typified by the site at Ma-chia-pang in Chia-hsing, northern Chekiang,[119] has been recognized by Wu Shan-ch'ing in at least eight additional sites in southern Kiangsu, in the areas of Nanking, Shanghai, Ch'ang-chou, Wu-chiang, and Wu Hsien.[120] This is, again, flat, low country, drained by the lower Yangtze, its many small tributaries, and a number of lakes between the Yangtze and the Chekiang River, the largest being lake T'ai Hu. In contrast to the Ch'ing-lien-kang country, with its essentially northern Chinese climate, the Ma-chia-pang country is definitely southern Chinese in climate and vegetation. There is no question, now, that the inhabitants of the sites of this phase were rice growers, since remains of rice grains have been brought to light from the site at Sung-tse in Shanghai (lower stratum) and from Ts'ao-hsieh-shan in Wu Hsien.[121] Bones of cattle, deer, boar, fox, and fish, and turtle shells, fragments of bamboo and wood, and a carbonized water-caltrop shell (*Trapa* sp.) found at the Ma-chia-pang site[122] attest to the diversified utilization of other resources. In fact, the amount of bones found here is staggering: about a metric ton of bones was uncovered from a test trench in an area of only 50 square meters. Among the cattle bones, those of water buffalo (*Bubalus* sp.) were identified, suggesting that the most important domestic animals here was the water buffalo rather than the pig as in the north.

Settlements of this phase are located on low mounds or directly on the river banks. Houses were rectangular, with a hardened floor, timber posts, and wattle-and-daub walls. The posts were reinforced with planks

119. *KK* 1961 (7), 345–51, 354.
120. *WW* 1973 (6), 51. See also *KK* 1974 (2), 109–15.
121. *KKHP* 1962 (2), 28. *WW* 1973 (6), 57.
122. *KK* 1961 (7), 351.

and splints, probably because the ground soil tended to be soft in marshy surroundings. Reed and bamboo mats are seen with mud fragments, presumably from wall and roof furnishings. Burials were placed apart from the dwelling area. They were placed singly, heading north or northeast. A vast majority of the bodies were laid out in a prone posture. At the Ts'ao-hsieh-shan site, some of the bodies had their faces buried in red bowls placed beneath the head, recalling the Erh-chien–site practice in northern Kiangsu.

Pottery again consisted of sandy and fine wares, handmade, red in color, often slipped in red. The most common vessel forms are round-bottomed beakers, large-mouthed bowls, *tou* with unperforated ring feet or ring feet with small holes near the base. *Ting* tripods were rare, mostly with broad, flat legs. No painted pottery has been found. Finely polished jade rings began to appear in tombs. Among other implements, bone points, awls, chisels, needles, and stone arrowheads and flat axes with a large hole at the center of the blade are conspicuous.

A single radiocarbon date has been obtained from the lower stratum at Sung-tse, in Shanghai, which at 5190 ± 100 B.P. gives a calibrated range of 4190–3880 B.C., about the same time span as the radiocarbon date at Ta-tun-tzu in the north.

Comment

Half a century ago, when Neolithic cultures began to be discovered in China, the overriding concern of the archaeologists at the time was, How did they come about? Today, this remains our overriding issue, although the overall outlook is drastically different. Scholars used to worry about proving or disproving that the Chinese Neolithic was derived from the Near East. Now the question concerns the detailed process whereby the terminal Palaeolithic people expanded their reliance upon food plants and eventually came to domesticate some of them for principal food sources.

Presently available archaeological evidence points to two regions where the initial switch from the Palaeolithic to the Neolithic way of life occurred, namely the Huang Ho basin of North China, where millets were the center of attention, and the southeastern coastal areas, where there was probably a greater dependence on roots and tubers. Even though the minute links are not yet completely available, there can be no question now that the Yang-shao and the Ta-p'en-k'eng cultures grew indigenously from their respective Palaeolithic bases. The fact that both the initial phase of the Yang-shao culture and the Ta-p'en-k'eng culture were characterized by cord-marked pottery (with incised designs) suggests some kind of interrelationship of the two, but in view of the very different material inventories in general, it does not appear that either can be regarded as a derivative of the other. The Yang-shao culture was wholly confined to North China, but the Ta-p'en-k'eng culture resembles in some respects the Hoabinhian culture of Vietnam and the rest of Indo-China, so much so that many issues would depend on a consideration of both cultures.

The third earliest Neolithic center, the Huai Ho and lower Yangtze plains, is at the moment the least known but, perhaps because of this, the most tantalizing. The early date of this culture—in the fifth millennium B.C.—is the least firmly established of the three, and we do not yet have any inkling as to its precedents. No initial prototypes are suggested in local data, and no Palaeolithic cultures have been unequivocally established on these plains. In fact, there is a real question whether the plains were too marshy—if not mostly submerged—for habitation until the time of Ch'ing-lien-kang occupation. Therefore, until a precedent foundation can be shown to exist here, the Ch'ing-lien-kang and related cultures in the Pacific seaboard must have come from one or both of the other centers—down the Huang Ho from Yang-shao (probably of the pre-Pan-p'o phase) or down the hills and up the coast from Ta-p'en-k'eng.

Comparing Ch'ing-lien-kang and Ma-chia-pang phases with Yang-shao and Ta-p'en-k'eng, one easily sees that the greater resemblance lies with Yang-shao, especially in terms of the red ware, the painted pottery, the tripod type, and the stone knife. Ch'ing-lien-kang, more than Ma-chia-pang, would not be out of place if it were regarded, if only for the sake of argument, as another Yang-shao phase. Its resemblance to the Hou-kang phase has been mentioned before. We would be on even firmer ground if data became available on the kinds of crops that were being cultivated.

On the other hand, there are strong reasons also to tie the Ch'ing-lien-kang and Ma-chia-pang phases to cultures to their south. The first is rice. Botanically, wild rice is known to have grown in monsoon Asia from Bengal to the Yangtze,[123] and the Ta-p'en-k'eng culture, rather than Yang-shao, would be the more likely greenhouse for the early stages of its domestication. Secondly, physical anthropological studies of Neolithic skeletons from Shantung and northern Kiangsu[124] have shown that the

123. T. T. Chang, "The origin, evolution, cultivation, dissemination, and diversification of Asian and African rices," *Euphytica* 25 (1976), 425–41.

124. *KKHP* 1972 (1), 91–122; 1973 (2), 91–125; 1974 (2), 125–40.

populations in this area (of a slightly later stage than the initial Ch'ing-lien-kang and Ma-chia-pang phases) show a greater morphological resemblance to those further south (especially modern Polynesians) than those in the nuclear area of North China, even though all are classed within the Mongoloid phylum.

It would be premature to conclude from the above that the Huai Ho and lower Yangtze Neolithic culture was derived from either Yang-shao or Ta-p'en-k'eng. As yet, one can only say that perhaps both contributed to the population of this lowland area and to its first farming culture.

4 : *The Lungshanoid Cultures*

If the interrelationship of the earliest Neolithic cultures in the middle Huang Ho basin, the Pacific seaboard, and the southeastern coastal area is as yet unclear, there can be no question about the mutual similarity of these cultures in the next stage. After approximately 3200 B.C., similar cultural transformations took place in all three areas, bringing about a series of Neolithic cultures broadly like one another all across China. We refer to these as the Lungshanoid cultures, their name being derived from the site at Lung-shan-chen in Shantung, where a Neolithic culture of this type was first discovered in 1928. The Lungshanoid development is a seeming paradox: everywhere there is credible archaeological evidence that demonstrates a local or regional continuity of culture from the previous foundation—which varied from area to area—to the new Lungshanoid—which exhibits broad similarities across different areas. And everywhere one recognizes two major stages of cultural development: an early Lungshanoid phase, seemingly transitional, and a late Lung-shan phase, in which the earlier peaceful and largely egalitarian village life had been transformed into a warlike and ranked society preparatory for the formation of civilization and the state.

How did this seeming paradox come about? What accounts for the similarities of cultures of widely divergent ancestries? Why did the Lung-shanoid development march toward the rise of civilizations? In attempting to resolve the issues, we are faced with a difficult challenge posed by Chinese archaeology in the 1970s. Let us briefly review the Lungshanoid problem in a historical perspective.

Classification of Neolithic Cultures in North China

The period around 1920 can be called a turning point in the study of ancient China. The history of China before the Three Dynasties had been a legendary account of the sage kings; after 1920 it became a true history of China's cultural development from the Stone Age to civilization, based upon archaeological evidence. This change in the basic orientation of historiography occurred in a context of scholarly skepticism of legends that stemmed partly from the May Fourth Movement of 1919 but was directly brought about by a series of significant archaeological discoveries at that time. These included the excavation of Palaeolithic implements in the Ordos in 1920 and of painted-pottery sites at Yang-shao-ts'un, Honan, and Sha-kuo-t'un, Liaoning, in 1921–22—discoveries that helped fill the historiographic void with new empirical data. In view of the fact that Chinese elements plainly occurred in the newly found Painted Pottery culture and, also, that the human skeletal remains at these sites were quickly pronounced "proto-Chinese" by physical anthropologists, scholars of ancient China at once undertook to seek in the Painted Pottery culture the genesis of the ancient civilizations of the land. The two archaeological sites first established in scientific scholarship were Yang-shao-ts'un and Hsiao-t'un (the site of the last Shang dynasty capital, which was not excavated until 1928), and the names Yang-shao and Hsiao-t'un soon became landmarks of ancient Chinese history and historiography. Andersson, excavator of the Yang-shao-ts'un site, dated the Yang-shao culture from 2200 to 1700 B.C. in the belief that it immediately preceded the historical civilizations.

It is true that elements of the Shang civilization at Hsiao-t'un can be found at Yang-shao-ts'un, but exactly how far apart were the two? Li Chi, for the first time, undertook to make a detailed comparison between the Yang-shao and the Hsiao-t'un cultures, arriving at the following conclusions: the culture with painted pottery was earlier than the Shang; the Shang culture as represented by the site Hsiao-t'un was derived from one with which the Yang-shao culture was only indirectly related.[1]

Problems naturally arose about the ethnic identity of the Yang-shao culture in terms of ancient texts—now that it was shown not to be directly ancestral to the Shang—and about the direct antecedents of the Shang in archaeological terms. Hsü Chung-shu suggested that the Yang-shao culture could probably be identified with the Yü-Hsia people of the ancient texts and that the Hsiao-t'un culture was probably derived from the eastern coastal portions of North China, the "circum–Pohai Bay area that probably cradled the first Chinese civilization."[2]

It was at this time, when speculations were being ventured that the Shang's antecedents were derived from Shantung and its environs, that a new type of Neolithic culture was discovered in Shantung. In 1928,

1. Li Chi, *An-yang fa-chüeh pao-kao* 2 (1930), 337–47.
2. Hsü Chung-shu, *An-yang fa-chüeh pao-kao* 3 (1931), 523–57.

seven years after the excavation of Yang-shao-ts'un, a so-called Black Pottery site was discovered by Wu Chin-ting (G. D. Wu; a native of Shantung and pupil of Li Chi) at Ch'eng-tzu-yai, near the town of Lung-shan in the heart of this eastern province.[3] The site was not excavated until 1930–31 when the Institute of History and Philology, Academia Sinica, whose excavations at An-yang were forced to a halt in 1930 by outbreaks of civil disturbance in Honan, gave it concentrated attention. Two ancient cultural layers were uncovered at Ch'eng-tzu-yai—a Neolithic assemblage in a lower stratum and Eastern Chou types in an upper stratum.[4]

The Neolithic culture exhibited several remarkable characteristics. Its pottery included pieces that were thin, hard, lustrous, and black, drastically different from the painted red sherds at Yang-shao-ts'un. Its stone inventory, though broadly similar to the Yang-shao, contained a number of new types, and its abundant shell artifacts were also distinctive. Thus, in the Neolithic archaeology of North China, appeared the concept of a Black Pottery (Lung-shan) culture to contrast with the Painted Pottery (Yang-shao) culture. Moreover, in the new type of culture there were features that indicated close connections with the Shang, especially oracle bones and a village wall constructed by the *hang-t'u* method. Thus it appeared that the prototype of the first civilization of China was located about where scholars speculated it should be. In his preface to the Ch'eng-tzu-yai report, Li Chi made the following observations:

> Because these black-pottery sites are scattered in Shantung and the eastern part of Honan, the central point most likely is in the Shantung region. To what degree they are related to the painted pottery cultures of the northwest and the north, we as yet have no way of knowing. But that there are two independent complexes, and that the development in each area manifested temporal differences is very clear. In the culture of the earliest period of Chinese history as represented at Yin-hsü, according to all our experience, not only was bone divination bound in with all the mental life of that time but also the practice of bone divination probably had a very great motivating influence on the early evolution of Chinese writing. Although the divination bones at Ch'eng-tzu-yai manifested no writing, nevertheless, the pottery sherds of that time period included some

3. Wu Chin-ting, *BIHP* 1, fasc. 4 (1930).
4. Li Chi et al., *Ch'eng-tzu-yai*, Nanking, 1934.

which bore symbols, and one could see that the lower-stratum Ch'eng-tzu-yai culture had already freed itself completely from the "Dark Ages." All this gives us a strong hint, namely that the single most important element composing China's earliest historic culture was evidently one which developed in the east.... If we can take the Ch'eng-tzu-yai black-pottery culture and search out the sequence of its expansion and the exact extent of its sphere, we can then settle the greater part of the history of the dawn period in China.[5]

This new view of culture history quite naturally served to bridge the gap between the historic and the prehistoric. In the Neolithic archaeology of the 1930s the Painted Pottery culture of western Honan, Shansi, Shensi, and Kansu, and the Black Pottery culture of eastern Honan and Shantung came to be regarded as a pair of opposing, parallel cultures of the "late" Neolithic period that immediately preceded the rise of the Shang civilization. This view was strengthened by discoveries of the Black Pottery culture sites after Ch'eng-tzu-yai: Hou-kang in An-yang, in 1931;[6] Kao-ching-t'ai-tzu in An-yang[7] and Ta-lai-tien in Chün Hsien,[8] in 1932; Liu-chuang in Chün Hsien, in 1933;[9] T'ung-lo-chai in An-yang, in 1934;[10] Liang-ch'eng-chen in Jih-chao;[11] and Tsao-lü-t'ai and Hei-ku-tui in Yüng-ch'eng,[12] in 1936—all of them in eastern Honan and Shantung. Furthermore, similar finds were reported from Shou Hsien in northern Anhwei in 1934,[13] Liang-chu near Hangchow in northern Chekiang in 1936,[14] and Yang-t'ou-wa near Port Arthur on Liaotung Peninsula in 1933,[15] extending the Lung-shan domain to much of the Pacific coast from Pohai Bay to Hangchow Bay. Thus the two-culture theory became

5. *Ibid.*, pp. xv–xvi, trans. by Kenneth Starr, Yale University Publications in Anthropology, no. 52 (1956), pp. 21–22.

6. Liang Ssu-yung, *An-yang fa-chüeh pao-kao* 4 (1933), 609–25; *Essays Presented to Ts'ai Yüan P'ei*, part 2 (1935), 555–67.

7. Wu Chin-ting, *An-yang fa-chüeh pao-kao* 4 (1933), 627–33; *TYKKPK* 1 (1936).

8. Liu Yao, *TYKKPK* 1 (1936), 69–89.

9. *Ibid.*, pp. 254–55.

10. *Ibid.*, p. 255.

11. *Ibid.*, p. 255.

12. Li Ching-tan, *Chung-kuo k'ao-ku hsüeh-pao* 2 (1937), 83–120.

13. Wang Hsiang, *Chung-kuo k'ao-ku hsüeh-pao* 2 (1937), 179–250.

14. Shih Hsin-keng, *Liang-chu*, Hang-chou, West Lake Museum, 1938.

15. Kanaseki Takeo et al., *Yang-t'ou-wa*, Archaeologia Orientalis, ser. B, no. 3, Tokyo, 1943.

entrenched in the Neolithic archaeology of North China, with the Lung-shan of the east designated as the progenitor of the Shang civilization.[16]

Soon after the discovery of the new Black Pottery culture, however, archaeologists began to be puzzled by the following phenomena that seemed somewhat at odds with the above view. Remains of both cultures were found at a number of sites in northern Honan and, without exception, Yang-shao culture remains were found from layers lower—and thus earlier—than the Lung-shan remains, a sequence of culture first established by the famous Hou-kang stratigraphy where Yang-shao, Lung-shan, and Shang culture remains were found in temporal succession (fig. 67). At many sites in western Honan, on the other hand, remains of both cultures were discovered in the same layers without discernible relationship of stratification. Liang Ssu-yüng attempted to explain these by suggesting that the Lung-shan culture intruded into western Honan from the east, thus effecting the appearance of "mixed culture sites" in that area.[17]

If the archaeological data before the Sino-Japanese War of 1937–45 could be explicated within the two-culture framework and the puzzling phenomena described above could be explained away by the idea of mixed cultures, new data brought to light during the war could no longer be treated according to these views. The puzzling finds were the Lungshan-like gray pottery remains discovered by Shih Chang-ju in the Wei River valley of Shensi in 1943.[18] In an article published in 1952 discussing the Neolithic cultures of North China, Professor Shih attempted to solve the dilemma by adding a third—the Gray Pottery culture—to the Neolithic potpourri.[19]

The 1950s, however, witnessed the beginning of a drastic revision of the Neolithic classification, which was attempted from two different but complementary approaches: the synthesizers tried to revise the old framework to accommodate both the old and the new data, which could no longer be adequately encompassed within the older structure; the field-workers attempted to analyze the new data and design a new framework on this basis. As late as 1957, when T'ung Chu-ch'en attempted to summarize the Neolithic materials of the Huang Ho and the lower Yangtze valleys to that date,[20] he still adhered to the two-culture theory. Two

16. See, e.g., Li Chi, *The Beginnings of Chinese Civilization*, and Cheng Te-k'un, *Prehistoric China*.

17. *Essays Presented to Ts'ai*, pt. 2, pp. 560–61.

18. Shih Chang-ju, *BIHP* 27 (1956), 205–323.

19. *Ta-lu tsa-chih* 4 (1952), no. 3, 65–75.

20. T'ung Chu-ch'en, *KKHP* 1957 (2).

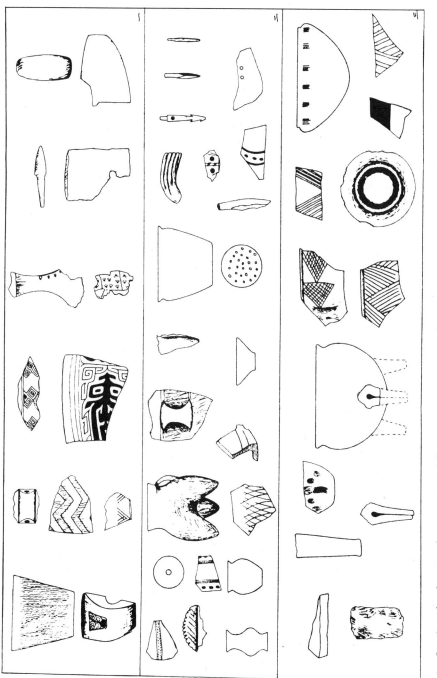

67. Stratigraphy showing the succession of the Yang-shao (*lower*), Lung-shan (*middle*), and Shang (*upper*) cultures at the Hou-kang site, An-yang, northern Honan. (From Liang Ssu-yüng, *Essays Presented to Mr. Ts'ai Yüan P'ei on His 65th Birthday*, Institute of History and Philology, Academia Sinica, 1935, vol. 2, p. 555.)

years later, several scholars independently proposed a new scheme of classification under which the Yang-shao and the Lung-shan were considered two successive stages of development of the same culture rather than two cultures of different origin.

Among the first to plant the seeds of doubt about the two-culture theory were several foreign scholars who, as relatively impartial observers, were less bound by loyalty to the orthodox views than their Chinese colleagues and less hesitant to question and criticize when confronted by new evidence from the field. In reviewing the archaeological developments in China in the early 1950s, the late Lauriston Ward reported, "Excavations of prehistoric sites ... are stated to show that black pottery is found everywhere in the same levels as painted pottery, thus indicating that earlier views about two separate Neolithic cultures in the North China plain, the Yang-shao or Red Pottery culture and the Lung-shan or Black Pottery culture, may have to be seriously modified."[21] The significance of the divergence—chronological or cultural—between the two ceramic cultures was also questioned by two Japanese scholars, Mizuno Seiichi and Sekino Takeshi, in 1953, at the Fourth Far Eastern Prehistory Congress at Quezon City in the Philippines.[22]

At this time, as Ward pointed out, Lungshan-like remains were discovered at K'o-hsing-chuang in 1951 and A-ti-ts'un in 1953, both near Sian in Shensi, from a layer between a Painted Pottery stratum below and a Western Chou stratum above.[23] Similar findings in an identical stratigraphic situation were made in southern Shansi.[24] These discoveries made untenable the old two-culture theory and led me, among others, to ponder anew the whole scope of cultural classification in Neolithic North China, seeking answers to the following questions:

1. Could the Gray Pottery cultures of Shansi and Shensi be contemporary and comparable with the Black Pottery culture of Shantung?
2. If the answer is affirmative, is it possible that the Lung-shan culture and all Lungshan-like ("Lungshanoid") cultures belong to a developmental level subsequent to the Yang-shao culture of Chung Yüan?

21. L. Ward, in *Current Anthropology*, W. T. Thomas, ed., University of Chicago Press, 1956, pp. 89–90.

22. Mizuno, "Prehistoric China: Yang-shao and Pu-chao-chai," and Sekino, "On the black and grey pottery of ancient China," *Proc. 4th Far Eastern Prehist. Congr. 1953*, vol. I, fasc. I, 1956.

23. *KKTH* 1955 (1); 1956 (2).

24. *WWTKTL* 1956 (10).

3. If so, how does one explain the so-called mixed sites of western Honan?

4. What is the nature of the similarity and difference between the Yang-shao and the Lung-shan cultures both in first principle and in final analysis?

Starting from this lack of biased premises, we took on the two-culture theory as hypothesis rather than historic fact and came to call a regional culture precisely a regional culture rather than a standard type with which cultures of other regions had to conform. More specifically, the Lung-shan culture of Shantung was to be regarded as a regional cultural phase in Shantung, but it was not to be used *a priori* as an absolute standard for a "Lung-shan culture" for all of North China. In this view, a new frame of reference for the Neolithic archaeology of North China was inevitable. In two papers published in 1959, "Chronology of the Neolithic Cultures in China"[25] and "Chinese Prehistory in Pacific Perspective: Some Hypotheses and Problems,"[26] I have argued that the Lungshanoid cultures throughout North China constituted a horizon for all of North China that must be placed stratigraphically above the whole scope of the Yang-shao culture, and that the differences between the two cultures were developmental (table 7). From such a perspective the following scheme of levels has been developed:[27]

1. *Incipient agriculture.* The transitional stage from food gathering to food producing in the nuclear area; the evidence for this level of culture remains merely circumstantial.

2. *The establishment of village farmers.* The Yang-shao culture, described in chapter 3.

3. *The expansion of advanced village farmers from the nuclear area to new frontiers.* The Lungshanoid formative stage during which advanced farmers broke through the natural habitat barriers of the cultigens to expand rapidly toward the fertile plains and river valleys of the east and the southeast. Many Yang-shao elements (especially the painted pottery) remained intact, but innovations emerged. A surprising degree of cultural uniformity could be seen at the sites of this level, to which belonged the so-called mixed culture sites.

4. *The formation of local cultures.* The Lung-shan cultures of various regions assumed distinctive local characters as a result of permanent

25. *BIHP* 30 (1959), 259–309.

26. *Harvard Jour. Asiatic Studies* 20 (1959), 100–49.

27. See "China," in *Courses Toward Urban Life,* Robert J. Braidwood and Gordon R. Willey, eds., Viking Fund Publications in Anthropology, no. 32 (1962).

Table 7

Yang-shao and Lungshanoid Cultural Contrasts

Yang-shao	*Lungshanoid*
Shifting settlement; repetitive occupation	Permanent settlement; relatively permanent occupation
Pigs and dogs as principal domestic animals	Cattle and sheep sharply increased in addition to pigs and dogs
Largely confined to the nuclear area; indicative of stable population density?	Far-reaching expansions into eastern plains, Manchuria, central and South China; indicating population pressure from permanent settlement and great productivity and greater degree of interaction?
More symmetrical edges than asymmetrical on all edged tools; more circular and oval cross sections; indicates extensive use of the wood-felling complex for field clearance	More asymmetrical edges than symmetrical; more rectangular cross sections; indicates extensive use of carpenters' tools (adzes, chisels, antler wedges)
Rectangular, single-holed or double-notched stone knives characteristic; indicates more game hunting and use of longitudinal cutting tools	Semilunar and double-holed, or sickle-shaped stone knives and shell sickles characteristic; indicates more extensive use of harvesting tools
Pottery handmade	Beginning of wheel-made pottery; indicates intensified crafts specialization
None	Scapulimancy; indicates intensified occupational specialization
No defensive works; few artifacts exclusively for fighting	Appearance of *hang-t'u* village walls and weapons; indicates necessity for fortification and means for offensive action
Burial practice showing age and sex differentiation	Growing number of otherwise differentiated burials; possibly indicates more rigidly constituted classes
Community patterns showing little evidence of major social stratification	Concentration of jade artifacts at isolated spots in one site; indicates more intensive status differentiation
Art associated with domestic crafts (ceramics)	Art not conspicuously associated with domestic crafts; possible association with theocratic crafts (?)

Table 7 [continued]

Yang-shao	Lungshanoid
Utility wares (cord-mat-basket pattern) characteristic	Ceremonial wares (eggshell forms and fine, well-made cups, fruit stands and shallow dishes) characteristic
"Fertility cult" characteristic	Evidence of institutionalized ancestor cult; ceremonials far beyond merely agricultural; possibly associated with specialized groups of people

settlement, isolation, and varying adaptive tendencies. This is the level of the Lung-shan cultures of Shantung, Honan, Shansi, Shensi, and so forth.

This developmental sequence in essence agreed with—and, indeed, sank into relative insignificance in the face of—the new interpretations given the data by several field archaeologists in China. In 1959, An Chih-min proposed to derive the Lung-shan cultures of Honan, Shansi, and Shensi from the Yang-shao culture of the same area, and Shih Hsing-pang sought to explain their differences in terms of economic and societal changes.[28] In 1960 Hsü Shun-ch'en positively stated that "recent discoveries of the sites transitional in nature have demonstrated that the Yang-shao and the Lung-shan were successive cultures of the same sequence rather than a pair of parallel cultural systems."[29] In "Archaeology of New China," published in 1962 and purporting to sum up results in China during the preceding decade, the authors made the following statement:

> With regard to the interrelationship of the Yang-shao and the Lung-shan, in the past they were generally regarded as cultures of different origins. New discoveries in the last decade gradually forced a change in this view. Particularly as a result of the discovery of the Miao-ti-kou II culture, the hypothesis has been generally accepted by archaeologists that the Lung-shan cultures of the Chung Yüan were developed out of the Yang-shao culture.[30]

It must be noted that the above quotation refers merely to the Lung-shan culture of the Central Plain (Chung Yüan), leaving the issue of the

28. *KK* 1959 (10).
29. *WW* 1960 (5), 39.
30. *Hsin Chung-ko ti k'ao-ku shou-hu*, Peking, Wen Wu Press, 1962, pp. 20–21.

origins of the Lungshanoid cultures in the eastern coastal areas more or less dangling. My own scheme, on the other hand, emphasized the similarities between the Lung-shan cultures of Chung Yüan and the Lungshanoid cultures of the Pacific seaboard, giving rise to the hypothesis that the entire Lungshanoid represents a radiation from out of a Yang-shao base in Chung Yüan. To both of these hypotheses of Lung-shan developing out of Yang-shao—one of a narrow scope and the other of a broader one—there were notable dissensions. Li Chi, for example, insisted on emphasizing the distinctive features of the Lung-shan cultures in eastern China, refusing to see any of the Lung-shan cultures as a Yang-shao derivative.[31]

It has been recognized, since the Lungshanoid hypothesis was presented, that chronology is of the essence. In the previous edition of this volume, I had pointed out that to adequately describe and explain the nature of the interrelationship of the Yang-shao and the Lung-shan cultures in terms of the above development sequence, the Lungshan-like cultures must be proved later in time than the Yang-shao culture as a whole, and regional chronologies of the Lungshan-like cultures must be established to show that those cultures within the sphere of the Yang-shao distribution were ancestral to those outside it. At the time of that writing (1967), the only available absolute chronology pertaining to any of the Lungshan-like cultures was in Taiwan, where such culture was shown to begin around 2500 B.C.[32]

Radiocarbon dates from Neolithic China have become available since 1972, and the chronological situation they point to does not exactly fit the conditions specified above. What the radiocarbon dates, still few and less than adequate for a definitive solution, seem to point to is a picture comprising the following parts: (1) the interrelationship of the Yang-shao and the Lung-shan cultures in the Chung Yüan remains as it was viewed in the 1960s—namely, that the Lung-shan culture in Chung Yüan developed out of the Yang-shao culture through an intermediate, transitional stage of the Miao-ti-kou II culture; (2) the Ch'ing-lien-kang and some related cultures, heretofore classified as Lungshanoid, now appear to emerge in the eastern Pacific seaboard at an earlier time; (3) the later stages of the Ch'ing-lien-kang and related cultures—including the Ta-wen-k'ou culture of Shantung, the Liu-lin and Hua-t'ing-ts'un phases of northern Kiangsu, the Pei-yin-yang-ying and Sung-tse phases of southern Kiangsu and northern Chekiang, the Ch'ü-chia-ling culture of Hupei,

31. Li Chi, *Bull. Dept. Arch. Anth.* 21/22 (1963), 1–12.
32. K. C. Chang et al., *Fengpitou, Tapenkeng, and the Prehistory of Taiwan.*

and the Ts'ao-hsieh-tun culture of Taiwan—are found to be not only similar to one another and to the Miao-ti-kou II culture of Chung Yüan but also largely contemporaneous. I propose to refer to these cultures and their immediate descendants as the Lungshanoid cultures, divisible into earlier (Lungshanoid) and later (Lung-shan) phases.

Largely from the radiocarbon chronology, a new pattern of Neolithic interrelationships in China is now emerging—a pattern that is providing new and broader information on the old Yang-shao–Lung-shan interrelationship. It suggests that, for the earlier periods of the Chinese Neolithic, three centers are now discernible, their interrelationship having been discussed in the previous chapter. Beginning about 3200 B.C., their descendant cultures came to exhibit an increasing tendency toward similarity to one another, resulting in, first, the earlier Lungshanoid cultures and phases and, later, the various local Lung-shan cultures.

The Earlier Lungshanoid Cultures

Although their first manifestations must be traced to the western Honan "mixed-cultures sites," the Lungshanoid cultures were not identified until a series of sites with Lung-shan characteristics *and* painted pottery was found in eastern and southeastern coastal China. Under Lungshanoid we may group the Miao-ti-kou II culture of Honan (including the mixed-culture sites), eastern Shensi, and southern Shansi; the Ta-wen-k'ou culture of Shantung; the later phases of Ch'ing-lien-kang and related cultures of the Huai Ho and the lower Yangtze; the Ch'ü-chia-ling culture of the lower Han River; and the so-called Painted Pottery cultures of Chekiang, Fukien, Taiwan, and Kwangtung. All these cultural phases, each restricted to its own limited area of distribution, shared a number of significant features, as will be discussed later. Largely speaking these phases are all characterized by painted pottery but differ substantially from the Yang-shao, and the features on which they differ from the Yang-shao are similar to those of the Lung-shan. In time they were without exception demonstrably earlier than the Lung-shan cultures wherever they occurred with these cultures, and they are ancestral to the latter in each region. Space does not allow a detailed description of each of the Lungshanoid cultures, but the following summaries of five of the most important of them will suffice for the purpose of this volume.[33]

33. Much of the following summary was based on *Hsin Chung-kuo ti k'ao-ku shou-huo*, pp. 15, 20, 28, 30–32. New data that have appeared after the publication of the book have also been incorporated.

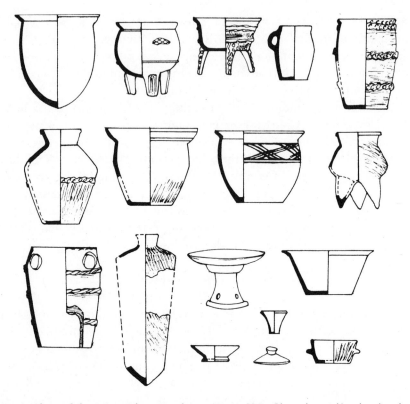

68. Artifacts of the Miao-ti-kou II culture. (From *Hsin Chung-kuo ti k'ao-ku shou-huo*, Peking, Wen Wu Press, 1962, p. 18.)

The Miao-ti-kou II Culture

Known from the nuclear area (western Honan, southern Shansi, and eastern Shensi), the Miao-ti-kou II culture (fig. 68) is best represented by the upper stratum of Miao-ti-kou in Shan Hsien, Yang-shao-ts'un in Mien-ch'ih Hsien, and Wang-wan in Lo-yang, Honan; Ch'üan-hu-ts'un in Hua Hsien and Heng-chen-ts'un in Hua-yin Hsien, Shensi; and P'an-nan-ts'un in P'ing-lu Hsien, Shansi. The Miao-ti-kou stratigraphy shows that this phase of culture was later in time than the Yang-shao, and the Wang-wan and Heng-chen-ts'un stratigraphies indicate that it was earlier than the Honan and Shensi Lung-shan cultures.

In addition to the chipped stone knives with side notches common at Yang-shao sites, there appeared in this phase polished semilunar and sickle-shaped knives and shell knives, indicating a more advanced agriculture. Double-pronged wooden cultivating implements (*lei*) are known from their impressions in the earth. Bones of domestic chicken are found along-side those of dogs and pigs. Stone net sinkers and stone and bone arrow-heads are found widely.

Pottery was manufactured mainly by the coiling technique. Occasional wheel-made pieces are reported; the technique of polishing and retouch-ing pottery by rotation was apparently known then, though the true potter's wheel at this time is doubtful. The pottery paste is usually coarse and gray. Decoration was most often done by impression—basket, cord, and check marks occurred—and secondarily by applique and incision. Painted pottery still occurred widely, the major type being a large, deep, reddish bowl painted in black in the upper portions. A small amount of thin, hard, lustrous black pottery was found. Aside from bowls, jars, and pots, the shapes of pottery included tripods and some ring-footed vessels. The tripods include *ting* and *chia* but not *li*.

The "transitional" nature of the Miao-ti-kou II pottery is of particular significance; it has caused many scholars to embrace the view that the Honan Lung-shan pottery could have been derived from the Yang-shao:

> Many pottery forms seem to have evolved out of the Yang-shao forms, particularly the cup, pot, pointed-bottomed jar, and the *ting* tripod. The pointed-bottomed jars are typical of the Yang-shao culture; this type of jar, similar to the finds at Miao-ti-kou II, is also found in Yang-shao-ts'un, Mien-ch'ih Hsien, and at Heng-chen-ts'un in Hua-yin Hsien, Shensi, all closely related to but different from the Yang-shao stage forms. The small cups slipped in red pigment are typical of this site but possibly related to the coarse small cups of the Yang-shao stage. . . . In short, the ceramics of Miao-ti-kou II exhibit features transitional from the Yang-shao to the Lung-shan.[34]

At the Miao-ti-kou site 145 human burials, mostly single, were found; the bodies had been arranged in regular rows and were in a stretched, supine position with heads to the south. Grave furnishings were minimal. At the Wang-wan site near Lo-yang, among 39 burials two were prone, rather than supine, one showing evidence of having both hands bound at the time of burial.[35]

---

34. *Miao-ti-kou yü San-li-ch'iao*, 1959, pp. 110–11. For other local sequences demon-strating a continuous development of Yang-shao/Miao-ti-kou II/Honan Lung-shan cul-tures, see the reports on Wang-wan, Loyang (*KK* 1961, no. 4) and Kao-yai, Yen-shih (*KK* 1964, no. 11).

35. *KK* 1961 (4), 177.

The Hua-t'ing Culture

In the Huai Ho plain of northern Kiangsu and southern Shantung is a series of interconnected lakes and small rivers. Beginning in the 1950s, archaeological sites yielding similar remains, shown to be earlier than the Lung-shan culture in the same general area, have been unearthed on river terraces, mounds, and isolated hills. The most important sites (fig. 65) are those at Hua-t'ing-ts'un in Hsin-i, northern Kiangsu, discovered in 1952 and excavated in 1952 and 1953;[36] Kang-shang-ts'un in T'eng Hsien, southern Shantung, also discovered in 1952 but excavated in 1961;[37] Ching-chih-chen in An-ch'iu[38] and Hsi-hsia-hou in Ch'ü-fu,[39] both in southern Shantung and discovered in 1957; Liu-lin in P'i Hsien, northern Kiangsu, discovered in 1959;[40] Ta-wen-k'ou in T'ai-an Hsien, southern Shantung, also discovered in 1959;[41] Ta-tun-tzu in P'i Hsien, northern Kiangsu, discovered in 1962;[42] Yeh-tien in Tsou Hsien, southern Shantung, discovered in 1965;[43] and Ta-fan-chuang in Lin-i, southern Shantung, discovered in 1973.[44]

The prehistoric remains at these sites apparently were those of a single culture with common characteristics, although internal variation and change can be clearly discerned. But this culture has been referred to by various labels, in large part as the result of an accident. Since the sites in Kiangsu were for the most part investigated by archaeologists from the Nanking Museum, whereas those in Shantung were studied by archaeologists in Shantung, the provincial boundary assumed an undue influence on the naming of the culture. The sites in Shantung have been grouped under the label "Ta-wen-k'ou culture,"[45] while other archaeologists prefer a subdivision into three successive phases (Ch'ing-lien-kang, Hua-t'ing, and Liu-lin).[46] Chinese archaeologists recognize this terminological confusion,[47] and we can expect that new and better classificatory schemes

36. *WWTKTL* 1956 (7), 23–26.

37. *KK* 1963 (7), 351–61.

38. *KKHP* 1959 (4), 17–29.

39. *KKHP* 1964 (2), 57–104.

40. *KKHP* 1962 (1), 81–102; 1965 (2), 9–47.

41. *Ta-wen-k'ou*, Peking, Wen Wu Press, 1974. This site has sometimes been referred to as Pao-t'ou, after Pao-t'ou village, in Ning-yang Hsien.

42. *KKHP* 1964 (2), 9–56.

43. *WW* 1972 (2), 25–30.

44. *KK* 1975 (1), 13–22, 6.

45. Tseng Chao-yüeh and Yin Huan-chang, *Chiang-su sheng ch'u-t'u wen-wu hsüan chi*, Peking, Wen Wu Press, 1963, p. 4.

46. *KKHP* 1964 (2), 47–48. Wu Shan-ch'ing, *WW* 1973 (6), 49.

47. An Chih-min, *KK* 1972 (6), 40.

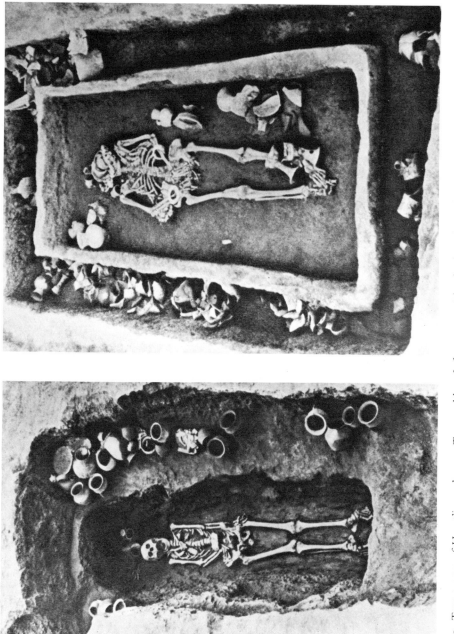

69. Two graves of Hua-t'ing culture at Ta-wen-k'ou. *Left*, a grave with *erh-ts'eng-t'ai*; *right*, a burial chamber outlined by wooden logs. (From *Ta-wen-k'ou*. Peking, Wen Wu Press, 1974.)

will appear with additional data and analytic research. For the purpose of this volume, I will do two things: (1) identify sites of the Ch'ing-lien-kang phase (Ch'ing-lien-kang, Erh-chien-ts'un, and perhaps Tzu-ching-shan in P'eng-lai) as being the type sites of a Ch'ing-lien-kang culture, at the head of the known chronological sequence in this area; and (2) group all the other sites (principally Liu-lin, Hua-t'ing and Ta-wen-k'ou) into a single culture, tentatively referred to as the Hua-t'ing culture—Hua-t'ing-ts'un being the first discovered and excavated site of the whole group.* Ch'ing-lien-kang culture has been described in the last chapter. There is little question that Hua-t'ing culture represents a further growth of the Ch'ing-lien-kang culture, and it underwent a growth process of its own, with Liu-lin at the earlier end of the process and Ta-fan-chuang at the later end. No radiocarbon dates are yet available from this entire culture, but one may make an educated guess and place it between late fourth millennium and middle third millennium B.C.

Most of the Hua-t'ing sites are burial sites (fig. 69), and as burial sites they share the following features: they are mostly single burials, with bodies supine and heads pointing east (except for Liu-lin, where the heads point north); the graves are rectangular pits, some with an erh-ts'eng-t'ai ("second level platform or ledge"), namely, a ledge around the burial pit formed by a larger opening on top; similar pottery and tools were used as grave furnishings; and there is wide disparity in the amount of grave furnishings between different burials, probably suggesting a beginning of significant social ranking. This last feature is of particular interest for our understanding of the Lungshanoid cultures in terms of their social developmental status. In some graves only a single pottery vessel accompanied the dead, but in others there were many more pottery vessels, tools, ornaments, and/or sacrificial animals (pigs in Ta-wen-k'ou and dogs at Liu-lin, for example): grave furnishings numbered more than 180 at Ta-wen-k'ou, 40 or 50 at Yeh-tien, and 85 at Ta-fan-chuang. In many of the burials it is shown that the custom of tooth extraction (usually of the lateral incisor) was practised (fig. 70).

Artifacts and other remains found from the graves at the sites of the Hua-t'ing culture indicate a culture with agriculture (inferred from such agricultural implements as ax, bone sickle, and deer-incisor cutter) and domestic animals (pigs, dogs, cattle, and sheep). Characteristic items also include certain distinctive pottery-vessel forms, turtleshells (both carapaces and plastrons) as containers and arm-guards, bone spatulas (as food servers) and bone combs (for hair restraint), and jade ornaments, widely used (fig. 71).

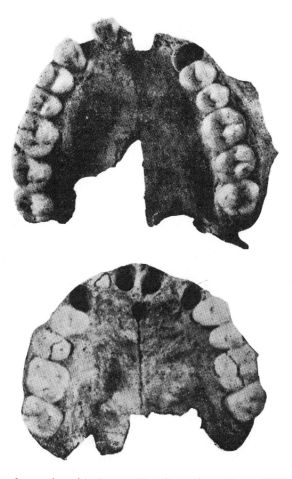

70. Extraction of upper lateral incisors in Hua-t'ing culture (From *KKHP* 1974, no. 2, pl. 3.)

Pottery of the Hua-t'ing culture underwent appreciable change within the culture's duration. For most of the period pottery was handmade, but wheel-made pottery appeared in later stages. Red ware, of fine paste or sandy, was predominant, but in later stages gray ware became more important. The pottery surface was largely left plain, but some were impressed (by cord or basket) or incised. Painted pottery was more conspicuous in earlier stages, including designs similar to the Miao-ti-kou phase of Yang-shao culture; and polished black pottery, some extremely lustrous and thin, increased in quantity in later periods. Incised symbols or signs have been found on a few sherds of this culture (fig. 72). In vessel forms, the Hua-t'ing culture may be characterized as the culture of *ting*

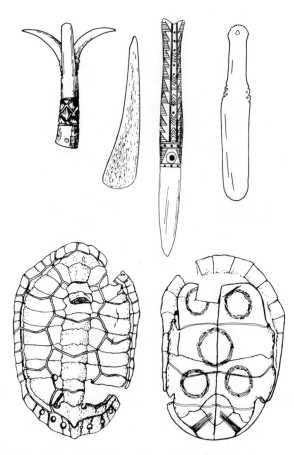

71. Bone and shell artifacts of Hua-t'ing culture. (From *KKHP* 1964, no. 2; *KKHP* 1965, no. 2; *Kiangsu ch'u-t'u wen-wu hsüan chi*, Peking, Wen Wu Press, 1963.)

tripods (bowls or jars with three legs), *kui* tripods (water jar with three hollow legs, a large handle, and a large spout), *tou* (bowl on pedestal or ringfoot) with elaborate designs formed by holes cut in the hollow pedestal, beakers with lugs, and small cups on high and thin pedestals (fig. 73). Most of these forms are also characteristic of the Lung-shan culture of Shantung, which was undoubtedly a direct descendant.[48]

The Pei-yin-yang-ying Culture

Southern Kiangsu and northern Chekiang is another low, fertile land of many waters, primarily the lower Yangtze, Lake T'ai, and the lower

48. *KK* 1963 (7), 360, 377–78.

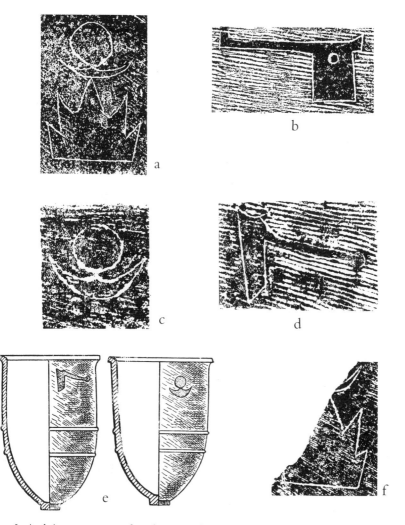

72. Incised signs on pottery found at Hua-t'ing culture sites: (a–e) Ling-yang-ho, in Chü Hsien; (f) Ch'ien-chai, in Chu-ch'eng. (From *Ta-wen-k'ou*, Peking, Wen Wu Press, 1974.)

Chekiang (Ch'ien-t'ang) River (fig. 65). The earliest prehistoric culture here is the one represented by the Ma-chia-pang site in Chia-hsing, northern Chekiang, which was discussed in the last chapter. The next stage of the area's prehistory is represented by two well-known and highly important sites, namely Pei-yin-yang-ying at the heart of Nanking city,[49]

49. *KKHP* 1958 (1), 7–23. Wu, *WW* 1973 (6), 52–53.

73. Pottery types of Hua-t'ing culture. (From *Ta-wen-k'ou*, Peking, Wen Wu Press, 1974; *KK* 1975, no. 1; *KKHP* 1962, no. 1; *KKHP* 1964, no. 2.)

and Sung-tse in Ch'ing-p'u Hsien, in the southwestern part of Shanghai city.[50] Remains from these two sites indicate a broadly similar culture, which is tentatively referred to as the Pei-yin-yang-ying culture, but there is also appreciable diversity between the two sites, which Wu Shan-ch'ing regards as being indicative of chronological difference.[51]

The prehistoric site at Pei-yin-yang-ying, located at a staff dormitory area of Nanking University, was discovered in the 1930s, but excavation at the site, by archaeologists from Nanking Museum, did not begin until 1955. Four seasons of work have since taken place, and two occupational phases have been distinguished. The earlier phase, which is used to typify the Pei-yin-yang-ying culture, is represented by a cemetery, in which 276 burials have been unearthed. All graves were single burials, the bodies mostly lying supine, with the head pointing northeast. Many graves were furnished with tools, ornaments, and pottery, some lavishly. A few graves indicate prone- and flexed-postures or secondary burials. Stones are characterized by flat, perforated hoes or axes, adzes, knives with multiple perforations, and various ornaments (rings, beads, tubes, pendants, and so forth, of jadelike materials and agate). Pottery was mostly of a sandy or fine red ware, often slipped in red, some painted in dark red with designs. Other decorations were incised, impressed, and appliquéd. Principal vessel forms are *ting* tripods, bowls on low ring feet, *tou* on medium-high and perforated pedestals, and water pots with handle and spout. Gray and black pottery of fine paste was also found but in small quantities (fig. 74).

The Sung-tse site, discovered in 1958 and excavated in 1960–61 by

50. *KKHP* 1962 (2), 1–28.

51. *WW* 1973 (6), 53–55. Other sites of the same type are reported in *KK* 1959 (9), 479; 1963 (6), 308–18.

74. Artifacts of the Pei-yin-yang-ying phase. (From *Hsin Chung-kuo ti k'ao-ku shou-huo*, Peking, Wen Wu Press, 1962, p. 29.)

staff members of the Shanghai City Cultural Relics Commission, contained occupational debris or burials from three successive stages. The earliest stratum yielded remains that have been compared with the Ma-chia-pang culture described in the previous chapter, and the uppermost stratum belonged to the Eastern Chou period. The middle stratum, which contains the culture in question, produced a cemetery in which 51 graves were excavated. All burials were single, supine, with the head pointing to the southeast. Again pottery, tools, and ornaments constituted the bulk of grave furnishings. The pottery exhibits sandy and fine red ware, but black and gray wares increased to more than a third of the total. Many pottery vessels were made on a wheel, and a few sherds were incised with symbols or signs (fig. 129). Principal vessel forms are *ting* tripods, *tou* bowls on pedestals, beakers, and small-mouthed jars.

The Ch'ü-chia-ling Culture

In 1954 a new Neolithic culture was discovered at a site near Ch'ü-chia-ling village in Ching-shan Hsien, eastern-central Hupei, in the lower Han-shui basin—a culture characterized most conspicuously by eggshell-thin potsherds and clay spindle whorls with painted decorative designs.[52] In the twenty years since, sites yielding broadly similar remains have been brought to light in the plains and river valleys of the middle Yangtze from easternmost Szechwan to easternmost Hupei and of the middle

52. *WWTKTL* 1955 (4). *KKTH* 1956 (3), 11–21.

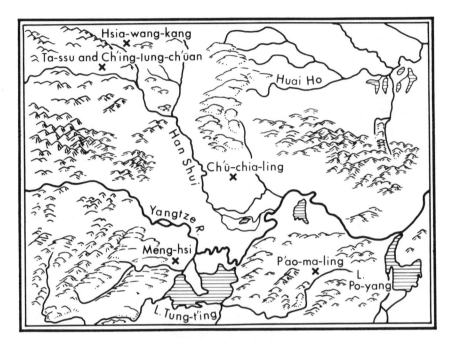

75. Map showing principal sites of Ch'ü-chia-ling culture.

and lower Han-shui drainage from southernmost Honan down to its confluence with the Yangtze, an area about 550 kilometers east-west and 400 kilometers north-south, covering the whole province of Hupei and parts of Honan, Szechwan, Hunan, and Kiangsi (fig. 75). The most important sites are, in addition to Ch'ü-chia-ling itself,[53] Hsia-wang-kang in Hsi-ch'uan, Honan,[54] Ta-ssu and Ch'ing-lung-ch'üan in Yün Hsien, northwestern Hupei,[55] Meng-hsi in Li Hsien, northern Hunan,[56] and P'ao-ma-ling, near Shan-pei-ts'un, in Hsiu-shui, northwestern Kiangsi.[57]

On the basis of stratigraphic information from the northern sites (in Hsi-ch'uan and Yün Hsien), it seems quite clear now that the Yang-shao culture of a Pan-p'o–related phase reached south to at least this area— that is, to the mountain valleys of the upper Han-shui. It is from this Yang-shao foundation that a new—Lungshanoid—culture, referred to here as the Ch'ü-chia-ling, had sprung. The new culture was followed, in the

53. *Ching-shan Ch'ü-chia-ling*, Peking, Science Press, 1965.
54. *WW* 1972 (10), 6–15, 28.
55. *KK* 1961 (10), 519–30.
56. *WW* 1972 (2), 31–38.
57. *KK* 1962 (7), 353–67.

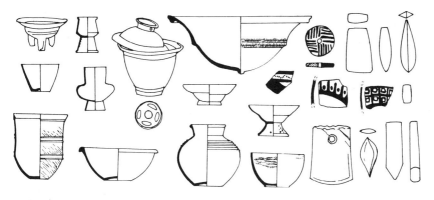

76. Artifacts of the Ch'ü-chia-ling culture. (From *Hsin Chung-kuo ti k'ao-ku shou-huo*, Peking, Wen Wu Press, 1962, p. 29.)

northern part of the region at least, by the Lung-shan culture of the Honan variety. Radiocarbon dates from the Huang-lien-shu site in Hsi-ch'uan (4100 ± 90), Ch'ü-chia-ling (4030 ± 100, 4080 ± 160), and P'ao-ma-ling (4160 ± 90) can be calibrated to the 2980–2490 B.C. range, placing the Ch'ü-chia-ling culture comfortably within the 3200–2500 B.C. range given to the earlier Lungshanoid cultures.

The Ch'ü-chia-ling culture was undoubtedly one of rice farmers. Remains of carbonized rice and of rice straws and shells used as tempering material for wall plasters have been found widely.[58] At the P'ao-ma-ling site, four peanut seeds were reported along with remains of rice and mountain peaches.[59] Bones of dogs and pigs occurred at many sites, and clay models of sheep, chickens, ducks, and geese have been uncovered at some localities. Stone implements include axes, adzes, harvesting knives, and arrowheads.

The most characteristic find of the culture is its pottery. Red or gray ware, the Ch'ü-chia-ling pottery is above all distinguished by its painted spindle whorls; eggshell-thin black or black-slipped pottery, some of which is painted in red or purple; and a group of distinctive vessel shapes—including deep bowl with wide, flared rim and ring foot, *ting* tripod with short round legs or with flat legs extending parallel to the body wall, and *tou* and jar with long cylindrical neck, bulging belly, and high ring foot (fig. 76).

58. Ting Ying, *KKHP* 1959 (4), 31–33. *KK* 1961 (10), 523.
59. *KK* 1962 (7), 365, 367.

77. Pottery at the Feng-pi-t'ou site, Taiwan. (Collection, National Taiwan University.)

The Feng-pi-t'ou and T'an-shih-shan Cultures
of the Southeast Coast

Scattered remains of painted pottery and associated artifacts have been collected from Fukien (e.g., the site at T'an-shih-shan) and Kwangtung, but the best known site is Feng-pi-t'ou of southwestern Taiwan.[60]

Prehistoric remains on the Feng-pi-t'ou hills, at the southern end of the Feng-shan tableland southeast of the city of Kao-hsiung in southern Taiwan, about one kilometer from the coast, were known toward the end of World War II, but the site was not extensively excavated until early 1965. The earliest culture at the site, characterized by cord-marked pottery, belongs to the early prehistoric horizon of southern coastal China described at the beginning of chapter 3. From 2500 to 400 B.C. the site was a settlement of considerable magnitude, occupied by people engaged in farming, hunting, fishing, and shellfish gathering. The pottery at the site has two main phases of development: an earlier phase characterized

60. K. C. Chang et al., *Fengpitou, Tapenkeng, and the Prehistory of Taiwan.*

by cord-impressed red pottery of fine paste in a variety of shapes, including *ting* tripods and *tou* with high, cutout pedestals; and a later phase characterized by pottery of coarse paste with impressed, incised, and painted decorative patterns (fig. 77). The later phase also contained a considerable number of thin, hard, lustrous, wheel-made black potsherds. Shellmounds constitute a large part of the deposits of the later phase; in one of these was found a single burial, stretched, supine, head to the south. The T'an-shih-shan site at the mouth of the Min River in northern Fukien has yielded remains almost identical with those of the late phase in Feng-pi-t'ou.[61] The radiocarbon dates both from the late phase at Feng-pi-t'ou and from T'an-shih-shan place the sites in the 2000–500 B.C. range, which would place the earlier (red ware) phase of Feng-pi-t'ou at about 2500 B.C. Thus, the typologically earlier Lungshanoid cultures in Fukien and Taiwan began several hundred years later than in the more northern areas.

The Lungshanoid sites described above under the five regional headings (fig. 78) are for the most part recent discoveries, still requiring detailed analysis and comparison, and it is apparent that each culture is distinctive. However, we find that the following common denominators unite the various cultural phases in this vast area.

1. All these cultures were based mainly on an agricultural subsistence which was supplemented to various extents by fishing, hunting, and gathering. Remains of rice characterize many sites of these cultures in the Han-shui, Huai Ho, and Yangtze valleys and to their south, in significant contrast to the Yang-shao culture of Chung Yüan with millet as its staple crop. It is notable that the only site in the north where evidence of rice has been reported is in Yang-shao-ts'un itself—a Miao-ti-kou II culture site according to its stone inventory and pottery wares. This probably indicates an influence from the south, where rice cultivation most likely was first mastered.

2. All these cultures had polished stone implements that included, as major distinctive types, rectangular adzes, perforated knives, and sickles. If we assume the primary use of adzes was for carpentry rather than tree felling, and the use of knives and sickles was for harvesting stalked plants, this would suggest agriculture of considerably advanced levels.

3. At the sites of these cultures there were greater numbers and varieties of bone, horn, and shell artifacts than at the Yang-shao sites.

61. *KKHP* 10 (1955), 53–68. *KK* 1961 (2), 669–72, 696; 1964 (12), 601–02, 618; 1965 (4), 192–98.

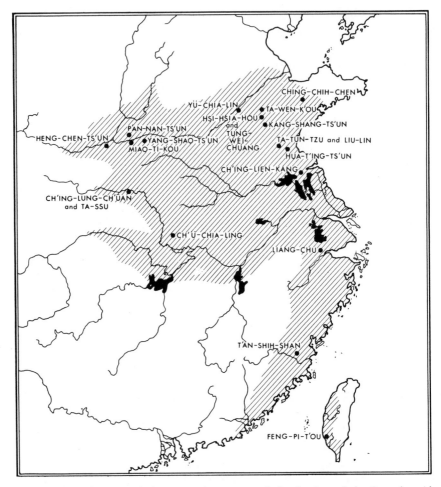

78. Lungshanoid sites and the approximate area of distribution of the Lungshanoid cultures.

4. The most significant common features of the sites are their pottery remains. The pottery at all these sites is a mixture of impressed, incised, and painted patterns. If one compares these sites with both the classical Yang-shao and the classical Lung-shan cultures, their pottery must be placed between the two groups.

In these Lungshanoid cultures the pottery shapes, though different in detail, shared several basic forms: *ting* tripods with solid legs, *tou* with cut-out ring feet, *kui*-type jars (wide mouthed, ring footed, two-loop or strap handles), and the wide occurrence of lids. Pottery from all sites was mostly handmade (mostly from coils) in earlier stages, and at all sites there is evidence that the rim and the ring foot were polished on turntables of fast rotation. The homogeneous nature of the black pottery found at all sites indicates a highly sophisticated level of paste preparation and kiln control. Evidence of potter's wheel is seen toward the end of the earlier Lungshanoid cultures.

5. All the burials at these sites were single, with the body stretched and supine.

6. All these cultures occupy a comparable chronological position. In terms of relative stratification, the Miao-ti-kou II and the Ch'ü-chia-ling cultures are between the Yang-shao and the Lung-shan cultures. The other cultures are outside the Yang-shao sphere and cannot have direct stratigraphic relationship with it, but wherever Lung-shan cultures were known the other cultures preceded the Lung-shan. In absolute dates, the culture in Taiwan persisted into the late first millennium B.C., but in Chung Yüan the same cultures must have begun no later than the fourth millennium.

7. Finally, these cultures not only physically adjoin one another but their distribution follows a pattern determined by the river valleys and seacoasts. The Miao-ti-kou II culture flows down the Huang Ho and the Han-shui to the area of the Ch'ü-chia-ling and Hua-t'ing cultures. The Ch'ing-lien-kang culture directly adjoins the Ma-chia-pang and the Pei-yin-yang-ying cultures to the south, which in turn are connected with the Ch'ü-chia-ling culture through the Yangtze. Feng-pi-t'ou of Taiwan is widely separated from the cultures of the lower Yangtze, but the early Lungshanoid culture of Chekiang and Fukien helps bridge the gap. In other words, each of the Lungshanoid cultures occupied a natural geographical division of eastern or southeastern China and was interconnected with the areas of the other cultures by a web of waterways that plainly played significant roles in the lives of the inhabitants.

Accordingly, we can say with confidence that the cultures described above constitute a well-defined horizon in the archaeological sense. Each possessing its own distinctive features, these cultures nevertheless shared a number of basic and significant characteristics. How did these similarities come about? What was the relationship of these earlier Lungshanoid cultures with the precedent cultures of their area of distribution—Yang-shao, Ch'ing-lien-kang and Ma-chia-pang, and Ta-p'en-k'eng, the cultures described in chapter 3?

Let us take a look at these cultures region by region. In Honan, Shensi, and Shansi, the derivation of the Miao-ti-kou II culture from Yang-shao has been commented on before. In Shantung and northern Kiangsu, the Hua-t'ing culture exhibits many of the characteristic features—in ceramics and stones—of the Ch'ing-lien-kang phase, and the same can be said of the Pei-yin-yang-ying culture of southern Kiangsu and Chekiang in relation to the Ma-chia-pang phase. The Ch'ü-chia-ling culture of the middle Yangtze is shown by the Yün Hsien and the Hsi-ch'uan sequences to have been derived, at least in good part, from the Yang-shao culture in southern Honan. Thus, all these earlier Lungshanoid cultures have been shown to have sprung probably from their respective antecedent cultures. The only seeming exception is the Feng-pi-t'ou culture, which is much more strikingly similar to the Lungshanoid cultures in eastern coastal China than to the Ta-p'en-k'eng culture antecedent in its own area.

How can this apparent dilemma—striking similarity among contemporaneous cultures seemingly derived from different ancestors—be resolved? Although there cannot be definitive answers to this question now, when these cultures are only beginning to be understood and pertinent issues are just beginning to be identified, several phenomena are highly suggestive.

The earlier Lungshanoid sites are large, thick, and densely spread over a wide and continuous area of much of China, which points to a period of considerable population size and density. The use of the potter's wheel and the manufacture of eggshell pottery both indicate a significant degree of industrial specialization, and the burial patterns plainly point to the beginning of a ranked society. The successful planting of rice and the use of a broader range of food resources undoubtedly gave these farmers a greater ability to adapt to a greater variety of environments in central and south China. All these indications point to a period of societal development that favored increased interaction (including trade) and mobility. The earlier Lungshanoid period, from about 3200 to 2500 B.C., was thus a period of rapid expansion of all Neolithic cultures, during which they came into contact and interacted with each other. In this connection we may also recall our observation, at the end of the previous chapter, about the possible interrelationships of the Yang-shao, Ta-p'en-k'eng, and Ch'ing-lien-kang/Ma-chia-pang cultures (table 8).

Formation of Late Neolithic Local Cultures and the Threshold of Chinese Civilization

As stated above, the significant similarity of the Lungshanoid cultures indicates a rapid process of diffusion, migration, and interaction. But unless such processes kept repeating themselves—or, even, despite any repetition of such processes—localization and regionalization of the

Table 8

Regional Grouping and Chronology of Lungshanoid Cultures

Years B.C.	Hupei	Shensi	Honan	Shantung N.Kiangsu	S.Kiangsu N.Chekiang	Southeast Coast
	Shang	W.Chou	Shang	Shang	Hu-shu culture	T'an-shih-shan culture
1850	Lung-shan culture	Shensi Lung-shan culture	Lung-shan culture	Lung-shan culture	Liang-chu culture	Feng-pi-t'ou culture
2500	Chü-chia-ling culture	Miao-ti-kou II culture	Miao-ti-kou II culture	Hua-t'ing culture	Pei-yin-yang-ying culture	
3200	Yang-shao culture	Yang-shao culture	Yang-shao culture	Ch'ing-lien-kang culture	Ma-chia-pang culture	Ta-p'en-k'eng culture
4500						

Table 9

Contrasts between the Chung Yüan and Coastal Lung-shan Cultures

Chung Yüan	*Coastal*
Pottery mainly characterized by gray ware manufactured by paddle-and-anvil technique; cord and basket marks often impressed on exterior surface by paddles	Pottery characteristically black and lustrous, many made or retouched by wheel; circumferential ridges and incised patterns common, but impressed decorations rare; occasional painted decorations
Major shapes of pottery vessels are *kuan* jars and *li* tripods with short, hollow legs; *ting* tripods extremely rare; *kui* jars and *tou* have low ring feet	Major shapes of pottery vessels are *ting* tripods, *kui* tripods, and *tou* with high and cut-out ring feet; *li* tripods extremely rare
Sites usually on low terraces of river valleys	Sites usually on low terraces in the plains, and often on mounds
Bronzes absent; microliths rare	Persisted into period when bronzes occurred; finely made microlithic implements often seen in northern part

Lungshanoid cultures were unavoidable. Broadly speaking the local Lung-shan cultures can be grouped into an interior and a coastal group. The interior group of Chung Yüan exhibited a greater degree of change from the Lungshanoid horizon and was probably the progenitor of the Shang and Chou civilizations. Coastal Lung-shan cultures, on the other hand, were continued and differentiated phases of the Lungshanoid prototypes, and these gave rise to other civilizations parallel to the Shang and Chou of North China. The most important contrasts between the two groups are exemplified in table 9.

The best known Lung-shan cultures of the Chung Yüan group at the present time are the so-called K'o-hsing-chuang II culture and the Hou-kang II culture. Those of the coastal group are the so-called classical Lung-shan culture and the Liang-chu culture. The major characteristics of these four Lung-shan cultures are given below.[62]

The Shensi Lung-shan Culture (K'o-hsing-chuang II Culture)

Confined to Shensi, southern Shansi, and westernmost Honan, this culture is best known from the sites of K'o-hsing-chuang and Mi-chia-yai,

62. Mainly based on *Hsin Chung-kuo ti k'ao-ku shou-huo*, pp. 16–21, 31–32.

near Sian, and at Heng-chen-ts'un in Hua Hsien, Shensi. At Heng-chen-ts'un, remains of this culture were found above the Miao-ti-kou II layer; and at Chang-chia-p'o, also near Sian, the culture is shown to antedate the remains of Western Chou. Largely contemporary with the Lung-shan culture and perhaps the early phases of the Shang civilization of Honan, the Shensi Lung-shan culture's relationship with the Western Chou and its chronological position relative to the Shang are important topics for further study.

Remains of ten semisubterranean houses were found at K'o-hsing-chuang. The houses have a single room or two adjoining rooms. The double houses, with two rectangular rooms or an interior round room and exterior square room, are particularly distinctive. The floor inside the house was paved with habitation debris and compacted from use. Pocket-shaped storage pits, each with a bottleneck opening and an enlarged chamber about 4 meters in diameter, are also characteristic.

Of the implements found at the sites, most are for agriculture, but hunting and fishing gear still occurred. These included knives, adzes, axes, spearheads of stone; fishhooks, arrowheads, and spatula-like artifacts of bone; and spindle whorls of clay. Shell objects are absent. Among the animal bones at the site of K'o-hsing-chuang, those of dog, pig, cattle (*Bos* sp.), water buffalo (*Bubalus* sp.), sheep (*Ovis* sp.), rabbit, and water deer were identified. All but the deer and rabbit were domesticated, showing considerable progress from the Yang-shao. About 80 percent of the pottery is gray in color. Black sherds like the coastal Lung-shan pieces are no more than 1 percent. Most of the impressed decorations were cord- or basket-marked, and check-stamped pieces are rare. There are occasional painted sherds (dark red on red slip). In shape, *li* tripods with single handles, cord-marked *kuan* jars, and cord-marked *chia* tripods are most common. *Ting* tripods are extremely rare. Most of the vessels were built by hand from coils, and some of the *li* tripods were apparently molded. A very few sherds exhibit evidence of the wheel (figs. 79 and 80).

A double burial, of a man and a woman, was found at Heng-chen-ts'un; it has six pots. At the site of K'o-hsing-chuang bodies were sometimes buried in abandoned storage pits, each pit having from one to five skeletons. Another important trait of the culture is the use of sheep scapulae for divination; burned shoulder blades of sheep were found.

Honan Lung-shan Culture (Hou-kang II Culture)

Sites of this culture are known from most of Honan and the southern portions of Shansi and Hopei. The Wang-wan (near Lo-yang) stratigraphy indicates that the Honan Lung-shan culture followed the Miao-ti-kou II

79. Pottery of the K'o-hsing-chuang (Shensi Lung-shan) culture: (a), *ting*; (b, c) *chia*; (d, e) *l*
(f) *kui*; (g–i) *kuan*; (j) lid. (From *KK* 1959, no. 10, pl. 2.)

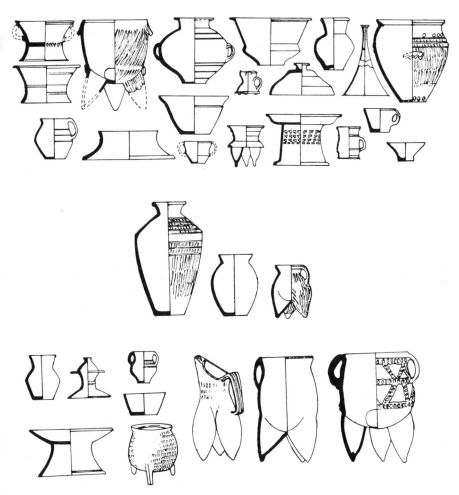

80. Artifacts of the Shensi and Honan Lung-shan cultures: *lower*, Shensi; *upper*, Honan; *middle*, shared. (From *Hsin Chung-kuo ti k'ao-ku shou-huo*, Peking, Wen Wu Press, 1962, p. 18.)

culture in time, and the Hou-kang (An-yang) stratigraphy places this culture between the Yang-shao culture, below, and the Shang civilization, above. Radiocarbon dates from Wang-wan (3830 ± 90 B.P.), Tz'u Hsien (3935 ± 95), and Hou-kang (3800 ± 90) are in the 2680–2160 B.C. range.

The stone inventory of the Honan Lung-shan culture is basically identical with that of the Miao-ti-kou II, but the chipped knives with side notches are absent. In addition to wooden *lei*, bone spades are found in considerable numbers. The most significant difference in tool inventory from the

Shensi Lung-shan culture is the wide use of shell artifacts in Honan. Among the bones of domestic animals, those from the pig were most numerous. The discovery of stone and bone arrowheads, shells of mollusks and snails, stone sinkers, and fishhooks indicates the continuing importance of fishing, hunting, and gathering in the Honan Lung-shan subsistence.

A rectangular semisubterranean house was found at the site of Hui-tsui in Yen-shih, the floor and walls having been hardened by fire. Round houses were excavated at Hou-kang, the floors plastered in white, limy clay. Some pottery remained handmade, but wheel-made pieces increased in number (fig. 80). (At the site of San-li-ch'iao, Shan Hsien, wheel-made and wheel-touched pieces account for one fifth of the total sherds.) Red ware decreased and black ware increased. The typical eggshell black pottery is also known. Cord impression was the leading decoration and basket-marked pottery followed, but there was also a noticeable increase of check-stamped pieces. In shape there was a greater variety than in Miao-ti-kou II, including *tseng* steamers, *li* and *kui* tripods, handled jars, and cups. There are many corded *li* tripods with single handles, but fewer *chia* and *ting* tripods.

Only scattered remains of human burials have been found; most are similar to the Miao-ti-kuo II pattern, with very few grave furnishings. At the site of Chien-kou, near Han-tan in southern Hopei, human bodies were found in abandoned pits and wells. No fewer than ten skeletons were found in a round pit only 1.5 meters in diameter. These include people of all ages who were placed in the pit without any discernible order or pattern but who were covered with a layer of burned clay. Five skeletons were found in an abandoned well; some were decapitated and others had died struggling. This seems to indicate an intervillage raid, something yet to be found in the peaceful Yang-shao village settlements.

The Classical Lung-shan Culture

The so-called classical or typical Lung-shan culture, typified by the Ch'eng-tzu-yai and Liang-ch'eng-chen sites, is in fact a local Lung-shan–type culture that centered in Shantung and extended north to Liaotung Peninsula and south to northern Kiangsu. In Shantung alone some hundred sites have been excavated.[63] At Ch'eng-tzu-yai, the first site excavated, the village was surrounded by a wall of *hang-t'u* construction (fig. 81).

The only radiocarbon dates have come from a site at Lü-ta, in Liaotung Peninsula, one (3890 ± 90 B.P.) fits the time range of the other later Lung-shanoid sites, but the other (3030 ± 90 B.P.) seems a bit too late.

63. *KK* 1963 (7), 377.

81. *Hang-t'u* village wall of the Ch'eng-tzu-yai site, Shantung. (From Li Chi et al., *Ch'eng-tzu-yai*, Nanking, Institute of History and Philology, Academia Sinica, 1934, pl. 5, pic. 2.)

The tool inventory includes highly polished stone axes, adzes, knives, sickles, arrowheads, spearheads, and bone harpoons. The square stone adzes and chisels are especially distinctive. Some stone implements were carved animal-mask designs similar to those found on Shang bronzes (fig. 82). At a number of sites very finely chipped microliths (scrapers and arrowheads) were found, apparently related to the microlithic industry of the north.

Pottery was characteristically wheel-made and accounted for over 50 percent of the sherds at some sites (fig. 83). The large numbers of jet-black, thin, highly polished pottery and extremely thin (eggshell) pieces of black pottery are the hallmarks of the Shantung Lung-shan culture. In addition to black and gray sherds, red and white wares also occurred. The most common shapes of vessels are *kui* tripods (tripods with three fat, hollow feet, long body, spout, and single handle) and *ting* tripods with the so-called ghost-face legs. Also common are *tou* with high cut-out ring feet, cups, and bowls. Such common Chung Yüan Lung-shan shapes as *li* tripods, *chia* tripods, and *tseng* steamers are totally absent or extremely

82. Animal-mask designs on stone adz at Liang-ch'eng-chen site, Jih-chao, Shantung. (From *KK* 1972, no. 4, p. 56.)

rare. The pottery is generally plain and highly polished; decorations were mostly circumferential ridges and incisions. Impressed patterns of any kind were very rare.

Burials are widely found. Those at Ching-chih-chen, placed in rows, are single burials, with the body supine, stretched, and the head pointing east. Rich grave furnishings accompanied the dead. Burned shoulder blades of cattle were found, apparently for divination.

The Hangchow Bay Lung-shan Culture (Liang-chu Culture)

Previously grouped with the generalized Lung-shan culture, sites of this culture are now known from northern Chekiang in the lower Ch'ien-t'ang River and Lake T'ai and are sufficiently understood through a series of new excavations (at Liang-chu, Lao-ho-shan, and Shui-t'ien-pan near Hangchow, Ch'ien-shan-yang near Wu-hsing, and Ma-chia-pang near Chia-hsing) to be grouped into a separate, local, Lung-shan–culture phase.

Remains of the Liang-chu culture from a site in Chia-hsing[64] are dated by radiocarbon (3830 ± 95 B.P.) to the 2550–2170 B.C. range, but the Ch'ien-shan-yang site has yielded a date (4560 ± 100 B.P.) that would push the culture back to the 3470–3210 B.C. range. This latter date does not fit the overall chronological picture formulated on the basis of other

64. *KK* 1974 (4), 249–50.

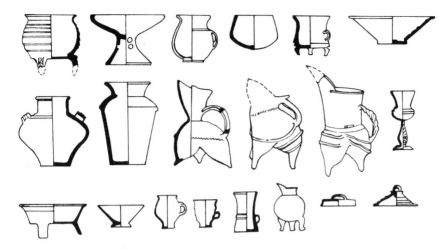

83. Artifacts of the classical Lung-shan culture. (From *Hsin Chung-kuo ti k'ao-ku shou-huo*, Peking, Wen Wu Press, 1962, p. 18.)

dates, and the Ch'ien-shan-yang stratigraphy has been seriously called into question.[65]

Agriculture of advanced levels was in evidence at many sites. At Ch'ien-shan-yang, remains of rice grains (of both *ting* and *keng* varieties) were found, alongside remains of certain species of peach (*Prunus persica*), melon (*Cucumis melo*), water caltrop (*Trapa natans* or *T. bispinosa*), peanut (*Arachis hypogaea*), possibly sesame (*Sesamum indicum* or *S. orientale*), and possibly beans (*Vicia faba*). Among these the peanut, a well-known early American species, is of particular interest.[66] Of the agricultural implements, the flat and perforated spades are identical with the Ch'ing-lien-kang type. In addition, there are the so-called winged implements of cultivation, rectangular and semilunar knives with holes, and sickles. A large, coarse-paste, point-bottomed jar was found together with a wooden pestle, possibly a grain-pounding apparatus. Among the bones of domestic animals, water buffalo, pig, dog, and sheep are recognized. Considerable numbers of water-buffalo bones were identified at Ma-chia-pang.

65. An Chih-min, *KK* 1972 (6), 40–41.

66. *KKHP* 1960 (2), 84–85. The stratigraphy of the remains of peanuts has been questioned—rightly, it now seems from the radiocarbon disconformity—by a number of scholars who are skeptical of the early date of peanuts in China (Ho Ping-ti, *Huang-t'u yü Chung-kuo nung-yeh ti ch'i-yüan*, Hong Kong, Chinese University, 1969, pp. 205–09; J. R. Harlan and J. M. J. de Wet, *Current Anthropology* 14 [1973], p. 54). But see the earlier discussion on peanuts at P'ao-ma-ling in Kiangsi.

84. Artifacts of the Liang-chu culture. (From *Hsin Chung-kuo ti k'ao-ku shou-huo*, Peking, Wen Wu Press, 1962, p. 29.)

Remains of net sinkers, wooden floats, and wooden paddles indicate considerable familiarity of the inhabitants with water crafts and fishing. A variety of wild animals (deer, boar, fox) and aquatic species (fish, mollusks, and turtles) have been identified at Ma-chia-pang.

By chance of preservation, the wooden artifacts of this culture are well known; these include remains of house structures, boats, tools, and utensils. Stone and bone artifacts are also highly developed. Black pottery of fine, soft paste is highly characteristic of the Liang-chu culture (fig. 84); the vessels are constructed by the wheel technique. High luster on the surface was produced by polishing. The shapes include jars with double lugs, *tou*, shallow dishes, *ting* tripods, and *tui* pots, but *li* tripods are again absent. Most of the ring feet found have cut-out designs and are further decorated by circumferential ridges. In addition, red and gray wares of a variety of pastes are also seen here, both handmade and wheel-made. Many of the sandy wares are decorated with cord and basket impressions. Occasional painted pieces occur. Some potsherds bear incised symbols (fig. 129).

House remains have been found at Ch'ien-shan-yang and Shui-t'ien-pan. These were built on flat ground and are rectangular in shape, ranging in size from 5 to 20 square meters. Walls were built from wattle and daub on timber posts. The roof was probably gabled. Ma-chia-pang has thirty burials; most single but prone. A few are supine or flexed.

Other Lung-shan Cultures

The cultures above (two in the Chung Yüan group and two in the coastal group) are obviously from widely separate regions, but they

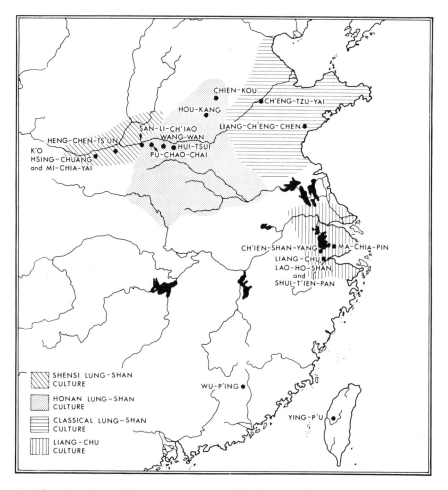

85. The major sites and the approximate areas of distribution of the various local Lung-shan cultures.

are all referred to as Lung-shan cultures because they were apparently derived from the common Lungshanoid horizon, they still share a number of characteristic features, and presumably they continued intercommunication. They all had advanced agriculture and their general cultural makeup was highly complex. It is very probable that the Honan Lung-shan culture was ancestral to the Shang civilization; that the Shensi Lung-shan culture was related to the antecedents of the Western Chou culture; that the Shantung Lung-shan culture was related to the so-called Eastern I peoples in the historical texts; and that the Liang-chu culture was largely ancestral to the subsequent Yüeh culture characterized by geometric-stamped pottery. In other words, the local Lung-shan cultures apparently laid the foundations for the civilizations and ethnic groups in the dawn of ancient China.

In addition to the above, other Lung-shan–type cultural assemblages are known from elsewhere (fig. 85). The Gray Pottery culture of the lower Fen Ho valley of Shansi, still very inadequately known, appears to resemble the Shensi Lung-shan culture. The Gray and Black Pottery sites in the upper Huai Ho, in southeastern Honan and northern Anhwei, are largely similar to the Honan Lung-shan culture but contain elements traceable to southern Shantung and northern Kiangsu.

More problematic is the extent of the Lung-shan distribution in the southern direction. Much of this will be discussed in the next chapter. The pregeometric Gray Pottery culture of Kiangsi, the Neolithic cultures of Szechwan and western Hupei in the Yangtze Valley, and the Neolithic cultures of the southwest all exhibit strong resemblance to the Lung-shanoid horizon and to some Lung-shan phases. The sites of Wu-p'ing in Fukien and of Ying-p'u in Taiwan are unquestionably related to the coastal group of the Lung-shan cultures. Many features of the Ying-p'u pottery—especially the jars with lugs, the ring-footed *tou*, and the sandy-pottery *ting* tripods—recall the Liang-chu culture; and the widespread practice of prone burials in central Taiwan in a black pottery context is traceable to the site of Ma-chia-pang. Carbon-14 dates from Ying-p'u place the Lung-shan–type culture in Taiwan in the late second millennium B.C., just a few hundred years later than its counterpart across the Taiwan Strait.

5 : The Spread of Agriculture and Neolithic Technology

Efforts have been made in the last two chapters to trace the developments of the Neolithic farmers in North, South, and eastern China. In other areas, a basically hunting-fishing subsistence persisted. During various periods in some regions, the hunter-fishers were exposed to advanced farming cultures and adopted for local use many Neolithic technological elements, such as polished stone tools and pottery, thus giving rise to cultural phases that can be described as sub-Neolithic. In other regions the hunter-fishers adopted the new ways of life and became part- or full-time farmers. Such cultural transformations took place from the time that Yang-shao and Ta-p'en-k'eng farmers first appeared in the nuclear areas through the subsequent Lungshanoid expansion and early historic periods. The discussion of such transformations is placed here—between the description of the Lungshanoid and the discussion of the emergence of historical civilization in North China—because the cultures in question are classified as "Neolithic." Actually, farming was not introduced into some regions until after historical civilization had already begun in North China. This will become clear in the following sections, each dealing with a separate historical region (fig. 86).

Northern Shensi, Shansi, and Hopei

Since the provincial boundaries have shifted back and forth several times during the present century, a geographical clarification of the title of this section is in order. In general terms, the area referred to is simply the northern part of North China proper and the southern fringes of Inner Mongolia, a region of relatively high altitude, with a steppe vegetation, drained by the northernmost section of the Huang Ho, its many small tributaries, and the upper reaches of several rivers in the alluvial plains in the northwestern part of the Pohai Bay area. It is a relatively arid and barren area at present, though oases, parklands, and large and

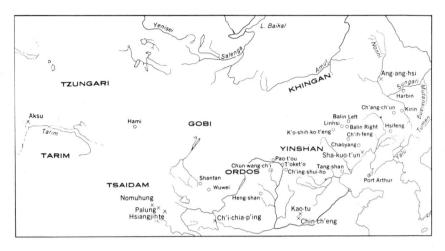

86. Important prehistoric sites (x) and cities near which important prehistoric sites have been found (o) in Inner Mongolia, Sinkiang, and Manchuria.

small basins with stable water supplies may have characterized the landscape during the prehistoric period.[1]

The Ordos area in northern Shensi and southern Inner Mongolia Autonomous Region is famous for its Upper Palaeolithic industries, and recent discoveries in the neighborhood of P'ien-kuan Hsien in northwestern Shansi and Ch'ing-shui-ho Hsien in southern Inner Mongolia appear to indicate Mesolithic assemblages characterized by microblade artifacts and points and scrapers of "Mousterian" flakes, features resembling the Sha-yüan assemblage of the lower Wei-shui valley in central Shensi.[2] Small arrowheads, small elongated scrapers, and microblades have been found in the Hei-liu-t'u-ho valley in Heng-shan Hsien, in what may be a nonceramic context.[3] Ceramic assemblages, with and without evidence of agriculture, have been unearthed widely in Ch'ing-shui-ho, Chünwang-ch'i, and Pao-t'ou.[4] The pottery is red, brown, or gray, of a fine or coarse paste; the red ware is often painted in black pigment, but cord

1. For a survey of the Neolithic cultures of this area, see *WW* 1961 (9), 5–7; *KK* 1962 (12), 658–71; *Nei Meng-ku ch'u-t'u wen-wu hsüan chi*, Peking Wen Wu Press, 1963.

2. *VP* 3 (1959), 47–56. An Chih-min, *KK* 1959 (10), 560.

3. *KKHP* 1957 (2), 11.

4. Egami and Mizuno, *Inner Mongolia and the Region of the Great Wall*, Archaeologia Orientalis, ser. B, no. 1 (1935). J. Maringer, *Contribution to the Prehistory of Mongolia*, Stockholm, 1950. *KKTH* 1955 (5), 9–13. *WWTKTL* 1957 (4), 26–28. *KKHP* 1957 (1), 9–20; 1959 (2), 1–13; 1960 (1), 9–22. *WW* 1961 (9), 6, 12–13. *KK* 1963 (1), 9–11, 51–52, 55.

marking is characteristic of the red pottery. Bowls, jugs, and basins are common forms, but *li* tripods also occur occasionally. The stone industries contain two clear-cut traditions: chipped microliths, in the form of blades, flakes, arrowheads, scrapers, and awls; and polished stone implements, including such agricultural tools as mortars and pestles, hoes, knives, and sickles, in addition to axes and adzes. It is apparent that the Yang-shao technology and subsistence patterns must have been introduced among the Microlithic hunter-fishers of this area, and the Neolithic ways of life may have persisted here well into the historic periods.[5] Subsequent arid conditions apparently did not favor the growth of civilization in the Ordos, and these Neolithic peoples were followed by steppe nomads.

To the east of the Ordos, in northern Shansi and southern Inner Mongolia, a nonceramic assemblage has recently been found in Chahar Right Central Banner, but its age is uncertain.[6] Microlithic finds in a ceramic context have been discovered as far south as Chin-ch'eng Hsien and Kao-tu Hsien in southeastern Shansi.[7] But Yang-shao type sherds have been found in southeastern Shansi and western Hopei,[8] and microlithic assemblages mixed with Yang-shao–type red sherds have been uncovered in Shansi and Hopei.[9] Microlithic elements were still very conspicuously present in the Lungshanoid assemblages at Ta-ch'eng-shan in northern Hopei.[10] It seems likely, therefore, that this area had a microlithic substratum into which Yang-shao and Lungshanoid elements were introduced, with or without agriculture.

The Liao Ho Valley, Eastern Mongolia, and Southern Manchuria

The Liao Ho drainage is divided into two well-defined sections: the upper Liao Ho valley in eastern Inner Mongolia and western Liaoning, with two major tributaries—Hsi-liao, or Sharamurun, and Lao-ha—which drain the eastern fringes of the Mongolian plateau; and the lower Liao Ho valley of the southern Manchurian erosion plain, immediately

5. *WW* 1961 (9), 10–13. *KK* 1962 (2), 72–75; 1965 (10), 487–95.

6. *KK* 1975 (1), 23–26.

7. *KK* 1959 (2), 63.

8. *KKTH* 1955 (1), 45–46. *WWTKTL* 1955 (11), 73–76. *KK* 1959 (2), 63; 1962 (12), 658–71.

9. *KKTH* 1958 (6), 45–46. *KK* 1959 (2), 63; 1959 (7), 332–37. *WWTKTL* 1953 (5/6), 143–52.

10. *KKHP* 1959 (3), 21–22.

87. Pottery types at the Neolithic site at Hung-shan-hou, Ch'ih-feng. (From *Ch'ih-feng Hung-shan-hou*, Tokyo and Kyoto, Society for East Asian Archaeology, 1938, pls. 33, 36.)

north of Pohai Bay. The known cultural history of this region can be summarized as follows: no preceramic industries have been found from the early postglacial period; there are cultural assemblages characterized by microlithic industries mixed with Yang-shao and non–Yang-shao ceramic features, some of which definitely show evidence of agriculture and animal domestication, while others conspicuously lack such evidence; after these sub-Neolithic and Neolithic phases, in a large part of this area there were occupations of a nomadic kind of culture with assemblages similar to those on the Ordosian steppe.

The best-known prehistoric site in the Lao-ha River valley is Hung-shan-hou near Ch'ih-feng, discovered by Torii Ryūzō in 1908 and investigated by other scholars in 1924, 1930, and 1935.[11] Two phases of occupation have been distinguished here, the Painted Pottery and the Red Pottery. The Red Pottery phase contains bronze artifacts and other Eastern Chou affinities, and the Painted Pottery phase has been synchronized with the Yang-shao stage in North China. This Painted Pottery phase undoubtedly has a northern Microlithic and sub-Neolithic cultural base, as indicated by microliths and brownish coarse pottery with loop and lug handles and combed, dented, and rocker-stamped designs. Yang-shao influence

11. Hamada Kosaku and Mizuno Seiichi, *Ch'ih-feng: Hung-shan-hou*, Archaeologia Orientalis, ser. A, no. 6 (1938). *KKHP* 1958 (3), 25–40.

is strongly suggested by remains of thin-walled, handmade, orange-red pottery of a fine texture, characterized by bowl and small-necked jar forms and painted in geometric patterns in dark red and black pigment. Agriculture is indicated by the remains of stone hoes, spades, knives, pestles and mortars. Cattle, sheep, pig, and horse bones were also found, as well as many spindle whorls of clay and artifacts of shell, bone, antler, and teeth (fig. 87).

In 1943, what was probably a later settlement was found in the nearby village of Tung-pa-chia, also in Ch'ih-feng Hsien.[12] Stone and ceramic remains again indicate a northern Microlithic and sub-Neolithic base, but black pottery and *ting* tripods are found, possibly indicating Lung-shanoid or later influences from North China rather than Yang-shao. The most significant feature of this site is that the whole village was surrounded by a wall of rocks. The village fortification and the arrangement of houses inside the compound, which indicated the existence of a paramount chief in the village, seem to suggest that a tightened social organization also came into being in this part of China after the stage of the first farmers, as was the case in North China proper.

Sites in the Sharamurun River valley have been widely found in Lin-hsi Hsien, K'o-shih-k'o-t'eng Banner, Balin Left Banner, and Balin Right Banner.[13] Microlithic implements were found in most of the cultural assemblages, and the predominant pottery is brownish-gray or red in color, coarse in texture, and characterized by combed and dentated decorative designs. Rocker-stamped pottery, seen at the site of Hung-shan-hou, is especially distinctive in this area.[14] Evidence of contact with North China consists of rare painted sherds and a number of *li* tripods, probably introduced at different times. Remains of polished stone hoes, spades, and large pestles and mortars at most of the sites suggest the prevalence of agriculture. At the Fu-ho-kou-men site in Balin Left Banner, remains of shoulder blades of sheep or deer, burned for divination purposes ("oracle bones"), were found with rocker-stamped pottery and birch bark (fig. 88).[15] Radiocarbon dating of birch bark remains gives a date of 4600 ± 100 B.P.,[16] which, when calibrated, indicates a true date of 3560–3240 B.C. This is the earliest known date of scapulimancy in China, or anywhere, a custom which assumed great importance in the Shang civilization.

12. *KKTH* 1957 (6), 15–22.
13. See *n*4 above.
14. *KK* 1964 (1), 1–5.
15. *Ibid.*, p. 3
16. *KK* 1974 (5), 336.

88. Pottery, stone implements, and oracle bone at Fu-ho-kou-men site, Balin Left Banner, Liaoning. (From *KK* 1964, no. 1, pl. 1.)

In the lower Liao Ho valley on the southern Manchurian plains, a cultural sequence similar to that of the upper Liao can be postulated. Cultural assemblages found here show a mixture of microlithic implements; polished stone axes, knives, and sickles; combed ware, painted pottery, black pottery, checker-impressed sherd, .id *li* tripods.[17] A northern sub-Neolithic base characterized by microliths and combed pottery can be assumed, and Huang Ho Neolithic influences seem to have reached this area in successive waves, as indicated by the predominantly Yang-shao elements in the Sha-kuo-t'un site[18] and the predominantly Lungshanoid features at Shao-hu-ying-tzu-shan in Ch'ao-yang Hsien.[19] The Liaotung Peninsula also seems to have had a similar sequence, although it does not appear to have been exposed to the Yang-shao culture but, rather, appears to have been heavily influenced by the Classical Lung-shan, as shown at the site of Yang-t'ou-wa.[20] Shellmound sites near Port Arthur and on the islets off the tip of Liaotung Peninsula show clearly a native cultural substratum with microliths and the combed brown pottery of the area.[21]

It is still too early to say whether the Liao Ho valley was populated during Mesolithic periods, for evidence is completely lacking. It is possible, however, that a significant population of this area was achieved by the Microlithic hunter-fishers of the northern part of China, whose culture was enriched by the introduction of North Chinese Neolithic technology or agriculture or both. A Neolithic way of life prevailed here until the Eastern Chou and Han periods, when nomadic tribes roamed on the upper Liao Ho steppes, and Han-Chinese settlements began to penetrate this region from North China.

The Sungari Valley

The Neolithic cultural substratum of the Sungari Valley in central Manchuria[22] is represented by the microlithic and nonceramic assemblages

17. *KKTH* 1955 (6), 13–16; 1956 (6), 19–25; 1958 (1), 1–4.

18. Andersson, *PS*, ser. D, 1 (1923).

19. *KKTH* 1956 (6), 19–25.

20. Burnished red potsherds similar to sherds of the Yang-shao stage in North China were reported from Wen-chia-t'un in the Port Arthur region of the southern Liaotung peninsula, but these were uncovered from a Lungshanoid context. See Kanaseki et al., *Yang-t'ou-wa*, Archaeologia Orientalis, ser. B, no. 3, 81 *n*6.

21. *KK* 1961 (12), 689–90; 1962 (2), 76–81; 1962 (7), 345–52.

22. K. C. Chang, *Southwestern Jour. Anthropol.* 17 (1961), 56–74. *KK* 1961 (10), 557–67, 568–76.

in the Harbin area, apparently a continuation of the Upper Palaeolithic in the north, and by the microlithic and ceramic assemblages at Ang-ang-hsi and other sites in the lower Nonni Valley [23] and a series of sites in the lower Mu-tan-chiang.[24] The ceramic features as well as stone and bone inventories, characterized by flat-bottomed pottery and bone harpoons and needle cases, are linked with the sub-Neolithic cultures on the Pacific coast.

Distinct Huang Ho Neolithic influences on the sub-Neolithic substratum are seen in the southwestern part of this area, around the cities of Kirin and Ch'ang-ch'un, where millet agriculture and pig domestication as well as pottery tripods, polished stone knives, and stone sickles have been found.[25] Prehistoric agriculture, however, penetrated as far north at least as the Mu-tan-chiang valley, where at the Tung-k'ang site remains of millets (*Setaria italica* and *Panicum miliaceum*) and stone knives were found from cultural strata dated to the early centuries of our era.[26] The same cultural traditions continued in this area even when the Han dynasty and later civilizations became firmly established in the Liao Ho valley and Chinese cultural elements appeared in the native artifactual inventories.[27]

The T'umen Valley

The T'umen Valley of southeastern Manchuria has an early cultural history similar to that of the northern and eastern Sungari in that the sub-Neolithic cultural substratum is strongly marked, and although the impact of Huang Ho civilization is shown by occasional import items, hunting-fishing continued to be the principal mode of subsistence during most of its early cultural history.[28]

23. For Ang-ang-hsi, see Liang Ssu-yüng, *BIHP* 4 (1932), 1–44. A. S. Loukashkin, *GSoC Bull.* 11 (1931), 171–81, and *China Jour.* 15 (1931), 198–99. *KK* 1960 (4), 15–17; 1974 (2), 99–108. For other sites in the Nonni Valley, see *KK* 1961 (8), 398–403, 404–06; 1961 (10), 534–43.

24. *KK* 1960 (4), 20–22. Komai Kazuchika, *Kōkogaku Zasshi*, 24 (1934), 11–16. Komai Kazuchika and Mikami Tsuguo, *Kōkogaku Zasshi* 26 (1936), 487–96. *KKHP* 7 (1954), 61–75. Okuda Naoshige, *JZ* 54 (1939), 459–63. V. V. Ponosov, *Bull. Inst. Sci. Research, Manchukuo* 2 (1938), 23–30. *KK* 1960 (4), 23–30; 1961 (10), 546–51; 1965 (1), 4–5, 24; 1975 (3), 158–68.

25. *KKTH* 1955 (2), 5–12. *KKHP* 1957 (3), 31–39. *KK* 1960 (4), 31–34. *WW* 1973 (8), 55–62, 63–68.

26. *KK* 1975 (3), 159, 165.

27. *KKHP* 7 (1954), 61–75. Wen Ch'ung-i, *BIE* 5 (1958), 115–210.

28. An Chih-min, *Hsüeh yüan* 2 (Nanking, 1948), 26–36. *KKHP* 1957 (3), 31–39. *KKTH* 1956 (6), 25–30. *KK* 1961 (8), 411–24; 1965 (1), 42–43. *WW* 1973 (8), 69–72.

Kansu and Sinkiang

Geographically, western Kansu, Chinghai, and Sinkiang are parts of a huge steppe, desert, and oasis belt extending from the Caspian and Black seas in the west to the upper Huang Ho valley in the east. This has proved to be a frequently used corridor for the transmission of cultural ideas and for trade between the East and theWest during historical periods. Scholars have therefore had some grounds for speculating that there may have been a similar route of cultural diffusion during the earlier period, whereby the first ideas of agriculture and the first ideas of civilization could have been transmitted from the Near East and Central Asia to the Huang Ho valley.[29] This conjecture, however, remains to be borne out by actual archaeological findings in the area.

From a Huang Ho terrace near Chung-wei in Ninghsia Province, Teilhard de Chardin and C. C. Young in 1930 discovered remains of chipped implements which they regarded as Upper Palaeolithic and prob-ably of the Ordosian tradition.[30] Nonceramic assemblages which may be of relatively recent periods have been located by the same scholars near Hami in eastern Sinkiang, apparently of the Microlithic horizon.[31] Since these sites remain unexcavated, the Mesolithic stratum has yet to be established. But microlithic implements in association with pottery have been collected widely in southern Ninghsia, Chinghai, and Sinkiang, and even pebble tools predominate in one or two known assemblages in a ceramic context, such as the site of Aksu.[32] The pottery found in some of the sites has no definitely discernible counterpart in the rest of China, but painted sherds have been collected from many parts of the Chinese north-west (fig. 89), and in the eastern fringes of this region they occur in Neolithic assemblages.[33] As far as the available archaeological record goes, we are sure of the following three facts: (1) archaeological assemblages that can be considered Neolithic are confined to the part of Kansu east of Chiu-ch'üan Hsien and the eastern part of Chinghai in the Huang-shui valley,

29. E.g., Carl W. Bishop, *Antiquity* 28 (1933), 389–404; *Origin of the Far Eastern Civilization*, Washington, Smithsonian Institution, 1942.

30. *GSoC Bull.* 12 (1932), 103–04.

31. *Ibid.*

32. Folke Bergman, *Archaeological Researches in Sinkiang*, Stockholm, Bokförlags Aktiebolaget Thule, 1939, pp. 13–37. P. Teilhard de Chardin and C. C. Young, *GSoC Bull.* 12 (1932), 83–104. *KK* 1959 (3), 153–54; 1959 (7), 329–31; 1962 (4), 170–71; 1964 (5), 227–31, 241; 1964 (7), 333–41; 1964 (9), 475; 1965 (5), 254–55. *WW* 1960 (6), 22–31; 1962 (7/8), 11–15, 80.

33. See, in *n*32 above, Bergman; Teilhard and Young; *WW* 1962 (7/8); *KK* 1964 (7); and *KK* 1965 (5).

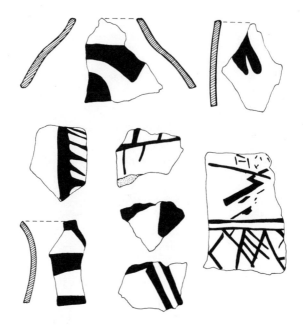

89. Painted sherds from the Astana site in Sinkiang. (From *KK* 1964, no. 7, p. 341.)

and these are definitely extensions of the Kansu Yang-shao culture; (2) the ceramic assemblages in Sinkiang and western Chinghai contain elements which indicate that a native microlithic and sub-Neolithic substratum may have persisted in this region into early historical times; and (3) the ceramic assemblages that contain the so-called painted pottery in Sinkiang and western Chinghai are probably late in time, in most cases considerably later than the Neolithic of North China, as indicated by the metal objects sometimes associated with them. Andersson declared in 1943 that "as far as the Yang Shao time is concerned, Sinkiang remains an unknown quantity."[34] Extensive investigations in Sinkiang since 1943 have failed to warrant any significant changes in this view, except by suggesting that, during the Yang-shao stage of the North China Neolithic, Sinkiang played little if any role in the shaping of cultural history in areas east of it.

But the Yang-shao farmers definitely brought the food-producing way of life into eastern Kansu and the Huang-shui valley in eastern Chinghai. After the Lungshanoid farmers evolved in the nuclear area to the east, the Yang-shao stage in Kansu and eastern Chinghai seems to have been gradually replaced by several new cultures whose origins remain unclear but which seem to have some sort of connection with the sub-Neolithic

34. *BMFEA* 15, 280.

90. Pottery of the Ch'i-chia culture. (From *Sekai kōkōgakū taikei*, Tokyo, Heibonshya, 1960, vol. 5, pl. 54.)

and possibly Neolithic peoples to the north and west in the steppe regions. Three such cultures can now be defined—the Ch'i-chia, the Shan-tan (or Ssu-pa), and the Tsaidam (or No-mu-hung).

The Ch'i-chia culture, named after its type site at Ch'i-chia-p'ing in Ning-ting Hsien in the T'ao Ho valley of eastern Kansu, was discovered in 1923 by Andersson, who regarded it as the earliest Neolithic culture in Kansu, from which the Yang-shao culture in Kansu and Honan was ultimately derived.[35] This thesis has proved to be completely fallacious. Stratigraphical evidence in the entire area of its distribution has shown that the Ch'i-chia culture followed the Kansu Yang-shao culture but preceded the Chou strata in the upper Wei-shui as well as several other contemporary local Aeneolithic cultures to the west.[36] Its area of distribution is confined to the valleys of the T'ao, the upper Wei-shui, and the upper Hsi-han-shui, all in the eastern part of Kansu, but remains of Ch'i-chia culture type are known from Ninghsia and Inner Mongolia.[37] Its pottery is characterized by yellow and buff ware with combed or incised decorative designs and

35. Andersson, *Preliminary Report on Archaeological Research in Kansu*, GSuC, Mem., ser. A, no. 5; *Children of the Yellow Earth*, London, Kegan Paul, Trench & Trubner, 1934; *BMFEA* 15.

36. The stratigraphical position of the Ch'i-chia culture over the Kansu Yang-shao culture layers has been observed in a number of sites in the T'ao-ho valley and the upper Wei-shui; see Hsia Nai, *KKHP* 3 (1948), 101–17; *KKTH* 1956 (6), 9–19; 1958 (5), 1–5; 1958 (7), 6–16; 1958 (9), 36–49; *KK* 1959 (3), 138–42, 146.

37. *KK* 1962 (1), 22; 1964 (5), 232–33, 244; 1973 (5), 290–91.

91. Fabric impressions on pottery (*left*) and remains of millet (*right*) found at the Ch'i-chia culture site at Ta-ho-chuang, Yüng-ching Hsien, Kansu. (From *KKHP* 1974, no. 2, pl. 6.)

especially by a kind of flat-bottomed jar with a constricted neck, flared mouth, and two large vertical loop handles on the shoulder (fig. 90). Painted pots are seen occasionally, and cord marks are another surface feature. Remains of millet and fabric impressions on pottery were found at the Ta-ho-chuang site in Yüng-ching Hsien (fig. 91); oracle bones of sheep scapulae at Ta-ho-chuang and Ch'in-wei-chia in Yüng-ching; oracle bones of cattle, sheep, and pig scapulae at Huang-niang-niang-t'ai in Wu-wei Hsien; and copper ornaments and small objects at all three sites.[38] Bones of dogs, pigs, cattle, and sheep and remains of hemp have also been found.[39] All these go to show that the Ch'i-chia was a culture of advanced farmers, among whom domesticated animals were of apparently greater importance than they were in much of the rest of North China.[40]

At the Huang-niang-niang-t'ai site in Wu-wei, rectangular house floors plastered with white limy clay were uncovered; near or within the houses round or square hearths had been built (fig. 92). Surrounding the houses were storage pits of various shapes. From the houses and storage pits twenty-three copper implements and copper slugs were recovered, including knives, awls, chisels, and rings. An analysis of a knife and an awl disclosed that copper accounts for over 99 percent of the total metal used in their manufacture, with impurities (lead, tin, etc.) less than 0.4 percent.[41]

38. *KKTH* 1958 (7), 6–16. *KKHP* 1960 (2), 59–60; 1974 (2), 29–61; 1975 (2), 57–96. *KK* 1960 (3), 9–12; 1961 (1), 6.

39. Margit Bylin-Althin, *BMFEA* 18 (1946), 457–58.

40. For an argument about the relative importance of agriculture and animal husbandry in the Ch'i-chia culture, see *KK* 1961 (1), 3–11; 1961 (7), 388–89.

41. *KKHP* 1960 (2), 53–70.

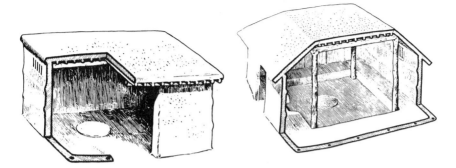

92. Reconstructions of Ch'i-chia culture houses at Ta-ho-chuang, Yüng-ching, Kansu. (From *KKHP* 1974, no. 2, pp. 36–37.)

Villages of the Ch'i-chia culture incorporate their own burial areas. Two cemeteries have been found at Ch'in-wei-chia, one in the southwestern part of the site and one in the northeastern part. Twenty-nine burials were located in 1960 in the northeastern cemetery in an area about 100 meters square, arranged in three north-south rows, all with heads to the west. Twenty-four of the tombs are single burials, but the other five contained two adults each, a male and a female. The male skeleton lies stretched, and the female, at his left, is flexed (fig. 93). All tombs contained grave goods of stone and pottery artifacts and the lower jaws of pigs, the last item ranging in number, in individual tombs, from one to fifteen. The southwestern cemetery yielded eight burials from a lower stratum and ninety-nine burials from an upper stratum, the latter arranged in six rows running northeast-southwest, with the head end invariably pointing toward the northwest. The overwhelming majority of the tombs are again single, and they were all furnished with grave goods—pottery vessels, stone and bone tools, ornaments, oracle bones, and pigs' lower jaws.[42] The significance of these burial patterns for an understanding of the Ch'i-chia social organization is obvious. At the Ta-ho-chuang site, rings of small rocks were discovered on the ground—possibly a religious construction—near which were the burials of sacrificial animals.

Two radiocarbon dates from Ta-ho-chuang (3540 ± 90, 3570 ± 90) place the site in the 2150–1780 B.C. range, making the copper artifacts of the Ch'i-chia culture one of the earliest-dated metal finds in China.[43] Without question, Ch'i-chia represents the culture of farmers, and their farming

42. *KK* 1964 (6), 267–69. *KKHP* 1975 (2), 57–96.
43. *KK* 1972 (1), 55.

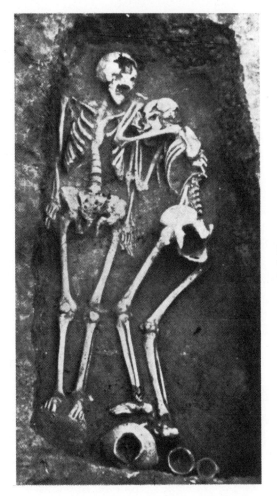

93. A double burial at the Ch'i-
chia culture cemetery at Ch'in-
wei-chia, Lin-hsia, Kansu. (From
KK 1964, no. 5.)

tradition was probably introduced from the Yang-shao culture. But there
is plenty of room for dispute about its cultural affiliations. Its similarities
to the Yang-shao, the Lungshanoid cultures in the Wei-shui area, and
Western Chou civilizations have been noted,[44] but these could easily be
accounted for by cultural contacts during various time periods. It is possible
that in this area, which is adjacent to the dry steppes of northwest China
and Inner Mongolia, and where the climatic conditions of the present time
tend to be on the arid side, the Yang-shao farming culture was not well
adapted and was replaced by cultural phases having a native sub-Neolithic

44. *KK* 1959 (3), 138–42, 146; 1959 (7), 323–25, 345; 1959 (10), 517; 1961 (1), 10.

base but receiving considerable cultural influence from the Yang-shao farmers. The nature of its contemporary cultural phases and the many local cultural traditions which followed the Ch'i-chia seem to indicate this possibility.

In Shan-tan, Min-lo, Yüng-ch'ang, and Chiu-ch'üan counties of central Kansu, immediately northwest of the Ch'i-chia area, there was probably another cultural phase contemporary with and possibly related to the Ch'i-chia. This could be named the Shan-tan culture, after its type site discovered in 1948 at Ssu-pa-t'an in Shan-tan Hsien. This culture is characterized by agriculture, stone phallus models, and a distinctive kind of pottery of a coarse texture, often painted in very thick pigment, which makes the designs stand out in relief. The basic form of pottery is again the double-handled jar. This may very well be a regional branch of the Ch'i-chia, but its distinctive pottery painting and the large number of phallus models seem to warrant its consideration as a separate culture.[45]

The Tsaidam culture is thus far represented by three sites in No-mu-hung, Pa-lung, and Hsiang-jih-tê counties of northwestern Chinghai, south of the Tsaidam basin.[46] These were discovered in 1959 and are characterized by houses with mud-wall enclosures, urn burials, a large number of bone and horn artifacts, wool fabrics, plain pottery jugs and basins with straight walls, and tent rings of sandbags. Copper objects were found at one of the sites. These remains apparently indicate a food-producing culture leaning toward animal domestication and nomadic life, but the rarity of metal objects seems to provide grounds for synchronizing this cultural phase with the Ch'i-chia to the east. This is borne out by the single radiocarbon date obtained at the site—3670 ± 90 B.P.

Stratigraphic evidence in eastern Kansu and eastern Chinghai shows that the Ch'i-chia culture was followed by several small local cultural phases which carried on the painted pottery tradition. These possessed metallurgy and had some inclination toward animal domestication. They include the well-known phases of Andersson's Hsin-tien, Ssu-wa, and Sha-ching "cultures" and the newly identified "T'ang-wang culture," all of which will be discussed in a later chapter.

The Southwest

The greater Chinese southwest includes the Red Basin of Szechwan and the hills and plateaus of Kwangsi, Yunnan, Kweichow, and western

45. *KKHP* 1959 (3), 7–15.
46. *WW* 1960 (6), 37–40. *KK* 1961 (1), 16. *KKHP* 1963 (1), 17–44.

Kwangtung, on the upper reaches of the Yangtze, the Pearl, the Mekong, the Salween, and the Irrawaddy rivers. When farmers began to appear in the rest of China and while a good deal of "revolutionary" activity was going on there, pottery and polished stone implements also began to appear in the southwest. There is no question that the Neolithic cultures of the southwest continued from the Mesolithic cultural substratum of the area, [47] a condition also prevailing in Indochina,[48] but the life and society of these peoples are little-known archaeologically. In the beginning of chapter 3 I mentioned the probability of a horticultural beginning in the Neolithic period of South China and Southeast Asia characterized by cord-marked pottery, and it appears quite likely that agriculture and a fully Neolithic industry and culture emerged in the southwest long before the full impact of the later Chinese historical civilizations was felt in this region. It is significant to note that the middle Yangtze Valley provided the only major point of contact between the North China nuclear area and Neolithic South China known in the archaeological record, and the cultural exchanges between these two regions—in whichever direction—must have been frequent and significant. The fact that the Yang-shao sites in southwest Honan exhibit significant "local" characteristics[49] may suggest that the upper Han-shui valley and the middle Yangtze in western Hupei and eastern Szechwan provided a route for significant contact between the beginning agricultural phases of North China and those of Southeast Asia. Further information on Neolithic cultures from this area may shed light on the whole range of problems of agricultural origins in the Far East, but at this time excavated sites that are demonstrably earlier than or contemporary with the Yang-shao culture have yet to be reported.

Neolithic sites in the southwest are yet few, but there are many characteristic features that indicate an early separation from Neolithic North China in cultural style. Evidence of agriculture notwithstanding, most of the southwestern Neolithic sites show the great importance of fishing or mollusk collecting or both, but hunting does not appear to be very signi-

47. Cheng Te-k'un, *Archaeological Studies in Szechwan*, Cambridge Univ. Press, 1957. *WWTKTL* 1958 (3), 69–71. R. Maglioni, *Hongkong Naturalist* 8 (1938), 211. W. Schofield, *Proc. 3rd Far Eastern Prehist. Congr.* (1940), p. 259. D. J. Finn, *Hongkong Naturalist* 7 (1936), 258. K. C. Chang, *Ta-lu tsa-chih* 9 (1954), 4–8. *KKHP* 1959 (4), 1–15.

48. Henri Mansuy, *Stations préhistoriques dans les cavernes du massif calcaire de Bac-Son (Tonkin)*, Mémoirs du Service Géologique de l'Indochine, no. 11, fasc. 2, 1924; *Nouvelles decouvertes dans les cavernes du massif calcaire de Bac-Son (Tonkin)*, Mém. Serv. Géo. l'Indochine, no. 12, fasc. 1, 1925.

49. *KK* 1962 (1), 23; 1965 (1), 1–3.

ficant since stone arrowheads and other hunting implements are as a rule rare. The stone inventories include the highly characteristic shouldered axes, remains of which have been unearthed from Ya-an in Sikang, in the west, to the island of Hainan in the east.[50] The ceramics are characterized by the long persistence of corded red ware, the abundance of flat-bottomed and concave-bottomed forms, and the wide use of shell and grit temper. Painted pottery, black pottery, stone knives and sickles, and pottery tripods, which may be indicative of North China influences, are all present at various sites but are relatively rare. Geometric ware similar to that of the southeast is seen only along the eastern fringes of this region, while the characteristic southeastern stone implement, the stepped adz, is not present at all. Aside from these generalizations, well-documented excavated materials are available at only a few regions in the whole area.

To begin in the Yangtze Valley between I-ch'ang (Hupei) and Pa-tung (Szechwan), in the Hsi-ling-hsia area that was the eastern gateway to the Red Basin, fifty-four early sites investigated in 1960 have been grouped into five categories, ranging in date, according to the estimates of the investigators, from Neolithic to Han.[51] At the three sites in the first category (Neolithic), chipped and polished stone implements were found alongside a variety of pottery (fig. 94). Four kinds of ware are recognized: coarse red (30 percent), coarse brown (30 percent), fine red (15 percent), and fine black (15 percent). The coarse wares were tempered with fibers and shell powders. A few were painted in red or black. Bowl and urn shapes predominated, and a variety of ring feet occurred. The high ring feet were often decorated with cut-out patterns or circumferential ridges. A large number of incised, clay pot-supporters was found, recalling similar finds in Indochina and the Yüan-shan culture of Taiwan.[52] These characteristic features of the Neolithic sites in the Hsi-ling-hsia area suggest a culture of considerable distinctiveness, but its ceramics cannot be earlier than the Lungshanoid Ch'ü-chia-ling culture to the east and northeast.

50. The shouldered ax has been discovered widely in the Chinese southwest: Szechwan (Cheng, *Archaeological Studies in Szechwan*, p. 60); Yunnan (*KK* 1959, no. 4, 175; Wu Chin-ting et al., *Yunnan Ts'ang Erh ching k'ao-ku pao-kao*, Lichuang, National Museum, 1942, p. 37); Kweichou (*KKTH* 1956, no. 3, 48–50; *WWTKTL* 1955, no. 9, 67–69); Sikang (*WWTKTL* 1958, no. 9, 48–49); Kwangsi (*WWTKTL* 1956, no. 6, 58–59; *KK* 1964, no. 1, 591; 1965, no. 6, 313); Kwangtung (*WWTKTL* 1956, no. 11, 42; 1957, no. 6, 9–12; *KKTH* 1956, no. 4, 5–6); and Hainan (*KKTH* 1956, no. 2, 38–41).

51. *KK* 1961 (5), 231–36. For similar finds in this area, see *WW* 1959 (5), 75.

52. W. H. Sung, *Bull. Dept. Arch. Anth.*, National Taiwan Univ., no. 9/10 (1957), 137–45.

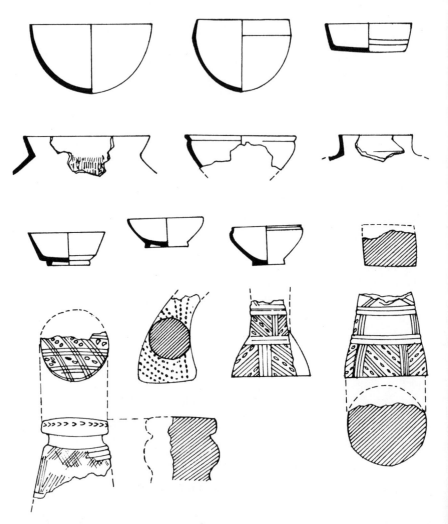

94. Artifacts at the Neolithic site at Yang-chia-wan, in the Hsi-ling-hsia Gorge region of western Hupei. (From *KK* 1961, no. 5, p. 233.)

Farther upstream on the Yangtze is the site of Ta-hsi (Huo-pao-hsi) in Wu-shan, easternmost Szechwan, on a terrace at the junction of two rivers.[53] Among the finds excavated here in 1959 are chipped and polished stone axes, hoes, chisels, scrapers, clay spindle whorls, and bone needles; stone arrowheads and bone spear points; a large number of fishbones; and an elaborate assemblage of stone, bone, jade, and shell ornaments. The

53. *WW* 1961 (11), 15–21, 60.

pottery at the site resembles the Hsi-ling-hsia wares described above, including sandy red, fine red, and black pottery. Some painted sherds of jars, bowls, and urns occurred. In shape, *ting* tripods and ring-footed vessels (including *tou*) again suggest Lungshanoid features of the Ch'ü-chia-ling culture. During a late phase of the occupation, a part of the site served as a cemetery. The bodies in the burials—all single—were stretched and supine. Grave goods varied and a few had peculiar furnishings: two dishes, one on each side of the breast; three painted jars, one on top of the other, lying between the legs; a piece of ivory placed beneath the head; fishbones found in the mouth; a dog.

Not far to the west, along the Yangtze, Neolithic remains have been located in an area approximately 1 kilometer in length on the terraces of both banks of the Han-ching-kou River near Chung Hsien.[54] These remains, investigated by the Szechwan Museum in the middle and late 1950s, were concentrated in six clusters on the western bank and one on the eastern. The sites on the western bank, apparently residential settlements, have yielded a large number of sand-tempered, corded ceramics of the *li*-tripod and pointed- and round-bottomed-jug forms, together with small numbers of gray and black sherds. Basket impression and checker stamping are both seen on some sherds, and some of the rim sherds are painted in black pigment. Stone axes, adzes, chisels, hoes, and pestles, chipped, chipped and polished, and totally ground, have been discovered, together with remains of horses, sheep, pigs, and deer, a human skull, a large number of fishbones, and many mollusk shells. Oracle bones and a bronze arrowhead were found, possibly from a late occupation. The site on the eastern bank, 100 by 50 meters in size, has produced a large number of pebbles, blanks, and finished stone tools from what was possibly a workshop site, near a dwelling house. Seen as a whole, the Chung Hsien sites again show significant similarities to the late Yang-shao and early Lungshanoid stages in southwestern Honan and Hupei, but such similarities are fewer here than in the sites farther downstream, described above.

Other than the Szechwan sites,[55] and in addition to a few finds in Kweichou and Tibet,[56] only in Yunnan are significant numbers of Neolithic localities known in the literature. Both in the extreme northeast[57]

54. *KK* 1959 (8), 393–97; 1962 (8), 416–17. *KKTH* 1958 (5), 31–32.

55. Other than the above sites on the Yangtze in eastern Szechwan, Neolithic sites are also known from the northwestern part of the Red Basin where Kansu-style painted pottery has been found. See *KK* 1965 (12), 614–18; *WW* 1974 (5), 91–92.

56. *WW* 1973 (1), 61–62. *KK* 1975 (5), 310–15.

57. *KK* 1962 (10), 529–30, 534.

and the extreme south, [58] distinctively local remains are known, but the best-investigated areas are around Lake Tien in the east and Lake Erh in the west. No fewer than nine Neolithic sites were located in 1958 on the eastern shore of Lake Tien in central eastern Yunnan.[59] Most of these can be described as shellmounds or kitchen middens, consisting of compact layers of molluscan shells (most of which had been knocked open) mixed with a large number of potsherds, some stone implements, and a few shell artifacts. The implements consist of shouldered axes, net sinkers with constricted waist, perforators, and grinding stones. Potsherds from the middens have been grouped into four classes:

(1) Red ware of fine texture, predominantly handmade (coiled), tempered with paddy husks. This pottery is generally of small size, with a plain surface, in the form of cups, small bowls, and shallow dishes with flat or concave bases; it makes up a large percentage of the sherds uncovered from such sites.

(2) Gray ware with grit or shell temper, made on wheels and sometimes slipped and then burnished. Pottery of this class, generally larger in size, includes jugs with straight or flaring mouths, basins with two handles, and concave-based cups; its incised or impressed decoration includes feather patterns, lozenges, wavy parallel lines, crosshatches, basket designs, and rows of dots.

(3) Yellow-slipped ware with grit or shell temper, wheel- or mold-made, in the forms of basins, cups, and ring-footed vessels.

(4) Orange ware with grit or shell temper sometimes decorated with cord marks and checker impressions.

Stone arrowheads were found here, but the remains of rice grains and husks imprinted or embedded in the pottery of the first class suggest the importance of rice farming. Further research on the shores of the lake in 1960 brought to light additional sites of the same culture.[60]

Terraced fields were identified by Wu Chin-ting in the Ta-li region near Lake Erh during the late thirties at the sites of Ma-lung and Fo-ting, on the slopes of the Tien-ts'ang Mountains.[61] Natural creeks must have been utilized here for irrigation, and semisubterranean houses have been excavated. Differing from the Lake Tien region, however, the Ta-li pottery is characterized by spouted jars, *ting* tripods, and stamped designs.

58. *KK* 1963 (6), 337; 1963 (10), 573–74; 1965 (11), 588–89.
59. *KK* 1959 (4), 173–75, 184. *WWTKTL* 1957 (11), 47.
60. *KK* 1961 (1), 46–49.
61. Wu Chin-ting et al., *Yunnan Ts'ang Erh ching k'ao-ku pao-kao.*

Stone sickles and the absence of kitchen middens in the Ta-li area further distinguish it from the Tien-ch'ih phase, and some archaeologists contend that the latter might have been slightly earlier in time.

Satisfactory stratigraphic evidence indicates that such Neolithic farming settlements appeared in the southwest after the Mesolithic and sub-Neolithic cultures but prior to the metal civilizations to be described in a later chapter. The cultural relationship of this area with North China was unquestionably very close, as is indicated by the stone inventories and the stylistic similarities in ceramics and by the crops planted in both of these regions. Such Neolithic cultures provided a background for the appearance of the subsequent indigenous civilizations in the middle of the first millennium B.C. under the strong influence of the Eastern Chou civilization in the areas to the north and the east.

General Conclusions

The brief descriptions of the emergence of pottery and agriculture in central and South China demonstrate the pattern of cultural growth in these regions. Clearly, the hunting-fishing Mesolithic populations for the most part continued to occupy their original habitat after the Neolithic ways of life began in several areas of China, and among them the technology of ceramics and stone polishing gradually emerged. Agriculture and animal domestication emerged or were introduced into some of these regions, and the Neolithic transformation process took place slowly. The whole process and pattern of cultural assimilations can be elaborated and clearly understood when some of the early cultural history of the regions adjacent to China is taken into consideration. While a lengthy discussion of these adjacent regions is not possible in this volume, some general remarks will prove helpful.

The northern Asian regions west and north of the Huang Ho valley and immediately adjacent to it can be grouped on the basis of vegetation and topography into three groups: the steppe-desert zone of Central Asia, Sinkiang, Mongolia, and southwestern Siberia; the taiga zone around Lake Baikal and the upper Lena, the Selenga, and the Amur rivers; and the Pacific coast from the Sea of Okhotsk down to and including Korea. Sub-Neolithic and Neolithic cultures in these regions more or less follow similar subdivisions.[62] The taiga culture may be omitted from discussion for the present since the region directly adjacent to it, northernmost

---

62. C. S. Chard, *Anthropologica* 2 (1960), no. 2, 1–9.

Manchuria, which is separated from Lake Baikal by the Khingan Mountains, is archaeologically unexplored.[63] The available archaeological evidence from central Manchuria in the Sungari Valley, as mentioned above, indicates more direct affiliations with North China and the Pacific coast than with the taiga zone to the north. As Chester Chard has pointed out, "it is to be expected that Manchuria, except probably the western portion, would show its closest affinities with North China on the one hand and the Pacific coast of Siberia on the other, and stand in contrast to Siberia and Mongolia."[64]

The northwestern part of China, extending from eastern Mongolia through Sinkiang, is the eastern portion of the steppe-desert belt that consists of Russian Turkestan and the eastern European steppes as well as northwest China, and the Microlithic cultural assemblages from the latter region resemble the Kelteminar complex to the west. This complex is characterized by microblade implements that show considerable elaboration but are rarely retouched bifacially and seems to suggest a whole series of local cultures adapted to a similar natural environment. According to A. A. Formozov, the "best witness for the ethnic diversity of this large culture area is the variation of pottery types found within it."[65] On the Chinese periphery, pottery elements in association with microlithic implements can be classified into three groups: those that show connections with the Huang Ho valley, such as some of the painted pottery and the *li* and *ting* tripods; those that show connections with the Kelteminar complexes in southwestern Siberia and Kazakhstan, such as the combed and some of the incised pottery; and those that do not show affiliations with either, such as the brownish and plain-surfaced wares of eastern Mongolia. This may lead to the conclusion that the microlithic assemblages in the northern frontiers of China, instead of belonging to a single cultural complex (such as the so-called Gobi culture),[66] may represent a series of local survivals of the Upper Palaeolithic hunting-fishing cultures which adopted ceramic and other Neolithic technological traits compatible with their local environment and cultural ecology from China and from their northern and western neighbors. Some of these groups in more favorable environments had even adopted agriculture and animal domestication. This process as observed in northern frontiers of China is parallel,

63. See *KK* 1972 (4), 20–23, for a site found in 1964 in the taiga area of northwestern Heilungkiang.

64. *Northeast Asia in Prehistory*, Univ. of Wisconsin Press, 1974, p. 61.

65. *American Antiquity* 27 (1961), 87.

66. Cheng Te-k'un, *Prehistoric China*, p. 52.

for example, to that seen in the eastern Caspian areas where pottery and food production were introduced from the nuclear area of Iran, leading to a series of food-producing assemblages such as the Jeitun culture of Jeitun-Tepe and Anau near Ashkhabad.[67] The steppe zone undoubtedly also served as a route of cultural movement and diffusion between the high cultural centers in the east and west. In the current archaeological record, we see two radiating centers—one in the Iraq-Iran area and the other in the Huang Ho—which spread their influence across the intervening steppes from opposite directions and made scattered contacts. We do not see, however, that the steppe zone during the sub-Neolithic and the Neolithic stages served as a route of significant cultural transmission from one of the high culture centers to the other.

The influence of the steppe culture phase tapers off toward the east and is only weakly felt in southern and central Manchuria, which may legitimately be classed, during the sub-Neolithic and Neolithic stages, with the Pacific coast traditions. During the several millennia before the Christian era, the regions, in northeastern Asia, of Manchuria, Korea, and the Maritime Province of the U.S.S.R. can probably be said to have belonged to a single culture area characterized by flat-bottomed and straight-walled pottery, shell collecting, fishing, and sea-mammal hunting, as well as a distinctive complex of bone artifacts, such as barbed and (occasionally) toggle harpoons, bone armor, and needle cases made of bird bones.[68] This phase of culture is of considerable antiquity on the islands off the coast and in scattered areas on the coast. The sub-Neolithic cultures in the Sungari and T'umen valleys appear to be the interior phases of this same tradition. It is upon such a tradition that the Neolithic farmers' cultural influences were imposed from the Huang Ho valley to the southwest. Farming, however, seems to have been introduced only into the middle Sungari, where the environment permitted it, while elsewhere in northern and eastern Manchuria the archaic hunting-fishing cultures persisted into historic periods.

In South China, the early Recent hunter-fishers were apparently part of the widespread population whose cultural remains, discovered throughout all of mainland Southeast Asia, bear striking resemblances from region to region. This culture has been named the Hoabinhian after its type region. It has been suggested that in northern Indochina the Hoabinhian horizon, characterized by crude pebble choppers, was followed by a Bacsonian

67. M. E. and V. M. Masson, *Cahiers d'histoire mondiale* 5 (1959), 15–40.
68. A. P. Okladnikov, *Proc. 32nd Int. Congr. of Americanists*, 1958, pp. 545–56.

horizon, a continuation of the previous Hoabinhian but with the addition of ceramics and partially polished stone implements. How a horticultural beginning was accomplished in this cultural horizon and what its relationship was with the nuclear area of North China are important areas of further inquiry.[69]

69. See K. C. Chang, *Antiquity* 44 (1970), 175–85. In recent years, because of the very important finds of pottery and plant use—and even of bronze implements—from very early horizons in Thailand, there has been much discussion of the Southeast Asia—North China interrelationship. See, e.g., W. G. Solheim, "Remarks on the Neolithic in South China and Southeast Asia," *Journal of the Hong Kong Archaeological Society* 4 (1973), 25–29; and my comments, in *Jour. Hong Kong Arch. Soc.* 5 (1974), 34–38. Before the Neolithic cultures in the Chinese Southwest are better known, speculations on this topic would be premature. But this will surely be an issue that will engage our attention in the years to come.

6: The Emergence of Civilization in China

History and Archaeology in the Study of Ancient China

Despite the quality and complexity that distinguish the ancient civilizations from their more barbarous antecedents, these early civilizations continue to be the object of archaeological research, since they are known to us primarily through their material remains: ruins, implements, utensils, and the visual arts. Nevertheless, with the emergence of the Shang in North China, Chinese archaeology advances into a new phase, for in some important aspects the archaeology of the ancient civilizations differs significantly from that of their Palaeolithic and Neolithic predecessors. Civilizations are the outcome of major qualitative developments of culture, as were the other major qualitative transformations before them (e.g., the first use of tools and the invention of agriculture), but in this evolution which produced civilizations, social, political, and economic organizations played especially significant roles. In grasping the essence of ancient civilizations, therefore, the archaeologist must give special emphasis and attention to the articulation of his data as well as to the empirical aspects of the data themselves. Moreover, in most civilizations the first written records emerged. As Christopher Hawkes has pointed out, when texts become available, the scholar must be responsible to them as well as to the archaeological data.[1]

The Shang, the builders of the first verifiable civilization in China, were also the first literate people of Asia east of the Urals. In the royal court of the Shang there were archivists and scribes who recorded important events of the state. With brush and ink, they transcribed characters onto slips of bamboo or wood, and bound them together into book form (the so-called *ts'ê*). We know of these books, however, only through reference to them in other contexts, for they have not yet been found.[2]

1. *Amer. Anthropologist* 56 (1954), 155–68.

2. Some inscribed carapaces of turtles bore holes, and some scholars speculate that they were strung together into *ts'e*. See *WWTKTL* 1954 (5), 25; and Y. L. Liu, "The tortoiseshell *ts'e* of the Yin period," *Soochow University Journal of Chinese Art History* 2 (1973), 11–38.

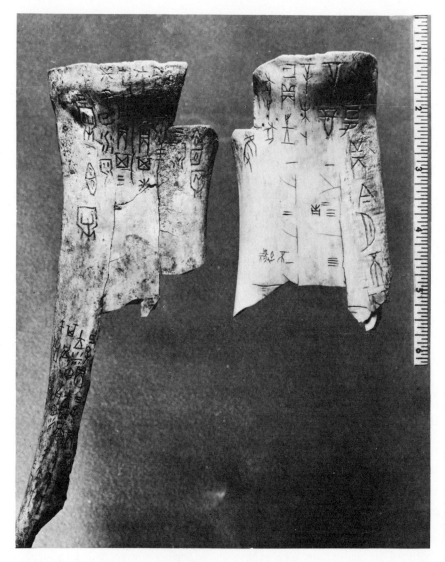

95. Oracle bones of the Shang dynasty excavated from Hsiao-t'un, An-yang, Honan. (Collection, Academia Sinica; photo courtesy of *Life* magazine.)

Aside from occasional inscriptions on pottery and other artifacts, the known written records of the Shang that have been preserved intact to this day are primarily of two kinds: records of divination incised on the shoulder blades of animals (mainly oxen) (fig. 95) and on turtleshells—the two principal media of divination—and signs of possession and offering cast on bronze vessels (fig. 96). The former are known as the *chia ku wen*

96. Inscriptions cast on a bronze vessel of the Shang period excavated in Ch'ang-ch'ing, Shantung. (From *WW*, 1964/4, p. 47.)

(turtleshell and bone scripts), and the latter are known as *chin wen* (bronze scripts). The study of each kind of script is a highly specialized field of learning.[3]

The written records of the Chou, successors to the Shang at the center of the political stage of ancient China, are scarcely more abundant at the beginning. The custom of bone and turtleshell divination—scapulimancy and plastromancy—was continued by the Chou with much less interest; the practice of inscribing bones and turtleshells was in general discontinued and thus the *chia ku* scripts were no longer a source of textual information for the Chou. On the other hand, the bronze scripts of the Chou have longer texts than the Shang bronzes, often recording the political and ritual contexts in which the vessels were made and offered (fig. 97). The

3. For a comprehensive and authoritative survey of the pre-Ch'in literature, see Tsien Tsun-hsün, *Written on Bamboo and Silk*, Univ. Chicago Press, 1962. See also Hsü Cho-yün, *Ancient China in Transition*, Stanford Univ. Press, 1965, pp. 183–92.

97. A Western Chou inscription cast on a bronze vessel excavated at Chang-chia-p'o. (From *Ch'ang-an Chang-chia-p'o Hsi Chou t'ung-ch'i ch'ün*, Peking, Wen Wu Press, 1965, pl. 8.)

chin wen, therefore, became a major source of the Chou textual information. In addition, there have been rare discoveries of inscribed silk and bamboo and jade tablets (fig. 98), but the texts are in most cases short and the information they contain inconsequential.

Although archaeologically found Chou texts are scarce, literacy expanded to the local states during the second half of Chou history—the Eastern Chou period—and many more books, archives, and other written materials came into being throughout China. Many of these survived the Chou and were transcribed onto the newly invented paper during the Han dynasty. Known as the pre-Ch'in texts, these became a part of

98. Inscribed bamboo tablets excavated from Ch'u tombs at Chiang-ling, Hupei. (From *WW* 1966, no. 5.)

the traditional literary heritage of China that was handed down through the subsequent two millennia of her historical period. Including such important volumes as the annals of the various states (e.g., *Ch'un ch'iu* and *Chu shu chi nien*), the "Book of History" (*Shu ching*), and the "Book of Odes" (*Shih ching*), the pre-Ch'in texts were the principal source from which Ssu-ma Ch'ien compiled his *Shih chi*, the first comprehensive and objective history of China, in the beginning of the first century B.C. As sources of information, however, these pre-Ch'in texts are full of problems. Because of the Ch'in upheaval, all of these documents did not survive into the Han dynasty intact; many had to be restored by Han scholars, many of whom had their own axes to grind and points to make and had been known to speak their own minds through their ancients. Each book must therefore be authenticated, section by section or even sentence by sentence, in order to be used as a piece of pre-Ch'in textual material. Moreover, few of these texts are accurately dated, and owing to the scale of cultural change during the periods they represent, the date must be carefully estimated, often on very circumstantial evidence. In the last few years, a number of texts, on silk and bamboo tablets, have been discovered in early Han tombs, essentially supporting the current versions of the same texts.[4] Archaeology may yet produce important textual data for the pre-Ch'in period.

Thus, the study of ancient China can be divided into a prehistoric and a historic segment. For the study of prehistory, scholars must rely exclusively on archaeology, but the historical archaeologist has the advantage of the textual information that was available for both the Shang and Chou periods. Since the textual information pertains primarily to political and ritual aspects of the Shang-Chou cultures, aspects that are important concerns of civilizational studies, it is apparent that research into Shang and Chou culture and society cannot be a purely archaeological task.

It does not, however, necessarily follow that in the study of Shang and Chou China the archaeologist cannot play an independent part. All three main sources of textual information pertaining to the Shang and Chou are highly specialized fields of learning, each containing countless unsolved problems, many of which are perhaps unsolvable. To undertake research in depth in one of these fields one must become a chiakuologist, a chinwenologist, or a pre-Ch'in text specialist. Among the scholars of the last group there are even those who devote their lives to the study

---

4. The principal sites are Ma-wang-tui in Ch'ang-sha and Lin-i in Shantung. For Ma-wang-tui (tomb no. 3), see *WW* 1974 (7), 39–48; *KK* 1975 (1), 47–57, 61. For Lin-i, see *WW* 1974 (2), 15–35; 1974 (12), 11–24.

of single books. The archaeologist cannot be expected to become master of all these specialized fields, nor should he wait until all the textual information becomes known and all its problems solved before he undertakes his own study. On the other hand, many archaeological problems of ancient China are not only independent of textual study but are capable of contributing solutions to textual problems. The study of Shang and Chou China, therefore, calls for active and close collaboration between the archaeologist and the historian. Each must be aware of the other's results and conclusions and undertake his own research with them in mind, but he cannot be expected to be minutely responsible for the other's data and issues. In dealing with Shang and Chou China in this volume, I adhere strictly to my role as an archaeologist. Textual information and historical conclusions will be used only when and if they contribute to a better archaeological understanding.

A related issue in this connection is the matter of pre-Shang history. There may be two meanings to the phrase. The first refers to written records dated to an earlier period than the Shang. Since such records do not exist at present, and the problem is purely hypothetical, it requires no further discussion. The second meaning refers to the personages and events, recorded in Shang and Chou texts, that were regarded by the Shang and Chou themselves as having existed or taken place before their era.

Such data, collectively referable as the myths and legends of the Shang and Chou, are part of the material for the study of the Shang and Chou themselves, highly useful for an understanding of their views of cosmology and history. Undoubtedly they also included oral traditions that had been handed down from remote antiquity to the Shang-Chou period and are thus truly reflective of pre-Shang events and conditions. Two such events, the rise of the Huang Ti era and the whole history of the Hsia dynasty, are illustrative.

The exact nature of Huang Ti, the celebrated Yellow Emperor, and the history of his career are subjects of numerous studies. His supposed accession took place in 2697 B.C. He was the greatest of the cultural heroes of ancient China, and to him are credited the invention of all the essential elements of the civilization. He was also the greatest war hero of the Flower People, from whom all subsequent dynasties claimed descent. These stories are perhaps more important symbolically than historically: Huang Ti was more a symbol of an era than an actual ancestor.

During the Age of Shen Nung, men cultivated food and women wove clothing. People were governed without a criminal law and prestige was built without the use of force. After Shen Nung, however, the strong began to rule over the weak and the many over the few. Therefore, Huang Ti administered internally with a penal code and externally with armed forces. ["Hua-ts'ê," in *Shang chün shu*]

Thus is described a major transition of Chinese society from self-contained peaceful villages to warlike states with centralized government. Shen Nung ushered in an era with farming villages, but Huang Ti was responsible for the rise of cities and the state. These tales anticipated the modern archaeologists in giving due recognition to the Neolithic and the urban revolutions as epoch markers of ancient history. How the ancient Chinese arrived at these notions is unimportant. It is significant that portions of the pre-Shang history in Shang-Chou texts contain grains of historical judgment that would have met the approval of a Gordon Childe.

The records concerning the Hsia dynasty are of more than symbolic importance. A royal genealogy of the Hsia is known fragmentarily from pre-Ch'in texts and in organized form in *Shih chi*. Tales about particular kings, events during the reigns of several, and the detailed process in which the Shang overthrew the Hsia are recorded in Ssu-ma Ch'ien's *Shih chi*, whose credibility in recording some true history of the Three Dynasties is amply demonstrated by the reliability of its Shang and Chou portions. Was there a Hsia dynasty as well? If so, what was its archaeological equivalent? These questions cannot yet be answered. Historians generally believe that the Hsia centered in southern Shansi and northwestern Honan,[5] precisely the area of the earliest phase of the Shang civilization as manifested in archaeological remains (see below). The Hsia dynasty could be a local facies of the Honan Lung-shan culture, or it could be represented by the remains (or some of the remains) believed to be early Shang. Until written records (such as divination records containing names of kings) are found in which such issues are elucidated, the identity of the Hsia will remain a mystery in ancient Chinese history.

In any event, both archaeological and legendary Chinese prehistory preceded the Shang dynasty. Earlier chapters have described the former, which ends where the Shang and Chou began. In other words, from two opposite directions Chinese prehistory and history meet at the beginning of the Shang civilization. The legendary prehistory is certainly contained

5. Hsü Chung-shu, *An-yang fa-chüeh pao-kao* 3 (1931). Hsü Liang-chih, *Chung-kuo shih-ch'ien-shih hua*, Hong Kong, Asia Press, 1954, pp. 197–230. Ting Shan, *BIHP* 5 (1935), 89–129.

in the archaeological prehistory and may enrich and amplify it. A proper study of it, however, must be left to other volumes.[6]

The Shang and the Chinese Civilization

As was made clear in chapter 4, by the time of the Lung-shan cultures at the beginning of the second millennium B.C., the foundation for civilization—essentially defined as a combination of city life, metallurgy, writing, and great art style made possible by a highly stratified society—had been well laid in several regions of China, prominent among them being Honan, Shantung, Kiangsu, and Hupei. In the past, we had tended to underestimate the level of societal growth in many of these regions, and we concentrated our attention on Honan as the sole birthplace of Chinese civilization. Archaeological data brought to light since the mid-1960s are fast changing our understanding of the real situation. It now looks as if incipient civilizations developed along parallel lines—in an interrelated way, without doubt—in all of these regions. But the Honan civilization still commands our special attention, because it was the earliest to emerge in the archaeological record and is by far the most literate and archaeologically the richest. It is the civilization of the Shang dynasty, the second historical dynasty—after the Hsia—but the first that has been archaeologically verified.

The earliest Chinese civilization was apparently not confined to the Shang dynasty, a dynasty geographically centering in Honan and its immediate surroundings only. Archaeological sites with Shang-type remains have been found in a much wider area—from Hopei and Shansi in the north to central Shantung in the east and to Hunan and Kiangsi in the south. But here, as we have said just above, we must come to grips with textual history and treat the archaeological data within the Shang territory, as defined in texts, separate from data elsewhere. In this chapter we deal with the archaeology of the Shang dynasty, along with contemporary sites outside the Shang dynastic domain in North China—Shansi, Shantung, and northern Kiangsu—and in the Yangtze Valley.

In describing the Shang archaeology we must, at the outset, make

6. For mythology in ancient China, see Marcel Granet, *Danses et légendes de la Chine ancienne*, Paris, Félix Alcan, 1926. Henri Maspero, *Jour. Asiatique* 204 (1924), 1–100. Bernhard Karlgren, *BMFEA* 18 (1946), 199–365. Derk Bodde, "China," in *Mythologies of the Ancient World*, New York, Doubleday, 1961. Yang K'uan, *Ku shih pien* 7 (1941). Hsüan Chu, *Chung-kuo shen-hua yen-chiu ABC*, Shanghai, Shih-chieh Book Co., 1929.

very careful distinctions between the following terms: *Shang dynasty* is the political dynasty whose life history has been described in detail in historical texts and whose powers were instrumental in changing the archaeological landscape of North China during the second millennium B.C. The *Shang state* is the governmental instrument of the Shang dynasty with a territorial definition largely incorporating the modern provinces of Honan, southern Hopei, western Shantung, and northern Anhwei. The *Shang period* is the period, approximately 1750–1100 B.C., when the Shang dynasty ruled much of North China. The *Shang civilization* is defined here as the civilization in China, with distinctive features, largely coterminous with the Shang dynasty, although its beginning dates should be extended (by about 100 years, to 1850 B.C. as an arbitrary figure) to incorporate the immediately precedent period. The Shang civilization definitely includes the civilization of the Shang dynasty but should not be restricted to it. Outside the Shang state there were other states and perhaps other forms of society with a civilization comparable to the Shang's, and these were all parts of the Shang—or Chinese—civilization. The term *Shang people*, often encountered in history books, will not be used here. The people sharing the Shang civilization are the Chinese people; to call them the Shang people could be misunderstood since all of them did not live under the Shang rule. There could be a Shang people from which the Shang rulers sprang, but it could not be recognized archaeologically.

Major Sites of the Shang

The archaeological sites in Honan, western Shantung, and southern Hopei probably represent settlements within the territory of the Shang state, but the boundary of the state was not fixed and must have varied from time to time. Other sites outside this area will also be included as Shang sites as long as they exhibit the characteristics of the civilization (fig. 99). The best known sites are in the following regions.

1. Yen-shih

The first "king" who founded the Shang dynasty is known as T'ang or Ta I. T'ang overthrew the Hsia dynasty and made Po the capital of his new state in 1766 B.C. The location of Po is uncertain; according to some scholars it is identified with places in easternmost Honan and adjacent western Shantung, but according to others it was near the modern city

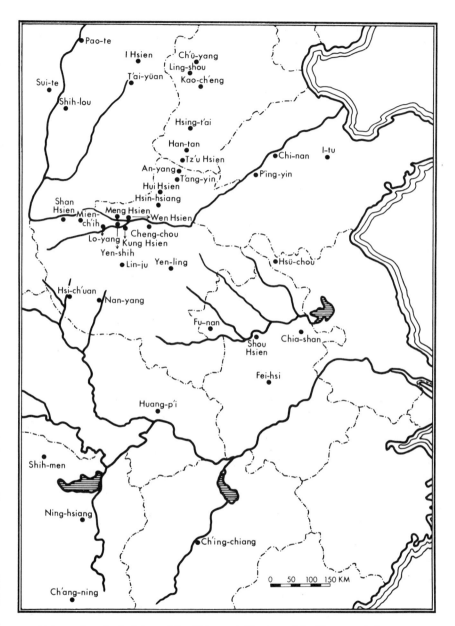

99. Major archaeological sites of the Chinese civilization of the Shang period.

of Yen-shih in northwestern Honan. Shang sites were not found in the Yen-shih area until 1958,[7] but in the last decade and a half new data have accumulated in this region to indicate the existence here of a Shang settlement of major proportions at an early stage within the Shang period.

Yen-shih and the neighboring Lo-yang are the two major cities in the Lo-yang basin of western Honan, surrounded on all sides by low mountain ranges and drained by the rivers I and Lo, tributaries of the Huang Ho to the north. In the area of Yen-shih fourteen archaeological localities are known that date from the Shang period,[8] but only at the sites of Erh-li-t'ou,[9] Kao-yai,[10] and Hui-tsui[11] are brief descriptions of the excavated material available (fig. 100). The site of Kao-yai is of special significance in revealing a Neolithic stratigraphy of Yang-shao–Lungshanoid–Lung-shan sequence that suggests a continuous cultural development paralleling that of the Wang-wan site in neighboring Lo-yang.[12] From the Shang stratum at Kao-yai a bronze knife was discovered.

At the Erh-li-t'ou site a developmental sequence continues from Kao-yai and suggests that out of the Honan Lung-shan culture grew an early phase of the Shang culture that can be referred to as the Erh-li-t'ou phase, which was apparently ancestral to the later Shang phases known at Cheng-chou and An-yang. More than 8,000 square meters of the site were excavated between 1959 and 1964, with impressive results leading to speculation that perhaps the T'ang capital of Po has been uncovered here. Additional data of great importance were obtained in the 1970s, and work at the site is continuing.

Archaeological remains of the Erh-li-t'ou phase occur in an area approximately 1.5 kilometers wide, north to south, and 2.5 kilometers long, east to west, and of higher elevation than the surrounding land. These remains are found in cultural layers, occasionally as much as 3 meters thick, stratigraphically sandwiched between Lung-shan remains, below, and Shang remains of the Erh-li-kang phase, above. The layout of the settlements is not yet clear, but it is known that a large "palace foundation" was located at the center of the site; around the foundation on all sides were found "house floors, storage pits, wells, kilns, bronze-casting

7. *WW* 1959 (12), 41–42.

8. *KK* 1963 (12), 649.

9. *KK* 1959 (11), 598–600; 1961 (2), 81–85; 1965 (5), 215–24; 1974 (4), 234–48; 1975 (5), 302–09.

10. *KK* 1964 (11), 543–47.

11. *WW* 1959 (12), 41–42. *KK* 1961 (2), 99.

12. *KK* 1961 (4), 175–78.

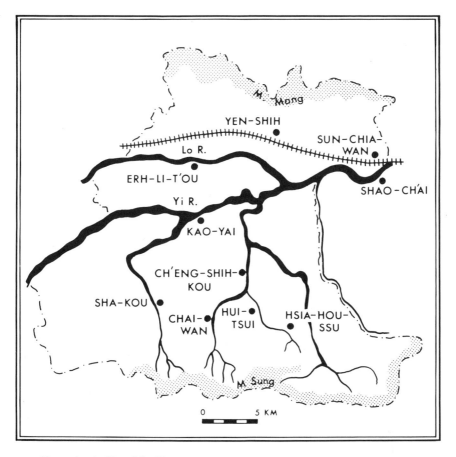

100. Shang sites in Yen-shih, Honan.

clay molds, fragments of crucibles, stone materials, and bone materials.
It looks as if the Erh-li-t'ou site was of a scale of an ancient capital city,
and not just an ordinary natural village."[13] About 500 meters to the east
of the palace foundation another complex of house foundations and
elaborate burials was located in 1972–73.[14] Obviously we are only beginning to understand the settlement pattern of the place.

Excavations of the site now distinguish four components of the Erh-
li-t'ou phase, designated as I, II, III, and IV, from early to late. The division
is basically a stratigraphical one, but ceramic changes provide the most
consistent criteria:

13. *KK* 1974 (4), 234.
14. *KK* 1975 (5), 302.

Pots and urns of I are mostly flat-bottomed, some having slightly protruding rims around the base, whereas those in III are round-based. In I there was 14 percent fine black pottery, which decreased to 9.5 percent in II, and only 3 percent in III. In I, basket impressions predominated, and checker-stamped and fine-cord-impressed patterns also occurred . . . . In II fine-cord impressions predominated, and there were basket impressions, large, checker stampings, various impressed patterns, both positive and negative "string" patterns, and appliquéd designs. Wine vessels such as *ho*, *chüeh*, and *ku* began to occur in II, together with a single four-footed square *ting*. In IV, coarse-cord impressions became the most numerous, and "pockmarks" were seen widely on pottery interiors. Pottery *li* tripods and large-mouthed *tsun* beakers began to appear in significant numbers. There were also some changes in vessel shapes.[15]

Pottery of IV is typologically intermediate between III and the Erh-li-kang phase. *Li* increased in IV relative to urns but were not yet a majority vessel as in Erh-li-kang. The *tsun* beaker of IV has its mouth and shoulder of about equal diameter, unlike the III *tsun* with smaller mouth or the Erh-li-kang *tsun* with larger mouth.[16]

Radiocarbon dates are available for components I and III. The former is 3470 ± 95 or (calibrated) 2080–1690 B.C. The later is 3105 ± 90 or (calibrated) 1590–1300. Component III is in fact the most important period at the Shang site since the bulk of the archaeological finds of particular significance, including the "palace" foundation, most architectural features (houses, pottery kilns, wells, a pebble-paved walk), burials with jades and cinnabar, bronzes and bronze metallurgical remains, and incised signs on pottery, are all dated to this period, whereas remains dated to I and II consist of only a few storage pits, burials, and house floors of a basically Neolithic type. Many Chinese archaeologists are now convinced that the Shang settlement at Erh-li-t'ou was in fact the site of Po, the capital city of King T'ang, the founder of the Shang dynasty. According to the orthodox chronology, the dynasty was founded in 1766 B.C., which would fall within component I at the site according to the radiocarbon date. If the site did not reach the peak of its activities until III, which is carbon-dated to only 1590–1300 B.C., then perhaps the chronology should be shortened. T'ung Chu-ch'en, in fact, regards III as early Shang and I as

15. *KK* 1965 (5), 221–22.
16. *KK* 1974 (4), 246.

101. Erh-li-t'ou palace foundation, west side (view from south). (From *KK* 1974, no. 4, pl. 2.)

Hsia.[17] But since the excavation at the site is only beginning, further speculation at this time would be quite futile.

The palace foundation at the center of the site is the earliest-known such structure in Chinese history (fig. 101, 102). It is in fact an earthen platform—108 meters long east-west and 100 meters north-south, oriented north-south, about 8° to the west—on which various other structures were built to form a compound: a building (30.4 by 11.4 meters) on a smaller platform (36 by 25 meters), in the north; walls with roofed corridors, along the sides; and a large door with nine columns, in the south. The surface of the larger platform has been destroyed, but 80 centimeters of the platform still remained over the original ground level. It was built of *hang-t'u* layers about 4.5 centimeters thick, and three layers of river-worn pebbles lay underneath the *hang-t'u* in the area directly under the smaller, second-level platform. Post holes of various sizes outline rectangular structures with timber-reinforced wattle-and-daub walls and probably sloping roofs supported by separate smaller posts. Rocks were placed at the base of most columns and posts. Pottery water-pipe sections (fig. 103) were found in storage pits north of the platform, probably having to do with some architectural feature of the palace. The word '*palace*'

17. *WW* 1975 (6), 29.

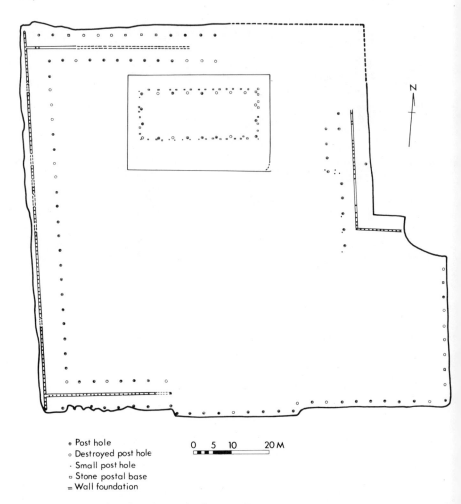

Post hole
Destroyed post hole
Small post hole
Stone postal base
Wall foundation

0   5   10   20 M

102. Erh-li-t'ou palace foundation plan. (From *KK* 1974, no. 4.)

(*kung tien*), incidentally, is used by the excavators advisedly, in light of its architectural features that are identical with those of the palaces of kings and noble people in later historical ages. The Erh-li-t'ou building evidently served people in the highest reaches of the Shang society, although there is no proof to necessarily associate it with the royalty itself.

About 50 meters south of the foundation are three clusters of smaller house floors. Eleven houses have been excavated, rectangular in ground plan (one over 9 meters long east-west), with stamped earth floors and stone post bases. At various parts of the site are three pottery kilns, two

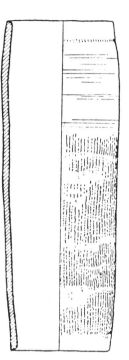

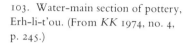

103. Water-main section of pottery, Erh-li-t'ou. (From *KK* 1974, no. 4, p. 245.)

water wells, several dozen human burials, and hundreds of storage pits. Many of the burials have recognizable grave pits and grave goods, and the bodies in them are all stretched, lying supine or on one side. The grave goods included various kinds of pottery (drinking vessels, cooking wares, containers, and serving vessels and dishes), a bronze bell, and ornaments of turquoise, jade, and shell. The burials without grave goods are mostly found in habitation layers and storage pits, and the bodies are in various postures such as squatting, flexed, or stretched. Some were apparently victims of some sort, with hands tied and perhaps buried alive; some had heads or parts of the limbs missing. These burials indicate most vividly a stratified society in which members of a lower class were sometimes victims, perhaps of religious ceremonies.

Large numbers of pottery vessels at the site distinguish the Erh-li-t'ou phase as stylistically intermediate between the Honan Lung-shan culture and the later Shang phases. The paste of the pottery varies from very fine to very coarse and ranges in color from white and light yellow to red, gray, and black. Parts of the same vessel were often made in different ways: handmade, modeled, coiled, and wheel-made. Decorations were mostly impressed with cord, basket, and check designs, and appliquéd and

104. Pottery of the Erh-li-t'ou phase of Shang civilization from the Erh-li-t'ou site, Yen-shih, Honan. (From *KK* 1965, no. 5, pls. 1–4.)

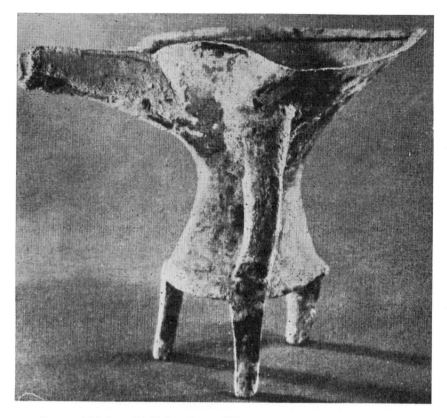

105. Bronze *chüeh* from Erh-li-t'ou. (From *KK* 1975, no. 5, pl. 9.)

incised patterns are also found. Among the incised patterns are stylized animals such as dragons, serpents, fishes, and *t'ao-t'ieh*. In shape the vessels include pots, basins, and various kinds of ring-footed forms and tripods (*ting, li, chia, chüeh, ho, kui,* etc.). On the interior of the rims of some *tsun* vessels are incised signs of various shapes that may have been some kind of script. Of special significance is the appearance of specialized wine-serving vessels (*chüeh, chia, ku, ho, kui,* etc.), mostly found in graves with furnishings, indicating a leisurely social class (fig. 104).

Among the implements found at Erh-li-t'ou are hoes, sickle knives, and flat spades of stone, shell, and bone; arrowheads and spearheads of stone, bone, shell, and bronze; bone harpoons; fishhooks of bone and bronze; and clay sinkers and spindle whorls. Shoulder blades of oxen and sheep with burned marks are found, but no elaborate preparation or inscriptions are in evidence. There are also various art objects and orna-

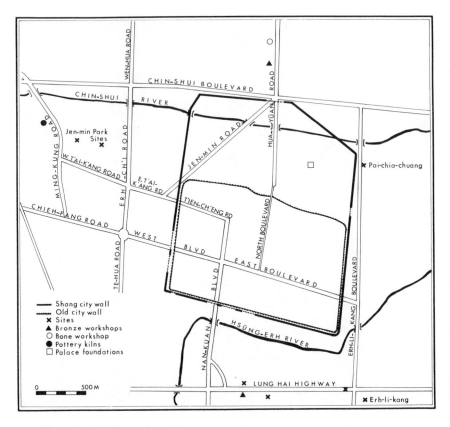

106. Shang sites in Cheng-chou, Honan.

ments of clay, stone, jade, turquoise, bronze, and shell. It is significant
that bronze artifacts are few and simple (knives, a chisel, awls, fishhooks,
a bell, and two *chüeh* wine servers [fig. 105]), but fragments of clay crucibles, bronze slugs, and clay molds indicate a bronze foundry at this site.
Many bone fragments and half-finished bone artifacts tell of a developed
bone industry.

Stratigraphic evidence at the site and at other sites with remains of the
Erh-li-t'ou phase shows that this was earlier than the Erh-li-kang phase
(to be described below); in fact, it is the earliest verifiable phase of a full-
fledged Shang civilization with bronze metallurgy (of possibly a more
primitive state), advanced forms of symbols on pottery, a Shang art,
large *hang-t'u* structures, a highly stratified burial pattern, and specialized
handicrafts. In pottery, the impressed decorations and such forms as *ku*,
chia, *tou*, and deep pots suggest a very close relationship with and probably

direct descent from the Honan Lung-shan culture of the area. The importance of the Yen-shih sites cannot be exaggerated.

Remains of the Erh-li-t'ou phase have been located at the Tung-kan-kou site in neighboring Lo-yang.[18] The distribution of similar remains elsewhere will be described below.

2. Cheng-chou

Discovered in 1950, the Shang remains in the vicinity of Cheng-chou, northern Honan (fig. 106), are still being excavated and studied. Enough has been discovered, however, for An Chin-huai to conclude that the "Shang dynasty remains, except for those found in scattered spots in the western suburbs of Cheng-chou, are mostly concentrated within the ancient city site of Cheng-chou and its vicinity. Shang settlements spread continuously in an area of about 40 square kilometers, from Feng-huang-t'ai in the east, to Hsi-ch'eng-chuang in the west, and from Erh-li-kang in the south to the north of Tzu-ching-shan."[19] Before the Shang, the area of Cheng-chou was occupied by both Yang-shao and Lung-shan farmers, whose remains have been unearthed at Ta-ho-ts'un, Lin-shan-chai, Niu-chai, Ko-ta-wang, and other sites. Immediately subsequent to, and apparently evolving out of, the Honan Lung-shan culture were strata of the earlier stages of the Shang. The Shang history of settlement seems to be divisible, according to available evidence, into five stratigraphic phases,[20] as shown in table 10.

The Shang-chieh phase, thus far represented only by the site at Shang-chieh in the westernmost portions of Cheng-chou, is on the very border line between the Honan Lung-shan culture and the Shang. At the site several floors were found, all but one rectangular in shape. Over thirty storage pits, most with oval-shaped openings, were excavated. Among the artifacts, the polished stone spades and multiperforated knives particularly recall Lung-shan forms. In ceramics, jugs, *tou* fruit stands, bowls, basins, *li* tripods, and wide-mouthed jars are characteristic Shang items, but the flat-bottomed jugs with a high body resemble Lung-shan forms (fig. 107). No metal objects have been unearthed here. Ox and pig bones that had been utilized for oracle purposes were found, but evidence of preparation before heat application is lacking. Five human burials were

18. *KK* 1959 (10), 537–40.

19. An Chin-huai, *WWTKTL* 1957 (8), 17.

20. Cheng Te-k'un, *Shang China*, p. 28. Tsou Heng *KKHP* 1956 (3). Honan Wen-huachü, *Cheng-chou Erh-li-kang*, Peking, Science Press, 1959. *KKTH* 1958 (9), 54–57. *KK* 1960 (6), 11–12, *WW* 1961 (4/5), 79–80. *KKHP* 1973 (1), 65–91.

Table 10

Shang Culture Phases at Cheng-chou, Honan

Jen-min Park Phase	Jen-min Park III
	Ko-ta-wang III
Upper Erh-li-kang Phase	Erh-li-kang II
	Jen-min Park II
	Pai-chia-chuang II
	Nan-kuan-wai III
	Tung-chai III
Lower Erh-li-kang Phase	Erh-li-kang I
	Jen-min Park I
	Pai-chia-chuang I
	˙ Nan-kuan-wai II
	Tung-chai II
	Ko-ta-wang II
Lo-ta-miao Phase	Lo-ta-miao
	Nan-kuan-wai I
	Tung-chai I
	Ko-ta-wang I
Shang-chieh Phase	Shang-chieh

located. Two of them have clearly outlined, rectangular grave pits; one has a "waist-pit" (see p. 357) containing bony remains of animals, and the other has two pieces of cowrie-shaped bone objects. The other three burials were found in habitation layers, and their unpatterned postures suggest that the bodies were thrown without ceremony into amorphous pits.[21]

Four sites so far can be grouped into the second, or Lo-ta-miao, phase. All seem to have been residential villages, but pottery kilns were also uncovered at Ko-ta-wang. Stratigraphy shows conclusively that this phase was chronologically situated between the Lung-shan and the Lower Erh-li-kang phase, although the relative dating between the Lo-ta-miao and the Shang-chieh phases is still typologically based. (At the Nan-kuan-wai site, remains of the lower stratum are seen to be earlier than the Lower Erh-li-kang phase—see below—and seem to have distinctive

21. *KK* 1960 (6), 11–12; 1966 (1), 1–7.

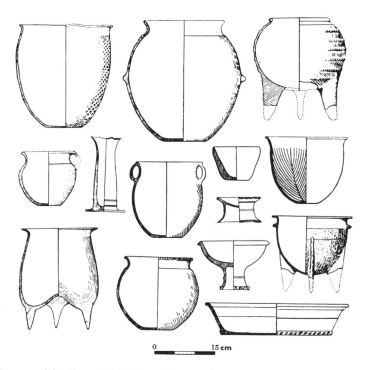

107. Pottery of the Shang-chieh phase, Shang civilization, from the site of Shang-chieh, Cheng-chou, Honan. (From *KK* 1966, no. 1, p. 5.)

features.[22] Its relationship with the Lo-ta-miao phase still has to be worked out). Metal objects are lacking in the cultural remains of this phase. In the cultural inventory, typical Shang traits increased, but there were still many Lung-shan features such as the great number of shell artifacts, bone hairpins with awl-shaped heads, pocket-shaped storage pits (which had become rare, however), and the generally unprepared oracle bones. Some diagnostic ceramic features are the round-bottomed and cord-marked jugs with high and nearly vertical bodies, vessels with large mouth openings, small basins and jars, and jugs with checker impressions. This stage is again known only imperfectly, but there is no question of its existence.[23]

Cheng-chou of the Lower Erh-li-kang phase seems to have stepped

22. *KKHP* 1973 (1), 91.

23. *KKHP* 1957 (1), 56–58. Hsia Nai, *China Reconstructs* 6 (1957), 20. *KKTH* 1955 (3), 18; 1958 (2), 6–8; 1958 (9), 54–57. *WWTKTL* 1957 (10), 48–51. *KKHP* 1958 (3), 41–62.

suddenly into increased activity and expanded the size of its settlement. Sites of this phase contain dwelling houses, burials, workships, and a city wall.[24] It has been suggested that during this stage dwelling quarters and burials of the aristocrats were inside the city wall, and that the city itself was the center of living and administration, but that the commoners' residences, the cemetery, craft shops, and farming fields were outside the wall. According to literary records, the ancient Shang kings changed their capital sites several times before finally settling at Yin, the site of the present city of An-yang. One of these earlier capitals, four capitals before An-yang, is said to have been the city of Ao, or Hsiao, probably in the vicinity of the present town of Ying-tse, about 15 kilometers northwest of Cheng-chou. Intensive investigations were undertaken during the 1950s in the neighborhood of Ying-tse, but they failed to turn up any Shang dynasty remains. In Cheng-chou, however, a full-fledged city site has been located, dating to the Lower Erh-li-kang phase, which as will be shown, is considerably earlier than the dynastic phase of An-yang stratigraphy. Some scholars have suggested, therefore, that Cheng-chou may have been the site of the ancient capital of Ao.[25]

The Shang city wall was roughly rectangular in shape, with a total perimeter of 7,195 meters and an enclosed area of 3.2 square kilometers. The maximum height of the surviving wall is 9.1 meters and the maximum width at the base is 36 meters. The wall was built in successive compressed layers, each of which has an average thickness of 8 to 10 centimeters. On the surface of each layer are clear depressions made by the pestles used for compressing, and the soil making up the wall is hard and compact (fig. 108). The inner structure shows that it was built at two different periods, both within the time of the Shang, possibly corresponding to the Lower and the Upper Erh-li-kang phases. The wall was apparently used and mended during subsequent historic periods, but a new wall was built during the Han dynasty around a smaller enclosure.[26] The Shang wall shows without doubt that the city of Cheng-chou during the Shang dynasty was of considerable importance and was constructed only with major effort. An Chin-huai[27] estimates the original wall to have been

24. Honan Wenhuachü, *Cheng-chou Erh-li-kang. WW* 1961 (4/5), 73–80. *KKHP* 1957 (1), 53–73.

25. An Chin-huai, *WW* 1961 (4/5), 73. But see Liu Ch'i-i, *WW* 1961 (10), 39–40; An Chih-min, *KK* 1961 (8), 448–50.

26. *WW* 1961 (4/5), 73–74. Hsia Nai, *China Reconstructs* 6 (1957) 18–19. *KKHP* 1957 (1), 58–59.

27. *WW* 1961 (4/5), 77.

108. *Hang-t'u* wall of Shang city at Cheng-chou (*upper*) and layers with pits (*lower*). (Photo by author, 1975.)

10 meters in average height, with an average width of 20 meters, which—multiplied by the total length of 7,195—required 1,439,000 cubic meters of compressed soil or (by a ratio of 1 to 2) 2,878,000 cubic meters of loose soil. Experiments carried out by archaeologists show that an average worker produces per hour 0.03 cubic meters of earth by means of a bronze pick, or 0.02 cubic meters by means of a stone hoe. An concludes that to build the whole city wall of Cheng-chou, including earth-digging, transporting, and compressing, required no less than 18 years, with 10,000 workers working 330 days a year. This impressive figure, even though roughly calculated, indicates that Cheng-chou of the Shang dynasty was no ordinary town.

The enclosure apparenly marks the center of administration and ceremony. Since it overlaps the present city site of Cheng-chou and has therefore been only spottily excavated, the layout of this site is not completely understood. But enough has been found to provide some ground for speculation. In the northeastern portion of the Shang city an area of concentrated clusters of hang-t'u floors, about 300 meters (east-west) by 150 meters (north-south), was located in 1973–74, and large floors and large post-holes, "palatial" in proportions, were excavated. In 1974, among the floors a section of a ditch was found, into which about a hundred human skulls were dumped, mostly sawed off across the eyebrow and ear portions, presumably raw materials for bone manufacture (fig. 109).[28] At the northwestern corner of the city site a large house floor has been identified with a compressed, burned-hard, lime-plastered floor, with post holes 14 to 35 centimeters deep, 19 to 34 centimeters across. Such large buildings have not been found outside the city area. North of this building a platform of compressed earth was found. It is of an incomplete length 25.5 meters east to west, and an incomplete width 8.8 meters north to south. This reminds us of the earth altar at the center of Hsiao-t'un in the An-yang area. From a test trench in the northern part of the enclosure, south of the Tzu-ching-shan, archaeologists found (in addition to potsherds) bone artifacts, stone implements, and scores of jade hairpins of excellent workmanship. Only two or three hairpins of this kind have ever been found in the vast area outside the enclosure.[29]

Outside the city enclosure there were many residential sites and handicraft workshops, which can be attributed chronologically to the Lower and Upper Erh-li-kang stages. Two bronze foundry sites have been found

28. WW 1974 (9), 1–2.
29. WW 1961 (4/5), 78–79.

109. Human skulls found in ditch in Shang palace in Cheng-chou. (Photo by author, 1975. Originally published in *WW* 1974, no. 9, p. 2.)

thus far; one, north of Tzu-ching-shan, is approximately 100 meters north of the city wall, and the other about 500 meters south of the wall at the point of the present South Gate (Nan-kuan). The workshop to the south covers an area of 1,050 square meters and has yielded crucibles of pottery, clay molds for both vessels and weapons, bronzes, debris of melted ocher, charcoal, and other stone and pottery remains. They are assigned to the Lower Erh-li-kang phase.[30] The bronze foundry remains to the north are significantly connected with one of four stamped-earth house foundations: on the floor of the house is a layer of fine-grained and hardened, copper-containing, light-green earth with some dozen conical depressions, each containing a layer of melted copper; outside the house is another area of verdigris 0.1 to 0.15 of a meter thick; a heap of clay molds and relics of crucibles was placed beside a door connecting two rooms inside the house; a big lump of copper ocher was found 10 meters west of the house. This site belonged to the Upper Erh-li-kang phase.[31] The last find is especially interesting, indicating that the bronzesmiths of the Shang dynasty lived in stamped-earth houses and thus seem to have

30. *KKHP* 1957 (1), 56. Hsia Nai, *China Reconstructs* 6 (1957), 20.
31. *WWTKTL* 1957 (6), 73–74.

enjoyed a higher privilege than the common folk, who had to be satisfied with semisubterranean houses.

Approximately 50 meters north of the Tzu-ching-shan bronze foundry was a bone workshop. It is a good-sized pit, possibly of the Lower Erh-li-kang phase, containing over a thousand pieces of sawed and polished, finished bone artifacts (arrowheads and hairpins), half-finished bone pieces, bone fragments used as raw materials, rejected pieces of bone, and eleven grinding stones. The bones are from human beings (about 50 percent), cattle, deer, and pigs.[32]

A pottery kiln site of the Erh-li-kang phases has been located on the west side of the Ming-kung Road, about 1,200 meters west of the Shang city wall. In an area of 1,250 square meters, archaeologists have located fourteen kilns, near which are storage pits containing unfired and misfired pottery, pottery-making paddles and anvils, and stamps. Among the kilns are stamped-earth house foundations, which may have been the houses of the potters.[33] Since all the pottery found at this site is of fine clay texture, there were presumably other kiln quarters for the manu-facture of sand-tempered culinary wares, hard pottery, glazed pottery, and/or white pottery.

At Erh-li-kang, many large, coarse-textured pottery jars were found, on the inner surface of which is a layer of white substance, which may indicate that they were containers for a kind of alcoholic beverage. The possibility that this was a wine-making industrial quarter has been sug-gested.[34]

Besides those listed above, a large quantity of other kinds of remains has been unearthed both inside and outside the city enclosure. House foundations have been located at Pai-chia-chuang.[35] Scattered water ditches have been found at Erh-li-kang, Pai-chia-chuang, Nan-kuan-wai, and the region on the west side of the Ming-kung-lu.[36] These ditches average 1.5 to 2.5 meters in width and 1.5 meters in depth. Those near Pai-chia-chuang have rows of small round depressions along both sides of the bottom. More than two hundred storage pits have been located throughout the area. Besides cultural debris and occasional pig and human

32. *KKHP* 1957 (1), 58. Hsia Nai, *China Reconstructs* 6 (1957), 21.

33. *KKHP* 1957 (1), 57. Hsia Nai, *China Reconstructs* 6 (1957), 19. *WWTKTL* 1955 (9), 64–66; 1956 (10), 50–51.

34. *WW* 1961 (4/5), 78. For a suggested origin of wine making in the Neolithic period of North China, see Li Yang-sung, *KK* 1962 (1), 41–44.

35. *WWTKTL* 1956 (4), 3–5. *KKHP* 1957 (1), 57.

36. *KKHP* 1957 (1), 58.

110. Bronze ceremonial vessels excavated at Shang city in Cheng-chou. (From *Exhibition of archaeological finds in the People's Republic of China*, Washington, D.C., 1975.)

III. Square bronze *ting* found in Cheng-chou in 1975. (From *WW* 1975, no. 6, pl. 1.)

skeletons, some of the pits contain large numbers of dog or cattle burials and apparently had some ceremonial significance.[37] Burials have been located at Erh-li-kang, Tzu-ching-shan, Pai-chia-chuang, and Jen-min Park and are particularly numerous at the last two sites.[38] Some of the burials at Pai-chia-chuang (Upper Erh-li-kang phase) are described as large graves, with grave furnishings and (in two cases) human sacrifices; the others are small graves, which are numerous at the sites above named, and contain little or no grave furnishing. At Tu-ling, 300 meters to the west of the Shang city, a burial of two large (86.4 kilograms and 64.25 kilograms in weight) *ting* quadrupods was found in 1974 (fig. 111).[39]

These remains indicate that during the Erh-li-kang phases the city at Cheng-chou was a major political and ceremonial center. The population was apparently very large, in view of the extent of cultural distribution, the nature of settlement, and the depth of deposits (1 meter average, with a maximum depth of 3 meters). The artifacts found here include not

37. *WWTKTL* 1957 (8), 19. *KKHP* 1957 (1), 58.
38. *WWTKTL* 1957 (8), 19. *KKHP* 1957 (1), 70–71.
39. *WW* 1975 (6), 64–68.

only stone, bone, shell, and bronze implements and vessels, as well as utilitarian pottery, but also bronze ceremonial vessels (fig. 110, 111), glazed pottery, hard pottery, white pottery, jade and ivory artifacts, and three pieces of incribed oracle bone. The dating of the inscribed bones is uncertain, but it has been suggested that they were intrusive from later strata and do not antedate the An-yang sequence of oracle records. The city enclosure was apparently occupied by a ruling aristocracy, while the craftsmen and farmers inhabited mainly the suburbs surrounding the city site. It is indeed highly probable that the traditional Shang capital of Ao was located here.

The Shang city life apparently continued into the final, Jen-min Park phase of the Cheng-chou sequence, for large graves of this phase have been located in the park, a short distance west of the Shang city wall.[40] Aside from the findings here, however, remains of the Jen-min Park phase have thus far been found only in the upper stratum of the Ko-ta-wang site and in Ming-kung-lu.[41] Whether this results from incomplete exploration of the area or indicates diminishing activities during this final phase of the Shang dynasty, when the political center of the aristocracy had shifted away from the city of Ao, is a problem awaiting solution.

Some characteristic features of the Lower and Upper Erh-li-kang and the Jen-min Park phases are listed in table 11[42] (fig. 112).

Table 11

Characteristic Features of Erh-li-kang and Jen-min Park Phases of the Shang Culture at Cheng-chou

Lower Erh-li-kang Phase: The pottery has relatively thin walls, fine tempering materials, fine cord marks, and is generally well made; the characteristic ceramic forms are *li* tripods with elongated bodies, rounded rims curving outward and downward, high feet with long conical ends; *hsien* tripods with fine tempering materials and breast-shaped feet; *chia* tripods with out-turned rims; *kuan* jugs with fine cord marks and thin bodies; *tsun* jars with squat bodies and short collars; *ting* tripods with basin- or bowl-like bodies; *tou* fruit stands with shallow dishlike bodies. Oracle bones are similar to the Lo-ta-miao forms, and bone hairpins are of the conical-head type.

40. *KKTH* 1955 (3), 16–19. *WWTKTL* 1954 (6), 32–37. *KKHP* 1957 (1), 70–71.

41. *KKHP* 1958 (3), 41–62. *KK* 1965 (10), 500–06.

42. Honan Wenhuachü, *Cheng-chou Erh-li-kang. KKHP* 1956 (3), 77–103; 1957 (1), 53–73.

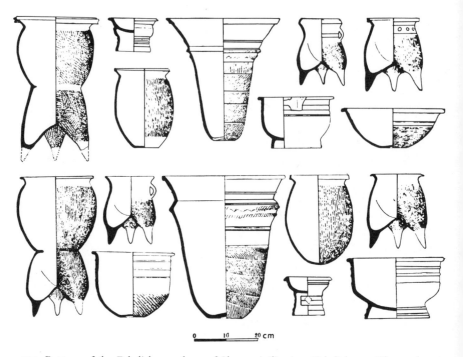

112. Pottery of the Erh-li-kang phase of Shang civilization, Erh-li-kang, Cheng-chou, Honan. (From *Hsin Chung-kuo ti k'ao-ku shou-huo*, Peking, Wen Wu Press, 1962, p. 45.)

Upper Erh-li-kang Phase: Pottery of this phase is similar to the previous phase, but the tempering materials are generally coarser, the bodies thicker, and the cord marks made of thicker strands. Many of the Lower Erh-li-kang ceramic forms continued into this phase, but some of the forms that were initiated during the previous phase now became prevalent, such as the *li* tripods with angular and up-turned rims, *hsien* tripods with coarser cord marks and conical feet, *chia* tripods with in-turned rims, *ting* tripods imitating bronze forms, *tou* with bottoms considerably higher than indicated by the external contours (false-bodied *tou*), and *tsun* jars with elongated bodies and long collars. Oracle bones and bone hairpins are similar to the previous phase.

Jen-min Park Phase: The ceramic style has changed markedly, and the pottery is largely of coarse tempering material, thick bodies, large-stranded cord marks, and crude workmanship. Few Erh-li-kang phase forms remain, while squat and short-footed *li* tripods, *tou* with low pedestals, *p'o*, *yü*, and *yu* vessels appeared. There also appeared bone hairpins with carved heads. Most of the oracle bones are turtleshells, and the preparation was elaborate. The large graves containing human victims and rich furnishings which appeared in the Upper Erh-li-kang phase continued here.

113. Huan River north of Hsiao-t'un village. (Photo by author, 1975.)

3. An-yang

From King T'ang to King Ti Hsin, seven Shang capitals were recorded in the literature—Po, Hsiao (Ao), Hsiang, Keng (Hsing), P'i, Yen, and Yin.[43] The locations of the first six, although generally assumed to be in northern Honan and its immediate neighborhood, are uncertain; the possibility that Po has been uncovered near Yen-shih and that the Shang settlements near Cheng-chou are the remains of Ao has been discussed above. There is no question that the ruins of the last Shang capital, seat of power for twelve kings from P'an Keng to Ti Hsin, for an alleged 273 years until the fall of the dynasty, are situated on both banks of the Huan River (fig. 113) northwest of the modern city of An-yang, northern Honan. They have been known to historians for ages past and were referred to as Yin Hsü, the Ruins of Yin, by Ssu-ma Ch'ien in Shih chi (chap. "Hsiang Yü pen chi").[44] But it was not until 1899, when the remains of

43. For a recent review of the problem relating to the various Shang capitals, see Ch'ü Wan-li, Bulletin, College of Arts, National Taiwan University, no. 14 (1965), 105–09.

44. Miyazaki Ichisada—in Tōyōshi kenkyū 28 (1970), 265–82, and 29 (1970), 275–80— contends that the present archaeological site northwest of An-yang was in fact the mortuary site of the Shang kings, whose administrative center was located far to the southeast.

inscribed oracle bones were known to have been found in this area, that the Ruins of Yin were brought to the attention of scholars.[45] From 1928 to 1937, fifteen seasons of scientific excavation were undertaken in this region by the National Research Institute of History and Philology.[46] Since 1950, small-scale but intensive diggings have taken place continuously.[47] Shang remains are now known in the An-yang region from no fewer than seventeen sites, covering an area of approximately 24 square kilometers (fig. 114).[48]

The importance of the An-yang excavations in the history of archaeology in China cannot be exaggerated.[49] The scale of the work, time, money, and man power devoted to the excavations, and the scientific precision of the digging are still surpassed only rarely in China. And it was the An-yang excavation that settled, once and for all, the controversial problem of the existence of this dynasty, previously accredited only by legends. It was also the first site given a date in the earliest segment of Chinese written history, and it thus ties written history to the prehistoric Neolithic cultures. However, work was interrupted by the Sino-Japanese War leaving many sites in the An-yang group only partially excavated, and results have yet to be completely published. The center of Shang studies has tended to shift from An-yang to Cheng-chou, where a longer

45. For a history of the archaeology of the area, see Tung Tso-pin, *Chia-ku-hsüeh wu-shih nien*, Taipei, I-wen, 1955; Kaizuka Shigeki, *Kodai Yin tegaku*, Tokyo, Misuzu Shobo, 1957.

46. It is impossible to provide an exhaustive bibliography for the An-yang material here, but much of the original published material can be found in the following series of publications: *An-yang fa-chüeh pao-kao*, 4 vols. 1929–1933; *T'ien-yeh k'ao-ku pao-kao* 1936; *Chung-kuo k'ao-ku hsüeh-pao*, vols. 2–4 (1938–50); *Archaeologia Sinica*, vol. 2 (Hsiao-t'un) and vol. 3 (Hou-chia-chuang); and the *Bulletin of the Institute of History and Philology*, Academia Sinica, various numbers. Because of national and international events since 1937, much of the An-yang material excavated before the war remains unpublished. See also recent syntheses of the remains at An-yang by Li Chi (*An-yang*, Seattle, University of Washington Press, 1976) and S. Umehara (*Yin Hsü*, Tokyo, Asahi Shinbunsha, 1964).

47. *KKHP* 5 (1951); 1955 (1); 1958 (3). *WWTKTL* 1958 (12). *KK* 1960 (6); 1961 (2); 1964 (8); 1972 (2); 1972 (3); 1972 (4); 1972 (5); 1975 (1).

48. Following historians, archaeologists often refer to the period of Shang when An-yang (Yin) was the capital as the "Yin period" and to the remains found here as Yin remains. For historians, it seems reasonable to make such a subdivision, but the remains at An-yang were deposited during a period that was probably longer than the 273 years when An-yang was the capital site. I shall use the word Shang throughout for the entire period and use archaeological phases to designate chronological segments, of which Yin is one.

49. See Li Chi, "Importance of the An-yang discoveries in prefacing known Chinese history with a new chapter," *Annals Acad. Sinica* 2 (1955), 91–102.

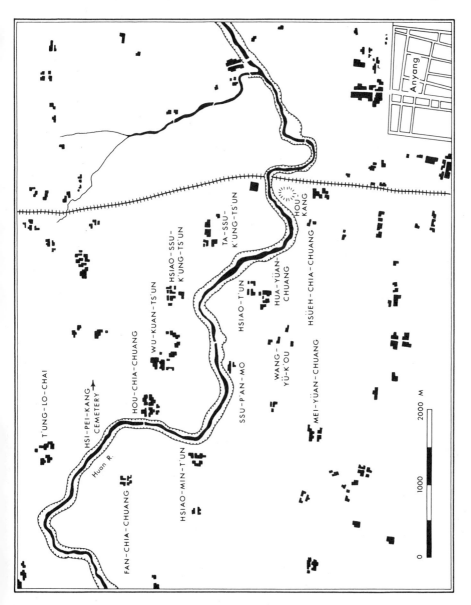

114. Shang sites at An-yang, Honan.

sequence has been uncovered and a series of preliminary and final reports has been made available. An-yang's fundamental importance, however, can never be doubted. Among other things, the oracle bone inscriptions from this area furnish much indispensable information concerning Shang culture and society that other Shang sites may never be able to match.

115. Wheat field near Hsiao-t'un village today, under which Shang palaces were excavated. Tree-lines near horizon indicate course of Huan River. (Photo by author, 1975.)

Similar to the settlement pattern of the Shang sites at Cheng-chou, the Shang sites of the An-yang region were apparently articulated into a complex network of specialized parts.

The Yin palaces south of the Huan Ho (near the modern village of Hsiao-t'ü) constituted the center of the Yin Hsü, surrounded on all sides by habitation clusters, workshops, and tombs. North of the Huan Ho, with Wu-kuan-ts'un and the area north of Hou-chia-chuang [Hsi-pei-kang] as a center, there was the area of the royal cemetery, burials of noblemen, and many thousand sacrificial burials, an area also encircled by Yin settlements and burials. Conditions of cultural deposits indicate that the neighborhood of Hsiao-t'un was the region of the greatest abundance, and on its outskirts were settlements of varying sizes. Remains at these settlements do not occur in a continuous area, but the distribution of the settlements was fairly dense. Distances between settlements became greater as groups moved away from the center. Palaces and the royal cemetery were apparently under the direct control of the ruling class, and the settlements surrounding Hsiao-t'un were probably habitations of [noblemen and the common people]. The latter classes were buried near where they lived, resulting in the intermixture of living and burial remains, although it is possible that [the noblemen] had their own cemeteries also. In the neighborhoods of the settlements were many workshops. For instance, large bronze foundry sites have been found at Miao-p'u-pei-ti and Hsiao-min-t'un, and bone workshops were identified at Pei-hsin-chuang and Ta-ssu-k'ung-ts'un. Even in the area of the palaces, many clay molds and bone materials were found. These may suggest that handicrafts were carried out under the direct control of the [upper classes], and that workshops often occurred in habitation areas [of the settlements] but were not necessarily concentrated in [special industrial] quarters.[50]

All this goes to show that the entire An-yang group formed a tightly organized unit, and the presence of the Royal House in this group is symbolized by the administrative and ceremonial center near Hsiao-t'un and the "royal cemetery" at Hsi-pei-kang.

The excavated part of the site at Hsiao-t'un (figs. 115, 116) is divided into three sections—A, B, and C. Section A, the northernmost, consists of fifteen parallel, rectangular houses built on stamped-earth foundations. Section B, in the middle, includes twenty-one large houses, rectangular or square, built on stamped-earth foundations, and accompanied by a number of burials. These houses are arranged in three rows on a north-south axis, the central row consisting of three large houses and five gates. Section A and section B are separated by a square stamped-earth foundation (of pure loess), which is thought to be a ceremonial altar. Section C, at the southwestern corner of the site, consists of seventeen stamped-earth foundations, arranged according to a preconceived plan and again accompanied by burials. Under the foundations in section B is a complicated system of underground water ditches. The entire area of the Hsiao-t'un settlement includes about 10,000 square meters. According to the interpretation of Shih Chang-ju, section A was probably the dwelling area of the settlement, section B the royal temples, and section C a ceremonial quarter. It is noteworthy, however, that these three sections seem to have been constructed during different time intervals, in the order A, B, and C.[51] In view of the large scale of the construction, the elaborate planning of the houses, the extensive sacrifice of humans in the construction of the temples and the ceremonial altar, the innumerable in-

50. An Chih-min et al., KK 1961 (2), 65.

51. Shih Chang-ju, Yin-hsü chien-chu i-ts'un, Taipei, Academia Sinica, 1959.

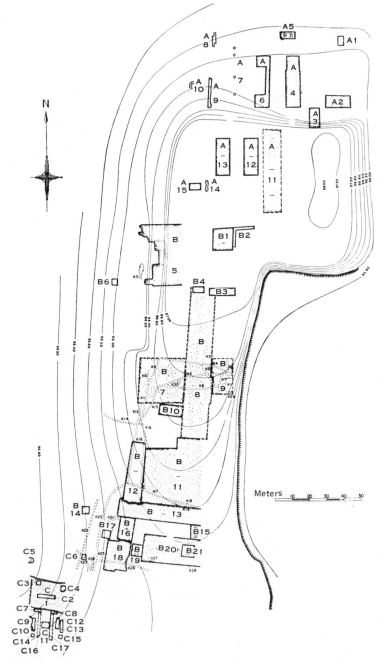

116. Shang house floors at the site of Hsiao-t'un, An-yang. (After Shih Chang-ju, *Yin Hsü chien-chu i-ts'un*, Taipei, 1959, fig. 4.)

117. Side view of *hang-t'u* layers of a Shang house floor at Hsiao-t'un, An-yang, Honan. (After Shih Chang-ju, *Yin Hsü chien-chu i-ts'un*, Taipei, 1959, pl. 11.)

scribed oracle bones found at the site, and the mode of construction in stamped earth (fig. 117) in contrast to the ordinary semisubterranean dwellings, it appears reasonable to assume that this settlement was the center of the Royal House of the Yin dynasty. These palaces and temples, as Tung Tso-pin describes them,

> were all above-ground houses with stamped-earth foundations and stone-pillar supporters [fig. 118]. Although they were constructed of wattle and daub, these structures looked glorious and solemn enough [fig. 119]. Near these foundations are often semisubterranean pit houses, about 4 meters in diameter and the same in depth. These were presumably the service area of the Royal House subordinates. Inside the pit houses are round or rectangular bins several meters deep, possibly places of storage.[52]

These service areas included bronze foundries, stone and bone workshops, and pottery kilns. But some of these pit houses must also have

52. Tung Tso-pin, *Ta-lu tsa-chih* 5 (1950), 12.

118. *Hang-t'u* floor with stone post bases of a Shang house at Hsiao-t'un, An-yang. (From Shih Chang-ju, *Yin Hsü chien-chu i-ts'un*, Taipei, 1959, pl. 9.)

served as domiciles. It is apparent that this Hsiao-t'un site served the same function as the city enclosure of Cheng-chou, but remains of a city wall have not been found. Nevertheless, it must be remembered that the Hsiao-t'un site was not completely excavated and that the excavators presumably did not look specifically for a city wall. Since the city walls appeared at Cheng-chou before the Hsiao-t'un phase and continued into later historical periods, I would not be surprised if more intensive future investigations find that this site also had a walled enclosure.

Hsi-pei-kang, near Hou-chia-chuang and including the area north of Wu-kuan-ts'un, is best known for its burial complex, which includes 11 large graves (the royal cemetery) and 1,222 small graves, although dwellings and workshops have also been found here (fig. 120). The eleven large tombs (fig. 121) are grouped into a western cluster of seven and an eastern cluster of four, happily coinciding in number with the eleven kings from P'an Keng to Ti I who ruled from An-yang. (The last king at An-yang, Ti Hsin, was supposedly burned to death when the capital fell to the Chou invaders.) Although it cannot yet be fully established that these were the kings' graves, we know that they were constructed on a large scale, with elaborate ceremonial procedures, and their furnishings repre-

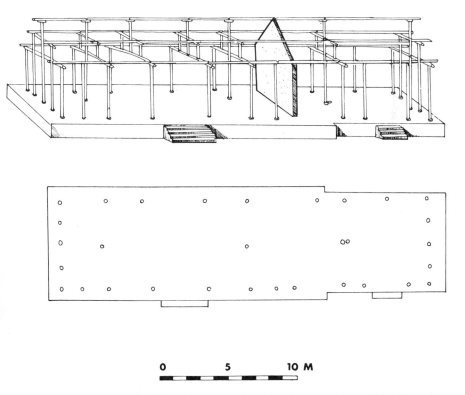

0   5   10 M

119. Reconstruction of a Shang house at Hsiao-t'un, An-yang. (From Shih Chang-ju, *Annals of Academia Sinica* 1, 1954, p. 276.)

120. Cotton field at Hsi-pei-kang today. (Photo by author, 1975.)

sent the highest achievements of Shang technology and art.[53] According
to the estimates of Li Chi, the earth-digging alone required at least seven
thousand working days for each of the large graves of Hsi-pei-kang.[54]
All the graves are square or oblong, oriented north-south, with long ramps
on two (north and south) or four sides. The best known of the tombs,
no. 1001, is shaped like a cross in ground plan and forms a pit about 10
meters deep, with slightly sloping walls (fig. 122). The mouth of the pit
is 19 meters long, north to south, and 14 meters wide. A ramp leads from
the ground to the bottom of the grave pit on each of the four sides; the

53. A full report of the Hsi-pei-kang excavations is being prepared by Kao Ch'ü-hsün
of the Academia Sinica in Taipei, and six of the large tombs have been fully described in
Archaeologia Sinica 3 (Hou-chia-chuang), nos. 2–8 (1962–76). A large tomb excavated in
1950 is described in Kuo Pao-chün, *KKHP* 5 (1951). Preliminary and general descriptions
of the royal cemetery as a whole are available in Kao Ch'ü-hsün, *Bull. Dept. Archaeol.
Anthropol.*, Natl. Taiwan Univ., no. 13/14 (1959), 1–9; Paul Pelliot, "The Royal Tombs
of An-yang," in *Independence, Convergence, and Borrowing in Institutions, Thought, and Art*,
Cambridge, Harvard Univ. Press, 1937; and Tung Tso-pin, *Ta-lu tsa-chih* 1 (1950),
15–18.
54. Li Chi's preface to Shih Chang-ju, *Yin-hsü chien-chu i-ts'un*, p. iii.

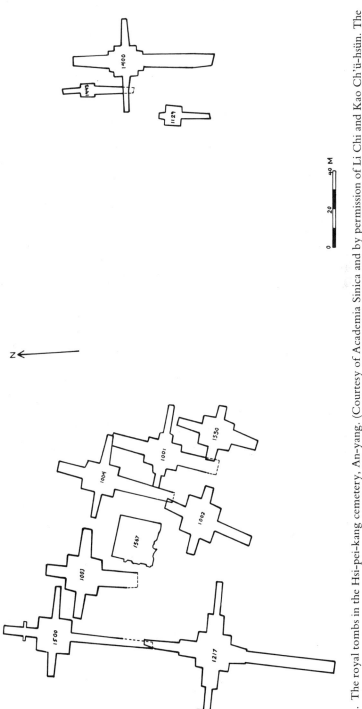

121. The royal tombs in the Hsi-pei-kang cemetery, An-yang. (Courtesy of Academia Sinica and by permission of Li Chi and Kao Ch'ü-hsün. The fourth tomb in the eastern sector, excavated in 1950, is not included.)

122. Grave pit of royal tomb no. 1001 at Hsi-pei-kang, An-yang. (From Liang Ssu-yung and Kao Ch'ü-hsün, *Hsi-pei-kang 1001 ta mu*, Nankang, Institute of History and Philology, Academia Sinica, 1962.)

southern ramp, the longest, measures about 30 meters. Within the pit a wooden chamber was built; the chief coffin of the tomb was probably placed in the center. Many sacrificial burials occurred in various spots within the pit but were concentrated within the chamber itself and in the southern ramp. Some of the sacrifices were provided with coffins and small grave pits, but most were without either coffin or pit, and many were separate burials of heads and trunks (fig. 123). The tomb was abundantly furnished with stone, jade, shell, bone, antler, tooth, bronze, and pottery artifacts, including many that are the best examples of Shang art (fig. 124).[55] Li Chi has listed the following as the most significant contributions of the Hsi-pei-kang excavations to Shang archaeology: (1) importance of pisé (rammed-earth) construction in Shang architecture; (2) Shang burial institutions and the organization of manpower as indicated by the construction of single tombs; (3) the reality and magnitude of sacrificial burials; (4) the high level of achievement of the Shang material

55. Liang Ssu-yung and Kao Ch'ü-hsün, *Archaeologia Sinica* 3 (Hou-chia-chuang), no. 2 (tomb 1001), 1962.

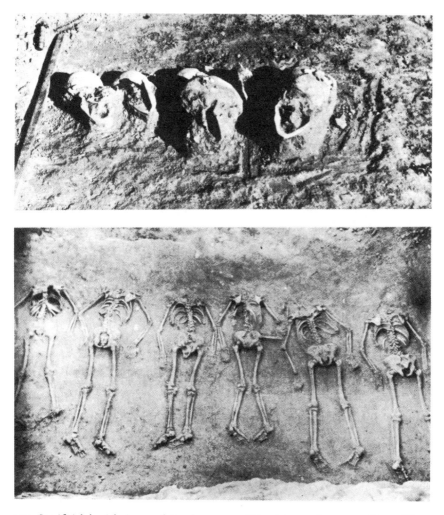

123. Sacrificial burials in royal tomb 1001 at Hsi-pei-kang, An-yang. (From Liang Ssu-yung and Kao Ch'ü-hsün, *Hsi-pei-kang 1001 ta mu*, Nankang, Institute of History and Philology, Academia Sinica, 1962.)

culture and the extent of leisure of the ruling class; (5) the discovery of stone sculptures and the sophistication of the decorative art; and (6) the representative products of bronze industry.[56] To these we must add a point of chronological significance. If these eleven tombs were those of the kings and if these tombs can be chronologically seriated among them-selves and together with Hsiao-t'un's habitation remains,[57] then there

56. Li Chi, preface to *Yin-hsü chien-chu i-ts'un*.
57. Li Chi, *Bull. Inst. Hist. Philol.*, Acad. Sinica, no. 29 (1958).

124. Stone sculptures from royal tomb 1001 at Hsi-pei-kang, An-yang. (From Liang Ssu-yung and Kao Ch'ü-hsün, *Hsi-pei-kang 1001 ta mu*, Nankang, Institute of History and Philology, Academia Sinica, 1962.)

is a complete sequence of artifacts and arts available at An-yang that covers the entire range of 273 years when An-yang was the royal capital. Therefore, the Hsi-pei-kang tombs represent a solid chronological segment of the Shang civilization and their sequence provides a basis for the study of cultural change within the segment.

Furthermore, if the Hsi-pei-kang tombs began with P'an Keng, then at the site of Hsiao-t'un the habitation floors and storage pits that are considered on typological grounds to be earlier than tomb 1001 must belong to an earlier period than P'an Keng, the so-called pre-dynastic period of Hsiao-t'un.[58] In other words, in An-yang there is the segment of 273 years that can be referred to as the Yin or Hsi-pei-kang phase with which Hsiao-t'un II was contemporaneous. Hsiao-t'un I, therefore, must predate the Yin phase. The details of these Hsiao-t'un phases cannot be known until all the excavated materials become available.[59] But excavations at other sites in the An-yang area are revealing. At a spot south of Hsiao-t'un Village (Hsiao-t'un-nan-ti), a 430 square meter area was opened in 1973, bringing to light many important artifacts, including 4,821 pieces of inscribed oracle bones. The artifacts are grouped into two phases, the earlier Shang (or pre-dynastic) phase and the later Yin phase. The Yin phase is further divided into Early, Middle, and Late periods, covering the entire dynasty span of some 250 to 300 years.[60] At Ta-ssu-k'ung-ts'un, remains of habitation floors and burials (fig. 125) were found, and at least two stages of occupation were distinguished.[61] A piece of oracle bone dated to King Wu Ting's reign, or thereabouts, was discoverrd from the earliest stratum, suggesting that the entire Ta-ssu-k'ung-ts'un sequence can be placed within the Hsi-pei-kang phase. At Mei-yüan-chuang, two cultural strata were recognized, the upper layer similar to the Hsiao-t'un phases but the lower layer similar to Cheng-chou's Lower Erh-li-kang.[62] Thus, at An-yang the following stratigraphical sequence has been suggested: Mei-yüan-chuang 1, the earliest; Hsiao-t'un 1 and Hsiao-t'un-nan-ti Shang phase, possibly of the same phase or slightly later; and Hsi-pei-kang, contemporary with Hsiao-t'un II, Hsiao-t'un-nan-

58. Li Chi, *The Beginnings of Chinese Civilization*, Univ. of Washington Press, 1957.

59. V. C. Kane—in *Ars Orientalis* 10 (1975), 93–110—has attempted a chronological arrangement of the An-yang materials on the basis of an evolutionary sequence of the styles of the bronzes.

60. *KK* 1975 (1), 27–46. Cf. Tsou Heng, "Shih lun Yin Hsü wen-hua fen ch'i," *Peking University jen-wen hsüeh pao* 1964 (4), 37–58; 1964 (5), 63–90.

61. *KKHP* 9 (1955), 25–90. *KK* 1961 (2), 65–66; 1964 (8), 380–84.

62. An Chih-min et al., *KK* 1961 (2), 65.

125. A chariot burial at Ta-ssu-k'ung-ts'un, An-yang. (From *KK* 1972, no. 4.)

ti (Early, Middle, and Late Yin), Mei-yüan-chuan II, and Ta-ssu-k'ung-ts'un I and II (table 12.).

Little is known concerning Shang sites in An-yang other than the above. But information is available at the sites of Hou-chia-chuang-nan-ti, Hou-kang, Hsüeh-chia-chuang, and Kao-lou-chuang.[63] Remains of house floors, burials of varying scales and degrees of richness, bronze, pottery, and bone workshops, and storage pits have been reported from these sites, suggestive of the nature of the settlements in the An-yang group other than Hsiao-t'un and Hsi-pei-kang. All these sites are dated within the Hsi-pei-kang range.

The Yin settlement at An-yang may be summarized as follows: prior to the time of P'an Keng (1384 B.C., according to T. P. Tung's chronology), who made An-yang his capital, the Shang had already occupied the An-yang area. At any rate, at Hsiao-t'un,[64] Hsüeh-chia-chuang[65] as well

63. Tung Tso-pin, *TYKKPK* 1 (1936), 91–166. Shih Chang-ju, *Liu t'ung pieh lu* 1 (1945), 1–26. *KKHP* 1960 (1). Chao P'ei-hsin, *KK* 1960 (6). Chou Tao and Liu Tung-ya, *KK* 1963 (4), 213–16, 220. *KK* 1972 (3), 14–25; 1972 (5), 8–19. Chao Hsia-kuang, *WWTKTL* 1958 (12), 31. Liu Tung-ya, *KKTH* 1958 (8), 23–26.

64. Li Chi, *The Beginnings of Chinese Civilization*, p. 45. Tsou Heng, *KKHP* 1956 (3), 77–103.

65. Liu Tung-ya, *KKTH* 1958 (8), 23–26.

Table 12

An-yang Stratigraphy and Chronology

B.C.	Mei-yüan-chuang	Hsiao-t'un	Hsiao-t'un-nan-ti	Ta-ssu-k'ung-ts'un	Hsi-pei-kang
—1200—	II	II Dynastic	Late Yin	II	Eleven royal tombs
—1300—			Middle Yin		
	I		Early Yin	I	
14th cent. P'an Keng Removal		I Pre-dynastic	Shang		

as Mei-yüan-chuang remains were found that are similar to the Erh-li-kang phases of Cheng-chou. These are mostly of a domiciliary nature, but a bronze industry had already been established here.[66] Whether the other settlements had been occupied cannot be established at present because of the lack of stratigraphic evidence. From the time of P'an Keng (so says the traditional history, which is supported by oracle bone records), the An-yang area was the capital of the Royal House of the Shang dynasty. Most of the settlements of the An-yang group were probably occupied by the people of Yin and by nobility connected with the Royal House. Royal palaces and ceremonial centers were constructed at Hsiao-t'un and Hou-chia-chuang-nan-ti, and the cemeteries of the royal family were constructed at Hsi-pei-kang (and Wu-kuan-ts'un) and Hou-kang. The individual settlements were probably more or less self-sufficient in terms of basic subsistence and handicrafts, but as far as the control of the economy, political administration, and religious and ceremonial affairs is concerned, the entire An-yang settlement group appears to have formed a single unit.

Other Shang Sites

Yen-shih, Cheng-chou, and An-yang are centers of Shang archaeology, and each has yielded finds of unique significance in terms of not only Shang archaeology but also Shang history. But archaeological sites where Shang remains have been recognized and which have been assigned a Shang date are now numerous, and they are distributed in a large part of China proper—from central Shansi and Hopei in the north to northern Hunan and Kiangsi in the south, or even beyond (fig. 99). None of the sites have been excavated to the degree seen at Yen-shih, Cheng-chou, and An-yang, but quite likely other sites will be shown by future investigations to be as important or in some way even more so. A brief summary of available information is given below in each of the major areas of distribution.

1. *Northwest Honan and southern Shansi.* This is the section of the Huang Ho valley from the big bend (at the Shensi-Honan border) to the vicinity of Cheng-chou, including the Lo River basin and some of the source rivers (such as the River Ju) of the Huai Ho. Shang sites in this area appear to possess the greatest time depth, from the earliest levels of the Erh-li-t'ou phase to the end of Shang, and at several places these levels exhibit a continuity from the Honan Lung-shan culture. Both Yen-shih and Cheng-

66. Shih Chang-ju, *Yin-hsü chien-chu i-ts'un.*

chou are in this area. Other sites include Ch'i-li-p'u in Shan Hsien,[67] Lu-ssu in Mien-ch'ih,[68] Chien-hsi in Meng Hsien,[69] Hsiao-nan-chang in Wen Hsien,[70] a series of sites in the neighborhood of Lo-yang,[71] Shao-ch'ai in Kung Hsien,[72] and Mei-shan in Lin-ju.[73]

Remains characterized as the Erh-li-t'ou phase occur in Shan Hsien, Yen-shih, Lo-yang, Kung Hsien, and Cheng-chou,[74] and they have further been identified in the lower Fen Ho valley in southern Shansi, in the regions of Ho-chin, Chi-shan, Hsin-chiang, and Hou-ma.[75] This area—southern Shansi and northwesternmost Honan—is traditionally believed to be the territory of the Hsia dynasty. The relationship of the earliest segment of the Shang civilization—the Erh-li-t'ou phase—with the legendary Hsia dynasty is now an important issue in Chinese archaeology.[76]

2. *Central Shansi and Shensi.* Shang-style bronze vessels and weapons are said to have been found in Shih-lou, in western central Shansi in the Huang Ho valley, before the Liberation. Assemblages of these finds, mostly chance discoveries, have now been reported all along the Yellow River valley as far north as Pao-tê, and important finds are now available from several localities (Erh-lang-p'o,[77] T'ao-hua-chuang,[78] Hou-lan-chia-kou,[79] and I-tieh[80]) in Shih-lou, Pao-tê,[81] and also Sui-tê in Shensi, across the river from Pao-tê.[82] Isolated finds of Shang-like remains have also been identified in the Fen Ho valley of central Shansi, such as T'ai-yuan[83] and I Hsien.[84] The cultural context of these Shang-style bronzes

67. *KKHP* 1960 (1), 25–47.
68. *KK* 1964 (9), 435–40.
69. *KK* 1961 (1), 33–39.
70. *WW* 1975 (2), 88–91.
71. *KKHP* 9 (1955), 91–116; 1956 (1), 11–28. *KKTH* 1955 (5), 26. *KK* 1959 (10), 537–40.
72. *WW* 1975 (6), 29.
73. *KK* 1975 (5), 285–94.
74. *WW* 1975 (6), 29.
75. *WW* 1972 (4), 2. *KK* 1962 (9), 459–64.
76. *WW* 1972 (4), 2; 1972 (10), 2–3; 1975 (6), 29.
77. *WWTKTL* 1958 (1), 36.
78. *WW* 1960 (7).
79. *WW* 1962 (4/5), 34–35.
80. *KK* 1972 (4), 29–30. *WW* 1974 (2), 69.
81. *WW* 1972 (4), 62–64.
82. *WW* 1975 (2), 82–87.
83. *WW* 1972 (4), 2.
84. *Ibid.,* pp. 67–68.

is almost entirely unknown, and we have absolutely no idea how they came about in this area.

3. *Northern Honan and southern Hopei.* This is the plains area of the lower Huang Ho valley with An-yang as its center, extending northward along the eastern side of the T'ai-hang mountains. Known Shang sites in this area include Lu-wang-fen in Hsin-hsiang,[85] several sites in Hui Hsien,[86] Ch'ao-ko in T'ang-yin,[87] Chieh-tuan-ying in Tz'u Hsien,[88] Chien-kou-ts'un in Han-tan,[89] Yin-kuo-ts'un, Ts'ao-yen-chuang and several other sites in Hsing-t'ai,[90] T'ai-hsi-ts'un in Kao-ch'eng,[91] Pei-chai-ts'un in Ling-shou,[92] and Feng-chia-an in Ch'ü-yang.[93] An assemblage of bronze vessels found in Liaoning, much further to the north, has also been described as Yin or at least from the "border period between Yin and Chou."[94]

Of these, the Hui Hsien, Hsing-t'ai, and Kao-ch'eng sites are of especial importance in light of the extensive nature of the distribution of remains over wide areas, suggesting the possibility of large urban complexes of the kind that we see in Cheng-chou and An-yang. The Kao-ch'eng finds have received additional attention because of a bronze halberd with iron blade, pottery with incised signs, remains of lacquerware (which has also been identified in An-yang[95]), and peach and apricot pits believed to have been collected for medicinal purposes.

4. *Shantung.* According to survey data up to 1972, Shang remains are said to have been reported from the entire province except for the district of Tê-chou in northernmost Shantung.[96] The best known of the Shang sites, however, are two that were discovered many years ago and where

85. *KKHP* 1960 (1), 51–60.

86. Kuo Pao-chün, Hsia Nai, et al., *Hui Hsien fa-chüeh pao-kao*, Peking, Science Press, 1956. *KKTH* 1957 (2), 32–35. *KK* 1965 (5), 235.

87. *WWTKTL* 1957 (5), 86.

88. *KK* 1974 (6), 356–72.

89. *KK* 1961 (4), 197–202.

90. *WWTKTL* 1956 (9), 70; 1956 (12), 53–54; 1957 (3), 61–63; 1958 (10), 29–31. *KKHP* 1958 (4), 43–50. *KK* 1959 (2), 108–09. *WW* 1960 (4), 42–45, 60.

91. *KK* 1973 (1), 25–29; 1973 (5), 266–71. *WW* 1974 (8), 42–49, 50–53, 54–55; 1975 (3), 57–59.

92. *KK* 1966 (2), 107–08.

93. *KKTH* 1955 (1), 39–44.

94. *KK* 1973 (4), 225–26, 257; 1974 (6), 364–72; 1975 (5), 274–79.

95. *KK* 1961 (2), 75.

96. *WW* 1972 (5), 3; see also *KK* 1961 (2), 86–93.

new investigations have revealed important data. These are Ta-hsin-chuang, in the eastern suburb of Chi-nan,[97] and Su-fu-t'un, northeast of I-tu.[98] The Su-fu-t'un cemetery was excavated in 1965–66 and four Shang tombs were found. Tomb no. 1, the only tomb described in publications thus far, closely resembles the royal tombs at Hsi-pei-kang: The tomb pit is rectangular, 8.25 meters deep, about 15 meters north-south and 10.7 meters east-west, oriented north-south 3° to the west. It has four ramps, a cross-shaped wooden chamber surrounded by reconstituted "second-level platforms" and with two successively excavated pits at the bottom. The entire grave was heavily furnished with bronzes (including two large axes with *t'ao-t'ieh* faces), pottery, jade objects, stone ornaments, and 3,790 cowrie shells. (The grave was plundered before, and many whole bronze vessels have presumably been removed.) In addition, skeletons of forty-eight humans and six dogs, all sacrificial victims, were found in various parts of the grave—in the pits at bottom, on the second-level platform, and at the base of the southern ramp. This is the largest Shang tomb yet outside An-yang (fig. 126).

5. *Huai Ho plain in Honan, northern Kiangsu, and Anhwei.* The Huai Ho plain in eastern Honan, southwesternmost Shantung, and northern Kiangsu and Anhwei is potentially an important area for Shang archaeology because most historians have placed Po—T'ang's capital—in the environs of Shang-ch'iu in easternmost Honan, and the ancient inhabitants in this area are known to be among the staunchest allies of the Shang at the time of their rebellion against the Chou, after Wu Wang's death. But despite the fact that the Huai Ho area was an early target of Shang archaeologists,[99] Shang sites here are not yet very many. Shang remains have been reported at Fu-kou in Yen-ling, central Honan;[100] several sites in the Hsü-chou area of northern Kiangsu, especially Kao-huang-miao[101] and Ch'iu-wan;[102] sites in Fu-nan,[103] Shou Hsien,[104] and

97. F. S. Drake, *China Journal* 31 (1939), 77–80; 33 (1940), 8–10. *WW* 1959 (11), 8–9; 1972 (5), 3. *KK* 1959 (4), 185–87; 1973 (5), 272–75.

98. *Chung-kuo k'ao-ku hsüeh-pao* 2 (1947), 167–77. *WW* 1972 (8), 17–30.

99. *Chung-kuo k'ao-ku hsüeh-pao* 2 (1947), 83–120, 179–250.

100. *KK* 1965 (2), 94–96.

101. *KKHP* 1958 (4), 7–17. *KK* 1960 (3), 25–29.

102. *KK* 1973 (2), 71–79; 1973 (5), 296–98. *WW* 1973 (12), 55–58.

103. *WW* 1959 (1), inside cover; 1972 (11), 64–66. *The Exhibition of Archaeological Finds of the People's Republic of China*, Peking, 1974, p. 18.

104. *Chung-kuo k'ao-ku hsüeh-pao* 2 (1947), 250. Li Chi, *BIHP* 23 (1951), 612.

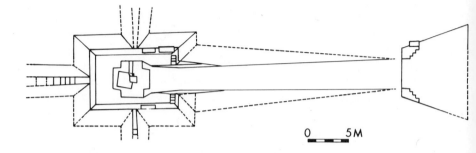

0   5M

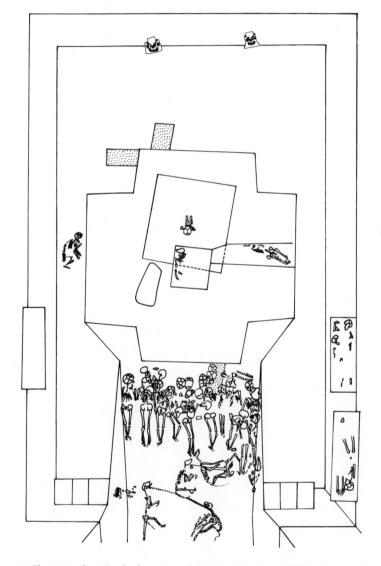

126. Shang tomb at Su-fu-t'un, I-tu, Shantung. (Based on *WW* 1972, no. 8.)

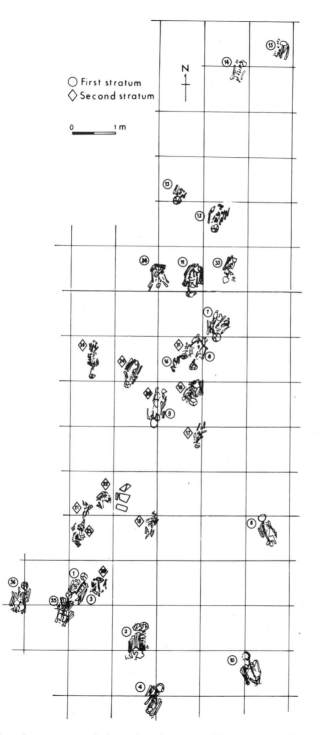

Chia-shan[105] in northern Anhwei, and even in Fei-hsi in central Anhwei at the Yangtze drainage.[106]

The materials in this area have not been described in archaeological publications in great detail, and our knowledge about the Shang civilization in the Huai Ho plain is extremely limited. But the Fu-nan bronzes are of such a style (a combination of *early*-looking "trumpet-mouthed" *tsun*, the nonseparation of the decorative motif from a *lei-wen* background—supposedly an *early* feature—and the high relief decor commonly regarded as a *late* feature) and have such idiosyncratic casting techniques that some observers are convinced that they were the products of a local metallurgical industry.[107] At the Ch'iu-wan site, a burial area (fig. 127) was excavated in 1965 in which twenty skeletons, two isolated skulls, and twelve dog skeletons were found in an area of some 75 square meters, at the center of which was a cluster of four large rocks erected together on the ground (fig. 128). All the human skeletons were prone, with flexed lower limbs, most with arms bound behind the back. Clearly this is a scene of human sacrificial rituals, and several commentators have used textual evidence to show that the find represents a Shê (Earth deity) rite involving human sacrifice, well-known among the Eastern I people of ancient China.[108] Hsü-chou is located in the area of the Shang state of P'eng, and the Ch'iu-wan find clearly points to a local civilization which is comparable to the Shang of Honan to the extent of its social stratification and in which there was undoubtedly a metallurgical industry capable of producing vessels with the area's own decorative style.

6. *The Han-shui and middle Yangtze valleys.* Originating in southern Shensi, the Han-shui connects the northern province of Honan with the middle Yangtze basin in eastern Hupei, and throughout Chinese history it has been an important avenue of communication between the north and the south. At its mouth it opens into the central Chinese lacustrine basin, now drained by the middle Yangtze and the two largest lakes of China, Tung-t'ing in the west and Po-yang in the east; in ancient times most of this region was covered by Great Lake Yün-meng. In recent years Shang remains and Shang sites have been unearthed in this whole area in significant numbers, extending the distribution of the Shang civilization in a southern direction to a hitherto unexpected extent.

To begin, in southwestern Honan in the upper Han-shui valleys, Shang

105. *WW* 1965 (7), 23–25.
106. *The Exhibition of Archaeological Finds*, p. 18.
107. V. C. Kane, *Archives of Asian Art* 28 (1974/75), 80. *WW* 1972 (11), 64–66.
108. *KK* 1973 (5), 296–98. *WW* 1973 (12), 55–58.

128. Burial area of Shang date at Ch'iu-wan, Hsü-chou, Kiangsu. (From *KK* 1973, no. 2.)

sites are known at Shih-li-p'u in Nan-yang[109] and at Hsia-wang-kang in Hsi-ch'uan.[110] The Shang remains at Hsia-wang-kang have been compared with the early Shang remains of the Erh-li-t'ou phase, the first such remains identified outside the northwestern Honan–southern Shansi area. Further down the Han-shui, bronze vessels and weapons of Shang types were discovered in at least three localities in Huang-p'i, near the confluence of the Han-shui and Yangtze in central Hupei: the most important of these were five tombs and two storage pits opened in 1963 at P'an-lung-ch'eng, and a town wall and palace foundations excavated at the same locality in 1974.[111] The walled town site at P'an-lung-ch'eng, according to Hsia Nai's description,

> had a large palace consisting of a hall of four bays girded by a continuous corridor. On the four sides outside the corridor were 43 large post holes originally holding wooden posts for supporting eaves. The layout is very similar to Shang palaces described in ancient records, and to the early Shang palace unearthed at Erlitou.
>
> A tomb found outside the city contained an inner and outer wooden coffin which, though rotted, still retained their shape. The exterior

109. *KK* 1959 (7), 370.

110. *WW* 1972 (10), 13–14.

111. *KKTH* 1958 (1), 56–58; 1958 (9), 72–73. *KK* 1964 (8), 420–21. Hsia Nai in *China Reconstructs* 24 (1975), no. 11, 40–41.

of the outer coffin is engraved with exquisite animal-mask and thunder-cloud designs. They are China's earliest extant wood carvings. More than 60 funerary objects of bronze, jade and pottery were also exhumed. Two bronze *yüeh* (axes) bore dragon and cicada designs. All these indicate that the person buried in the tomb was a high-ranking slave-owner. In the same tomb were found skeletons of three immolated slaves.[112]

The tombs brought to light earlier (in 1963) were rectangular pit-graves with *erh-ts'eng-t'ai* and *yao-k'eng*, and the bronze artifacts included ceremonial vessels (*ting, li, chia, chüeh, ku*) and weapons (spearheads, *ko* halberds, knives, axes, and arrowheads) decorated with animal-mask and dragon patterns. Many of these vessels, as well as a bronze *chüeh* tripod from the Yang-chia-wan site and three bronze *ko* halberds, are similar to the same types of the Erh-li-kang phase.

Further south, on the eastern and southern shores of the Great Lake, pottery with Shang forms and decorative patterns has been reported from a prehistoric site at Tsao-shih, in Shih-men, northern Hunan,[113] and Shang-type bronze vessels have been discovered in Ning-hsiang and Ch'ang-ning in the Hsiang River valley of central and southern Hunan.[114] Although there is no question that these bronze vessels are of Shang type, some of them exhibit strong local features, and we are not at all clear about the circumstances under which the finds were made. The same may be said of the reported Shang finds upstream along the Yangtze to Szechwan. The late Shang and early Western Chou civilizations appear to have had some contact with the Szechwan Neolithic, as indicated by the remains of *li* tripods of gray and cord-marked ware, and sherds of *tou* of a Bronze Age style[115] found in the Yangtze Valley in the extremely eastern end of Szechwan, where it adjoins Hupei. Some authors maintain the Shang culture reached as far as the Min River valley, as shown by such sites as Shui-kuan-yin in Hsin-fan Hsien.[116] This view is perhaps given support by the bronze *ko* halberds and ceremonial vessels with animal-mask decorations discovered at Chu-wa-chieh in P'eng Hsien.[117]

112. Hsia Nai, *op. cit.*, p. 41.

113. *KK* 1962 (3), 144–46.

114. *KK* 1963 (12), 646–48. *WW* 1960 (3), 75. *The Exhibition of Archaeological Finds*, p. 18.

115. *KK* 1959 (8), 399–400.

116. *Ibid.*, p. 401.

117. *WW* 1961 (11), 30.

The nature of the Shang influence in this area remains to be clarified, however, by additional excavated evidence.

Further down the Yangtze, an extremely important Shang site was discovered in 1973 near the village of Wu-ch'eng in Ch'ing-chiang Hsien, northwestern Kiangsi.[118] Here, "a house floor, 48 storage pits, 13 burials, 1 pottery kiln, and more than five hundred artifacts including bronzes, stones, pottery, primitive porcelain, jades, and bronze-casting stone molds" were found. Pottery contains Erh-li-kang types, and includes glazed varieties that can be described as porcelain.[119] There are only three bronze objects: a knife, a *ko* halberd, and an ax. But the existence of stone molds—at least thirty-five larger fragments—unquestionably indicates a local bronze foundary for the production of implements and weapons. Also noteworthy are the written characters incised (and occasionally impressed) on pottery and some of the stone molds. Thirty-nine characters have been identified, and they occur singly or in groups of twelve, seven, five, and four. According to T'ang Lan,[120] a few of the characters are identical with Shang characters at An-yang, but most (especially earliest ones) are unrecognizable. At this site remains are said to scatter in an area of 4 square kilometers, but so far only a little over 1,100 square meters have been excavated. Future finds will undoubtedly disclose a civilization of complexity and distinctiveness that may be broadly comparable with the Shang but may also exhibit heretofore completely unknown dimensions.

Time and Space Definitions of the Shang Civilization and the Problem of its Origins

Shang history according to written records can be subdivided into four segments: legendary ancestors, from Ti K'u to Wang Hai; early ancestors, from Shang Chia to Shih Kui—the first six ancestors in the ritual genealogy recorded in the oracle scripts; the dynastic period from T'ang to Yang Chia, when the Shang were rulers of China but before they moved to An-yang; and the dynastic period from P'an Keng to Ti Hsin, when An-yang was the royal capital. Three dates are therefore of crucial significance in the chronology of the Shang: the accession of T'ang, the removal of the Shang capital to An-yang under P'an Keng, and the fall of the Shang dynasty under Ti Hsin. Exact dates for these

118. *WW* 1975 (7), 51–71.
119. *Ibid.*, pp. 77–82.
120. *Ibid.*, pp. 72–76.

events are still being debated among historians, but no conclusions have been reached.[121] However, in this volume I shall adopt some round figures: 1750 B.C. for T'ang's accession, 1400 B.C. for P'ang Keng's move to An-yang, and 1100 B.C. for the fall of the Shang dynasty. For our purposes here, where broad chronological segments are adequate for studies of trends of cultural development and of cultural relationships, it is not necessary to take sides in this technical debate.

Before the Shang sites at Cheng-chou were excavated, the An-yang culture was the sole representative of the Shang civilization, and our understanding of it was accordingly restricted and conditioned.[122] Since those excavations, however, the Cheng-chou sequence, by virtue of its long and seemingly complete stratigraphy, has been used by archaeologists as the yardstick by which other Shang sites are measured. Tsou Heng, for instance, has classified the cultural remains at Hsiao-t'un of the An-yang group into three stages: pre–Hang-t'u, Hang-t'u, and post–Hang-t'u. The Hang-t'u phase of An-yang, according to Tsou, can be synchronized with the Jen-min Park phase of Cheng-chou, whereas the pre–Hang-t'u was earlier than the Jen-min Park phase but later than the Upper Erh-li-kang phase, and the post–Hang-t'u phase was later than the Jen-min Park phase of Cheng-chou.[123] The earliest phase at Hsing-t'ai, according to T'ang Yün-ming, was probably earlier than the Erh-li-kang phases, but the later phases correspond to them.[124] For other sites, the terms Erh-li-kang and Hsiao-t'un are used freely for similar chronological and classificatory purposes. Carrying this scheme to the extreme, Cheng Te-k'un boldly attempts to synchronize all of the Shang sites, which he divides into five groups: Proto Shang, Early Shang, Middle Shang, Late Shang, and Post Shang.[125]

It is true that cultural remains similar to this or that phase of the Cheng-chou sequence are found elsewhere, and this may have chronological

121. For a survey of some pertinent arguments, see K. C. Chang, "Relative chronologies of China to the end of Chou," in Robert Ehrich (ed.), *Chronologies in Old World Archaeology*, Univ. of Chicago Press, 1965. Two new articles on the subject matter are Chou Fa-kao, *Journal of the Institute of Chinese Studies of the Chinese University of Hong Kong* 4 (1971), no. 1, 173–205; and Ho Ping-ti, *Journal of the Chinese University of Hong Kong* 1 (1973), 17–35.

122. E.g., H. G. Creel, *The Birth of China*, London & New York, Reynal & Hitchcock, 1937; Li Chi, *The Beginnings of Chinese Civilization*, Seattle, Univ. of Washington Press, 1957.

123. Tsou Heng, *KKHP* 1956 (3), 77–103.

124. See Cheng Te-k'un, *Shang China*, p. 27.

125. *Ibid.*, p. 37.

significance. Until a number of sites other than Cheng-chou and An-yang are excavated intensively, however, it would be impossible for us to claim that the fivefold subdivision of the Shang sequence at Cheng-chou, as it is known at a certain period in the history of Shang archaeology, is universally valid. For the time being, I believe that we are better off to confine discussion of the chronological development of the Shang culture to the few sites whose stratigraphy is reasonably well established.

The archaeological remains uncovered at the various Shang sites described above were plainly left during a long period that can be subdivided into a number of segments or phases according to the change of artifacts and styles. Stratigraphic evidence at Yen-shih, Cheng-chou, and An-yang, the three most important Shang sites both in the amount and quality of remains and in terms of the chronological information they provide, appears to warrant the tentative and broad correlation of the various phases indicated in table 13. In other words, speaking of the total area of distribution of Shang sites in North China, three phases of Shang civilization are definitely indicated: *Erh-li-t'ou*, earliest; *Erh-li-kang*; and *Yin*, the phase of Yin Hsü occupation by the Royal House. Further subdivisions can certainly be made. For instance, several components occurred at the site of Erh-li-t'ou, at least Shang-chieh and Lo-ta-miao phases can be distinguished in Cheng-chou before Erh-li-kang, and the Yin phase contained at least the minor subphases at Ta-ssu-k'ung-ts'un. These problems, however, require further study on the basis of additional information that is not yet adequate. For the time being, we can only speak of the following broad stages of the development of the Shang civilization.

The Erh-li-t'ou Phase

As of now, Shang sites classified with the Erh-li-t'ou and the Shang-chieh and Lo-ta-miao phases have been known in Shan, Lo-ning, I-yang, Lo-yang, Sung, I-ch'uan, Yen-shih, Teng-feng, Lin-ju, Kung, and Cheng-chou, all in northwestern Honan south of the Yellow River in an area drained by the Huang Ho and its tributaries I and Lo and the neighboring River Ju, an upper tributary of the Huai Ho.[126] Sites with similar remains have been reported in southern Shansi in the lower Fen Ho valley, and also from the Hsia-wang-kang site in Hsi-ch'uan, southwestern Honan. *Shih chi* states that the removal of P'an Keng to An-yang involved the crossing of the Yellow River, and it is likely that prior to P'an Keng all Shang capitals were south of the river, although historians by no means

126. *KK* 1965 (5), 223.

Table 13

Tentative Correlation of Shang Culture Phases at Major Sites

PHASES	YEN–SHIH LO–YANG	CHENG–CHOU	AN–YANG
ca. 1100 YIN	LATE SHANG SITES LO–YANG	JEN–MIN PARK	HSI–PEI–KANG HSIAO–T'UN II
— ca. 1400 —		UPPER ERH–LI–KANG	
ERH–LI–KANG	ERH–LI–KANG PHASE LO–YANG	LOWER ERH–LI–KANG	HSIAO–T'UN I MEI–YÜAN–CHUANG I
— ca. 1650 —	TUNG–KAN–KOU	LO–TA–MIAO	
ERH–LI–T'OU ca. 1850	ERH–LI–T'OU	SHANG–CHIEH	

agree on this point. If T'ang indeed rose at the present site of Erh-li-t'ou, it appears probable that this earliest Shang phase represents the period immediately before and after the founding of the dynasty, a possibility that suggests a tentative date of 1850–1650 B.C. for the Erh-li-t'ou phase of the Shang civilization. As discussed above, the only available radiocarbon dates do not fit in too well with this estimation, and we must take an extremely cautious and open attitude toward the dating of this phase.

The important characteristics of the Erh-li-t'ou phase are: large *hang-t'u* floors of palatial buildings; division of human burials into those with grave pits and grave goods and those without them, some of the latter seeming to be sacrificial victims; the manufacture of bronze implements (knife, awl, fishhook, and bell) and ritual vessels; the incision of complex symbols on pottery; divination by the shoulder blades of oxen and sheep; the occurrence in graves of pottery wine utensils; the large numbers of stone, bone, and shell hoes, spades, and sickles; remains of domestic pigs, oxen, sheep, and horses; and bone shops and bronze foundries. Characteristic also is a distinctive group of pottery vessels and decorative patterns that was absent both in the Lung-shan culture before the Erh-li-t'ou phase and in the Erh-li-kang phase after it (shallow dishes with three legs; flat-bottomed basins; characteristic types of *ting, tou, ho, kui, ku, chüeh, chiao*; "filters"; steamers; deep pots with vertical walls; *ting* with single handles; square *ting* with four legs; *chia* with handles; large check marks; a variety of impressed designs; developed appliquéd designs; dotted patterns on the vessel interiors). The forms and modes of some pottery vessels (especially those of wine vessels such as the lids and handles of *ho*) give the impression that metal types were being imitated—the occurrence of bronze vessels in this phase is now an archaeological reality. All these features point to a highly stratified, complex society and a culture with advanced agriculture and handicrafts, perhaps some rudimentary form of writing, and definitely a bronze industry at perhaps a lower level of achievement than that of the An-yang bronzes.

Available data of the Erh-li-t'ou phase reveal a stage of cultural development intermediate to the Honan Lung-shan culture and the more advanced Shang civilization of later phases. This stage certainly has great bearing on the problem of origin and the process of growth of the Shang culture.

> The Erh-li-t'ou type of culture apparently grew out of the foundation of the Honan Lung-shan culture, having absorbed elements of the Shantung Lung-shan culture. Some pottery types of this phase were common in both the Honan and the Shantung Lung-shan cultures, such as the flat-bottomed basins and *kui* tripods. Some types find antecedents in the Shantung Lung-shan culture, such as the shallow dishes with three legs and the *kui* tripods. Other types and decorations grew out of Honan Lung-shan proto-forms, such as the "filter," *ku*, deep pots with vertical walls, *weng*, *tou*, *chia*, and the basket, check, and cord marks.[127]

The problem of Shang origins in the light of recent work at the Erh-li-t'ou phase sites is discussed below.

The Erh-li-kang Phase

By the time of the Erh-li-kang phase, Shang sites had already attained their maximal distribution, north as well as south of the Yellow River. Significantly, the pottery at the Yangtze Valley sites in Huang-p'i and Ch'ing-chiang is regarded as being of Erh-li-kang types, and may suggest that Shang civilization accomplished its geographic spread during the Erh-li-kang period. If we use the Lower Erh-li-kang phase of Cheng-chou as the type site of this Shang phase and use the beginning of the capital status of An-yang to mark its upper end, then the Erh-li-kang phase of the Shang civilization can be placed between 1650 and 1400 B.C. If the site at Cheng-chou was indeed the capital city of Ao, the supposed date Ao was made a capital (1557 B.C.) falls within this time span.

Aside from new types and modes of pottery there is relatively little in

127. *Ibid.*

the Erh-li-kang phase that is significantly different from the previous one. *Hang-t'u* constructions and bronze foundries existed, the latter producing primarily small and simple implements and ornaments but also some ceremonial vessels, some of considerable size. No writing other than pottery scripts has been found, and divination was carried out by means of shoulder blades of oxen and sheep. The pattern of settlement clearly indicates an urban network decisively different from the Neolithic village pattern. Since the Erh-li-t'ou phase is not well known it is difficult to assess how much progress it had achieved, but there is no question that it was still at a more primitive level, compared with the Yin phase, as far as cultural complexity and artistic achievement are concerned.

The Yin Phase

This is the phase represented by the Hsi-pei-kang royal tombs, dated to the period of 1400 to 1100 B.C. The center of the state had shifted north of the Yellow River and there was a notable decline of cultural intensity at Cheng-chou, but the distribution of remains of this phase appears to be the same as in the previous phase. This is the phase of the oracle scripts (whose remains are virtually confined to An-yang), divination by turtle shells, advanced bronze metallurgy, and artistic climax.

Placed into the above chronological framework, Shang sites show an early concentration in northwestern Honan (and adjacent regions) but a rapid spread throughout their larger area of distribution by the Erh-li-kang phase. This time-space arrangement of Shang sites is of significance for the origin of the Shang civilization. We have seen not only that the earliest (Erh-li-t'ou phase) Shang sites are confined to the Yellow River valley of northwestern Honan, but also that in this area there is demonstrable continuity and growth process from the Honan Lung-shan culture to the Shang civilization. The Lung-shan period, as described in chapter 4, already saw the beginning of a movement toward social ranking and differentiation, and the Shang civilization of the Erh-li-t'ou phase represents a further—qualitatively transforming—push into a stage of development in which the state form of government and the sharp distinction of economic classes became characteristic. Archaeological evidence available to date has convincingly placed the origin phase of the Shang civilization into Erh-li-t'ou and at northwestern Honan.

The subsequent Erh-li-kang phase of the Shang civilization indicates *both* the Shang civilization's geographic spreading *and* the transformational process from Lung-shan barbarism to Shang civilization in each individual region in which such sites are found. The broad comparability of Erh-li-kang–type pottery across China from Shansi to Kiangsi suggests a sphere of interaction in which cultural influence from the central Shang civilization must have been dominant. On the other hand, Shang civilization of the Erh-li-kang phase had a geographical expanse much greater than the Shang state as defined either by textual data or by references in the oracle bone inscriptions,[128] and by this time it is obvious that states other than Shang, possessing civilizations broadly similar to Shang but also characterized by regionally distinctive features, must have also come into existence. Various Lung-shan cultures throughout China provided the precedent background for various local civilizations and states to form, although the influence from the central Shang may have in some cases provided a necessary stimulus. Archaeological studies, to compare the Shang civilizations in various areas of China, and textual studies of Shang data, to reveal the nature of the interactions between the Shang and the other states, will be the necessary steps before the interrelationship of the various Shang civilizations can be fully understood.

But the fact that there were various centers of precivilizational development in China prior to the rise of the Shang is sufficient to suggest that the Shang origins are not likely to be monolithic and monogenetic and that the cultural continuity (mainly in ceramics and architecture) from Lung-shan to Shang in northwestern Honan does not wholly explain the origin of the Shang civilization. Looking at Shang civilization as a whole, one may easily single out the following cultural traits as being characteristic and important in separating Shang from its Neolithic predecessors:[129]

—urbanism
—palatial as opposed to domestic architecture
—human sacrifice
—the sharp contrast of social classes as symbolized by the above at both ends of the spectrum

128. The geographic expanse of the Shang state as determined from oracle bone inscriptions is not always large. Paul Wheatly (*Pivot of the Four Quarters*, Chicago, Aldine, 1971, p. 62) has pointed out that "the frequency with which the recorded Shang government was either at war with far from remote neighbors or repelling tribal raids at no great distance from the ceremonial center affords some indication that the effective political unit for which records survive was not large." See Ch'en Meng-chia, *Yin Hsü p'u ts'e tsung shu*, Peking, Science Press, 1956; Li Hsüeh-ch'in, *Yin tai ti li chien lun*, Peking, Science Press, 1959; Tung Tso-pin, *Yin li p'u*, Li-chuang, 1945; Li Ya-nung, *Yin tai shê-hui sheng-huo*, Shanghai, Jenmin Press, 1955.

129. Cf. Li Chi, *The Beginnings of Chinese Civilization*, p. 15.

—ceremonial and artistic complex of the aristocracy, consisting of
burials in wooden chambers with second-level platforms, rich
grave furnishings, stone sculpture, jade ornaments and para-
phenalia, and use of turtle shells (especially plastrons) for divination
—bronze metallurgy
—new war patterns (capture of prisoners and use of horse-drawn
chariots)
—an elaborate writing system

None of the above has been fully traced into the Lung-shan period in
northwestern Honan, and we cannot see this part of Honan as a closed
area within which the entire growth process of Shang civilization took
place. To give a more complete picture of the Shang origins, attempts
must be made to search for the origins of the Shang innovations listed
above. Some of these (e.g., urbanism, palaces, war captives, economic
classes) represent societal transformations and do not necessarily have a
step-by-step history. But others have been illuminated by recent archaeological finds, and they amply indicate that many more peoples and
cultures in China than the Honan Lung-shan may have had a hand in
contributing to the Shang growth. In the words of both Li Chi[130] and
Ling Shun-sheng,[131] the Shang civilization was "polygenetic" in its origin.

One of the most important recent discoveries in Chinese archaeology
concerns the history of Chinese writing. On the basis of an "archaic"
script on bronzes during the Shang period, students of ancient Chinese
writing have long speculated about a writing system in China predating
the Shang,[132] but no clear evidence of any such system had been found.
In recent years, on prehistoric pottery in many parts of China, incised
signs or symbols that may have been makers' or owners' marks have
been found. These include those at the Yang-shao sites in Pan-p'o-ts'un[133]
and Chiang-chai,[134] both in eastern Shensi (fig. 51); the Hua-t'ing (Ta-
wen-k'ou) culture sites in Shantung (fig. 71);[135] the Pei-yin-yang-ying

130. Li Chi, "Yin hsü t'ung-ch'i wu chung chi ch'i hsiang-kuan chih wen-t'i," *Papers
Presented to Dr. Ts'ai Yüan P'ei on His 65th Birthday*, Peiping, Academia Sinica, 1933,
pp. 73–104.

131. Ling Shun-sheng, "Chung-kuo ku-tai hai-yang wen-hua yü Ya-chou ti-chung-
hai," *Hai-wai tsa-chih* 3 (1954), no. 10, 7–10, Taipei.

132. Tung Tso-pin, *Ta-lu tsa-chih* 9 (1952), 348–58. T'ang Lan, *KKHP* 1957 (2), 7–22.

133. *Hsi-an Pan-p'o*, Peking, Wen Wu Press, 1962, p. 197.

134. *WW* 1975 (8), 82.

135. *Ta-wen-k'ou*, Peking, Wen Wu Press, 1974, pp. 117–18.

culture site at Sung-tse in Shanghai;[136] and the Feng-pi-t'ou site in south-ern Taiwan (fig. 129).[137] These finds remind us of similar occurrences of pottery symbols at Ch'eng-tzu-yai in Shantung,[138] at Liang-chu in Chekiang,[139] and at several late Neolithic sites in Hai-feng, eastern Kwang-tung and Hong Kong[140]—all found in the 1930s but hitherto largely ignored because of the rarity of these things at the time. Since these symbols invariably occur singly, they might have been easily dismissed as potters' marks of some kind, without significance as ancient writing, if not for the fact that similar marks have also been found on pottery of the Shang period (fig. 130) at Erh-li-t'ou,[141] Erh-li-kang,[142] An-yang,[143] Hsia-wang-kang in Hsi-ch'uan,[144] T'ai-hsi in Kao-ch'eng,[145] and Wu-ch'eng in Ch'ing-chiang.[146] We know for a fact that the Shang used writing extensively, and many of the pottery symbols are in fact identical with oracle-bone inscrip-tion characters, making it clear that the Shang pottery symbols were a part of the total Shang writing system. It is unlikely that the Neolithic Chinese were totally literate in the sense that the Shang Chinese were. But many palaeographers and historians are now convinced that the pottery symbols of Neolithic China provided the Shang writing system with an important early source of script, especially in the area of numerals and ordinals.[147]

Bronze metallurgy underwent apparent development from a more primitive stage (in which the principal archaeological remains are small tools such as awls, chisels, and adzes, and the ritual vessels that were cast

136. *KKHP* 1962 (2), 7, 11.

137. K. C. Chang et al., *Fengpitou, Tapenkeng, and the Prehistory of Taiwan*, 1969, pp. 95, 100.

138. Li Chi et al., *Ch'eng-tzu-yai*, 1934, Pl. 16.

139. Shih Hsin-keng, *Liang-chu*, 1938, p. 25. Ho T'ien-hsing, *Hang Hsien Liang-chu-chen chih shih-ch'i yü hei t'ao*, Shanghai, 1937, pp. 6–8.

140. R. Maglioni, *Archaeological Discovery in Eastern Kwangtung*, Hong Kong Archaeo-logical Society Reprint, 1975, p. 111. D. J. Finn, *Hongkong Naturalist* 4 (1933), no. 1, 60–63; W. Schofield, *Proc. 3rd Far Eastern Prehist. Congr.*, 1938, 236–84.

141. *KK* 1965 (5), 222.

142. *KKHP* 8 (1954), 77; 1957 (1), 68. *Cheng-chou Erh-li-kang*, Peking, Science Press, 1959, fig. 31. *KKHP* 1973 (1), 84.

143. Li Chi, *Hsiao-t'un t'ao-ch'i*, Taipei, 1956, pp. 123–48.

144. *WW* 1975 (7), 60.

145. *WW* 1974 (8), 50–53.

146. *WW* 1975 (7), 56–58.

147. Li Hsiao-ting, *Nanyang University Journal* 3 (1969), 1–28; *BIHP* 45 (1974), 343–94. Kuo Mo-jo, *KK* 1972 (3), 2–13. Yü Hsing-wu, *WW* 1973 (2), 32–35. Cheng Te-k'un, *Journal of the Chinese University of Hong Kong* 1 (1973), 41–58. Ho Ping-ti, *Cradle of the East*, pp. 223–67.

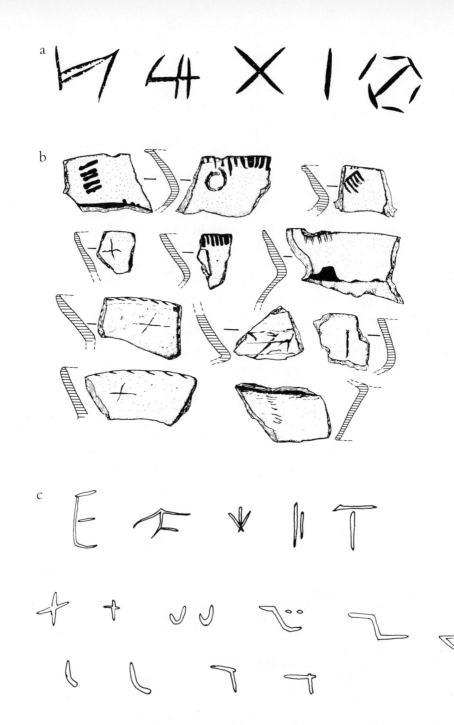

129. Incised signs on Neolithic pottery: (a) Liang-chu (from Shih Hsin-keng, *Liang-chu*, Hang-chou, 1938, p. 25); (b) Feng-pi-t'ou (from K. C. Chang, et al., *Fengpitou, Tapenkeng and the Prehistory of Taiwan*, Yale University Publications in Anthropology, no. 73, New Haven, 1960, p. 100); (c) Hai-feng (from R. Maglioni, *Archaeological Discovery in Eastern Kwangtung*, Archaeological Society of Hong Kong, 1975 reprint, p. 111); (d) Ch'eng-tzu-

d

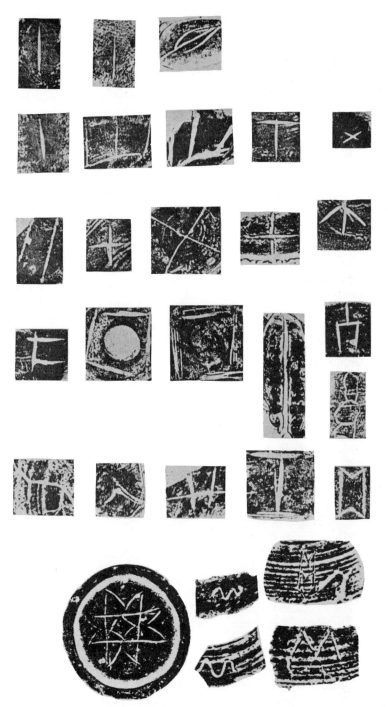

e

yai—only the top three signs have been assigned to the Neolithic stratum, while the others are alleged to be Eastern Chou (from Li Chi et al., *Ch'eng-tzu-yai*, Nanking, Institute of History and Philology, Academia Sinica, 1934, pl. 16); (e) Sung-tse, Shanghai (from *KKHP* 1962, no. 2, p. 7).

130. Some Shang pottery writings. *Left*, Wu-ch'eng, Kiangsi (from *WW* 1975, no. 7, p. 76); *upper right*, Cheng-chou (from *KKHP* 1973, no. 1, p. 84); *lower right*, Kao-ch'eng (from *WW* 1974, no. 8, p. 50.)

were thin, angular, undecorated, and of rough surface) to the mature An-yang stage during the Shang period itself. The primitive, early bronze casting of the Erh-li-t'ou phase was in all likelihood derived from an even more primitive prototype in the Lung-shan cultures. There is as yet no evidence of such prototypes within Honan Lung-shan itself, but the Shan-tung Lung-shan culture has yielded finds of small bronze plates,[148] and many of its pottery forms have long been regarded as possible imitations of metal originals. Copper objects have been found at sites of the Ch'i-chia culture in Kansu as described earlier, in chapter 5. Even though the precise steps of the development of bronze metallurgy remain to be better substantiated by future archaeological evidence, we are on firm ground in attributing the source of this Shang cultural complex to Neo-lithic cultures within North China. After exhaustive research into the technological details of ancient Chinese bronzes, Noel Barnard and Sato Tamotsu came to the conclusion that "as a consequence of this exercise it has become increasingly evident that the very practice of metallurgy it-self was in all probability the result of an indigenous discovery, and one entirely independent of influences from other cultural spheres."[149] In earlier editions of this book, I had felt obliged to comment on the attempts, invariably unsuccessful, to look for the origin of Chinese bronze metal-lurgy in western Asia. Now the question is no longer *whether* bronze metallurgy began indigenously in North China: it is, rather, *where* and *how*.

The horse-drawn chariot is the only Shang—late Shang—innovation that may have originated in the Near East, where an almost identical complex of chariot parts occurs archaeologically centuries earlier.[150] This awesome weaponry must have increased the Shang's military powers and thereby played an important, but by no means decisive, role in the further development of the Shang state. However, thousands of miles of land, archaeologically sterile insofar as any horse-drawn chariots are concerned, still separate Shang China and the contemporary Near East, and before one can actually demonstrate that a diffusion took place,

148. These were discovered at the Ta-ch'eng-shan site in T'ang-shan in Hopei. See *KKHP* 1959 (3), 33.

149. *Metallurgical Remains of Ancient China*, Tokyo, Nichiōsha, 1975, p. 83. See also Noel Barnard, *Bronze Casting and Bronze Alloys in Ancient China*, Tokyo, Australian National University and Monumenta Serica, 1961.

150. M. V. Dewall, *Pferd und Wagen im Frühen China*, vol. 1, Bonn, Saarbrücker Beiträge zur Altertumskunde, 1964. Hayashi Minao, *Minzokugaku-Zasshi* 23 (1959), 39–40; 24 (1960), 33–57; *Tōhōgakuhō* 29 (Kyoto, 1959), 155–284.

efforts should not be spared to explore the antecedent history of this particular cultural complex within China itself.[151]

There is no question about scapulimancy being something that the Shang inherited from the Lung-shan culture. Archaeology has established without a doubt that the use of animal shoulder blades (deer, pig, sheep) for divination was widespread in China, from the Ch'i-chia culture in the west to the Lungshanoid cultures of Honan and the Pacific seaboard at the time level prior to the rise of the Shang. (The earliest archaeological find of scapulimancy occurs at Fu-ho-kou-men in Balin Left Banner, Chaowuta League, Liaoning.)[152] But "plastromancy," involving the use of turtle plastrons, appears to be a Shang innovation, and the Shang's valued use of turtle shells does not have an archaeological antecedent in the Honan Lungshan culture, but it was indeed foreshadowed by the use of turtle shells in the Hua-t'ing culture. At both Ta-wen-k'ou and P'i Hsien, polished shells (both plastrons and carapaces) of turtles were found, some perforated or with remains of ribbons or cinnabars on them, and they were probably used as containers.[153] Also probably derived from the Hua-t'ing culture were the tremendously generous use of grave goods, the construction of wooden chambers in burials, and the placement of grave goods on the so-called 'second-level platforms,' which were all part of the Shang burial custom and were also prominently displayed in the Hua-t'ing culture burial sites. In fact, this reminds us of the fact that the only hang-t'u structures of the Lung-shan period have been found in Shantung (Ch'eng-tzu-yai) and northern Honan (Hou-kang, An-yang) rather than western Honan. Recall our discussion of the Lung-shan studies, where it was shown that the Pacific seaboard was for a long time regarded as the birthplace of the Shang civilization. As Li Chi reemphasized in a recent paper, "in the earlier half of the Shang history, the capital city of the state moved eight times from Ch'i to Ch'eng T'ang, most of them located within the territory of Shantung."[154] Even now, at a time when archaeologists seem to agree that Shang civilization's development began in western Honan with the Erh-li-t'ou phase, T'ang Lan continues to stress the fact that T'ang's capital, Po, has been regarded by most historians

151. Certain finds in the Southern Urals have been considered by Stuart Piggott to provide a link between the Near East and China. However, the dates of these finds may be too late to serve that purpose. See Antiquity 48 (1974), 16–24; 49 (1975), 289–90.

152. P. C. Chang, BIHP 37 (1967), 827–79. KK 1964 (1), 3.

153. KKHP 1964 (2), 29. Ta-wen-k'ou, 1974, p. 103.

154. Bull. Dept. Arch. and Anth. 21/22 (1963), 2.

to be located in the area "north of Shang-ch'iu, Honan, and south of Ts'ao Hsien, Shantung."[155]

How are we to reconcile, on the one hand, the historian's inclination toward the east for Shang's ancestry and the archaeological importance of the Pacific seaboard insofar as a number of Shang innovations are concerned (*hang-t'u*, turtleshells, tomb construction, bone carving, jades), and, on the other hand, the archaeological fact of the Shang development from western Honan in the Erh-li-t'ou phase? This, I think, is the key to the issue of the origin of Chinese civilization, and its answer may well lie in the interrelationship of the Hsia and Shang dynasties. This is the topic of a separate treatise and cannot be discussed here further.[156]

Content and Style of the Shang Civilization

The earliest strata of the Shang civilization known at present in the form of the Erh-li-t'ou phase of western Honan are not adequately known, but it is already clear that by this time (ca. 1850 B.C.) the Neolithic economy had begun to give way to the formation of settlement groups as self-contained units. Bronze metallurgy was already well started, and at some sites one sees the beginning of a highly intensified and sophisticated aristocratic complex.

By the time the city wall was constructed at Cheng-chou, perhaps around 1650 B.C., there can no longer be any doubt that Chinese urbanization was mature and that a Shang style of Chinese art and culture is manifest in the archaeological record. Because the term *urbanization* is somewhat arbitrarily defined in the archaeological literature,[157] we must carefully characterize the nature of city life of the Shang dynasty in North China. The foremost feature of the Shang sites is that individual villages were organized into intervillage networks in economy, administration, and religion. Each group depended upon others for specialized services and offered services in return. There was a political and ceremonial center (a walled enclosure in the case of Cheng-chou), where the royal family and

155. *WW* 1973 (7), 7.

156. K. C. Chang, "Kuan-yü Yin-Shang wen-ming ch'i-yüan yen-chiu shang ti i-ke kuan-chien wen-t'i" [A key question pertaining to the study of the origin of the Shang civilization], in *Papers Presented to Dean Emeritus Shen Kang-po on His Eightieth Birthday*, College of Arts, National Taiwan University, 1976, pp. 151–69.

157. V. G. Childe, *Town Planning Review* 21 (Liverpool, 1950), 3–17. See also R. J. Braidwood and G. R. Willey, eds., *Courses Toward Urban Life*, Viking Fund Publications in Anthropology, no. 32, 1962.

the nobles resided. It apparently served as the nucleus of the group and, when the capital of the dynasty was located there, as the center of political and economic control of the whole kingdom. Surrounding and centripetal to this nucleus were industrial quarters with high degrees of specialization, and farming villages. Goods apparently circulated among the various villages, with the administrative center serving also as the center for redistribution. The population of the entire settlement group was considerable, as indicated by the spatial dimensions and by the quantity and complexity of the cultural remains, and the social stratification and industrial specialization of the populace were highly intensified. We find in Shang China no physical counterparts to such large population and architectural configurations as Ur of Mesopotamia, Mohenjo-Daro on the Indus, and Teotihuacan of Mexico, yet the Shang capital sites performed all the essential functions of a city, indicating a definite break from the Neolithic community pattern. This basic Shang city pattern continued on into later historic periods. During the Eastern Chou period the capital sites grew into large commercial and political urban centers, as will be described in the next chapter.

Purely from an archaeological perspective, the populace of a Shang city seems to have been divided into three major groups: the aristocracy, the craftsmen, and the farmers.

The aristocracy. Archaeological excavations, oracle-bone inscriptions, and historic records have jointly established the fact that the Shang capitals at Cheng-chou and An-yang were seats of a powerful centralized government in control of a number of settlement groups scattered over a part of North China. At one or a few of the sites within a same settlement group, an aristocratic complex of artifacts and architecture can easily be recognized. In architecture, this includes ceremonial altars, rectangular house structures with stamped earth floors, stone pillar foundations, and in some cases, stone sculptures used as pillar bases. Such sites have a complex system of graves, including tombs of gigantic dimensions and sophisticated structure, evidence of human sacrifice and accompanying burials of animal victims and horse-drawn chariots. This aristocratic complex is often associated with a sophisticated ritual complex, manifested by human sacrifice, animal sacrifice, scapulimancy, and ceremonial vessels of pottery (e.g., white pottery) and bronze. Horse and chariot fittings and other apparatuses for ritual use help to mark the distinctions of status, along with such artifacts as prepared and inscribed oracle bones, white, hard, glazed pottery, elaborately carved bone hairpins, jade weapons, and bronze ceremonial and household utensils. Groups of bronze and pottery vessels for use in wine drinking and serving occurred in the Shang burials for the first time. Remains of cowrie shells, probably used as a medium of exchange, may also be significant. Writing is mainly associated with the aristocracy, as are highly developed decorative arts like the *t'ao-t'ieh* style, mosaic designs, and stone and bone sculptures and engravings. Discovery of such artifacts points to a strongly consolidated aristocracy that was definitely absent prior to the Shang.

From the oracle inscriptions and the historic records, a little is known about the Royal House, the rule of succession to the throne, and the political relationships between the various settlement groups. Mythological sources relate that the Royal House of the Shang dynasty was a grand lineage by the name of Tzu, attributed to a divine birth in Ssu-ma Ch'ien's *Shih chi*, volume 3:

> The mother of Ch'i, founder of the Yin dynasty, was called Chien Ti, a daughter of the tribe Yu Jung and second consort of Emperor K'u. Basking with two companions, Chien Ti saw an egg fall from a black bird and swallowed it. She then became pregnant and gave birth to Ch'i.

The grand lineage occupied a central position in the state's political, economic, and ceremonial structures, which were expressed and maintained with elaborate and solemn ancestor-worship rites. There is little question about the relationship between the ancestor-worship rites performed by and for the grand lineages and the origin myths of the descent of these lineages. According to the ancestor-cult calendar worked out from the oracle inscriptions, Li Hsüeh-ch'in has been able to generalize that among thirty-five kings of the Shang dynasty, whose rules of succession are relatively clear, the throne was assumed by sons for eighteen generations, and for seven generations (ten kings) it was taken over by brothers.[158]

The settlement groups that were not under the direct rule of the monarch were administered by lords appointed by the central government. The lords were relatives of the monarch (sometimes junior sons), high officials who made great contributions to the cause of the Royal House, and the de facto rulers of regions that paid tribute to the central government but were out of the reach of the royal forces, and whose administrative status had to be recognized.[159]

158. Li Hsüeh-ch'in, *Wen-shih-chê* 1957 (2), 21–37. For a new hypothesis on the rules of royal succession in the context of the kinship system, see Chang Kwang-chih, *BIE* 15 (1963), 65–94. *BIE* 35 (1973), 111–27.

159. Hu Hou-hsüan, *Chia-ku-hsüeh Shang-shih lun ts'ung*, vol. 1, Ch'i-lu Univ., 1944.

The central government and the local governments thus formed a tightly organized hierarchy, with the king at the top, assisted by officials of a royal court and priests. Communications between the various settlement groups and the central administration were possible with the aid of a highly developed system of writing and a standardized currency. Raids and warfare between states were frequent, as judged by the war records in the inscriptions, the abundant remains of weapons, the sacrificial use of what were apparently war captives, and the chariots. The centralized power of government is most clearly indicated by the control of manpower. In addition, public works began to appear to a significant extent. The *hang-t'u* structures at Hsiao-t'un and Cheng-chou, such as the walled enclosure and the temples and altars, were probably built by large groups of people, organized and directed by administrative agencies. The construction of the large royal tombs at Hsi-pei-kang, An-yang, is of particular interest in this connection.

The social institutions that governed the aristocracy and its auxiliary groups, as indicated by the archaeological evidence and the oracle bone inscriptions, were as follows: Marriage in the royal family was as a rule monogamous. The families of the Royal House, the nobility, and some of the craftsmen were of the extended family type, probably patrilineal. Beyond the family, unilinear lineages may have been prevalent among the nobility and some of the craftsmen; these were possibly segmentary lineages based on patrilineality and primogeniture (see below). The lineage system may have been related to a part of the class structure. The kinship terminology of the royal family was possibly of the generation type.

The organization of the royal family is relatively clear. According to the Shang calendar of rituals, as recorded in the oracle-bone inscriptions, each king had one particular spouse.

> *P'i* [grandmothers and female ancestors] were partnered to *tsu* [grandfathers and male ancestors], *mu* [mothers] partnered to *fu* [fathers], and *fu* [daughters-in-law] partnered to *tzu* [sons]. Each man usually had only one official spouse. Among all the fathers, one, and one only, had an especially supreme status, and his spouse also had supreme status. The family descent and the calendar of rituals were both based on patrilineality.[160]

The families of the nobility seem to be of the extended type. Their domiciles can be represented by the foundation A4 at Hsiao-t'un, which is 28.4

---

160. Li Hsüeh-ch'in, *Wen-shih-chê* 1957 (2), 36.

meters long and 8 meters wide and is divided into two large halls and eleven small rooms, all connected by doors.[161]

There is little question that lineages existed during the Shang dynasty. In Shang times the principle of primogeniture played an important role, and the order of seniority of birth was duly symbolized in the order of rituals and the classification of temples and altars into grand and lesser lines.[162] It is therefore possible that the so-called *tsung-fa* system of kinship, well known to be characteristic of the Chou dynasty, had already started in the Shang stage. This system is characterized above all by the close correlation of political status with kinship descent; i.e., an individual's rank within the clan is determined by his consanguineous proximity to the alleged main line of descent.

The highly organized ceremonial patterns of the Shang dynasty essentially carried on the Neolithic heritage, as indicated by an institutionalized ancestor worship, the practice of scapulimancy, and the elaboration of ceremonial objects, especially vessels. But by Shang times, the ceremonial structure of society had been very much intensified and was unmistakably tied up with the aristocracy. Priests, whose main duty was probably to divine and foretell events, served the royal court; the elaborate and sophisticated ceremonial bronze vessels were apparently used for rituals performed for the Royal House according to an annual calendar, mainly rituals of ancestor worship; the ceremonial center of the An-yang settlement group was spatially identified with the administrative center (Hsiao-t'un); and large-scale human and animal sacrifice was offered for the royal family.

In this manner the ceremonial structure was possibly correlated with the kinship structure on the one hand and with the economic system on the other. Ancestral worship was stressed and the calendar of ancestral worship rituals was carefully scheduled, as a reminder and reinforcement of the rules of primogeniture, the supremacy of the grand lineages, and the ramification of the lesser lineages, which became more and more degraded with each succeeding generation. The king, at the top of the hierarchal clan, was the supreme ruler of the kingdom and of the clan and also the focus of attention for all rituals. The relationship among the various settlement groups of the Shang kingdom was thus not only economically based (concentration and redistribution) but also accounted for in terms of kinship, and sanctioned and reinforced by rituals.

161. Shih Chang-ju, *Annals Acad. Sinica* 1 (1954), 267–80.
162. Hu Hou-hsüan, *Chia-ku-hsüeh Shang-shih lun ts'ung* 1, 16.

The craftsmen. At the Shang cities, craftsmen were physically identified with both farmers and the aristocracy, since the industrial quarters were distributed among the farming villages in the suburbs as well as near the palatial nuclei. Our knowledge about these men is rather limited, but we know that industry was a minutely specialized affair, that each settlement group had a number of industrial centers at the service of the aristocracy to provide for the whole settlement, that the craftsmen probably enjoyed a higher status than the farmers by virtue of their special skill and knowledge, and that various handicrafts may have been tied to kin groups. It is mentioned in the "Chronicle of the Fourth Year of Ting Kung" (of Lu state in the Spring-Autumn period) in *Tso chuan* that "after Wu Wang [of the Chou] conquered the Shang, Ch'eng Wang established the regime and selected men of wisdom and virtue and made them feudal lords to protect the royal Chou." To each of the lords Ch'eng Wang is said to have given a number of *tsu* (thought to be equivalent to minimal lineage), and the names of the *tsu* mentioned here included words for a drinking utensil, pottery, flag, and pots and pans. This passage shows that during the Shang dynasty, handicraft was possibly a kin-group affair. Some of the lineages specialized in particular branches of handicrafts either as a supplement to agriculture or full time. The Cheng-chou potters, as mentioned above, seem to have devoted full time to a special kind of pottery, whereas other kinds of ceramics probably were the business of other groups. The skills and special technical knowledge were probably passed down within the kin groups and because of this, the members of the group may have enjoyed certain privileges that the farmers did not have. At Cheng-chou the bronzesmiths and potters lived in above-ground, stamped-earth houses which were usually associated with the nobility. The bronzesmiths' dwellings found in the region north of Tzu-ching-shan in Cheng-chou consist of four houses:

> Each house is partitioned by a wall into two rooms. The two rooms are connected by a door. The two rooms may both have had a door to communicate with the outside, or only one of them may have had. Each room has an earth platform by the door, and a fireplace.[163]

Furthermore, these four houses are arranged according to a definite plan, and each is separated from the next by a distance of 10 or 11 meters. These facts may indicate that the bronzesmiths' families were of the extended type, and that their households belonged to the same patrilineage, a con-

163. Liao Yüng-min, *WWTKTL* 1957 (6), 73.

clusion in complete agreement with the historic records concerning the lineage-occupation linkage.

Ground houses have also been uncovered at An-yang in association with the bronze technology. In 1959 and 1960 at the site of Miao-p'u-pei-ti, southeast of Hsiao-t'un, a number of ground-house floors were located, many of which were associated with clay molds. A large floor (more than 8 meters long and 4 meters wide), partitioned into two rooms, was built on a layer of *hang-t'u*, and the walls were also constructed by the *hang-t'u* technique. Posts were based on rocks here in the same manner as in the Hsiao-t'un palaces and temples. In the house, near the entrance, is a gourd-shaped pit, probably a hearth. Surrounding the floor were many piece molds of clay and fragments of crucibles, indicating a close connection with bronze work.[164]

From the large number of piece molds as well as the remains of clay models, crucible fragments, and the bronze artifacts themselves, the techniques of bronze making are well understood. Flat bronze implements such as knives and *ko* halberds were probably manufactured with the aid of a single mold or a two-piece mold into which molten copper and tin were poured. Hollow implements of plain form, such as axes, were also relatively simply made, with an outer mold and an inner core. The complicated vessels, especially large ones and those with cast decorative designs (a square *ting* from An-yang is 137 centimeters high, 110 centimeters long, 77 centimeters wide, and 700 kilograms in weight), involved a more complex process.

A bronze casting is simply a replica in bronze of a model created in another medium. In the Western tradition this model has typically been made of wax on a clay core, then sheathed in a solid clay outer mold, melted out and replaced with molten bronze [the so-called lost-wax method]. In ancient China, on the contrary, it appears that the model was made of *clay* (and perhaps of other infusible materials such as wood) around a clay core and that the outer mold was not solid and continuous but segmented. This segmentation (making the outer mold a "piece mold") was necessitated by the fact that the baked clay model, unlike its wax counterpart, could not be melted out but had to be removed bodily. Thus when the mold segments have received the imprint of the model they are detached from it, the model is broken or scraped away from the core, and the mold segments

164. An Chih-min et al., *KK* 1961 (2), 67.

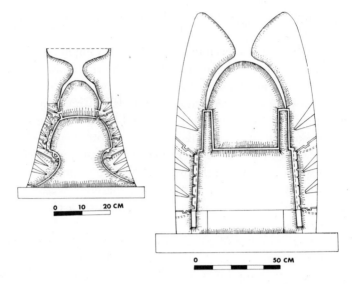

131. Clay molds for casting bronze vessels, Shang period. (From Shih Chang-ju, *BIHP* 26, 1955, pp. 113, 117.)

are reassembled around the core ready to receive the molten bronze in the now hollow interstice between the two.[165]

This multiple piece-mold process of the Shang (fig. 131) is what has convinced Noel Barnard that bronze metallurgy emerged independently in China,[166] but Wilma Fairbank goes so far as to see it as a far more complex application of the rudimentary bronze metallurgical principles for processing ores and alloying, heating, and pouring the metal, made possible by the superior ceramic craftsmanship of the Chinese.[167]

Perhaps the high social status apparently enjoyed by the bronzesmiths resulted from the association of bronze artifacts with the upper class. During the Yin phase of the Shang civilization at least, the bronze artifacts were made for the most part for exclusive purposes like ceremonies, warfare, and hunting. On the other hand, practically all the tools and implements for such basic subsistence purposes as agriculture and domestic utility continued to be made of wood, stone, clay, or bone. In all likelihood

165. Wilma Fairbank, *Archives of the Chinese Art Society of America* 16 (1962), 9. For detailed analyses of the bronze metallurgy of the Shang, see Noel Barnard, *Bronze Casting and Bronze Alloys in Ancient China*, Tokyo, Monumenta Serica Monograph no. 16 (1961); Shih Chang-ju, *BIHP* 26 (1955), 95–129.

166. Barnard, *op. cit.*, pp. 59–62.

167. Fairbank, *op. cit.*, pp. 10–11.

the industrial specialization at this time was tightly correlated with status differentiation.

Archaeologically substantiated handicrafts (whose "workshops" have been discovered) include manufacture of bronzes, pottery, and stone and bone artifacts, and possibly wine making. Other professions that can be inferred from archaeological remains or have been mentioned in the oracle bone inscriptions include carpentry, sculpture, earth construction, masonry, manufacture of drinking utensils, chariots, and weapons, tailoring, fabric making, and flag making.[168] Their extent of specialization seems to vary, and they had clienteles of differing social status.

The farmers. Shang subsistence was based on agriculture and supplemented by hunting and fishing. Remains of crops of the Shang period have been found at Cheng-chou, An-yang, and Hsing-t'ai, but have not been specified. From the oracle-bone inscriptions it can be determined that millet (probably both *Setaria* and *Panicum*), rice, and wheat were planted.[169] Little is known about the cultivation techniques except that stone hoes, spades, and sickles were used, as well as a kind of large wooden digging stick which may have been pushed by men or pulled by cattle and dogs and was possibly a prototype of the plow.[170] Two crops of millet and rice were harvested each year, and irrigation was probably employed,[171] although it has not been satisfactorily demonstrated that the water ditches discovered at An-yang and Cheng-chou are connected with irrigation. Those at Hsiao-t'un, at least, are not likely to have been related to irrigation. Fertilizers may have been used, but this again is by no means certain.[172] An elaborate agricultural calendar was developed.[173] Other archaeological finds connected with farming include pestles and mortars. Among the cultivated materials for fabrics were hemp[174] and silk.[175] In the domestica-

168. Li Chi, *The Beginnings of Chinese Civilization.* Li Ya-nung, *Yin-tai shê-hui sheng-huo,* Shanghai, Jenmin Press, 1955. Amano Motonosuke, *Tōhōgakuhō* 23 (1953). Shih Chang-ju, *BIHP* 26 (1955). Li Chi, *BIHP* 23 (1951), 523–619. Hsia Nai, *China Reconstructs* 1957 (12). Li Chi, *Hsiao-t'un t'ao-ch'i.* Yü Yü, *WWTKTL* 1958 (10), 26–28.

169. Hu Hou-hsüan, *Chia-ku-hsüeh Shang-shih lun ts'ung* 2 (1945), 134. Yü Hsing-wu, *Tung-pei ta-hsüeh jen-wen hsüeh pao* 1 (1957), 81–107.

170. Hu, *Chia-ku-hsüeh* 2 (1945), 134.

171. *Ibid.*

172. Hu Hou-hsüan, *Li-shih yen-chiu* 1955 (1). *WW* 1963 (5), 27–31, 41.

173. Tung Tso-pin, *Yin li p'u,* Institute of History and Philology, Academia Sinica, Li-chuang, 1945.

174. Li Chi, *An-yang fa-chüeh pao-kao* 3 (1931), 466. Iwama, *Manshu gakuhō* 4 (1936), 1–7.

175. Amano Motonosuke, *Tōhōgakuhō* 1 (1955). Vivi Sylwan, *BMFEA* 9 (1937), 119–26. Hu Hou-hsüan, *WW* 1972 (11), 2–7, 36.

tion of animals the Shang carried on the Neolithic heritage (pigs, dogs, cattle, sheep, horses, and chickens), with some additions (water buffalo) and modifications (such as the use of dogs, cattle, and sheep for sacrifice and horses for chariot warfare).[176]

Fishing is indicated by fishbones,[177] fishhooks, and the scripts for fish-nets and fishhooks. Hunting is indicated by the large quantity of wild-animal bone remains (tiger, leopard, bear, rhinoceros, deer, water deer, hare, etc.), by the remains of stone and bronze arrowheads, by the hunting records in the oracle-bone inscriptions, and by the animal designs in the decorative art. However, the part played in the basic subsistence by hunting may not have been very significant. According to Li Chi, the "game huntings mentioned in the ancient inscriptions were evidently pursued for pleasure and excitement rather than for economic necessity. . . . Such pursuits were the monopolies of a privileged class."[178]

There is no question that agriculture was the basis of Shang subsistence, or that the techniques were highly developed and the yield considerable. In the suburbs of Cheng-chou and An-yang, the many residential hamlets were presumably occupied by farmers who tilled the fields in the neigh-borhood. One controversial point among Shang specialists is whether the direct participants in agricultural production were free farmers or slaves. It is known that slaves suffering from malnutrition, possibly war cap-tives,[179] were sacrificed in the construction of palaces, temples, and royal tombs, were buried dead or alive with the royal body in the royal tomb, and that their bones were used for the manufacture of artifacts. But whether slaves were the sole laborers in the farming fields is not known. Amano suggests that during the Yin dynasty there were two kinds of fields: the royal field, cultivated by slaves under centralized management, and the clan fields cultivated by the lower classes of clan members.[180]

Created and sustained by people of all these categories, in concert if not in harmony, the Shang civilization by the Yin period at the latest achieved both distinction and greatness, placing it among the civilized giants of the

176. Shih Chang-ju, *Bull. College of Arts, Nat'l. Taiwan Univ.*, no. 5 (1953), 1–14.

177. Chao Ch'üan-ku et al., *KKHP* 1957 (1), 63. Wu Hsien-wen, *Chung-kuo kao-k'u hsüeh pao* 4 (1949), 139–43.

178. Li Chi, *Bull. Dept. Archaeol. and Anthropol.*, Nat'l. Taiwan Univ., no. 9/10 (1957), 12.

179. Mao Hsieh-chün and Yen Yen, *VP* 3 (1959), 79–80. For human sacrifice, see Hu Hou-hsüan, *WW* 1974 (7), 74–84; 1974 (8), 56–72.

180. Amano Motonosuke, *Shigaku Kenkyu* 62 (1956), 11. See also Chang Cheng-lang, in *KKHP* 1973 (1).

ancient world. It can best be recognized through its art and religion—those complexes of culture through which the Shang expressed their minds about the world around them and indicated to us how the various aspects of their lives could be articulated.

For much of the Shang religion and ritual we must resort to the information that only written records provide,[181] but archaeology is rich in religious symbols and ritual art. Shang domiciles, palaces, temples, and tombs alike were invariably square or oblong, governed in orientation by the four cardinal directions and dominated in design by a persistent attempt at symmetry. The ancestral temples in section B at Hsiao-t'un were constructed in two north-south rows facing each other east and west, with an earthen altar at the northern end to provide focus; the Hsi-pei-kang royal tombs, neatly square and angular themselves, formed an eastern and a western half. In the decorative art of the bronzes "there is never any asymmetry,"[182] and in inscribing the plastral shells of turtles after a divination the messages were repeated on the left and the right sides.[183] As shown in the *chia ku* scripts, the world was considered square, and each of the four directions probably had its own symbolic color and certainly its own deity with its own name; winds blown from the four directions were the deities' agents, and countries beyond the kingdom were grouped into four directional classes.

Above the four directional deities—and also the deities of sun, moon, earth, mountains, clouds, rivers, and other natural beings—was a Shang Ti, Supreme God on High, who presided over a court consisting usually of five ministers. He was all-powerful, controlling human affairs large and small, but he was never directly sacrificed to or specifically located. With all deities and, especially with Shang Ti, ancestors of the royal lineages were in constant and easy communication, and plastromancy and scapulimancy were the means by which living persons achieved communication with the ancestors in the other world. Probably carrying on an ancient shamanistic tradition, the Shang had access to the other world through animal agents. In death, the nobleman's living possessions were buried with him in his chamber of eternal rest; in life, he burned animal bones to reach the ears of his ancestors and performed ancestral worship rites, using utensils covered with animal images.

Shang art, in other media as well as in bronze, was an art that primarily

181. Ch'en Meng-chia, *Yin Hsü p'u-tz'u tsung-shu*, Peking, Science Press, 1957, pp. 551–603.

182. B. Karlgren, *BMFEA* 34 (1962), 16.

183. Ch'en Meng-chia, *op. cit.*, p. 13.

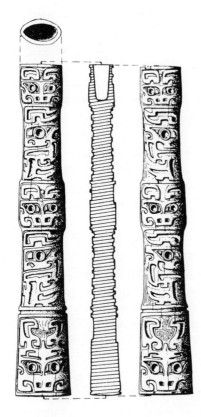

132. Shang bone carving excavated from Hsiao-t'un, An-yang. (From Li Chi, *The Beginnings of Chinese Civilization*, Seattle, Univ. Washington Press, 1957, p. 30.)

worked with animal motifs.[184] Images and forms of animals—serpent, dragon, phoenix, owl, falcon, tiger, sheep, oxen, buffalo, cicada, elephant, rhinoceros—and their bodily parts, in realistic or stylistic motifs, permeated Shang ritual art on bronze vessels, stone sculptures, bone, jade, and ivory carvings, white pottery, plastic clay, and wood carvings with stone and bone inlays (fig. 132). Human images constituted another significant category of artistic work (fig. 133). The interrelationship of animal and human images in Shang art is an interesting topic whose significance, however, will not become explicit until after we have observed, in the next chapter, how it changed during the subsequent Chou period.

Bernhard Karlgren has isolated a number of bronze decorative motifs and analyzed the distribution patterns of these motifs in the total decor of complete vessels of Shang types.[185] Finding that some motifs tend to be

184. B. Karlgren, *BMFEA* 34 (1962), 16.
185. *BMFEA* 9 (1937), 1–117; 34 (1962), 1–28.

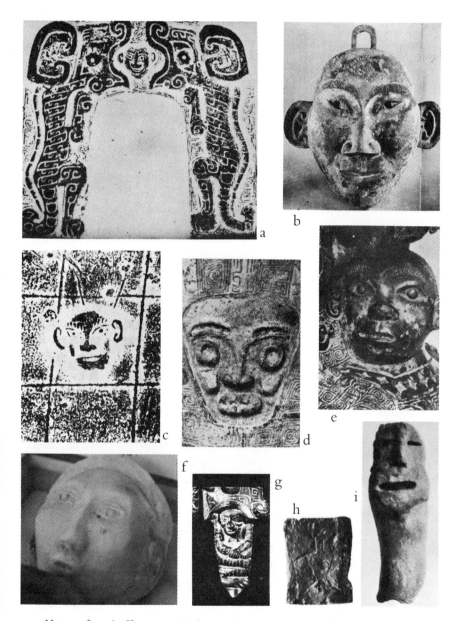

133. Human faces in Shang art: (a) bronze, from An-yang (Li Chi, *The Beginnings of Chinese Civilization*, Seattle, Univ. of Washington Press, 1957, pl. 1); (b) bronze, from An-yang (*Life*, 29 September 1961); (c) bronze, presumably from An-yang (*KK* 1964, no. 11, p. 592); (d, e) bronze, presumably from An-yang (*Sekai Bunkashi Taikei*, Tokyo, Katokawa, 1958, vol. 15, p. 26); (f) plaster impression from a pottery mold found at Wang-yü-k'ou, An-yang (photo by author at An-yang Field Station, Institute of Archaeology; originally published in *KK* 1959, no. 5, p. 272); (g) bronze (collection of the Freer Art Gallery, Washington, D.C.); (h) clay, from Erh-li-t'ou, Yen-shih, Honan (*KK* 1965, no. 5, pl. 3); (i) clay, from Shang-chieh, Cheng-chou (*KK* 1966, no. 1, pl. 1).

associated with one another but are excluded from other motifs, Karlgren
has constructed two contrasting styles that he calls A and B, each consisting
of a number of motifs. Both A and B styles were components of the same
Shang art, for "the intimate connection between all the classes of both
styles is emphasized by a series of 'neutral' elements which constitute
constantly recurring paraphernalia of the bronze decor and which appear
in various classes of both A style and B style vessels."[186] But Karlgren also
believes that they were perhaps chronologically distinct (A being earlier
than B in the beginning) or that they were perhaps the art styles of two
contending social groups of the ruling class, each claiming a style exclusive
to its own families of artisans. An analysis of the bronze motifs of vessel
assemblages discovered in Shang graves has convinced me that the A and
B styles were indeed not only favored by different artisans in making the
bronze vessels but were also favored by different social groups who selected
these ceremonial paraphernalia for burial with their dead members, because
all bronze vessels found in each grave tend to exhibit either A or B style
preferences.[187]

These studies may have revealed a significant key to the meaning of a
number of apparently interrelated phenomena of Shang art, archaeology,
and history. The late Tung Tso-pin[188] was the first scholar to discover
the significant internal criteria that enabled the oracle texts, fragmentary
and disjointed, to be placed in a chronological sequence within the 273 years
of their history at An-yang. In so doing, he was the first to bring into focus
the cyclical changes of the Shang institutions—ritual calendar for one, and
court etiquette for another—which he characterized as two contending
traditions. I have come to notice the cyclical pattern of distribution of the
temple designations of the Shang kings and their spouses in their genealogical sequence, and from this I have worked out a dualistic scheme of
royal succession whereby two parallel but different groups within the
Royal House alternated in ascent to the throne.[189] This would not only
provide a basis for an interpretation of the A and B styles of Shang bronzes
and the two institutional traditions in the *chia ku* scripts but also explain
why Hsiao-t'un had two parallel rows of temples and Hsi-pei-kang had

186. *BMFEA* 34 (1962), 18. See Max Loehr, *Archives of the Chinese Art Society of America*
7 (1953), for a different classification of bronze styles in An-yang.

187. Kwang-chih Chang, *Jour. Asian Studies* 24 (1964), 45–61. *Symposium in Honor of
Dr. Li Chi on his Seventieth Birthday* (Taipei, Ch'inghua Journal), pt. 1, 1965, pp. 353–70.

188. *Yin li p'u*, Li-chuang, 1945.

189. Kwang-chih Chang, *BIE* 15 (1963), 65–94. See also the many articles, pro and
con, discussing the problem raised therein, in *BIE* 19 (1965), and 21 (1966).

two clusters of royal tombs. The genealogical duality of the Shang kings would dictate a division of the eleven Shang kings at An-yang (again excluding the last king, who presumably was not buried in the same manner as his eleven predecessors) into a left (eastern) cluster of four and a right (western) cluster of seven, which is exactly what we find at Hsi-pei-kang. Many of these dualistic phenomena are identical with the essential features of the so-called *chao mu* institution of the Chou, a point worthy of attention in discussing the Shang-Chou cultural identity in the next chapter.

7 : Further Developments of Civilization in North China to 221 B.C.

The nucleus of the Shang civilization—in the sense of being the civilization of the Shang state—was probably confined to the northern third of Honan and some of its immediate surrounding areas. While in the past the Shang were regarded as being an island of civilization surrounded by a sea of Neolithic and sub-Neolithic barbarians, my current view is that other comparable civilizations also sprang up in other regions of China, especially toward the latter stages of the Shang dynasty. Most of these regions will be discussed in the next two chapters, but one of them must be described here, for a civilization that emerged in the Wei-shui valley, later known as the Chou, replaced the Shang after they were weakened by long and exhausting military involvement with some Huai Valley powers. Until the unification of China under Shih Huang Ti of the Ch'in dynasty in 221 B.C., North China was the stage of the Chou.

The nine hundred years of the Chou period constituted an exciting epoch for the student of early China because, during it, all aspects of Chinese civilization throughout the country underwent some fundamental changes that brought about the end of formative Chinese antiquity and the beginning of imperial China and its "traditional" pattern, which was to last for the next two thousand years. A comprehensive description and discussion of Chou China is impossible in a brief chapter. Moreover, it would require much greater use of the written records—of which there are many—than the nature and scope of this volume would justify. But there are compelling reasons for some discussion of this period. First, the literary records of the period are still fragmentary and incomplete, and many aspects of the Chou civilization must depend upon the archaeological data, as will become self-evident below. Furthermore, the next two chapters will discuss the emergence and development of civilizations and states in other parts of China, which took place in ways interrelated to the history and expansion of the northern Chinese civilizations. Without a brief description of events in the north during the Shang and Chou periods, contemporary events elsewhere in China become difficult to understand; nor could we even engage in a chronological study of these peripheral, but highly important, civilizations, most of which were illiterate during the initial phases.

A few historical dates are important for this chapter. According to the traditional Chinese chronology, the conquest that caused the fall of the Shang and raised the Chou to the center of North China's historical stage took place in 1122 B.C. Historians are not in agreement on this date, however, and no fewer than ten other dates have been suggested for this important historical event: 1116, 1111, 1070, 1067, 1066, 1050, 1047, 1030, 1027, and 1018.[1] Since the ancient Chinese calendrical system is still imperfectly known, the selection among these eleven different dates is more or less a matter of convenience—depending upon which date suits each author best for any particular historical problem. For the purpose of discussing civilizational and societal trends on a macroscopic scale, a precise dating of the conquest is of secondary importance; I shall use 1100 B.C. as an approximation.

The Chou period is ordinarily divided into the Western and Eastern Chou. The former designates the period during which the royal capitals of the Chou were located in the Wei-shui valley of Shensi, of which Hao, near Sian, was the best known and probably the most important. Eastern Chou refers to the period following the removal, in 771 B.C., of the royal capital to Lo-yang in western Honan, under the reign of P'ing Wang. Eastern Chou is divisible into two minor periods, Ch'un-ch'iu, or Spring and Autumn, and Chan-kuo, or Warring States. The dividing date between these two stages is variously set at 481, 478, 468, 453, and 403. For our purpose, round figures are again sufficient: 770 for the beginning of the Eastern Chou and 450 for the beginning of the Warring States period. These are all political events, but for cultural-historical studies other subdivisions are often made, as will be made clear below.

Chou Before the Conquest

In the study of early China few topics are more difficult to define than the interrelationship of the Shang and the Chou. In his famous essay *Yin Chou chih-tu lun* ("On the Institutions of the Yin and the Chou"),

---

1. Tung Tso-pin, *Bull. College of Arts*, Nat'l. Taiwan Univ., no. 3 (1951), 178. Chou Fa-kao, *Harvard Jour. Asiatic Studies* 23 (1960–61), 108–12. *Jour. Inst. Chinese Studies of the Chinese University of Hong Kong* 4 (1971), no. 1, 173–205. Ho Ping-ti, *Jour. Chinese Univ. of Hong Kong* 1 (1973), 17–35.

Wang Kuo-wei, one of the most brilliant and literate scholars of modern China, argued that "the changes and revolutions in Chinese politics and culture have never been greater than those that took place between Yin and Chou." The capitals of the ancient rulers from the Five Emperors to the Shang had been in the east, according to Wang; only the Chou arose in the west. But the shift from Shang to Chou was more than a change in ruling clans or capitals; "in essence, it signifies the fall of old institutions and the rise of new ones; the fall of old cultures and the rise of new ones."[2] Wang enumerated the following new institutions and cultures of the Chou that distinguish them from their Shang predecessors: the system of political succession by the primary son of the primary wife, which gave rise to the *tsung-fa* lineage and the mortuary system, both of which in turn were at the root of the *feng-chien* ("feudal") system; the plan of the ancestral temples; and the marriage taboo within the clans. In the same vein, the late Fu Ssu-nien divided the ancient ethnic groups of China into the western Hsia and the contrastive eastern I, thus making the conquest an outcome of a perennial ethnic conflict—a triumph of the Chou, a Hsia tribe, over the Shang, a I tribe.[3]

There is no question that the conquest was a political upheaval of the first magnitude which affected the total alignment of the political map of ancient China. Nor is there any doubt that the ruling families of the Shang (Tzu) and of the Chou (Chi) came from different parts of North China with somewhat different subcultural heritages. To what extent the conquest was an event of "cultural" significance in the total picture of ancient Chinese history, however, is a highly debatable point. Did the Chou have a separate civilization of their own that was comparable to the Shang in magnitude and intensity but was different in style and replaced the Shang civilization after the conquest? Or was the Chou civilization primarily a local manifestation of the Shang, so that the conquest resulted merely in its propagation? To answer these questions we must take a look at the Chou culture before the conquest to see how far it had developed and how different it was from the Shang. What happened after the conquest and what contributions the Chou brought to Chinese civilization will be described in the following sections of this chapter.

The legendary ancestor of the Chou rulers, known as Hou Chi or Ch'i. had his own myth of birth. According to Ssu-ma Ch'ien,

2. Wang Kuo-wei, *Kuan T'ang chi lin*, Taipei, I-wen Press, 1956, p. 116 (original publication 1923).

3. Fu Ssu-nien, *Ch'ing-chu Ts'ai Yüan-p'ei hsien-sheng liu-shih-wu sui lun-wen chi*, Peiping, Institute of History and Philology, Academia Sinica, 1933, pt. 2, pp. 1093–134.

Hou Chi's mother, a daughter of the tribe Yu-i, was known as Chiang Yüan. Chiang Yüan was the first consort of Ti K'u. Once Chiang Yüan was out in the field and saw a giant's footprint. She was delighted and desired to fit her own foot into it. She did so and she became pregnant. After the usual interval of time, she gave birth to a child, Ch'i. ["Chou pen chi" in *Shih chi*]

The "Book of Odes" locates the birthplace of Hou Chi at Yu-i, which has been identified with several places in the middle Wei-shui valley of Shensi and the lower Fen Ho valley of Shansi. In any case, it has been well established that, at the latest, the Chou had settled in the Wei-shui valley by the reign of T'ai Wang, who is said to have moved to Ch'i, near the modern city of Pao-chi, in the middle Wei-shui valley. T'ai Wang was the great-grandfather of Wu Wang, under whom the conquest was accomplished. Thus, for at least four generations, during the latter part of the Shang dynasty, the seat of the state of Chou was the Wei-shui valley of Shensi.

Archaeological excavations of the lower Fen Ho and Wei-shui valleys have established the fact that the ancient cultural sequence in these regions is a succession of Yang-shao Neolithic, Lung-shan Neolithic, and Western Chou. Western Chou remains in the Wei-shui valley were identified and excavated by Hsü Ping-ch'ang, Su Ping-ch'i, and Shih Chang-ju during the 1930s and 1940s,[4] but it was not until the early fifties that the Neolithic-Chou sequence began to be clearly defined and formulated. At K'o-hsing-chuang, near Sian, Su Ping-ch'i and Wu Ju-tso grouped the early cultural remains, according to stratigraphic evidence, into three classes: Yang-shao, Lung-shan, and Chou, and characterized the Chou stratum as follows:[5]

Gray pottery with relatively homogeneous color, wheel marks, angular rims, and clearly defined, decorative cord marks confined to the body parts of vessels; *li* tripods with low feet, low collars, and nearly flat bottoms; basins, *tou*, and plain jugs with undecorated surfaces.

Nine localities in the neighborhood of Sian are assigned by Su and Wu to the Chou stratum; these are characterized by deep cultural deposits,

4. Shih Chang-ju, *BIHP* 27 (1956), 205–323. Su Ping-ch'i, *Tou-chi-t'ai Kou-tung-ch'ü mu-tsang*, Peiping, National Academy of Peiping, 1948. Hsü Ping-ch'ang and Ch'ang Hui, *Bull. Peiping Acad. Sci.* 4, no. 6.

5. *KKTH* 1956 (2), 36.

rectangular pits, graves containing human sacrifices, and relatively concentrated habitations.

The important question at the moment is not whether the Chou civilization was later in time than the Neolithic stage, which is certainly the
case, but whether we can identify, in archaeological remains, the period
of the Western Chou before their conquest of the Shang. We know from
chia ku scripts that during the Yin phase of the Shang period the Chou
were referred to as a powerful subordinate state to be reckoned with.
Archaeological remains of Shang types have been located in the Wei-shui
valley in a Neolithic context,[6] but archaeological remains of the Chou
demonstrably contemporary with the Shang have been wanting. Ritual
bronzes and large tombs of the Chou period have long been known in
the Wei-shui valley, but all that have been found thus far seem to date
within the latter part of the Western Chou dynasty.[7]

If there was a Chou civilization comparable in magnitude and intensity
with the Shang civilization in Honan, its ruins and relics should exist at
least around the capitals of Wen Wang and Wu Wang, probably in an
area southwest of the modern city of Sian on the banks of the Feng River.
The modern village of Chang-chia-p'o and its environs have yielded the
largest amount of relics dating to the Western Chou period. Between
1955 and 1957 a habitation area and a number of human burials were
excavated; two occupational components were distinguished at the habitation area, and the tombs have been grouped into five stages. The early
occupational stratum of the habitation area antedates the earliest burials,
which have been dated to Ch'eng and K'ang—the two kings who reigned
immediately after Wu Wang—according to the typology of the bronze
vessels found in the tombs, which is comparable with bronze vessels of
known date. The site therefore must have been inhabited before King
Ch'eng. Since the region was not a major Chou area until Wen Wang,
it is possible that the early habitation component of the Chang-chia-p'o
site can be dated to Kings Wen Wang and Wu Wang, that is, to the Chou
immediately before and after the conquest.[8] The cultural remains at the
site thus have a direct bearing on the level of culture of the Chou at that
time.

6. Shih Chang-ju, *BIHP* 27 (1956), 315. Hsu I, *WWTKTL* 1956 (3), 65.

7. The only existing inscribed bronze vessel that could date from the pre-conquest
period of Western Chou history is the so-called T'ien-wang kui. See Sun Tso-yün,
WWTKTL 1958 (1), 29–31; Ch'ien Po-ch'üan, *WWTKTL* 1958 (12), 56–57; Sun
Tso-yün, *WW* 1960 (5), 50–52; Yin Ti-fei, *WW* 1960 (5), 53–54.

8. Wang Po-hung et al., *Feng-hsi fa-chüeh pao-kao*, Peking, Wen Wu Press, 1962.

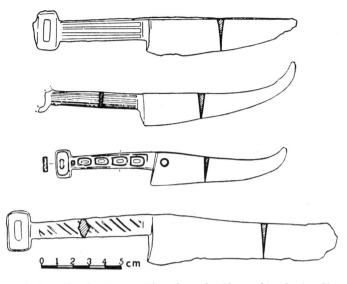

134. Bronze knives of early Western Chou from the Chang-chia-p'o site, Sian, Shensi. (From *Feng Hsi fa-chüeh pao-kao*, Peking, Wen Wu Press, 1962, p. 83.)

Archaeological remains uncovered from this early habitation stratum indicate very strongly that during its occupation—which probably contained the period of Chou before the conquest—the Chou was already a bronze-making culture with a sophisticated social organization. Many bronze implements were found at the site, including a socketed ax, fifteen knives, sixty-two arrowheads, and several horse and chariot fittings. The knives are characteristically bent, with a concave back, and are equipped with a square loop at the end (fig. 134), distinct from the common Shang types at Hsiao-t'un; and the arrowheads also differ from the Hsiao-t'un types in minor features.[9] It is not clear from the report of the site whether these bronze implements came from the early stratum or from a later occupation (also Western Chou but near the end), but from the early occupation four pieces of clay molds (for casting horse and chariot fittings) were excavated, indicating that during the early period the Chou were not only bronze casters in the Shang tradition but also horse-chariot warriors. Also from the early period was a workshop that manufactured only hairpins and arrowheads of bone and antler. The bone hairpins are of several types, but all have counterparts in the specimens from Hsiao-t'un and Hsi-pei-kang.[10]

9. Compared with Hsiao-t'un types described in Li Chi, *Bull. College of Arts*, Nat'l. Taiwan Univ., no. 4 (1952), 179–240.

10. Li Chi, *BIHP* 30 (1959), 1–69.

Apparently the Chang-chia-p'o village of the early Western Chou period provided some essential services to the men of the upper classes whose center of activity was in the cities nearby (Feng or Hao or both), which remain to be discovered. Presumably a great deal more will be known about the level of achievement of Chou civilization when these city sites have been unearthed, but the new data from Chang-chia-p'o suffice to show that the Chou before the conquest had already achieved a level much higher than the Neolithic K'o-hsing-chuang culture (Shensi Lung-shan culture) of the same area, from which, or from a culture similar to which, the Chou were apparently derived. It would indeed be strange if the Chou, who were able to overthrow the powerful government of the Shang dynasty at An-yang, were still at a barbarous Neolithic level of culture and came empty-handed into the Shang legacy.[11]

Major Sites of the Chou

For a civilization like the Chou, whose temporal duration was close to a millennium and whose areal expanse covered most of China, it is no longer possible to enumerate all the important archaeological sites, nor is it necessary to describe even the most characteristic. But the nucleus of the Western Chou civilization, located in the neighborhood of Sian, Shensi, must be discussed. By the time the royal capital had shifted to Lo-yang in western Honan, a series of local states had risen to eminence, each achieving its own subcivilization within a common Chou Chinese frame-work. The archaeological data from the Lo-yang area must of course be described, and some local subcivilizations whose archaeological data are abundant will be included. Then, using data from these areas and from other sites throughout China, I shall discuss several of the most important archaeological aspects of the developmental trends of the Chou civilization.

The Sian Area

From Hou Chi to Wu Wang, five or six capitals of the Western Chou dynasty were recorded in historical literature. Of these, the last one, Hao, was the most important, not only because it provided the center stage for Wu Wang's conquest, but also because it served as the seat of power for twelve kings from Wu Wang to Yu Wang for a period of 351 years

11. See Magdalene von Dewall, *Symposium in Honor of Dr. Li Chi on His Seventieth Birthday* (Taipei, *Ch'ing-hua Journal*), pt. 2, 1966, pp. 1–68, for a discussion of the "creative" aspects of the Chou as against the Shang according to the Hsin Ts'un finds.

(1122–771 B.C.). The exact location of Hao has been described in historical records, and there is little question that it was in an area southwest of the modern city of Sian, in Shensi Province, on the east bank of the River Feng, a small tributary of the Wei-shui in the north. On the west bank of the same river is said to be the site of Feng, Wen Wang's capital for only fifteen years. Although the capital was moved across the river to Hao, Feng remained the site of the royal temples. The well-drained plain west of Sian, located between the Tsinling Mountains in the south and the Wei River in the north, was thus the center of the Royal Chou until they came to an end in 771 B.C.[12] The Han historian Pan Ku, writing toward the end of the first century of the present era, praised this region thus,[13]

> In abundance of flowering plants and fruits it is the most fertile of the Nine Provinces
>
> In natural barriers for protection and defense it is the most impregnable refuge in heaven and earth
>
> This is why its influence has extended in six directions
> This is why it has thrice become the seat of imperial power

The last line "refers to the successful use of the area as a center of power by the Chou who launched from this plain their conquest of the Shang, by the Ch'in, the creators of unified empire, and by the great Han during the first two centuries of their rule."[14]

The archaeological investigations of the Chou settlements in the Feng/Hao area began in the 1930s, but it was not until the 1950s that this region was given the concentrated effort it deserves. Sites containing Western Chou remains appear to cluster in two loci on both banks of the Feng (fig. 135). One is on the west bank from K'o-hsing-chuang in the northeast to Feng-ts'un in the southwest, in an area about 5 kilometers east-west and 2.5 kilometers north-south, a site approximating the location of the old capital Feng in the literature. The other, coinciding with the location of Hao, is on the east bank from Lo-shui-ts'un in the north to south of Tou-men-chen, covering an area about 4 kilometers north-south and 1.5 east-west. Outside these two clusters, isolated remains and ruins have been

12. Shih Chang-ju, *Ta-lu tsa-chih t'eh-k'an*, vol. 1, Taipei, Ta-lu Tsa-chih Shê, 1953. *KK* 1963 (4), 188–97.

13. Translated and quoted by Arthur F. Wright, *Jour. Asian Studies* 24 (1965), 668–69.

14. *Ibid.*, p. 669.

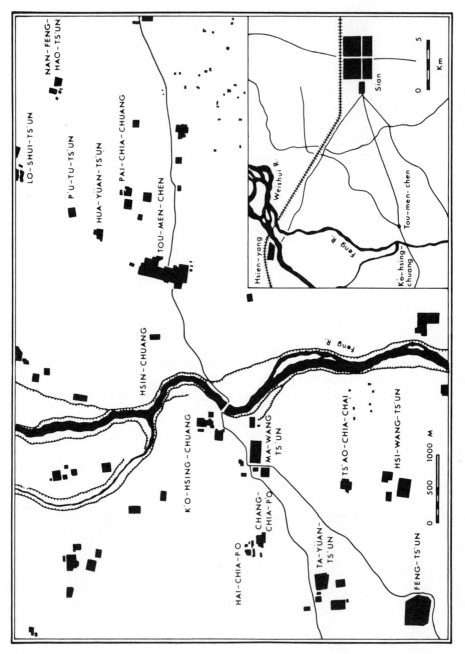

135. Villages on the banks of the river Feng southwest of Sian, Shensi, where important Western Chou sites have been discovered.

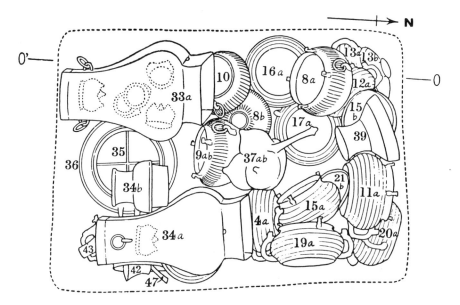

136. A hoard of Western Chou bronze vessels found at Ma-wang-ts'un, Sian. (From *Ch'ang-an Chang-chia-p'o t'ung-ch'i ch'ün*, Peking, Wen Wu Press, 1965, p. 12.)

found throughout the neighborhood.[15] For the sake of convenience, I refer to the cluster of sites on the west and east banks as the Feng and Hao areas respectively.

The Feng area has yielded a large number of Western Chou remains as a result of intensive excavations since 1955. The area west of the village of Chang-chia-p'o is the best known: dwelling remains, 136 tombs, and 4 horse-drawn chariot burials excavated in 1955–57;[16] dwelling remains, 4 burials, and 1 chariot burial in 1960;[17] and a large tomb with ceremonial bronzes in 1964.[18] East of Chang-chia-p'o in the vicinity of the village of Ma-wang-ts'un, dwelling remains were brought to light during 1959–60;[19] a hoard of 53 bronze vessels (11 of which were inscribed) was uncovered in 1961 (fig. 136),[20] a large tomb with 28 bronze vessels was investigated in 1963,[21] and a hoard of 25 bronzes (many inscribed) was

15. Hsü Hsi-t'ai, *KK* 1962 (6), 306–07.

16. Wang Po-hung et al., *Feng-hsi fa-chüeh pao-kao. KK* 1959 (10), 516–30; 1964 (9), 441–47, 474.

17. *KK* 1962 (1), 20–22.

18. *KK* 1965 (9), 447–50.

19. *KK* 1962 (6), 307–09.

20. *Ch'ang-an Chang-chia-p'o Hsi Chou t'ung-chi ch'ün*, Peking, Wen Wu Press, 1965.

21. *KK* 1963 (8), 413–15.

uncovered in 1973.[22] North of Ma-wang-ts'un, in the K'o-hsing-chuang area, habitation remains and 51 tombs of the Western Chou period were excavated during 1955–57.[23] Southwest of Chang-chia-p'o, near the village of Ta-yüan-ts'un, habitation remains, wells, and burials were excavated during 1959–60.[24] We know that habitation debris is scattered throughout the area; that "workshops" for bone, pottery, bronze, and tile have been found at various localities; that tombs of various kinds with furnishings of varying degrees of luxuriousness (including a few with up to four human sacrificial victims for a single tomb) are scattered throughout; and that chariot burials were constructed presumably to accommodate some departed noblemen. The remains in the whole area range in date from possibly the Wen Wang reign through the end of the Western Chou. Apparently this Feng area was a major center of cultural activity during the entire Western Chou period, and the royal capital of Feng is perhaps still buried, to be brought to light in the future. Until that happens, however, the pattern and history of settlement west of the Feng River remains unknown.

It is significant, however, that the 182 tombs in the Chang-chia-p'o and K'o-hsiang-chuang area excavated during 1955–57 by the Institute of Archaeology (Academia Sinica, Peking) were apparently constructed throughout the span of the Western Chou's some 330 years, and the typology of artifacts and tomb construction here constitutes a complete sequence of development that can well serve as a standard scale for other Western Chou sites in the vicinity and beyond. Five major typological phases have been distinguished, primarily on the basis of ceramic types (fig. 137), and habitation remains throughout the Feng area have been cross-dated with the tombs accordingly.

Compared with the Feng area, there are fewer archaeological remains in the Hao area. Historical records relate that during the T'ang dynasty the construction of K'un-ming Lake in the royal gardens destroyed a good part of the ancient ruins of Hao, which could account for the relative scarcity of remains of Western Chou date, but exploration is only just beginning. Large tombs with ritual bronze vessels dating to the reign of Mu Wang in the early part of Western Chou were uncovered in 1954 and 1955;[25] and large areas of habitation and burial remains have been

22. *KK* 1974 (1), 1–5.
23. Wang Po-hung et al., *Feng-hsi fa-chüeh pao-kao. KK* 1959 (10), 516–30.
24. *KK* 1962 (6), 309.
25. *KKHP* 8 (1954); 1957 (1), 75–85.

Type / Period / Type tomb		Li	Kuan	Kui	Tou	Yü
I	M 178					
	KM145					
II	KM69					
III	M 157					
IV	M453					
V	M 147					

137. Characteristic pottery types of the five stages of Western Chou tombs in the area of Sian, Shensi. (From *Feng-hsi fa-chüeh pao-kao*, Peking, Wen Wu Press, 1962.)

located from Pai-chia-chuang in the south to Lo-shui-ts'un in the north.[26] If this was indeed the old site of Hao, further investigations in the area and of the interrelationship between the Hao government center and the Feng temple area of the Royal Chou will be extremely revealing and important for Western Chou archaeology.

Other Western Chou Sites

Prior to the establishment of the Chou in the Sian area, the Chou ancestors are said to have emerged either in the upper Wei-shui valley in western Shensi[27] or in the Huang Ho valley in southern Shansi.[28] In either area the available archaeological data cannot push back the time of the Western

26. *KK* 1963 (8), 403–12.
27. Shih Chang-ju, *Ta-lu tsa-chih t'eh-k'an*, vol. 1.
28. Ch'ien Mu, *Yenching Jour. Chinese Studies* 10 (1926), 1,955–2,008.

Chou civilization (as known in its earliest manifestation at Chang-chia-p'o, Sian), and the Neolithic sites characterized by the gray corded pottery (of the K'o-hsing-chuang culture) everywhere preceded the known Western Chou remains. The initial base of the Western Chou in the Wei-shui valley and in southern Shansi and in the Shang territory of western and northern Honan constituted the area of effective control of the new Western Chou dynasty immediately or some time after the conquest about 1100 B.C.

Events that took place during the decade after the conquest were highly important in shaping the subsequent developments. Wu Wang captured Wu Keng, crown prince of the Shang dynasty, but let him continue to head the fallen dynasty at Yin under the tutelage of Princes Kuan, Ts'ai, and Huo, three of Wu Wang's many brothers. The Shang, however, continued to claim the loyalty of the people in the old Shang territory in eastern Honan, Shantung, and northern Anhwei. Seven years after the conquest, Wu Wang died. His successor, Ch'eng Wang, was young, and he ascended the throne under the regency of his uncle Chou Kung, another younger brother of Wu Wang. Taking advantage of the unstable situation, Prince Kuan and Wu Keng, with the support of the former Shang vassal states in the east, rebelled against the new regime. Thereupon Chou Kung embarked on a series of moves that resulted in the thorough subjugation of all the Shang territory. First, having recaptured Yin and executed Prince Kuan and Wu Keng, he appointed another brother, Prince K'ang, the Duke of Wei, to rule the old Shang royal territory; second, he moved farther east and conquered the state of Yen in western Shantung, where he created the state of Lu and appointed his son Po Ch'in its duke; third, he built an eastern capital at Lo-yang in western Honan to facilitate total control of the eastern parts of North China. Thus, Wu Wang merely conquered the Shang dynasty, but Chou Kung unified the Shang and Chou territories into a Chou China. The regimes immediately after Chou Kung, those of Ch'eng (Chou Kung stepped down when the boy was old enough to rule) and K'ang, were the peaks of Western Chou royal power, reaching beyond the areas of the Shang and the Chou into the north (as far as Inner Mongolia) and the south (beyond the Yangtze Valley).

Archaeological assemblages of bronzes—the surest indications of the political and ritual aspects of the Chou regime—have been unearthed in the old Chou domain of Shensi and Shansi, in the old Shang territory of Honan and Shantung, and also in areas farther north and south (fig. 138). These have been dated—by means of inscriptions, typology, and context

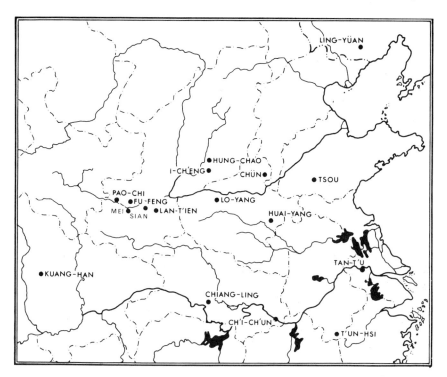

138. Major sites of the Western Chou.

—from shortly after the conquest to the reigns of the last Western Chou kings. In most cases they came from tombs, but in a few instances hoards of bronze vessels were found, probably indicating the burial of ritual treasures at times of upheaval. In the Shensi and Shansi region they included such significant finds as those in Pao-chi,[29] Mei Hsien,[30] Ch'i-shan,[31] Fu-feng,[32] Chou-chih,[33] Ch'ang-wu,[34] Ching-yang,[35] and Lan-t'ien,[36]

29. Su Ping-ch'i, *Tou-chi-t'ai Kou-tung-ch'ü mu-tsang.* KK 1963 (10), 574–76. Umehara Sueji, Kyoto Tōhō Bunka Kenkyu So, Research Report, no. 2, 1933. WW 1975 (3), 47–48, 72–75.

30. WWTKTL 1957 (4), 5–9. WW 1972 (7), 2, 3–4.

31. WW 1972 (6), 25–27. KK 1976 (1), 31–38.

32. *Fu-feng Ch'i-chia-ts'un ch'ing-t'ung-ch'i ch'ün,* Peking, Wen Wu Press, 1963. KK 1962 (2), 88–91, 1963 (10), 574–76. WW 1961 (7), 59–60; 1963 (9), 65–66; 1972 (6), 30–35; 1972 (7), 9–12; 1973 (11), 78–79; 1975 (8), 57–60.

33. WW 1975 (7), 91.

34. WW 1975 (5), 89–90.

35. WW 1972 (7), 5–7.

36. WW 1960 (2), 5–10; 1960 (8/9), 78–79. KK 1960 (5), 33–36.

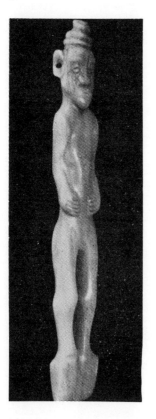

139. A carved human figure of jade from a
Western Chou tomb in Ling-t'ai, Kansu.
(From *WW* 1972, no. 12.)

in Shensi;[37] Hung-chao[38] and I-ch'eng[39] in Shansi; and Ling-t'ai in Kansu
(fig. 139).[40] In the old Shang domain Western Chou finds occurred in
Lo-yang,[41] Chün Hsien,[42] Hsin-cheng[43] and Huai-yang[44] in Honan; and
Tsou Hsien in Shantung.[45] Farther north, Western Chou tombs with
bronze vessels, chariots (fig. 140), and human victims have been found near

37. Reports of other important Shensi bronzes of Western Chou date include *Ch'ing-
t'ung-ch'i t'u shih*, Peking, Wen Wu Press, 1960; *WW* 1963 (3), 43–45; 1964 (7), 20–27;
1965 (7), 17–19; 1966 (1), 1–6; *KK* 1965 (3), 152.

38. *WWTKTL* 1955 (4), 46–52; (8), 42–44.

39. *WW* 1963 (4), 51–52. *KK* 1963 (4), 225.

40. *WW* 1972 (12), 2–6. *KK* 1976 (1), 39–43.

41. *KKTH* 1955 (5), 30. *KK* 1959 (4), 187. *WWTKTL* 1955 (5), 116–17; 1955 (6),
124. *Lo-yang Chung-chou-lu*, Peking, Science Press, 1959.

42. Kuo Pao-chün, *Chün Hsien Hsin-ts'un*, Peking, Science Press, 1964.

43. *WW* 1972 (10), 66.

44. *KK* 1964 (3), 163–64.

45. *KK* 1965 (11), 541–47.

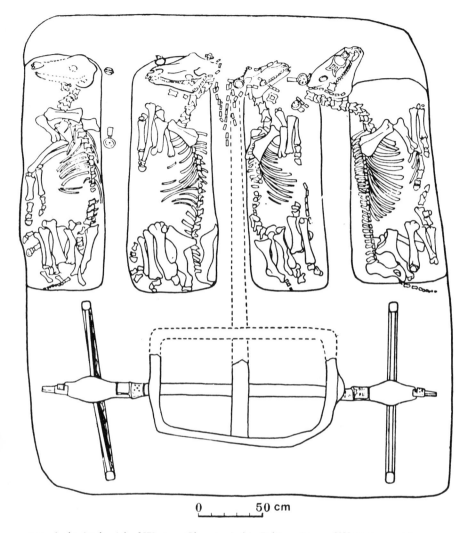

0   50 cm

140. A chariot burial of Western Chou period in Peking. (From *KK* 1974, no. 5.)

Peking,[46] and a bronze assemblage was found in Ling-yüan in Liaoning.[47] It is even said that the masked horses at Chang-chia-p'o were probably the prototype of those at Pazyryk.[48] In the south, whole bronze assemblages of western Chou types are known from Tan-t'u in Kiangsu,[49] T'un-

46. *KK* 1974 (5), 309–21.

47. *WWTKTL* 1955 (8), 16–27.

48. John F. Haskins, *Archives of the Chinese Art Society of America* 16 (1962), 92–96.

49. *WWTKTL* 1955 (5), 58–63; 1956 (1), 45–46. T'ang Lan, *KKHP* 1959 (2), 79–84.

hsi in Anhwei,[50] Ch'i-ch'un[51] and Chiang-ling[52] in Hupei, and Kuang-han in Szechwan,[53] that is, throughout the Yangtze Valley. A bronze *ho* with rather convincing Western Chou decorative patterns has recently been reported from western Kwangtung.[54] The glazed pottery from T'un-hsi is so similar to that at Chang-chia-p'o in technique of manufacture and mineral composition that some scholars were convinced the Chang-chia-p'o pottery was imported from the south.[55] Recent findings of glazed pottery ("porcelain") from Western Chou tombs near Lo-yang,[56] as well as from a number of Shang sites, testify to the chronological priority of the north, but the T'un-hsi find was still a significant indication of the extent of Western Chou contact and communication in the southern direction. Further discussion of the south will be undertaken in the final chapter.

Other than indicating the extent of the Western Chou civilization, these sites and their various remains are of varying importance in the study of ancient China. Many bronzes are inscribed: one more inscribed bronze vessel means one more piece of textual material for the study of Western Chou society and history. The bronzes found in archaeological sites provide a body of data that not only helps to identify the thousands of unauthenticated ritual bronze vessels of the same period in public and private collections but also provides a contextual background for the study of cultural associations and chronology. With these data, old and new, that furnish a series of bronze assemblages from the beginning to the end of Western Chou, historians and art historians, as well as archaeologists, have a source of information far exceeding that provided by the pre-Ch'in texts. In addition to the bronzes and their inscriptions, these sites also tell scholars about the developments of technology, art, and burial customs, aspects that will be dealt with in some detail in the following sections.

The Lo-yang Area

Lo-yang in western Honan, like Sian, has been a city of great significance throughout Chinese history and served as the capital of the empire repea-

50. *KKHP* 1959 (4), 59–90.
51. *KK* 1962 (1), 1–9.
52. *KK* 1963 (4), 224–25. *WW* 1963 (2), 53–55.
53. Cheng Te-k'un, *Hsieh-ta Jour. Chinese Studies* 1 (1949), 67–81.
54. *WW* 1975 (11), 94.
55. *KK* 1961 (8), 444–45.
56. *WW* 1972 (10), 25.

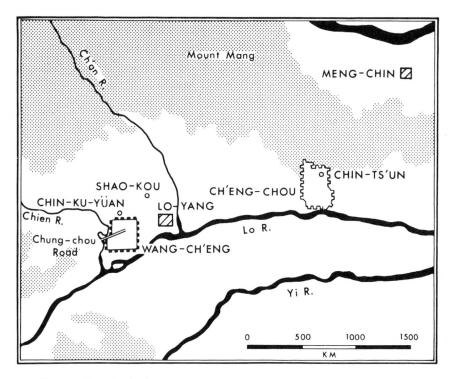

141. Eastern Chou sites in the Lo-yang area, Honan.

tedly. The sites of the Lo-yang city (fig. 141) during the various dynastic periods were not identical but were all situated in an area south of Mang Mountain where two small rivers, Chien in the west and Ch'an in the east, flow southward into the River Lo, a tributary of the Huang Ho. The present walled city of Lo-yang is on the west bank of the Ch'an, but most of the early ruins of Lo-yang occur in the suburban areas to its east and west. The city was built by Chou Kung at the site of an existing Shang settlement after his eastern military campaign and apparently consisted of two separate sites, Wang Ch'eng and Ch'eng Chou. Wang Ch'eng was in the western suburb of modern Lo-yang on the eastern bank of the River Chien, and Ch'eng Chou was east of Lo-yang, east of the River Ch'an. During the Han dynasty, a new and smaller enclosure was built in the Wang Ch'eng area and was known as Ho-nan; the Han capital of Lo-yang was probably built at the site of Ch'eng Chou in the east.

Although the twin cities of Lo-yang were constructed at the beginning of Western Chou, archaeological remains dating from Western Chou are relatively few in the Lo-yang area and are largely known at three or four localities in the western,[57] northern,[58] and eastern [59] suburbs of modern Lo-yang. All of these are tombs. Remains of the Eastern Chou period increase noticeably in the Lo-yang area, which became the seat of the Royal Chou after 771 B.C. When additional data from the Western Chou period become known, especially data concerning Wang Ch'eng and Ch'eng Chou, a comparison between the Western Chou and the Eastern Chou cities of Lo-yang will be interesting.

Major Eastern Chou remains at Lo-yang are known from four archaeological loci: the Wang Ch'eng walls, the Chung-chou Road, Shao-kou on the Wang Ch'eng side, and Chin-ts'un on the Ch'eng Chou side. The walls of Wang Ch'eng were outlined during 1954–58;[60] a study of the Chou relics in relation to the city wall brings to light for the first time some aspects of the pattern of urbanism in a Chou royal capital and will be described below. The tombs at both Shao-kou[61] and Chin-ts'un[62] are dated to the Warring States period. The Chin-ts'un tombs were particularly prolific in fine specimens of art and vessels with inscriptions pertaining to affairs of various states, attesting to the continuing role of the Royal Chou as the center of some ritual and social transactions throughout North China.

Eastern Chou sites along the Chung-chou Road[63] are of special significance in yielding remains dating from the Eastern Chou period of more than half a millennium and providing a master sequence against which other Eastern Chou sites can be measured for chronological placement. In the 1950s a new urban expansion project took place in the western suburbs of Lo-yang, and a main road, Chung-chou-lu, was constructed between the old walled city of modern Lo-yang and the new housing area, from the western bank of the Ch'an River to the eastern bank of the Chien River; it cuts across the middle of the Wang Ch'eng city site. In 1954 and 1955, archaeologists investigated the Chung-chou Road for

57. *Loyang Chung-chou-lu*, pp. 139–40. KK 1961 (4), 178.

58. *KKTH* 1955 (5), 30. KK 1959 (4), 187; 1972 (2), 35–36. *WWTKTL* 1955 (5), 116–17; 1955 (6), 124. *WW* 1964 (9), 54–55; 1972 (10), 20–28.

59. Kuo Pao-chün and Lin Shou-chin, *KKHP* 9 (1955), 104–08.

60. *KKHP* 1959 (2), 15–36.

61. *KKHP* 8 (1954), 127–62.

62. William C. White, *Tombs of Old Lo-yang*, Shanghai, Kelly & Walsh, 1934. S. Umehara, *Rakuyō Kinson Kobo shūei*, Kyoto, Hayashi Press, 1936.

63. *Lo-yang Chung-chou-lu*. KK 1974 (3), 171–78.

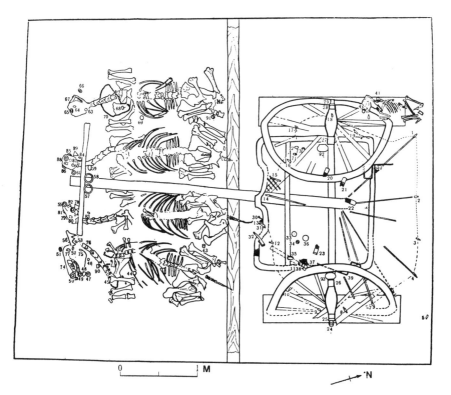

142. A chariot burial found at Chung-chou-lu in Lo-yang. (*KK* 1974, no. 3.)

a distance of 2,100 meters to the east from the eastern bank of the Chien, exposing an east-west cross section of the Eastern Chou city. Yang-shao, Shang, and Chou (both Western and Eastern) storage pits were found, but the largest group of remains consisted of 260 burials of the Eastern Chou (fig. 142). On the basis of stratigraphy and the association patterns of some characteristic pottery vessel types, Su Ping-ch'i, An Chin-min, and Lin Shou-chin have grouped the 260 tombs into seven periods (dates are approximate and furnished by the present author): (1) Early Spring Autumn (770–670 B.C.); (2) Middle Spring Autumn (670–570); (3) Late Spring Autumn (570–470); (4) Early Warring States (470–400); (5,6) early and late Middle Warring States (400–300); (7) Late Warring States (300–220) (fig. 143). This is the longest single typological sequence of Eastern Chou archaeological remains to date, and many other Eastern Chou sites in North China can be placed according to this sevenfold scheme on the basis of their bronze and ceramic types.

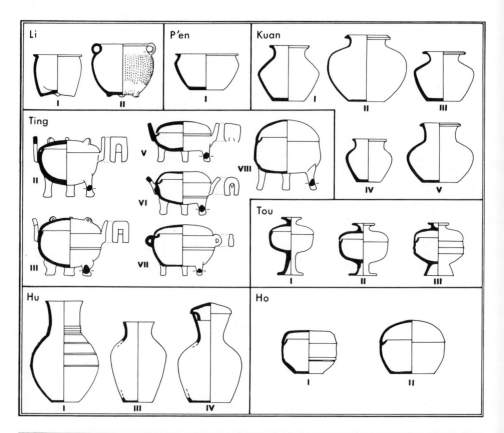

Periods \ Associations	Li – P'en – Kuan	Ting – Tou – Kuan	Ting – Tou – Hu	Ting – Ho – Hu
I	I – I – I I – I – II			
II	II – I – II			
III	II – I – III II – I – IV	II – I – III II – I – IV		
IV		II – I – V	II – I – I II – II – I III – II – I	
V		V – II – V	V – II – I V – II – III	
VI		VI – III – V	VI – III – III	
VII		VII – III – V	VII – III – III	VII – I – III VIII – II – IV

143. Characteristic pottery types of the seven stages of Eastern Chou tombs of Chung-chou-lu, Lo-yang. (Based on *Lo-yang Chung-chou-lu*, Peking, Science Press, 1959.)

Other Eastern Chou Sites

The eighth and seventh centuries B.C. were a great turning point in the ancient history of China—a turning point that was probably of even greater consequence than the Wu Wang and Chou Kung conquests of the eleventh century in long-term developmental trends of the Chinese civilization. The Royal Chou's power had weakened toward the beginning of the eighth century to such an extent that the growing pressure of the warlike mounted nomads in the northwest became unbearable, and the capital had to be moved, in 771 B.C., to Lo-yang. In inverse proportion to the dwindling status of the Royal Chou, the local lords of the feudal states—appointed in the beginning of the Western Chou dynasty mainly from among the royal brothers and relatives—grew more prosperous, mighty, and independent. The archaeological remains of the Eastern Chou period (fig. 144) show this new trend of development in several ways. Rich assemblages of bronzes and other artifacts, found at large habitation sites and in lavishly furnished tombs, are now commonplace throughout China. Many inscribed pieces show they were made for the state courts and local lords, in contrast to the Western Chou pieces which concerned either the Royal Chou themselves or their relatives. It is now no longer practical to describe or enumerate the sites of the period under a simple heading of "Eastern Chou"; rather, important finds must be referred to the states to which they belonged (fig. 145). The number of walled-city sites, now scattered over the country, drastically increased, testifying to the growing localization of political and military affairs. Data for the following discussion of cultural developments must be selective, for my purpose here is not to compile a complete catalogue of archaeological finds. A number of classical or extremely important sites, however, must not be left unmentioned.

In the *area of Chin*—the biggest of the Eastern Chou states, which includes modern southern Shansi, southern Hopei, and northern Honan and which broke up around 450 B.C. into three smaller states, Chao, Wei, and Han—large and well-known Eastern Chou sites are the most numerous. In the region of Chao[64] are two well-known sites found before

---

64. Reference to the regions of Chao, Wei, and Han is for the purpose of identifying the location of sites and does not necessarily indicate that the sites were within these states, which were not formed before 453 B.C. For an approach to the discrimination among these three states according to weapons, see Huang Sheng-chang, *KKHP* 1974 (1), 13 ff.

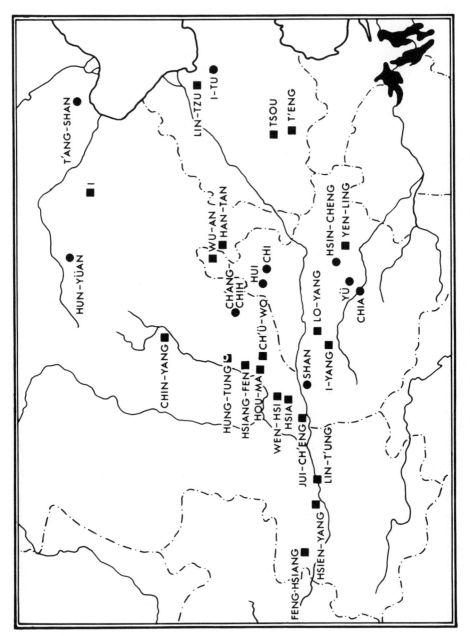

144. Major sites of the Eastern Chou civilization: *circles*, tombs only; *squares*, city ruins.

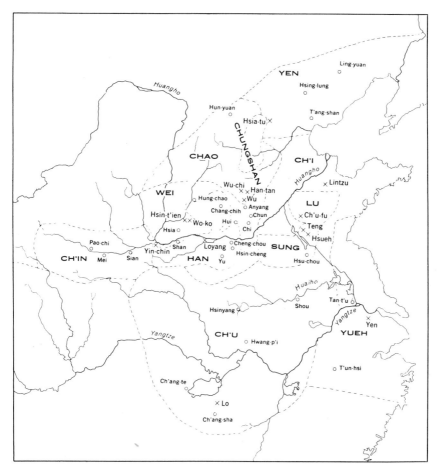

145. Important Bronze Age sites in China in relation to the boundaries in the Warring States period, at approximately 350 B.C. (State boundaries drawn after Yang K'uan, *Chan Kuo shih*, Shanghai, Jenmin Press, 1957.)

World War II, Li-yü-ts'un in Hun-yüan, northern Shansi,[65] and Han-tan, in southern Hopei.[66] Li-yü-ts'un, a tomb of the Warring States period discovered by accident in 1923, was one of the earliest sites found in modern Chinese archaeology and is often used to illustrate the Warring States types of bronzes. The Han-tan city site, Chao's capital from 386 to 228 B.C., was briefly investigated before the war, and recent work around it has uncovered many contemporary remains of various kinds.

65. Shang Ch'eng-tso, *Hun-yüan i-ch'i*, Shanghai, 1936.

66. Komai Kazuchika and Sekino Takeshi, *Han-tan*, Archaeologia Orientalis, ser. B, no. 7, 1954.

The region of Wei in southern Shansi and northern Honan includes the remains of an important urban complex near the town of Hou-ma, Shansi,[67] and a series of tombs at Liu-li-ko and Ku-wei-ts'un in Hui Hsien[68] and Shan-piao-chen in Chi Hsien,[69] northern Honan. The tombs here provide some of the best examples of Warring States artifacts, and the bronze vessels and iron implements are used as type specimens of the period. The city site of Hou-ma consists of a complex of earthen enclosures, a ceremonial locus, farming villages, and workshops, and it is perhaps one of the three or four best-known city sites in the archaeology of ancient China.

Farther south in the region of Han, there are the important tombs at Fen-shui-ling in Ch'ang-chih,[70] and three well-known bronze assemblages in tombs in Hsin-cheng,[71] at Pai-sha in Yü Hsien,[72] and at T'ai-p'u-hsiang in Chia Hsien.[73] Of these, the Hsin-cheng bronzes were among the earliest found of the Chou period (1932), and their dating problem has engaged the attention of scholars for many years.

Important sites in the area of Chin must include the burials at Shang-ts'un-ling in Shan Hsien, westernmost Honan.[74] Inscribed bronzes found here ascribe the burials to the state of Kuo, a small state annexed by Chin in 655 B.C., thus providing a rare find that dates during the crucial period from late Western Chou through the early Spring Autumn period.

In the *area of Yen* northeast of Chin, the city site of Hsia-tu in I Hsien, central Hopei,[75] furnishes information of city life in the state, and the burials at Chia-ko-chuang, near T'ang-shan in northern Hopei,[76] contained bronze vessels that well attest to the occurrence of some of the finest art of the Eastern Chou in the northernmost area of China proper. In the *area of Ch'i* in Shantung, east of Chin, the city site of Lin-tzu[77] and the burials

67. See below, pp. 324–27.

68. Hsia Nai et al., *Hui Hsien fa-chüeh pao-kao*, Peking, Science Press, 1956. Kuo Pao-chün, *Shan-piao-chen yü Liu-li-ko*, Peking, Science Press, 1959.

69. Kuo Pao-chün, *op. cit.*

70. *KKHP* 1957 (1), 103–18; 1974 (2), 63–84. *WW* 1957 (12), 77; 1972 (4), 38–44. *KK* 1964 (3), 111–37.

71. Carl W. Bishop, *Chinese Jour. Science and Arts* 3 (1925), 72–74. Sun Hai-p'o, *Hsin-cheng i ch'i*, K'ai-feng, 1937. Kuan Po-i, *Cheng chung ku-ch'i t'u-k'ao*, Shanghai, Chung-hua Book Co., 1940. *KK* 1964 (7), 368; 1973 (6), 372–80. *WW* 1972 (10), 32–40.

72. *KKHP* 7 (1954), 87–101.

73. *WWTKTL* 1954 (3), 60–62; 1954 (5), 38–40.

74. Lin Shou-chin et al., *Shang-ts'un-ling Kuo Kuo mu-ti*, Peking, Science Press, 1959.

75. See below, pp. 335–39.

76. *KKHP* 6 (1953), 57–116.

77. See below, pp. 339–41.

at Su-fu-t'un in I-tu[78] provided the initial impetus of Eastern Chou archaeology in that part of China. In the *area of Ch'in* in Shensi, west of Chin, perhaps the recent discovery and excavations of several city sites, including the principal state capital at Hsien-yang, are most noteworthy.[79] In the *area of Ch'u* in Hupei, Anhwei, and Hunan, tombs in Shou Hsien and Ch'ang-sha are the most outstanding. These, and other Eastern Chou sites of South China, will be described in chapter 9.[80]

The archaeological data unearthed at the Chou sites characterized above, and at many other sites that cannot be mentioned here,[81] are a treasure trove that will probably engage many archaeologists and historians in lifetimes of study. Drawing on some of the pertinent material, I shall discuss only those important aspects of the development of the Chou civilization that are of general significance for the purpose of this book. A full treatment of Chou archaeology is not intended, nor is any attempt made here to use the written materials for a comprehensive history of Chou society and culture.

Development of Cities

In the last chapter the characteristics of the first cities in North China were described; the Shang cities were shown to have consisted physically of an aristocratic center, in the shape of a walled enclosure of pounded earth, in which the aristocratic and ceremonial buildings and structures were located, and the area around this enclosure, where specialized industrial quarters and farming villages were dispersed. When we trace these constituents of Shang cities in time, a number of persistent traditions can be shown to have continued throughout the span of the Chou dynasty, such as the wall of stamped earth, the ceremonial and palatial platform, and the aristocratic center. The basic pattern of urban organization, however, underwent some important changes with time.

In the history of city development, unfortunately, archaeological materials are totally lacking for the entire Western Chou period. This hiatus is not fatal, however, for the culture during this interval of approximately three hundred years is known from other kinds of remains, to be

78. Ch'i Yen-p'ei, *Chung-kuo k'ao-ku hsüeh-pao* 2 (1947), 167–71.

79. See below, pp. 344–45.

80. Among the sites described will be the earlier tomb of the marquis of Ts'ai, dating to a period before the Ch'u annexation of the Shou Hsien area. See *Shou Hsien Ts'ai-hou mu ch'u-t'u i-wu*, Peking, Science Press, 1956.

81. Cheng Te-k'un, *Archaeology in China*, vol. 3, *Chou China*, Cambridge, Heffer, 1963, includes very useful summaries of other Chou sites throughout China.

discussed later in this chapter. Moreover, as we shall see, the basic change
in the pattern of urbanization seems to have come after the beginning of
the Eastern Chou period.

There is no question that the Western Chou aristocracy were city
builders. The poem "Wen Wang yu sheng" in the section "Ta ya" of
Shih ching describes how Wen Wang built the city of Feng, and Wu
Wang built the city of Hao. Lo-yang was, according to Tso Lo chieh in
I Chou shu, situated between the River Lo in the south and Chia Mountain in the north and consisted of two enclosures of considerable dimensions.
The city enclosure was apparently again built of layers of stamped earth,
the construction of which was described vividly in the poems "Hung yen
chih shih and "Mien p'ien" (in the "Ya" sections of *Shih ching*), which are
generally regarded as containing reliable data from the Western Chou
period. As described above, the Chou cities at Sian and Lo-yang consisted
of two neighboring enclosures, one in the west, the other in the east,
separated by a river. The significance of this is not clear.

During the Eastern Chou period, when a series of local states came of
age, the number of cities certainly increased greatly and they expanded
throughout North China. Oshima Riichi has been able to list, from *Tso
chuan* and *Kung-yang chuan*, seventy-eight cities that were built during the
Ch'un-ch'iu period from 722 to 480 B.C. These include twenty-seven
cities in the state of Lu, twenty in Ch'u, ten in Chin, four in Cheng, three
in Ch'i, two in Sung, and one each in Chu, Ch'en, Wu, and Yüeh, extending in area throughout North China and the lower and middle Yangtze
Valley.[82] There were presumably other cities in these and other states
that were not recorded in the two sources Oshima has consulted. Archaeological surveys and excavations have thus far located and explored the
remains of the following cities of the Eastern Chou period (see fig. 144).

Lo-yang, Honan (probable site of Wang Ch'eng, Royal Chou). The royal
city of Lo-yang as it was during the Eastern Chou dynasty has only begun
to be explored; the results published thus far are preliminary.[83] The city
wall of the Eastern Chou period has been outlined, although only the
northern wall, the northern sections of the western and eastern walls,
a southern section of the western wall, and a western section of the southern
wall have been located (fig. 146). These walls made an enclosure approximately square in shape, 2,890 meters long on the northern side. The walls
were built in stamped-earth layers, averaging about 5 meters wide at the

82. Oshima Riichi, *Tōhōgakuhō* 30 (1959), 53.
83. *KKHP* 1959 (2), 15–34. *KK* 1961 (4), 216.

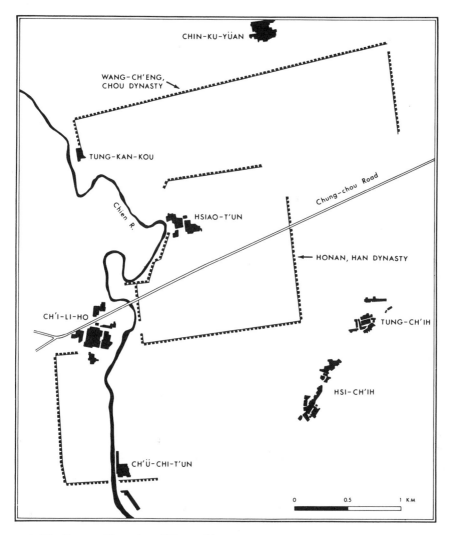

146. The Eastern Chou city of Wang-ch'eng, near Lo-yang, Honan. (Based on *KKHP* 1959 no. 2, facing p. 16.)

base, with a surviving height of 1.5 to 4 meters. Excavations carried out within the enclosure tend to show that important buildings were located in the southern or central part of the enclosure, as indicated by many stamped-earth house floors and a large amount of tiles (both flat and semicylindrical types) and eave tiles with *t'ao-t'ieh* and *yün* patterns. A pottery kiln area and one adjacent house foundation were located in the northwestern section of the enclosure; southeast of the kiln area there was

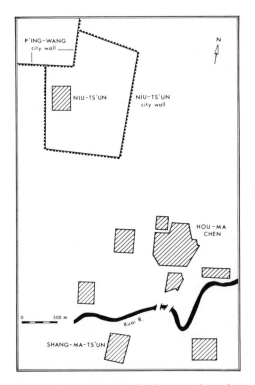

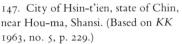

147. City of Hsin-t'ien, state of Chin, near Hou-ma, Shansi. (Based on *KK* 1963, no. 5, p. 229.)

a bone factory, and, farther south, a factory for making stone ornaments. Water ditches have been identified at scattered spots within the city. Associated cultural remains show that the city was built before the middle of the Ch'un-ch'iu period and was continuously in use until the later phases of the western Han dynasty, when a smaller enclosure within the former Lo-yang site was constructed. This Han Dynasty town is known as the seat of Honan county.[84]

Hou-ma, Shansi (probable site of Hsin-t'ien, state of Chin). The ruins of two old cities northwest of Hou-ma in southern Shansi were found in 1957. Fieldwork is still actively going on there and walls of additional city sites are being discovered within the same complex, but a general idea about the setup of the first two cities can be obtained from a series of preliminary reports.[85] These ruins have been dated to a late phase of the Ch'un-ch'iu period, with one of the two probably succeeding the

84. *KKTH* 1955 (1), 9–21.
85. *WWTKTL* 1957 (10), 55–56; 1958 (12), 32–33. *WW* 1959 (6), 42–45; 1960 (8/9), 11–14; 1961 (10), 25, 31–34; 1962 (4/5), 37–42, 43–54; 1966 (2), 1–3; 1972 (1), 63–69; 1972 (4), 27–37; 1972 (8), 31–38; 1973 (6), 62–65; 1975 (5), 1–26. *KK* 1959 (5), 222–28; 1962 (2), 55–62; 1963 (5), 229–45; 1973 (3), 185–91.

other, and are identified with the city of Hsin-t'ien, one of the capitals of of the prince of Chin (fig. 147).

The two cities adjoined each other diagonally. The one in the northwest has been called the Old City of P'ing-wang, named after a village nearby, and the one in the southeast, the Old City of Niu-ts'un, after a village of that name. Most of the walls of Niu-ts'un have been located in an enclosure 1,340–1,740 meters north-south and 1,100–1,400 meters east-west, forming a rough rectangle with an oblique northern wall. Only the southeastern corner of P'ing-wang, which intruded into the northwestern corner of Niu-ts'un, has been found and its general outline is still unknown. Both cities were built in stamped-earth layers by means of the pisé technique, but the surviving walls, completely covered under the ground, are only about 1 meter high. The earth making up the wall is fairly pure, and each stamped layer is about 6 centimeters thick. The cities seem to have been built on top of a cemetery area of early Ch'un-ch'iu period but were intruded into both by tombs of the Warring States period and by vehicle roads constructed during the Warring States and western Han. It seems probable, therefore, that the two cities were built successively during a later period of the Ch'un-ch'iu.

The only remains within the enclosures are a road section in Niu-ts'un and two platforms, one in each city, on which relics of buildings were found. The platform of P'ing-wang is in the southern part of the enclosure, but since the northern wall of this city has not been found the precise location is not clear. It was built on three levels. The bottom level is 75 meters square, oriented according to the four cardinal directions. Only the top of this level, which is of stamped-earth construction, has been excavated. A stamped-earth rectangle, 30 meters wide and over 20 meters long, adjoins the center of the southern side of the bottom level and is attached to a sloping ramp, about 6 meters wide and over 20 meters long, extending toward the south. The second level is about 4 meters above the ground; the central portion of its southern side is sloping. The third level is situated atop the northern portion of the second level, making a rectangle 35 meters north-south and 45 meters east-west. Fragments of tiles and a stone block, possibly a pillar foundation, were found on the top level of the platform. The whole platform is 8.5 meters high, consisting entirely of compactly stamped pure earth. The Niu-ts'un platform, in the northern part of the center within the city enclosure, is a square 52.5 by 52.5 meters and 6.5 meters high, composed of compactly stamped earth. Remains of buildings, such as fragments of tiles, are found on top of the platform, which has a depth of over 1 meter. The northern side of the platform is vertical, and the southern side forms a slope. Investigators of the site call both of these platforms palace foundations. Apparently the buildings atop the platforms were of considerable dimensions, facing south, and accessible by long ramps extending from the top of the platforms toward the bottom and the south.

A section of ditch 6 meters wide and 3 to 4 meters deep, possibly the remains of a defensive watercourse surrounding the city, was found outside the south wall of Niu-ts'un.

Outside of the Hsin-t'ien cities, but in the immediate neighborhood, a variety of other remains of approximately the same age have been found. Three foundries were located south of Niu-ts'un, over 200 meters apart. Tens of thousands of fragments of clay mólds and remains of crucibles were found. At one of the foundries the molds were used exclusively for the manufacture of such implements as spades and chisels and *pu* coins; at another foundry only molds for the making of belt hooks and carriage fittings were uncovered. The third one, the largest, has seventeen semi-subterranean houses, and clay piece molds for making bronze vessels, implements, and weapons. Remains here were left during two occupations, the earlier dating from the late Spring Autumn period and the later from early Warring States. Three bone manufactories have been located in the Hou-ma group, two in the neighborhood of the foundries, the other over 1,000 meters to the southeast. Wastes and raw materials, mostly deer bones, constitute the bulk of recovered remains at these three spots. A pottery kiln area has been located 1,000 meters southeast of Niu-ts'un; kilns are concentrated within an area of about half a square kilometer, some of them adjoining. The pots found in and near the kilns are of the same types as those found in the Niu-ts'un city area.

A residential village, also of the same age, was approximately 5 kilometers east of Niu-ts'un. The dwellings were all semisubterranean, 1.4 to 1.5 meters deep into the ground and 2.4 by 3 meters or 3 by 4 meters in dimension. The doors always face south and have stairways to the ground. Each house has a small niche in the interior wall, some divided into two levels. The upper part of the house was apparently built with wooden beams and covered with tiles. These houses are always in clusters and are accompanied by storage pits and sometimes by wells. Potsherds, shell saws, shell knives, bone hairpins, and bronze awls were found in and near the houses. Storage pits have been found at most of the sites in the Hsin-t'ien area; some were apparently for grains and soybeans, remains of which have been found.

Three groups of animal burials have been located: 0.5 kilometers south, 2.5 kilometers southeast, and 3 kilometers east of Niu-ts'un. These were oval pits, arranged regularly in groups, in which skeletons of horses (many), sheep (relatively few), and cattle (rare) were excavated. The animals seem to have been tied and placed upside down alive in the pits. Associated with the skeletons were bronze ornaments and jade artifacts. From the south-eastern complex of sacrificial pits, discovered at the end of 1965, more than six hundred brush- and red-ink-inscribed stone and jade tablets were excavated. These are regarded as pledges of allegiance between states, which were buried in several dozen pits as a part of an allegiance ritual.

About 2 kilometers south of the Niu-ts'un city an Eastern Chou cemetery was excavated in 1961. Bronzes and pottery found in the tombs (fourteen were opened) are of types ranging from late Western Chou through the middle Warring States. This cemetery was possibly related to the city ruins to its north, and its earlier date may suggest existence in this area of previous city structures that are yet to be located. Another cemetery area was found near Ch'iao-ts'un, its most striking feature being the large numbers of sacrificial human victims, many with an iron choker attached to the neck.

The Hsin-t'ien cities near Hou-ma, as described above, strongly recall the cities of the Shang dynasty in their basic constitution. The enclosures were probably the seats of aristocracy and state religion, and the farming and handicraft hamlets were located in the surrounding suburbs. The investigators have concluded, rightly I think, that these were no ordinary cities but the capitals of princes. They have attempted to identify these ruins as the Hsin-t'ien city of Chin, capital of thirteen Chin princes, on the basis that their geographic location matches the description given to this city in the historic records.

Chin-yüan, Shansi (probable site of Chin-yang, state of Chin). Besides Hsin-t'ien, four other walled towns dating from the Spring Autumn period in the area of Chin have been located in Shansi in the Fen Ho valley. These are, from north to south, the city ruins in Chin-yüan, Hsiang-fen, Ch'ü-wo, and Wen-hsi. All of them are known only through preliminary work, and none approaches Hsin-t'ien's magnitude.

Near the modern town of Chin-yüan, southeast of T'ai-yüan, remnants of an Eastern Chou city wall found in 1961 indicate an enclosure of *hang-t'u* construction, probably square, oriented north–northeast to south–south-west, about 2,700 meters long north–south. The investigators identify it with the city of Chin-yang of the state of Chin.[86]

Chao-k'ang Chen, Hsiang-fen, Shansi (probable site of Chiang, state of

86. *WW* 1962 (4/5), 55–58.

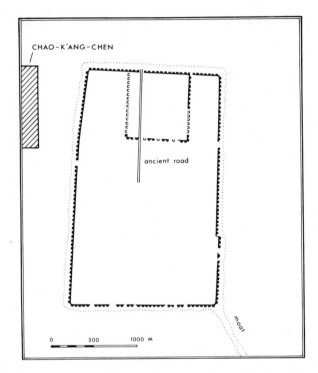

148. City of Chiang, state of Chin, near Hsiang-fen, Shansi. (Based on *KK* 1963, no. 10, p. 544.)

Chin). Beginning in 1960, investigations undertaken east of Chao-k'ang Chen, in the southwestern corner of Hsiang-fen, have disclosed a rectangular *hang-t'u* enclosure, 2,600–2,700 meters long north-south, 1,530 meters wide in the north and 1,650 meters wide in the south. A moat closely encircled the entire city wall. A smaller enclosure, approximately 800 meters square, is inside at the north-central part, its northern wall identical with the northern wall of the larger enclosure (fig. 148). The location of the site suggests the Chin city of Chü or Chiang, sometime capital of the state.[87]

Ch'ü-wo, Shansi (probable site of Wo-kuo, state of Chin). A city site of the Eastern Chou period with a double enclosure was found in 1956 about 1 kilometer southwest of Ch'ü-wo in southern Shansi, 8,700–11,200 meters east of the city of Hsin-t'ien, described above. The inner enclosure is a square of about 1,100 meters to a side, but the southern wall has been eroded by the River Kuai and only 600 to 1,000 meters of the east and west walls are left (fig. 149). The walls have a remaining height of 1–3 meters,

87. *KK* 1963 (10), 544–46.

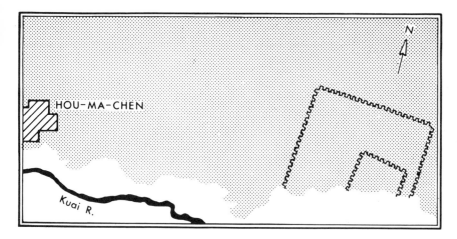

149. City of Wo-kuo, state of Chin, near Ch'ü-wo, Shansi. (Based on *WW* 1960, no. 8/9, p. 15.)

are about 12 meters wide at the base, and are composed of stamped earth in layers 6 centimeters thick. The outer enclosure now has only the northern and western walls left, the former over 3,100 meters long and the latter 2,600 meters. The distance between the northern walls of these two enclosures is about 1,400 meters. Preliminary surveys at this site show that cultural remains are abundant within the inner enclosure, including some tiles and pottery of the Hsin-t'ien type, and also a large number of tiles which are probably of Warring States and Han dynasty date. The location of this site coincides with the description given in historic records for the city of Wo-kuo, capital of the state of Chin before it was moved to Hsin-t'ien, although the ruins that have been found here seem to date from later periods.[88] West of the city site a Warring States tomb containing human sacrificial victims has been found.[89]

Wen-hsi, Shansi (probable site of Ch'ing-yüan, state of Chin). A square *hang-t'u* enclosure, about 980 meters to a side, was located about 17.5 kilometers northeast of Wen-hsi, southwestern Shansi. Remnants of the city wall exhibit clear signs of pisé construction: a ditch was dug, filled with layers of compact clay to make the base, and then the wall, about 10 meters wide, was built up in layers of clay rammed between two planks tied together by ropes. Around the wall were remains of an ancient moat (fig. 150). Within the wall Lung-shan Neolithic, Eastern Chou, and Han relics were found.[90] The Eastern Chou city may correspond to Ch'ing-

88. *KK* 1959 (5), 222–23.
89. *WW* 1960 (8/9), 15–18.
90. *KK* 1963 (5), 246–49.

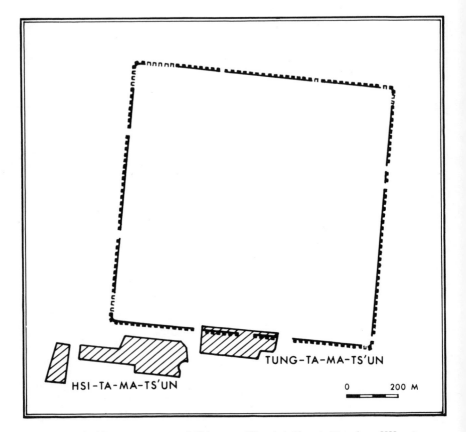

150. City of Ch'ing-yüan, state of Chin, near Wen-hsi, Shansi. (Based on *KK* 1963, no. 5, p. 246.)

yüan, a fort town of importance in the Chin defense against the nomads from the west.

Hsia Hsien, Shansi (probable site of An-i, state of Wei). Around 450 B.C. Chin was split into three separate states, Chao in the north, Wei in the middle, and Han in the south. The cities described above probably began under the Chin regime, but they continued to be in use during the Warring States period and even later. Other than Chin-yang, which fell within Chao's boundaries, all the others became cities of the state of Wei. In addition, ruins of three or four other cities, which can be dated no earlier than the Warring States,[91] have been located in the Wei area, including

91. See *KK* 1959 (11), 604–05, for the probable site of Yin-chin, state of Wei, near Hua-yin, Shensi, in addition to the three sites described below.

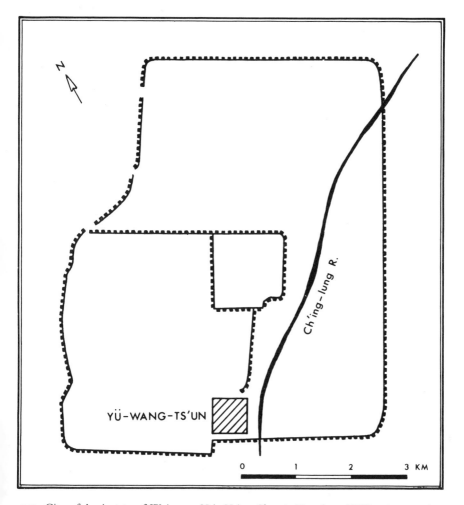

151. City of An-i, state of Wei, near Hsia Hsien, Shansi. (Based on *WW* 1962, no. 4/5, p. 61.)

the probable site of the state capital at one time, An-i. This is the site of Yü-wang-ch'eng, about 7 kilometers northwest of Hsia Hsien, southwestern Shansi, investigated in 1959, 1961, and 1962. It consists of three enclosures. The largest is oriented north-northeast and south-southwest, is trapezoidal, and is about 4,500 meters long (north-south) and 2,100 meters wide on the south side. Remnants of a moat were found nearby. Its southwestern quarter forms a second enclosure, and the third—smallest —enclosure is at the center of the site (fig. 151). The investigators believe that the largest and smallest enclosures were the original Warring States

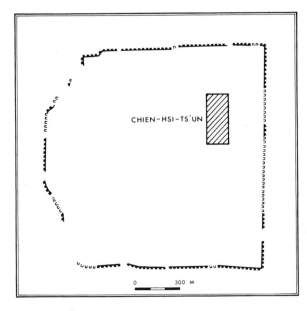

152. City of Wei-ch'eng, state of Wei, near Jui-ch'eng, Shansi. (Based on *WW* 1962, no. 4/5, p. 60.)

city and that the smallest enclosure was probably the site of palatial structures.[92]

Jui-ch'eng, Shansi (probable site of Wei-ch'eng, state of Wei). A square (about 1,000 meters to a side) *hang-t'u* enclosure of an Eastern Chou town site was located north of Jui-ch'eng, southwestern Shansi (fig. 152). Tiles, pottery, and tombs of Warring States types were found inside. It is suggested that this was the ruins of Wei-ch'eng, another Wei capital city.[93]

Hung-tung, Shansi (probable site of Yang, state of Wei). An early town site was investigated in 1962 southeast of Hung-tung in southern Shansi. Rectangular, it is 1,300 meters long (east-west) and 580 meters wide (north-south). Remains of pottery and tiles were found inside, concentrated in the western and central parts, and burials were located northwest of the city. It is possibly the ruins of Yang, a small town ruled by a Wei minister.[94]

I-yang, Honan (probable site of I-yang, state of Han). A square *hang-t'u* enclosure, about 1,400 meters to a side, was found in 1959 northwest of

92. *WW* 1962 (4/5), 61–64. *KK* 1963 (9), 474–79.
93. *WW* 1962 (4/5), 59–61.
94. *KK* 1963 (10), 547–49, 552.

I-yang, western Honan. Tiles and potsherds of Warring States types occurred on the surface inside.[95]

Han-tan, Hopei (probable site of Han-tan, state of Chao). Three city sites are probably attributable to the state of Chao, namely, Han-tan, Wu-ch'eng, and Wu-chi, all in the southern part of Hopei.

The name of Han-tan was first mentioned in *Tso chuan*, the tenth year of Ting Kung (500 B.C.), and was the capital city of Chao from 386 (the first year of Ching Hou) to 228 B.C., when the troops of Ch'in conquered the city and terminated the state. This old city of Han-tan, known throughout Chinese history to be about 4 kilometers southwest of the present city of Han-tan in southern Hopei, was investigated by a group of Japanese and Chinese archaeologists in 1939.[96]

The ruins of Han-tan consist of two adjoining enclosures, with a possible third to the north. The city proper is roughly square, about 1,400 meters to a side. An eastern annex, using the eastern wall of the city proper as its western wall, is about half the size. A section of a wall over 520 meters long, possibly the remains of a second annex, has been found, which extends from the northern wall of the city proper northward. The wall, of *hang-t'u* construction, is given a reconstructed height of over 15 meters and a base width of over 20 meters. Each of the walls of the city proper has one to three openings, near which are scattered tiles and bricks. These were probably the gates of the city. Within and near the enclosures are remains of sixteen earth platforms, ten of which are of considerable dimensions. At the middle of the city proper, four platforms are located along the north-south axis. The first one from the south, known among the natives as Lung T'ai, is the largest; it is 13.5 meters high, 210 meters (east-west) by 288 meters (north-south) at the base, and 105 meters (east-west) by 130–140 meters (north-south) at the top. On its flat surface no cultural remains of any significant amount have been found. The second platform, north of Lung-t'ai, is 4.5 meters high and 49 by 51 meters in size. On top of it were found two parallel rows of stone pillar foundations, lying north-south, and, outside of these, two more rows of bricks. These are thought to be the remains of two corridors, on top of which was probably a second floor. The platform to its north, 3 meters high and 60 by 70 meters in size, has no stone foundations. On it were fragments of tiles, pottery, knife coins, and a small number of other bronze and iron implements.

95. *KK* 1961 (1), 32.

96. Komai Kazuchika and Sekino Takeshi, *Han-tan*, Archaeologia Orientalis, ser. B, no. 7, 1954.

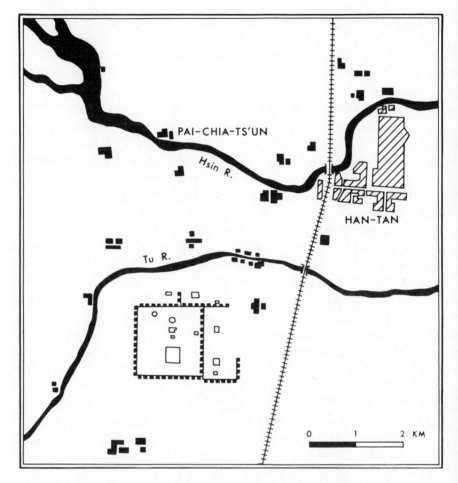

153. City of Han-tan, state of Chao, near Han-tan, Hopei. (From Sekino Takeshi, *Han-tan*, Tokyo and Kyoto, Society for East Asian Archaeology, 1954, fig. 2.)

The northernmost platform of this row is round, with a diameter of 62 meters and a height of 7.5 meters Two square platforms are located in the eastern annex, again along the north-south axis, slightly to the west of the middle. The other platforms, all rectangular or square except for one which is round, are scattered in and around the city (fig. 153). Bricks and tiles are found atop all the platforms; the eave tiles and pottery types date the city site to the Warring States period.

A cemetery of this period was excavated in 1957 and 1959 in the Pai-chia-ts'un area north of the Chao city. Forty-nine tombs and six chariot burials were excavated. Of the twelve lavishly furnished tombs, five have yielded sacrificed humans. One tomb had an earthen mound above the ground.[97]

Wu-ch'eng, Hopei (probable site of Wu-ch'eng, state of Chao). The ruins of Wu-ch'eng, found recently, form a rough square enclosure, about 1.1 kilometer to a side. The wall, with a remaining height of 6 meters and a base width of 12 meters, is constructed of stamped-earth layers, each 8–11 centimeters thick. Five or six openings are located in the western and northern walls, which are intact. A water ditch, 20–30 meters in length, was found along the northern wall. Cultural remains within the city, consisting of tiles, eave tiles, potsherds, *pu* coins, spindle whorls, and bronze arrowheads, are mostly of the Warring States type, with some Han dynasty forms. Urn burials of infants have been excavated in an eastern part of the city.[98]

Wu-an, Hopei (probable site of Wu-chi, state of Chao). Two ancient city ruins are known southwest of Wu-an Hsien, southern Hopei. The one in the west, near the town of Wu-chi, was investigated in 1956. The earthen walls, again of stamped earth, 8–13 meters wide and with a remaining height of 3–6 meters, form a roughly rectangular enclosure, 889 meters east-west and 768 meters north-south. A paved road led through one gate in each wall. Residential remains, wells, pottery kilns, and burials were found in the western part of the enclosure and indicate a date of Eastern Chou through Western Han.[99]

I Hsien, Hopei (probable site of Hsia-tu, state of Yen). Hsia-tu, near I Hsien in central Hopei, was an important city of the state of Yen, possibly occupied between 697 and 226 B.C. It was investigated and excavated in 1930,[100] 1957,[101] 1958,[102] 1961–62,[103] and 1964–65,[104] turning out to be perhaps the best excavated and described of all the Chou cities (fig. 154).

The city was a rectangular *hang-t'u* enclosure, about 8 kilometers long east-west and 4 kilometers wide north-south, separated in the middle by

97. *KK* 1959 (10), 531–36; 1962 (12), 613–34.

98. *KK* 1959 (7), 354–57.

99. *KKTH* 1957 (4), 43–47. *KK* 1959 (7), 338–42, 343–45.

100. Fu Chen-lun, *Kuo-hsüeh chi-k'an* 3, Peking University, 1932, pp. 175–82. *KKTH* 1955 (4), 18–26.

101. *WWTKTL* 1957 (9), 61–63.

102. *KK* 1962 (1), 10–19, 54.

103. *KKHP* 1965 (1), 83–106; 1965 (2), 79–102.

104. *KK* 1965 (11), 548–61; 1965 (11), 562–70; 1975 (4), 228–43. *WW* 1965 (9), 60; 1975 (6), 89–91.

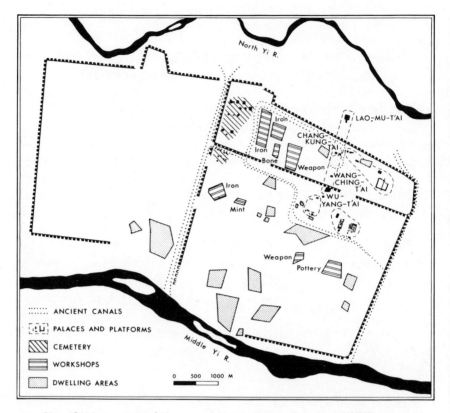

154. City of Hsia-tu, state of Yen, near I Hsien, Hopei. (Based on *KKHP* 1965, no. 1, fig. 1, following p. 84.)

a north-south wall with a water ditch ("canal") on its west into an eastern and a western half. Another partition wall further separated the eastern city into a northern section of about a third and a southern section of two thirds. Gates and garrison barracks were associated with the walls. A section of the western wall, almost 40 meters thick, excavated in 1957, exhibits its *hang-t'u* structure clearly: the core of the wall was constructed first and then the exterior and interior faces were added. Two planks were placed on edge a little distance apart and loose earth was filled in between, the boards were tightened with ropes, mats were placed on top of the earth which was pounded to compact it, and then the ropes were cut and the boards removed. When the core of the wall was done, the same procedure was repeated for the outside and inside layers. Sections of walls were thus built successively one on top of the other until the desired height was reached.

The western city, although dating from the Warring States period, was

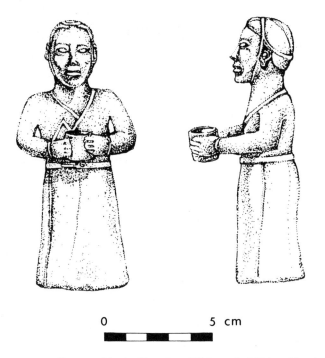

0   5 cm

155. Bronze statuette discovered in the Yen city of Hsia-tu, in I Hsien, Hopei. (Based on *WW* 1965, no. 2, p. 43.)

apparently built later than the eastern city. Only two dwelling houses, some tombs, and a number of weapons were found in it; possibly it was a defensive adjunct to an existing city. The major activities of the Hsia-tu life took place in the eastern city, which was clearly divided into four functional regions: palatial, industrial, dwelling, and burial.

The palatial area is in the northern part of the eastern city and has yielded remains of large structures on *hang-t'u* platforms, ground structures, bricks, and elaborately decorated tiles and eave tiles. There are remains of four large platforms, forming a north-south line. These, referred to by the local inhabitants as Wu-yang-t'ai (the southernmost), Wang-ching-t'ai, Chang-kung-t'ai, and Lao-mu-t'ai (the northern most), were all rectangular, built in *hang-t'u* layers, and of various sizes and heights. The largest, Wu-yang-t'ai, has a remaining height of 11 meters, divided into two levels, the base about 140 meters east-west and 110 meters north-south. On top of these platforms are remains of tiles, burned clay, and fragments of wattle and daub. Clay water-pipe sections, presumably used for drainage, were found on Wu-yang-t'ai, and a bronze human statuette was found in the vicinity (fig. 155). Archaeologists who ex-cavated the site believe that these four platforms and the old structures

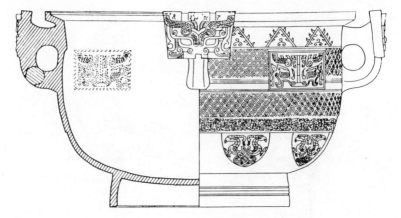

156. Yen pottery *chien* with bronze vessel-style decorative patterns, excavated from a burial mound in the city of Hsia-tu, near I Hsien, Hopei. (From *KKHP* 1965, no. 2, p. 89.)

on top of them were the dominating features of the city. Three clusters of rectangular house floors (*hang-t'u* built, with large post holes containing chicken and animal bones) surrounded Wu-yang-t'ai on its northeastern, southeastern, and southwestern sides. These houses were built at ground level, but each cluster had a large house constructed on a platform several meters high.

The industrial region forms a belt west and south of the palatial region in the eastern city. Three iron workshops, two weapon manufactories, a coin mint, a pottery kiln area, and a bone workshop were identified within the belt. Slugs, wastes, molds, kilns, tools, and other handicraft artifacts were found alongside storage pits, dwelling floors, wells, and remains of buildings and utensils.

Surrounding the palatial complex and the industrial belt were remains of dwelling houses and domiciliary artifacts, especially abundant in the southwestern, central, eastern, and northeastern parts of the eastern city.

At the northwestern corner of the eastern city was the burial area. Twenty-three burial mounds were identified, divided into two groups by the partition wall. North of the wall are thirteen mounds, arranged in four rows one row of four and three rows of three. South of the partition are ten mounds, arranged in two rows of five. These are all pit graves, richly furnished with pottery (some very elaborately decorated in imitation of bronze vessels; fig. 156), a few bronzes, and stone and shell artifacts; they are equipped with ramps and are capped with *hang-t'u* mounds. Throughout the city a number of small pitgraves were found, in which iron chokers and leg-irons were associated with the skeletons. These were presumably graves of people with very different social status from the masters of the burial mounds. South of the city, a cemetery of Warring States date was located in 1964; its relation with Hsia-tu remains to be determined.

A network of water ditches completes the layout. In addition to the long ditch separating the two cities, a section of a moat was located outside the east wall, and two ditches continue from the central "canal" into the eastern city. One in the north separated the cemetery from the palatial and industrial regions. The excavators believe that these ditches were constructed to isolate (and facilitate the defense of) the central part of the city, to provide water for the households and industries, for communication, and for drainage.

A city of this magnitude was certainly no ordinary town; its well-planned total layout, the palatial complex, the interrelationship of the different quarters, and the pattern of arrangement of tombs are rare features among the known ruins of the contemporary cities and are indicative of the level of cultural and societal achievement of Yen.[105]

Lin-tzu, Shantung (*probable site of Lin-tzu, state of Ch'i*). The ruins of a Warring States city, identified as the Ch'i capital of Lin-tzu, were investigated by Sekino in 1940 and 1941 and by the Shantung Bureau of Culture in 1958, 1964–66, and 1971.[106] The city consists of two enclosures of stamped-earth walls (fig. 157). The larger one, rectangular in shape, is approximately 3,300 meters east-west and 5,200 meters north-south. At the southwestern corner of the large enclosure a smaller one was built, about 2,200 meters north-south and 1,400 meters east-west. The walls were massive affairs, ranging from 25 meters to 43 meters wide at the base. Eleven gates were located, six for the larger enclosure and five for the smaller. The entire wall, 14,158 meters in length, was surrounded by small natural streams and moats. Seven major roads were identified within the larger city and three roads in the small enclosure, and each had at least an underground sewer.

A mound built of *hang-t'u* layers—referred to as Mound of Duke Huan, the most prominent of the Ch'i dukes—is seen within the smaller enclosure, slightly west of center in its northern part. Fourteen meters high and 86 meters long north-south, it has an oval base and three steps on each

105. For the remains of another possibly Yen town, Hsü-shui, Hopei, see *KK* 1965 (10), 540.

106. Sekino Takeshi, *Chugaku kōkōgaku kenkyū*, University of Tokyo, Institute for Oriental Culture, 1956, pp. 241–94. *KK* 1961 (6), 289–97. *WW* 1972 (5), 45–54.

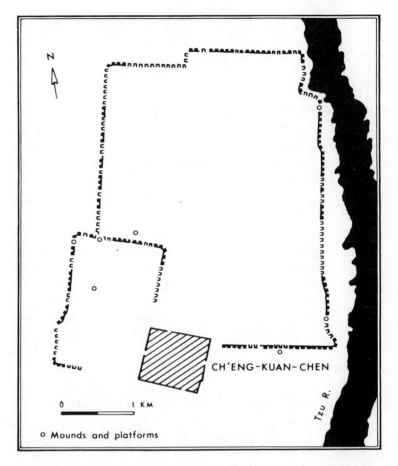

157. City of Lin-tzu, state of Ch'i, near Lin-tzu, Shantung. (Based on *KK* 1961, no. 6, p. 289.)

side, gentle on the south and steep on the rest. Remains of tiles were collected on the top of the mound and many *hang-t'u* floors were identified in the area surrounding. These are probably remains of a palatial complex. Another smaller mound, 30–40 meters to a side, is located in the northeastern part of the small enclosure. Other mounds have been reported, one at the northeastern corner of the large enclosure and the others outside the city area.

Cultural relics have been discovered all over the city, including tiles, eave tiles, bricks, potsherds, knife coins, coin molds, bronze arrowheads, and so forth. Six localities are considered iron workshops, two within the smaller city and four in the larger city. In addition, two bronze foundries (one in the small city and one in the large), one coin mint (small city),

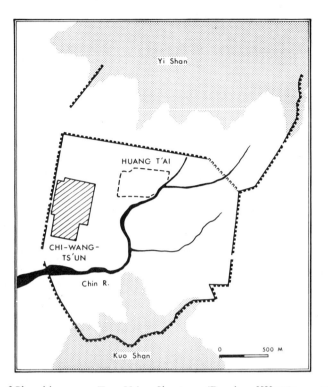

158. City of Chu-ch'eng, near Tsou Hsien, Shantung. (Based on *KK* 1965, no. 12, p. 623.)

and some bone workshops (large city) were identified in various parts of the city, as were two cemeteries (large city). According to Sekino's estimates, the dimensions of the city and the amount of cultural remains indicate a population of scores of thousands of households.

Tsou Hsien, Shantung (probable site of Chu-ch'eng, state of Chu). Investigated in 1964, a *hang-t'u* enclosure of Chou and Han occupation was located about 10 kilometers south of Tsou Hsien in Shantung, in a small valley about 1,200 meters wide, between the I and the K'uo mountains. Roughly rectangular, the northern and the southern sections of the east and west city walls were built on the low foothills. At the center of the enclosure is an earthen platform 500 by 250 meters, referred to by local inhabitants as Huang-t'ai (fig. 158). Remains of pottery, tiles, and pottery-making implements have been collected inside the enclosure. This was possibly the Chu-ch'eng site, capital of the small state of Chu from 615 to 281 B.C.[107]

107. *KK* 1965 (12), 622–27.

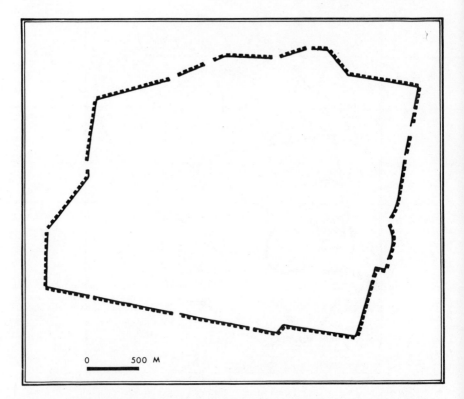

0   500 M

159. City of Hsüeh, near T'eng Hsien, Shantung. (Based on *KK* 1965, no. 12, p. 628.)

T'eng Hsien, Shantung (probable sites of Hsüeh-ch'eng and T'eng-ch'eng, states of Hsüeh and T'eng). Two *hang-t'u* city enclosures of Eastern Chou date, one south and the other southwest of T'eng Hsien in southern Shantung, were investigated by Sekino Takeshi during World War II[108] and by the Institute of Archaeology in 1964.[109] The former site was probably the ruins of the ancient city of Hsüeh (fig. 159); and the latter was possibly the ruins of T'eng (fig. 160), both small states of Eastern Chou. Both were *hang-t'u* structures, roughly rectangular. An earthen platform was found at the northeastern corner of T'eng, seemingly a focal spot of intensive cultural activities.

Yen-ling, Honan (probable site of Yen-ch'eng, state of Cheng). A rectangular *hang-t'u* enclosure, about 1,600 meters long (north-south) and 800 to 1,000 meters wide (east-west), was found in 1961 northwest of Yen-ling,

108. Sekino, *op. cit.*
109. *KK* 1965 (12), 627–33.

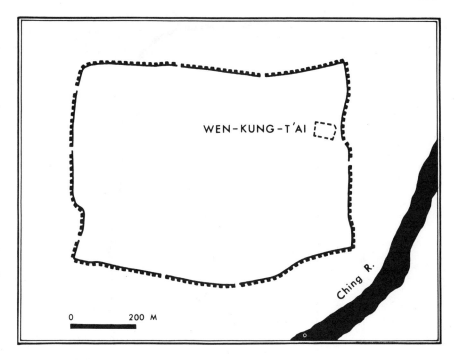

WEN-KUNG-T'AI

Ching R.

0   200 M

160. City of T'eng, near T'eng Hsien, Shantung. (Based on *KK* 1965, no. 12, p. 632.)

central Honan. A smaller enclosure (148 by 184 meters) was located in the northeastern part of the city, and a habitation area occurred in the southeastern part. Remains of corded tiles and *li* tripods found on the surface of the site indicate a Spring Autumn dating, and it has been identified with the Yen-ch'eng city of the state of Cheng of the early Eastern Chou period.[110]

Lin-t'ung, Shensi (probable site of Li-yang, state of Ch'in). Investigated in 1963 and 1964, the ancient city site 12.5 kilometers northeast of the present town of Li-yang, in Lin-t'ung Prefecture, eastern Shensi, consists of ruins forming a rectangular enclosure about 2,200 meters long north-south and 1,800 meters wide east-west. Segments of *hang-t'u* walls were identified and one north-south main street across the entire length of the city and two parallel east-west streets across the width were traced. Remains collected and excavated in the city included architectural relics, pottery, tiles, well rings, sewers, and kilns of Eastern Chou types. North of the city area a segment of an ancient irrigation ditch was found, and two

110. *KK* 1963 (4), 225–26.

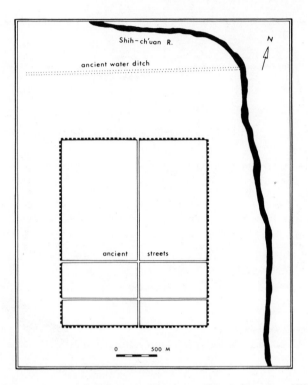

161. City of Li-yang, state of Ch'in, near Lin-t'ung, Shensi. (Based on *WW* 1966, no. 1, p. 12.)

mounds were located south of the city (fig. 161). The investigators of the site believe this was probably the ruins of Li-yang of Ch'in State, capital from 383 to 350 B.C.[111]

Hsien-yang, Shensi (probable site of Hsien-yang, state of Ch'in). From 1959 to 1963, archaeological investigations were carried out in an area east-northeast of the modern city of Hsien-yang, eastern Shensi, on the northern bank of the River Wei, an area believed to be the site of the ancient city of Hsien-yang, important capital of the Eastern Chou state of Ch'in from which the conquest of China, completed in 221 B.C., originated. Two segments of *hang-t'u* walls were located, but the outline of the entire city remains to be worked out. In the northern part of the ruins twelve house floors were excavated, some built on *hang-t'u* platforms. One house has the base parts of the walls left; these were plastered and painted with polychromic murals. Bronze vessels, iron nails, and bone artifacts were

111. *WW* 1966 (1), 10–16.

found in some of the houses. In the same area are many remains of clay pipes, probably the relics of an ancient network of underground drainage. In addition, wells, pottery kilns, and storage pits were found throughout the ruined area, yielding pottery, bronze and iron artifacts, and tiles. Urn burials of children occurred at a spot in the eastern part.[112]

Feng-hsiang, Shensi (probable site of Yüng-ch'eng, state of Ch'in). South of Feng-hsiang, central Shensi, in an area 4.5 kilometers long east-west and 2 kilometers wide north-south, was a ruined city of Eastern Chou period identified with the Yüng-ch'eng city, an early capital of the state of Ch'in. Pottery, tiles, and clay sewage pipes were found; some of the eave tiles have inscriptions indicating their use on palatial structures.[113]

Summary. In Chinese archaeological studies of the Chou period attention is often focused upon tombs and their yields of works of art, whereas habitation sites—cities and villages—are sometimes neglected. For the study of cultural and societal change during the Chou period, however, the cities provide a focus for studies of the various aspects of the Chou civilization. For this reason I have undertaken a rather detailed summary of all the printed information that is known to me concerning the Chou cities.[114] In assessing its significance in the development of city life in North China, however, the nature of the data must be constantly borne in mind. Among the scores of Eastern Chou cities we know from history, the above twenty or so represent a mere fraction. Of those that have been described, only the ruins at Hou-ma and I Hsien have been intensively excavated, so that the available information is sketchy and uneven. Their chronological positions are not all certain, and these cities belonged to different states which must have had distinctive cultural characteristics within the general framework of the North China civilization of the Chou period. Some of these cities were probably royal or princely capitals, while others were presumably provincial towns or even fortified villages. Undoubtedly their natures were not universally the same, and their basic constitutions not always comparable.

Even so, some broad general trends of city growth can be ascertained from the data, which include some major cities of not only the Royal

---

112. *KK* 1962 (6), 281–89. *WW* 1964 (7), 59.

113. *KK* 1963 (8), 419–22.

114. I have excluded references in publications to possible Eastern Chou sites so brief that the data cannot be relied upon as well as sites whose dating from the Eastern Chou is doubtful. Examples are the Ch'ü-fu site of Shantung (see Komai Kazuchika, *Archaeological Research Reports* 2, 1951, Tokyo University, Faculty of Letters) and the Ku-ch'eng site in Yen-shih, Honan (see *KK* 1964, no. 1, 30–32).

162. *Hang-t'u* layers of a section of the Eastern Chou city near Lo-yang, Honan. (From *KKHP* 1965, no. 2, pl. 2.)

Chou but also all the important states such as Chin, Chao, Wei, Han, Yen, Ch'i, Cheng, and Ch'in. Many were probably the state capitals at one time or another. The data should be adequate for a contrastive analysis between the earlier cities of the Shang dynasty and the general patterns of the Eastern Chou city ruins.

There are some observable constants in the city history from the Shang through the beginning of the Han dynasty. (1) The cities were always located on level plains near waterways. (2) They tended to be walled. (3) The city wall was in all cases constructed of stamped earth (fig. 162), and the technique of *hang-t'u*, or pisé, construction remains identical throughout the period. (4) The majority of the cities were oblong or square, though in rare cases they were rather irregular. (5) The orientation of the city enclosure and the ceremonial and palace structure was constantly guided by the four cardinal directions, with an emphasis upon the north-south axis. (6) Earthen platforms or mounds always served as the foundations of structures which were politically and/or ceremonially important and prominent (fig. 163). (7) The basic constitution of specialized quarters is constant to all the cities where excavated data are sufficient for an understanding of their functional layout: a city always consisted of

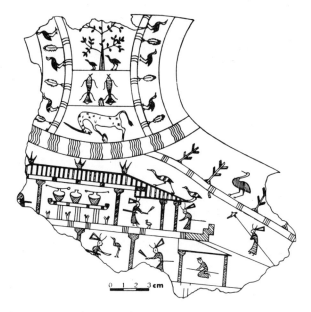

163. Decorative patterns with scenes of platforms and rituals on a bronze vessel excavated from a Warring States period tomb at Fen-shui-ling, Ch'ang-chih, Sansi. (*KKHP* 1957, no. 1, p. 109.)

a number of parts, no one of which could be considered totally independent in terms of economy, political organization, or religion.

There are obviously also some profound differences and changes. Some of these are in the area of architecture, such as the beginning of the use of tiles (fig. 164) during the Western Chou period and of bricks during the Warring States period. Others, however, reflect socioeconomic changes, one of the most important of which has to do with the general layout of the city and its interior subdivisions.[115]

The Shang city of Cheng-chou had a walled enclosure as its administrative and ceremonial nucleus; the nature of the remains inside is not altogether clear, but outside the enclosure industrial quarters and residential and farming villages were dispersed in a wide area, without apparent planning. The city of An-yang had the same arrangement: settlements of various kinds were spread in a wide area along the banks of the River

115. Cf. Li Ya-nung, *Chung-kuo ti nu-li-chih yü feng-chien-chih*, Shanghai, Hua-tung Jen-min Press, 1954, pp. 138–46; Oshima Riichi, *Tōhōgakuhō* 30 (1959); Miyazaki Ichisada, *Asiatica*, Studies in Oriental History, vol. 1 (1957), 50–65; *Essays in Oriental Studies, Jubilee Volume on the Fifteenth Anniversary of Tōhōgakukai*, Tokyo, Tōhō Gakkai, 1962, pp. 342–57; Paul Wheatley, *Pivot of the Four Quarters*, Chicago, Aldine, 1971.

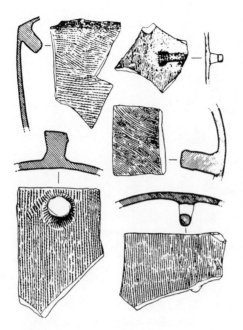
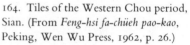

164. Tiles of the Western Chou period, Sian. (From *Feng-hsi fa-chüeh pao-kao*, Peking, Wen Wu Press, 1962, p. 26.)

Huan, and the royal temples of Hsiao-t'un and the royal tombs at Hsi-pei-kang provided the focus of the ruined area. The essential contrasts within the city area, then, are those between the aristocratic nucleus and the rest of the community. This basic pattern seems to be retained by the Chin State capital at Hsin-t'ien as late as the second half of the Ch'un-ch'iu period. In ancient literature pertaining to the Chou, this contrast appears to be reflected in several terms which are not, however, always clearly definable. The city as a whole seems to have been referred to as *i*, a general term for settlements of all sizes and kinds that began to appear in the oracle-bone inscriptions. The *i* physically has two divisions: *tu*, or *kuo*, where *chün-tzu* ("gentlemen") lived, and *pi*, occupied by *min* ("folk") or *yeh-jen* ("people of the field").

A new layout of the city began to appear—in the case of Lin-tzu, for example—toward the end of the Ch'un-ch'iu period. In addition to a walled enclosure which housed the aristocratic center, a larger enclosure within another wall included the industrial quarters along with residences and commercial streets, in layouts that show careful and total planning. In Lo-yang, as far as the available archaeological record goes, this change involved simply an enlargement of the enclosure to include some residential and industrial quarters that were formerly outside the city. But in most cases, an inner enclosure was built. In most of the Eastern Chou cities there now were three contrasting spatial units within the city: aristocracy in a small enclosure of a special area; industrial and commercial quarters in a larger enclosure; and the farming fields outside the city wall. In *Mencius*, this triple division is made clear in the following quotation:

[If so, then] the gentlemen scholars would be anxious to serve in Your Excellency's court, the farmers would be anxious to till Your Excellency's land, and the merchants would be anxious to store their goods in Your Excellency's market.

In the "Ch'i yü" section of *Kuo yü*, the same divisions are given as administration (*kuan-fu*), market (*shih-ching*), and fields (*t'ien-yeh*). In some of the lesser cities that were not capital seats of the princes, such as the Wu-chi city described above, the aristocratic center may not have been a major center within the city; but the same principle, that of the walled enclosure including industries and residences as well as the aristocracy, still held. When there was a double enclosure, the outer wall was referred to as *kuo*, and the inner as *ch'eng*. Both terms can be applied to the wall when there is only a single enclosure.

This change in the city layout during the Eastern Chou period, which archaeological materials have amply substantiated, is surely significant. In the first place, it is apparent that the more people there are enclosed within a walled area, engaging in specialized activities, the fewer there are to participate directly in farming the fields outside the enclosure. Such large Warring States cities as Lo-yang (ca. 3,000 meters square), Lin-tzu (ca. 4,000 meters square), and Hsia-tu (ca. 8,000 by 4,000 meters) presumably housed a considerable population of remarkable density. This indicates, among other things, the existence of a highly developed technology, advanced cultivating techniques, and sophisticated administration.

Secondly, the new layout symbolized the growing importance and increasing specialization of the handicrafts. Cheng-chou and Hou-ma cities have produced evidence that minute subdivisions within the manufacture of bronze artifacts alone were already developed. The new city layout further intensified this specialization by enclosing the industrial quarters within the control and protection of the walled city itself. Inscriptions on pottery often indicate the names or groups of the manufacturers, perhaps suggesting a more private kind of ownership of manufactured goods and a more commercial nature of the industrial undertakings. In the third place, commercial streets, which had not been seen before, now form an important part of the city structure. Historic records show that jewelry, curios, furs and leathers, fabrics and clothing, salt, drugs, food, and wine were all purchased at stores in the Warring States cities, where inns, restaurants, gambling houses, and brothels were also found. The widespread appearance of state currency[116] and the construction of roads shown in the archaeological data further testify to the important role played by commerce in the cities. And finally, the enlarged enclosure and the moats surrounding the city indicate a growing need for defense against invasions. In "Tsa-shou-p'ien" of *Mo Tzu*, Mo Tzu listed five conditions under which a city could not defend itself: when a large city had a small population; when a small city had a large population; when a large population had an insufficient food supply; when the market area was too far from the administrative center; and when the wealth and the wealthy were outside the city wall. Thus a prevailing principle of urban planning during the latter part of the Eastern Chou was apparently to enclose the market, the industries, and the wealth within the city wall for defensive purposes.

Other aspects of Chou cultural history, important to the history of city development in North China, will be discussed below.

Technology

Throughout the Shang and Chou periods stone, bone, antler, and shell remained among the principal materials for implements in the villages, and bronze making was an essential industry. The Chou bronzes continued to be manufactured by the piece-mold method, but new techniques appeared during the Eastern Chou period. Remains of four furnaces were found in 1959 at Hou-ma; the base of the furnaces was round, about 70 centimeters in diameter. Beginning in the late Spring Autumn and early Warring States periods, techniques were developed to cast the body and the appendages of the vessels separately, as is shown by bronzes in the Chung-chou Road sequence. Appendages (handles, lugs, legs, etc.) were cast first and then attached to the clay body mold before the molten bronze was poured into the mold; or the body was manufactured first, and clay molds for appendages were applied to the body before casting; or they were made separately and then welded together. Another development was the very fine casting of decorative patterns by means of copper, gold, and silver pieces attached to the bronze surface.[117] The clay piece molds at the Hou-ma site also show that the negative decorative patterns on

116. Wang Yu-ch'üan, *Wo kuo ku-tai huo-pi ti ch'i-yüan ho fa-chan*, Peking, Science Press, 1957. Cheng Chia-hsiang, *Chung-kuo ku-tai huo-pi fa-chan shih*, Peking, San-lien, 1958. For some major recent discoveries, see *WW* 1972 (5), 55–59; *KK* 1974 (1), 6–15.
117. *Hsin Chung-kuo ti k'ao-ku shou-huo*, Peking, Wen Wu Press, 1962, p. 65.

the piece molds were often impressed on the clay with stamps,[118] resulting in decorated bronzes of identical design, something that has not been found among the Shang and Western Chou assemblages. This, plus the intensified specialization (different kinds of artifacts being made at different foundries and the separate casting of bodies and appendages of vessels), indicates that handicrafts in general and bronze making in particular were becoming increasingly sophisticated and commercial.

In addition to the advances in bronze making during the Eastern Chou period, there were other considerable or even revolutionary advances in other technologies during the latter half of the Eastern Chou period: highly developed iron metallurgy and extensive use of iron for implements; the use of iron plows, possibly drawn by cattle; and sophisticated, intensive irrigation systems.[119]

Umehara suggested that the bronzesmiths of the Shang dynasty probably already had some chemical knowledge of iron and had a practical mastery of its use, as is shown by the chemical analysis of some An-yang bronze artifacts.[120] A recent find of a bronze *ko* halberd with an iron blade at the Shang site in Kao-ch'eng, Hopei, initiated a series of discussions about whether it was or wasn't worked from a meteorite.[121] There is little question, however, that bronze was the only significant material for making metal artifacts throughout the Shang, Western Chou, and early part of the Eastern Chou periods. It is significant that during this long interval (1750 to 500 B.C.) bronze was used primarily for ceremonial vessels and weapons and thus was in the service, so to speak, of the aristocracy. Huang Chan-yüeh stated in 1957:

> Bronze agricultural implements of Shang and Chou that have been excavated by archaeologists up to this date consist of only three Shang dynasty spades (found in An-yang, Cheng-chou, and Lo-yang, respectively), and no more than ten adzes and axes. . . . Extensive excavations undertaken by the Institute of Archaeology, Academia Sinica, in recent years in such regions as Feng, Hao, and Lo-yang, where there was intensive activity during the Western Chou dynasty, have so far failed to turn out either a single piece of iron or an agricultural imple-

118. *KK* 1962 (2), 59.

119. For general discussions on some aspects of these problems, see Sekino Takeshi, *Chugaku kōkōgaku kenkyū*; Joseph Needham, *The Development of Iron and Steel Technology in China*, London, Newcomen Society, 1958; Wang Chung-shu, *KKTH* 1956 (1), 57–76; Li Chung, *KKHP* 1975 (2), 1–20.

120. Umehara Sueji, *Shina kōkōgaku runkō*, Tokyo, Kōbundō, 1929, pp. 179–80.

121. *KK* 1973 (5), 266–71. *WW* 1974 (8), 42–44; 1975 (3), 57–79. *KKHP* 1975 (2), 1.

ment made of bronze. On the other hand, the agricultural implements and handicrafts tools that have been found there consist of stone adzes, stone axes, stone knives, shell knives, shell sickles, bone needles, and bone chisels. Weapons, however, except for some bone and shell arrowheads, were all cast in bronze. . . . We have, thus, reason to believe that the principal agricultural implements during the Western Chou dynasty were basically wooden and stone; there were some that were made of bronze, but these are rare and of secondary importance and supplementary nature.[122]

To my knowledge, this statement has thus far not been invalidated by more recent discoveries. Starting with the Warring States period, however, the wide use of iron implements is amply substantiated by archaeological discoveries of remains of this period from all over China.

Recent archaeological discoveries indicate a highly noteworthy phenomenon. Namely, tombs dated before the Warring States, whenever and wherever the dating is certain, do not contain iron artifacts. Every cemetery of the Warring States period and the Han dynasty, on the other hand, yields some amount of iron artifacts, with almost no exceptions; in some cases the amount is even considerable. This is certainly not accidental. . . . It is therefore our studied opinion that, as a new, significant raw material of implement manufacture, the use of iron began toward the end of the Ch'un-ch'iu period and the beginning of the Chan-kuo period.[123]

This is confirmed by the first occurrence of iron objects in period IV (early Warring States) of the Chung-chou Road sequence at Lo-yang.[124] It would be strange, however, if iron technology suddenly began in the Warring States period without antecedent, and archaeological evidence in the area of Ch'u (see chapter 9) shows that iron implements began to appear in the earliest Ch'ang-sha tombs, many of which date from the late Spring Autumn period. It seems very likely that the emergence of iron metallurgy as a major industry for toolmaking should be placed in the sixth century B.C. at the latest, although the techniques probably were not perfected and widely used until the fifth century, as far as archaeological evidence is concerned.

122. *KKHP* 1957 (3), 106. For a discussion of agricultural implements made of bronze, see M. Amano, *Chūgoku nogyō-shi kenkyu*, 1962.

123. *KKHP* 1960 (1), 82–83.

124. *Lo-yang Chung-chou-lu*, p. 146.

Moreover, as soon as iron implements began to appear in significant quantity in archaeological assemblages, both cast iron (pig iron) and wrought iron appeared at the same time. Sekino pointed out some time ago that many iron implements excavated before World War II in southern Manchuria and Korea which had been dated to the Warring States period had been cast, according to laboratory analysis. He speculated that the same technique must have been developed in North China.[125] A recent metallographical study of four iron implements from the Warring States period (excavated from Hopei, Liaoning, and Hunan) shows that they were all cast and confirms Sekino's speculation.[126] The significance of this fact in Old World iron prehistory has been discussed by Sekino,[127] Joseph Needham,[128] and Nikolaas van der Merwe.[129] The discussions by the last author are the most up-to-date and concise; with his kind permission, passages from his work are quoted below:[130]

Cast iron is a brittle alloy of iron with a carbon content ranging between 1.5 per cent and 5 per cent, which occurs in two forms— white iron and grey iron.... The best known attribute of cast iron is its melting point (ca. 1,150°C), which is lower than that of steel (ca. 1,400°C) or wrought iron (1,535°C) and allows it to be cast in the molten state. While the discovery of iron casting added a significant new dimension to the existing techniques of iron metallurgy, the real significance of cast iron involves the economics of iron production. The metal yield from the ore is greater when cast iron is manufactured, while steel can be mass-produced through oxidation of the carbon in cast iron—a procedure which is considerably less laborious than cementation. Wrought iron can be manufactured in the same way by carrying the oxidization a step further; this is known as the *indirect process.*

Although cast iron may have a melting point as low as 1,130°C, depending on its carbon content, this temperature must not be confused with the much higher temperature at which it is produced. A number of variables combine to make a temperature as high as 1,400°C a requirement for the production of cast iron....

125. Sekino Takeshi, *Chugaku kōkogaku kenkyū*, pp. 187–88.

126. *KKHP* 1960 (1), 73–87.

127. *Ibid.*, pp. 189–91.

128. See *n*119, above.

129. *Carbon-14 Dating of Iron*, University of Chicago Press, 1969.

130. *Ibid.*, pp. 26–27, 46–48. This work also reports a C-14 date of an iron object excavated from Chin-ts'un, Lo-yang, in the Royal Ontario Museum collection.

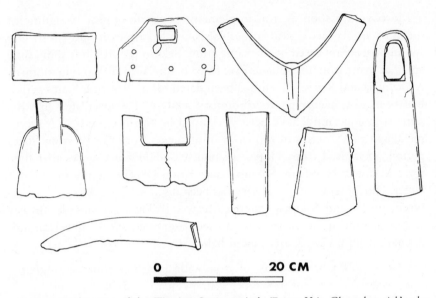

165. Iron implements of the Warring States period. (From *Hsin Chung-kuo ti k'ao-ku shou-huo*, Peking, Wen Wu Press, 1962, p. 61.)

The solution of the problems described here requires a sophistication in furnace construction and operation which took the Europeans more than 3000 years to develop; only in China was the appropriate furnace in use before the Christian era. . . . The early development of this [indirect] process can be said to have taken place almost exclusively within the borders of China, where the history of iron metallurgy followed a radically different course from that of the countries to the west. . . .

It is possible that the early Chinese iron smelters may have known how to produce iron in a bloomery furnace; however, the evidence for it is entirely lacking. The blast furnace seems to have been the mainstay of Chinese iron metallurgy from the very beginning. It is significant that there seem to be no Chinese words for the reduction of iron ore in a solid form; the words for smelting, *chu* and *yeh*, refer to the production of iron in its liquid form. It can therefore be assumed that the early occurrences of wrought iron were probably the result of the firing of cast iron; the fact that the Chinese words for cast iron (*sheng t'ieh*) and wrought iron (*shu t'ieh*) mean "raw iron" and "ripe iron," respectively, supports this view of the indirect process as the basic tradition of Chinese metallurgy. The technological and economic factors which made possible this early production of cast iron have

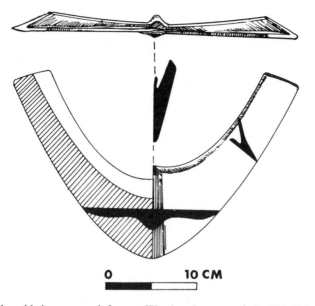

166. Iron plow blade excavated from a Warring States tomb in Hui Hsien, Honan. (From Hsia Nai et al., *Hui hsien fa-chüeh pao-kao*, Peking, 1956, p. 92.)

been explored by Sekino and Needham. The most important of these are probably to be found in an early sophistication in the control of heat: Chinese artisans of the 7th century B.C. possessed great skill in the casting of intricate bronze objects and were able to fire pottery at high temperatures. . . . The initial production of cast iron was reinforced by the invention of double-cylinder bellows with reciprocating motion (4th century B.C.), the double-acting (push-pull) cylinder bellows (2nd century B.C.), and the application of water power to these bellows in the 1st century A.D. A reinforcing result . . . is the fact that the rendering of cast iron from ore allows for the mass production of the full range of alloys at a highly efficient rate. Thus iron became the metal of the Chinese peasantry and found its early and large-scale use in the fashioning of agricultural implements.

The use of cast iron for agricultural implements is undoubtedly a highly significant event in Chinese economic history. The common types of implements during the latter part of the Eastern Chou period included axes, adzes, chisels, spades, sickles, and hoes (fig. 165); the plow was manufactured, but was relatively rare and does not seem to have been effective enough to replace the spade and hoe as a cultivating tool. The

167. Cattle plowing; Han dynasty murals from Shantung. (From *KK* 1964, no. 7, p. 356.)

earliest iron plows that are well documented archaeologically come from the Warring States tombs at Ku-wei-ts'un, in Hui Hsien, northern Honan.[131] These are flat, V-shaped iron pieces which probably were mounted on wooden blades and handles to serve as working edges (fig. 166). The width of each arm, measured from two complete specimens, averages 18 centimeters. In view of its relatively small size and its mounting device, which could not have been too secure, this primitive plow was probably not capable of turning over the soil to any considerable depth.[132] There is no archaeological evidence that cattle were used to draw the plows. Cattle-drawn plows of considerable size, capable of deep plowing, did not appear in the archaeological record until the middle of the western Han dynasty (fig. 167).

However, with the advent of new, iron cultivation implements, revolutionary changes must have occurred. There is no question that they are more effective and efficient than stone and bone implements, and their development must have been related to the growth of population in the cities. Another of the most significant and consequential of the changes, which may or may not be related to the use of iron implements, is that irrigation techniques became highly elaborate and intensified during the

131. Kuo Pao-chün et al., *Hui Hsien fa-chüeh pao-kao*, p. 91.
132. *KKHP* 1957 (3), 105. *KK* 1964 (7), 355–61.

latter part of the Eastern Chou period. Literary sources indicate that both Shang and Western Chou practiced irrigation to some extent, but the earliest reference to irrigation on a large scale appeared in 563 B.C. in the state of Cheng of central Honan.[133] *Hsün tzu* recorded state officials who specialized in this phase of agriculture, and Li Ping's construction of irrigation works in Szechwan during the Warring States period is well known. The only piece of archaeological evidence of the construction of irrigation ditches is the one described for the Ch'in city of Li-yang above. The significance of large-scale waterworks during the Eastern Chou period to agricultural production and thus to political organization should not be overlooked.[134]

Burial Customs

Since our knowledge of the Chou period is in most cases derived from tombs, a typological sequence of the burial customs during this dynastic interval is fairly well established. Some highly pertinent aspects may be mentioned at this juncture.

Throughout the span of both Shang and Chou periods, cultural constants are met continually in the burials. A typical tomb can be described as follows (fig. 168): The deceased was interred in a rectangular pit (*shu hsüeh*, or "vertical pit"), slightly or much larger than the size of the body, excavated to a considerable depth. The walls of the pit were vertical or sloped slightly inward or outward. Frequently, about half a meter before the desired depth was reached, a smaller pit was continued to the bottom, which left a ledge around the lower pit for the placement of grave goods (*sheng-t'u erh-ts'eng-t'ai*, or "raw earth second-level platform"). In some cases, the pit was dug clear to the bottom on all four sides, but a ledge of fresh earth was built around the lower part of the pit (*shu-t'u erh-ts'eng-t'ai*, or "ripe earth second-level platform"). Sometimes niches were dug into the walls for the placement of goods. The floor and the walls were often plastered, and the walls were sometimes painted, occasionally with drapery designs like the inside of a bed or room. At the center of the bottom in many pits was a small square pit (*yao-k'eng*, or waist pit, since it was located below the waist of the body) in which an animal, usually a dog, was buried. Then, the bottom and the lower walls of the pit were lined with wooden planks to form a chamber (*kuo*), in which the body was placed in

133. Hsü Chung-shu, *BIHP* 5 (1935), 255–69.
134. See, e.g., K. A. Wittfogel, "The theory of Oriental society," in M. H. Fried, ed., *Readings in Anthropology*, vol. 2, New York, Crowell, 1959.

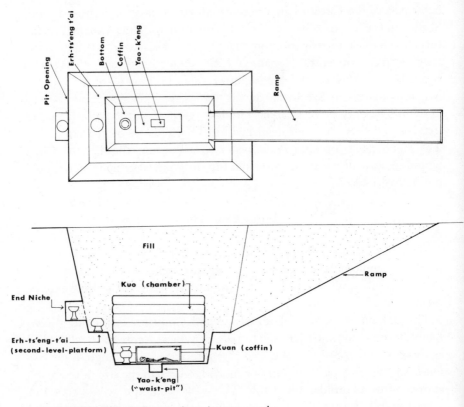

168. A typical Chinese Bronze Age pit-grave tomb.

a wooden coffin (*kuan*). Grave goods, consisting of utensils, ornaments, weapons, food in containers, and so on, were placed in the coffin, outside the coffin in the wooden chamber, or outside the chamber on the ledge or in the wall niches. The pit was then filled with earth, often pounded in layer by layer. Many larger graves had, in addition to these elemental components, one, two, or four ramps that ran from the ground to the floor level of the pit. Bodies of sacrificed humans and animals, and sometimes chariots, were buried in various spots in the tomb (in the wooden chamber, outside in the pit, on the ledge, under the floor of a ramp, or in the fill) or outside the pit in separate graves nearby, depending on the size and elaborateness of the burial.

Many of these features of a typical Shang or Chou burial (of the upper class) were apparently manifestations of a prevailing ancestor worship and a deep belief in life in the afterworld. On the other hand, details and features of the tomb construction, the posture and orientation of the dead,

and the nature and amount of grave goods were presumably more significant of cultural traditions and styles or of the societal status of the dead
than they were of religious beliefs.

In tomb construction, the basic vertical pit pattern prevailed throughout,
although variations were plentiful. This basic pattern is exemplified by
the graves of Shang,[135] Western Chou,[136] and the early part of Eastern
Chou.[137] At Pai-sha in Yü Hsien and Pi-sha-kang in Cheng-chou, both
in Honan, the tombs dated to the end of the Ch'un-ch'iu and the beginning
of the Chan-kuo were still exclusively of this vertical pit pattern.[138] Later
in the Chan-kuo period, however, another style of tomb construction
began to appear, the so-called *tung-shih-mu*, or "cave-chamber graves".
For such graves a vertical pit was dug as usual, but a cave was excavated
into one of the pit walls, and the coffin was placed in this chamber instead
of at the bottom of the pit (fig. 169). At the Warring States cemetery near
Shao-kou in Lo-yang, there were sixteen cave-chamber graves as against
forty-three vertical pit graves.[139] Of the 112 Warring States graves at the
Pan-p'o cemetery near Sian, only 11 retained the old vertical pit pattern;
the rest were of the cave-chamber variety.[140] According to Kuo Pao-chün
and Lin Shou-chin, an evolutionary sequence of change from the traditional
pit grave to the new cave-chamber tombs took place during a short
interval within the latter part of the Warring States.[141] Although many
wall niches in graves of this period contained grave goods, there was a
tendency to enlarge the niche and place the body in it and to place the
grave goods in the pit itself. When both grave goods and the body were
placed in the niche, it had to be enlarged into a chamber, and the pit itself
was reduced in size and importance to the role of shaft or ramp. In the
Chung-chou Road sequence of Lo-yang, of the 260 Eastern Chou graves,
only 4 are of the cave-chamber type. One of these is too poorly preserved
to be dated, but all the others are dated to period VII, the last period. It is
conceivable that the inhabitants of Lo-yang, still the Royal Chou strong-
hold, were more resistant to change than were the people of other areas of
North China, but the number of wall niches in the Eastern Chou graves

135. Kao Ch'ü-hsün, *Bull. Dept. Archaeol. Anthropol.*, Nat'l. Taiwan Univ., no. 13/14
(1959). Shih Chang-ju, *BIHP* 23 (1953), 447–87.

136. *KKHP* 8 (1954), 110–13; 1957 (1), 75–77. *WWTKTL* 1955 (4), 49. Kuo Pao-chün,
TYKKPK 1 (1936), 167–200.

137. E.g., Lin Shou-chin et al., *Shang-ts'un-ling Kuo-kuo mu ti*, pp. 3–4.

138. *KKHP* 7 (1954), 89.

139. *KKHP* 8 (1954), 130.

140. *KKHP* 1957 (3), 67–70.

141. *KKHP* 9 (1955), 109–10.

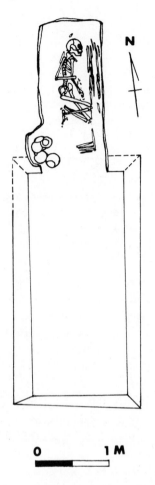

169. A Warring States cave-chamber tomb, at T'ai-shan-miao, Lo-yang. (From *KKHP* 9, 1954, p. 110.)

0   1 M

tells an interesting story. Of all the datable graves on the Chung-chou Road, ten were of the Western Chou; six had waist pits, but none had a wall niche. There are neither waist pits nor wall niches in graves of period I of Eastern Chou; wall niches begin to appear in period II and continue through period VII (table 14). Most of the niches are in the north wall, although they also occur on the other three sides. These facts indicate that the cave-chamber tomb of the late Eastern Chou probably did evolve out of the pit grave by the conversion of the wall niche into a burial chamber. The new mode of construction may merely represent a fashion of the time, which, in combination with bricks, completely replaced the vertical pit graves during the following Han dynasty as the principal mode of tomb

Table 14

The Increase of Wall Niches in Tombs of the Pit-Grave Type
During the Chou

	Period	Total Graves	Graves with Wall Niches	(%)
Western Chou		10	0	0
Eastern Chou	I	6	0	0
	II	30	3	10.0
	III	37	2	5.40
	IV	26	5	19.23
	V	15	3	33.33
	VI	22	7	31.81
	VII	26	10	38.46

construction. Use of bricks of a hollow variety for the construction of the tomb chamber was also a late Warring States innovation.[142]

A related item has to do with the earthen mound built on top of the grave after the pit was filled. Historical records and many local traditions relate to burial mounds of the Eastern Chou period, but those in the city of Yen Hsia-tu are the only known graves with earthen mounds that have been excavated (fig. 170). Confucius, of the Spring Autumn period, was quoted as saying, "I hear that in ancient times the dead were interred but no mounds were built." Ancient times to Confucius were apparently the Shang and Western Chou periods. The Hsi-pei-kang royal tombs of the Shang dynasty probably had no mounds, and Kuo Pao-chün, who specifically looked for evidence of mounds at the Western Chou cemetery at Hsin-ts'un in Chün Hsien, Honan, found none for that period.[143] Until there is definitive evidence to the contrary, it appears that the custom of building mounds atop a burial was another innovation of the Eastern Chou period.

The posture and orientation of the corpse pose special and difficult problems. Throughout most of Shang and Chou, the stretched-out posture predominated. The Shang and Western Chou burials, however, are differentiable into supine and prone groups. Among the Shang burials at Ta-ssu-k'ung-ts'un excavated in 1953, 89 have enough bone remains to

142. *Lo-yang Chung-chou-lu*, tables 3–11. Honan Bureau of Culture, *Cheng-chou Erh-li-kang*, 1959, pp. 80–81.

143. *TYKKPK* 1 (1936), 174.

170. A burial mound in the city of Hsia-tu, Yen. (From *KKHP* 1965, no. 2, p. 102.)

determine that 67 were supine and 22 prone.[144] Of the 109 Western Chou tombs at Chang-chia-p'o and K'o-hsing-chuang, near Sian, 70 bodies were supine, 39 prone.[145] All the bodies in these two groups are stretched out; the prone burials, though in the minority, account for a considerable percentage (25 percent of the Ta-ssu-k'ung-ts'un group and 36 percent of the Sian group) and cannot be dismissed as mere exceptions. Obviously, during the Shang and Western Chou periods, these two postures had a significant contrast that must have had to do with the social and ritual status of the dead.

This contrast, however, was replaced by another contrasting pair of burial postures at the beginning of the Eastern Chou—the stretched and the flexed postures (fig. 171). Burials with a flexed or contracted posture were not absent in Western Chou burials. The late Western Chou tomb at P'u-tu-ts'un, near Sian, contains three bodies, two of which were flexed.[146] Among the eighteen early Western Chou tombs at Fang-tui-ts'un in Hung-chao, Shansi, four flexed burials are found.[147] At the late Western Chou and early Eastern Chou cemetery at Shang-ts'un-ling, 221 graves contain recognizable skeletons, 44 of which are flexed.[148] However, there is no question that the flexed posture was relatively rare during this period. Among the 109 burials in the Sian group at Chang-chia-p'o and

144. *KKHP* 9 (1955), 27–71.
145. Wang Po-hung et al., *Feng hsi fa-chüeh pao-kao*, p. 116.
146. *KKHP* 1957 (1), 76.
147. Wang Chi-sheng, *WWTKTL* 1955 (4), 49.
148. Lin Shou-chin, *Shang-ts'un-ling Kuo-kuo mu-li*, p. 4.

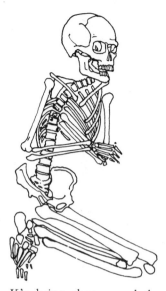

171. A flexed burial of the Warring States period at Pan-p'o, Sian. (From *KKHP* 1957, no. 3, p. 71.)

K'o-hsing-chuang and the 10 burials at Chung-chou Road of Lo-yang of the Western Chou period, not a single flexed burial occurred. Along the Chung-chou Road, in contrast, of 256 Eastern Chou tombs, 215 are contracted, and the stretched bodies are a distinct minority. Moreover, the flexed posture became a predominant manner of burial with the beginning of the Chung-chou Road sequence (the beginning of the Spring Autumn period). Of six period I tombs, five are flexed; of thirty period II tombs, twenty are flexed; after this time stretched burials are exceptions. It is evident that the flexed posture and burial in wall niches and cave chambers were related: it was easier to place a flexed body in a small niche or cavity. Since flexed burials preceded the cave-chamber burials, the former may be said to have influenced the latter development but they cannot be explained by it. Burial in Han dynasty tombs again favored a stretched posture, which must be related to the enlargement of the cave-chambers in Han tombs.

The problem of the orientation of the tomb and of the corpse is even more perplexing; one finds all sorts of variations but no clear-cut regularities that change with time. All the Yin tombs of the Hsi-pei-kang group were south–north oriented, but since all of them had been robbed during early historic times and no skeletons of the tomb masters were left at the time of excavations, the orientation of the corpses is a matter for speculation. During the Chou dynasty, in all its various subphases, both north–south and east–west orientations are found, and in the former case the head is sometimes oriented toward the north and sometimes toward the south.

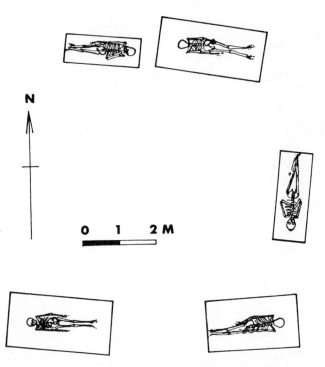

172. Five Western Chou burials near Sian. (From *Feng-hsi fa-chüeh pao-kao*, Peking, Wen Wu Press, 1962, p. 116.)

It is tempting to make a case here for a correlation of the orientation with the posture of the corpse or with the status of the dead person, but generalizations should not yet be made.

It is evident, however, that in the interpretation of burial remains from both Shang and Chou periods the scholar must bear in mind that the burial ritual was to transport the deceased from the world of the living to the world of the dead, a transportation that involved his social and ritual status as well as his worldly possessions. The meaning of the posture and the orientation of the dead person must be sought in terms of his ritual and social importance. An indication of this is the spatial position of his tomb in relation to the tombs of his contemporaries. The possible meaning of the arrangement of the royal tombs in An-yang in the two east-west clusters has been mentioned before. Among the Western Chou tombs at Chang-chia-p'o and K'o-hsing-chuang, a particular layout is especially interesting. The corpses in five tombs, which contained artifacts of apparently a single period, were positioned head to head and feet to feet, as shown in figure 172. Similar clusters are not rare among the early Western

N

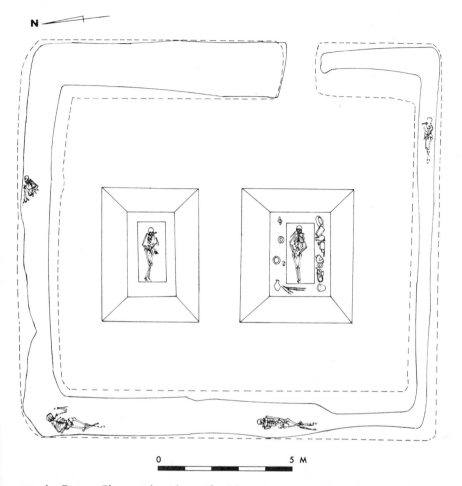

0   5 M

173. An Eastern Chou tomb with sacrificed humans, excavated near Hou-ma, Shansi. (From *Hsin Chung-kuo ti k'ao-ku shou-huo*, Peking, Wen Wu Press, 1962, p. 71.)

Chou tombs.[149] The large burial mounds of Hsia-tu, it may be recalled, were also placed in regular rows.

Also to be accounted for by the social and ritual status of the dead person as well as by the fasion of the times are the amount and nature of the grave goods. The contrast in social levels cannot be more vividly demonstrated in archaeology than it is by burials. Among the Chung-chou Road burials of the Eastern Chou, for instance, the very few rich graves have large pits, double wooden chambers, many bronzes, and much

149. Wang Po-hung et al., *Feng-hsi fa-chüeh pao-kao*, pp. 115–16.

pottery; the very poor ones have no shaped pits, no coffins, and no grave goods. The roles played by the various burials in each of the royal tombs in An-yang are well known. But changes can be observed between tombs of different periods. The typology of the grave goods of course goes with the burial chronology, and the changes in this respect during the Chou period will be discussed below. Another important shift concerns the human retainers. Of 182 Western Chou tombs in the Chang-chia-p'o and K'o-hsing-chuang group, 9 contained sacrificed humans. Of more than three thousand tombs of the Warring States period known by 1962, from various parts of China, only about a dozen have sacrificed retainers (fig. 173).[150] On the other hand, in tombs of the late Eastern Chou period large numbers of figurines were substituted for human beings. In the north these images were made of clay and, occasionally, of lead; wooden ones prevailed in the south. The implications of this change from humans to figurines, in terms of the social and economic history of the Shang and Chou periods, are self-evident.

Artifacts

The study of artifacts (of stone, bone, jade, pottery, bronze, and iron) of the Shang and Chou periods is the hallmark of Chinese archaeology. Sites and tombs were not excavated and examined in their totality until less than sixty years ago, but individual works of art have been the object of scholarly research in China for the past two thousand years, and as material for study there are as many artifacts in artistic collections as there are in archaeological assemblages brought to light under scientific supervision. There are many studies of Shang and Chou artifacts, and they are admirably treated in many textbooks of Chinese archaeology and art history.[151] For the present purpose, our discussion must be highly selective, and it is concerned largely with bronzes. Stone and bone implements of the Shang and Chou do not materially differ from their Neolithic prototypes except in a few special cases, and iron artifacts began only toward the end of the period. Ceramics is highly important, to be sure, and its chronological uses have been demonstrated by the Sian and Lo-yang sequences

150. *Hsin Chung-kuo ti k'ao-ku shou-huo*, p. 70.

151. See, e.g., Chu Chien-hsin, *Chin shih hsüeh*, Shanghai, Commercial Press, 1940. Jung Keng, *Shang Chou i-ch'i t'ung-k'ao*, Peiping, Yenching University, 1947. William Watson, *Ancient Chinese Bronzes*, Rutland, Vt., Tuttle, 1962. Cheng Te-k'un, *Chou China*, Cambridge, Heffer & Sons, 1963. Max Loehr, *Relics of Ancient China*, New York, Asia Society, 1965.

of Western and Eastern Chou tombs. But research in ceramics has been much less extensive, and in many ways it must be based on a thorough understanding of the bronze vessels, for many forms and decorations of the pottery in the Chinese Bronze Age were manifest imitations of their bronze counterparts.

The central problem for the study of bronzes is the formulation of types.[152] The abundant data on the chronology of Shang and Chou archaeological sites provide a solid basis for a chronological arrangement of the occurrences and changes of individual types of bronzes throughout the period in question. Furthermore, it is possible to examine the history of change of individual modes that compose the types, as well as the history of change of whole assemblages of artifacts consisting of types in association. Since my purpose here is not the history of bronze types, modes, and assemblages per se but is rather the examination of aspects of the history of Shang and Chou civilizations as revealed by these studies, I shall confine the discussion to the general problem of type formulation and some significant developmental trends in the history of bronze artifacts.

The formulation of types of Chinese bronzes has its own conventions. In Chou and Han texts there are numerous references to bronze utensils, and some bronze vessels name themselves in their inscriptions. The identification of their "native lexicons" with the actual bronze types would be an important terminological problem of general anthropological interest. But scholars can hardly choose to use or not use the native terms for the types, for ever since the Sung dynasty there has been a standard terminology in the Chinese antiquarian and archaeological literature, consisting of lexicons taken from the Chou and Han texts. A tripod with three solid legs, for instance, is a *ting*, and one with hollow legs a *li*. Moreover, since these terms in their textual contexts refer to artifact types in regard to use but not to form, these terms carry implicit meaning of use. A *tou*, for instance, refers to a container for food (mostly meat) used for ritual purposes, and a *chüeh*, also a tripod with three solid legs, immediately calls to mind a ritual wine cup. Therefore, the standard Chinese terminology for the bronzes of Shang and Chou is by definition "functional," presumably ideal and useful for the purpose of archaeological reconstruction of the ancient culture and society. The question, however, is whether

152. For "type" and "mode," the definitions of Irving Rouse are adopted in this section. See his *Prehistory in Haiti: A Study in Method*, Yale University Publications in Anthropology, no. 21 (1939).

the identification of the Chou and Han terms with actual artifact types
is correct (except for cases where the vessels are named in their inscriptions).
Another complicating factor is the problem of hierarchy of taxa. A *tsun*,
for instance, often refers to a bronze vessel of a specific form, but on other
occasions it includes all classes of ceremonial vessels. With these considerations, Li Chi, in his studies of the bronze vessels of An-yang, has sought to
establish a separate system of terminology based exclusively on the shape
of the lower part of the vessel, a system that he used first to classify the
pottery of Hsiao-t'un.[153] Thus the Shang bronzes at Hsiao-t'un were first
grouped into the following five "orders"; *round-bottomed*, 1 vessel; *flat-
bottomed*, 2 vessels; *ring-footed*, 34 vessels; *tripod*, 36 vessels; *quadrupod*, 3
vessels; and *lid-shaped*, 6 pieces. Under each order, the traditional terms
are adopted for finer characterizations—*ting*-shaped, *chüeh*-shaped, and so
forth. This new system based on shape is used entirely for description and
has proved useful. The traditional terminology, however, continues to be
used. In the current Chinese archaeological literature, the ancient terms are
used freely when the artifacts can be typed with certainty or near certainty;
when they cannot, descriptive terms such as those coined by Li Chi are
used. Although there is a considerable confusion of terms in Chinese
archaeology, especially in the classification of bronze and ceramic vessels,
the following categories of some of the most common bronze artifacts
are more or less in general use (fig. 174):

1. Cooking and dining vessels: ting, li, yen, fu, kui, hsü, tui, tou
2. Drinking vessels: chüeh, chiao, chia, ho, tsun, ku, chih, yu, kuang,
   i, niao shou tsun, hu, lei, shuo
3. Water utensils: p'an, i, chien, yü, p'en, cheng, chu, wan
4. Musical instruments: cheng, jao, chung, to, ling (varieties of bell),
   ku (drum)
5. Weapons: ko (halberd), chi (halberd), mao (spear), shih (tsu)
   (arrow), chien (sword), fu (ax), tao (knife)
6. Horse and chariot fittings
7. Mirrors and belt hooks

Some of these types occurred throughout the Shang and Chou periods,
but in some intervals they exhibited variations in mode. Others occurred
only during certain intervals. The occurrence and variation of these types,
either singly or in association, during the different periods of Shang and
Chou are, therefore, significant. For example, *ting* and *ko* are two types

---

153. Li Chi, *Chung-kuo k'ao-ku hsüeh-pao* 3 (1948), 1–99; *Hsiao-t'un t'ao-ch'i*, Taipei,
Institute of History and Philology, Academia Sinica, 1956.

TING   LI   YEN (HSIEN)   TUI   TOU

 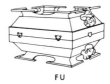

KUI   FU

CHÜEH   CHIAO   CHIA   HO   TSUN

KU   CHIH   YU   HSI-KUANG   I

P'AN   CHIEN

HIAO-TSUN   HU   LEI   I   YÜ

174. Major types of Shang and Chou bronze vessels.

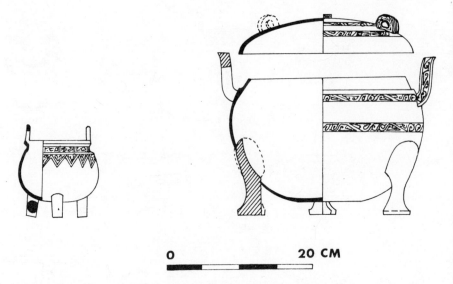

0   20 CM

175. *Ting* tripods: *left*, Shang period (from Li Chi, *KKHP* 3, 1948); *right*, Warring States period (from Kuo Pao-chün, *Shan-piao-chen yü Liu-li-ko*, Peking, Science Press, 1959, p. 11).

that are almost universal at Shang and Chou sites, but the changes in mode are chronologically significant. All *ting* consist of three components: body, two handles, and three legs. In Shang and early Western Chou periods, the two handles were placed on the rim, and the three legs were straight. Later, the handles were sometimes lowered to the body and had to be bent, and the legs were made thicker and bent to resemble the legs of animals (fig. 175). The earlier *ko* halberd consisted merely of a cutting blade and a flat hafting tongue, but as time went on the lower edge at the end of the blade extended downward to accommodate an increasing number of holes for greater security of hafting, and the tongue became increasingly pointed to change from a purely hafting device to an auxiliary part of the weapon (fig. 176).

Other types of bronze artifacts occurred only at a certain time in the Shang and Chou periods, and their occurrence alone is chronologically significant. Bronze swords, mirrors, and belt hooks, for instance, were most commonly found in tombs of the Warring States period, and it used to be thought that they were innovations at that time. Recent reports and discoveries have pushed the first occurrence of swords to the late Western Chou or initial Eastern Chou period,[154] that of the mirror to the Shang

154. Lin Shou-chin et al., *Shang-ts'un-ling Kuo kuo mu-ti. Lo-yang Chung-chou-lu.* Lin Shou-chin, *KKHP* 1962 (2), 75–84.

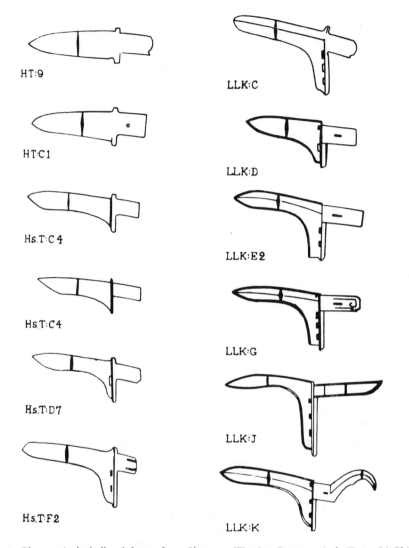

HT:9

HT:C1

Hs.T:C4

Hs.T:C4

Hs.T:D7

Hs.T:F2

LLK:C

LLK:D

LLK:E2

LLK:G

LLK:J

LLK:K

176. Changes in *ko* halberd forms from Shang to Warring States period. (From Li Chi, *The Beginnings of Chinese Civilization*, Seattle, Univ. of Washington, 1957, p. 57.)

period (fig. 177),[155] and that of belt hooks to the early Spring Autumn period.[156] The earlier finds, however, are not the same as the later varieties, and there is no question that these types did not become prevalent until the middle of Eastern Chou.

The decorative art of the bronzes is another area of research in which

155. Kao Ch'ü-hsün, *BIHP* 29 (1958), 658–719.
156. *Lo-yang Chung-chou-lu*, pp. 145–46.

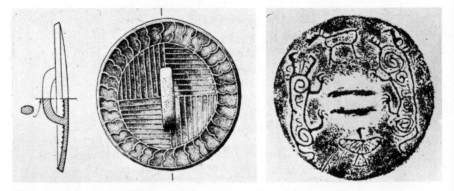

177. Bronze mirrors: *left*, Shang (from Kao Ch'ü-hsün, *BIHP* 24, 1958, p. 689); *right*, Western Chou (from *Shang-ts'un-ling Kuo kuo mu-ti*, Peking, Science Press, 1959, p. 27).

extensive data have been accumulated. Most of the decorative motifs of Shang and Chou bronzes are derived from the animal world; floral patterns did not occur significantly until the late Eastern Chou.[157] Again, individual motifs occurred in different periods or underwent changes throughout the era. The most characteristic single motif of Shang and early Western Chou bronzes is the *t'ao-t'ieh* face (without the lower jaw) of a mythical creature. During the latter half of the Western Chou and the early part of Eastern Chou, the most characteristic motif is the *ch'ieh-ch'ü* pattern, a pair of interlocked serpents. After this, the latter part of the Eastern Chou is most distinguished by the *p'an-ch'ih* design of many interlocking small serpents. Also characteristic of this last period are scenes of rituals on bronze vessels, which provide material for the study of the architecture, garments, ceremonial paraphernalia, and other aspects of life of the Warring States period (figs. 178, 179).

In the early 1930s Kuo Mo-jo and Bernhard Karlgren, probably independently studying the bronze vessels of the Shang and Chou dynasties, arrived at very similar methodologies and conclusions.[158] Their aims were to arrange the Shang and Chou bronzes into a chronological order and, from this, to study the problems of stylistic evolution. "We shall try first," Karlgren states, "to classify the inscriptions in their chronological order, without any side glances at the types of the vessels; and once this literary chronology has been established we shall use it as a means for classifying

157. Bo Gyllensvärd, *BMFEA* 34 (1962), 29–47.

158. Kuo Mo-jo, *Liang Chou chin-wen-tz'u ta-hsi*, Tokyo, Bunkyūdō, 1932; *Ku-tai ming-k'ê ts'ung-k'ao*, 1933; *Liang Chou chin-wen ts'u ta-hsi t'u-lu*, Tokyo, Bunkyūdō, 1934. Bernhard Karlgren, *BMFEA* 6 (1934); 8 (1936).

178. Principal decorative motifs in Shang and Chou bronze art: *top*, T'ao-t'ieh; *bottom left*, Ch'ieh-ch'ü; *bottom right*, P'an-ch'ih.

the vessels, their types and decoration, in chronological groups."[159] In similar fashion, Kuo Mo-jo attempted to subdivide the Chinese Bronze Age into five stages:[160]

1. *Stage of Beginnings:* a hypothetical stage in which bronzes first appeared in China. The time was possibly "late Hsia" dynasty and early Shang dynasty. The place was possibly the lower courses of the Yangtze and Huai Ho, where copper mines were known in early historic periods. The bronze metallurgy in the Huang Ho valley, according to Kuo, may have been introduced from this area.

159. *BMFEA* 8 (1936), 10.

160. *Liang Chou chin-wen tz'u ta-hsi t'u-lu; Ch'ing-t'ung shih-tai*, Chungking, Wen-chih Press, 1945.

179. Interlocking serpents on lacquerware found from late Chou tomb at Fen-shui-ling, Ch'ang-chih, Shansi. (From *KKHP* 1974, no. 2.)

2. *Stage of Florescence:* late Shang-Yin and early Chou dynasty, including the reigns of Kings Ch'eng, K'ang, Chao, and Mu. The characteristic artifacts were *ting*, square *i*, lidless *kui*, *tsun*, *yu*, *chüeh*, *chia*, and *tuo*. *Li* and *chung* were present but rare. *Fu*, *hu*, *p'an*, and *i* were absent. The artifacts were either completely decorated or not at all. The characteristic designs included *k'ui-lung*, *k'ui-feng*, *t'ao-t'ieh*, elephant, and *lei-wen*—the *t'ao-t'ieh* and the *lei-wen* being predominant. In general, the decorative patterns were "primitive" in character. In inscriptions, the composition was simple and succinct, and the calligraphy solemn and grave. The form of the vessels tended to be "heavy and solid," without any exhibition of "frivolity."

3. *Stage of Decadence:* from the middle of the Western Chou dynasty, including the reigns of Kings Kung, I, Hsiao, and I, through the middle of the Ch'un-ch'iu period. In bronze artifacts, *ting*, *li*, *kui*, *fu*, *chung* (bell), *fu*, and the like, grew in quantity; the square *i*, *yu*, *chüeh*, *chia*, *ku*, and the like, became extinct; and *p'an*, *i*, *hsü*, and *hu* began to appear. The decorations were thin-line geometric patterns made by shallow incisions and engravings. The *lei-wen* became rare, and the elephant pattern disappeared. The *ch'ieh-ch'ü* pattern replaced the *t'ao-t'ieh* as the leading decorative motif, and the *t'ao-t'ieh* was demoted to the feet of *ting* and *kui* vessels. *K'ui-lung*, *k'ui-feng*, and *p'an-k'ui-wen* became deformed. In inscriptions, the characters became "relaxed" and random, including some cursive forms. The form of vessels was simple and crude but was "emancipated from the primitive style and mythological tradition."

4. *Stage of Renaissance:* from the middle of Ch'un-ch'iu through the end of Chan-kuo. In artifact types, *tui* and *cheng* appeared, *pien-chung* became popular, *li* and *yen* became rare, and *hsü* was extinct. In decoration, the incisions and engravings became shallower and thinner. Repetitive motifs were widely applied with molds. The patterns included a great variety of motifs. Most accessory ornaments were realistic animals. In inscriptions the composition tended to rhyme, and the characters, a part of the total decor, were refined, regularly arranged, and placed conspicuously. In form the artifacts were light, convenient, and style conscious—indicating, according to Kuo, the commercialization of the bronzes during this period.

5. *Stage of Decline:* after the end of the Chan-kuo period. Bronze vessels became simple and coarse but practical and convenient. Decorative patterns became a rarity. Most of the inscriptions were incised rather than cast, and pertained to weight, volume, or names of the manufacturers rather than to history or morality. Bronze mirrors and coins prevailed, but otherwise iron served as the raw material for artifacts.

Karlgren's classification closely parallels this scheme of Kuo Mo-jo's. Omitting Kuo's stage of Beginnings and stage of Decline, which are beyond the temporal scope of the Yin and Chou anyway, Karlgren sub-divides the Yin and Chou bronzes into three classes:[161]

1. *Archaic*, further divisible into Yin, prior to 1122 B.C.; and Yin-Chou, 1122 to ca. 950 B.C.
2. *Middle Chou*, ca. 950 to 650 B.C.
3. *Huai*, ca. 650 to 200 B.C.

Thus, both in time and in definition, Karlgren's Archaic class is identical with Kuo's Florescence; his Middle Chou is analogous to the Decadence stage; and his Huai coincides with Kuo's Renaissance. In addition, Karlgren has painstakingly worked out a list of stylistic criteria which characterize each of his classes.

Kuo and Karlgren have thus demonstrated that the political subdivisions of Chou into such categories as Western Chou, Ch'un-ch'iu, and Chan-kuo are not necessarily meaningful in the evolution of artifacts and art. Instead, three well-marked artistic and typological stages are discernible. The first is the early part of the Western Chou, up to the reign of King Kung, or roughly the year 950 B.C. The bronze art of this stage, called Yin-Chou by Karlgren, "in all essentials an epigonous art,"[162] "was still essentially the same as that of the Yin, with but small innovations."[163]

The second stage, from the middle of Western Chou (ca. 950 B.C.) through the middle of the Ch'un-ch'iu period (ca. 650 B.C.)—Kuo's stage of Decadence or Karlgren's Middle Chou style—witnessed a

> sudden, complete and fundamental change in the art tradition in China. It is characterized on the one hand by a ruthless abolition of the whole array of Yin elements . . . on the other hand by the introduction of a series of new elements, most of which were entirely unknown in China before that time, and some of which had cropped up but sporadically, in exceptional cases, anterior to 947.[164]

Kuo characterizes the art of this stage as "degenerate," and Karlgren describes it as "poor and mediocre."[165] The latter has further attempted

161. *BMFEA* 9 (1937), 5.
162. *BMFEA* 8 (1936), 139.
163. *Ibid.*, p. 89.
164. *Ibid.*, p. 116.
165. Karlgren, *BMFEA* 13 (1941), 4.

180. Decorative patterns on a Warring States–period vessel excavated from the site at Shan-piao-chen, Chi Hsien, Honan. (From Kuo Pao-chün, *Shan-piao-chen yü Liu-li-ko*, Peking, Science Press, 1959, fig. 11.)

to explain the sudden appearance of a whole series of new stylistic motifs as the "result of the widening of the sphere of Chinese civilization from the Shensi and Honan centers to large districts of China north of the Yang-tze"[166] where contacts with alien peoples were made and new artistic inspirations were received.

On the basis of the Middle Chou style, an artistic renaissance occurred in the middle of the Ch'un-ch'iu period (ca. 650 B.C.) which gave rise to a new style, the Huai.[167] Karlgren characterizes this style as a self-conscious art, a "highly sophisticated one working with all the paraphernalia and tricks of a pompous baroque," and one that is "keen on a brilliant impression of richness and variety." He states that "during the 7th–3rd centuries B.C. the Chinese world was already sufficiently advanced in culture to allow a conscious artistic renaissance movement, which incorporated elements now already ancient and venerated in the new pompous baroque art."[168] Also, fresh artistic inspirations resulting from the expanding sphere of the North China civilization and increased contacts with the Ordos area in the north gave impetus to the development of the Huai style. The warfare scene, for instance, is common to the Huai (fig. 180)

166. *BMFEA* 8 (1936), 146.
167. *Ibid.*, p. 90.
168. *BMFEA* 13 (1941), 4.

0   1   2
cm

181. A bronze plaque of the Eastern Chou period from an Eastern Chou tomb at K'o-hsing-chuang, Sian. (From *Feng-hsi fa-chüeh pao-kao*, Peking, Wen Wu Press, 1962, p. 139.)

and the Ordos; both of these styles, furthermore, contained such curious and specific elements as pear-shaped cells or figures, comma-shaped figures, circles on the bodies of animals, and so forth, indicating an exchange of artistic ideas during this period (fig. 181).[169]

These studies of Kuo Mo-jo and Bernhard Karlgren are of great importance to an understanding of cultural growth during the Chou period in North China. For the entire time span of the Western Chou dynasty, archaeological discoveries are few and mostly confined to tombs. We must therefore depend largely upon such studies of bronze vessels for an insight into the problems of cultural change during this period. However, as several decades have elapsed since these studies were published, we might ask what, if any, major strides have been made to bring the Kuo and Karlgren material up to date. The answer is that potentially useful data have been found in great quantities, but studies utilizing these new data are unfortunately lacking. Many details can now be added, however, to the Kuo and Karlgren schemes and many others should be modified, sometimes quite drastically. I will give a few examples.

First, several graves have been excavated in recent years, such as P'u-tu-ts'un (Sian) and Li-ts'un (Mei) in Shensi, and Fang-tui-ts'un and Tung-pao (Hung-chao) in Shansi, that are attributed to the early part of the Western

169. Karlgren, *BMFEA* 9 (1937), 102–11.

Chou period.[170] Bronze vessels found in these tombs are indistinguishable from Yin pieces both in form and in decoration; in fact, in most cases these are dated to the Western Chou by inscriptions. On the other hand, two out of the four Yin-Chou style innovations claimed by Karlgren, namely, bent ear and *p'an*, were found, as pointed out by Karlgren himself, at An-yang; their Yin dynasty dating, which was doubted by Karlgren, is no longer doubtful since the An-yang finds at Hsi-pei-kang are now well dated stratigraphically. Thus only two of Karlgren's Yin-Chou innovations are left—hook projections and tail-raising birds. To these, Ch'en Meng-chai would add the following as exclusively Western Chou but not Yin traits: *kui* with four ears; *kui* with square supports; independent square or rectangular vessel supports (the so-called *chin*); bent handle of *tou* (or *shuo*); projecting flanges; some combinations of vessels that differ from the Yin pattern; and the absence of some Yin decorative patterns.[171] These traits, whether valid or not, do not occur universally among Western Chou vessels; among the early Western Chou tombs enumerated above we find evidence of only one of these new elements, the bent handle of *tou*, which was found at an early Western Chou tomb at P'u-tu-ts'un.[172] I think we can positively say that the bronze art of early Western Chou was a continuation of the Yin bronze art. Karlgren justifies his separation of the Yin-Chou art from the Yin on the basis of the innovations.[173] But, as he himself points out, there were greater and more significant innovations within the Yin style. Karlgren attacks T'ang Lan for making divisions of art history on the basis of political considerations alone. What then are his own grounds (besides political considerations) for not subdividing his Archaic style into more stages (such as Max Loehr's Styles I–V) than Yin and Yin-Chou? The present evidence shows that the Archaic style of bronzes of the Florescence stage (Yin and early Western Chou) is a continuous development; it can certainly be further subdivided, but the segment that is described as Yin-Chou by Karlgren is not stylistically significant enough to indicate either that the Chou art was different from the Shang art, or that the Chou people made any real contribution to their Shang heritage after the conquest.

Another important fact concerning the Western Chou bronzes is their widespread geographic distribution. Not only have they been found in an

170. *KKHP* 8 (1954), 109–26. *WWTKTL* 1955 (4), 46–52; 1957 (4), 5–9; 1957 (8), 42.
171. *KKHP* 9 (1955), 138. *WWTKTL* 1955 (5), 65.
172. *KKHP* 8 (1954), 120.
173. *BMFEA* 9 (1937), 96.

area ranging from Liaoning in the north to Anhwei and Kiangsu in the south[174] but we also find that funeral assemblages of typically early Western Chou types found at Yen-tun-shan in Tan-t'u, Kiangsu, can be dated to the reign of King Ch'eng or of King K'ang at the latest.[175] The fact that during the early period of Western Chou the Chou sphere of cultural influence had already become so wide seems to be in strong support of Karlgren's contention that the emergence of the Middle Chou style was the result of this widening of territory and, consequently, the greater extent of cultural contacts and exchange of new artistic ideas. This is, however, more apparent than real. Unless and until it can be demonstrated that the new Middle Chou elements pre-existed (either in bronzes or in some other media) in other regions in China, which archaeological data from regions outside the nuclear area of the Chou do not yet indicate, the basic dynamics of the emergence of this new style in North China must be sought elsewhere. Cultures and civilizations in regions both north and south of North China contemporary with the Western Chou will be described in the following chapters. Both the Western Chou assemblages and the native cultural contexts show that the Middle Chou style, in elements and in total, was not apparent anywhere in these areas before the cultural impact of the Chou civilization.

As far as North China is concerned, two of the most important discoveries of bronzes of the Middle Chou style are from tombs at P'u-tu-ts'un, Sian, near those mentioned above of the early Western Chou stage,[176] and from a large cemetery at Shang-ts'un-ling in Shan Hsien, western Honan, possibly of the state of Kuo.[177] The former assemblage is dated to shortly after the reign of King Mu, whose name was mentioned in the inscriptions, and the latter is placed at the end of Western Chou and the beginning of the Ch'un-ch'iu period. Thus, these two discoveries chronologically mark both the beginning and the end of the Middle Chou style and the Decadence stage as defined by Karlgren and Kuo respectively. Typologically, they do the same. The P'u-tu-ts'un find includes such Archaic elements as *ku*, *chüeh*, *yu*, and *ting* with vertical ears and cylindrical legs. But bells, *ting* with curved legs, and the *ch'ieh-ch'ü* pattern (a variety of Karlgren's "broad band"), which are all diagnostic of Karlgren's Middle Chou style, had already appeared. It is indeed possible that some

174. Higuchi, *Tōyōshi-kenkyu* 16 (1957), 40–61.
175. *WWTKTL* 1955 (5), 65.
176. *KKHP* 1957 (1), 75–85.
177. Lin Shou-chin et al., *Shang-ts'un-ling Kuo kuo mu-ti*.

of the Archaic elements of this group may have been relics or antiquities at the time of the burial, and vessels that happened to be placed in one grave are not necessarily "contemporary" in the usual archaeological sense. However, this cannot explain both Archaic and Middle Chou elements combined in one vessel. A *lei* and a *ho*, for instance, have both the hanging blade of Karlgren's Archaic style and the *ch'ieh-ch'ü* of his Middle Chou style. Such combinations lead us to conclude that the Middle Chou did not replace the Archaic style suddenly and completely, as Karlgren has suggested. A transitional period, around the time of Kings Kung and Mu, perhaps, may have existed before the Middle Chou style became mature and well established. The Shang-ts'un-ling cemetery, on the other hand, shows a well-defined Middle Chou style of bronzes which had already foreshadowed the succeeding Huai style with such typical elements as the *t'ao-t'ieh* and the mirror. In many other aspects also, such as the type of weapons and modes of burial, the Shang-ts'un-ling find pushes many of the Huai elements back in time.

Our knowledge of the stylistic evolution of the Chou bronze vessels can be supplemented considerably by a study of the evolution of bronze weapons in North China,[178] but for a full understanding of the meaning and significance of the stylistic changes, formal analysis alone will hardly suffice. Chinese bronzes as a source of information in Shang and Chou society are only beginning to be tapped. In discussing the stylistic differtiations of Shang bronzes we have already mentioned the sociological significance of the A and B styles of Karlgren revealed by the association of artifact and stylistic types.[179] In the Chung-chou Road sequence of Lo-yang, the chronological importance of the association of vessel types during different periods has already been described. Such association studies should also be undertaken from a sociological perspective.

In period I [of the Eastern Chou sequence of Chung-chou Road] *ting* occurred only in large graves with bronzes, but *ting* appeared in graves of middle size with only pottery goods in period II and in graves of small size with only pottery goods in period III. Pottery *ting* appeared in period II only in graves of middle size with only pottery goods, but they appeared in large graves during period IV.[180]

178. Chou Wei, *Chung-kuo ping-ch'i shih kao*, Peking, San-lien, 1957. *KK* 1961 (2), 111–18. Hayashi Minao, *Chugaku In-shō jidai no buki*, Kyoto University, Inst. Humanistic Sciences, 1972.

179. See p. 294, above.

180. *Lo-yang Chung-chou-lu*, p. 145.

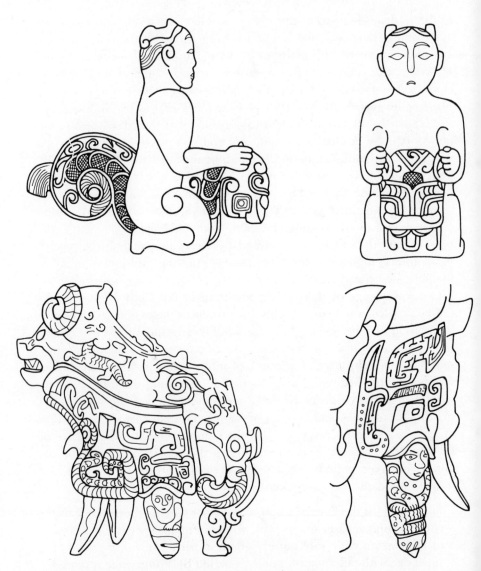

182. Changing relationship of man and animal in Shang and Chou bronze art: *top*, carved jade figurine from a Warring States tomb in Lo-yang (after *KK* 1959, no. 11, p. 657); *bottom*, leg of *kuang* of the Shang type (from *Sekai bijutsu zenshū*, Tokyo, Katokawa, 1962, vol. 12, p. 167).

The *ting* was central in the ritual vessel complex of Shang and Chou periods, and the ritual vessel complex was an unequivocal marker of the upper class. This ancient ritual tradition was maintained in period I (the beginning of Eastern Chou), but soon afterward it broke down entirely, and the vessel-type alignment within a grave changed completely. This may indicate a major change of social status alignment from the Western Chou to the Eastern Chou.[181] Another example of the functional study of stylistic shift during the Shang and Chou is the changing relationship between man and animal in both the mythology and the decorative art of this period (fig. 182).[182] It provides an insight into basic attitudes of the Shang and Chou peoples toward their world and thus furnishes a clue to the interrelationships of the various aspects of that world, aspects whose changes throughout the period have been described above (table 15).

General Conclusions

In the foregoing passages, information about the development of cities, technology, burial customs, and artifacts has been presented to fill in the pattern of cultural growth during the Chou period. The question now is: What is the summation of all these data?

In speaking of the cultural growth during the Chou period in North China, literary records must be consulted to provide a complete picture. For the purposes of this volume, however, the archaeological data are sufficient to outline the high points and to relate the cultures of North China and the rest of the country.

The trends of cultural growth can be described in two ways. First, there was a constant tendency toward a greater degree of similarity of cultures throughout the geographic expanse of Chinese civilization. Second, there was an accelerated growth of the internal society, economy, and political organization. Moreover, these two phenomena are probably interrelated.

In speaking of the trend toward greater internal coherence of the Chou civilization, we agains face the problem of cultural definitions. In the first section of this chapter it was suggested that the "Western Chou people" during the Shang dynasty may have been no more than a group of local inhabitants under Shang rule who were within the expanse of the Shang civilization. To be sure, the Western Chou had their subcultural characteristics, but the "conquest" in 1122 B.C., whereby the Chou replaced the Shang as China's masters, cannot be called a conquest by an alien people having an alien culture. It was, in fact, from all evidence, no more than an internal struggle for power. The notion that the conquest of the Shang by the Chou represents the triumph of the Western Hsia over the Eastern I, as has been suggested by Fu Ssu-nien, is correct only if the Hsia and the

181. *Hsin Chung-kuo ti k'ao-ku shou-kuo*, p. 69.
182. K. C. Chang, *BIE* 16 (1963), 115–46.

Table 15

Some Aspects of Interrelated Changes of Chinese Civilization in
Its Formative Stages

Dates (B.C.)	Dynastic & Predynastic periods	Technology	Settlement patterns	Political forms	Mythological types	Some religious concepts	Art styles	Animals
206	Han	Iron	Political-ritual-commercial-industrial cities plus farming hamlets	Empire	Clan origins Heaven-Earth separation Cosmogonic origins Heroes as saviors	Total separation of world of gods from world of ancestors God's supreme authority challenged Individual virtues and merits stressed	Late Chou	"Hunting scenes" Animals being subdued Conventionalized animal motifs
221	Ch'in							
450	Warring-States (Eastern Chou)			competition of local powers (State)				
	Spring-Autumn (Eastern Chou)	Bronze	Administrative-ceremonial centers plus farming and industrial satellites			World of gods ≠ world of ancestors God goes to Heaven King rules Earth as God's agent by virtue of te	Middle Chou	Conventionalized animal motifs
770	Western Chou				Clan origins		Yin-Chou	
1100	Yin (Shang)		(urbanization)	total royal power (Chi Tzu Te)		Supreme Being (Shang Ti) Identification of Shang Ti with ancestors of Tzu World of Gods = world of ancestors	Yin (Archaic)	Scripts with animal compounds Scapulimancy Potency in art
1400		Stone						
1700	Lung-shan		Permanent farming villages	Villages	?	Institutionalized ancestor cult	Lungshanoid	
	Yang-shao		Shifting farming villages			Fertility cult	Yang-shao	
	Mesolithic		Camps					

I are considered no more than geographical variants of the same Chinese people.

There is no archaeological evidence for significant change in the basic pattern of Chinese civilization in North China immediately after the conquest. The Western Chou took over the Shang culture in bronze metallurgy, burial rites, and decorative art in virtually unaltered forms. Karlgren's Yin-Chou elements plus Ch'en Meng-chia's Western Chou innovation in the style of bronze vessels involved no basic changes in cultural beliefs and artistic styles. Changes inevitably occurred but are of the kind that would take place over any period of time under normal incentives during the development of a culture.

Nor, in the sense defined a few paragraphs back, did the Western Chou gain any new territory during the first years of the dynasty. The sphere of cultural influence may have been expanded, compared to the Shang, but the Western Chou territory was wider than the Shang mainly because the Western Chou had as a base Shensi and Shansi, which the Shang did not emphatically claim as being within their own state. In the south, we know from history that Huai Ho valley natives considered themselves akin to the Shang rulers and were continuously disaffected under the Chou rule. A widespread rebellion shortly after the conquest was soon subdued by the military expeditions of Chou Kung. Western Chou bronze assemblages found in Anhwei and Kiangsu, in the Huai region, bear out the historical records and indicate that Western Chou powers became established in this region. But as will be shown in a later chapter, the Huai River valley cultures during both the Shang and the early Western Chou dynasties maintained their own cultural identity. A significant breakdown of the native cultural traditions and the establishment of typical North China kingdoms did not take place in the Huai Ho valley and the Yangtze Valley until after the beginning of the Western Chou period. Contacts with alien peoples surrounding the Royal Chou and a resulting fresh impetus in artistic inspiration may only partially account for the emergence of the Middle Chou style. A more compelling explanation must be sought in the development of Chou civilization. The latter part of the Western Chou and the beginning of the Eastern Chou, the period covered by the Middle Chou style, was between the classical "Archaic" Yin and Chou civilization and the youthful, spirited Eastern Chou renaissance in style and revolution in technology and economy. The Middle Chou period thus represents a transitional stage wherein the classic styles began to give way to the innovations in all Chinese territory.

A new era in the history of North China began with the Eastern Chou.
In political history, ancient China consisted of the Shang and Chou dynasties; but in cultural history, the subdivision may be placed at the middle
of the Chou dynasty, dividing the Shang-Chou periods into two stages,
Shang and Early Chou, and Late Chou. Iron metallurgy was developed
in the Eastern Chou, and industrial specialization was very much intensified.
The old Yin and Western Chou pattern of urban constitution lingered on
for a while but, from the late Ch'un-ch'iu period on, new cities emerged
in all of North China. Here the importance of industry and commerce was
indicated by the physical incorporation of their quarters into the walled
city. Cultural contacts with foreign lands became very much more
frequent, particularly in the north. During the Eastern Chou period,
common cultural traits, including important elements of daily life, were
shared more and more by North China and the steppe nomads. In art,
too, we have seen that the Huai style shared a number of characteristic
traits with the Ordos and its adjacent cultures. The horse became a mount
as well as a draught animal, and swords came into wide use. Burial mounds
were fashionable, belt hooks were used for a new style of dress, and flexed
burials became important. These new cultural elements, and the old traits
that had gained in popularity at this time, are certainly indicative of the
wider circle of cultural contact and communication between North China
and the northern nomads, although the direction of flow of these exchanges
cannot always be ascertained.[183]

The Chou period is a crucial period for contemporary archaeologists of
China, for it is during this period—perhaps late Ch'un-ch'iu, around
500–550 B.C.—that the transition from the slave society to the feudal
society is said to have taken place.[184] The above analysis shows that, at
the beginning of the Eastern Chou, Chinese society underwent fundamental changes in every archaeologically pertinent respect, and this must
mark a transformational process of the first magnitude, whatever label
we come to use to capture the spirit of that process.

183. Kao Ch'ü-hsün, KKHP 2 (1947), 121–66. Karlgren, BMFEA 13 (1941), 1–125.
Kao Ch'ü-hsün, BIHP 23 (1951), 489–510.
    184. Kuo Mo-jo, "Chung-kuo ku-tai-shih ti fen-ch'i wen-t'i," KK 1972 (5), 2–7;
"Chung-kuo ku-tai-shih chiang-tso," Li-shih yen-chiu, 1975 (4), 133–41.

8: Farmers and Nomads
of the Northern Frontier

During the late second millennium B.C. and most of the first, various cultural transformations took place among the Neolithic farmers and sub-Neolithic hunter-fishers on the northern frontiers of the Shang and Chou civilizations. The processes and patterns of these transformations were greatly conditioned by events in the adjacent regions, mainly North China and the steppe regions to the west. Literary records of the Eastern Chou and Han periods refer to the peoples in these various regions by various names: the Wei-mo people in southern Manchuria and the Pohai Bay area; the northern Ti, Hu, or later, Hsiung-nu in the Yin Shan area between and including the upper Liao Ho and the Ordos; and the western Jung to the northwest.[1] To what extent this ethnic classification of the Eastern Chou and early Han periods was true for the northern frontier peoples and can be traced back in time is an ethnohistoric problem. The archaeological material, however, tends to bear out this subdivision, in that three regional cultural complexes can be distinguished for the Shang-Chou period in this area: the cist-grave builders of the Pohai Bay area and southern Manchuria; the mounted nomads and farmers north of the Great Wall; and the "Aeneolithic" Painted Pottery cultures in Kansu and Chinghai. The geographical distribution of these various cultures, their different ecological situations, and the diverse historical influences to which these groups was exposed are problems of great theoretical interest.

The Pohai Cist-Grave Builders

This cultural complex was centered in the area of the northern coasts of the Pohai, the lower Liao Valley, and the upper Sungari River. It was essentially a continuation of the old Neolithic cultures described in chapter 5, but numerous cultural elements of North China origin or affinity have also been found from archaeological assemblages dated to this period. The

1. See Lin Hui-hsiang, *Chung-kuo min-tzu shih*, 2 vols., Shanghai, Commercial Press, 1936.

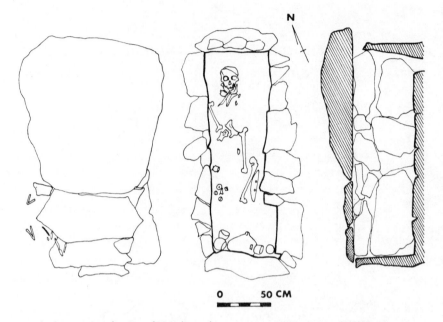

183. A cist grave at the site of Hsi-t'uan-shan-tzu, near Kirin. (From *KKHP* 1964, no. 1, p. 33.)

people represented were farmers and pig raisers, who made flat-bottomed pottery and polished slate and other stone implements, and buried their dead in cist graves (fig. 183). Hunting was apparently still extremely important, as shown by the large number of arrowheads, mostly chipped in the old Microlithic tradition.[2]

Archaeologically speaking, definite Shang remains in this area are rare. Several "white sherds" of Shang type have been reported at the Lao-t'ieh-shan site in the Port Arthur region at the tip of Liaotung Peninsula,[3] and the historic records indicate that the people in this area were among the so-called Eastern I groups, whose cultures were considered very close to the North Chinese. Chi Tzu, a brother of the last Yin monarch, is said to have led a group of Yin refugees into exile in northern Korea, where they established a civilization and taught the local inhabitants to raise silkworms and to farm. In the archaeological record, however, it is not until the Eastern Chou period that there is decisive evidence that North Chinese cultures of the historical period penetrated significantly into the Pohai Bay area and southern Manchuria. Metal objects such as axes, arrowheads,

2. K. C. Chang, *Southwest. Jour. Anthropol.* 17 (1961), 70–71.

3. Hamada Kosaku, *JZ* 44 (1929), 319–26. Umehara Sueji, *Tōa kōkōgaku kaikan*, Kyoto, Hoshino, 1947, p. 63.

spearheads, and ornaments of Eastern Chou type were found east from Liaotung peninsula (at such sites as Kao-li-chai and Mu-yang-ch'eng), and west to the upper Liao Valley (at such sites as the Red Pottery cemetery at Hung-shan-hou near Ch'ih-feng).[4] To the north, metal objects reached as far as the upper Sungari around the city of Kirin. Sites have been found here at which burials in pits lined with granite slabs (cist graves) are characteristic. A bronze dagger was found in a tomb at Ta-ch'ing-shan,[5] bronze knives and fishhooks occurred at the site of Ch'ang-shê-shan, and stone arrowheads and spearheads apparently imitating bronze prototypes have been found at the site of Liang-pan-shan, in the eastern suburb of Kirin.[6] In 1965, a whole cemetery was excavated at Cheng-chia-wa-tzu in the southeastern suburb of Shen-yang, where bronze tools, mirrors, horse fittings, as well as sheathed daggers were found.[7] Skeletal remains from the cist tombs at the Hsi-t'uan-shan site, southwest of Kirin, indicate that the inhabitants at this time were physically classifiable as "Tungusic," but the Cheng-chia-wa-tzu skeletons are said to exhibit a mixture of Siberian and northern Chinese features.[8] Stone imitations of metal swords and spearheads have been reported farther east, in the T'umen Valley, on the Pacific coast around Vladivostok, and in Korea and Japan.[9]

Settlements of Eastern Chou style are found at least as far away as northern Hopei. Stone molds, for instance, for making metal axes, knives, and spearheads (which were found at the Pao-shen-miao site near T'ang-shan), are dated to an earlier period than the Warring States.[10] These molds undoubtedly indicate a local metallurgy and point to a much more intensified acculturation of the natives by the oncoming North Chinese civilization than occurred among the peoples to the north who apparently continued the Neolithic way of life while adopting some cultural imports. However, by the end of the Han dynasty at the latest, highly sophisticated civilizations were recorded in Chinese annals in a large part of southern Manchuria.[11]

During the Eastern Chou and the following Han period, the southern

4. *Mu-yang-ch'eng*, Archaeologia Orientalis, no. 2, 1931. *Pi-tzu-wo*, Archaeologia Orientalis, no. 1, 1929. *KK* 1973 (6), 361.

5. *KK* 1974 (4), 276.

6. *KK* 1964 (1), 6–12.

7. *KKHP* 1975 (1), 141–55.

8. *KKHP* 1963 (2), 101–09; 1964 (1), 29–49; 1975 (1), 137–63.

9. K. C. Chang, *Southwest. Jour. Anthropol.* 17 (1961), 70. G. O. Andreev, *KKHP* 1958 (4), 36. J. E. Kidder, *Japan*, New York, Praeger, 1959, p. 93. Kim Jŏng-hak, *The Archaeology of Korea*, Tokyo, Kawade, 1972, pp. 163–66.

10. *KKHP* 7 (1954), 85.

11. Wen Ch'ung-i, *BIE* 5 (1958), 115–214.

Manchurian farmers apparently were also intruded upon by peoples and cultures from the steppes to the west. Whereas the influences from the Huang Ho during the Eastern Chou took the form of cultural infiltration and assimilation, the steppe nomads apparently took physical possession of territories in the lower Liao Valley, as shown by assemblages of cultural remains of steppe origin discovered in isolated regions of Liaoning Province. By the middle of the Western Han dynasty, however, Wu Ti's military expeditions were successful enough to have incorporated the entire area of southern Manchuria and northern Korea into the vast empire of Han, though even the Han forces at times could not withstand the fierce inroads of the steppe nomads.[12]

Farmers and Mounted Nomads North of the Great Wall

The Great Wall of China, which begins at Shan Hai Gate between Hopei and Liaoning in the east and ends at Chia Yü Gate in eastern Kansu in the west, was built during various periods of early Chinese history, but sections of it were begun during the Eastern Chou. It may be said to symbolize two ways of life—the agrarian of the Huang Ho valley to the south, and the nomadic of the steppes and deserts to the north—but the demarcation between the two was never as sharp and clear as the Great Wall itself, and the early history of the area north of it during the Shang and the Chou periods is complex and not at all well understood from the archaeological evidence.

The northern frontiers of the Shang and Chou civilizations of North China, embracing the area known at the present time as Inner Mongolia, western Liaoning, and the northern portions of Hopei, Shansi, and Shensi, were typically grasslands and plateaus. During early postglacial times, as shown in chapter 1, the region was drained by a great number of small rivers and large and small lakes and ponds. Today, many of these rivers and lakes are diminished in size or have dried up. It is, however, still not known when the desiccation process began in this part of China. In the Huang Ho valley, we know that desiccation was not widespread until after the Shang, and then only as a result of intensive deforestation combined with climatic deterioration. In the steppe zone of the north, large sedentary farming settlements seem to have existed at some spots as late as the Eastern Chou period, or even later, near water sources that are now dry. It appears, therefore, that during the Shang-Chou period the northern frontier experienced no desiccation catastrophic enough to have

12. *KKHP* 1956 (1), 29–42; 1957 (1), 119–26. *KKTH* 1956 (2), 54–59.

had a decisive effect upon the pattern of human settlement at that time.

Nevertheless, in many regions of the north where farming villages appeared during the Lungshanoid stages, a new way of life emerged during the period when the Shang and Chou civilizations thrived in the Huang Ho valley—a way of life in which the domestication of animals and the mobility of settlements became increasingly important. There were still farming settlements in the northeastern part of North China and in the Ordos, but animal herders had also appeared on the scene. We are not clear about the relationship between the farmers and herders. It is possible that farmers engaged in herding as a supplement or during some part of the year; it is also possible that farmers and herders were symbiotic occupants of the steppes and the oases. The possibility also exists that the northern farmers and herders were hostile toward each other and may have been of different cultural origins and traditions. Soon after the Shang-Chou period, nomads began to dominate the northern steppes. Farming lands shrank and in many places disappeared altogether. This process, however, took a whole millennium to complete.

The eastern and western parts of the Great Wall must be distinguished in order to study the prehistory of the area north of it during the Shang and Chou periods, for their histories and their archaeological cultures appear to differ. The eastern part refers to the upper courses of the Liao River, in the provinces of Liaoning, northern Hopei, and eastern Inner Mongolia; the western part refers to the area of Ordos, namely, the western part of Inner Mongolia in the Huang Ho valley in the former province of Suiyüan.

In the east, significant excavations took place in 1960 at the sites of Yao-wang-miao and Hsia-chia-tien, near the city of Ch'ih-feng.[13] Two cultural phases are distinguishable: *Lower Hsia-chia-tien*, including the site of Yao-wang-miao and the lower stratum of the site of Hsia-chia-tien, and *Upper Hsia-chia-tien*, typified by the upper stratum of the site of that name. The Lower Hsia-chia-tien phase, which has a wide distribution throughout the upper Liao Valley, is characterized by a distinctive stone inventory (polished cylindrical axes, flat hoes, shouldered hoes, flat perforated axes, knives, and microliths) and by ceramic ware (sand-tempered gray pottery, in the forms of *li* and *yen*). Copper and bronze artifacts and foundry remains have also been uncovered at its sites. Layers of this phase are known to have been intruded into by a Western Chou bronze assemblage at Ling-yüan in Liaoning, which indicates that the Lower Hsia-chia-tien culture was at

13. *KK* 1961 (2), 77–81. *KKHP* 1974 (1), 111–44. See *WW* 1973 (11), 44, for a discussion of the chronological issues at these sites.

least in part contemporary with the Shang civilization of North China.[14]

The Upper Hsia-chia-tien culture, typified by red and brown wares and a larger number of bronze artifacts and characterized by burial sites with slab cists, has a slightly larger area of distribution and has been dated to the Chou period.[15] The Western Chou civilization apparently had a deeper penetration than the Shang into this region, as shown by a group of typically Western Chou bronze vessels discovered in Ling-yüan,[16] and during the Eastern Chou period the Huang Ho civilization pushed extensively into the northern frontier, as shown by widespread intensive settlements where objects of Eastern Chou style remained, such as the so-called Red Pottery settlement at Ch'ih-feng, the best known of the Upper Hsia-chia-tien sites.[17] The intensity of Chou acculturation of this region is shown by an iron workshop discovered at Hsing-lung in northern Hopei. At this site eighty-seven pieces of molds for casting iron or bronze hoes, sickles, axes, chisels, and cart fittings were excavated, indicating that during the Warring States period, to which the site has been dated, iron foundries as well as Chinese stylistic imports were brought into eastern Inner Mongolia.[18] However, the frontier position of the Inner Mongolian province of the Eastern Chou civilization is clearly demonstrated by the presence of many cultural traits that point either to the Microlithic substratum or to the contemporary northern cultures. Such traits include, for instance, slab graves, the brownish-red, flat-bottomed pottery prevalent during the Neolithic period of the same area, stone battle-axes, and microlithic implements, which persisted even into Han dynasty sites.

At some of the Eastern Chou period settlements of the Upper Hsia-chia-tien culture in eastern Inner Mongolia there is already emphasis upon the domestication of animals. At Hung-shan-hou, for example, considerable numbers of cattle bones were found at the site, though the predominant mode of subsistence may still have been farming.[19] By the latter half of the Eastern Chou, however, a nomadic life better adapted to the steppe environment appears to have prevailed in a large part of eastern Inner

14. *KK* 1962 (12), 658–71; 1975 (2), 99–101.

15. *Ibid.*

16. *WWTKTL* 1955 (8), 16–27.

17. Hamada Kosaku and Mizuno Seichi, *Ch'ih-feng Hung-shan-hou*, Archaeologia Orientalis, ser. A, no. 6, 1938. Lower Hsia-chia-tien remains, however, have also been found at the site, whose stratigraphy was probably not clearly recognized at the time of the 1930s excavations.

18. *KKTH* 1956 (1), 29–35.

19. *KKHP* 1958 (3), 25–40.

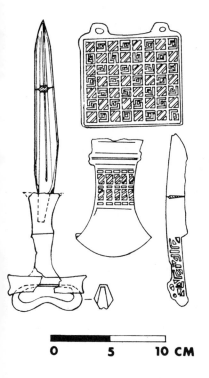

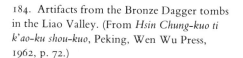

184. Artifacts from the Bronze Dagger tombs in the Liao Valley. (From *Hsin Chung-kuo ti k'ao-ku shou-kuo*, Peking, Wen Wu Press, 1962, p. 72.)

0   5   10 CM

Mongolia, as shown by the recent discovery of a series of so-called Bronze Dagger tombs. The tombs probably represent a regional and temporal phase of the Upper Hsia-chia-tien culture and are typified by the site of Nan-shan-ken, in Ning-ch'eng Hsien, Inner Mongolia.[20] These tombs, in which remains of a T-shaped bronze dagger are characteristic, have been located primarily in the lower Liao Valley in southern Manchuria;[21] they yield, besides the daggers, bronze weapons (halberds, helmets, and arrow-heads), horse fittings, implements, mirrors, and ornaments (animal-style pendants, buttons, and beads) (fig. 184), together with stone artifacts (including microliths and rare agricultural implements) and pottery. These remains apparently indicate a mounted culture, based for subsistence upon herding and hunting-fishing, with little farming. It must have had a close cultural affiliation with the western part of the Chinese steppe belt, even though many Eastern Chou types of artifacts, such as halberds, spearheads, and knives, have been found, by which the above steppe finds are dated. A study of the skeletal materials from Hsia-chia-tien (upper stratum) and

20. *KK* 1962 (5), 272. *KKHP* 1973 (2), 27–38; 1975 (1), 117–40.
21. *KKHP* 1960 (1), 63–70. *KK* 1964 (1), 44–45; 1964 (6), 277–85; 1975 (4), 226–27.

Nan-shan-ken is reported to indicate that the ancient inhabitants in this area show an essential physical affinity with the contemporary residents of North China.[22]

A recent discovery of sixty-three graves dated to Western Han, but apparently a continuation of the basic cultural tradition of the Eastern Chou nomads, is abundant in cultural remains and particularly revealing as to the inhabitants' mode of subsistence. This cemetery was found in 1956 at Hsi-ch'a-kou in Hsi-feng Hsien, in northeastern Liaoning. All the graves in the group were single burials, and each was accompanied by weapons, horse fittings, pottery, and ornaments. Horse teeth were collected from many of the graves, and three horse skulls were found buried on top of a hill within the cemetery area. The human bones were entirely decomposed, but some remaining teeth show that aged people were rare among the dead. Many of the bronze ornaments depicted cattle, horses, sheep, dogs, and camels. These and other bits of evidence have led to the conclusion that

> This tribe [whose members were buried in this cemetery] belonged to a nomadic people, and pastoral nomadism occupied a principal position in the social economy. The bronze ornamental plates found from the graves indicate that horse, cattle, sheep, and camel were the major domestic animals in this society. The horse in particular, as evidenced by finds of teeth and skulls, was highly important both economically and militarily and was the basic means for transportation and warfare, as shown by the horse teeth and skulls. The large amount of handmade, sand-tempered pottery, the persisting use of a small quantity of microliths, the hunting dogs and hunting falcons portrayed on the bronze ornamental plates, some microlithic arrowheads, a great variety of bronze and iron arrowheads, and remains of fur clothing all indicate that these northern peoples engaged in hunting and pastoral nomadism.[23]

A similar culture, also among a militant people, emerged in the Ordos area in the western part of Inner Mongolia. Among the so-called Ordos bronzes, most of which can best be described as "stray finds," pieces occur that bear close similarities to the Shang bronzes.[24] In the Altai Mountains and the Minusinsk area of the upper Yenisei Valley, the Karasuk culture is usually considered a product of direct Shang stimulation, but in the

22. KKHP 1975 (2), 157–69.
23. WW 1960 (8/9), 20.
24. Max Loehr, Artibus Asiae 14 (1951), no. 1/2.

185. Animal art in Ordos bronzes excavated from Zungar, Inner Mongolia. (From *WW* 1965, no. 2, pl. 6.)

Ordos the process of introduction of Shang and Western Chou civilizations is not known.[25] By the Warring States[26] and Han[27] periods, however, the complex of Ordos bronzes became recognizable in the archaeological record. It was characterized by bronze weapons and ornamental horse fittings that unmistakably indicate a mounted nomadic culture and by an ornamental art in which animals (sheep, deer, horse, wolf, and a variety of birds) are prominent (fig. 185). The culture of the Ordos bronzes differs from the Bronze Dagger Tomb culture of eastern Inner Mongolia in the style of artifacts, but it represents the same kind of militant nomadic life of the steppes.

For the gradual replacement of farmers by herders in the northern frontiers, several probable causes can be discerned. First, the high grassland of the northern frontier had never been as favorable to agriculture as the fertile plains and river valleys of the Huang Ho or the lower Liao drainage systems. At present it has an extremely continental climate, cold and arid, with long winters. During and after the climatic optimum of early post-Pleistocene times, the continentality of the climate in this area may have been less severe, but the difference is probably one of degree. Second, and this may be the principal factor, during the first millennium B.C. a mobile

25. K. V. Jettmar, *BMFEA* 22 (1950). B. Karlgren, *BMFEA* 17 (1945). For possible Western Chou influence in the area, see *WW* 1961 (9), 6.

26. *WW* 1959 (6), 6; 1959 (6), 276–77; 1965 (2), 50–51. *KK* 1962 (12), 644–45.

27. *WWTKTL* 1957 (4), 29–32. *KKTH* 1956 (2), 60–61. *WW* 1965 (2), 44–45.

and militant culture known as the Scythian appeared in the steppe zone of the heartland of Asia. By the end of the eighth century B.C., the Scythians and related complexes had replaced the Late Timber culture in southern Russia, the Late Andronovo culture in Kazakhstan, and the Karasuk culture in the Altai Mountains and the Minusinsk basin.[28] Karl Jettmar has pointed out that by the time the Maiemiric period appeared in the Altai to replace the Karasuk Culture, the whole steppe zone of Asia, from the Pannonic steppes to China, had been unified into a pattern characterized by mounted warfare.[29] This common Eurasian steppe culture—characterized by a mobile settlement pattern, by a subsistence mode based principally upon the herding of sheep, cattle, and horses, by mounted militancy, and by an animal-oriented style of art—was apparently built upon an ecological adjustment to the steppe environment, and a number and variety of ethnic and cultural elements must have participated in this pattern.[30] However, the wide similarities must have resulted primarily from historical contacts among peoples, and the rapid and expansive cultural flow was greatly facilitated by the steppe environment and the mobile way of life.

The appearance of numerous so-called steppe nomads in the vast steppe belt of Eurasia, in 700 B.C., was coincident with the wide expansion of the Eastern Chou civilization toward the north and the south. Cultural exchange between the Huang Ho and the steppes and taigas in the north had been a constant phenomenon since the Palaeolithic period, but now such contacts took the form of conflicts between the farmers and the nomads. These conflicts often resulted in warfare and were amply recorded in the historical sources dated to the Eastern Chou and Han periods. The Great Wall symbolizes these conflicts and demarcates the two ways of life. Under such circumstances it is small wonder that herders' remains have been documented archaeologically on the northern frontier of Eastern Chou China and the Han Empire. Farmers, who found the new colonies not highly favorable for their settled way of life in the first place, were no match for the militant nomads and gradually gave way to the new masters of the steppe. As far as the Chinese steppes are concerned, physical anthropological evidence does not indicate that the nomads,

28. See Karl Jettmar, *Art of the Steppes*, New York, Crown, 1967, for an up-to-date summary of the pertinent data and an extensive bibliography.

29. Jettmar, *BMFEA* 23 (1951), 148.

30. Ralph M. Rowlette, "Early Phases of Horse Nomad Cultures of the Eastern Terminus of the Eurasiatic Steppe," term paper for Anthropology 111, Cambridge, Harvard University, 1960.

whose cultural remains have been widely found and clearly bear cultural affinities to the steppe cultures toward the west, were "intrusive" ethnic elements. We can therefore regard the hostility as one between two ways of life, although it is not unlikely that foreign ethnic elements were responsible for some of the cultural groups whose archaeological remains have been found. The Great Wall marks the resistance of the agrarian residents, but in spite of it, mounted warfare, certain burial customs, and many stylistic motifs in the decorative art were introduced into North China to enrich and provide variety to the Eastern Chou cultural life and artistic style.

The "Aeneolithic" Painted Pottery Cultures of Kansu

The site of Yang-shao-ts'un in western Honan was discovered in 1920 by Liu Ch'ang-shan, a field assistant of J. G. Andersson. In 1921 Andersson investigated the site himself, finding, among other things, some painted pottery which he considers to be related to the Painted Pottery cultures of Anau and Tripolye. In 1923–24 Andersson made an extensive survey in the area of eastern Kansu, presumed to be the area linking the east with the west. In the Huang Ho valley in eastern Kansu around the city of Lan-chou, and in the valleys of the T'ao Ho and the Huang-shui (Hsi-ning Ho), Andersson found a considerable number of early culture sites. Grouping these into six stages, he considers them to be the linear succession of a "Painted Pottery culture" tradition and gives consecutive dates B.C. to each of the six stages.[31] Andersson's Kansu chronology, in its final modified version, is as follows:[32]

Late Stone Age:
        Ch'i Chia (2500–2200)
        Yang Shao (Pan–shan) (2200–1700)
        Ma Ch'ang (1700–1300)

Bronze Age:
        Hsin Tien (1300–1000)
        Ssu Wa-Ch'ia Yao (1000–700)
        Sha Ching (700–500)

The Introduction to this volume might have been a more appropriate place for this chronological table, for such a succession of stages in Kansu

31. Andersson, GSuC, Mem., ser. A, no. 5 (1925).
32. BMFEA 15 (1943), 295.

is of little more than historical interest. I have cited it here, however, because this scheme is still adopted by some writers of books and articles dealing with prehistory. Archaeological materials collected since Andersson offered his six-stage theory have proved it to be erroneous except for the fact that the Late Stone Age was earlier than the Bronze Age. Otherwise there is no reason whatever to adhere to Andersson's scheme. The Ch'i-chia stage, as shown in a previous chapter, followed the Yang-shao instead of preceding it. The chronologically linear succession of his three Bronze Age stages is not proven; rather, it has been demonstrated that after the Ch'i-chia stage there were probably several contemporary cultural assemblages such as Hsin-tien, Ssu-wa, and Sha-ching in the eastern Kansu area. Some of these may be slightly earlier or later than the others, but all of them overlapped in time and cannot be considered successive "stages" of a single culture. With these two major shifts of classification, Andersson's absolute dates become obsolete; he sees the whole sequence as ending around 500 B.C., which, according to Andersson's authority, Bernhard Karlgren, is when iron came into use in North China.

Archaeological materials that have accumulated since the early twenties in eastern Kansu show that the first farmers who occupied eastern Kansu were the Yang-shao of the Kansu subdivision, a derivative of the Yang-shao peoples in the nuclear area. These were followed by peoples of the Ch'i-chia culture, corresponding in time to the Lungshanoid cultures to the east but possibly of a different ethnic strain and probably of a distinctive cultural tradition. Between the Ch'i-chia and the Ch'in civilization, which swept into this region and made it a part of the Ch'in Empire, and contemporaneous with the Shang and the Chou civilizations in the middle and lower Huang Ho valley, the area in eastern Kansu was occupied by several contemporary or overlapping cultures: Hsin-tien, Ssu-wa, and Sha-ching (fig. 186).

The Hsin-tien Culture. Archaeological assemblages of the Hsin-tien culture have been recognized in the lower T'ao Ho valley north of the town of Lin-t'ao, the Huang Ho valley around the city of Yüng-ching, and the lower Huang-shui valley east of the town of Lo-tu.[33] They consisted of some stone implements, copper and bronze objects, and, above all, a distinctive ceramic style characterized by coarse red and gray fabrics, white and red slip, and geometric patterns painted in black pigment. The pottery was handmade by means of the coiling technique and a beater. Both the coiled surface and the cord impressions produced by the beater

33. *KK* 1958 (9), 47; 1959 (7), 379.

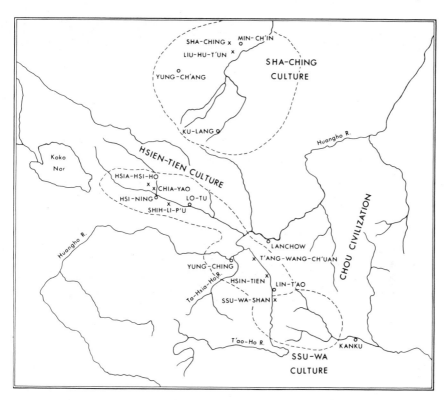

186. Aneolithic cultures in Kansu.

were then smoothed over with wet fingers. The black paintings were simple and robust, executed freehand in bands around the shoulder and the middle circumference of the pot; the designs were mostly curvilinear and round. The pottery is characterized by a distinctive demarcation between the body and the collar, a large mouth, and one or two large vertical handles attached to the middle part of the pot with one end connected to the body and the other attached to the rim or below the rim.[34] Within this culture, at least two phases are distinguishable: Hsin-tien phase A, centering in the T'ao Ho valley; and Hsin-tien phase B, concentrated in the Huang Ho valley near the city of Yüng-ching. Two other ceramic phases, T'ang-wang, near Yüng-ching, and Chia-yao (classified by Andersson with the Ssu-wa culture), both in the lower Huang-shui, may also be related to the Hsin-tien culture.

Hsin-tien phase A, the classical Hsin-tien phase recognized by Anders-

34. Wu Chin-ting, *Prehistoric Pottery in China*, pp. 105–06.

son, is represented by dwelling sites at Hui-tsui, T'ao-sha Hsien, and Chi-chia-ch'uan, Lin-hsia Hsien; and by the cemetery at Hsin-tien (Hsin-tien locality A), T'ao-sha Hsien. Burial sites of this phase have also been found in Lin-t'ao, Lin-hsia, and other localities in T'ao-sha.[35] The Hui-tsui dwelling site was on a high terrace surrounded by deep ravines and was probably highly advantageous for defense purposes. Andersson believes that the natural topography of this site was essentially the same as it is today.[36] From this locality, pottery, stone and bone implements, beads, half a cowrie shell, a bronze knife, and a bronze button were discovered by Andersson. The bronze knife has very similar counterparts among the Yin knives, and Wu Chin-ting finds some of the meander designs on the pottery reminiscent of North China bronze patterns.[37] A wu-shu coin of the Han dynasty was found, but Andersson considers it intrusive. The pottery is coarse and highly porous, mostly of a gray or red color. The vessels were coiled, beaten, and then smoothed over with wet fingers. Two forms predominate—round-bottomed bowls and big-mouthed, high-collared jars with two handles. The handles are all vertical, either placed at the belly at the maximum diameter of the piece or below the rim with one end attached to the rim or the upper part of the collar and the other end to the shoulder. The bottoms are predominantly concave. On the whole, the pots are relatively small, with an average height and diameter of 15 centimeters. The surface designs consist of the beaten cord marks that were not obliterated, incisions, scratched short parallel lines, and paintings in black pigment. The painting is largely confined to the shoulder and collar parts, consisting of simple geometric designs of forcefully but freely executed thick lines, such as horizontal black bands, narrow wavy lines, triangles, meanders, and N-shaped patterns. Some conventionalized anthropomorphic and zoomorphic patterns are also present. The Chi-chia-ch'uan site has yielded a similar ceramic ware, as well as a semisubterranean rectangular house, a number of storage pits, and a flexed burial.[38]

Hsien-tien phase B is represented by three localities in Yüng-ching Hsien: Chang-chia-tsui, Han-chia-tsui, and Wa-cha-tsui.[39] In the same area, assemblages of Hsin-tien phase A were also found. It is probable that these two phases were chronologically successive, with B the earlier

35. Andersson, BMFEA 15 (1943), 167–79. KK 1962 (2), 69–71.
36. BMFEA 15 (1943), 168.
37. Prehistoric Pottery, London, Kegan Paul, Trench & Trübner, 1938, p. 106.
38. KK 1962 (2), 69–71.
39. KKHP 1957 (2). KK 1959 (4).

of the two, although no stratigraphic evidence has been uncovered to confirm this view.[40] At the Chang-chia-tsui site, eighty-six round and rectangular pits were excavated, packed within a small area and yielding deep cultural debris. Chipped stone axes with ground edges, stone spades, knives (rectangular or notched), spindle whorls, perforated disks, and mortars and pestles were collected, along with bone spades, needles, awls, combs, ornaments, and two fragments of bronze or copper. Among the pottery remains, some red and gray pieces with a fine texture were noted, but most are of a kind of brick-red ware tempered with sand or powdered pottery. They were also coiled and smoothed over and burnished, like the pottery of phase A, but on the whole they have a finer paste and there is a greater proportion of white slipped specimens. For surface decoration, cord marks, applied ridges, beaten checkers, and paintings are reported. The painting is again done in black pigment, but a few red patterns are found. The designs consist of parallel lines, deformed S-shapes, double spirals, N-shaped patterns, chevrons filled with parallel lines, sun patterns, crosses, and X-shaped patterns; most are common to both phase A and phase B, but others bear strong resemblance to the T'ang-wang phase. The vessels are more elongated, with larger handles than their phase A counterparts, and the bottoms are uniformly flat rather than concave. In addition to jugs and bowls, pans, mugs, and *ting* and *li* tripods are also common (fig. 187).[41]

Closely related, if not practically identical, to the Hsin-tien phase B is a ceramic phase that has been termed the T'ang-wang style.[42] The type site of this style is Shan-shen, near T'ang-wang-ch'uan, in Tung-hsiang Hsien, Kansu, in the lower T'ao Ho valley, but pots and sherds of the same style have been collected at other sites near Yüng-ching, in Lin-t'ao Hsien in the lower T'ao Ho, and along the lower Huang-shui east of Lo-tu.[43] The site of Shih-li-p'u near Hsi-ning in Chinghai, found by Andersson, who classified it with the Ma-ch'ang phase of the Kansu Yang-shao horizon, yielded pottery that shows no relation whatsoever to the Ma-ch'ang[44] but bears unmistakable resemblance to the T'ang-wang style. The pottery is characterized by red ware of coarse paste, tempered with powdered pottery and occasionally with sand. Most of the sherds and pots are plain or corded cooking ware, but some of them were

40. *KKHP* 1957 (2), 30.
41. *KKHP* 1957 (2), 30. *KK* 1959 (4), 182–83.
42. *KKHP* 1957 (2), 23–27.
43. *KKHP* 1957 (2), 23–27. *KK* 1959 (7), 379. Andersson, *BMFEA* 15 (1943), 160–61.
44. K. C. Chang, BIHP 30 (1959), 298.

187. Pottery of the Hsin-tien phase B, Kansu. (From *KKHP* 1957, no. 2, facing p. 33.)

burnished and painted in black pigment. The surface was first smoothed over (thus obliterating the coil marks) and then, very often, slipped in red. Black patterns were executed on the slipped surface, most confined between two parallel lines around the belly, and consisting of spirals and whorls. Additional geometric patterns, such as S-shaped designs, parallel oblique lines, N-shaped designs, meanders, and chevrons filled with parallel lines, adorn parts of the rest of the pot on the collar, shoulder, or handle. The forms include jars with two or four vertical handles, single-handled mugs, *tou*, and *li* tripods. The most conspicuous feature in vessel forms is the very large loop handle, often higher than the mouth (fig. 188). Both in form and in decoration, the T'ang-wang style is closely similar to the Hsin-tien phases, particularly phase B, to which some investigators would assign this style altogether.[45]

In the same area of distribution is another ceramic phase typified by the site of Chia-yao, which was grouped by Andersson with the Ssu-wa culture but is considered by many other fieldworkers as an independent culture.[46] I believe that it is neither, but that it should be regarded as a ceramic phase related to that of Hsin-tien, which we may call the Chia-yao phase. The type sites, Chia-yao and Hsia-hsi-ho, were first discovered in 1923–24 by Andersson in the valley of a tributary of the Huang-shui in Hsi-ning Hsien, Chinghai.[47] The Chia-yao (Ch'ia-yao, K'a-yao) site, a cemetery, yielded thirteen skeletons which lie stretched on their backs, most with the head west. Some of the corpses had been sprinkled with red ocher. Eight burials were found at Hsia-hsi-ho, another burial site across the river. The vessels found in the graves have flat or (more rarely) concave bases, big bellies, and collars of varying length. The saddle-shaped mouth occurs on some of the pots. Most of the jars are equipped with two vertical handles, of the shoulder or collar type. Four-handled jars, with two large collar handles and two small shoulder loops, are also present. The surface of the pottery is brick-red or grayish, mostly plain, but corded specimens are also reported. Andersson recorded no painted specimens.

In addition to pottery, in the Chia-yao and Hsia-hsi-ho graves, were found perforated stone disks, bone awls, plates, arrowheads, turquoise beads, clay spindle whorls, bronze buttons, folded buttons, links, openwork funnels, a knife, and some "rectangular objects." Andersson classifies these assemblages as Ssu-wa solely on the basis of some jars with saddle-

45. *KK* 1959 (4), 184.
46. Andersson, *BMFEA* 15 (1943), 222. But see *KKTH* 1956 (6); and *WW* 1960 (6), 36.
47. Andersson, *BMFEA* 15 (1943), 185–97.

188. Pottery of the T'ang-wang style, Kansu. (From *KKHP* 1957, no. 2, pls. 1–3, following p. 32.)

shaped mouths, which are characteristic of the Ssu-wa culture. This classification is dubious. It appears to me that the Chia-yao assemblages resemble the Hsin-tien phases more closely than the Ssu-wa culture for the following reasons: (1) the saddle-shaped mouth is not common and is also found in the Hsin-tien phases, which may indicate cultural contacts with the Ssu-wa; (2) large collar handles, some of which are higher than the rim, are present; (3) four-handled jars are found; (4) concave bases are represented; and (5) geographically the Chia-yao phase is separated from the Ssu-wa region by a considerable area occupied by the Hsin-tien. This classification—with Hsin-tien instead of Ssu-wa—is strengthened by the result of new investigations since 1959 in Huang-chung Hsien and near the city of Hsi-ning, which brought to light thirty-one localities of the Chia-yao phase.[48] Among the pottery remains were coarse red sherds tempered with powdered pottery and occasionally with sand or mica. These were coiled, some slipped (in red or, rarely, grayish-white), and painted, corded, appliquéd, incised, or combed. The painting was done in black pigment, in designs of zigzags, triangles, and spirals. In form, the pottery is characterized by a wide mouth and large and small vertical handles, mostly on the collar part of the jar. A few *li* tripods are found. Concave bottoms occurred quite frequently. In addition, some stone, horn, and bronze artifacts were also found. Among the bronzes, the *ko* halberds, buttons, and two-winged arrowheads are said to resemble Chou types.[49] The close similarity of this Chia-yao assemblage to the T'ang-wang phase of the same region has been noted,[50] and there is some speculation that the T'ang-wang phase was probably the proto–Chia-yao, so to speak. At any rate, the Chia-yao phase is shown to be related to the Hsin-tien phases by the new finds, in the following aspects: temper of powdered pottery, coiling, red slip, black pigment in painting, and spiral designs. It is thus possible that the Hsin-tien B phase and the T'ang-wang style represent an earlier stage of the Hsin-tien culture, evolving into the Hsin-tien A phase in the T'ao Ho valley and into the Chia-yao phase in the Huang-shui valley.

The Ssu-wa culture. This culture is now represented by over a dozen archaeological sites in the upper T'ao Ho valley, south of Lin-t'ao Hsien, and in the upper Wei-shui tributaries in eastern Kansu.[51] The type locality

48. *WW* 1960 (6), 35–36. *KK* 1964 (9), 475–76.
49. *KK* 1959 (7), 380.
50. *Ibid.*, p. 379.
51. *KKTH* 1956 (6), 15; 1958 (9), 47. *KK* 1959 (7), 327, 380; 1963 (1), 48.

of this culture is the Ssu-wa-shan cemetery in Lin-t'ao Hsien, discovered by Andersson in 1924.[52] The pottery remains in the eight burials here are plain, rather large, and brick-red or red in color. The shape of the vessels is characterized by jars with saddle-shaped mouths; some *li* tripods were found, and these also have saddle-shaped mouths. The body of the vessels is essentially oval, which has led Wu Chin-ting to conclude that the pots are designed to be easily portable.[53] Two vertical handles are attached to the upper part of the vessel. On the collar between the two handles there is in some cases an indented appliquéd ridge. The average height of the vessels is 24 centimeters. They are coarse, sand-tempered, and handmade and smoothed out while still wet. Wu also observes that "every characteristic of the pottery seems to testify that the Ssu-wa culture is not Chinese, though it might have been influenced by that culture."[54] In addition to pottery, Andersson found an armlet of bronze, a perforated axe, and two goat horns. According to Andersson the goats were probably domesticated.[55]

The Ssu-wa-shan site was again investigated in 1945 by Hsia Nai, who excavated six additional burials. Three ways to dispose of the dead were distinguished by Hsia in his data: cremation and ash urns; interment of the dorsal and stretched type; and probably secondary burials. These burial customs, Hsia contends, indicate that the Ssu-wa-shan people were not Han Chinese but were possibly the Ch'iang recorded in Chinese annals.[56] Pottery similar to Andersson's finds was uncovered by Hsia, who also recognized the use of the coiling technique and of powdered-pottery tempers. A stone and a clay ball were collected, possibly slingstones. On the surface of a potsherd, impressions of grains were noted.[57]

More sites of the Ssu-wa tradition were investigated in the T'ao Ho and upper Wei-shui valleys in 1956,[58] 1957,[59] and 1958.[60] In 1957, some painted sherds were discovered in the Ssu-wa assemblages, with such patterns as concentric semicircles, meanders, and other geometric designs executed in black. Stone implements associated with the Ssu-wa pottery

52. Andersson, *BMFEA* 15 (1943), 179–85.
53. *Prehistoric Pottery*, p. 107.
54. *Ibid.*
55. *BMFEA* 15 (1943), 185.
56. *KKHP* 4 (1949), 96.
57. *Ibid.*, pp. 106–07.
58. *KKTH* 1956 (6), 15.
59. *KKTH* 1958 (9), 45.
60. *KK* 1959 (7), 327.

were mostly chipped, including edge-ground axes, knives with side notches, and shouldered axes.

The Sha-ching culture. Approximately 200 kilometers north of Lan-chou, in the arid land between the Huang Ho and the Ch'i-lien Mountains, lies the eastern segment of the so-called Ho Hsi corridor, drained by the Pai-t'ing River. Ecologically, this region is on the border between the Huang Ho valley and the steppe but is still on the south side of the Great Wall. During the final Neolithic period, the area contained the Shan-tan (or Ssu-pa) culture, described in chapter 5. When the Ch'i-chia culture in the Huang Ho and T'ao Ho valleys to the south gave way to the Aeneolithic Hsin-tien and Ssu-wa phases described above, the arid land in the north was occupied by a different cultural tradition, the Sha-ching. Archaeological remains of this culture have been located in Min-ch'in, Yüng-ch'ang, and Ku-lang counties.[61] It is typified by the archaeological sites at Sha-ching-ts'un, in Min-ch'in (Chen-fan) Hsien, which were discovered in 1923–24 by Andersson.[62] These consist of a fortified dwelling site, Liu-hu-t'un, and a cemetery. The former was a mud-walled fortress, 50 meters in diameter. Found inside were a *li* tripod, some handled high bowls, a steatite pan, some bone artifacts (needles, arrowheads, etc.), a bronze knife, a bronze prismatic arrowhead, and a piece of golden string. The cemetery is 260 meters to the west, and in it over forty burials were excavated. The skeletons lay on their backs, stretched or slightly flexed. The pottery was reddish—containing sand or mica for temper—beaten, and red-slipped. Some of the pots were painted in red pigment, and the favorite designs were horizontal lines, triangles, and bird figures. In form, two shapes are characteristic, handled mugs with vertical walls and small jars with two small shoulder loops. The bodies and the collars of the jars are not distinctively demarcated. In addition to pottery, Andersson found in the burials stone and turquoise beads, marble rings, perforated stone objects (similar in shape to the banner stones of the eastern United States), cowrie shells (all ground flat and open at the back), and copper and bronze artifacts including a spearhead, an arrowhead (with square cross section), a ring, a knife tip, a flat three-lobed piece with spiral design on the front and a bridge on each of the end lobes on the back (similar to an object found in a Warring States grave in Luan-p'ing, Hopei), tubes which were annulated at the ends and widened and smooth in the center (identical with objects found in the Ordos), and a button.

61. *KKTH* 1956 (6), 16.
62. Andersson, *BMFEA* 15 (1943), 197–215.

The chronological position of the above three cultures is stratigraphically clear insofar as they can be shown to be earlier than the Han dynasty but later than the Ch'i-chia culture in the same area. Stratigraphical evidence at Chang-chia-tsui and Wu-chia in Yüng-ching Hsien shows that the Hsin-tien culture was definitely later than the Ch'i-chia,[63] and that at Ssu-wa-shan the Ssu-wa culture was subsequent to the Ma-chia-yao phase of the Kansu Yang-shao culture.[64] Furthermore, the saddle-mouthed jars sometimes found in the Hsin-tien assemblages indicate that the Hsin-tien and the Ssu-wa at least overlapped in time.[65] Some idea of the absolute dating of these approximately contemporary cultures can be derived from the typology of the *li* tripods found in these assemblages (most of which are said to be of the Yin-Chou types), from the metal objects of Yin, Chou, and Ordosian affinities, and from the fact that within the Ssu-wa, which adjoined the Western Chou civilization of the Wei-shui valley, cultural elements such as specific types of shouldered axes and side-notched stone knives have been found, which indicate contacts with the Chou. It seems reasonable to place the Kansu Aeneolithic cultures at the end of the second millennium and during the first half of the first millennium B.C., an interval long enough for subdivisions to be made, such as the development of the Hsin-tien phases (Hsin-tien B and T'ang-wang to Hsin-tien A and Chia-yao).

If, as is shown, the Hsin-tien, Sha-ching, and Ssu-wa were approximately contemporary cultures, what are they exactly in terms of archaeological nomenclature? Archaeologically all three cultures are known primarily by their ceramics. The following characteristics are common to all of them: in shape, jars with vertical handles predominate, and the handles include both the small-belly and large-collar varieties, seeming, in these aspects, to carry on the basic ceramic forms of both the Pan-shan stage and the Ch'i-chia culture *in the same area*; pottery of all three cultures was coiled and beaten, with the roughened surface mostly smoothed out; ceramic painting is seen in all three, although it occurs only rarely (as recorded thus far) in the Ssu-wa; the painted designs are geometric and conventionally realistic in all three, and the lines are robust and the patterns simplistic. In shape and in decorative painting, the minimum denominators common to all three cultures, still sufficiently specific in terms of style to make cultural historic connections, are of such a basic nature as to lead us to suspect that

63. *KKTH* 1956 (6), 15.
64. *KKHP* 4 (1949), 74.
65. *KKTH* 1956 (6), 15; 1958 (9), 47.

they may have been three different regional phases of the same culture, one that carries on the basic ceramic features of both the Kansu Yang-shao and the Ch'i-chia culture in the area of eastern Kansu. It must also be noted that it is not at all impossible that some of the late Kansu Yang-shao phases and the Ch'i-chia culture overlapped in time in the marginal regions of this area, which may have resulted in a mutual influence or even a merging of styles.

On the other hand, many ceramic stylistic features set the Hsin-tien, the Ssu-wa, and the Sha-ching cultures apart from one another and from their local predecessors, a fact that also finds support from the little information available on their respective cultural contexts. In subsistence patterns, all three cultures appear to have been based on agriculture, but animal domestication may also have played an important role in the Ssu-wa, as indicated by remains of goat horns and the shape of pottery that may well have been designed for a mobile life, as Wu suggested. In burial customs, the Hsintien and Chia-yao used red ochers, the Ssu-wa had cremation, and the Sha-ching placed some of the dead in a somewhat flexed posture. In ceramics, the red pigment for painting and the flat-bottomed mugs are distinctive of the Sha-ching culture, whereas both the Ssu-wa and the Hsin-tien stressed large-handled jars with well-defined bodies and collars, and both used powdered pottery for tempering material. To what extent these differences in culture and technology indicate ethnic differences or diverse "origins" is an open question.

9: Early Civilizations in South China

The Tsinling Mountains and the Huai Ho did not form a barrier to an agrarian way of life, as the Gobi Desert did, but they do mark off the southern from the northern ecological zone, and the ancient civilizations divided by these formations had to adapt to very different climatic conditions. At present, most of South China receives more than fifty inches of rainfall annually, but north of the Tsinling there is a drop to twenty inches or less. In the Yangtze Valley the growing season continues for 250 days of the year, but in the delta of the Huang Ho the season is 225 days and even less west of the delta.[1] Two or three thousand years ago these figures may have been different, but the north-south difference must have been there, and the climatic contrast would account for many of the cultural distinctions between North and South China. The early civilizations in South China were largely based upon rice cultivation, whereas millet was the staple food in the north. Moreover, the emergence of civilizations in South China took place on the foundation of its own advanced, Neolithic farming cultures, although cultural stimulations from other civilizations— primarily those of the Shang and Chou of North China—must have provided an initial or crucial impetus. For these reasons, as well as for convenience, the civilizations in South China are described in a separate chapter, even though in many cases the southern civilizations may be regarded as regional variants of the Shang and Chou civilizations described in chapters 6 and 7.

The Huai Ho Plain

We have seen in chapter 6 that important Shang sites have been located in the Huai Ho plain in eastern Honan, northern Kiangsu, and northern Anhwei. Considering the area's importance in the Shang's legendary beginnings and in their oracle records, there is good reason to expect

1. George B. Cressey, *Land of the 500 Million*, New York, McGraw-Hill, 1955, pp. 66, 69.

many more Shang sites to be found in the future, some of which may shed light on the process in which the Shang civilization came about, both here and in general.

Two archaeological sites in northern Kiangsu, both considered to date from Western Chou, sharply contrast the life of the elite with that of the lower class. A tomb at Ta-ts'un in Hsin-hai-lien City yielded seven bronze ritual vessels, including two large *ting*, two small *ting*, and three *yen*.[2] At the Chiao-chuang site, in Tung-hai Hsien, seven burials were excavated, but only one contained grave furnishings, consisting of two pottery vessels.[3] At the latter site, the only bronze artifacts were knives and arrowheads, but archaeologists have also found a stone-lined well and remains of rice of the *keng* variety (*Oryza sativa* sub sp. Keng Ting).[4]

The Huai River provided the name for the Huai style, so it is not surprising that these plains are an important archaeological region for the Eastern Chou period. Finds attributed to Ch'u will be described later under the Yün-meng Basin. An assemblage of bronze vessels found in Shu Hsien, central Anhwei, could be the relics of the ancient state of Shu (657–615 B.C.).[5] But the most important discoveries for the period in question are those of the state of Ts'ai.

According to *Shih chi*, Ch'u invaded Ts'ai and forced the marquis Chao to move his capital to Chou-lai in 493 B.C. Chou-lai is generally agreed to have been in the neighborhood of Shou Hsien. Ssu-ma Ch'ien also reported that in 447 Ts'ai was finally overthrown by the Ch'u, who, in 241, in the reign of King K'ao-lieh, moved their capital to Shou-ch'un, southwest of the present town of Shou Hsien. An Eastern Chou tomb discovered in 1955 at Shou Hsien, in which over five hundred artifacts have been found, including bronze vessels with inscriptions mentioning the marquis of Ts'ai, can thus be dated to the narrow temporal interval between 493 and 447 B.C., although exactly who this marquis of Ts'ai might have been (five marquises had Chou-lai for their capital before the fall of the marquisate under the Ch'u) is a controversial subject.[6]

2. *KK* 1961 (6), 321–23.

3. *WW* 1975 (8), 45–56.

4. The report of a study of the rice remains at the site by the Research Institute of Agronomic Science of Kiangsu Province contains the following information: "Before the Great Proletarian Cultural Revolution, the Institute discovered wild rice in the mountainous region at Yün-t'ai in Tung-hai and collected specimens, which have since been identified as the *keng* variety. The cultivated *keng* rice found this time in Tung-hai may well be related to the wild rice in question" (*WW* 1975, no. 8, 60).

5. *KK* 1964 (10), 498–503.

6. *Shou Hsien Ts'ai-hou mu ch'u-t'u i-wu*, Peking, Science Press, 1956.

The tomb is a rectangular earthen pit, oriented north-south, 8.45 meters long north-south, and 7.1 meters wide east-west. Remains of a lacquered wooden coffin were found at the center of the tomb; the skeleton had disintegrated but, according to the position of the jade ornaments and a bronze sword presumably worn at the side, the body was probably buried with its head to the north. A skeleton was found at the southeastern corner of the grave, probably a sacrificed victim. Pottery, lacquer, and bronze vessels, musical instruments, weapons, and horse and chariot fittings were buried in various places within the grave. Some of the vessels were inscribed, indicating that the master of the tomb was a Ts'ai marquis. Typologically, the decoration and the shape of the bronze artifacts present another example of the Huai style and, since they are precisely dated, they can also be taken as a type assemblage for the bronzes of the late Ch'un-ch'iu and early Chan-kuo periods.

Two other large tombs, also in the area of Shou Hsien, were excavated in 1958–59, yielding a total of 112 bronze artifacts. Inscriptions on the bronze weapons found in one of the tombs (approximately 5 by 4 meters at the opening and 3 by 2 at the bottom, with *erh-ts'eng-t'ai* and a northern ramp) suggest that this was the tomb of Marquis Sheng of Ts'ai (enthroned 471 B.C., died 457).[7]

The Lower Yangtze and the Southeastern Coast

In chapter 4 it was shown that the Lungshanoid farmers were responsible for the development of rice agriculture and a Lungshanoid cultural style in the eastern part of South China—the part that is drained by the middle and lower Yangtze, the Huai Ho, and many small rivers along the southeastern coast and that consists of the present provinces of Anhwei, Kiangsu, Hupei, Kiangsi, Chekiang, Fukien, Taiwan, and the eastern part of Kwangtung. The Lungshanoid in South China is an authentic horizon in the sense used by American archaeologists—a highly homogeneous style of artifacts brought into a large area by a rapid or even explosive expansion. In eastern South China, the Lungshanoid and the Lung-shan cultures were followed by another highly homogeneous and even more widespread horizon, the Geometric.

The name *Geometric*, used in archaeological literature to refer to the impressed designs on pottery in this area of this horizon, is used here to designate the horizon style primarily characterized by the geometric

7. *KK* 1963 (4), 204–12.

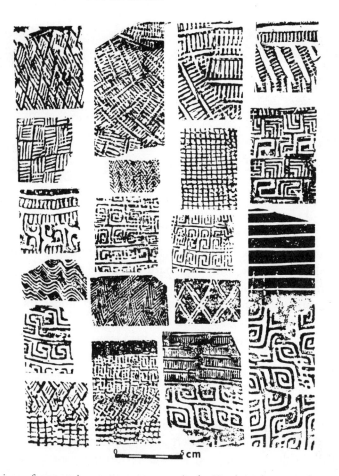

189. Rubbings of geometric patterns on pottery in the Hu-shu culture, southeast China. (From *KKHP* 1958, no. 1, p. 79.)

stamping manifested in the pottery remains. Both pottery stamps and geometric patterns (such as checkers, parallel lines, and wavy lines) appear in the Lungshanoid horizon, but in the Geometric horizon, geometric stamping dominated the ceramic decoration, was used far more extensively than before, and had greatly diversified design motifs. The color of the Geometric wares is predominantly red or grayish; the ware is handmade, beaten, and hard fired. The beater also served as a stamp for decorative designs, which include a long list of such geometric, basic patterns as checkers, chevrons, crosshatches, meanders, spirals, triangles, quadrangles, and circles (fig. 189). In shape, small-mouthed and flat- or round-bottomed urns predominate (fig. 190), though to some extent all

190. Pottery urns with stamped, geometric decorative patterns in the Hu-shu culture. (From *KKHP* 1958, no. 1, pl. 3.)

Lungshanoid forms are continued. This new ceramic style of South China can certainly be linked with the "hard ware" of the Shang pottery, and the Geometric horizon in eastern South China was apparently a development of the local Lung-shan substratum, in part under the continuous stimulation of the Shang and Chou cultural impacts.

In addition to the new ceramic style, the Geometric horizon carries over from the Lungshanoid Neolithic essentially the same cultural traditions of the area, such as the stone inventories (among which the stepped adz is the most characteristic) (fig. 191),[8] agricultural crops (primarily rice), habitation patterns (dwellings on mounds or on wooden piles, a feature which appears to be mainly environmentally oriented), and other aspects of the material culture. However, at least one other significant addition was made to the Lungshanoid foundation during the Geometric period, namely, bronze metallurgy. Small pieces of bronze objects have been found at many Geometric sites dated to a pre–Han dynasty period, and evidence of local bronze foundries has been discovered at many sites in southern Kiangsu.

The Geometric horizon spread over a wide area, largely the same as the Lungshanoid but including Hunan and more of Kwangtung and excluding most of Hupei. This horizon, however, occupied each of these regions far more intensively and lasted for a long time. For the entire area, the Geometric horizon started with the first influence of the Shang civilization from the north, probably during the middle of the second millennium B.C., and ended toward the end of the first millennium B.C., although geometric stamped pottery as a stylistic tradition of the area persisted

8. *KKHP* 1958 (3), 1.

191. Shouldered (*left*) and stepped (*right*) axes and adzes in the Neolithic period of the southeast. Excavated from Ta-p'en-k'eng, Taiwan.

throughout South China into the Han dynasty.[9] The Geometric horizon evolved in a number of different ways. At the beginning, the local communities in this area probably carried on the Lung-shan Neolithic ways of life, even though the new ceramic styling and some bronze metallurgy were introduced. In some regions, however, the local cultures developed into states similar to those of North China.

The late prehistoric culture in the lower Yangtze Valley in southern Kiangsu and central Anhwei, during the interval approximating the Shang and Chou periods, has been referred to as the Hu-shu culture, a term coined in 1959 by Tseng Chao-yüeh and Yin Huan-chang after the site at Hu-shu in Chiang-ning Hsien, Kiangsu.[10] The sites of this culture are on mounds

9. *KKHP* 1958 (1), 84.

10. *KKHP* 1959 (4), 47. For subsequent discussions of this culture, see *KK* 1962 (1), 32–37, 38–40; 1962 (3), 125–28, 133.

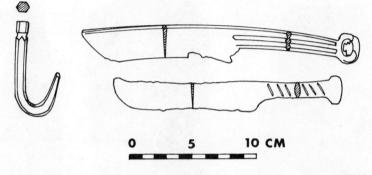

192. Bronze artifacts from the site of Suo-chin-ts'un, near Nanking. (From *KKHP* 1957, no. 2, p. 29.)

or low hills and hillsides, and the archaeological inventories are characterized by many distinctive common features in stone implements, ceramics, bone and antler artifacts, bronze metallurgy, house construction, scapulimancy, and burial customs. Among the ceramic remains, red and black pottery of a Lungshanoid heritage still constitute the majority, but geometric wares are important elements also.

Although the continuity from its Lung-shan antecedents is evident in the Hu-shu culture, important new elements appeared in addition to the geometric pottery. Bronze knives, arrowheads, axes, fishhooks, and handles and legs of bronze *ting* tripods have been found at a number of sites near Nanking (fig. 192) and Tan-t'u.[11] Pottery crucibles and fragments of bronze have been found from a lower stratum of this culture at Pei-yin-yang-ying, near Nanking, indicating the practice of bronze metallurgy in the local village communities. Shang- and Chou-type bronze arrowheads and knives as well as copper ores and pottery spoons (probably for bronze smelting) have been found at a number of sites in the I-cheng and Liu-ho area.[12] At the site of T'ai-kang-ssu near Hsi-shan-ch'iao, in Nanking, excavated in 1960, twenty-nine bronze artifacts, three pieces of oracle turtleshells, and stone, bone, and shell implements and pottery were discovered, together with ten burials. Some were headless bodies, some were heads only, and others had apparently tied legs.[13]

It is difficult to assess the extent to which the development of the Hu-shu culture may be attributed to Shang influence. Yin Huan-chang[14]

11. *KK* 1962 (1), 32–33.
12. *KK* 1962 (3), 128.
13. *Ibid.*, pp. 117–24.
14. *KKHP* 1959 (4), 54.

has singled out the following traits of the Geometric horizon in southern Kiangsu which he considers to be derived from Yin or early Western Chou influences: (1) in ceramics, such forms as *p'o, lei, li, yen, kui, yu, min,* and *tou,* such accessory parts as lugs, and such decorative designs as *yü* and *lei* patterns, cowrie, bands of triangles, and strings, all similar to the bronzes of the late Yin and early Chou; (2) in stone typology, stone halberds and stone arrowheads similar in form to the bronze halberds of the Yin and Chou dynasties and the bronze arrowheads excavated from Yin-Hsü; and (3) bronze knives, arrowheads, and handles and feet of the *ting* tripods of the late Yin and early Chou styles. According to Jao Tsung-i,[15] potsherds found in regions as far south as the Han-chiang valley in eastern Kwangtung resemble the "white pottery" of the Shang dynasty to such an extent in color and decorative designs as to suggest cultural influence. But even if not that far south, Shang influences unquestionably brought about the emergence of the Wu-ch'eng culture of Kiangsi—a culture that apparently grew out of a Geometric substratum. But Kiangsi is still some ways upstream from the Yangtze delta.

If the Shang civilization had come to the lower Yangtze at the very least, there cannot be any question that the Western Chou had also come this far. Groups of bronze vessels of probable Western Chou types have been discovered not only in the lower Yangtze Valley in Tan-t'u, I-cheng, and Nanking in southern Kiangsu but also from such southern localities as Ch'ang-hsing, on the western shore of T'ai-hu Lake in northern Chekiang, and T'un-hsi in southern Anhwei (fig. 193), in the upper reaches of the Ch'ien-t'ang-chiang (Chekiang River).[16] These bronzes exhibit either characteristic features that have been attributed to the Yin-Chou substage of the Archaic style according to North China criteria, or typical diagnostics of the Middle Chou style as defined by Bernhard Karlgren. Accordingly, these five sites can be grouped into two classes:

1. Early Western Chou: Tan-t'u and I-cheng finds, characterized by an Archaic style with features assumed to be Western Chou instead of Yin—four-eared *kui, p'an* with bent ears. These two sites are in the lower Yangtze in southern Kiangsu.
2. Late Western Chou or early Eastern Chou: Nanking, T'un-hsi, and Ch'ang-hsing finds, characterized by a typical Middle Chou style with local characteristics. The Nanking site is in the Yangtze

15. *Ta-lu tsa-chih* 8 (1954), 65–67.
16. *WWTKTL* 1955 (5), 58–62; 1956 (12), 31. *WW* 1960 (7), 48; 1965 (6), 52; 1973 (1), 62; 1975 (8), 87–88. *KK* 1960 (6), 41; 1961 (6), 321–23. *KKHP* 1959 (4), 59–87.

193. Bronze vessels of Western Chou types found at T'un-hsi, southern Anhwei. (From *KKHP* 1959, no. 4, pl. 1.)

Valley of southern Kiangsu, but the other two sites are farther south, in the Chekiang Valley in southern Anhwei and northern Chekiang.

These findings are of considerable importance for the study of Western Chou bronzes, and in connection with the present discussion their composition and geographical distribution are highly significant for the following reasons. The distribution of the bronzes of different ages indicates that the southbound expansion of the North Chinese cultural influences extended toward the south from the lower Yangtze to the Chekiang Valley during the span of the Western Chou dynasty. In addition to some bronze types that are so similar to their North China counterparts as to suggest importation from the north—a suggestion strengthened by the inscriptions of Western Chou characters on a *kui* vessel from the Yen-tun-shan site of Tan-t'u—there are other forms of bronze and other decorative designs on the vessels that find no counterparts in North China but must be considered as manufactured *in situ* and influenced stylistically by the local cultural tradition.

Some of the vessels [from the Tan-t'u group] are not identical with North China bronzes stylistically. For instance, the lid-knob and *ting* ears in the shape of standing animals . . . are rarely seen on North China bronzes. The body shape and the foot form of two small *ting* tripods resemble the pottery *ting* tripods of the [local Geometric horizon] cultures. The textile pattern on a pair of horn-shaped vessels and on several horse fittings is identical with the textile patterns on the local geometric stamped pottery. One can positively say that these bronzes were manufactured *in situ*, thus exhibiting some characteristic features of the local culture.[17]

At the T'un-hsi site, many ceramic remains found in association with the Western Chou type of bronzes are indistinguishable from the Geometric pottery discovered elsewhere in the same area in less glamorous contexts,[18] and the bronzes differ from North Chinese bronzes in decorative patterns, shapes, and sometimes even in type, as, for example, a special local kind of musical instrument. These distinctive features, if they mean the local manufacture of some bronzes, are significant indicators of the nature of the communities that were responsible for the making, use, and burial of these bronzes.

Another highly suggestive fact about these Western Chou bronzes is that, as they appear in the present archaeological record, they are isolated islands of high civilization surrounded by the sea of less advanced communities of the local Geometric horizon. In these communities, cultural elements indicative of Western Chou contacts, such as ceramic shapes, decorative designs, and the remains of bronze artifacts, are few and insignificant in comparison with the overwhelming majority of other remains found at the same sites, which consist of stone, bone, and shell implements of a local Neolithic tradition and ceramics of the geometric stamped style.

These facts suggest that the rise of some of the Western Chou civilizations in the lower Yangtze Valley may have been brought about by an elite class who established here a local technological and societal pattern after the North China model. The region of southern Kiangsu was known in Western Chou as the state of Wu and, according to local traditions, was the location of the burial place of two Western Chou princes, T'ai Po and Chung Yüng. These princes, according to Ssu-ma Ch'ien's *Shih chi* "escaped to the habitations of the Ching Man barbarians, tattooed

17. *KKHP* 1959 (4), 54.
18. *Ibid.*, p. 78.

themselves and cut off their hair [according to the local customs] to indicate their decision not to return.... They called themselves Kou Wu. The Ching Man people considered them as righteous men, and more than a thousand families followed their leadership." To what extent the details of this story are valid is debatable, but the story in its broad outline and the archaeological facts have jointly established the process of acculturation in this region by the Western Chou civilization.

Such events were not confined to the lower Yangtze and Chekiang valleys. Eastern Chou historical documents have recorded that many civilized kingdoms in southeast China had communications, transactions, and warfare with the Royal Chou and other northern Chinese states. Of these kingdoms, Wu of southern Kiangsu; Yüeh of Chekiang, Fukien, and Kwangtung; and Yen of southern Kiangsu are the best known. It is evident that such kingdoms emerged during the Western Chou dynasty, and the process described above may very well represent the initial phase of such an emergence. But in the archaeological record it was not until the Eastern Chou period that the remains of these early kingdoms in South China became widely found and substantially represented.

In the area of the Wu, a *hang-t'u* fortress of Spring Autumn date, consisting of two walled enclosures one inside the other, about 1,250 meters and 1,500 meters to a side respectively, was investigated in Yang-chou and identified as the town of Kan in historical records. Bronze weapons and geometric and glazed pottery were found associated with the site.[19] A cemetery in the upper most stratum of the Pei-yin-yang-ying site, probably dating from the Eastern Chou period, yielded finely polished stone artifacts and jade and opal objects in numbers varying widely from grave to grave—from over forty items to a single piece—which suggests sharply differentiated social status.[20] Such indications undoubtedly support the historical records of the Wu and Yüeh states in this and neighboring regions, although such states are yet to be identified precisely in the archaeological remains. Remains of stone plows, triangular in shape and closely similar to the iron plows of North China, have been unearthed in a Geometric horizon context at Yü-yao Hsien, Chekiang,[21] suggesting that the iron plow technology of the contemporary civilizations elsewhere had local imitations in the Hu-shu culture and its related phases. In fact, iron objects have been found from two tombs at Ch'eng-ch'iao

19. *WW* 1973 (12), 45–54.
20. *KKHP* 1958 (1), 7–18.
21. *WW* 1958 (11), 80.

in Liu-ho associated with bronze vessels very similar to the Ts'ai Hou tomb finds in Shou Hsien and, thus, dated to late Spring Autumn.[22]

Yen-ch'eng, the town of Yen, is a walled site south of Wu-chin (Ch'ang-chou), south of the Yangtze Valley in southern Kiangsu Province. It has three concentric walls called the outer wall, the inner wall, and the Tzu-lo or royal wall. The outer wall is an irregular circle, about 1,500 meters across, surrounded by a defensive moat. Both the inner wall and the royal wall make approximately square enclosures within the north-eastern part of the outer enclosure, with another protective moat surrounding the inner wall. Between the outer and inner walls, in the western part of the outer enclosure, is a row of three earthen mounds. The arrangement of this town is similar to some of the Eastern Chou cities in North China, as described earlier. Local traditions regard this town site as the remains of the capital of Yen, a Yüeh-related state in southern Kiangsu. Archaeological investigations were made at the site in 1935 and again in 1958, bringing to light a small amount of pottery, stone implements, bronze vessels, and wooden boats, but full-scale scientific excavations have yet to be carried out.

Pottery remains at the Yen site belonged to the Geometric variety, including nearly twenty whole urns covered with impressed geometric designs, some of which apparently were imitations of bronze patterns.[23] The bronzes, discovered in 1958, consist of three *tsun* vessels; a *p'an* with a handle, a spout, and three *ting*-like feet; a *p'an* with two wheel-feet and two animal-head handles; a set of seven portable bells; and an animal-shaped *i* vessel.[24] One hundred and fifty meters south of the spot where the bronzes were found, in the moat surrounding the inner wall, three dugout canoes were uncovered, one of which is 11 meters long and 90 centimeters wide at the top.[25]

The shape and decor of the bronze vessels find counterparts in the Huai style of North China, but many local characteristics are still highly conspicuous, such as the three-wheeled *p'an*, the *i* vessel with an animal-head spout, and the needle-shaped decorative designs on the *tsun* vessels. The associated Geometric pottery clearly indicates the basic cultural

22. *KK* 1974 (2), 116–20.

23. Wei Chü-hsien, *Chung-kuo k'ao-ku-hsüeh shih*, Shanghai, Commercial Press, 1937, p. 255. *KKHP* 1959 (4), 54. *WW* 1959 (4), 5, 54. For a similar find at Ch'i-chia-tun in Chin-shan, Shanghai, see *KK* 1973 (1), 16–24, 29.

24. *WW* 1959 (4), 5.

25. *WW* 1958 (11), 80.

affiliation of this town site. In any case, this find gives an interesting example of the Yüeh civilization in the Eastern Chou period.

By the time of Eastern Chou when civilizations flowered in the Wu and Yüeh strongholds of Kiangsu and Chekiang, evidence is widespread that bronze (and iron) metallurgy was established in the Geometric Ware sites of Kiangsi,[26] and bronze objects are found in Fukien[27] and Taiwan.[28] Habitation sites and tombs of the Warring States period have recently come to light in central Kwangtung in Shih-hsing in the north,[29] and near Canton in Tseng-ch'eng, Ch'ing-yüan, Ssu-hui, Te-ch'ing, and Chao-ch'ing in the south.[30] In all these southeastern coastal areas bronzes of the Warring States types were still found in association with stone implements of Neolithic type and with Geometric ware. At the habitation sites in Tseng-ch'eng and Shih-hsing, iron axes and hoe blades were found, indicating that by this time the use of iron for agricultural implements was widespread in the eastern part of South China. The construction of the tombs in Ch'ing-yüan and the general types of bronze vessels are in the Warring States pattern of the Chou civilization of the north, but the decorative patterns of the bronzes, the shapes of some bronze tools (such as the fan-shaped ax), and a dagger handle in the form of a human figure are distinctive local features (fig. 194). The hard, geometric-stamped urns at all these sites also indicate a local Neolithic background. According to Mo Chih and Li Shih-wen,[31] geometric stamped pottery was a long stylistic tradition in the area of Canton. Those with *k'ui*-shaped designs probably date from late Western Chou and the Spring Autumn period, and those with the *mi*-character ("Union Jack") designs were associated with iron implements and came from sites of the Warring States.

The Han-shui Valley and the Yün-meng Basin

Prehistoric and early historic cultures around the shores of the Great Lake, in the modern provinces of eastern and central Hupei and northern Hunan and northwestern Kiangsi, formed well-defined entities. One of these was the Lungshanoid Ch'ü-chia-ling culture of the Neolithic

26. *KK* 1962 (4), 172–81; 1965 (6), 265–67.

27. *KK* 1961 (4), 179–84.

28. Liu, *AP* 7 (1964), 217.

29. *KK* 1963 (4), 217–20; 1964 (3), 143–51, 160.

30. *KK* 1963 (2), 59–61; 1964 (3), 138–42, 143–51; 1975 (2), 102–08. *WW* 1973 (9), 18–22; 1974 (11), 69–77.

31. *KK* 1964 (3), 151.

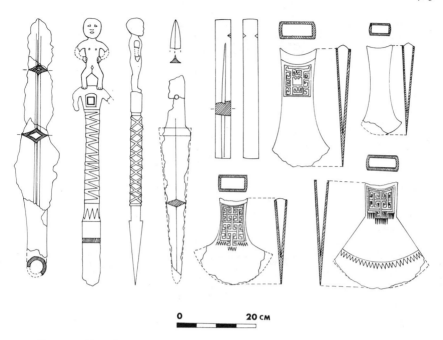

0   20 CM

194. Bronze artifacts from the Warring States tombs in Ch'ing-yüan, Kwangtung. (From *KK* 1964, no. 3, p. 141.)

period, discussed in chapter 4. The importance of this area in the archaeo-logy of the Shang civilization has been discussed in chapter 6.

Archaeological assemblages that have been referred to as Western Chou have also been found on the northern shores of the Great Lake, such as an assemblage of seventeen bronze vessels with inscriptions in a tomb near Wan-ch'eng in Chiang-ling, central Hupei,[32] and a village of timber struc-tures excavated in 1958 at the site of Wang-chia-tsui, northeast of Ch'i-ch'un, in eastern Hupei.[33] The Wang-chia-tsui site is of particular interest and import. Remains of an ancient habitation were found in an area about 30,000 square meters in size, where relices of timber structures were found in clusters in and around two small ponds. In the western cluster 109 wooden posts (0.2 meters in diameter) and remains of timber walls were brought to light, and three adjoining rooms (8 by 5 meters each) were restored, apparently three separate parts of a large, continuous structure. Remains of stairs were found. In the eastern cluster 171 posts were counted, but only two rooms were restorable. Other than pottery, which is Lungshan-

32. *KK* 1963 (4), 224–25.
33. *KK* 1962 (1), 1–9.

195. A fragment of a lacquered cup from the Western Chou site in Ch'i-ch'un, Hupei. (From *KK* 1962, no. 1, p. 7.)

like, and stone and clay artifacts, there were bronze arrowheads of the Shang and early Chou type, a bronze *chüeh* tripod, wooden containers, a lacquered cup (with bronze-vessel–type decorative patterns) (fig. 195), pieces of oracle bones and turtleshells, and remains of rice husks. The local character of this site is pronounced—witness the black pottery, paddy husks, and apparently a pile type of house construction—but the bronze vessel forms, bronze and ceramic decorative patterns, and the oracle bones very clearly indicate northern Chinese affiliations.

During the Chou period, particulary the Eastern Chou, the Han-shui valley was home to a number of small states, most supposedly having an origin from at least the Shang or Western Chou periods. One of these states is Tseng, which is now represented archaeologically by several assemblages of bronze vessels with inscriptions found in recent years in the upper and middle Han-shui valley from southern Honan (Hsin-yeh) to northern Hupei (Tsao-yang, Sui Hsien, Ching-shan).[34] But the most important state of the entire region was undoubtedly that of Ch'u. The state of Ch'u was the most powerful country in South China during the Chou period, and probably also the most civilized. Furthermore, this state was not only a political entity but also a cultural and ethnic one. In

34. *WW* 1972 (2), 47–53; 1973 (5), 14–20, 21–23. *KK* 1975 (4), 222–25.

the poem "Pi-kung," in the "Lu sung" section of *Shih ching*—literature dating possibly from an early period of the Chou dynasty—the peoples to the south are referred to as Ching and Shu. The inhabitants of the lower Han-shui valley in northern Hupei are known as Shu; Ching, originally the name of a plant which was also known as Ch'u, refers to the people living around Ching Mountain, thought to be in the present Nan-chang Hsien, near Hsiang-yang, Hupei Province. The names of Ch'u and Ching, therefore, were used interchangeably during the Chou period to designate the people in the lower Han-shui and the middle Yangtze valleys. The name of Ching seems to have appeared earlier than Ch'u, although Ch'u has since become widely used.[35]

The legendary beginnings of the Ch'u rulers were recorded in various literary records, but only around the time of Wen Wang of Western Chou did the genealogical record become historically established. Ssu-ma Ch'ien's *Shih chi* says that Ch'eng Wang of Western Chou made Hsiung I, the contemporary ruler of Ch'u, an earl to govern the people of Ch'u and made Tan-yang his capital. The exact geographical location of Tan-yang is disputed. Four hypotheses have been advanced to identify it as one of the following present-day locations: Tang-t'u, in central-eastern Anhwei on the Yangtze; Chih-chiang or Tzu-kui in western Hupei in the Yangtze Valley; the area between Shang Hsien in southeastern Shensi and Hsi-ch'uan in southwestern Honan, in the upper middle Han-shui valley.[36] Thus the majority of scholars believe that Tan-yang was somewhere in the Han-shui and middle Yangtze valleys, but the Tang-t'u theory, advanced by the authoritative *Han-shu ti-li-chih*, also deserves serious consideration. No matter where the original center of the political Ch'u may have been, by the beginning of the Eastern Chou period, under the reign of Earl Hsiung T'ung, the Ch'u state had already become a major power in central China. Hsiung T'ung went so far as to defy the Royal Chou authority and to call himself a king. From then on, throughout the Eastern Chou period, Ch'u was a major power to be reckoned with, not only in central China but in North China as well. At the peak of their power, the territory of the Ch'u extended from eastern Shensi east to the lower Yangtze Valley, as far north as the heart of Honan, and as far south as the Tung-t'ing Lake area in southern Hupei and northern Hunan. This powerful state was overthrown by the Ch'in dynasty in 223 B.C.,

35. Oyanagi Shigeta, *Tōhōgakuhō* 1 (1931), 196–228, Kyoto.
36. Hsü Hsün-sheng, *Chung-kuo ku-shih ti ch'uan-shuo shih-tai*, enlarged ed., Peking, Science Press, 1960, pp. 167–70. Ch'en P'an, "Proceedings of the International Conference of Historians of Asia, Hong Kong," vol. 3 (1964), prepublication print.

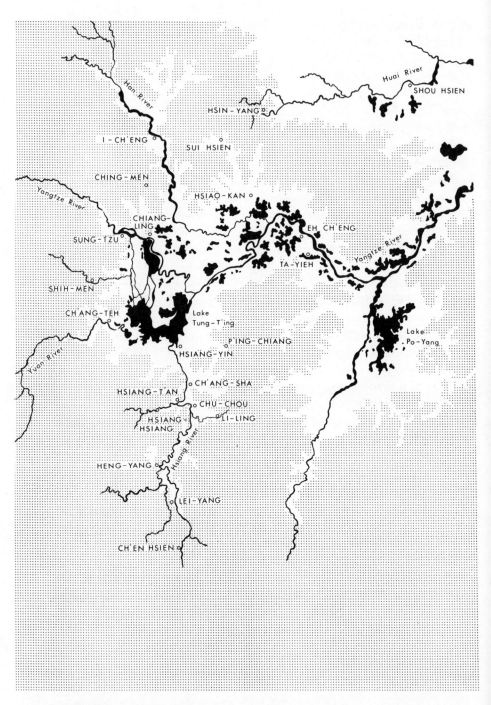

196. Principal cities in which Ch'u sites have been found. Dotted areas are over 100 meters in elevation. Solid areas are bodies of water, probably remnants of the ancient lake Yün-meng in the middle Yangtze area.

but the people and the culture maintained their distinct identity into the Han dynasty.

Cultural remains of the Ch'u dated to the Eastern Chou period have been found in a very wide area of the central part of South China, covering the Huai Ho valley in southeastern Honan and northern Anhwei and the Great Lake area of Hupei and Hunan (fig. 196). Ch'u remains over such a wide area bear out the literary tradition that the state of Ch'u expanded territorially around the beginning of the Eastern Chou, which is also suggested by the relative homogeneity of the cultural style represented by the relics from this region.

Under the state of Ch'u, town and city settlements were built that compare in urbanization with the northern Chinese cities described earlier, but habitation sites are few, and none has been thoroughly excavated. A Ch'u site of great promise is the walled ruins of Chi-nan-ch'eng, near the modern city of Chiang-ling on the Yangtze in central Hupei, traditionally held to be the site of Ying, Ch'u capital from 689 until 278 B.C. Clusters of burial mounds are found around the site, some of which have been excavated in recent years, but the walled town itself has yet to be investigated.[37] So far, only three walled sites have been explored by archaeologists: I-ch'eng in Hupei in the Han-shui Valley, and Shih-men and Hsiang-yin in northern Hunan. The I-ch'eng site, 2 by 1.5 kilometers, is the largest; remains of *li* tripods, *tou*, and *i-pi* coins were collected inside.[38] All that is known of the ruins at Shih-men is that the walled enclosure was rectangular and only 300 by 600 meters in size.[39] The Hsiang-yin site, 490 by 400 meters, was enclosed by *hang-t'u* walls, 14 meters wide and 3 high, traditionally believed to be the site of Lo, a small vassal state of the Ch'u. Cultural remains in association with the town site probably belonged to an early phase within the Eastern Chou period.[40] A dwelling site of a comparable period was found at T'ai-tzu-ch'ung near Ch'ang-sha, Hunan Province, where storage pits, pottery, and stone knives were collected.[41] Near the town of Weng-chiang in P'ing-chiang, northern Hunan, storage pits, pottery, iron axes, and bronze vessels, weapons, and implements, along with evidence of a bronze foundry, have been found, indicating a local workshop.[42] In Hupei, village remains with charac-

37. *WW* 1966 (5), 33–55.
38. *KK* 1965 (8), 377–82.
39. *KK* 1964 (2), 104–05.
40. *KKTH* 1958 (2), 10–14.
41. *WW* 1960 (3), 66.
42. *WWTKTL* 1958 (1), 39–41.

teristic *li* tripod sherds have been reported in Sui Hsien.[43] Needless to say, these discoveries are insufficient evidence of the kind of urbanism and civic and public structures that we can surely assume existed in the state of Ch'u. Painted scenes on lacquerware may give a notion about what some of their houses looked like (fig. 197).

The Ch'u sites so far discovered consist mainly of tombs. Within the province of Hunan alone, large numbers of Ch'u graves have been located in Ch'ang-sha, Hsiang-t'an, Hsiang-hsiang, Chu-chou, Li-ling, Heng-yang, Lei-yang, and Ch'en Hsien of the Hsiang River valley and in Ch'ang-te at the mouth of the River Yüan.[44] Of these sites Ch'ang-sha is the most prolific, having (by 1960) yielded twelve hundred individual graves dated to the Eastern Chou period.[45] Ch'ang-te[46] and Heng-yang follow in number of graves produced, with approximately a hundred each. In Hupei, the area where most of the capital sites of the Ch'u were located, the archaeology of this early civilization is only beginning, but important Ch'u tombs have already been reported from Chih-chiang,[47] Sung-tzu,[48] Chiang-ling,[49] and the Eh-ch'eng and Ta-yeh area of eastern Hupei.[50] Other than these two provinces, highly important Ch'u remains are known in Hsin-yang in Honan,[51] and Shou Hsien in Anhwei,[52] both in the Huai Ho valley. These centers of Ch'u finds outline the geographical extent of the Ch'u territory represented by archaeological remains—the four shores of the Great Lake Yün-meng, valleys of the three major rivers

43. *KK* 1959 (11), 635–36.

44. Kao Chih-hsi, *WW* 1960 (3), 33.

45. Hsia Nai et al., *Ch'ang-sha fa-chüeh pao-kao*, Peking, Science Press, 1957. Wen Tao-i, *KKHP* 1959 (1), 41–58; 1972 (1), 59–72. *KKTH* 1958 (9), 57–61; 1958 (12), 28–34. *KK* 1959 (12), 649–52. *WW* 1960 (1), 63–64; 1960 (3), 38–49, 51–56, 64–66; 1974 (2), 36–37; 1975 (2), 49–56. Jao Tsung-i, *Ch'ang-sha ch'u-t'u Chan-kuo tseng-shu hsin-shih*, Hong Kong, privately printed, 1958. Chiang Hsüan-i, *Ch'ang-sha Ch'u min-tsu chi ch'i i-shu*, Shanghai, Kunstarchäologie Society, 1949. Shang Ch'eng-tso, *Ch'ang-sha ku-wu wen-chien-chi*, Chengtu, Chin-ling University, 1939. Shih Shu-ch'ing, *Ch'ang-sha Yang-t'ien-hu ch'u-t'u Ch'u chien yen-chiu*, Shanghai, Ch'ün-lien Press, 1955.

46. *KK* 1959 (4), 207–08; 1959 (12), 658; 1963 (9), 461–73, 479.

47. *WW* 1972 (3), 65–68.

48. *KK* 1966 (3), 122–32.

49. *WW* 1962 (2), 56; 1964 (9), 27–32; 1966 (5), 53–55; 1973 (9), 7–17. *KK* 1972 (2), 67; 1972 (3), 41–48; 1973 (3), 151–61; 1973 (6), 337–44.

50. *KKTH* 1958 (8), 50–51. *KK* 1959 (11), 622.

51. *WWTKTL* 1957 (9), 21–22; 1958 (1), 5, 6–8, 15–23. *KKTH* 1958 (11), 79–80. *Honan Hsin-yang Ch'u mu ch'u-t'u wen-wu t'u-lu*, Honan, Jenmin Press, 1959.

52. *TYKKPK* 1 (1936). Liu Chieh, *Ch'u ch'i t'u shih*, Peiping, National Library of Peiping, 1935. O. Karlbeck, *BMFEA* 27 (1955). *WW* 1959 (4), 12. *KK* 1959 (7), 371–72.

197. Decorative scenes on Ch'u lacquerware, spread out, showing aspects of Ch'u life, Ch'ang-sha. (From *Ch'ang-sha ch'u-t'u ku-tai ch'i-ch'i t'u-an hsüan chi*, Peking, Historical Museum, 1954.)

that flow through or into the area (the Yangtze, Hsiang, and Han-shui), and the upper Huai Ho valley that is separated from the Yün-meng Basin by the Ta-peh Mountains. The cultural influence of the Ch'u civilization surely went beyond its territories, and evidence of such influence is seen clearly in northern Kiangsu in the east[53] and Szechwan and Yunnan in the west.

These finds show that the Ch'u built elaborate graves for their dead. All the tombs in the area were rectangular, earthen pit graves, with or without ramps. Some pits were narrower than others and may have been earlier in date. The orientation of the tombs was somewhat irregular, but heads to the north or the east were more common.

The bottom of the pit was often plastered with a layer of limy white clay, and around the pit walls a platform was sometimes built corresponding to the *erh-ts'eng-t'ai* of northern Chinese tombs. Niches or cavities in the wall were excavated for the storage of grave goods. At the center of the tomb, a wooden chamber was built, inside which a wooden coffin was placed. The coffin was often wrapped with cloths, probably a measure

53. *KK* 1960 (3), 29.

against moisture. Grave goods were placed inside the coffin or in the pit, and the whole pit was then filled with earth, sometimes compacted by stamping. Both the Shou Hsien and the Hsin-yang tombs were built in a similar manner, but the latter (two of which have so far been discovered) had a far more complicated wooden chamber structure and were divided into several sections.

Such elaborate burials indicate a highly stratified society and an advanced technology and economy, but direct evidence of farming techniques is limited to the occasional discovery of farming implements, including hoes and spades of iron.[54] There is no evidence of the use of the plow, which had begun both in contemporary North China and in the territory of Yüeh to the east. According to historical records, however, it is fairly certain that in the state of Ch'u as well as Yüeh, rice was cultivated and irrigated by both artificial and natural means. To the northerners of the Eastern Chou period as well as to those of subsequent historical periods, the rich natural resources in and south of the Yangtze Valley were objects of constant envy. Ssu-ma Ch'ien says in "Ho-chih lieh-chuan," *Shih chi*, that the "territory of the Ch'u and the Yüeh is vast but the population sparse. Rice is the staple food, and fish the main dish. The people *keng* with fire, and *ju* with water." There are various interpretations of the last sentence,[55] but, whatever the interpretation, the use of water for the cultivation of rice can be inferred. *Shih chi* also mentions the collection of mollusks for food, a practice substantiated by the shell-tempered pottery at one of the Sui Hsien sites in Hupei. In a tomb in Chiang-ling were found remains of chestnuts, fresh ginger, and sweet fennel; cherry, apple, and plum pits; melon seeds; and bones of fish, chickens, and animals.

In addition to agricultural implements, iron was employed to make axes, knives, adzes, weapons (swords, *chi* halberds, and arrowheads), and even ornaments (rings and belt hooks).[56] Lead was another metal melted by the Ch'u smiths, who fashioned it into mortuary money and covers for wooden handles. But as far as the archaeological data show, bronze was still the basic raw material for artifacts. In the tombs, bronze vessels (*ting* tripods, *tui* tripods, *hu*, and dippers), weapons (swords, *ko* halberds, and spears), horse and chariot fittings, belt hooks, mirrors,

54. *KKHP* 1959 (1), 43.

55. Nishijima Sadao, "The System of Rice Cultivation in Ancient China," in *Oriental Studies Presented to Sei (Kiyoshi) Wada*, Tokyo, Dainippon Yūbenkai Kōdansha, 1951, pp. 469–87. Amano Motonosuke, *Shigaku zasshi* 61 (1952), 58–61. Yoneda, *Shirin* 38 (1955), 1–18.

56. *KKHP* 1957 (3), 97–98.

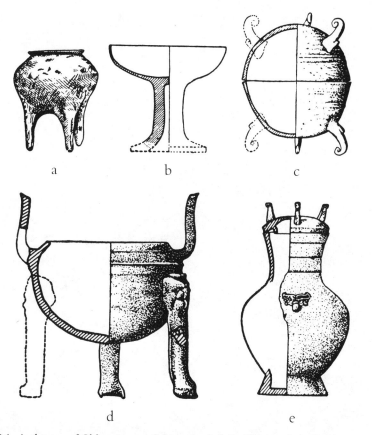

198. Principal types of Ch'u pottery of chronological significance, found in the tombs in Ch'ang-sha: (a) *li*; (b) *tou*; (c) *tui*; (d) *ting*; (e) *hu*. (From *Ch'ang-sha fa-chüeh pao-kao*, Peking, Science Press, 1957, various figures.)

musical instruments (such as *pien* bells, portable bells, and kettledrums), and even seals have been found in great numbers. A chemical analysis of some specimens of bronze[57] shows that the ratio of copper, tin, and various impurities was completely controlled. A large *ting* tripod unearthed from the Shou Hsien tomb is said to weigh nearly 400 kilograms,[58] indicating an advanced level of bronze metallurgy. The large number of bronze artifacts and their distinctive local features (such as the numerous stylistic motifs in the decoration and the inscriptions) rule out the possibility that these bronze artifacts were imports, and the bronze foundry site in P'ing-

57. *KKHP* 1959 (1), 48.
58. Liu Chieh, *Ch'u ch'i t'u shih*, p. 3.

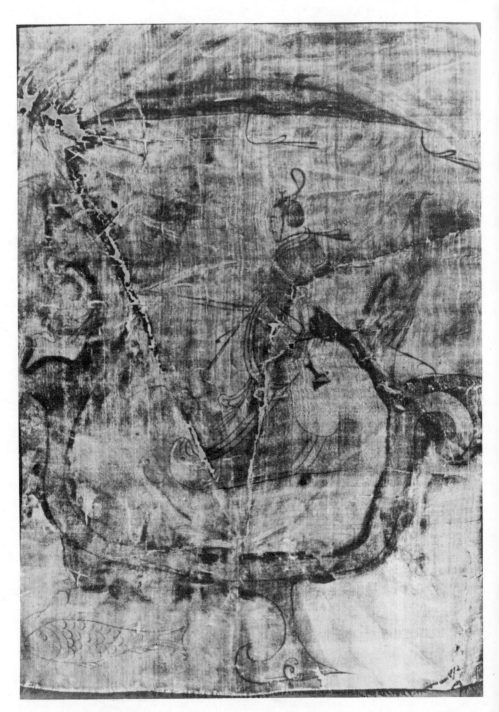

199. Silk painting found in a Ch'u tomb at Tzu-tan-k'u in Ch'ang-sha, Hunan. (From *KK* 1973, no. 7.)

chiang Hsien, Hunan, mentioned above, bears this out. A copper mine with elaborate shafts and remains of bronze and iron tools was found in Ta-yeh in 1965 and excavated in 1974; it is considered an important copper source of the Ch'u state.[59] Another copper mine of similar age was brought to light in 1973, but details are lacking.[60]

In addition to metallurgy of both bronze and iron, the Ch'u civilization was apparently highly developed in handicrafts, including ceramics, wood carving, carpentry, bamboo crafts, leatherwork, lacquerwork, silk and hemp weaving, and stone and jade crafts. The pottery is predominantly grayish or brownish in color, either of fine texture or tempered with sand, depending upon the kind of vessel and its purpose. Glaze was applied in some cases. The basic technique of manufacture was by wheel, although handmade and molded pieces occur not infrequently. Most of the pots are plain, but there is also decorated pottery, which is corded, stringed, incised, or painted in red, yellow, blue, white, or black, in spirals and geometric designs. *Ting* and *li* tripods, *hu*, *tou*, bowls, cups, stoves, urns, and so forth are all represented, and the occurrence of particular shapes seems to have some chronological significance (fig. 198). Bamboo mats, bows, suitcases, wooden combs, spears, leather remains, silk fabrics and silk paintings (fig. 199)[61] are among the extraordinary discoveries made in recent years. Bamboo was also cut into elongated slips for writing; dozens of these inscribed slips have been found in tombs in Ch'ang-sha, Chiang-ling, and Hsin-yang (fig. 98), along with remains of a writing brush and its container. Wood carving is another noted craft of the Ch'u, and wooden human and animal figurines, drums, animal tomb-guardians with antler horns (fig. 200), and carved boards have been found. Remains of wooden bases for the musical instrument *se* have been collected from the tombs at Hsin-yang and Chiang-ling (fig. 201). These relics vividly testify to the fact that industrial specialization had developed to a very considerable extent in this part of China during the Eastern Chou period, which is confirmed by the many names of handicraft products written on the bamboo tablets—probably lists of grave goods, many of which have since perished.

Supported by agriculture and industry of such high levels of complexity, the political and social organizations of the Chou were presumably also complex. No doubt Ch'u deserves the designation of "state," and the titles

59. *WW* 1975 (2), 1–12, 13–18, 19–25.
60. *KK* 1974 (4), 251–56.
61. *WW* 1973 (7), 3–4; 1974 (2), 36–40.

200. Wooden sculpture of a monster, excavated from a Ch'u tomb in Hsin-yang, Honan. (From *WW* 1957, no. 9, frontispiece.)

of king and earl must have been accompanied by corresponding political institutions. Archaeological evidence is lacking, but the remains of bronze coins (*i-pi-ch'ien*, or "ant-nose" coins)[62] and bronze scales and weights[63] show a good deal of social and economic sophistication. Moreover, the Ch'u was certainly a literary civilization, with writing still to be seen on bamboo tablets, weapons (fig. 202), bronze vessels, and silk clothing

62. *KK* 1973 (3), 192–96. *KKHP* 1973 (2), 61–88.
63. *KK* 1972 (4), 42–45.

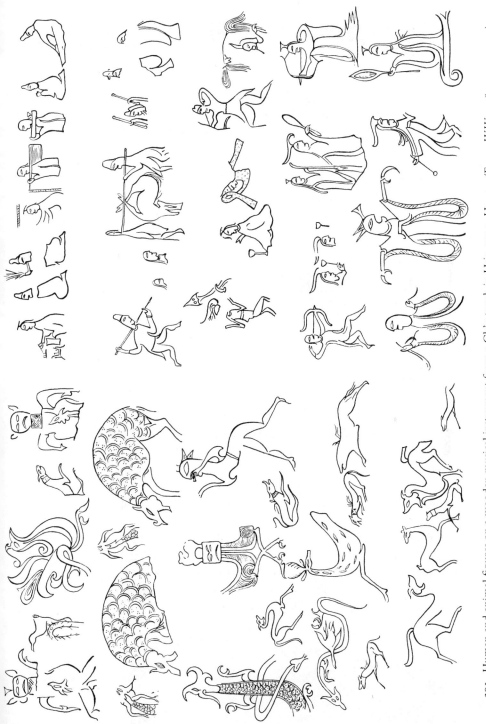

201. Human and animal figures on a wooden musical instrument from a Ch'u tomb in Hsin-yang, Honan. (From *WW* 1958, no. 1, p. 27.)

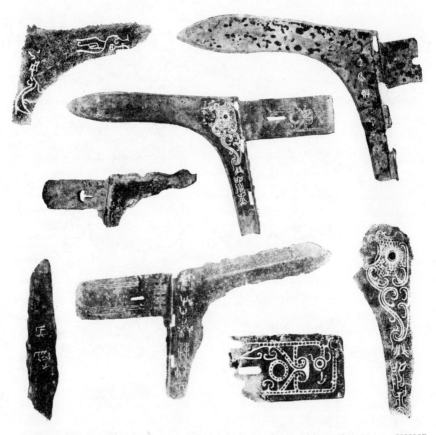

202. Decorated *ko* halberds excavated from Ch'u tombs in Ch'ang-sha. (From *KKHP* 1959, no. 1, pl. 11, following p. 60.)

(fig. 203). As in North China, the writing is composed of characters, many of which are identical with those used elsewhere in China. But unique characters, a distinctive calligraphy, and another distinctive system of character composition, mostly inscribed on weapons, indicate local characteristics. Kuo Mo-jo believes that during the Eastern Chou period, efforts were made to unify writing in the whole of China under the sovereignty of the Royal Chou, although various regional writing systems were still being used for certain specific purposes.[64]

Compared with contemporary North China, the Ch'u are also distinctive in being an especially religious-minded people. The Eastern Chou and Han saying, that the "Ch'u people are particularly superstitious," testifies

64. *WW TKTL* 1958 (1), 5.

203. Silk with paintings and inscriptions from a Ch'u tomb in Ch'ang-sha. (From *The Ch'u Silk in the Sackler Collections*, New York, International Arts Press. Reprinted by permission of the Sackler Foundation.)

to this fact. The elaborate burial customs indicate a highly complex system of ancestor worship. In *Ch'u tz'u*, a piece of genuine Ch'u literature handed down through subsequent historical periods, there is a long poem entitled "T'ien wen," in which Ch'ü Yüan, the alleged author and an officer of the king's court, asks a series of questions concerning the creation of the cosmos, of man, the various deities, and the legendary history of the Ch'u kings. It has been suggested that this poem was composed in the ancestral temple of the Ch'u ruler, on the interior walls of which pictures depicting the various myths and legends were painted, and that Ch'ü Yüan asked questions on various topics as he looked at these pictures. Ancestral temples of this nature have yet to be found. But among the Ch'u people there must have been beliefs concerning various spirits and deities, as indicated by the text of a silk writing,[65] and also by the remains of wooden animal tomb-guardians, wooden human figurines, and wooden human statues with protruding tongues and antler horns. Snake, phoenix, and dragon were favorite decorative motifs, and musical instruments (wooden and bronze drums, bells, various kinds of wooden and bamboo wind and string instruments, and pottery whistles) must have had some ceremonial use.

These descriptions of the Ch'u civilization suffice to show that it was basically identical with the Chou civilization of North China, but that distinctive characteristics are at the same time plentiful. Legends of the Ch'u, as recorded by North Chinese historians, say that the founders of the Ch'u were descended from Tuan Hsü, a grandson of the Yellow Emperor. One may be tempted to regard the Ch'u rulers as North Chinese and the ruled people as indigenous natives. This, however, was not necessarily so. Hsiung Ch'ü, an earl of Ch'u and a near descendant of the first earl, was quoted in *Shih chi* as saying: "We are barbarians." The Ch'u system of government closely followed that of the Chou dynasty, but according to the accounts in *Tso chuan* (first year of Wen Kung and thirteenth year of Chao Kung), the succession to the monarch of the earldom or, later, the kingdom seems to have favored a junior son rather than the primary son as in the Chou dynasty. The Ch'u language was somewhat different from the contemporary northern Chinese, as is shown by a few lexical elements recorded in North Chinese literature. In the archaeological remains, although the culture is shown to be basically the same as the

65. *WW* 1963 (9), 48–60; 1964 (9), 8–20. Jao Tsung-i, *Ch'ang-sha ch'u-t'u Chan-kuo tseng-shu hsin-shih*, Hong Kong, 1958. Noel Barnard, *The Ch'u Silk Manuscript*, Monographs on Far Eastern History, no. 5, Australian National University, 1973.

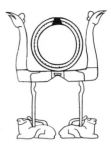

204. Wooden sculptures of tigers and birds, probably used as drum supports in the manner shown in the dancing scene at bottom, found in Ch'u tombs: *top*, Chiang-ling (from *WW* 1964, no. 9); *middle*, Hsin-yang (after *KKTH* 1958, no. 11, and *WW* 1964, no. 9); *bottom*, enlargment of a segment from a scene in Ma Ch'eng-yüan (*WW* 1961, no. 10).

Eastern Chou of North China, many distinctive local features are discernible, such as the characteristic writing styles, the special deities and ceremonies, the highly developed wood carving and bamboo crafts, the wooden drum frame consisting of a pair of birds and a pair of tigers (fig. 204), the bird motif in a distinctive style of decorative art (fig. 205), the great abundance of lacquerware, silk fabrics, mirrors, and swords, the tattooing of faces (fig. 206), and the different systems of currency (*Ying yüan* and *i-pi-ch'ien*). Many of these, as well as rice cultivation, can be attributed to the riverine and lacustrine environment, but others must indicate a distinctive Ch'u cultural style.

The widely distributed Ch'u remains show remarkable homogeneity in style, although regional phases are discernible within this vast territory.[66] Ch'u remains began to appear at the beginning of the Ch'un-ch'iu period and, as far as we know from the available material, underwent a similar sequence of change and development throughout the area. In the region of Ch'ang-sha, three well-defined stages can be distinguished both stratigraphically and typologically.[67]

1. *Early*: Ch'un-ch'iu and the beginning of Chan-kuo. Approximately one hundred tombs (among the more than twelve hundred in the area) belong to this stage and are characterized by smaller and narrower tombs than the later ones; wall niches mostly at the head end; a scarcity of ramps; in ceramics, three combinations: *li*-bowl–*hu-tou*-jug, *lei*-bowl–*tou*, or *hu*-bowl–*tou*-urn; *li* tripods of pottery; certain types of bronze weapons and vessels; some iron implements.

2. *Middle*: early Chan-kuo period. Over six hundred graves belong to this stage, characterized by a growing number of wider grave pits, side niches, and ramps; pottery *ting* tripods taking the place of *li* tripods; the appearance of pottery *tui* tripods; bronze vessels and weapons of later types; more iron implements.

3. *Late*: late Chan-kuo and the beginning of Western Han. Characterized by predominance of rectangular grave pits of great width; a growing number of side niches; the appearance of cave chambers and multiple burials; the use of clay to seal off the wooden chamber; complex wooden chamber structures; much painted pottery; more complex bronze artifacts; more iron implements and even iron weapons; the occurrence of stone *pi* rings; decorative inscriptions on bronze weapons.

66. Ch'en Meng-chia, Preface to *Ch'ang-sha ku-wu wen-chien-chi*, by Shang Ch'eng-tso, p. 10.

67. *KKHP* 1957 (4), 47–48; 1959 (1), 55–56. *KKTH* 1958 (9), 60–61; 1958 (12), 34. *WW* 1960 (3), 33–34. Hsia et al., *Ch'ang-sha fa-chüeh pao-kao*, p. 37.

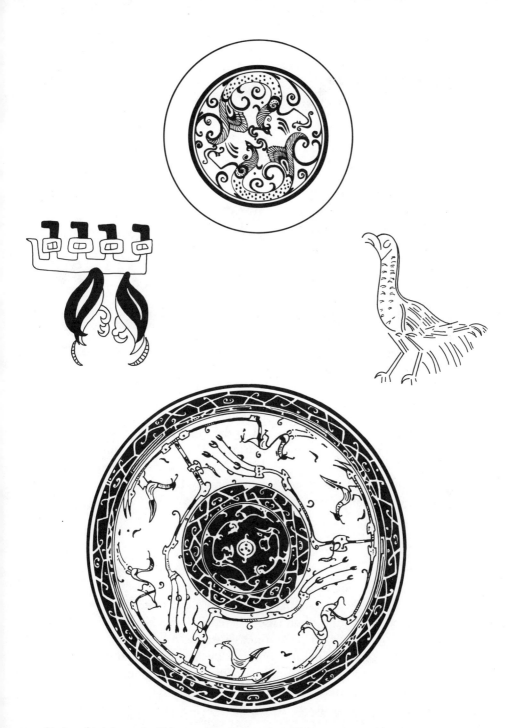

205. Various bird forms in Ch'u art: *left*, Ch'ang-sha, silk manuscript (after Shang Ch'eng-tso, *WW* 1964, no. 9); *right*, interior decoration of a winged cup (Singer Collection; drawing after Max Loehr, *Relics of Ancient China*, New York, Asia Society, 1965); *top and bottom*, Ch'ang-sha, paintted lacquered dishes (after *Ch'ang-sha ch'u-t'u ku-tai ch'i-ch'i t'u-an hsüan chi*, Peking, Historical Museum. 1954).

206. Wooden figures found in Ch'ang-sha. (First figure from *Ch'ang-sha fa-chüeh Pao-kao*, Peking, Science Press, 1957; all others from Chiang Hsüan-i, *Ch'ang-sha Ch'u min-tsu chi ch'i i-shu*, Shanghai, Mei-shu k'ao-ku hsüeh-she, 1950.)

A similar sequence can also be found in the burials of the Ch'ang-te area.[68] Ch'u graves in Hupei and in the Huai Ho valley are not yet susceptible to such chronological treatment. However, it is noteworthy that the Hsin-yang tombs, while probably dated to an early period comparable to Ch'ang-sha's Early stage,[69] contain many features that did not appear in Ch'ang-sha until later.

Early Civilizations in Szechwan

In the upper Yangtze Valley in the Red Basin (fig. 207), less is known about the beginning of civilization than in eastern and central South China, but the development may have been quite different. There was a long-established Mesolithic foundation here, and the Neolithic cultures are obviously characterized by distinctive styles. As described in chapter 6, very little is known of the area insofar as the Shang civilization is concerned, although Shang influence may be discerned in some archaeological assemblages of pottery and bronzes.

The western part of Szechwan, nevertheless, was definitely influenced

68. *KK* 1959 (12), 662.
69. *WWTKTL* 1958 (1), 5.

207. Early historical sites in Szechwan.

by the Western Chou civilization. Archaeological remains that can probably be dated to late Western Chou or early Eastern Chou have been discovered thus far in four counties: Han-chou (Kuang-han), Hsin-fan, Ch'eng-tu, and Mien-yang, in the P'ei, T'o, and Min River valleys. The T'ai-p'ing-ch'ang site in Kuang-han was discovered in 1931 and investigated in 1933 by David C. Graham of the university museum of West China Union University.[70] At this site, a habitation area was located, and a ceremonial pit was uncovered which contained over twenty stone disks of various sizes and a number of jade and stone ceremonial objects (circular *yüan*, square *tsung* tubes, *wan-kui*, etc.). Some stone implements and a large number of potsherds were brought to light from the habitation layer. The pottery was red or grayish, with corded or plain surface, and

70. David C. Graham, *Jour. West. Border Research Soc.* 6 (Ch'eng-tu, 1933/34), 114–31.

208. A ceremonial platform, possibly of the Western Chou period, found at Yang-tzu-shan, Ch'eng-tu, Szechwan. (From *KKHP* 1957, no. 4, p. 20.)

in such forms as high-stem *tou*, urns, and tripods. No metal artifacts have been found, but a red iron nugget, a fragment of iron ore, and a small lump of copper ore were collected from the cultural debris. Cheng Te-k'un thinks that the ceremonial pit and the cultural debris were of different ages, the former probably dating from the Eastern Chou and representing the remains of a mountain-worship ceremony (possibly the worship of Min Mountain, as recorded in *Shan hai ching*) belonging to the so-called "Aeneolithic period," dating from 1200 to 700 B.C.[71] Cheng's chronology is open to doubt. The stratigraphical relationship of the ceremonial pit and the habitation layers is not altogether clear, but they could very possibly be contemporary since jade and stone rings and plates similar to those found in the ceremonial pit have been unearthed in the cultural layer, and perhaps they should not be dismissed as "intrusive," as Cheng has called them. Recent findings of cultural remains probably dating from a comparable stage seem to confirm this, since stone and jade ceremonial objects and pottery—which resemble the objects found at T'ai-p'ing-ch'ang from both the pit and the cultural layer—have been shown to come from the same cultural stratum.

North of the city of Ch'eng-tu in the Min River valley is a low hill, known as Yang-tzu-shan. An earthen ceremonial platform was excavated on top of the hill in 1956. Since Warring States tombs were built into it, the platform must have been constructed some time earlier than the Chan-kuo period.[72] The platform is square and oriented northwest-southeast. It is constructed in three levels, measuring 31.6, 67.7, and 103.6 meters across, respectively, and has a total height exceeding 10 meters (fig. 208). Within the platform, stone disks and pottery remains similar

71. *Hsieh-ta Jour. Chinese Studies* 1 (Foochow, 1949), 67–81.
72. *KKHP* 1957 (4), 17–31.

to those of T'ai-p'ing-ch'ang were found. Similar pottery sherds have also been unearthed at the Pien-tui-shan site in Mien-yang Hsien, on the upper P'ei River.[73] High-stemmed *tou* vessels similar to those found in Kuang-han have been unearthed from the cultural strata at the site of Shui-kuan-yin in Hsin-fan Hsien, mentioned previously. At this site both habitation remains and burials have been found, but more than a single cultural stage is probably represented. Bronze arrowheads of the two-winged type, *ko* halberds of the Yin type, spearheads, axes, *yüeh* axes, and knives have been unearthed, but the overwhelming majority of the associated remains indicates a persisting Neolithic context.[74] This site has been given a Shang dynasty date mainly on the basis of the Shang type of *ko* halberds; but the same type of weapon has been found in as- sociation with typical Warring States inventories from the tomb at Yang- tzu-shan (intruded into the ceremonial platform described above), and this particular evidence is therefore of doubtful dating value.[75] Since the arrowheads and some of the pottery and other bronze weapons do not show characteristic Chan-kuo features, the Shui-kuan-yin site can probably be dated to either late Western Chou or early Eastern Chou, broadly contemporary with the T'ai-p'ing-ch'ang and Yang-tzu-shan ceremonial assemblages.

These archaeological discoveries in the western part of Szechwan indicate a cultural tradition, essentially a continuation of the local Neolithic, which was heavily influenced by the Western or early Eastern Chou civilizations of North China, and in which ceremonial structures and stone and jade ceremonial objects played significant roles, though metallurgy may not have developed locally to any considerable extent. In this part of Szechwan, megalithic structures have been noted in the historical literature and investigated by archaeologists; their correlation with archaeological remains is still not clear. Cheng Te-k'un[76] is inclined to correlate the megalithic monuments with the ceremonial pit at T'ai-p'ing-ch'ang, and this seems to be supported by the ceremonial platform at Ch'eng-tu. Such structures and objects certainly invite inferences regarding the religion and political authority of the people who left such remains, but further characterizations in cultural and social terms are impossible to make at the present time.

73. *Ibid.*, p. 30.
74. *KK* 1959 (8), 401.
75. *KKHP* 1956 (4), 6.
76. Cheng Te-k'un, *Archaeological Studies in Szechwan*, Cambridge Univ. Press, 1957, p. xiv.

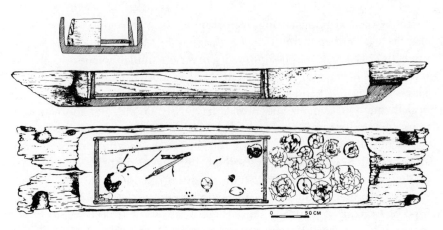

209. A boat coffin excavated at the Bronze Age site at Pao-lun-yüan, Chao-hua, Szechwan. (From *KKHP* 1958, no. 2, p. 81.)

Whatever the nature of the civilizations in Szechwan during the Western Chou and early Eastern Chou periods of North China, by the beginning of the Warring States period intensified civilizations appeared in many parts of the province, as indicated by archaeological remains abundant in bronze and iron artifacts, evidence of tightened political control, and writing. Three groups of metal-culture sites in Szechwan in the Warring States period can be discerned in the archaeological material: one represented by burials in the Chia-ling-chiang valley of eastern and central Szechwan; one centering in the valley of Min near the plains of Ch'eng-tu; and one confined to the extreme northwestern portion of the province, in the foothills and river valleys of the eastern Tibetan plateau. The former two groups, while exhibiting certain distinctive features, seem to have formed a single cultural tradition; whereas the third constitutes a separate culture of its own.

Two sites of the Chia-ling-chiang burials have been discovered so far: the Pao-lun-yüan cemetery in Chao-hua in north central Szechwan, and the Tung-sun-pa cemetery in Pa Hsien, near the confluence of the Chia-ling-chiang and the Yangtze, close to the city of Chungking.[77] At least thirteen individual burials, four of which are intact, have been brought to light at the Pao-lun-yüan site, and eighteen, with one completely preserved, at Tung-sun-pa. Both of these cemeteries were situated on river terraces. The individual graves, arranged in regular rows crowded

77. *KKHP* 1958 (2), 77–95. Szechwan Museum, *Szechwan ch'uan-kuan tsang fa-chüeh pao-kao*, Peking, Wen Wu Press, 1960.

into small areas, were rectangular earthen pits, perpendicular to the river-
bank. The pits were only just large enough to contain individual dugout
canoes which served as coffins. Each canoe was about 5 meters long and
1 meter wide, with a flattened bottom, two beveled ends, each with a
big hole, and a dugout cavity at the top, which contained the body as well
as grave goods (fig. 209). In several cases the canoe was so large that the
cavity served as a chamber into which a smaller coffin containing the
body was placed, together with grave goods, but these are believed to be
of a later type. Bronze, iron, stone, bamboo, and wooden artifacts, pottery,
lacquer, silk and hemp clothes, and clay and glass beads were uncovered
from the graves. Among the bronze artifacts are axes, spears, *ko* halberds,
arrowheads, vessels, mirrors, belt hooks, knives, seals, and scale weights,
mostly of the Warring States variety, but the most typical bronzes are a
willow-leaf-shaped sword and a socketed ax with a circular blade. The
blade of the sword is tapered toward the end to become a handle which is
lengthened with the addition of wooden splints and decorated with many
kinds of unusual designs, such as tiger heads, tiger-skin patterns, "hand-
and-heart" patterns, and writings (fig. 210). The hand-and-heart pattern
is seen only on the bronze swords, not only in these boat burials but
throughout the Szechwan area,[78] and is never used for other kinds of
weapons or vessels with the single exception of one spearhead. The other
decorative patterns are found on other kinds of implements and weapons.
Metallurgical analysis has shown that the bronzes in the boat burials
contain a lower quantity of tin than is usually found in Chinese bronzes,
and that the artifacts are therefore relatively soft. In several burials, bronze
pan-liang coins of the Ch'in dynasty were found, but these burials are
thought to be of a later phase than the rest. Iron artifacts are few and
consist only of knives and axes. The pottery is predominantly brownish
in color and sand tempered; in form it is characterized by a flat or round
bottom and by the use of ring feet. It is mainly wheel made, and painted
decorations are rare. A series of new finds, including tombs, further down
the Yangtze from Pa Hsien has been made in the P'ei-ling area, disclosing
additional materials similar to the above but including such typical Eastern
Chou items as sets of bronze bells.[79]

   The Warring States period sites in the Ch'eng-tu area include a cemetery
in P'eng-shan, a group of bronzes from Lu-shan,[80] and several groups of

   78. They are seen as far east as the Ch'ü-t'ang Gorge area of the Yangtze River in
Szechwan. See *KK* 1962 (5), 253.
   79. *WW* 1973 (1), 59; 1974 (5), 61–80, 81–83; 1974 (12), 62.
   80. *KK* 1959 (8), 439.

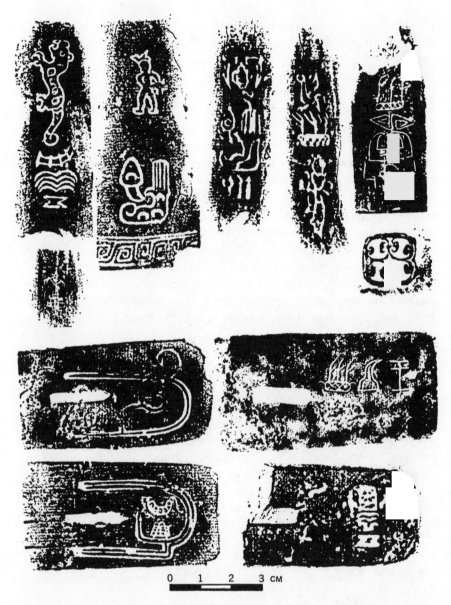

210. Designs on spearheads (*above*) and halberds (*below*) from the Eastern Chou and Han burials in the Chia-ling-chiang region of Szechwan. (From *KKHP* 1958, no. 2, p. 89.)

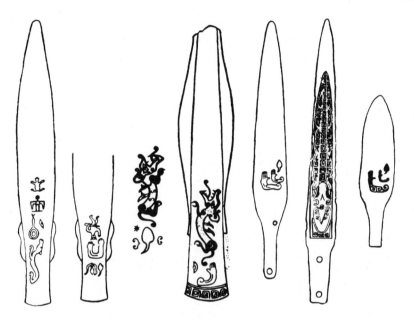

211. Decorated bronze swords and spearheads from the Pai-ma-ssu site, near Ch'eng-tu, Szechwan. (From *Shuo wen* 3, 1941, Shanghai.)

burials and habitation remains in the neighborhood of the city of Ch'eng-tu, such as Ch'ing-yang-kung, Yang-tzu-shan, Pai-ma-ssu, and one outside the southern city gate. Of these, P'eng-shan and the site at Pai-ma-ssu were discovered before and during World War II, and it has been reported that the heart-and-hand patterned bronze sword is characteristic of the Pai-ma-ssu burials[81] (fig. 211). Sand-tempered brown pottery similar to that of the Chia-ling-chiang sites is found at Ch'ing-yang-kung site in Ch'eng-tu, where a bronze knife, oracle bones, and turtleshells were also reported.[82] Generally speaking, however, the Warring States period cultural remains at Ch'ing-yang-kung indicate certain similarities to—or, more probably, continuities from—the period represented by the Shui-kuan-yin locality. The site outside the southern city gate of Ch'eng-tu was secondary burial, in association with which were pottery, some bronze vessels, weapons, and implements. Among the weapons is a type of *ko*, triangular in shape and having a tiger-head decoration, which is one of the most characteristic types of artifacts in the Ch'eng-tu area.[83]

81. Wei Chü-hsien, *Shuo-wen yüeh-k'an* 3 (1941), 1–29.
82. *KK* 1959 (8), 411–14.
83. *Ibid.*, pp. 449–50.

The Warring States burials at Yang-tzu-shan, north of the Ch'eng-tu city, were intrusive into, and hence subsequent in time to, the ceremonial square platform described above. A tomb, no. 172, that has been described in published reports, is of the usual Warring States type, with rectangular pit, wooden chamber, and a wooden coffin. The burial goods include gray pottery, bronze vessels, weapons, implements, mirrors, belt hooks, seals, horse and chariot fittings, lacquers, jades, precious ornaments, glass beads, and an iron tripod. Most of these are of the typical Warring States types seen in North China. It is, nevertheless, of particular interest that among the findings many characteristic features recall the Ch'u civilization to the east, such as the "bronze sword with jade-decorated handle, the t'ao-t'ieh pattern on the feet of the big ting tripods, the yen steamers divided into two parts, the shape and decor of the bronze lei, the decorative patterns of bronze spearheads and lacquer boxes, and the gold- and silver-inlaid decorative designs.[84] Furthermore, some features of this assemblage are said to have local characteristics: the shape of the pottery urns, the bronze vessel handles with stranded-cord designs, the white cement used to attach the gold and silver pieces of the inlay designs, the lack of any attempt to achieve symmetry in the decor, the bas-relief animals on the belt hooks, and the distinctive writing system. On the other hand, some decorative motifs, such as the moth-antenna pattern, find close relatives in the Dongson culture to the south. On the whole, the Yang-tzu-shan burial exhibits its Szechwan characteristics, but an increasingly strong influence of North Chinese traditions upon the native civilization is indicated toward the end of the Warring States period.

To the west of both of these two groups—Chia-ling-chiang and Ch'eng-tu—there was another cultural tradition, beginning no later than the final phases of the Chan-kuo period. This is represented by the finds at Li-fan (or Fan) and Kan-tzu in westernmost Szechwan, the region that begins to climb uphill toward the Tibetan plateau. At Li-fan, a large group of slab tombs (cists of slates) was excavated during World War II and in 1964, and from the burials pottery, bronzes, iron, glass beads, and coins were brought to light.[85] The interesting and instructive point concerning the Li-fan slab tombs is that among the grave goods cultural influences from more than a single direction are discernible. Contacts with the Chinese civilization of late Eastern Chou and Ch'in and Han dynasties are indicated by Chinese inscriptions (of the styles of the various

84. KKHP 1956 (4), 19.
85. KKHP 1973 (2), 41–59.

stages) and many types of pottery and bronze artifacts, including *pan-liang* and *wu-shu* coins.[86] On the other hand, cultural contacts with Kansu, directly north, are shown by some ceramic features, particularly the flat-bottomed jars with two large, vertical loop handles and the concave bottom of several jars "which [were hollowed out] with a sharp implement, probably of bamboo, when the paste was still wet,"[87] both of which recall the Hsin-tien ceramics described in the previous chapter. Moreover, the so-called Ordos bronze features are very strongly represented in (1) the large numbers of weapons and armor, which indicate the prevalence of close combat; (2) the small artifacts such as bells, buttons, tubes, rings, and plates; (3) the bronze kettles; (4) the dotted designs; and (5) the animal style represented by a bronze ring with three birds in relief. Glass beads, according to Cheng, suggest indirect contacts with western Asia via the steppe nomads. A group of similar bronze artifacts, among which the horse fittings are outstanding, has been found farther west, in the area of Kan-tzu.[88] This area of Li-fan and Kan-tzu is now inhabited by the Ch'iang people whose legends relate that a slate-tomb building people, called the Ko, occupied the region before the Ch'iang came.[89] These Ko may have been farmers, as Cheng suggests, but apparently their settlements were mobile and mounted warfare prevailed. This region is separated from the steppe nomads by a great expanse of land which was occupied by the farming peoples of Kansu during its "Aeneolithic" stage. Whether there were direct connections between the Li-fan region and the steppe, or whether any such connections were by way of the Chinese civilization, cannot be determined for certain until the intervening regions are better known archaeologically.

It is evident that these three groups of Warring States period cultures in Szechwan represent two principal cultural traditions. With the Li-fan and Kan-tzu finds being placed in a separate category, the Warring States period civilizations of both the Chia-ling-chiang and the Ch'eng-tu groups were probably the development of a single local culture, with intensive influences from North China and from the Ch'u of the middle Yangtze. Cheng Te-k'un points out that "Szechwan is fundamentally a

86. An iron object collected from a Li-fan slab tomb by Ling Shun-sheng of the Academia Sinica was sent to the Yale Radiocarbon Laboratory for age determination; it yielded a date of 2130 ± 100 B.P. (180 ± 100 B.C.). See Nicholaas van der Merwe, *Carbon-14 Dating of Iron*, p. 97.

87. Cheng Te-k'un, *Harvard Jour. Asiatic Studies* 9 (1946), 67.

88. An Chih-min, *KKTH* 1958 (1), 62–63.

89. Cheng Te-k'un. *Harvard Jour. Asiatic Studies* 9 (1946), 77.

marginal area, and the culture of this province had never been a result of independent development. It has always been under the influence of some neighboring culture."[90] Applied to the Warring States period, this statement must not be taken literally, for the many distinctively local stylistic characteristics make it hard to believe that all the Szechwan civilizations were nothing but imports from central and North China. Although the bronze and iron implements and weapons in this region closely follow North Chinese prototypes, they were apparently modified to conform to local beliefs, usages, and traditions. The hand-and-heart design, the characteristic writing and other decorative symbols on weapons, the tiger as a favorite decorative motif, the distinctive types of willow-leaf-shaped bronze swords and the circular-socketed *yüeh* axes, the triangular *ko* halberds, the bridge-shaped bronze "coins," the bronze seals with undeciphered signs,[91] and the boat burials and cliff burials (which have been found dating to the Han dynasty, but must have had a pre-Han background), all testify to the fact that the civilization of Szechwan had a distinctive and original spirit that is more than a mere imitation of North China prototypes, let alone a full-scale importation. Eastern Chou and Han literature refers to the ancient peoples dwelling in the Red Basin as the Pa and the Shu peoples; according to *Hua-yang-kuo chih*, compiled during the Chin dynasty, the Pa territory was in the eastern part of Szechwan, and the Shu territory in the western part, coinciding with the division made above into the Chia-ling-chiang and the Ch'eng-tu subareas, although a positive identification must await further findings and more precisely dated discoveries. To be sure, the Chia-ling-chiang and the Ch'eng-tu groups were probably only slightly different phases of the same cultural tradition, but nevertheless some differences can be enumerated between these two subareas. For instance, the circular-socket *yüeh* ax is relatively rare in the Ch'eng-tu area, but the same area is abundant in the triangular shaped *ko* halberds and in bird designs as decorative motifs, which are scarcely represented at all in the Chia-ling-chiang boat burials.[92] Feng Han-chi has convincingly shown that the Chia-ling and the Ch'eng-tu *ko* and swords can be distinguished by some minute and distinctive differences.[93] As a cultural complex, boat burials have so far not been found west of the Chia-ling Valley. Moreover, the eastern division of the Szech-

90. *Archaeological Studies in Szechwan*, p. xix.
91. *KK* 1959 (8), 439.
92. *KKHP* 1958 (2), 94.
93. *WW* 1961 (11), 33.

wan civilization appears to continue into the area of Hupei, and its relation with the Ch'u must have been highly intimate. Boat burials, for instance, have been recorded widely in the historical documents of South China, particularly the Ch'u and the Yüeh areas.[94] On the other hand, the western division of the Szechwan civilization shares with the contemporary civilization of Yunnan (Tien and the Dongsonian) many decorative motifs and implement types, as well as the kettledrum. This does not mean that the east-west subdivision of the Szechwan civilizations of the Chan-kuo period was clearly demarcated. Szechwan civilization as a whole shared with both the Ch'u and the Tien many stylistic characteristics. This civilization, furthermore, must have had a complex political organiza-tion and a sophisticated social stratification approaching the levels of a state structure. Throughout this civilization, the tiger played a prominent ritualistic role. In *Hou Han shu*, in the "Biography of the Southern Man," a story relates that when the paramount chief of the Pa died, his soul was reincarnated as a white tiger, and that the people made offerings of human victims to him, believing that tigers ate human blood. If this story was indeed that of the Szechwan people of that time, which is likely in view of the prevalence of tiger motifs in their civilization, it gives us an idea of some political and religious institutions existing among them at that time. Historical books say that the Pa-Shu civilization came under the control of the state of Ch'in in 329 B.C., over a century before the emperor of Ch'in conquered the whole of China, but the distinctive civilization of Szechwan apparently persisted, in quite undisturbed form, into the Ch'in and early Han dynasties until the time when the Han style of brick tombs appeared widely in the province.

Early Civilizations in Yunnan

Farther upstream along the Yangtze from the Red Basin is the high hilly plateau country of the Chin-sha-chiang valley, drained by the upper reaches of the Yangtze, the Red, and the Mekong rivers, where the modern provinces of Szechwan and Yunnan meet (fig. 212). This country, in-habited by Neolithic peoples as late as the first millennium B.C., was open to cultural influences from at least three sources besides the south: the Yüeh and the Ch'u civilizations to the east, which could gain access to this area via the Pearl River; the Pa-Shu civilization of Szechwan, a little way down the Yangtze; and the Li-fan and Kan-tzu hilly country to the

94. Ling Shun-sheng, *BIHP* 23 (1951), 639–64.

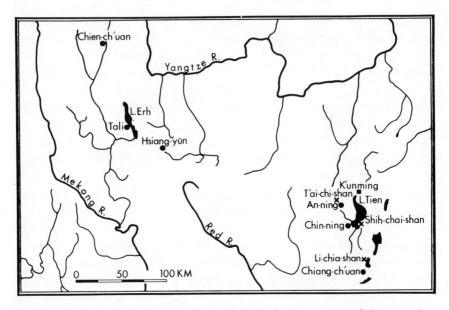

212. Bronze Age sites in Yunnan: *circles*, towns whereby sites are identified; *crosses*, sites located in villages or separately; *square*, capital of Yunnan.

north, which connects this area with the steppe zone in the far north. Since these last regions had no highly developed civilizations themselves until the Eastern Chou period, Yunnan was not exposed to the influence of the Shang and early Chou cultures. Archaeological evidence of any such influences, direct or indirect, is completely lacking.

The available archaeological record shows that civilization apparently came to Yunnan during the latter part of the Eastern Chou period, simultaneously with irrigated farming and the use of iron implements. In this connection, Wu Chin-ting's investigations during 1938–40 in Ta-li Hsien, in the Lake Erh and Tien-ts'ang Mountain area of western Yunnan a little way below the Chin-sha-chiang, are highly important.[95] At the site of Ma-lung, a protracted occupation by prehistoric inhabitants has been brought to light. During the period when the site was continuously inhabited by people of the same cultural tradition, a major change occurred which divided the culture of this site into two stages: the first is the Neolithic culture described in chapter 5; the second, although a continuation of the same cultural tradition, is marked by the simultaneous appearance of terraced fields, construction of water ditches—probably for irrigation

95. Wu Chin-ting et al., *Yünnan Ts'ang Erh ching k'ao-ku pao-kao*, Lichuang, National Museum, 1942.

purposes—construction of mud village walls, growing use of potters' wheels, and use of both bronze and iron as shown by remains of bronze objects, an iron fragment, and an iron sickle. This discovery, which has never received the recognition it deserves, is important in giving a basis for dating the appearance of metallurgy and irrigation in the area of Yunnan, and it suggests that societal changes (such as the beginning of fortification and the intensification of industrial specialization) were concurrent with the appearance of metallurgy and irrigation. The full implication of the latter innovations can be realized in two recently discovered sites, one in Chien-ch'uan, north of Ta-li, and the other in Hsiang-yün, south of Ta-li, both in the general area of Lake Erh.

A habitation site discovered in 1957 at Chien-ch'uan, between the Chin-sha-chiang valley and Lake Erh in northwestern Yunnan, is a pile village, built along the Hai-wei River, half on the bank, the other half submerged. Remains of agricultural implements and grains of rice, wheat, and millet were found, together with a large number of mollusk shells, animal bones, and fishhooks. Implements were mainly made of stone, including axes, adzes, sickles, chisels, scrapers, arrowheads, awls, spindle whorls, and grinding stones. Pottery is of the local Neolithic tradition, but the percentage of striking Lungshanoid types, such as lustrous black pottery, ring-footed vessels, high-stemmed *tou*, and perforated ring feet, is remarkably large for this area. Fourteen copper artifacts were found at the site, including axes, knives, chisels, rings, fishhooks, and ornaments, all hammered except for the axes, which were cast.[96] This site can be classified as essentially Neolithic in character, but it represents the first step taken by the early Yunnan civilization to achieve a full-fledged metal culture. A piece of wood found here has yielded a radiocarbon date of 3010 ± 90 B.P.[97] calibrated to 1480–1170 B.C.

At Ta-p'o-na Commune in Hsiang-yün, southeast of Ta-li, a burial area was discovered in 1961. A tomb, excavated in 1964, proved to be a rectangular pit grave, 4 meters deep, 7.5 by 2.5 meters at the mouth, and 7 by 2.2 meters at the bottom. A wooden chamber, about 3.75 by 1.85 meters in size, was built at the bottom of the pit from large timber posts and was plastered on the outside with a layer of very sticky, white limy clay. Inside the chamber was a bronze coffin, assembled from seven pieces, in the shape of a house with a gabled roof, standing on twelve short legs. The entire exterior of the coffin was cast with decorative patterns, those

96. *KKTH* 1958 (6), 5–12.
97. *KK* 1972 (5), 57–58.

213. A bronze coffin at Ta-p'o-na, in Hsiang-yün, Yunnan. (From *KK* 1964, no. 12, pp. 608–09.)

on the roof and the side walls were composed of geometric elements and those on the two walls at the ends consisted of various animal forms such as falcons, swallows, tigers, leopards, wild boars, deer, horses, and water birds (fig. 213). The coffin contained only a bronze stick and several pieces of limb bones; in the chamber and in the fill were found more than a hundred pieces of bronze artifacts and a few gray and orange sandy sherds. The bronzes included implements (hoes and plow blades, axes, knives); weapons (spearheads, swords, picks, fan-shaped axes, spear ends); vessels (*tsun* goblets, cups, dibbles, fruit stands, a cooking pot); spoons and two pairs of chopsticks; musical instruments (a kettledrum, two gourd-shaped *sheng*, a bell); models of houses, cattle, horses, sheep, pigs, dogs, and chickens; ornaments; and other miscellaneous items.[98]

Compared with the Chien-ch'uan site, the Ta-p'o-na bronze coffin indicates a far more advanced bronze-making culture; the casting of the coffin itself must have involved a complex metallurgical process. On the other hand, iron artifacts have not been found here, and the composition of the bronze artifacts appears to be uneven, uncontrolled, and less than effective (table 16), suggesting a more primitive stage of metal civilization

98. *KK* 1964 (12), 607–14.

Table 16

Percentage of Metals in Selected Ta-p'o-na Bronze Coffin Artifacts

	Copper	*Tin*	*Lead*	*Iron*
Coffin	89.60	5.02	2.25	
Hoe	92.77	0.19		
Adz	94.20	3.71		0.20
Spearhead	93.79	2.35	0.62	
Cooking pot	93.25			
Spoon	84.13	13.69		
Bell	79.96	16.34	trace	
Kettledrum	87.96	6.87	3.46	0.64
Gourd *sheng*	97.63	1.32	0.52	
Ring	79.60	14.75	2.89	
Horse figurine	93.80	1.92	1.12	

than the Shih-chai-shan finds to be described below. The culture must have been one with advanced agriculture and domesticated animals. The tomb construction (pit grave with a wooden chamber), some of the bronze vessel types (*tou* and bell), and the use of chopsticks are within the Chinese tradition of the Shang and Chou periods, but the form of the house, bronze kettledrum, the fan-shaped axes, and the decorative art characterize an essentially indigenous civilization, possibly antecedent to the Shih-chai-shan culture of eastern Yunnan. It is regarded as the culture of the K'un-ming people[99] or one of the Mi-mo tribes[100] described in *Shih chi* for the area of the southwest, and it has been placed within the middle Eastern Chou period.[101]

The sites in the area of Lake Erh of northwestern Yunnan have already shown a sequence of development of the Bronze Age civilization in Yunnan from the most primitive to more advanced, but the climax of this civilization occurred in the southeastern part of the province in the area of Lake Tien, not far from northern Vietnam, the country of the classical Bronze Age site at Dong-son. Bronze remains suggestive of Dong-son types have been known from various localities in Yunnan for a long time,[102] but few scholars were prepared for the truly spectacular finds

99. *Ibid.*, p. 614.

100. *KK* 1966 (1), 45, 46–48.

101. *KK* 1965 (9), 478–79.

102. Komai Kazuchika, "On stone implements and bronze artifacts of South China," in *Lectures on Anthropological and Prehistoric Topics*, vol. 19 (1940), Tokyo.

in the cemetery at Shih-chai-shan, in Chin-ning, and burial sites of the same culture in An-ning and Chiang-ch'uan, on and near the shores of Lake Tien. Shih-chai-shan, a small, low hill (about 20 meters high), is between Lake Tien to the west and the city of Chin-ning to the east. A Bronze Age cemetery was found on the eastern part of the hilltop, and four seasons of excavation were carried out between 1955 and 1960 by the Yunnan Provincial Museum. Thirty-four individual tombs were opened, and over four thousand pieces of artifacts have been brought to light.[103] A summary of the findings and their culture and society are given in table 17.

Table 17

Summary of the Tien Culture at Shih-chai-shan, Yunnan

Tombs: Mostly oriented E–W, with the head pointing to the east; simple earthen pits, without a regular plane, sometimes outlined by naturally placed rocks. When the body and grave goods were in place, the pit was filled with the dug-out earth or sandy earth mixed with pebbles. One tomb has fire-hardened walls, a wooden chamber, and an *erh-ts'eng-t'ai.* Remains of wooden coffins covered with lacquer and wrapped with cloths have been found in some graves.

Implements: Of the 706 implements reported in May 1959, 558 are bronzes, 92 iron, 43 stone, and 13 clay (spindle whorls). The bronze implements include 21 plows, 23 spades, 1 saw, 108 axes, 11 adzes, 23 chisels, 5 sickles, 26 knives, and a cylindrical object probably used for collecting mollusks. According to some depictions of the plow on the bronzes (fig. 214), it was probably hafted onto a bent wooden handle with a small crossbar at the end. One or two men pulled the plow with a rope, and another pushed from behind. The biggest plow found weighs 750 grams and is 29 cm long by 20 cm wide. Iron implements include adzes, axes (iron-edged), and knives.

Subsistence and Handicrafts: Agriculture was apparently practiced. Cattle, sheep, dogs, horses, chickens, and pigs are depicted in the decorative and plastic art;

103. *Yün-nan Chin-ning Shih-chai-shan ku mu ch'ün fa-chüeh pao-kao,* Peking, Wen Wu Press, 1959. *WW* 1959 (5), 59–61; 1975 (2), 69–81. *KK* 1959 (9), 459–61; 1963 (9), 480–85. For a perceptive analysis of the Shih-chai-shan art in terms of the ethnic components of the culture and the various ritual observances, see Feng Han-chi, *KK* 1961 (9), 469–87, 490; and 1963 (6), 319–29. English summaries of the remains of the site are available in Richard C. Rudolph, *AP* 4 (1960), 41–49; and Magdalene von Dewall, *Antiquity* 41 (1967), 8–21. A study in French, with extensive translations, is Michèle Pirazzoli-t'Serstevens, *La civilisation du royaume de Dian a l'époque Han,* Publications de l'Ecole française d'extrême-Orient, 1974.

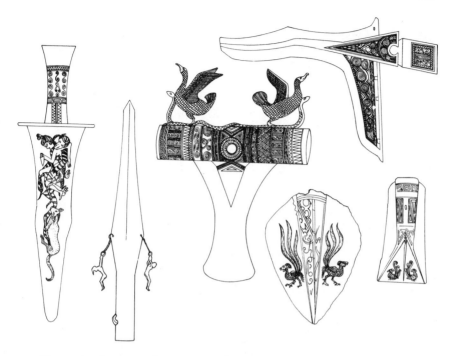

214. Bronze implements and weapons at the Tien site at Shih-chai-shan, Chin-ning, Yunnan. (From *Hsing Chung-kuo ti k'ao-ku shou-huo*, Peking, Wen Wu Press, 1962, p. 90.)

horses were used for riding and warfare, and cattle probably only ceremonially and for meat. Hunting with dogs was carried on. Handicrafts were highly developed, as shown by the wine ware, finely made bronzes, iron metallurgy, opal work, and leatherwork.

Trade and Currency: Hundreds of thousands of cowrie shells were found in drum-shaped containers. Plastic market scenes depicted the exchange of cattle and food (fig. 215). Some of the coins, mirrors, lacquers, crossbows, *ko* halberds, arrowheads, and *chi* halberds were identical with North China types of Eastern Chou and Han periods and were probably imports.

Weaving: A plastic bronze model shows a type of horizontal loom now widely seen in Southeast Asia. Hemp was probably cultivated.

Utensils: Sophisticated sets of daily utensils, of pottery or bronze.

Habitation: Pile dwellings, shown in plastic bronze models, have two stories (upper level for inhabitants and lower level for domestic animals) and thatched roofs (fig. 216).

Social Stratification: Three social classes are distinguished by the excavators

215. Market scene cast in the round on the top of a bronze vessel from a Tien tomb at Shih-chai-shan. (From *Yün-nan Chin-ning Shih-chai-shan ku mu ch'ün fa-chüeh pao-kao,* Peking, Wen Wu Press, 1959.)

according to the hairstyles and dresses of the human figurines in the plastic bronze models:

1. Aristocracy and the rich, the "owners of the cowrie shells." One of the tomb masters was particularly wealthy; he was accompanied by a *pien* bell set, jade objects, bronze *ting* tripod, four cowrie-shell containers, and a gold seal with four Chinese characters inscribed: *Tien Wang chih yin* (the Seal of King of Tien). Women apparently enjoyed higher status than men, or at least had special deference shown them, such as being carried sitting on stools, as is seen in the plastic bronze models.

2. Freemen, the commoners of the same group, serving as managers.

3. Slaves.

216. A ritual scene cast in the round on the top of a bronze vessel from a Tien tomb at Shih-chai-shan. (From *Yün-nan Chin-ning Shih-chai-shan ku mu ch'ün fa-chueh pao-kao*, Peking, Wen Wu Press, 1959.)

217. Battle scene cast in the round on the top of a bronze vessel from a Tien tomb at Shih-chai-shan. (From *Yün-nan Chin-ning Shih-chai-shan ku mu ch'ün fa-chüeh pao-kao*, Peking, Wen Wu Press, 1959.)

Warfare: A large number of weapons (fig. 214) is found, including some iron types. Most were of bronze, including 214 swords, 299 spearheads, 14 crossbows, and 266 arrowheads. Iron was used only to make swords, and these were protected by gold sheaths. Warfare is also depicted in plastic models, which show mounted horsemen and headhunters (fig. 217). Horse-and-chariot fittings of bronze are also abundantly represented.

Luxuries: Ornaments and objects of gold, silver, jade, opal, turquoise, and lacquerware.

Rituals: Many ritual scenes are depicted in bronze plastic models; e.g. one in which a pillar, with a snake coiling around it and a tiger at the top, is surrounded by people killing human victims. Several others show the ceremonial killing of cattle. Bronze kettledrums, many of which were found, figured importantly in rituals, as shown in figure 216. Some ritual participants wore feathered plumes,

218. Boats in the decorative scenes of the Shih-chai-shan bronzes. (From *WW* 1964, no. 12, p. 44.)

such as the cattle killer and the dancers. Priests and/or shamans played musical instruments, made gestures, and danced. The wooden boat (fig. 218) was another important element of the rituals. Cattle and peacocks apparently had some special ritualistic significance.

Art: The bronzes display extremely sophisticated decorative art, in plane or plastic forms. Dancing was probably part of the rituals. Musical instruments included bronze kettledrums, *sheng* panpipes, flutes, and *pien* bells.

A detailed account of the Shih-chai-shan culture is possible because the finds of representative art are abundant, and archaeologists can read, rather than interpret, the life of a people depicted in the bronze art. This pictorial account represents a lengthy period of occupation during which cultural changes occurred. The excavators have been able to distinguish four classes of tombs, which can be grouped into three stages. The first stage, probably dated to the late Chan-kuo period and the beginning of the Western Han, has relatively few iron implements, and no Chinese coins or other imported artifacts such as the mirrors, belt hooks, and bronze utensils which came later. The second stage, which can probably be dated by the Chinese coins to between 175 and 118 B.C., witnessed a growing incidence of mirrors, iron axes, and swords, and bronze implements made in the Chinese style. The third stage is dated by Chinese coins to late Western Han and early Eastern Han.[104]

Across the lake from Shih-chai-shan is another burial site of the same culture—T'ai-chi-shan, located west of the town of An-ning.[105] Seventeen tombs, all of the rectangular pit-grave type, were found. Most of the grave

104. *Yün-nan Chin-ning Shih-chai-shan ku mu ch'ün fa-chüeh pao-kao*, p. 133.

105. *KK* 1965 (9), 451–58. See M. von Dewall, *Antiquity* 41 (1967), 8–21, for a description and analysis of the site.

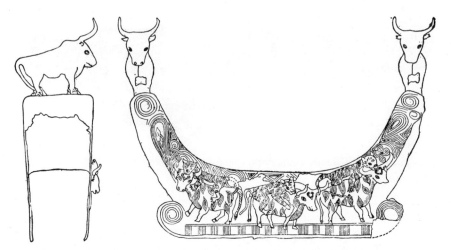

219. Bronze pillow from a Li-chia-shan tomb, Chiang-ch'uan, Yunnan. (From *KKHP* 1975, no. 2, p. 131.)

goods are pottery, but thirty-two bronze and iron implements of the Shih-chai-shan type also came to light. Much less lavishly furnished, the T'ai-chi-shan cemetery may have been the resting place of lesser noblemen or even commoners, in contrast to the kingly tombs of Shih-chai-shan, and it is therefore significant for its more balanced and complete depiction of the Tien civilization.

Over forty kilometers to the south of Shih-chai-shan near the town of Chiang-ch'uan and on the northern shore of a smaller lake, Lake Hsing-yün, another cemetery of the same period was found in 1966 on Li-chia-shan. Excavations in 1972 disclosed twenty-seven burials and more than a thousand archaeological objects. The burials are grouped into three types. The first, twenty-two tombs in all, was confined to the top of the hill and its surroundings, and the tombs contain characteristically Shih-chai-shan types of artifacts—drums, bronze pillows (fig. 219), shell containers, and so forth (figs. 220, 221). The second and third types, found on the slopes, did not contain the Shih-chai-shan types but yielded many tools, weapons, horse fittings, belt hooks, mirrors, and crossbow mechanisms of Han types. The excavators place the tombs of the first type from late Warring States period to early Western Han, and those of the second and third types from middle Western Han to early Eastern Han. Among the tombs of the first type, the quality and quantity of the grave furnishings vary sharply, indicating a stratified society of the Shih-chai-shan order.[106]

106. *WW* 1972 (8), 7–15. *KKHP* 1975 (2), 97–156

220. Bronze armor plates from a Li-chia-shan tomb, Chiang-ch'uan, Yunnan. (From *KKHP* 1975, no. 2, p. 121.)

221. Bronze stick terminal with human figure, from a Li-chia-shan tomb, Chiang-ch'uan, Yunnan. (From *KKHP* 1975, no. 2, pl. 20.)

The importance of the Shih-chai-shan, T'ai-chi-shan, and Li-chia-shan discoveries can hardly be over-emphasized. Their proximity to the classical site of Dong-son on the Gulf of Tonkin[107] and the many stylistic similarities that these three sites share indicate without question that they represent the same culture, characterized by the following stylistic elements: bronze kettledrums; fan-shaped and boot-shaped bronze axes; plastic bronze art as a decorative adjunct to ceremonial objects, artifacts of high prestige value (e.g., heads for sticks and tops of cowrie-shell containers), and similar weapon forms; cattle and peacocks as favorite decorative motifs, with ceremonial implications; and certain other distinctive decorative motifs such as connected concentric circles, whorls, moth-antenna designs, and S-shaped patterns.[108] In terms of society and

107. O. R. T. Janse, *Archaeological Research in Indo-China*, vol. 3, *The Ancient Dwelling-site of Dong-son (Thanh-Hoa, Annam)*, Bruges, Institut belge des hautes études chinoises, 1958.

108. K. C. Chang *BIE* 7 (1959), 56. Kobayashi Tomowo, *Kōkōgaku-zasshi* 26 (1936), 701–18.

economy, there is no question that the Dong-son culture had a highly sophisticated and stratified society and intensive industrial specialization. On the other hand, it seems to have had no writing, and the dwelling sites that have been found show no evidence of mature urbanization.

This highly developed civilization was apparently centered in Yunnan and the northern part of Indochina, but its influence was widely felt. Bronze drums have been found or recorded in most of South China,[109] including the regions of the Ch'u and the Pa-Shu civilizations, and Don-sonian elements have been identified from a large part of Southeast Asia.[110] The discovery at Shih-chai-shan, furthermore, shows that the initial stimulation which brought about the emergence of this civilization in Yunnan was mainly from the areas of Ch'u and Szechwan toward the end of the Eastern Chou period, approximately the fourth and fifth centuries B.C. Many bronze elements in the Shih-chai-shan cemetery also indicate direct influence from the Li-fan and Kan-tzu group of Eastern Chou and early Han bronzes, such as the vivid animal style of art depicted in small, single-motif art objects. Heine-Geldern believes that the Dong-son owed its impetus directly to the western Asian and European Bronze Age and Iron Age cultures.[111] The Li-fan and Kan-tzu group of Szechwan civilizations, however, certainly provided the immediate sources for any supposedly western Asian elements in the Dong-son culture, and a recently discovered group of slab burials in Te-ch'in in extreme northwestern Yunnan[112] brings the Li-fan type of culture into Yunnan itself.

General Conclusions

South China's prehistory and early history are full of intriguing problems; with the cultural framework outlined in chapter 5 and in the present chapter, many specific questions remain to be answered and a good many details of tremendous historical significance deserve more extensive

109. Ling Shun-sheng, *Bull. College of Arts, Nat'l. Taiwan Univ.*, no. 1, 1950. *KK* 1965 (1), 31–39. *WW* 1974 (1), 51–61. *KKHP* 1974 (1), 45–90.

110. H. R. Heekeren, *The Bronze-Iron Age of Indonesia*, The Hague, Martinus Nijhoff, 1958. R. J. Pearson, *BIE* 13 (1962), 27 ff. An etched carnelian bead found at Shih-chai-shan may even suggest trade or other connections with the Near East; see Hsia Nai, *KK* 1974 (6), 382–85.

111. Robert von Heine-Geldern, *Saeculum* 2 (1951), 225–55; and *Paideuma* 5 (1954), 347–423. See also his "Some tribal art styles of Southeast Asia: An experiment in art history," in Douglas Fraser, ed., *The Many Faces of Primitive Art*, Englewood Cliffs, Prentice-Hall, 1966, pp. 161–221.

112. *KK* 1975 (4), 244–48.

treatment than the space here can afford. In concluding the discussion of the emergence of civilizations in South China, a few paragraphs should now be devoted to this area as a whole, pulling together the fragmentary information given above to show the general tendency of its cultural development during the Shang and Chou periods of North China and the patterns involved in the process.

Attention must once more be directed to the native cultures of South China, which interacted with the influences from the Bronze Age and Early Iron Age civilizations of the Huang Ho valley to produce the civilizatons of this area. Two main cultural traditions played important parts in South China—the Lungshanoid farmers in eastern South China, and the southwestern Neolithic cultures in Szechwan and Yunnan. The Lungshanoid, as mentioned before, was probably a mixture of several cultural origins, among them the Ta-p'en-k'eng culture of the southeastern coastal area, the Yang-shao culture of North China, and perhaps the Ch'ing-lien-kang culture of the eastern seaboard. The southwestern Neolithic probably developed on the southwestern Mesolithic and sub-Neolithic base, perhaps in part under the Lungshanoid influence.

By the Lung-shan periods of the Neolithic, several areas of South China saw the interrelated rise of civilizations, which were largely confined to the middle and lower Yangtze Valley and the Huai Ho valley. State organizations came into being toward the end of this stage in the Huai Ho valley and probably in the middle and lower Yangtze, and late Western Chou and early Eastern Chou impacts probably reached as far south as the Chekiang Valley. Throughout eastern South China the introduction of metallurgy and the bronze and pottery arts of the Shang and Chou styles helped bring about the formation of the Geometric horizon.

By the Eastern Chou period, various southern states emerged on the basis of the earlier civilizations of the area, at least in part as a result of the Eastern Chou expansion, but they were subsequently incorporated, one after another, into the Ch'in and Han. The Eastern Chou expansion into South China was closely linked to the internal changes taking place in North China itself. Archaeological materials from the Eastern Chou states of South China indicate that iron implements were found from the begin-of these civilizations along with bronze implements, although the latter were far more abundant in most regions. The evidence from Ch'u and from Ta-li in Yunnan further suggests that the Eastern Chou expansion was probably also linked with the increased use of irrigation. It is thus apparent that the Eastern Chou civilization of North China not only changed its structure in its homeland but expanded geographically toward the north and the south.

The South China Neolithic cultures—already in Shang and early Chou times stimulated toward an intensive internal growth in some regions—swiftly grew into a metal-age culture under the suddenly accelerated impacts of the Eastern Chou of North China. In some regions, such as the Ch'u and Yüeh, where previous contacts with Shang and Western Chou were frequent and considerable, there were probably transitional stages between village and state, and upon this basis state organizations and a literate civilization flowered during the Eastern Chou period. In other regions, such as Yunnan, the Eastern Chou civilization found a primarily Neolithic base. With the sudden burst of metal culture and sophisticated art, these cultures were apparently boosted to a level approaching that of the great civilizations, but at the societal level these civilizations lacked urbanism and writing. The precise form of the Pa-Shu civilizations in terms of such typological classifications is not clear at the moment.

In addition to typological differences among the southern civilizations in the Eastern Chou period, there are also stylistic differences which may serve, among other things, in making cultural groupings. Many common cultural characteristics are found throughout South China, in contrast to the north, which may indicate that the southern civilizations contained some unifying factors, many of which were apparently the result of similar ecological adjustments to a similar natural environment, but some of which probably indicate a certain degree of historical connection. Common features in South China include, for instance, pile dwellings, rice cultivation, the tubular borer, burial in boats and on cliffs, and bronze kettledrums. Distribution of these and other traits, however, suggests that there were actually parallel cultural traditions rather than a single cultural area in South China during this time interval, and that the widespread occurrence of certain characteristic features was the result of cultural contacts or similar ecological conditions. At least the following different cultural traditions can be distinguished among the Eastern Chou civilizations in South China:

1. Wu and Yüeh: in the eastern and southern coastal areas
2. Ch'u: in the middle Yangtze and the western Huai Ho valley
3. Pa-Shu: in the Red Basin of Szechwan
4. The Li-fan and Kan-tzu assemblages of westernmost Szechwan
5. The Tien and related civilizations of Yunnan

The stylistic characteristics of these traditions have been enumerated above, and repetition is not necessary. The powerful expansion of the

Ch'in and Han empires brought all these cultural traditions under the same political system and civilization, but in different areas the actual process of assimilation, as well as its rate and tempo, apparently differed. These different traditions also had dissimilar relations with cultures and civilizations in areas outside of China. Historical and modern non-Han Chinese ethnic groups have claimed descent from the various cultural traditions of the Eastern Chou period. Discussions of these problems must be left out of the present volume, but there is material here for many future studies which could make significant contributions to our knowledge of the cultural history of Southeast Asia.

Conclusions and Prospect

The year 221 B.C. has been chosen as a terminal date for the present study of ancient Chinese archaeology for two reasons. First, the year marked the unification of China under Shih Huang Ti, the first emperor of the Ch'in dynasty (fig. 222), and the consolidation of the Chinese as a single people with a single culture and a sense of common nationality. The various local cultures which flourished in different parts of China up to this time were from the formative stage of Chinese civilization. Second, we find that for the various cultures before the Ch'in and the Han dynasties, either no historical record was kept at all or the historical documents that survive are fragmentary and far from complete. The basic data for a study of the culture, society, and history of prehistoric and early historic China are provided by archaeology. It is true that for a complete history of the Shang and Chou dynasties, literary records would have to be utilized to a far greater extent than has been done in this book, which includes them only when they render archaeological data more meaningful. But these historical documents have been neglected for other considered reasons. The data for the same periods from literary sources are readily available in many good books already in existence. The writing of a book which uses both historical and archaeological materials to the full may be highly desirable, but it cannot be undertaken at a time when the archaeological data, much made available only in very recent years, still need processing and interpretation. Moreover, archaeology and history, by virtue of their different source materials, tend to stress different aspects of the same cultural history, and the present book supplements rather than overlaps the works on ancient Chinese history that have made use of literary sources.

This book has thus presented a cultural historical framework within which most of the available archaeological data from the area of China can be interpreted. We have seen that human beginnings in China may now be pushed back to the lower Pleistocene, more than a million years ago, but good archaeological evidence begins with Peking man, Lan-t'ien

222. Tumulus at the tomb of Ch'in Shih Huang Ti in Lin-t'ung, Shensi. (Photo by author, 1975.)

man, and their contemporaries at the beginning of the middle Pleistocene, who are now shown to be capable of using fire and fashioning stone implements of some sophistication and variety. During the upper Pleistocene, perhaps fifty thousand years ago, modern man (*Homo sapiens*) appeared on the Chinese stage with a lithic industry that was so specialized it was capable of being adopted for efficient use in a variety of natural environments. This in turn led to a stage of culture, toward the end of the Ice Age, about ten thousand years or so ago, in which a great number of natural food sources were apparently tapped to provide a highly diversified diet.

The first agriculture in China, as elsewhere, evidently emerged in such a cultural stage. When, for one reason or another, exploitative activities were stepped up and more of each of the food sources was consumed, it was probably soon found that some sources were exhaustible more quickly than others and that productivity could be increased in some areas of nature by means of additional efforts or artificial modifications. Food plants were undoubtedly among those sources to which man could lend a hand. Being familiar with the nature of each of the wild food plants in their natural habitat, the first farmers are thought to be those Palaeolithic people who learned to manipulate some of the food plants to increase their productivity and who then came to rely more and more on these plants than on other sources of food.

It is probable that agriculture began essentially in this fashion, but quite independently, among the latest Palaeolithic hunter-fisher-gatherers of many parts of the world. In any event, the inhabitants of any region must learn to manipulate the native plants of that region to cross their own agricultural threshold. In the area of China, two agricultural centers may be discerned in the archaeological record of the early postglacial period, one the nuclear area of North China (east-central Shensi, southern Shansi, northern Honan) and the other the southeastern coastal area (Fukien, Taiwan, Kwangtung). The former, home of the Yang-shao culture, is characterized by its cultivation of millets (*Setaria* and *Panicum*), and the latter, home of the Ta-p'en-k'eng culture and its related manifestations (which possibly extended southwestward into Southeast Asia), is thought to have initiated the cultivation of many root and tuber crops, such as taro and yam, as well as a number of fruits. A possible third center, located in the lower Yangtze and the Huai Ho plain, is manifested in the archaeological Ch'ing-lien-kang and Ma-chia-pang cultures, the latter at least associated with cultivated rice (*Oryza sativa*). All three earliest farming cultures may be dated to the fifth millennium B.C. as far as the available archaeological data are concerned, but both Yang-shao and Ta-p'en-k'eng cultures almost certainly could be pushed back into the sixth millennium or earlier, whereas there is no evidence that the Ch'ing-lien-kang and Ma-chia-pang cultures are earlier than the fifth millennium.

As the earliest farming cultures continued to develop they eventually outgrew their regional universe, reached outward, and came to interact with similar cultures reaching out of other regional universes. Included under the Lungshanoid banner are such diverse cultures, in such far-apart regions, as the Miao-ti-kou II culture of Honan, the Hua-t'ing culture of Shangtung and northern Kiangsu, the Pei-yin-yang-ying culture of southern Kiangsu and northern Chekiang, the Ch'ü-chia-ling culture of southern Honan, Hupei, and northern Hunan and Kiangsi, and the Ts'ao-hsieh-tun culture of Taiwan.

Around the middle of the third millennium B.C., the various Lungshanoid cultures entered the Lung-shan stage. The Lung-shan cultures of the various regions increasingly exhibited local characteristics, and many of them displayed features of a ranked society (such as evidence of war, status differentiation, and industrial specialization, including incipient metallurgy). The Lung-shan cultures of Honan, Shantung-Kiangsu, lower Yangtze, and Han-shui–middle Yangtze were, at the very least, cultures in which a base existed for civilizational development. And very possibly civilizations

Table 18

Early Cultural Chronology of North China

STAGE	E. KANSU	CENTRAL SHENSI	W. HONAN	N. HONAN	SHANTUNG N. KIANGSU	DATES B.C.
HAN / CH'IN		CH'IN AND HAN EMPIRES				220
EASTERN CHOU	SHA-CHING / HSIN-TIEN / SSU-WA	EASTERN CHOU				750
WESTERN CHOU	SHAN-TAN	WESTERN CHOU			SHANG	1100
SHANG	CH'I-CHIA	SHANG	YIN / ERH-LI-KANG	YIN / ERH-LI-KANG		
LUNG-SHAN	PAN-SHAN MA-CH'ANG	K'O-HSING-CHUANG	ERH-LI-T'OU / HONAN	LUNG-SHAN	CLASSICAL LUNG-SHAN	1850
LUNGSHAN-OID	MA-CHIA-YAO		MIAO-TI-KOU II		HUA-T'ING	2500
YANG-SHAO	CHUNGYÜAN YANG-SHAO		MIAO-TI-KOU I / PAN-P'O	TA-SSU-K'UNG-TS'UN / HOU-KANG	CH'ING-LIEN-KANG	3200
			PRE-PAN-P'O			5000
MESOLITHIC		SHA-YÜAN, LING-CHING, ETC.				

HISTORIC — NEOLITHIC

did arise—in the form of stratified society with urbanism and metallurgy—in an interrelated manner, in all these areas more or less simultaneously. However, present evidence unmistakably indicates that the earliest Chinese civilization—the early Shang—came about first in the North Chinese nuclear area (i.e., southern Shansi and northwestern Honan), probably in the nineteenth or eighteenth century B.C. But immediately following it, civilizational forms (middle Shang) became widespread in the Yellow River valley, the Huai Plain, and the Middle Yangtze. It looks now as if the early Shang civilization's influence was to a significant extent responsible for the emergence of high civilizations in much of China. But the fact that these civilizations emerged so rapidly in such a vast area must in large part be due to the high level of societal development that had pre-existed in the Lung-shan cultures of these areas. In the twelfth century B.C., the Shang dynasty was replaced by the Chou dynasty as China's masters, but essentially the same civilization continued. By the middle of the Eastern Chou period a series of interrelated events and factors occurred, among which the highly developed iron metallurgy and intensified communications throughout the country were paramount. These made the Huang Ho tradition expand toward the north and the south, thus paving the way for the unification of China under the Ch'in and Han empires (table 18).

These events finally led to the unification of China, the history of which concludes this volume. It can clearly be seen that by the end of the Warring States period much of China was already unified culturally. From southern Manchuria to the coasts of Kwangtung, we encounter, for this period, variations of the same civilizational form and spirit, exemplified in the tomb construction patterns, in the remains of a bronze mirror and an iron sword, in the decorative patterns of pottery and bronzes, and in the forms of writing. The unification of China by the Ch'in and Han empires was not a conquest accomplished by a single powerful state and culture over an assortment of political groups and cultural traditions. Essentially this unification was a political follow-up to the cultural unification and the emergence of the Chinese national spirit—developments which were already in force toward the end of the Eastern Chou. These probably not only stimulated but also enabled—or at least facilitated—the political conquest that marked the year 221 B.C.[1]

---

1. See Wang Shih-min, *KK* 1973 (6), 364–71, for an archaeological viewpoint on the role played by Ch'in Shih Huang in Chinese unification.

The following remarks, prepared for a symposium on 'cultural regionalism in Eastern

(*footnote continued overleaf*)

In that year the state of Ch'i, in Shantung, the last remaining power of
the Warring States, was officially dissolved by General Wang P'en of the
Ch'in. But the actual political unification of China was more or less
continuous, for several centuries. The state of Ch'in claimed the status of
kingdom in 325 B.C. Four years before, it had already taken over Szechwan.
Many historians believe that the rich resources and high civilization of
Szechwan, which came under Ch'in control, were largely responsible for
the phenomenal rise of the Ch'in state and its overwhelming power. In
256 B.C., the Ch'in overthrew the Royal Chou. By 221 B.C., all the major
states in Central and North China, including Ch'u, Yen, Chao, Wei, Han,
and Ch'i, bowed to the military might of the Ch'in. However, the incor-

(footnote 1, p. 475, continued)

Chou China,' at the 1975 annual meeting of the Association for Asian Studies, serve to
amplify on this question of cultural unification at the end of the Chou period:

> To the archaeologist, who classifies cultures on the basis of degrees of similarity
> and difference between assemblages of objects, the issue being discussed here does not
> at all sound unfamiliar. Was Eastern Chou China characterized by unity or by diver-
> sity? To the archaeologist the answer is not difficult, but it cannot be tackled on an
> either-or basis. To say there was unity is not to deny that there was diversity, and *vice
> versa.*
>
> This fundamental issue in archaeological classification my Yale colleague Irving
> Rouse puts as follows: "In doing cultural classification, as in other kinds of classifica-
> tion, it is possible to be either a 'lumper' or a 'splitter'—to pay so little heed to the
> differences between one's assemblages that one groups a relatively large number of
> them into a single class, or to be so obsessed by the differences among them that one
> puts them into a relatively large number of classes, each containing a relatively small
> number of assemblages" (*Introduction to Prehistory*, New York, McGraw-Hill, 1972,
> p. 89).
>
> When and how much to lump and when and how much to split are often a matter
> of different levels of contrast and comparison that depends almost totally on the
> purpose of the classification. When I look at Eastern Chou China as a whole, which
> is continental in scope, I tend to be a lumper, believing that in classifying at a higher
> level of contrast one comes more readily upon those historical entities that are truly
> significant for the grasp of cultural similarities and differences, and the revelation of
> historical processes and cultural relationships of the higher magnitudes. From such
> a point of view I would tend to stress cultural unity in Eastern Chou China—both
> Spring-and-Autumn and Warring-States periods.
>
> Take, for example, the archaeological assemblages of the Warring-States period
> in northwestern Honan and those in central Hunan. There can be no question, from
> an archaeological perspective, that in these two regions rather distant from each other,
> we are dealing with variants of the same tradition. This tradition is manifested in all
> the major items of material culture that our spades encounter: rectangular town
> enclosures of pounded earth oriented according to the four cardinal directions;

poration of southern Manchuria[2] and southern Yüeh[3] came later. By the time of Han, what is now southern Manchuria, Inner Mongolia, and all of China proper was completely and directly dominated by the Han civilization. Sugimoto and Kano have listed the Han dynasty remains brought to light in China up to the mid-fifties.[4] Three things are already made clear by that list: (1) Han remains have been found in every province

(footnote 1, p. 476, continued)

rectangular pit-graves for the upper class deceased, richly furnished, with wooden chambers and coffins, again oriented in accordance with the cardinal directions; a Chinese script; similar dress styles; common pottery and bronze food vessel types, including *ting, li, hu, kuan,* and *tui*; similar weapons such as *chi, mao,* and *chien*; similar decorative motifs, particularly the numerous variants of the *p'an-ch'ih* pattern. When one compares this large tradition, encountered in both Lo-yang and Ch'ang-sha, with a contemporary non-Chinese tradition, such as Iron Age Greece or the Maya, there can be no question about the existence of a single, archaeologically defined, Eastern Chou, or Eastern Chou Chinese, civilization. In other words, there *was* cultural unity in Eastern Chou China.

But cultural unity is not cultural homogeneity or cultural uniformity. Certainly one cannot fail to recognize regional characteristics when one shifts his level of contrast downward a bit and his attention to more minute—though by no means unimportant—details. As we have pointed out, despite the obvious fact of the Ch'u of Ch'ang-sha being a part of Chou China, the Ch'u civilization, as revealed by archaeology, has its unique features. Some of these were apparently determined by an environment vastly different from North China, such as rice, as against millets, and the many other cultivated plants better grown in the warmer and wetter Yangtze valley. Others are purely—as far as we can judge—a matter of style, such as a characteristic Ch'u art.

Certainly one can agree with the participants of this symposium concerning the regional characteristics of the aspects of Eastern Chou civilization that have been analyzed. If unity has been exclusively stressed in the past and if unity has been equated with uniformity and homogeneity, then the papers here have performed an important service in bringing regional variations to the fore. But I really am not sure of the essential accuracy of the assertion that "China was really a patchwork of regional cultures, held together by elements of and in varying degrees assimilated to the Great Tradition," especially if China of the Eastern Chou period is included in this statement. The centripetal process that moved toward the unification of the formative cultures in ancient China began well before Eastern Chou—perhaps thousands of years before—and by Eastern Chou had become all but complete. To refer to the cultures of the various states in Eastern Chou China as "local cultures" without at the same time making clear that these were local variants of a larger cultural tradition is to take out the trees from the forest.

2. T'ung Chu-ch'en, *KKHP* 1956 (1), 26–43.
3. L. Aurouseau, *Bulletin de l'École française d'extrême-Orient* 23 (1923), 127–265.
4. *Tōyōshi-Kenkyu* 6 (1957).

of China proper and many regions in southern Manchuria, indicating the extent of the Han civilization within China; (2) in each province the number of Han dynasty sites is considerable, suggesting the intensity of the Han acculturation in some of the marginal provinces; (3) it is evident that the Han remains from all China represent a single major cultural tradition. Han sites discovered since then not only reinforce their conclusions but further indicate the civilization's extension into Inner Mongolia and Sinkiang.[5]

I have mentioned that the Ch'in and Han political unification was essentially a political follow-up to a cultural unification which had been developing for some centuries before 221 B.C. I did not mean to say, however, that the total cultural unification of China was completed in every region of the area by that date. Local civilizational elements persisted into the Han and subsequent historical periods in many regions, particularly in the southwest.[6] But the political control of these regions under the Han Empire certainly accelerated and intensified their cultural assimilation into the Han civilization.

My interpretation of the formative process of the Chinese civilization, summarized above, can be regarded as only a working hypothesis, for there are still many gaps in our knowledge. Many of the archaeological data have been made available so recently, and the amount of painstaking research demanded is so vast, that this hypothesis is at best a tentative arrangement of the material according to my perspective and judgment at this time. It is already clear that archaeology since 1920 has given us a new version of ancient China that was surely beyond imagination a mere fifty-six years ago. Although the massive amount of available data may be subject to differing interpretations, we can all agree that there are quite a few issues of great importance in the history of the Chinese people and their culture which archaeology has illuminated. It may be rewarding to take a look at some of these issues and see where we stand at the present.

There can be no question that archaeology has qualitatively expanded and enriched Chinese history in ways that only archaeology can. Archaeology has extended human history in China from the second millennium B.C. (if we do not count the mythological and legendary beginnings as authentic history) to probably the Lower and definitely the Middle Pleistocene period—going back at least half a million years; and it has

5. *Nei Meng-ku ch'u-t'u wen-wu hsüan-chi*, Peking, Wen Wu Press, 1963. *Hsin-chiang ch'u-t'u wen-wu*, Peking, Wen Wu Press, 1975.

6. K. C. Chang, *COWA Survey*, area 17, no. 1, 1959, p. 6. *Current Anthropol.* 5 (1964), 359, 368–75, 399–400.

extended it from the small area of China where a literature existed to all of China. It gives the Hsia history a shot in the arm, the Shang history new life, and the Chou history a much richer content. In fact, for all historical periods, archaeology extends Chinese history from select aspects to all facets of life and from essentially a record of the ruling class to a record which also includes the downtrodden. No ancient Chinese historiography is now possible without archaeology, and the same may be said for some aspects of later historiography as well.

Material culture is of course archaeology's forte, but one should not lose sight of the more qualitative aspects of Chinese civilization as well. Take, for example, the question of what is China or Chinese? Textual records give us insight on the point-of-view of the Chinese people themselves, but a study of the artifacts of the peoples in China and in the neighboring areas approaches the question of Chineseness at a classificatory level. Classifying is surely not without its controversial aspects, but at least students can define—perhaps variably, perhaps invariably—China and Chineseness in explicit language, according to explicit criteria that can be historically defined—that is, defined in ways best indicated by data of each period.

What then defines Chineseness? To enumerate is to repeat much of what has already been stated, and specific items are not as important as the fact of continuity—both spatial continuity of common characteristics and temporal continuity from one period to another. Spatial and temporal continuity may be ascertained for such vital items as specific food plants, agricultural implements, certain pottery forms and decorative styles, building techniques, specific domestic animals, and the like, and together these items are powerful proof of a people's common heritage. This shows that the continuity of individual items must also be accompanied—perhaps explained—by their continuing interrelationship. It can further be shown that many of them (for example, the items having to do with the production, preparation, serving, and storage of certain kinds of food) are interrelated in the sense of mutually deterministic, and all of them are interrelated, at a higher level of abstraction, in ways that may pertain to the special characters of Chinese soil, water, and wind. Archaeologists may differ in the precise ways to define *Chinese*, but no one can fail to recognize, in the archaeological record, a Chinese culture that differs significantly from all other cultures near and far.

When did this Chinese culture begin? Significant continuity links Palaeolithic assemblages in China from different periods despite marked changes from one period to the next, but in the archaeological record there is a conspicuous discontinuity from the Palaeolithic to the Neolithic. This by no means indicates a dislocation of either population or culture but results from the respective bodies of data from the two periods. These data are so different as to be almost incomparable. Namely, flaked lithic material and pottery cannot be compared in the study of continuity. There is good reason to believe that a Mongoloid population was the maker of the Chinese Palaeolithic cultures, and that essentially the same population (or populations) was responsible for the earliest agricultural experiments in this area. But until many more details are known about the culture of the Palaeolithic peoples, we have as yet no way to characterize a Chinese culture before agriculture and pottery appeared on the scene.

Where did Chinese culture begin, now that we know it began with agriculture? I used to think that Chinese culture began only in the nuclear area of North China, whence it gradually radiated outward to absorb the non-Chinese cultures on its peripheries into the Chinese tradition, which eventually extended throughout China in historical periods. Archaeological materials made available in the last few years have begun to convince me that such a view in fact reflects a historical bias. The radiating process in which the nuclear-area culture of North China came to assimilate many of its neighbors is not at issue. The question concerns the Chinese label. Now that we have been shown that there were parallel developments of Neolithic cultures in China, if we apply the continuity criterion and trace the Chinese culture up in time, we are compelled to see that cultural continuities extend into more than the nuclear area of North China. The Ch'ing-lien-kang and related cultures of the Pacific seaboard may have been derived, at least in part, from the nuclear-area tradition, but even if they were not they were obviously ancestral to the historical Chinese civilization, and they were as much Chinese as the Yang-shao. The Ta-p'en-k'eng and related cultures of the southeast coastal areas undoubtedly contributed, to later Chinese cultures, such items as native food plants and other useful plants, the use of tree-bark paper and possibly paper itself,[7] and at least some pottery and lithic forms. Moreover, in terms of spatial continuity these Neolithic cultures shared many characteristic artifacts and artifact attributes, and as we have stated before they may have been closely related in origin. They are all Chinese, and they and some of their affiliated cultures (yet to be fully understood) contrast with many neighboring contemporary cultures that are plainly non-Chinese in a classificatory sense.

7. Ling Shun-sheng, 'Bark-cloth, impressed pottery, and the invention of paper and printing,' Institute of Ethnology, Academia Sinica (Taipei), Monograph no. 3, 1963.

In the same sense of continuity (within) and contrast (without), all the regional cultures of the Shang period are parts of the Shang civilization—that is, the Chinese civilization of the Shang period—even though all of them were not a part of the Shang state and all were not referred to as Shang by the Shang themselves. The same holds true for the Chou civilization. The Ch'u, Yüeh, Pa, and Tien civilizations of South China, for example, were all demonstrably ancestral to Chinese civilization—an amalgamation of many strains from many sources—or at least to some portions or regional divisions of that civilization, and they are, thus, all Chinese in a classificatory sense.

I am not unmindful of the historical-linguistic dilemmas that are involved in such classificatory problems, but to claim that any of these civilizations were non-Chinese and were subsequently assimilated or expelled by the Chinese, who came out of a single nuclear area, is to fly in the face of the archaeological evidence in every case, where continuity with change is invariably the rule. This is not to deny that the nuclear area of North China played an important role in Chinese history, or that cultural-historical processes such as diffusion, migration, and conquest did not occur in China as elsewhere. But these processes are never as important as—and they themselves must ordinarily be explained in terms of—the adaptational process of the culture, which must always come to terms with its own resources.

If these views are essentially valid, we are then confronted with an amazing phenomenon, namely, that the Chinese culture has coincided, more or less, with the area of China as we now know it, ever since the beginning of the agricultural way of life and possibly, though as yet undemonstrably, before that. And within that area, despite many cultural exchanges with the outside world, the Chinese culture has for thousands of years not only persisted but also proved to be basically self-contained. Both phenomena—continuity and self-containment—are, as far as I know, unprecedented in world history, when the size of China is taken into account. The question "why" is obviously worthy of pursuit, but let me not pretend that I can resolve the issue within the next paragraph or the next page. China's size, abundant and varying resources, and geographical location outlined by seas and oceans on two sides and plateaus and deserts on the other two, may all have something to do with it, but let us leave that to more philosophically inclined historians.

To point out the self-containment aspect of the Chinese civilization's growth and to appeal to China's geographical self-sufficiency as a possible explanatory factor is not to say that Chinese civilization developed in isolation or that it can be understood outside its world setting. In the first place, it would be astonishing if it proved to be that China in all stages of its development did not participate in various larger spheres of interaction in the ancient world. Seas and oceans serve to conveniently outline the territorial limits of the land, but they also serve to facilitate, rather than hinder, communication in the directions of Southeast Asia and the Pacific; and the Silk Route through Sinkiang is a prime example of overcoming natural barriers when it is necessary or desirable to do so. Furthermore, ancient China and modern China overlap but do not coincide exactly, and present political borders were no barriers for the peoples living across them. Unfortunately, archaeologists in China and from each of her adjacent countries stop at their present borders, and few if any archaeological reports of sites in the border areas take into account the archaeological data on the other side. Of all the outside connections, China's relationships toward the south are the most interesting. Archaeology and ethnology have, in recent years, combined to point to Southeast Asia as being the site of a very old cultural stratum, and the relationship of North China to this ancient substratum will be one of the most important topics of research in the next decade. In determining this relationship, South Chinese archaeology will prove crucial, and one can almost predict that many surprises are in store for us in this field.

Finally, Chinese civilization and its growth process must share some if not all of its patterns with civilizations elsewhere, and scholars of comparative civilizations are interested in China not only for her uniqueness but also for the areas in which she exhibits universal patterns. In a recent issue of *Vertebrata Palasiatica*, Chang Shen-shui[8] has discussed the continuity of industrial typology in the Chinese Palaeolithic to rebuke the opinion of L. S. Vasiliev, who has attempted to attribute the "Mousterian" characteristics of the Ting-ts'un assemblage to its western Asian derivation. Chang is certainly right in stressing the continuity, and I was rather surprised at the clumsy recent efforts by Vasiliev to revive the theory of the west Asia origins of the Chinese civilization.[9] But I trust that Chang is fully cognizant of the comparability of some of the Ting-ts'un and Ordosian industrial features with the Mousterian technology and that he is mindful of the broad implications of this fact in Palaeolithic archaeology. Indeed, the use of Marxist historical materialism—a universal model—in the interpretation of Chinese prehistory and history, which prevails in China, is itself a statement with regard to looking at Chinese data in terms

8. *VP* 14 (1976), 1–5.

9. L. S. Vasiliev, *Narody Azii i Afriki* 1964 (2), 123–35; *Voprosy Istorii* 1974 (12), 86–102; *Problemy Genezisa Kitaiskoi Tsivilizatsii*, Moscow, Nauka, 1976.

of universal patterns. In the foreword of Ho Ping-t'i's recent book *Cradle of the East*,[10] which seeks to establish the essential autochthony of Chinese civilization, William H. McNeill maintains that such a view "requires Westerners to abandon their older opinion that all mankind followed essentially the same path to civilization—a view, incidentally, enshrined in Marxian teachings about the universal stages of social development from primitive communism to capitalist exploitation, and beyond." I fail to see the logic of this argument. Chinese self-sufficiency does not automatically negate any universal pattern to which Chinese data may be fitted. In fact, the great importance of Chinese archaeology lies precisely in the necessity of both understanding China in its own terms and understanding it in terms of cultural and societal universals. Rather than being an exception to the rule, China should help establish the rule in the first place.

10. University of Chicago Press and the Chinese University of Hong Kong, 1976, p. xv.

Appendix 1: Radiocarbon Dates
in Chinese Archaeology up to January 1976

Lab-No	Site	Sample	Associated Culture	B.P. [before 1950] (Half-life= 5568 ± 30)	B.P. [before 1950] (Half-life= 5730 ± 40)	B.C. (Half-life= 5730 ± 40)	Source
1. Palaeolithic Archaeology							
ZK-109	Shih-yü, Shansi	animal bone	Upper Palaeolithic	28,135 ± 1,330			5
ZK-136	Upper Cave, Chou-k'ou-tien	animal bone	Terminal Palaeolithic	18,340 ± 410			5
ZK-19	Tzu-yang, Szechwan	wood	Tzu-yang Palaeolithic(?) man	7,270 ± 130	7,485 ± 130	5,535 ± 130	2
ZK-256	,,	,,	,,	6,550 ± 120	6,740 ± 120	4,790 ± 120	4
2. Yang-shao Culture							
ZK-38	Pan-p'o-ts'un, Sian	charcoal	Pan-p'o phase, Yang-shao	5,890 ± 110	6,065 ± 110	4,115 ± 110	3
ZK-121	,,	,,	,,	5,730 ± 100	5,905 ± 105	3,955 ± 105	3
ZK-122	,,	,,	,,	5,670 ± 100	5,840 ± 105	3,890 ± 105	3
ZK-127	,,	carbonized fruit pit	,,	5,420 ± 100	5,585 ± 105	3,635 ± 105	3
ZK-134	Hou-kang, An-yang	charcoal	Hou-kang phase, Yang-shao	5,520 ± 105	5,680 ± 105	3,730 ± 105	4
ZK-76	,,	,,	,,	5,330 ± 100	5,485 ± 105	3,535 ± 105	3
ZK-110	Miao-ti-kou, Shan Hsien	,,	Miao-ti-kou phase, Yang-shao	5,080 ± 100	5,230 ± 100	3,280 ± 100	3
ZK-185	Ta-ho-ts'un, Cheng-chou	,,	Ch'in-wang-chai phase, Yang-shao	4,885 ± 100	5,025 ± 100	3,075 ± 100	4
ZK-108	Ts'ao-chia-tsui, Lan-chou	charcoal	Ma-chia-yao phase, Yang-shao	4,390 ± 100	4,525 ± 100	2,575 ± 100	3
ZK-21	Ma-chia-wan, Yung-ching	,,	Ma-ch'ang phase, Yang-shao	4,010 ± 100	4,135 ± 100	2,185 ± 100	2
ZK-25	Ch'ing-kang-ch'a, Lan-chou	carbonized wood	Pan-shan phase, Yang-shao	3,900 ± 100	4,015 ± 100	2,065 ± 100	2

Lab-No	Site	Sample	Associated Culture	B.P. [before 1950] (Half-life= 5568 ± 30)	B.P. [before 1950] (Half-life= 5730 ± 40)	B.C. (Half-life= 5730 ± 40)	Source

3. Ta-p'en-k'eng and Related Cultures

Lab-No	Site	Sample	Associated Culture	B.P. (5568±30)	B.P. (5730±40)	B.C. (5730±40)	Source
NTU-125	Ch'ien-yuan Cave, Ch'ang-pin, Taiwan	charcoal	Ch'angpinian, nonceramic	15,000+			7
NTU-70	Ch'ao-yin Cave, Ch'ang-pin, Taiwan	,,	,,	5,340 ± 260	5,500 ± 270	3,550 ± 270	6
NTU-69	,,	,,	,,	5,240 ± 260	5,400 ± 270	3,450 ± 270	6
NTU-71	,,	,,	,,	4,970 ± 250	5,120 ± 260	3,170 ± 260	6
SI-1229	Pa-chia-ts'un, Kui-jen, T'ai-nan, Taiwan	oyster shell	Ta-p'en-k'eng	5,480 ± 55	5,645 ± 60	3,695 ± 60	11
NTU-65	Fu-kuo-tun, Quemoy, Fukien	shell	Shell-impressed pottery (lower stratum)	6,310 ± 370	6,500 ± 400	4,550 ± 400	6
NTU-64	,,	,,	Shell-impressed pottery (middle stratum)	5,800 ± 340	5,970 ± 350	4,020 ± 350	6
NTU-63	,,	,,	Shell-impressed pottery (upper stratum)	5,460 ± 320	5,620 ± 330	3,670 ± 330	6
ZK-39	Hsien-jen-tung, Wan-nien, Kiangsi	,,	geometric pottery overlying layer of corded ware?	10,565 ± 240	10,870 ± 240	8,920 ± 240	4

4. Ch'ing-lien-kang Culture

Lab-No	Site	Sample	Associated Culture	B.P. (5568±30)	B.P. (5730±40)	B.C. (5730±40)	Source
ZK-90	Ta-tun-tzu, P'i Hsien, Kiangsu	charcoal	Ch'ing-lien-kang	5,625 ± 105	5,785 ± 105	3,835 ± 105	4
ZK-55	Sung-tse, Ch'ing-p'u, Shanghai	wood	Ma-chia-pang	5,190 ± 100	5,345 ± 105	3,395 ± 105	3

5. Lungshanoid Cultures

Lab-No	Site	Sample	Associated Culture	B.P. (5568±30)	B.P. (5730±40)	B.C. (5730±40)	Source
ZK-111	Miao-ti-kou, Shan Hsien, Honan	charcoal	Miao-ti-kou II	4,140 ± 90	4,260 ± 95	2,310 ± 95	3
ZK-91	Huang-lien-shu, Hsi-ch'uan, Honan	,,	Ch'ü-chia-ling	4,100 ± 90	4,220 ± 95	2,270 ± 95	3
ZK-169	Li-chia-ts'un, Hsi-hsiang, Shensi	,,	?	4,075 ± 95	4,190 ± 95	2,240 ± 95	4

Lab-No	Site	Sample	Associated Culture	B.P. [before 1950] (Half-life= 5568 ± 30)	B.P. [before 1950] (Half-life= 5730 ± 40)	B.C. (Half-life= 5730 ± 40)	Source
5. Lungshanoid Cultures [continued]							
ZK-125	Ch'ü-chia-ling, Ching-shan, Hupei	wood	Ch'ü-chia-ling	4,080 ± 160	4,195 ± 160	2,245 ± 160	4
ZK-124	,,	charcoal	,,	4,030 ± 100	4,145 ± 100	2,195 ± 100	4
ZK-51	P'ao-ma-ling, Hsiu-shui, Kiangsi	,,	Ch'ü-chai-ling?	4,160 ± 90	4,285 ± 95	2,335 ± 95	3
NTU-244	Ts'ao-hsieh-tun, Ts'ao-t'un, Taiwan	,,	Red Corded Ware	4,000 ± 200	4,120 ± 205	2,170 ± 205	8
6. Local Lung-shan Cultures							
ZK-200	Shang-p'an-wang, Tz'u Hsien, Hopei	shell	Honan Lung-shan	3,935 ± 95	4,050 ± 95	2,100 ± 95	4
ZK-126	Wang-wan, Lo-yang, Honan	charcoal	,,	3,830 ± 90	3,950 ± 95	2,000 ± 95	3
ZK-133	Hou-kang, An-yang	,,	,,	3,800 ± 90	3,910 ± 90	1,960 ± 90	4
ZK-78	Shuang-t'o-tzu, Lü-ta, Liao-ning	carbonized wood	Classical Lung-shan	3,890 ± 90	4,010 ± 95	2,060 ± 95	3
ZK-79	,,	,,	Classical Lung-shan?	3,030 ± 90	3,120 ± 90	1,170 ± 90	3
ZK-49	Ch'ien-shan-yang, Wu-hsing, Che-kiang	rice shell	Liang-chu?	4,560 ± 100	4,700 ± 100	2,750 ± 100	3
ZK-242	Ch'üeh-mu-ch'iao, Chia-hsing, Che-kiang	wood	Liang-chu	3,830 ± 95	3,940 ± 95	1,990 ± 95	4
7. Neolithic and Later Prehistoric Cultures of Northern North China							
ZK-89	Ying-ko-ling, Ning-an, Heilungkiang	charcoal	Neolithic	2,940 ± 90	3,025 ± 90	1,075 ± 90	4
ZK-88	,,	birch bark	,,	2,900 ± 120	2,985 ± 120	1,035 ± 120	4
ZK-188	Fu-ho-kou-men, Balin Left Banner, Chao-wuta L., Liaoning	,,	,,	4,600 ± 110	4,735 ± 110	2,785 ± 110	4
ZK-176	Chih-chu-shan, Ch'ih-feng, Liaoning	charcoal	Lower Hsia-chia-tien	3,855 ± 90	3,965 ± 90	2,015 ± 90	4

Lab-No	Site	Sample	Associated Culture	B.P. [before 1950] (Half-life= 5568 ± 30)	B.P. [before 1950] (Half-life= 5730 ± 40)	B.C. (Half-life= 5730 ± 40)	Source

7. Neolithic and Later Prehistoric Cultures of Northern North China [continued]

Lab-No	Site	Sample	Associated Culture	B.P. 5568	B.P. 5730	B.C. 5730	Source
ZK-61	T'a-li-t'a-li-ha, No-mu-hung, Chinghai	wood	No-mu-hung	3,670 ± 90	3,775 ± 90	1,825 ± 90	3
ZK-15	Ta-ho-chuang, Yung-ching, Kansu	charcoal	Ch'i-chia	3,570 ± 90	3,675 ± 95	1,725 ± 95	2
ZK-23	,,	,,	,,	3,540 ± 90	3,645 ± 95	1,695 ± 95	2
ZK-17	Chao-su, Sin-kiang	,,	ancient tomb	1,960 ± 90	2,015 ± 90	65 ± 90	2

8. Neolithic and Later Prehistoric Cultures in South China

Lab-No	Site	Sample	Associated Culture	B.P. 5568	B.P. 5730	B.C. 5730	Source
Y-1580	Feng-pi-t'ou, Kao-hsiung, Taiwan	shell	Shellmound (lower)	3,310 ± 80	3,410 ± 80	1,460 ± 80	10
Y-1581	,,	,,	,,	2,910 ± 80	3,000 ± 80	1,050 ± 80	10
Y-1649	,,	,,	,,	2,900 ± 120	2,990 ± 120	1,040 ± 120	10
Y-1578	,,	,,	,,	2,780 ± 80	2,860 ± 80	910 ± 80	10
Y-1584	,,	,,	,,	2,670 ± 80	2,750 ± 80	800 ± 80	10
Y-1648	,,	,,	,,	2,670 ± 60	2,750 ± 60	800 ± 60	10
Y-1577	,,	,,	Shellmound (upper)	2,440 ± 100	2,510 ± 100	560 ± 100	10
NTU-201	no. 30, P'u-li, Nan-t'ou, Taiwan	charcoal	Black Pottery	3,282 ± 98	3,380 ± 100	1,430 ± 100	8
NTU-203	,,	,,	,,	3,207 ± 96	3,303 ± 100	1,353 ± 100	8
NTU-202	,,	,,	,,	2,994 ± 90	3,084 ± 90	1,134 ± 90	8
NTU-200	no. 29, P'u-li, Nan-t'ou, Taiwan	charcoal	Black Pottery	2,381 ± 71	2,452 ± 70	502 ± 70	8
NTU-196	no. 21, P'u-li, Nan-t'ou, Taiwan	,,	,,	2,197 ± 66	2,263 ± 70	312 ± 70	8
NTU-195	,,	,,	,,	2,104 ± 63	2,167 ± 65	217 ± 65	8
NTU-243	Chuang-hou-ts'un, T'ai-wan	,,	,,	2,070 ± 104	2,132 ± 110	182 ± 110	8
Y-1630	Ying-p'u, T'ai-chung, Taiwan	,,	,,	2,970 ± 80	3,060 ± 80	1,110 ± 80	10
Y-1631	,,	,,	,,	2,810 ± 100	2,890 ± 100	940 ± 100	10
Y-1632	,,	,,	,,	2,250 ± 60	2,320 ± 60	370 ± 60	10
Y-1547	Yüan-shan, T'ai-pei, Taiwan	shell	Yüan-shan	3,860 ± 80	3,980 ± 80	2,030 ± 80	10

Lab-No	Site	Sample	Associated Culture	B.P. [before 1950] (Half-life = 5568 ± 30)	B.P. [before 1950] (Half-life = 5730 ± 40)	B.C. (Half-life = 5730 ± 40)	Source

8. Neolithic and Later Prehistoric Cultures in South China [continued]

Lab-No	Site	Sample	Associated Culture	B.P. (5568±30)	B.P. (5730±40)	B.C. (5730±40)	Source
Y-1548	,,	,,	,,	3,540 ± 80	3,650 ± 80	1,700 ± 80	10
Y-1549	,,	,,	,,	3,190 ± 80	3,290 ± 80	1,340 ± 80	10
Y-1551	Ta-p'en-k'eng, T'ai-pei, Taiwan	charcoal	,,	2,850 ± 200	2,940 ± 210	990 ± 210	10
Y-1498	,,	,,	,,	2,030 ± 80	2,090 ± 80	140 ± 80	10
ZK-98	T'an-shih-shan, Min-hou, Fukien	shell	T'an-shih-shan	3,005 ± 90	3,090 ± 90	1,140 ± 90	4
ZK-103	Hou-shan-kang, Tseng-ch'eng, Kwangtung	,,	Neolithic	3,920 ± 95	4,035 ± 95	2,085 ± 95	4
?	SOS (Nan-sha-k'eng), Hai-feng, Kwangtung	?	Geometric	3,117 ± 150	3,210 ± 155	1,260 ± 155	1
?	TAS (Nan-tung-k'eng), Hai-feng, Kwangtung	?	Geometric	2,944 ± 400	3,032 ± 410	1,082 ± 410	1
ZK-229	Ta-tun-tzu, Yuan-mou, Yunnan	charcoal	Neolithic	3,120 ± 90	3,210 ± 90	1,260 ± 90	4
ZK-10	Hai-men-k'ou, Chien-ch'uan, Yunnan	wood	Hai-men-k'ou	3,010 ± 90	3,100 ± 90	1,150 ± 90	3

9. Shang and Chou periods and Han

Lab-No	Site	Sample	Associated Culture	B.P. (5568±30)	B.P. (5730±40)	B.C. (5730±40)	Source
ZK-212	Erh-li-t'ou, Yen-shih, Honan	shell	early Shang	3,470 ± 95	3,570 ± 95	1,620 ± 95	4
ZK-257	,,	charcoal	,,	3,105 ± 90	3,195 ± 90	1,245 ± 90	4
ZK-86	Hsiao-t'un, An-yang, Honan	,,	Shang (with oracle bones)	2,980 ± 90	3,065 ± 90	1,115 ± 90	3
ZK-5	Wu-kuan-ts'un, An-yang, Honan	,,	Shang (royal tomb)	2,950 ± 100	3,035 ± 100	1,085 ± 100	2
ZK-162	Yeh-tien, Tsou Hsien, Shan-tung	,,	Chou?	2,725 ± 90	2,805 ± 90	855 ± 90	4
Y-1513	Lo-yang, Honan	iron	Warring-States	2,380 ± 80	2,450 ± 80	500 ± 80	10,12
ZK-252	Tiao-yü-t'ai, Po Hsien, Anhwei	wheat grains	gray pottery (late Chou?)	2,370 ± 90	2,440 ± 90	490 ± 90	4
ZK-67-0	Ch'iao-ts'un, Hou-ma, Shansi	human bone	Warring-States	2,260 ± 85	2,325 ± 85	375 ± 85	4

Lab-No	Site	Sample	Associated Culture	B.P. [before 1950] (Half-life= 5568 ± 30)	B.P. [before 1950] (Half-life= 5730 ± 40)	B.C. (Half-life= 5730 ± 40)	Source
9. Shang and Chou periods and Han [continued]							
ZK-3	Ku-wei-ts'un, Hui Hsien, Honan	wood	Warring-States	2,170 ± 80	2,240 ± 80	290 ± 80	2
Y-1511	Sian, Shensi	iron	Han	2,060 ± 80	2,120 ± 80	170 ± 80	10,12
ZK-142	Pei-yin-yang-ying, Nan-king, Kiangsu	charcoal	Hu-shu	3,390 ± 90	3,490 ± 90	1,540 ± 90	4
ZK-28	,,	,,	,,	3,055 ± 105	3,145 ± 105	1,195 ± 105	4
ZK-204	Ch'a-shan, Chin-shan, Shanghai	,,	Geometric	2,875 ± 90	2,960 ± 90	1,010 ± 90	4
ZK-27	Yen Ho, Yen-ch'eng, Wu-chin, Kiangsu	wood	Geometric	2,795 ± 90	2,875 ± 90	925 ± 90	4
ZK-1	Ch'ang-sha, Hunan	,,	Ch'u	2,330 ± 90	2,395 ± 90	445 ± 90	2
GC-W9	Ma-wang-tui, Ch'ang-sha, Hunan	,,	Han (tomb no. 1)	2,195 ± 95	2,261 ± 100	311 ± 100	9
GC-W8	,,	charcoal	,,	2,115 ± 95	2,178 ± 100	228 ± 100	9
ZK-172	,,	fruit pit	,,	2,055 ± 80	2,115 ± 80	165 ± 80	4
ZK-165	,,	charcoal	,,	2,035 ± 80	2,095 ± 80	145 ± 80	4
GC-W1	Man-ch'eng, Hopei	wood	Han	2,155 ± 95	2,220 ± 100	270 ± 100	9
ZK-6	Ch'ang-sha, Hunan	,,	,,	1,930 ± 80	1,985 ± 80	35 ± 80	2
ZK-243	Chi-nan-ch'eng, Chiang-ling, Hupei	,,	,,	1,820 ± 85	1,870 ± 85	A.D. 80	4
Y-1515	Chia-shan-chai, Li-fan, Szechwan	iron	,,	2,130 ± 100	2,195 ± 100	245 ± 100	10,12

Laboratory abbreviations

GC   Gui-yang Geochemical Research Institute, Gui-yang (Kuei-yang), Kweichou
NTU   Radiocarbon Laboratory, National Taiwan University, Taipei, Taiwan
SI   Radiocarbon Laboratory, Smithsonian Institution, Washington, D.C.
Y   Radiocarbon Laboratory, Yale University
ZK   Zhong-guo Kexueyuan Kaogu Yenjiuso Shiyenshi (Laboratory, Institute of Archaeology Academia Sinica, Peking)

Sources

1. Beyer, H. O. 1956. "Preliminary note (on eight papers on Chinese Archaeology and Early History)," *Proceedings of the 4th Far Eastern Prehistory Congress*, vol. 1, p. 86.

2. Chung-kuo K'o-hsüeh-yüan K'ao-ku Yen-chiu-suo Shih-yen-shih. 1972. "Fang-she-hsing t'an-su ts'e-ting nien-tai pao-kao (1)," *KK* 1972 (1), 52–56.

3. Chung-kuo K'o-hsüeh-yüan K'ao-ku Yen-chiu-suo Shih-yen-shih. 1972. "Fang-she-hsing t'an-su ts'e-ting nien-tai pao-kao (2)," *KK* 1972 (5), 56–58.

4. Chung-kuo K'o-hsüeh-yüan K'ao-ku Yen-chiu-suo Shih-yen-shih. 1974. "Fang-she-hsing t'an-su ts'e-ting nien-tai pao-kao (3)," *KK* 1974 (5), 333–38.

5. Chung-kuo K'o-hsüeh-yüan K'ao-ku Yen-chiu-suo Shih-yen-shih, Ku Chi-chui Tung-wu yü Ku Jen-lei Yen-chiu-suo Shih-yen-shih. 1976. "Ku-chih piao-pen ti t'an-shih-ssu nien-tai ts'e-ting fang-fa," *KK* 1976 (1), 28–30.

6. Hsü, Yuin-chi et al. 1970. "National Taiwan University radiocarbon measurements I," *Radiocarbon* 12, 187–92.

7. Hsü, Yuin-chi et al. 1973. "National Taiwan University radiocarbon measurements II," *Radiocarbon* 15, 345–49.

8. Hsü, Yuin-chi. Personal communication.

9. Kuei-yang Ti-ch'iu Hua-hsüeh Yen-chiu-suo T'an Shih-ssu Shih-yen-shih. 1973. "Chi-ko k'ao-ku yang-p'in ti fang-she-hsing t'an nien-tai ts'e-ting," *Geochimica* 1973 (2), 135–37.

10. Stuiver, Minze. 1969. "Yale natural radiocarbon measurements IX," *Radiocarbon* 11, 545–658.

11. Stuckenrath, Robert. 1972. Personal communication.

12. Van der Merwe, Nikolaas J. 1969. *The Carbon-14 Dating of Iron*. Chicago: The University of Chicago Press.

Appendix 2: Chinese Characters for Proper Names and Technical Terms

This appendix lists the Chinese characters, transliterations of which appear in the text. Characters for materials used in the footnotes and for such common geographical and historical names as Huang Ho, Yangtze, the provincial names, and the dynastic names and subdivisions (e.g. Shang, Chou, Chan Kuo, etc.), are not included.

A-ti-ts'un 阿底村
Aksu 阿克蘇
Amano Motonosuke 天野元之助
An Chih-min 安志敏
An Chin-huai 安金槐
An-ch'iu 安丘
An-i 安邑
An-ning 安寧
An-yang 安陽
An-yang fa-chüeh pao-kao 安陽發掘報告
Ang-ang-hsi 昂昂溪
Ao 隞
Astana 阿斯塔那

Balin 巴林

Chang Ho (R.) 漳河
Chang-chia-p'o 張家坡
Chang-chia-tsui 張家嘴
Chang-kung-t'ai 張公台
Chang Shen-shui 張森水
Chao 趙
Chao Hou (Ts'ai) 昭侯

Chao Kung (Lu) 昭公
chao mu 昭穆
Chao Wang (Chou) 昭王
Chao-ch'ing 肇慶
Chao-hua 昭化
Chao-k'ang-chen 趙康鎮
Chaowuta 昭烏達
Chen-fan 鎮番
Cheng 鄭
cheng 鉦、鑫
Cheng Te-k'un 鄭德坤
Cheng-chia-wa-tzu 鄭家窪子
Cheng-chou 鄭州
Chi 姬
chi 戟
Chi Hsien (Honan) 汲縣
Chi Hsien (Hopei) 薊縣
Chi Tzu 箕子
Chi-chia-ch'uan 姬家川
Chi-nan 濟南
Chi-nan-ch'eng 紀南城
Chi-shan 稷山
chia 斝
Chia Hsien 郟縣

chia ku wen 甲骨文

Chia Lan-p'o 賈蘭坡

Chia-hsing 嘉興

Chia-ko-chuang 賈各莊

Chia-ling-chiang (R.) 嘉陵江

Chia-shan 嘉山

Chia-yü-kuan 嘉峪關

Chiang 絳

Chiang Yüan 姜原

Chiang-chai 姜寨

Chiang-ch'uan 江川

Chiang-hsi-ts'un 姜西村

Chiang-ling 江陵

Chiang-ning 江寧

chiao 角

Chiao-ch'eng 交城

Chiao-chuang 焦莊

Chieh-tuan-ying 界段營

Chien (R.) 澗

chien 鑑、劍

Chien Ti 簡狄

Chien-ch'uan 劍川

Chien-hsi 澗溪

Chien-kou 澗溝

Chien-p'ing 建平

Chien-shih 建始

chih 觶

Chih-chiang 枝江

Chin 晉

chin 禁

chin shih hsüeh 金石學

chin wen 金文

Chin-ch'eng 晉城

Chin-men 金門

Chin-ning 晉寧

Chin-sha-chiang (R.) 金沙江

Chin-ts'un 金村

Chin-yang 晉陽

Chin-yüan 晉源

Ching 荊

Ching Hou (Chao) 敬侯

Ching Man 荊蠻

Ching-chih-chen 景芝鎮

Ching-shan 京山

Ching-ts'un 荊村

Ching-yang 涇陽

Chiu-ch'üan 酒泉

Chou Kung 周公

Chou K'un-shu 周昆叔

Chou shu 周書

Chou-chih 周至

Chou-k'ou-tien 周口店

Chou-lai 州來

Chu 邾

chu 枓、鑄

Chu shu chi nien 竹書紀年

Chu-ch'eng 諸城

Chu-chia-ch'iao 朱家橋

Chu-chou 株州

Chu-wa-chieh 竹瓦街

Chuang Tzu 莊子

chung 鐘

Chung Hsien 忠縣

Chung Yüan 中原

Chung Yüng 仲雍

Chung-chou-lu 中州路

Chung-kuo k'ao-ku hsüeh-pao
   中國考古學報

Chung-kuo K'o-hsüeh Yüan
   中國科學院

Chung-wei 中衛

Chü 聚

Chü Hsien 莒縣

chüeh 爵

Chün Hsien 濬縣

chün tzu 君子

Chün-wang-ch'i 郡王旗

Ch'an (R.) 滻、瀍

Ch'ang-chih 長治

Ch'ang-chou 常州
Ch'ang-ch'ing 長清
Ch'ang-ch'un 長春
Ch'ang-hsing 長興
Ch'ang-ning 常寧
Ch'ang-pin 長濱
Ch'ang-sha 長沙
Ch'ang-shê-shan 長蛇山
Ch'ang-te 常德
Ch'ang-wu 長武
Ch'ang-yang 長陽
Ch'ao-an 潮安
Ch'ao-ko 朝歌
Ch'ao-yang 朝陽
Ch'ao-i 朝邑
Ch'en 陳
Ch'en Hsien 郴縣
Ch'en Meng-chia 陳夢家
Ch'en-chia-wo 陳家窩
ch'eng 城
Ch'eng Wang 成王
Ch'eng-ch'iao 程橋
Ch'eng-chou 成周
Ch'eng-tu 成都
Ch'eng-tzu-yai 城子崖
Ch'i 齊、岐、契、棄
Ch'i Hsien 祁縣
Ch'i-lien Shan (Mt.) 祁連山
Ch'i Yen-p'ei 祁延霈
Ch'i yü 齊語
Ch'i-chia 齊家
Ch'i-chia-p'ing 齊家坪
Ch'i-ch'un 蘄春
Ch'i-li-p'u 七里舖
Ch'i-lin-shan 麒麟山
Ch'i-shan 岐山
Ch'ia-yao 卡約(甲窰)
Ch'iang 羌
Ch'iao-ts'un 喬村
ch'ieh-ch'ü 竊曲

Ch'ien-chai 前寨
Ch'ien-hsi 黔西
Ch'ien-shan-yang 錢山漾
Ch'ien-t'ang (R.) 錢塘
Ch'ih-feng 赤峯
Ch'in Ling (Mts.) 秦嶺
Ch'in Shih Huang Ti 秦始皇帝
Ch'in-huang-tao 秦皇島
Ch'in-wang-chai 秦王寨
Ch'in-wei-chia 秦魏家
Ch'ing-chiang 清江
Ch'ing-kang-ch'a 青崗岔
Ch'ing-lien-kang 青蓮崗
Ch'ing-lung-ch'üan 青龍泉
Ch'ing-p'u 青浦
Ch'ing-shui 清水
Ch'ing-shui-ho 清水河
Ch'ing-yang 慶陽
Ch'ing-yang-kung 青羊宮
Ch'ing-yüan 清遠、清源
Ch'iu-pei 邱北
Ch'iu-wan 丘灣
Ch'u 楚
Ch'u tz'u 楚辭
Ch'un ch'iu 春秋
Ch'ü Yüan 屈原
Ch'ü-chia-ling 屈家嶺
Ch'ü-fu 曲阜
Ch'ü-wo 曲沃
Ch'ü-yang 曲陽
Ch'üan-hu-ts'un 泉護村

Djalai-nor 札賚諾爾

Eh-ch'eng 鄂城
Eh-mao-k'ou 鵝毛口
Erh (L.) 洱(海)
Erh-chien-ts'un 二澗村
Erh-lang-p'o 二郎坡
Erh-li-kang 二里崗

Erh-li-t'ou 二里頭
erh-ts'eng-t'ai 二層台

Fang-tui-ts'un 枋堆村
Fei-hsi 肥西
Fen (R.) 汾
Fen-shui-ling 分水嶺
Feng 豐
Feng (R.) 澧
Feng Han-chi 馮漢驥
Feng Hu Tzu 風胡子
Feng-chia-an 馮家岸
Feng-chieh 奉節
feng-chien 封建
Feng-huang-t'ai 鳳凰臺
Feng-hsiang 鳳翔
Feng-pi-t'ou 鳳鼻頭
Feng-shan 鳳山
Feng-ts'un 馮村
Fo-ting 佛頂
fu 父、婦、斧、簠、鎛
Fu Ssu-nien 傅斯年
Fu-feng 扶風
Fu-ho-kou-men 富河溝門
Fu-kou 扶溝
Fu-kuo-tun 富國墩
Fu-nan 阜南
Fu-ning 阜寧

Ha-mi 哈密
Hai-feng 海豐
Hai-wei (R.) 海尾
Han 韓
Han Fei Tzu 韓非子
Han shu ti-li chih 漢書地理志
Han-chia-tsui 韓家嘴
Han-chiang (R.) 韓江
Han-ching-kou 崙井溝
Han-chou 漢州
Han-shui (R.) 漢水

Han-tan 邯鄲
Han-yüan 漢源
hang-t'u 夯土
Hao 鎬
Hei-ching-lung 黑景隆
Hei-ku-tui 黑孤堆
Hei-liu-t'u-ho (R.) 黑流兔河
Heng-chen-ts'un 橫陣村
Heng-shan 橫山
Heng-yang 衡陽
ho 盉
Ho Hsi 河西
Ho Hsü 赫胥
Ho Ping-ti 何炳棣
Ho-chin 河津
Ho-nan 河南
Hoabinh 和平
Hou Chi 后稷
Hou Han shu 後漢書
Hou-chia-chuang 侯家莊
Hou-chia-chuang-nan-ti
　　侯家莊南地
Hou-kang 後岡
Hou-lan-chia-kou 後蘭家溝
Hou-ma 侯馬
Hu 胡
hu 壺
Hu-shu 湖熟
Hua 華
Hua Hsien 華縣
Hua ts'e 畫策
Hua Yang kuo chih 華陽國志
Hua-t'ing-ts'un 花廳村
Hua-yin 華陰
Huai Ho (R.) 淮河
Huai I 淮夷
Huai-an 淮安
Huai-jen 懷仁
Huai-yang 淮陽
Huan (duke) 桓

Huan (R.) 洹
Huang Chan-yüeh 黃展岳
Huang Ti 黃帝
Huang-lien-shu 黃楝樹
Huang-niang-niang-t'ai 皇娘娘臺
Huang-p'i 黃陂
Huang-shui (R.) 湟水
Huang-ts'ai 黃材
Hui Hsien 輝縣
Hui-hsing-kou 會興溝
Hui-tsui (T'ao-sha) 灰嘴
Hui-tsui (Yen-shih) 灰嘴
Hun-yüan 渾源
Hung yen chih shih 鴻雁之什
Hung-chao 洪趙
Hung-shan-hou 紅山後
hung-ting wan 紅頂碗
Hung-tse (L.) 洪澤
Hung-tung 洪洞
Huo chih lieh chuan 貨殖列傳
Huo Shu 霍叔
Huo-pao-hsi 火爆溪

Hsi tz'u 繫辭
Hsi-chiao-shan 西樵山
Hsi-chiao-ts'un 西樵村
Hsi-ch'a-kou 西岔溝
Hsi-ch'eng-chuang 西成莊
Hsi-ch'ou 西疇
Hsi-ch'uan 淅川
Hsi-han-chuang 西韓莊
Hsi-han-shui (R.) 西漢水
Hsi-hou-tu 西侯度
Hsi-hsia-hou 西夏侯
Hsi-hsiang 西鄉
Hsi-liao (R.) 西遼
Hsi-ling-hsia 西陵峽
Hsi-ning (R.) 西寧
Hsi-pei-kang 西北岡
Hsi-shan-ch'iao 西善橋

Hsi-t'uan-shan 西團山
Hsi-wang-ts'un 西王村
Hsi-yin-ts'un 西陰村
Hsia 夏
Hsia Hsien 夏縣
Hsia Nai 夏鼐
Hsia-chia-tien 夏家店
Hsia-hsi-ho 下西河
Hsia-meng-ts'un 下孟村
Hsia-p'an-wang 下潘汪
Hsia-tu 下都
Hsia-wang-kang 下王岡
Hsiang 相
Hsiang (R.) 湘
Hsiang Yü 項羽
Hsiang-fen 襄汾
Hsiang-hsiang 湘鄉
Hsiang-jih-tê 香日德
Hsiang-t'an 湘潭
Hsiang-yang 襄陽
Hsiang-yin 湘陰
Hsiang-yün 祥雲
Hsiao 囂
Hsiao Wang 孝王
Hsiao-ch'iao-pan 小橋畔
Hsiao-lin-ting 小林頂
Hsiao-min-t'un 孝民屯
Hsiao-nan-chang 小南張
Hsiao-nan-hai 小南海
Hsiao-t'un 小屯
Hsiao-t'un-nan-ti 小屯南地
hsien 縣
Hsien-jen-tung 仙人洞
Hsien-yang 咸陽
Hsin-cheng 新鄭
Hsin-chiang 新絳
Hsin-fan 新繁
Hsin-hsiang 新鄉
Hsin-i 新沂
Hsin-min 新民

Hsin-tien 辛店
Hsin-t'ai 新泰
Hsin-t'ien 新田
Hsin-ts'ai 新蔡
Hsin-ts'un 辛村
Hsin-yang 信陽
Hsin-yeh 新野
Hsing 邢
Hsing-t'ai 邢台
Hsing-yang 滎陽
Hsing-yün (L.) 星雲
Hsiu-shui 修水
Hsiung Ch'ü 熊渠
Hsiung I 熊繹
Hsiung Nu 匈奴
Hsiung T'ung 熊通
hsü 盨
Hsü Chung-shu 徐中舒
Hsü Ping-ch'ang 徐炳昶
Hsü Shun-ch'en 許順湛
Hsü-ch'ang 許昌
Hsü-chou 徐州
Hsü-shui 徐水
Hsüan Yüan 軒轅
hsüan wen 弦紋
Hsüeh-chia-chuang 薛家莊
Hsüeh-ch'eng 薛城
Hsüeh-fu-t'un 薛埠屯
Hsün Tzu 荀子

I 夷
I (R.) 易, 伊
i 彝, 匜
I Chou shu 逸周書
I Hsien 易縣、忻縣
I Shan 嶧山
I shih 逸史
I Wang 夷王、懿王
I-cheng 儀徵
I-ch'ang 宜昌

I-ch'eng 宜城、翼城
I-ch'uan 伊川
I-liang 宜艮
i-pi-ch'ien 蟻鼻錢
I-tieh 義牒
I-tu 宜都、益都
I-yang 宜陽、伊陽
I-yüan 沂源

jao 鐃
Jao Tsung-i 饒宗頤
Jen-min 人民
Jih-yüeh-t'an (L.) 日月潭
Ju (R.) 汝
ju 鬻
Jui-ch'eng 芮城
Jung 戎

Kai P'ei 蓋培
Kan 邗
Kan-ku 甘谷
Kan-tzu 甘孜
Kang-shang-ts'un 崗上村
Kao Ch'ü-hsün 高去尋
Kao-ch'eng 蒿城
Kao-ching-t'ai-tzu 高井臺子
Kao-huang-miao 高皇廟
Kao-hsiung 高雄
Kao-li-chai 高麗寨
Kao-lou-chuang 高樓莊
Kao-tu 高都
Kao-tui 高堆
Kao-yai 高崖
Keng 耿
keng 耕、粳
Kirin 吉林
Ko 戈
ko 戈
Ko-ta-wang 旭岙王
Ko-tzu-t'ang 鴿子堂

Ko-tzu-tung 鴿子洞

Kou Wu 勾吳

ku 觚、鼓

Ku Chi-chui Tung-wu yü Ku
  Jen-lei Yen-chiu Suo
  古脊椎動物與古人類研究所

Ku Chieh-kang 顧頡剛

Ku shih pien 古史辨

Ku-chiao 古交

Ku-hsiang-t'un 顧鄉屯

Ku-lang 古浪

Ku-wei-ts'un 固圍村

Kuai (R.) 澮

kuan 罐、棺

Kuan Shu 管叔

kuan-fu 官府

kuang 觥

Kuang-han 廣漢

Kuang-wu 廣武

Kuei-yang 桂陽

kui 鬹、殷

Kung 銎

Kung Ho 共和

kung tien 宮殿

Kung Wang 恭王

Kung Yang chuan 公羊傳

Kung-wang-ling 公王嶺

Kuo 虢

kuo 國、郭、槨

Kuo Mo-jo 郭沫若

Kuo Pao-chün 郭寶鈞

Kuo yü 國語

Kuo-chia Wen-wu Shih-yeh
  Kuan-li Chü
  國家文物事業管理局

K'ang Shu 康叔

K'ang Wang 康王

K'ao Lieh Wang 考烈王

K'ao-ku 考古

K'ao-ku hsüeh chuan-k'an
  考古學專刊

K'ao-ku hsüeh pao 考古學報

K'ao-ku t'u 考古圖

K'ao-ku t'ung-hsün 考古通訊

K'ao-ku Yen-chiu Suo
  考古研究所

K'o-ho 匼河

K'o-hsing-chuang 客省莊

K'o-shih-k'o-t'eng 克什克騰

K'o-tso 喀左

k'ui 夔

k'ui-feng 夔鳳

k'ui-lung 夔龍

K'un-ming 昆明

K'un-ming (L.) 昆明

K'uo Shan 廓山

Lai-pin 來賓

Lan-chou 蘭州

Lan-t'ien 藍田

Lao-ha (R.) 老哈

Lao-ho-shan 老和山

Lao-kuan-t'ai 老官台

Lao-mu-t'ai 老姆台

Lao-t'ieh-shan 老鐵山

Lee J. S. 李四光

lei 耒、罍

lei-wen 雷紋

Lei-yang 耒陽

li 鬲

Li Chi 李濟

Li Ching-tan 李景聃

Li Hsiao-ting 李孝定

Li Hsien 澧縣

Li Hsüeh-ch'in 李學勤

Li Ping 李冰

Li Shih-wen 李始文

Li Yu-heng 李有恆

Li-chia-shan 李家山

Li-chia-ts'un 李家村

Li-chiang 麗江

Li-ch'eng Hsien 歷城縣

Li-fan 理番

Li-ling 醴陵

Li-shih 離石

Li-ts'un 李村

Li-yang 溧陽

Li-yü-ts'un 李峪村

Li-yüan 梨園

Liang Ssu-yüng 梁思永

Liang-chu 良渚

Liang-ch'eng-chen 兩城鎮

Liang-pan-shan 兩半山

Liang-ts'un 梁村

Liang-wang-ch'eng 梁王城

Liao Ho (R.) 遼

Lien-yün-kang 連雲港

Lin Shou-chin 林壽晉

Lin-hsi 林西

Lin-hsia 臨夏

Lin-ju 臨汝

Lin-shan-chai 林山砦

Lin-t'ao 臨洮

Lin-t'ung 臨潼

Lin-tzu 臨淄

ling 鈴

Ling Shun-sheng 凌純聲

Ling-ching 靈井

Ling-shan 靈山

Ling-shou 靈壽

Ling-t'ai 靈台

Ling-yang-ho 陵陽河

Ling-yüan 凌源

Liu Ch'ang-shan 劉長山

Liu-chia-chuang 劉家莊

Liu-chiang 柳江

Liu-chuang 劉莊

Liu-ch'eng 柳城

Liu-ho 六合

Liu-hu-t'un 留胡屯

Liu-li-ke 琉璃閣

Liu-lin 劉林

Liu-tzu-chen 柳子鎮

Lo 羅

Lo (R.) 洛

Lo-han-t'ang 羅漢堂

Lo-ning 洛寧

Lo-p'ing 樂平

Lo-shui-ts'un 洛水村

Lo-ta-miao 洛達廟

Lo-tu 樂都

Lo-yang 洛陽

Lu 魯

Lu sung 魯頌

Lu-nan 路南

Lu-ssu 鹿寺

Lu-shan (Kiangsi) 廬山

Lu-shan (Szechwan) 蘆山

Lu-wang-fen 璐王墳

Luan-p'ing 灤平

Lung-hsi 隴西

Lung-shan 龍山

Lung-t'ai 龍台

Lü Ta-lin 呂大臨

Lü-ta 旅大

Ma-chia-pang 馬家浜

Ma-chia-wan 馬家灣

Ma-chia-yao 馬家窰

Ma-ch'ang 馬廠

Ma-ch'ang-yen 馬廠沿

Ma-lan 馬蘭

Ma-lang-chi-ts'un 馬郎磯村

Ma-lang-ch'uan-shan 馬郎船山

Ma-lung 馬龍

Ma-pa 馬壩

Mang (Mt.) 岷

Ma-wang-ts'un 馬王村

Ma-yü-kou 麻峪溝

Man-ch'eng 滿城
mao 矛
Mei Hsien 眉縣
Mei Hsien 湄縣
Mei-shan 煤山
Mei-yüan-chuang 梅園莊
Meng Hsien 孟縣
Meng-hsi 夢溪
mi 米
Mi-chia-yai 米家崖
Mi-mo 靡莫
Miao-p'u-pei-ti 苗圃北地
Miao-ti-kou 廟底溝
Mien p'ien 縣篇
Mien-ch'ih 澠池
Mien-yang 縣陽
Min (R.) 岷
min 民、皿
Min-ch'in 民勤
Min-lo 民樂
Ming-kung-lu 銘功路
Mizuno Seiichi 水野清一
Mo Chih 莫稚
Mo Tzu 墨子
Mo-ling 秣陵
mu 母
Mu Wang 穆王
Mu-tan-chiang (R.) 牡丹江
Mu-yang-ch'eng 牧羊城

Nan-chang 南漳
Nan-hai 南海
Nan-kuan-wai 南關外
Nan-ning 南寧
Nan-shan-ken 南山根
Nan-ta-kuo-ts'un 南大郭村
Nan-yang 南陽
Ni-ho-wan 泥河灣
niao shou tsun 鳥獸尊
Ning-ch'eng 寧城

Ning-hsiang 寧鄉
Ning-ting 寧定
Ning-yang 寧陽
Niu-chai 牛砦
Niu-ts'un 牛村
No-mu-hung 諾木洪
Nonni (R.) 嫩江
Nü Wa 女媧

Ordos 河套
Oshima Riichi 大島利一

Pa 巴
Pa (R.) 灞
Pa Hsien 巴縣
Pa-lung 巴隆
Pa-tung 巴東
Pai hu t'ung 白虎通
Pai-chia-chuang 白家莊
Pai-chia-ts'un 百家村
Pai-ma-ssu 白馬寺
Pai-sha 白沙
Pai-tao-kou-p'ing 白道溝坪
Pai-t'ing (R.) 白亭
Pan Ku 班固
Pan-ch'iao 板橋
pan-liang 半兩
Pan-p'o-ts'un 半坡村
Pan-shan 半山
Pao-chi 寶鷄
Pao-lun-yüan 寶輪院
Pao-shen-miao 雹神廟
Pao-te 保德
Pao-t'ou (Inner Mongolia) 包頭
Pao-t'ou (Shantung) 堡頭
Pei-chai-ts'un 北宅村
Pei-hsin-chuang 北辛莊
Pei-shou-ling 北首嶺
Pei-yang 北洋
Pei-yin-yang-ying 北陰陽營

pi 鄙
Pi kung 閟宮
Pi-sha-kang 碧沙岡
Pi-tzu-wo 貔子窩
pien chung 編鐘
Pien-chia-kou 邊家溝
Pien-tui-shan 邊堆山
Pin Hsien 邠縣
Po 亳
Po Ch'in 伯禽
Po-yang (L.) 鄱陽
pu 布

p'an 盤
P'an Keng 盤庚
P'an Ku 盤古
p'an-ch'ih 蟠螭
p'an-k'ui-wen 蟠夔文
P'an-lung-ch'eng 盤龍城
P'an-nan-ts'un 盤南村
P'ao-ma-ling 跑馬嶺
P'ei (R.) 浯
P'ei Wen-chung 裴文中
P'ei-ling 浯陵
p'en 盆
P'eng 彭
P'eng Hsien 彭縣
P'eng-lai 蓬萊
P'eng-shan 彭山
P'i 庇
p'i 妣
P'i Hsien 邳縣
P'ien-kuan 偏關
P'ing Wang 平王
P'ing-chiang 平江
P'ing-lu 平陸
P'ing-wang 平望
P'ing-yin 平陰
p'o 瓿
P'u-tu-ts'un 普渡村

San Huang 三皇
San-ho 三河
San-li-ch'iao 三里橋
San-men-hsia 三門峽
Sang-kan-ho (R.) 桑乾河
se 瑟
Sekino Takeshi 關野雄
Sian 西安
Sjara-osso-gol 薩拉烏蘇河
ssu 耜
Ssu-hui 四會
Ssu-hung 泗洪
Ssu-ma Ch'ien 司馬遷
Ssu-pa-t'an 四壩灘
Ssu-wa 寺窪
Ssu-wa-shan 寺窪山
Su Ping-ch'i 蘇秉琦
Su-fu-t'un 蘇埠屯
Sui Hsien 隨縣
Sui-tê 綏德
Sun-ch'i-t'un 孫旗屯
Sung 宋、嵩
Sung-tse 松澤
Sung-tzu 松滋
Sungari (R.) 松花江
Suo-chin-ts'un 鎖金村

Sha-ching 沙井
Sha-kang 沙崗
Sha-kuo-t'un 砂鍋屯
Sha-yüan 沙苑
Shan hai ching 山海經
Shan Hai Kuan 山海關
Shan Hsien 陝縣
Shan-pei-ts'un 山背村
Shan-piao-chen 山彪鎮
Shan-shen 山神
Shan-tan 山丹
Shang Chia 上甲
Shang Chün shu 商君書

Shang Hsien 商縣
Shang Ti 上帝
Shang-chieh 上街
Shang-ch'iu 商丘
Shang-ts'un-ling 上村嶺
Shao-ch'ai 稍柴
Shao-hu-ying-tzu-shan
  燒戶營子山
Shao-kou 燒溝
she 社
Shen Kua 沈括
Shen Nung 神農
Shen-yang 瀋陽
sheng 笙
Sheng Hou (Ts'ai) 聲侯
sheng-t'ieh 生鐵
sheng-t'u erh ts'eng t'ai 生土二層台
sheng-wen 繩紋
shih 矢
Shih Chang-ju 石璋如
Shih chi 史記
Shih ching 詩經
Shih Hsing-pang 石興邦
Shih Huang Ti 始皇帝
Shih Kui 示癸
Shih kuo 十過
Shih i chi 拾遺記
Shih-chai-shan 石寨山
shih-ching 市井
Shih-hsing 始興
Shih-li-p'u 十里舖
Shih-lou 石樓
Shih-men 石門
Shih-yü 峙峪
Shou Hsien 壽縣
Shou-ch'un 壽春
Shu 蜀、舒
Shu ching 書經
shu-hsüeh 豎穴
shu-t'ieh 熟鐵

shu-t'u erh ts'eng t'ai 熟土二層台
Shui-kuan-yin 水觀音
Shui-mo-kou 水磨溝
Shui-tung-kou 水洞溝
Shui-t'ien-pan 水田畈
Shun 舜
shuo 杓

Ta I 大乙
Ta ya 大雅
Ta-ch'eng-shan 大城山
Ta-fan-chuang 大范莊
Ta-ho-chuang 大何莊
Ta-ho-ts'un 大河村
Ta-hsi 大溪
Ta-hsia-ho (R.) 大夏河
Ta-hsin-chuang 大辛莊
Ta-kou 大溝
Ta-ku 大姑
Ta-lai-tien 大賚店
Ta-li (Shensi) 大荔
Ta-li (Yunnan) 大理
Ta-pieh-shan (Mt.) 大別山
Ta-p'en-k'eng 大坌坑
Ta-p'o-na 大波那
Ta-ssu 大寺
Ta-ssu-k'ung-ts'un 大司空村
Ta-ts'un 大村
Ta-tun-tzu 大墩子
Ta-wen-k'ou 大汶口
Ta-yeh 大冶
Ta-yüan-ts'un 大原村
Tai-hsi 代溪
Tan-t'u 丹徒
Tan-yang 丹陽
Tang-t'u 當塗
tao 刀
Tao Ch'ê 盜跖
Tê-chou 德州
Tê-ch'in 德欽

Tê-ch'ing 德慶

Teng-feng 登封

Ti 狄

Ti Hsin 帝辛

Ti I 帝乙

Ti K'u 帝嚳

Tien 滇

Tien Wang chih yin 滇王之印

Tien-ts'ang-shan (Mt.) 點蒼山

ting 鼎

Ting Kung 定公

Ting-ts'un 丁村

to 鐸

Torii Ryōzō 鳥居龍藏

tou 豆

Tou-men-chen 斗門鎮

tu 都

Tu-an 都安

Tu-ling 杜嶺

Tuan Hsü 顓頊

Tuan-chieh-ying 段界營

tui 敦

Tung Tso-pin 董作賓

Tung-a 東阿

Tung-chai 董砦

Tung-chuang-ts'un 東莊村

Tung-hai 東海

Tung-hsiang 東鄉

Tung-hsing 東興

Tung-kan-kou 東乾溝

Tung-k'ang 東康

Tung-pa-chia 東八家

Tung-pao 東堡

Tung-sun-pa 冬筍壩

tung-shih-mu 洞室墓

Tung-t'ing (L.) 洞庭

Tung-wei-chia 東魏家

tuo 鐸

T'ai (L.) 太（湖）

T'ai Po 太伯

T'ai P'ing yü lan 太平御覽

T'ai Wang 太王

T'ai-an 泰安

T'ai-chi-shan 太極山

T'ai-hang-shan (Mts.) 太行山

T'ai-hsi-ts'un 台西村

T'ai-kang-shan 太岡山

T'ai-p'ing-ch'ang 太平場

T'ai-p'u-hsiang 太僕鄉

T'ai-shan-miao 泰山廟

T'ai-tzu-ch'ung 太子冲

T'ai-yüan 太原

T'an-shih-shan 曇石山

T'ang 湯

T'ang Lan 唐蘭

T'ang Yün-ming 唐雲明

T'ang-shan 唐山

T'ang-wang 唐汪

T'ang-yin 湯陰

T'ao-hua-chuang 桃花莊

T'ao Ho (R.) 洮河

T'ao-sha 洮沙

t'ao-t'ieh 饕餮

T'eng Hsien 滕縣

T'eng-ch'eng 滕城

T'ien Wang kui 天亡設

T'ien wen 天問

T'ien-shui 天水

t'ien-yeh 田野

T'ien-yeh k'ao-ku pao-kao
　田野考古報告

T'o (R.) 沱

T'u-men (R.) 圖們

T'un-hsi 屯溪

T'ung Chu-ch'en 佟柱臣

T'ung-lo-chai 同樂寨

T'ung-tzu 桐梓

Tsa shou p'ien 雜守篇

Tsao-lü-t'ai 造律台
Tsao-shih 皂市
Tsao-yang 棗陽
tseng 甑
Tseng 鄫
Tseng Chao-yüeh 曾昭燏
Tseng-ch'eng 增城
Tsinling (Mts.) 秦嶺
Tso chuan 左傳
Tso Lo chieh 作洛解
Tsou Heng 鄒衡
Tsou Hsien 鄒縣
tsu 族、祖、鏃
Tsukada Matsuo 塚田松雄
tsun 尊
tsung 琮
tsung-fa 宗法
Ts'ai 蔡
Ts'ai Shu 蔡叔
Ts'ao Hsien 曹縣
Ts'ao-hsieh-shan 草鞋山
Ts'ao-hsieh-tun 草鞋墩
Ts'ao-yen-chuang 曹演莊
ts'ê 冊

Tzu 子
tzu 子
Tzu-ching-shan 紫荊山
Tzu-kui 秭歸
Tzu-lo-ch'eng 子羅城
Tzu-yang 資陽

Tz'u Hsien 磁縣

Umehara Sueji 梅原末治

Wa-cha-tsui 瓦碴嘴
Wa-kuan-tsui 瓦罐嘴
wan 盌
Wan Hsien 萬縣

Wan-ch'eng 萬城
Wan-ch'üan 萬泉
wan-kui 琬圭
Wan-nien 萬年
Wang Chia 王嘉
Wang Hai 王亥
Wang Hsiang 王湘
Wang Kuo-wei 王國維
Wang P'en 王賁
Wang Ssu-li 王思禮
Wang-chia-kou 王家溝
Wang-chia-tsui 王家嘴
Wang-chia-wan 王家灣
Wang-ching-t'ai 望景台
Wang-ch'eng 王城
Wang-wan 王灣
Wei 衛、魏
Wei Chü-hsien 衛聚賢
Wei-ch'eng 魏城
Wei Ch'i 衛奇
Wei-mo 濊貊
Wei-shui (R.) 渭
Wen Hsien 溫縣
Wen Hua Chü 文化局
Wen Kung 文公
Wen Wang 文王
Wen Wang yu sheng 文王有聲
Wen-chia-t'un 文家屯
Wen-hsi 聞喜
Wen-wu 文物
Wen-wu Kuan-li`Wei-yüan-hui
　文物管理委員會
Wen-wu ts'an-k'ao tzu-liao
　文物參考資料
weng 甕
Weng-chiang 甕江
Woo Ju-k'ang 吳汝康
Wu 吳
Wu Chin-ting 吳金鼎
Wu Hsien 吳縣

Wu Hsin-chih 吳新智
Wu Ju-tso 吳汝祚
Wu Keng 武庚
Wu Shan-ch'ing 吳山菁
Wu Ti 五帝、武帝
Wu Ting 武丁
Wu Wang 武王
Wu-an 武安
Wu-chi 午汲
Wu-chia 吳家
Wu-chiang 吳江
Wu-ch'eng (Hopei) 午城
Wu-ch'eng (Kiangsi) 吳城
Wu-hsing 吳興
Wu-kuan-ts'un 武官村
Wu-p'ing 武平
Wu-shan 武山、巫山
wu-shu 五銖
Wu-wei 武威
Wu-yang-t'ai 武陽台
Wuo-kuo 沃國

Ya-an 雅安
Ya-lu (R.) 鴨綠
Ya-p'u-shan 鴨蹼山
Yang 楊
Yang Chia 陽甲
Yang Chien-fang 楊建芳
Yang Chung-chien 楊鍾健
Yang Tzu-fan 楊子範
Yang-chia-wan 楊家灣
Yang-chou 揚州
Yang-lin-chi 楊林集
Yang-shao-ts'un 仰韶村
Yang-t'ou-wa 羊頭窪
Yang-tzu-shan 羊子山
Yao 堯
yao-k'eng 腰坑
Yao-wang-miao 藥王廟
yeh 冶

yeh-jen 野人
Yeh-tien 野店
Yen 燕、奄
yen 甗
Yen-ch'eng 奄城、鄢城
Yen-chia-ma-t'ou 顏家碼頭
Yen-erh-wan 雁兒灣
Yen-ling 鄢陵
Yen-shih 偃師
Yen-tun-shan 煙墩山
Yin 殷
Yin Chou chih-tu lun 殷周制度論
Yin Huan-chang 尹煥章
Yin Hsü 殷墟
Yin Shan (Mts.) 陰山
Yin Ta 尹達
Yin-chin 陰晉
Yin-kuo-ts'un 尹郭村
Ying 郢
Ying-p'u 營埔
Ying-tse 滎澤
Ying-yüan 郢爰
yu 卣
Yu I 有俟、有駘
Yu Jung 有戎
Yu Wang 幽王
Yu Yü-chu 尤玉柱
Yu-feng 游鳳
Yü 虞、禹
yü 盂
Yü Hsien 禹縣
Yü-chia-lin 于家林
Yü-wang-ch'eng 禹王城
Yü-yao 餘姚
Yüan (R.) 沅
yüan 瑗
Yüan K'ang 袁康
Yüan-chün-miao 元君廟
Yüan-ch'ü 垣曲
Yüan-mou 元謀

Yüan-shan 圓山
Yüeh 越
yüeh 鉞
Yüeh chüeh shu 越絕書
yün 雲
Yün Hsien 勛縣

Yün-meng 雲夢
yün-wen 雲紋
Yüng-ching 永靖
Yüng-ch'ang 永昌
Yüng-ch'eng 永城、雍城

Appendix 3: Chinese Archaeology, 1976

Nineteen seventy-six will surely be remembered as one of the most eventful years in the whole of Chinese history: the deaths of Chairman Mao, Premier Chou, and Marshall Chu; the elevation of Hua Kuo-feng to the top of the government and the party; the promulgation of the misdeeds of the Gang of Four at the highest levels of party leadership, and their subsequent arrest; and one of the most severe and murderous earthquakes in Chinese history. Under the circumstances, any archaeological work at all could be regarded as a notable accomplishment. It is, thus, all the more remarkable that 1976 saw the discovery and reportage of much very important archaeological data. A brief summary of selected 1976 reports follows.[1]

Fossil Man and Palaeolithic Archaeology

At the North China Quaternary Conference, held in P'ing-shan,[2] Hopei, in November 1975, Quaternary workers made a new attempt at correlating regional stratigraphies and dividing the Quaternary of North China on the basis of evidence and research new since 1964, the year of the Second All China Quaternary Conference.[3]

At a meeting held in June of 1976 to commemorate the centennial of Frederick Engels's essay "The Role of Labor in the Transition from Ape to Man," members of the Research Institute of Geomechanics of the Academy of Geological Sciences announced the results of their efforts to date the Yüan-mou teeth (p. 42) by palaeomagnetism. They dated the Yüan-mou formation at 1.5–3 million years and the Yüan-mou teeth at 1.7±0.1 million years.[4] These dates were based on more than 300 samples collected at 76 localities belonging to 28 strata in a 700-meter section. Palaeomagnetic dating of the same section was also carried out with similar results by workers at the

---

1. For this summary (written May 1977) the following issues of the periodicals have been consulted: *VP,* nos. 1–4; *KKHP,* nos. 1–2; *KK,* nos. 1–6; *WW,* nos. 1–12; *Hua Shih,* nos. 1–4. Thus, all of the principal 1976 archaeological publications are now included in our data base here.

2. For Chinese characters of names encountered here for the first time, see list at end of appendix.

3. *VP* 14 (2), inside back cover.

4. *Hua Shih* 1976 (4), 20–21, *VP* 1976 (4), 267.

Institute of Geology and at the Kuei-yang Institute of Geochemistry, Academia Sinica. The dates are important in establishing the lower Pleistocene beginnings of *Homo erectus* in China. A flaked stone said to be associated with Yüan-mou man was published recently.[5]

Three fossil teeth, possibly of *Homo erectus*, were excavated in 1975 from a cave in the Mei-p'u Commune in Yün Hsien, Hupei, in association with mammalian fossils and "stone flakes and pieces."[6] If verified, the Yün Hsien find would serve to link *Homo erectus* fossils of Yunnan (Yüan-mou) and North China (Peking and Lan-t'ien[7]).

Another human fossil, that of the right parietal of a child, was unearthed on 14 September 1976, at locality 100 of the Palaeolithic site at Ting-ts'un, the same locality where the three Ting-ts'un teeth were found in 1954.[8]

An important Upper Palaeolithic site was excavated in 1974 at Hsü-chia-yao in Yang-kao Hsien, northernmost Shansi.[9] The Palaeolithic types are considered to be within the Chou-k'ou-tien/Shih-yü tradition (p. 70), and the assemblage, dated to an early part of Malan loess stage, is seen as an important link between Chou-k'ou-tien and Shih-yü. The geological deposits in which the Hsü-chia-yao assemblage occurs are a part of the Ni-ho-wan stratum, raising the question of the geological subdivision (into Pliocene and lower, middle, and upper Pleistocene beds) of the Ni-ho-wan profile, which has often been attributed *in toto* to lower Pleistocene.

New Radiocarbon Dates of Neolithic and Early Historic Cultures

A large number of radiocarbon determinations has apparently been accumulating at the Laboratory of the Institute of Archaeology (ZK), but as of this writing only two new dates have been reported from this laboratory,[10] while a batch of significant new dates has just come out of the Radiocarbon Laboratory of Archaeology Specialization at the Department of History, Peking University (BK).[11] These dates are given below. (To save space, only the B.P. and B.C. dates based on the 5730 half-life are included).

North China

BK-76019 Yang-shao culture at Shuang-
           miao-kou, Teng-feng,
           Honan   6380 ± 150 B.P. 4430 ± 150 B.C.

5. *KK* 1976 (3), 155, fig. 2.
6. Wang Shan-ts'ai, in *VP* 14 (3), inside back cover.
7. See *VP* 1976 (3), 198–203, for a new analysis of the lithic assemblage of Lan-t'ien.
8. Hsin Hua She dispatch from T'ai-yüan, 22 November 1976, *VP* 1976 (4), 270.
9. *KKHP* 1976 (2), 97–114.
10. *WW* 1976 (8), 14; 1976 (12), 35.
11. *WW* 1976 (12), 80–84.

BK-76054
    +76055 (same as above)   6350 ± 200   4400 ± 200
BK-76020 (same as above)   5850 ± 110   3900 ± 110
BK-76003 Yang-shao culture at Ta-ho-
             ts'un, Cheng-chou, Honan   4800 ± 90   2850 ± 90
BK-76001 (same as above)   4550 ± 100   2600 ± 100
BK-76004 (same as above)   4500 ± 140   2550 ± 140
BK-75020 Ma-chia-yao phase at Chiang-
             chia-p'ing, Yüng-teng,
             Kansu   4500 ± 100   2550 ± 100
BK-75033 Pan-shan phase at Liu-wan,
             Lo-tu, Chinghai   4040 ± 100   2090 ± 100
BK-75009 Ma-ch'ang phase at Liu-wan,
             Lo-tu, Chinghai   3860 ± 90   1910 ± 90
BK-75012 (same as above)   3750 ± 100   1800 ± 100
BK-75028 Ma-ch'ang phase at Chiang-
             chia-p'ing, Yüng-teng,
             Kansu   3780 ± 90   1830 ± 90
BK-75017 (same as above)   3680 ± 90   1730 ± 90
BK-75010 Ch'i-chia culture at Liu-wan,
             Lo-tu, Chinghai   3840 ± 90   1890 ± 90
BK-75007 Shang civilization at T'ai-
             hsi, Kao-ch'eng, Hopei   3250 ± 100   1300 ± 100
BK-75075 Western Chou at Lu-ch'ang,
             Lung-shan, Ch'ang-p'ing,
             Peking   3070 ± 90   1120 ± 90

South and East China

ZK-92-0   Lower stratum, Hsien-jen-
             tung, Wan-nien, Kiangsi   8825 ± 240   6875 ± 240
BK-75057 Ho-mu-tu culture, layer 4,
             Ho-mu-tu, Yü-yao,
             Chekiang   6310 ± 100   4360 ± 100
ZK   (same as above)   5895 ± 115   3945 ± 115
BK-76022 Early Ch'ing-lien-kang cul-
             ture at Ts'ao-hsieh-shan,
             Wu Hsien, Kiangsu   5370 ± 110   3420 ± 110
BK-76023 Middle Ch'ing-lien-kang cul-
             ture at Wei-tun, Ch'ang-
             chou, Kiangsu   5300 ± 110   3350 ± 110

BK-75058 Ma-chia-pang phase, layer 2
       at Ho-mu-tu, Yü-yao,
       Chekiang   5050 ± 100   3100 ± 100

BK-75050 Neolithic culture at Shih-
       hsia, Ma-pa, Kwangtung   4020 ± 100   2070 ± 100

Other than the newly discovered Ho-mu-tu culture and its early dating, which will be discussed in some detail below, this list does not contain many surprises. If we calibrate them according to one or another of the dendro-chronological calibration charts and then plot them onto figure 31, p. 84, we will find that all of them mesh well with the previously known dates. (Fig. 31 is based on the chart by E. K. Ralph, H. N. Michael, and M. C. Han, in "Radiocarbon dates and reality," *MASCA Newsletter* 9, no. 1, 1973.)

Early Farmers

Important Neolithic remains were reported in all three of the early Chinese farming centers — north, south, and eastern coastal — and our understanding of these centers is enhanced by new radiocarbon dates.

The chronology of the Yang-shao culture (p. 119) has been strengthened by the new radiocarbon dates at both its earlier end (Shuang-miao-kou) and its later end (Ta-ho-ts'un). After calibration, the Shuang-miao-kou dates extend well back into the later half of the sixth millennium B.C., but the details of the site remain to be reported. Very rich burial sites were excavated in Lo-tu, Chinghai, yielding materials of both Pan-shan and Ma-ch'ang phases of the Kansu Yang-shao culture and of the Ch'i-chia culture.[12] Of particular interest are remains of wooden coffins and stone cists. Also of significance is new evidence that the Ch'i-chia culture represents a further development of the Ma-ch'ang culture.[13] The radiocarbon dates from this region provide new data on the relative sequence of Pan-shan, Ma-ch'ang, and Ch'i-chia.

In South China, very important new data of Ta-p'en-k'eng and related cultures (pp. 85–91) became available. A new site, the Tseng-p'i-yen Cave south of Kuei-lin in Kwangsi, was reported as having yielded cord-marked pottery, chipped and polished stone implements, bone and shell tools, human burials, and several thousand pieces of animal bones.[14] But the most significant new information pertains to an older site, Hsien-jen-tung in Wan-nien, Kiangsi (pp. 87–89). New materials from a 1964 excavation were reported,[15] including cord-marked pottery with incised decorations that remind us of the incised, cord-marked sherds from Ta-p'en-k'eng itself. A new Institute of

12. *WW* 1976 (1), 67–74; *KK* 1976 (3), 180–86; *KK* 1976 (6), 365–77.
13. *WW* 1976 (1), 69–70, *KK* 1976 (6), 352–55.
14. *KK* 1976 (3), 175–79.
15. *WW* 1976 (12), 23–35.

Archaeology radiocarbon date (ZK-92-0) from the lower stratum of the site places the early Neolithic culture of Hsien-jen-tung into the seventh millennium B.C. (p. 89). This culture is now being recognized at many sites throughout South China, including some previously classified as Mesolithic,[16] and it will surely be the focus of much archaeological attention in the near future.

Perhaps the most remarkable find reported in 1976 is the Ho-mu-tu site in the Tung-fang-hung Brigade, Lo-chiang Commune, Yü-yao Hsien, Chekiang Province, on the bank of the river Yao, south of Hang-chou Bay. More than 600 square meters of an ancient timber village site were excavated from November 1973 to January 1974. Four cultural strata were recognized. Layer 1 (from top) is seen to correspond to the middle stratum of the Sung-tse site, and layer 2 is correlated with the site at Ma-chia-pang in Chia-hsing. Thus, the cultures of layers 3 and 4 are stated to be "the earliest known Neolithic strata in the lower Yangtze valley and the southeastern coastal areas." The radiocarbon dates from layer 4 push the Neolithic culture of the lower Yangtze basin back in time to an even earlier horizon than that represented by Pan-p'o-ts'un.[17]

What makes Ho-mu-tu especially interesting is the nature of its remains as well as their date. Evidence is massive that the inhabitants engaged in the cultivation of rice (probably in irrigated fields) and the domestication of dog, pig, and probably water buffalo. Remains of rice were everywhere and included grains, husks, straws, and leaves, sometimes concentrated in layers about half a meter thick. Yu Hsiu-ling of the Agricultural College of Chekiang compared these rice remains with known varieties of modern rice, both domesticated and wild, and he has positively identified the rice here as *Oryza sativa* L. subsp. *hsien* Ting (=*indica* Kato).[18] Seventy-six hoe blades (*ssu*) made of animal shoulder blades and most likely used as tilling implements have been found from level 4 of the deposits. In addition, remains of water caltrop, gourd, sour date, and other fruits and nuts have been unearthed, along with bones of deer, turtles, rhinoceroses, and elephants. These items indicate the continued reliance on hunting and gathering, but there is no question that here, as early as the beginning of the fifth millennium B.C., the people had already engaged in rice farming of a fairly advanced level. Pollen analyses of soil samples collected at various spots at the site disclose a preponderance of various Gramineae species.

The artifacts found at Ho-mu-tu include bone, wood, and stone implements and pottery. Bone implements are the most numerous: in addition to bone hoe blades, also recovered were chisels, awls, needles, "whistles," spatulas, weaving shuttles, saw blades, arrowheads, and some items with

16. P'eng Shih-fan, *WW* 1976 (12), 15–22.
17. *WW* 1976 (8), 6–14.
18. *WW* 1976 (8), 20–23.

unknown uses. Wooden implements from the site include knives, spatulas, spears, handles, small sticks, and other types. Stone implements are few; common types are axes, adzes, and chisels. Objects that are artistic and decorative in nature include hairpins, stone beads, pendants and rings, a clay pig, a carved bone spatula, and four carved wooden cylindrical boxes.

Pottery is handmade, low-fired, and thick. The paste was tempered with large amounts of organic materials such as grass, crushed cereal straw and leaf, and husks of grains. These materials were carbonized by firing, giving the pottery a blackish color. Common types of vessels are cooking pots (round bottoms, carinated shoulders, flared or broad-rimmed mouths, with cord marks on the body and incised or punctated designs on the shoulder and the rim), jars (flat bottoms, one or two handles, cord marked or plain), deep and shallow basins, bowls, lids, and pot supports. Three painted pieces were found; these have dark brown designs painted on the usual cord-marked sherds that have been coated with a layer of clay wash. Several features of the pottery—rim shape, coarse paste, cord marking, and rim- and shoulder-incisions—remind us of the Ta-p'en-k'eng ceramics of the southeastern coasts. This point is of significance with regard to our discussion (p. 142) of the origin of the early farming cultures of the lower Yangtze basin. Further studies of the Ho-mu-tu site are eagerly awaited.

The new data from Hsien-jen-tung and Ho-mu-tu further confirm the importance of South China in the early Neolithic period. We are now even more anxious than ever to know the details of the pre-Pan-p'o period of the Huang Ho basin that has so far only been hinted at in the archaeological literature.

Shang Civilization

Important new finds were reported from both Yen-shih and An-yang. At the Erh-li-t'ou site in the general area of the palace foundation (p. 223), three pits were excavated in the autumn of 1975, bringing to light several bronze artifacts and many jades. The bronzes include two *ko* halberds, a *ch'i* halberd, a *chüeh* cup, a *ho* wine pot, and four discs. One of the discs has turquoise inlays, and the bronze vessels were apparently cast with piece molds. These constitute the earliest assemblage of Shang bronze ritual vessels and weapons so far discovered in China. The excavators date all three pits to period 3 in the Erh-li-t'ou stratigraphy, contemporary with the palace foundation.[19]

New materials of the Shang civilization came to light in An-yang in 1972–73[20] and 1975.[21] Particularly noteworthy finds include clay drainage pipes, house floors, jades, glazed pottery, lacquered pottery, and a piece of a mural on an interior wall of a house.

19. *KK* 1976 (4), 259–63.
20. *KK* 1976 (1), 61.
21. *KK* 1976 (4), 264–72.

Outside the nuclear area, Shang remains were reported in Shih-lou in Shansi,[22] Huang-p'i in Hupei,[23] Tu-ch'ang in Kiangsi,[24] and Li-ling in Hunan.[25] Of these, the P'an-lung-ch'eng site in Huang-p'i is the most noteworthy (p. 265). Excavations in 1963 and 1974 revealed a town wall of *hang-t'u* construction (290 meters north-south and 260 meters east-west), a palace foundation, many burials with sacrificed humans, a large number of bronze ritual vessels with shapes and decorations identical to Erh-li-kang types, clay impressions of wood carving, and pottery (including glazed types). They provide important data for the Shang civilization in the Han-shui and middle Yangtze valleys.

Chou Civilization

Remains of the Western Chou period were reported in Ch'i-shan,[26] Pao-chi,[27] and Fu-feng[28] in Shensi; Ling-t'ai in Kansu;[29] Peking;[30] and Li-shui in Kiangsu.[31] The many inscribed bronzes found in Shensi furnish important new documents pertaining to Western Chou history and society; and among the many archaeological remains the wooden burial chamber (radiocarbon dated to 3070±90 B.P.), the inscribed oracle shells of Peking, and the silk-fabric-impressed clay of Pao-chi are of exceptional interest.

A group of seven Warring States period tombs was reported at T'ao-hung-pa-la, in Hang-chin Banner, Ikjou League, Inner Mongolia. "These are all oblong earthen shafts containing [single burials] without any coffin. The tomb furniture consists mostly of bronze implements and ornaments of various materials, with only a few pieces of pottery. Of particular interest is the presence of numerous animal (horse, ox, and sheep) skulls and limb bones near the tomb entrances."[32] The archaeologists who reported on the find suggest that the tombs were those of the nomadic Hsiung-nu people.

22. *WW* 1976 (2), 94.
23. *WW* 1976 (1), 49–55; 1976 (2), 5–46.
24. *KK* 1976 (4), 273.
25. *WW* 1976 (7), 49–50.
26. *KK* 1976 (1), 31–38; *WW* 1976 (5), 26–59; 1976 (6), 40–44.
27. *WW* 1976 (4), 34–63.
28. *WW* 1976 (6), 51–65.
29. *KK* 1976 (1), 39–48.
30. *KK* 1976 (4), 246–58.
31. *KK* 1976 (4), 274.
32. *KKHP* 1976 (1), 131–44. (Quoted English ,passage original, p. 144).

List of New Chinese Characters

Ch'ang-p'ing 昌平
Chiang-chia-p'ing 蔣家坪
Hang-chin 杭錦
Ho-mu-tu 河姆渡
Hsü-chia-yao 許家窰
Liu-wan 柳灣
Lo-chiang 羅江
Lu-ch'ang 鹿場
Mei-p'u 梅鋪
P'ing-chiang 平江

Shih-hsia 石峽
Shuang-miao-kou 雙廟溝
T'ao-hung-pa-la 桃紅巴拉
Tseng-p'i-yen 甑皮岩
Tu-ch'ang 都昌
Tung-fang-hung 東方紅
Wei-tun 圩墩
Yang-kao 陽高
Yü-yao 餘姚
Yüng-teng 永登

Recommendations for Further Reading

The references cited in this volume are given in full in the footnotes, which constitute an intensive bibliography for the field of ancient Chinese archaeology up to the end of 1976. The following list is in two parts. The first gives titles of periodicals and serial publications, wherein the overwhelming majority of the original data are reported. The second part consists of a highly selective minimum of titles which are recommended for their wide coverage and general significance; it can also be used as a reading list for a graduate course in the archaeology of ancient China.

Major Periodicals and Serial Publications

Archaeologia Orientalis, series A and B, Tokyo and Kyoto, Toa-Koko-Gakukwai.

Archaeologia Sinica, Nanking and Taipei, Institute of History and Philology, Academia Sinica.

Archaeologia Sinica, new series, Taipei, Institute of History and Philology, Academia Sinica.

Chung-kuo k'ao-ku hsüeh pao, no. 2–4, 1937–49, Nanking, Institute of History and Philology, Academia Sinica.

Chung-kuo ku chi-chui tun-wu yü ku jen-lei yen-chiu suo chuan-k'an, Peking, Science Press.

K'ao-ku, 1959– , Peking, K'ao-ku Tsa-chih she.

K'ao-ku hsüeh chuan-k'an, series A, B, C, and D, Peking, Science Press.

K'ao-ku hsüeh pao, no. 5– , 1951– , Peking, Science Press.

K'ao-ku t'ung-hsün, 1955–58, Peking, Science Press.

Vertebrata Palasiatica, vol. 1 (1957)– , Peking, Science Press.

Wen-wu, 1959– , Peking, Wen Wu Press.

Wen-wu ts'an-k'ao tzu-liao, 1950–58, Peking, Wen Wu Press.

Other Important Titles

Aigner, Jean S., "Relative dating of North Chinese faunal and cultural complexes," *Arctic Anthropology* 9 (1972), no. 2, 36–79.

Amano Motonosuke, "Yintai no nōgyo to shakai kozo," *Shigaku kenkyū* 62 (1956), 1–16.

———, "Chugaku Kodai nōgyo no tenkai-Kahoku nōgyu no keiseikatei,"

Tōhōgakuhō 39 (1959), Kyoto.

An Chih-min, "Chung-kuo shih-ch'ien shih-ch'i nung-yeh," *Yenching Social Studies* 2 (1949), 37–58.

An Chih-min, comp., *Chung-kuo shih-ch'ien k'ao-ku-hsüeh shu-mu*, Peking, 1951.

Andersson, J. G., "Preliminary Report on Archaeological Research in Kansu," *GSuC, Memoirs*, ser. A, 5 (1925).

——, "Selected Ordos Bronzes," *BMFEA* 5 (1933), 143–54.

——, "Researches into the Prehistory of the Chinese," *BMFEA* 15 (1943).

An-yang fa-chüeh pao-kao, Peiping, Institute of History and Philology, Academia Sinica, 1929–33.

Barnard, Noel, "Bronze Casting and Bronze Alloys in Ancient China," *Monumenta Serica Monograph* 14 (1961), Australian National University and Monumenta Serica.

——, *The First Radiocarbon Dates from China*, rev. and enlarged, Monographs on Far Eastern History, vol. 8, Australian National University, 1975.

Barnard, Noel, editor, *Early Chinese Art and Its Possible Influence in the Pacific Basin*, 3 vols., New York, Intercultural Arts Press, 1972.

Barnard, Noel, and Sato Tamotsu, *Metallurgical Remains of Ancient China*, Tokyo, Nichiōsha, 1975.

Black, Davidson; P. Teilhard de Chardin; C. C. Young; and W. C. P'ei, "Fossil Man in China," *GSuC, Memoirs*, ser. A, 11 (1933).

Boule, M.,; H. Breuil; E. Licent; and P. Teilhard de Chardin, *Le Paléolithique de la Chine*, Archives de l'Institut de Paléontologie Humaine, Memoire no. 4 (1928).

Chang Kwang-chih, "New Evidence on Fossil Man in China," *Science* 136 (1962), 749–60.

——, "Prehistoric Archaeology in China: 1920–60," *Arctic Anthropol.* 1 (1962), no. 2, 29–61.

——, *Early Chinese Civilization: Anthropological Perspectives*, Cambridge, Harvard University Press, 1976.

——, "Chinese palaeoanthropology," in *Annual Review of Anthropology*, 1977, Palo Alto, Annual Reviews.

Chang Kwang-chih, co-editor, *COWA Survey and Bibliography, Area 17 Far East (China and Formosa)*, no. 1 (1959), no. 2 (1961), no. 3 (1963).

Chang Kwang-chih and collaborators, *Fengpitou, Tapenkeng, and the Prehistory of Taiwan*, Yale University Publications in Anthropology, no. 73, 1969.

Cheng Te-k'un, *Archaeological Studies in Szechwan*, Cambridge University Press, 1957.

——, *Archaeology in China*; vol. 1, *Prehistoric China*, 1959; supplement to vol. 1, *New Light on Prehistoric China*, 1966; vol. 2, *Shang China*, 1961; vol. 3, *Chou China*, 1963; Cambridge, Heffer.

——, "The Beginning of Chinese Civilization," *Antiquity* 47 (1973), 197–209.

Chung-kuo Ko-hsüeh-yüan K'ao-ku Yen-chiu Suo, *Hsin Chung-kuo ti k'ao-ku shou-huo*, Peking, Wen Wu Press, 1962.

Chung-kuo K'o-ksüeh-yüan Ku Chi-chui Tung-wu yü Ku Jen-lei Yen-chiu Suo, *Shensi Lan-t'ien hsin-sheng-chieh hsien-ch'ang hui-i lun-wen chi*, Peking, Science Press, 1966.

Creel, H. G., *The Birth of China*, New York, Ungar, 1937.

———, *The Origins of Statecraft in China*; vol. 1, *The Western Chou Empire*; University of Chicago Press, 1970.

Finn, D. J., *Archaeological Finds on Lamma Island near Hong Kong*, University of Hong Kong, 1958.

Foreign Language Press, *Historical Relics Unearthed in New China*, Peking, 1972.

Hayashi Minao, *Chugaku In-shō jidai no buki*, Kyoto University Institute of Humanistic Science, 1972.

Ho Ping-ti, *Huang-t'u yü Chung-kuo nung-yeh ti ch'i-yüan*, Hong Kong, Chinese University, 1969.

———, *The Cradle of the East*, Chinese University of Hong Kong, and University of Chicago Press, 1976.

Hu Hou-hsüan, *Chia-ku-hsüeh Shang-shih lun ts'ung*, 2 vols., Ch'eng-tu, Ch'i-lu University, 1944, 1945.

———, *Yin-hsü fa-chüeh*, Shanghai, Hsüeh-hsi-sheng-huo Press, 1955.

Jung Keng, *Shang Chou i-ch'i t'ung-k'ao*, Peking, Yenching University, 1941.

Karlgren, Bernhard, "Yin and Chou in Chinese Bronzes," *BMFEA* 8 (1936).

———, "New Studies on Chinese Bronzes," *BMFEA* 9 (1937).

———, "Huai and Han," *BMFEA* 13 (1941).

Kuo Mo-jo; Young Chung-chien; P'ei Wen-chung; Chou Ming-chen; Woo Ju-k'ang; and Chia Lan-p'o, *Chung-kuo jen-lei hua-shih ti fa-hsien yü yen-chiu*, Peking, Science Press, 1955.

Kuo Pao-chün, *Chung-kuo ch'ing-t'ung ch'i shih-tai*, Peking, Sanlien Books, 1963.

Li Chi, *The Beginnings of Chinese Civilization*, University of Washington Press, 1957.

———, *Anyang*, University of Washington Press, 1976.

Liang Ssu-yüng, "The Lungshan Culture," *Proc. 6th Pacific Science Congress* 4 (1939), 69–79.

Loehr, Max, "Ordos Daggers and Knives," *Artibus Asiae* 14 (1951), 77–162.

———, *Chinese Bronze Age Weapons*, University of Michigan Press, 1956.

———, *Relics of Ancient China*, New York, Asia Society, 1965.

———, *Ritual Vessels of Bronze Age China*, New York, Asia Society, 1968.

Maringer, John, *Contribution to the Prehistory of Mongolia*, Stockholm, 1950.

Mizuno Seiichi, *Yinshū seidoki to gyoku*, Tokyo, Nihon Keizaishinbun Sha, 1959.

Movius, Hallam L., Jr., *Early Man and Pleistocene Stratigraphy in Southern and Eastern Asia*, Papers of the Peabody Museum, vol. 19, Cambridge, Harvard University, 1944.

———, "The Lower Palaeolithic Cultures of Southern and Eastern Asia," *Transactions of the American Philosophical Society*, n.s. 38 (1949), pt. 4.

———, "Palaeolithic Archaeology in Southern and Eastern Asia, Exclusive of India," *Cahiers d'Histoire Mondiale* 2 (1955), 257–82, 520–53.

Needham, Joseph, *Science and Civilization in China*, vol. 1, Cambridge University Press, 1954.

——, *The Development of Iron and Steel Technology in China*, London, Newcomen Society, 1958.

Oshima Riichi, "Chugaku kodai no shiro o tsuite," *Tōhōgakuhō* 30 (1959), 39–66.

P'ei Wen-chung, *Chung-kuo shih-ch'ien shih-ch'i chih yen-chiu*, Shanghai, Commercial Press, 1948.

Sekai kōkōgaku taikei; vol. 5, *Eastern Asia: Prehistoric Period*; vol. 6, *Eastern Asia: Shang and Chou Periods*; Tokyo, Heibonshya, 1958, 1960.

Sekino Takeshi, *Chugaku kōkōgaku kenkyū*, University of Tokyo, Institute for Oriental Culture, 1956.

Shantung Sheng Wen-wu Kuan-li-ch'ü and Chi-nan-shih Po-wu-kuan, *Ta-wen-k'ou*, Peking, Wen Wu Press, 1974.

Shih Chang-ju, *K'ao-ku nien piao*, Yangmei, Institute of History and Philology, Academia Sinica, 1952.

Szechwan Museum, *Szechwan ch'uan-kuan tsang fa-chüeh pao-kao*, Peking, Wen Wu Press, 1960.

Teilhard de Chardin, P., *Early Man in China*, Peking, Institut de Géo-Biologie, 1941.

Tseng Chao-yüeh, et al., *Chiang-su sheng ch'u-t'u wen-wu hsüan chi*, Peking, Wen Wu Press, 1963.

Umehara Sueji, *Yin Hsü, Ancient Capital of the Shang Dynasty at Anyang*, Tokyo, Asahi Shinbunsha, 1964.

Von Dewall, Magdalene, "The Tien Culture of South-west China," *Antiquity* 40 (1967), 8–21.

Watson, William, *Archaeology in China*, London, Parrish, 1960.

——, *China Before the Han Dynasty*, New York, Praeger, 1961.

——, *Ancient Chinese Bronzes*, Rutland, Vt., Tuttle, 1962.

——, *Early Civilization in China*, London, Thames & Hudson, 1966.

——, *Cultural Frontier in Ancient East Asia*, Edinburgh University Press, 1971.

——, *Ancient China*, Boston, New York Graphic Society, 1974.

Wei Chü-hsien, *Chung-kuo k'ao-ku-hsüeh shih*, Shanghai, Commercial Press, 1937.

Wheatley, Paul, *The Pivot of the Four Quarters*, Chicago, Aldine, 1971.

White, W. C., *Bronze Culture of Ancient China*, Toronto, Royal Ontario Museum, 1956.

Wu, G. D., *Prehistoric Pottery in China*, London, Kegan Paul, Trench & Trübner, 1938.

Wu, C. T.; C. Y. Tseng; and C. C. Wang, *Yünnan Ts'ang Erh ching k'ao-ku pao-kao*, Lichuang, National Museum, 1942.

Yunnan Museum, *Yün-nan Chin-ning Shih-chai-shan ku-mu-ch'ün fa-chüeh pao-kao*, Peking, Wen Wu Press, 1959.

Index

Index entries are alphabetized word by word according to the following order of initials and (where initials are lacking) finals: a, b, c, ch, ch', d, e, f, g, h, hs, i, j, k, k', l, m, n, o, p, p', q, r, s, sh, t, t', ts, ts', tz, tz', u, v, w, y.